Barefoot Journeying

The Autobiography
of a
Begging Friar

Benedict M. Ashley, O.P.

NEW PRIORY PRESS

EXPLORING THE DOMINICAN VISION

**Dedicated to My Natural Family,
My Mother, Bertha
and My Father, Arthur
and
My Dominican Family**

Barefoot Dominic, 1974, by Fr. Thomas McGlynn, O.P.

"When the blessed Dominic
went to Rome with the witness,
whenever he left a city or village
he always took his shoes off
and carried them
under his arm...."

–*Testimony of Fra Buonviso,*
August 9, 1233

Contents

Poems

Introduction

A very long life – such as the remarkable one that our author has lived – does not guarantee that the individual has used those many years well. Benedict M. Ashley, O.P. has used his many years – almost a century now – to advance the Kingdom of God as a priest philosopher-theologian. But before turning his life to Jesus Christ (he was be baptized in 1938) and entering the Dominican Order in the 1940s (he was ordained in 1948), Ashley was a follower of Marx, not the Master. His autobiography, *Barefoot Journeying*, could very well be titled *From Socialism to the Savior*. In these pages you will find Ashley's "conversion story" told in both prose and poetry. It is good that these many poetic writings are included, because they give us great insight into the mind and heart of a man who started off with the hope of being a novelist and poet while at the University of Chicago in the early 1930s.

I first met Fr. Ashley in August of 1988, when I was assigned to be his graduate research assistant after enrolling at the Pontifical John Paul II Institute for Studies on Marriage and Family (Washington, DC), to study for an STL degree. As the cliché goes, "It seems just like yesterday." I was privileged to take six courses with Ashley and, as a Father Michael J. McGivney Fellow, to work with him on various writing projects for two academic years. What impressed me most about him was his humility, despite the incredible breadth and depth of his learning. We students would often lament that when Fr. "Benny" passes, a great deal of knowledge and wisdom would pass with him. Thankfully, our esteemed teacher has lived two plus decades since those early days of the "JPII Institute" – with Ashley the original "pillar" on which it stood – and his nearly two dozen books and hundreds of articles will live on even longer.

To read Fr. Ashley's intellectual autobiography is to immerse oneself in a virtual "Who's Who" of Twentieth and early Twenty-First century Catholicism. From his birth in May 1915, during the First World War, to the second decade of the Third Millennium, we encounter the figures of his teachers Mortimer J. Adler and Robert Maynard Hutchins in the "Great Books" program at the University of Chicago. We meet other teachers such as Waldemar Gurian and

Yves Simon at the University of Notre Dame (where Ashley received a doctorate in political philosophy in 1941). We come in contact with his Dominican conferees William H. Kane, William A. Wallace, and James A. Weisheipl in the 1950s (a decade when Ashley would study for a doctorate in philosophy at the Aquinas Institute, earning it in 1951). From there, we move on to the 1960s and the Second Vatican Council and the events and debates surrounding it, notably the encyclical on birth control, *Humanae vitae* (1968). Ashley then takes us all the way up to our present day, with its own debates, especially over the foundations of morality, biotechnology, and secularism.

What may impress the reader the most is the deep familiarity with and respect for modern science that is on display in the pages of Ashley's memoir. Already, in the early 1950s, Ashley was collaborating with his fellow Dominicans in founding the Albertus Magnus Lyceum (1951-1969) – a think tank of sorts to bring modern science and theology into dialogue. For these "River Forest School" Thom-ists, modern science is largely continuous with Aristotelian natural philosophy/natural science. Further, they argued, St. Thomas' metaphysics must be grounded in a sound philosophy of nature lest it lack a solid foundation. Ashley is still thinking about these questions, evidenced by some of his most recent books, *The Way toward Wisdom* (2006) and *How Science Enriches Theology* (co-authored with John Deely, 2012).

But Ashley has also taken the thought of St. Thomas and applied it fruitfully in the areas of the body-person, moral theology, bioethics, and psychology to cite just a few areas. His *Theologies of the Body* (1985/1995), is a massively learned work that ranges over, from the perspective of many different fields, the different understandings of the human person – in ancient philosophy, Christianity, secular humanism, and modern science among others. Ashley's *Living the Truth in Love* (1996) is what he calls "a biblical introduction to moral theology," that is organized by the four cardinal virtues and the three theological virtues, which themselves are coordinated with each other. *Health Care Ethics*, now in its fifth edition (2006), is Ashley's (and his late co-author Kevin O'Rourke) major contribution to theological bioethics. And *Healing for Freedom*, to be released sometime in 2013, is Fr. Ashley's effort to bring to bear "a Christian perspective on personhood and psychotherapy."

Barefoot Journeying will also bring the reader into contact with Aristotle and St. Thomas Aquinas – Ashley's two favorite philosophers. As well, Ashley's family and many friends such as Herbert Schwartz and Leo Shields are spread out across this autobiography like the Great Plains of Kansas and Oklahoma, from where he was born and raised. As with all stories of friends and family, there is much joy as well as much heartbreak – the "trials," as he calls them. You will read of this and more here. Many know Ashley only in his many public roles: for example, as priest, author, teacher, lecturer, educator, and administrator. In the following pages, you will come to know him in a more personal way as he reveals himself decade-by-decade.

In describing the events of his life, Fr. Ashley is brutally honest about his faults and sins. He does not hide any of the less-than-noble actions of his life – but not in the fashion of a contemporary "Tell All" book, where every salacious detail is recorded. As befits his priestly vocation, Ashley wants you to learn about the virtues of his life, to understand his theological thought and Dominican spirituality, to meet his friends and those who have influenced his life, and not get caught up in the *peccata* that blur the image of God in man. But more importantly, he wants you to meet our "wisest and best friend" (S.T., I-II, Q. 108, a. 4) that he has come to know these last six and a half decades – the one who has transformed him. That friend is Jesus Christ.

I hope my revered former teacher and friend takes this introduction as the tribute I intend it to be. I am honored and blessed to have been asked to write it. But even more blessed to have known him and studied with him.

Mark S. Latkovic, S.T.D.
Sacred Heart Major Seminary, Detroit, MI
December, 2012

Part I
Atheism Bumps into God: A Conversion Story

Chapter 1 - Poetic Empiricism

The "God Delusion"

The "New Atheism" of Richard Dawkins, Daniel C. Dennet, Sam Harris, Christopher Hitchens and Victor J. Stenger, among others,[1] confirms St. Thomas Aquinas' view that atheism, whenever it historically erupts, always presents two fundamental objections to God's existence: (1) that the universe is self-explanatory and (2) that it is filled with too many evils to have a good Creator. The first of these is the more fundamental, since the second presupposes that there is some reason to think God exists; while the first implies that theism is simply unintelligible. Yet a careful reading of these currently popular authors shows that it is this argument from evil that concretely motivates most atheists' absolute convictions. But why are they so blind to the classical arguments for God's existence?

Elsewhere I have responded to this new wave of atheism in abstract philosophical or scientific terms,[2] but when any of us comes to the absolute convictions on which his or her whole life depends we must also face up to the concrete experience of reality that each of us has as a unique person. The term "empiricism" is from the Greek for "experience" and in the broad sense refers not only to external sensation, but also to the work of our internal senses and our affects ("feelings") best expressed in fine literature and especially in poetry. Modern scientists, however, are often by their scientific education cut off from reality by their habits of abstract mathematical modeling. Thus paradoxically their mathematicism, which for Plato and neoplatonism poetically led upward to the spiritual world of the Ideas, centered on the Idea of the One or Good, that is, on God, blinds them to the Design Argument for his existence.

Hence in this book I have, with considerable embarrassment and only with the urging of my religious superior decided to relate the story of my own conversion to the Catholic faith as a concrete example of how poetry and science can support each other. My purpose is to encourage the reader to review her or his own personal choice of a "worldview and value system" and see if it is really and honestly the truest available. I call this "poetic empiricism" because poetry by its emphasis on "experience" keeps us in touch with reality better than does the telescope, the tube, and the computer.

When my superior urged me to write this memoir he suggested I start it with a reference to something he had once heard me say, namely, "According to family tradition my great-great grandfather on my mother's side was burned at the stake by Native Americans and his wife scalped and left for dead." I cannot verify this family tradition, but often dreamed as a child of being similarly taken captive and thus felt both the fire and the knife. At 94, however, and a member of the religious Order of Preachers, once notorious as Inquisitors who sent heretics to the stake, I also felt its fires when my Provincial asked me to write this. Reviewing one's life can burn deep. As I have written I have been concerned in talking about myself to show atheists why the All Merciful God is indeed the source of all reality.

My only sibling, six years my elder, was Richard Moore Ashley born March 13, 1909. I was born May 3, 1915 in Neodesha (Osage for Smoky-With-Mud-Water), a town of about 3,000 located in southeastern Kansas at the confluence of the Fall and Verdigris Rivers.[3] Native American lore has always formed my mental landscape and Neodesha for me is associated with two images, the burial Mound of Little Bear, the Osage chief who died in 1867, and the wild persimmons I picked as a boy on my uncle Joe Kammerer's, farm near the Mound. So sweet, those orange persimmons, but, if not quite ripe, how they puckered your lips!

My mother had hoped to pair her son Richard with a daughter whom she planned to name "Alicia," but when I also turned out male she named me "Winston" after Winston Churchill (not the British statesman but the St. Louis novelist then famous) and "Norman" for my grandfather. When I eventually became a Catholic for a baptismal name I took "Joseph" and when I became a Dominican friar as my "religious name" I took "Benedict Mary," which I have retained, though to take a religious name, and especially a feminine, devotional one, has, since Vatican II in the Catholic Church, become politically incorrect.

I was told that the doctor who delivered me used forceps so that I came from the womb with my head strangely pulled out, like the statues of King Tut. My mother recollected how the doctor patted it back into shape. Then, because I was rather slow to begin talking, my mother used to cry, fearing I would prove idiotic. I soon made up for lost time, as the loquacity of this book will testify.

My parents used to tell this story on me. One day my eight-year-old brother came home without me. When my parents anxiously inquired where he had left Wint, he replied, "I chained him in the sewer with my dog chain." Dick had indeed chained me in a large sewer pipe that workmen had been laying in an open trench in the street. When to tease me my parents told this story the punch line was always, "And when we rushed down to unchain you, you cried and cried. You preferred the sewer to home!"

I myself do not remember that friendly sewer, but I seem to remember another very early event. I was told that when I was about two I jumped off the front porch, but landed unharmed. This crash-landing came back to me later in dreams as an attempt to fly. In the dreams I saw under the porch where I took off a wooden lattice-work, a feature of no house in which we later lived. Not till I was ten did we again visit that house in Neodesha and behold I immediately recognized that porch with its latticework! Furthermore, that house was somehow connected in my mind with a dream I had repeatedly when six or seven. I dreamt that I was sitting at the window in its parlor when a wagon drew up before the house with two strange Indians, a man and a woman. It seemed they were coming to take me away. I screamed for my mother, feeling she had abandoned me. It was a scene of sheer terror until each time I awoke.

When I was two and a half we moved to Blackwell, Oklahoma, a town of 10,000.[4] where my father had a new job as the chief accountant of the Blackwell Zinc Smelter. Blackwell was just another farm town in wheat country, but the smelter had been built there to exploit the abundant natural gas from nearby wells in refining the ores mined in the Tri-State area of Oklahoma, Kansas, and Missouri. My Dad always claimed that it was the biggest smelter in the whole world exclusively for zinc, with twin hundred-feet smokestacks spewing out yellow smoke over the wheat fields, poisoning crops and cattle. For a time we lived at the west edge of town and in full view of the smelter, so that the view of those two smokestacks raised in the western sky with their clouds of pollution adding to the colors of the sunsets, already spectacular in the plains, is one of the most deeply impressed images in my brain.

Yet Blackwell was a pleasant, friendly, if rather bleak, town in the Cherokee Strip, once part of an Indian reservation, until it was opened to white settlement in the famous Cherokee Run of 1893. I like small towns, as later I was to love Dubuque, IA, although one of my Dominican confreres said, "If I had only six months to live, I would move to Dubuque, so that it would seem like six years."

In an early poem of mine I tried to capture this landscape:

HARVEST NOON

The wheat harvest is whirling in yellow hot hours,
the dense grain is falling in hot yellow showers,
at field fences yellow sunflowers
twirl and bend to the west.

The round stubble is shining in yellow new lanes,
the grain left is rippled in dense hot plains,
and bends to the whirl of the binder's vanes
bundled in even rows.

Standing grain falls in an even rain
that slows when the binder slows,
slows and turns.

Green squares of clashing corn,
the fallow field is yellow now,
yellow even the pale oats,
and even now alfalfa bloom
breathes tender under the darker green,
green squares of rustling half-grown corn,
sweet the clover
on the even wind burning
which slows and turns.

Evenly over the harvesters sweat black and burnt bending,
the wind burns and
turns the binder down the fields.

Under the wind the grain yields ripples,
spread way down the bright fields splash
into the bright blue even sky,
the dark trees hang high in the wind

that turns and burns.

The wheat harvest is burning in hot yellow lanes
of dense grain
up to the fences where twirl the yellow sunflowers
through yellow hot sun and yellow hours
the yellow shining stubble plains
spread and turn against the west
and burn.

The west burns blue.

I even remember Armistice Day, November 11, 1918 in Blackwell. A neighbor runs into our house to tell us something important, then noise and excitement. It meant just that to me. My mother's youngest brother, Uncle Harry, was in the army, but my Dad, with a family and an industrial job, was not drafted in World War I, nor were my other two maternal uncles who worked in the oil drilling business. Similarly in World War II my brother Richard and I escaped the draft. Some have viewed with suspicion the fact that it was in the very year of the World War II draft that I piously entered the Dominican Order.

I remember also that my Aunt May and Uncle Hick and their three little daughters, my cousins, had also moved from Neodesha to live near us. Uncle Hick was a foreman in the Blackwell smelter but got fired for activity in the labor union and had to return with his family to Neodesha. My father, belonging to the clerical staff was not involved and thought my uncle crazy to oppose the management. Dad was always a Republican, his politics formed by The *Kansas City Star* and *The Saturday Evening Post*.

Other impressions of 1918-1919 include an eclipse of the sun that we watched through a smoked glass, how I learned to cut out pictures from magazines with scissors, and the great influenza epidemic. We were all sick and there was a strange woman who came to help us but who burned the breakfast toast. They also used to tell me that when at about three I was given a Santa Claus doll, I chortled with delight, then promptly, for reasons unknown, ran into the bathroom and threw Santa into the toilet! I myself remember two emotional reactions. When they played on the phonograph a record called, "The Herd-Girl's Dream," I loved to dance around the room and then lie down on the floor as if asleep. I also was very distressed at the sadness of Stephen Foster's "Old Black Joe" and, if it was played, I would run out of the room with my hands over my ears.

Only when I was four or five did my world open up into something large, bright and coherent. We had moved to another house, then to a third that was on the Main Street of town but near the northern outskirts. Not far beyond it was a bridge over the Chikaskia River, an inconsiderable tributary of the Salt Creek fork of the Arkansas River, itself tributary to the great Mississippi.[5] The house had a large backyard and there were fields beyond. This landscape gave me a sense of the immense flat openness of the plains and its still wider sky, often filled with great heaped-up gleaming white clouds. To this day my mental compass of the four directions is the north, south, east and west of that house on North Main Street.

In the backyard was an empty garage chicken-house onto the top of which I could climb to sit and survey the world. I especially recall the great pleasure of vision that I found in the green fields, the flowers, the rising sun, the lightning in the distant clouds on summer nights. But I was also sometimes frightened by events. One day a summer grass fire threatened our house. Dogs barked and jumped on me. I was panicked when I saw a runaway horse. Yes, there were still a few horses and wagons to be seen in town, in this case a horse and wagon belonging to the Jewel Tea Company vendor was startled by a dog and plunged down the street dragging the anchor—weight the driver had put out.

It was a little before that, I believe, that something still more surprising happened. Our family had gone to a movie and as we walked home, my parents were discussing something and I asked a question about what they were saying. I don't remember what the question was about, but as I asked it, for the first time I was suddenly acutely aware of myself as a self-conscious, rational, free person. Of course, I did not have the words for that sudden realization, but at that moment I woke up from what had been before only a stream of impressions as in a dream. I was faced with the overwhelming sense of being myself. I was touching "the age of reason."

Yet I was still very much a child. My brother took me to school the first day. I wore a sailor suit with a drop seat and when I went to the restroom did not get it buttoned up right. My mother had kept me with a Buster Brown haircut, already out of fashion and only reluctantly let me have a regular short haircut after I complained about the fun the other boys made of me. I was small and rather cute and the girls who seemed bigger than me made a fuss over me, which was both flattering and frightening.

Mostly I liked school and my teacher, a nice elderly woman. On George Washington's birthday we were to have a flag drill, the climax of which was to march through the cloakroom and back into the classroom. I looked forward to that march carrying a little flag, but also dreaded the day because I was assigned to recite a poem and was afraid I would make foolish grimaces during my performance. The night before, as I undressed for bed, my mother said, "What are those red spots?" and chicken pox solved my dilemma. Later in the 1970s I had a painful case of shingles and the doctor told me that it was a reemergence of that childhood chicken pox virus.

The most painful incident I remember, though, was the trouble I had learning the alphabet. My mother had not tried to teach me, because a teacher friend had told her it was best to leave that to school. But Mrs. M. sent home a note that Mother was to practice me in my ABC's. I thought "Elomenopee" was the name of single letter, because the "Alphabet Song" we sang went very fast when we came to LMNOP. As we sat in the swing on our front porch in the bright Oklahoma sun my Mother drilled me, but I kept making dumb mistakes. She got irritated and I think may have reverted to her original fears that I was an idiot. Of those days the best time was when some seed I had planted in our garden (after ruthlessly tearing up things planted by my brother) grew up into great beautiful sunflowers and tall Indian corn with colored ears.

For a time I had some boys my age to play with and began to feel myself part of a gang, but when I was in second grade we moved again, this time to a larger house in town in walking distance of a grade school where I attended second and third grades, and then when I was five and six still another nearby school. I don't know why, but in this new neighborhood there were no children my age to play with and my childhood from then on never again seemed very happy all the way through high school.

Dad

For this unhappiness I cannot use the explanation, so fashionable today, that my Dad and Mother, as I always called them, "abused" me. They were faithful to each other and were loving and truly self-sacrificing parents. As I grow older my gratitude to them increases constantly. My parents had the defects they themselves had suffered in their own upbringing and this necessarily affected me, but they also had great gifts and they gave them to me and my brother as generously as they knew how.

My father, Arthur Burton Ashley, was nicknamed for some reason "Chink," although his parents had called him "Archie." He was born August 29, 1880 at Golden, IL, and raised in Lewistown, IL. Family tradition claimed his forbears had emigrated from the Carolinas in the area of the Ashley River. All I am sure is that William Dye Ashley and Martha Staten were my paternal grandparents with sons, Judson, Reuben, John, Oscar, and Robert, and my father, Arthur, and daughters Minnie Grafton, Alice Patterson, and Nettie Hadsall. Grandpa Ashley was a Civil War veteran on the Union side and, according to tradition, his grandfather was in the American Revolution. Recently, however, a friend whose hobby is genealogy traced my father's line and discovered that I am a descendant of the notorious First Earl of Shaftesbury,[6] satirized as the evil counselor Achitophel (2 Samuel, Chapters 14-15) in John Dryden's satire Absalom and Achitophel.

> Of these the false Achitophel was first;
> A name to all succeeding ages curst:
> For close designs and crooked counsels fit,
> Sagacious, bold, and turbulent of wit,
> Restless, unfix'd in principles and place,
> In pow'r unpleas'd, impatient of disgrace.

Shaftesbury (Ashley-Cooper) was Lord Chancellor of England and largely responsible for the expulsion of the last Catholic King of England, James II. He gave two of his sons large properties in what is now South Carolina but they did not remain rich for long and their male descendants were blacksmith's and farmers who moved to Kentucky and then to Illinois. I never met any of my father's family, except one of his brother's, because only once, on his honeymoon, did my father return home after he moved west to Kansas and Oklahoma. He had only a high school education and, after working for a brief time in a St. Louis shoe factory, he became a self-trained accountant. After St. Louis he moved to Neodesha, a town of about 3,000 in southeast Kansas where there was a newly discovered oil field, a refinery, and a smelter. There he worked as an accountant in the office of the Granby Mining and Smelting Company and married Bertha Moore, June 9, 1908. It was in May, 1918 that the Arthur Ashley's moved to Blackwell.

Dad was a rather small man, just my own height, 5 foot 6 inches but, unlike me, very athletic, and as old photos show, quite handsome. In spite of his small size he had played football in high school. He was to die back in Neodesha to which he and my mother returned after his retirement. The editor of the Neodesha *Register*, who had known Dad when Dad first lived there wrote an obituary which said,

> Arthur Ashley was a fine man and splendid citizen and he had the goodwill and highest respect of all who knew him. Back in the days when he was employed at the smelter here he was one of Neodesha's top ranking tennis players, a sport that he enjoyed immensely and he participated in many tennis tournaments in those days and won a number of trophies. The publisher of the *Register*, who also played tennis fairly well back in those halcyon days, always had the utmost respect for the skill of Arthur Ashley, who was then the master on the local courts.

When tennis became too strenuous for his mild heart problem, Dad took up golf, and while I was in grade school he played after work every afternoon available. When the weather excluded golf he spent the late afternoons at the local pool hall, where he was very popular with his fellow players.

In spite of his love of sport, however, Dad was no mere "jock." He had an inquiring mind, especially about scientific questions. When he found I had the same curiosity, he brought home from the by-products of the smelter some samples of mercury (we never thought of the possibility of poisoning) and also of the rare element gallium with which to experiment at home. He had a shorthand typewriter like those used by court stenographers, binoculars, a small telescope, and various other gadgets that I played with. As I grew older Dad and I often had lively discussions—"arguments" my mother called them—about current topics, arguments that were extremely stimulating to me.

Dad was hard working, generous with his small income, and he made us a decent, lower-middle class living, but he was never able to get ahead in business. He made small investments in property that had promise of producing oil, but the holes were always dry. Blackwell had its class system, and my mother was bitter about the fact that although my father played golf and went duck shooting with his bosses who found him very convivial, they never voted him in as a member of the local country club to which the town elite belonged.

I owe great gratitude to Dad for all this mental stimulus and for the very real sacrifices he made for me, especially sending me on his low salary in Depression years to college and his evident pride in my scholastic ability and my first efforts to be a writer. Yet my father in one important respect failed me: Dad did not give me the help he had given my six-year older brother in becoming a regular boy. Why he did not seem to realize this, I am not sure. I needed help to learn how to relate to other kids and to engage confidently in boy's sports as Dick did. I even dreaded any situation in which I would have to throw or catch a ball!

I admired and envied the athletes, yet avoided physical effort and felt utterly incompetent in any sport. The nearest I came to participating in school sports was for a brief time to be a member of the high school football "pep team." School provided little in formal physical training until the required high school course in "gym" and I got myself excused from that on the plea that my physician had detected I had a slight heart murmur. I did teach myself to walk on stilts and that effort was an important positive event for me, proof that I could learn physical skills if I really tried, but somehow I did not go on to do more. The result of this incompetence, along with my increasing bookishness, soon led my schoolmates definitively to label me "a sissy," a horrible title that reinforced what it contemptuously condemned.

Mother

Until I recently (see note 6) learned about my father's ancestry, I knew more about my mother's family with which we remained in contact than I did about my father's. One of my mother's sisters, my Aunt Vivian, a red-haired, very social person, belonged to the Masonic Eastern Star. In order also to gain admittance to the Daughters of the American Revolution Aunt Viv did considerable research on our family tree. She was able to dig up the genealogical data that my mother later left me in her own notes. If the Bible gives so much space to listing "begats," no matter how boring, why should I not put down such scattered facts about my origins as I have at hand? I cannot forget that I, like all of us, are part of the great web of human inheritance, of original blessing and of original sin.

Norman Landfair Moore, my maternal grandfather, of the fourth generation of his family in this country from Ireland, was born April 7, 1842, in Blairstown, PA and died December, 17, 1902 at Neodesha, KS.[7] Grandfather Moore was a private in the U.S. Civil War company E, 40th regular Pennsylvania Infantry Volunteers and in Company C, 3rd Regular Reserve Corps, Eleventh Regiment. He first married Lydia Delitha Blocher, March 26, 1868 and had two daughters Laura Elizabeth and Julia, who were always called "Dood" and "Dod," because when they were babies that was the way they pronounced their own names. After Lydia's death Norman married a second wife, Laura Jane Dawson, born July 20, 1858, my grandmother. In all this my only boast is that I had ancestors on both sides who fought in the Revolutionary and Civil Wars.

My maternal grandmother, Norman Moore's second wife, Laura Jane Dawson Moore, was born at Tarr Farm, Westmoreland County, PA, July 20, 1858, died and was buried at Neodesha, KS, Feb. 28, 1926. She married the widower Norman Moore Ashley in 1878 after his service in the Civil War and while he was a superintendent of drilling in the oil fields of Pennsylvania.[8] According to one account he took part in drilling the very first oil well in the U.S.A. at Titusville, PA in 1859. Yet in spite of their relative prosperity in Pennsylvania, the Moore and Dawson families in order to claim Civil War veterans' homesteads moved to Farnum in western Nebraska in 1885. Charity Jane Dawson, my great-grandmother died there Jan 12, 1904. My mother, born near Farnum October, 23, 1886, as the next to youngest of Norman and Laura Jane's children, used to tell me how as a girl she often rode without a saddle to herd their cows, and how, since the Nebraska prairie was almost treeless, she helped collect as fuel buffalo "chips" left by the great herds of bison, then only recently exterminated.

On those dry fields, not yet irrigated, Grandpa Norman Moore failed at farming and moved his family by covered wagon to Neodesha, KS, where he could again work in the oil fields, since the first oil well west of the Mississippi had been drilled there recently. At one time he was also the constable of Neodesha, but his health was poor and the family suffered from real poverty, so that only one daughter, my Aunt May, was able to graduate from high school. My mother left school after the eighth grade (not unusual in those days) and she and May had to go to work on the local newspaper, my mother as a proofreader. Aunt May married a smelter worker and they had three daughters. Mother's other sister, my Aunt Vivian, worked in a candy store and then married a railroad engineer, who was burned to death in a train wreck, leaving her widowed with two children to support by becoming a practical nurse.

Grandpa Moore died in 1902 of a heart attack, but Grandma had his Civil War pension and owned two frame houses on Wisconsin St., Neodesha, in one of which she lived, while renting the other. As a child of ten or so I visited there and remember its old fashioned furnishings, the sofa with lion claw feet, the big kitchen in which most of the living was done, and a parlor for visitors. The toilet was outdoors. It was covered with honeysuckle vines and had a wasps' nest under its eaves.

Two of my uncles, Herbert and Roland, who were twins, became workers in the oil field like their father. The third, Harry, was a clothing store clerk who was drafted in World War I and after his return married a lady, the propriety of whose previous life left my mother and aunts highly suspicious. This marriage failed and Uncle Harry became a Christian Science reader in Wichita, KS where he was to die.

Thus my mother was raised in respectable poverty. Although the Moores had only meager formal education as did most midwesterners at that time, they were intelligent people. I remember Grandmother Moore's visits to us in Blackwell when I was about eleven. She was a frail woman, with wrinkled hands whose soft skin I liked to touch, but she had bulging, staring eyes, the result of a very noticeable goiter. A very gentle lady, who read a great deal, she used to play rummy with me and often let me beat her at that game. Her death in 1928 after a long illness in the farm house of my Aunt Vivian where with my mother I visited her was my first experience of the strange reality of death, as I could hear from her darkened bedroom where she lay in a morphine-induced delirium that she was moaning, "Mamma! Mamma!"

Yet there was a marked division in the Moore family, on the one hand between my redheaded, socializing Aunt Viv, and my three uncles, who were hard drinkers, convivial and extraverted, and on the other hand my Aunt May and Mother who resembled Grandma, rather introverted, withdrawn, and I would now say somewhat neurotic and lacking in self-esteem. I will explain later how this neuroticism affected my mother in married life and through her affected me. I was a big boy before I could cut my own meat at table and always had to let my mother cut it for me. I used to sit on her lap until after I had begun school and I was always very dependent on her for everything. This she never discouraged.

I remember my mother as beautiful and her photos confirm my memory. She had a pleasantly round face, was a little plump, and had soft brown eyes and a lovely smile. I remember how she liked to catch a basin of rainwater so as to have "soft" water with which to wash the great mass of her lustrous, brown hair, which she wore long, late into the flapper age of the 1920s after this was very much out of style. She was always conscious of the poverty in which she had grown up and hated to spend any money on herself. Only once in my childhood, when her envy was aroused by a next door neighbor who was always showing off her new clothes, did Mother go out to purchase some dresses at a department store and those dresses lasted for years. She usually wore only housedresses that she had ordered from a mail catalogue.

While my dad's fundamental outlook was optimistic, my mother, like my Aunt May and Grandma Moore, was a pessimist. Although very friendly to people she met, she avoided meeting strangers, and seldom left the house and the garden where she grew many flowers, except when forced to go to the dentist or doctor, or on a Sunday during the hot Oklahoma summer on cool evening drives with my father and me in the country. The great embarrassment for me was that when other parents attended school or social functions with their kids she would never make an appearance. Either my father had to go with me, or I had to make excuses. Her explanation for this was usually, "I have nothing to wear."

Her absences at school events deeply embarrassed me when I was in the third to fifth grades. Along with being a "sissy," it is the main reason I remember my childhood as unhappy. I believe that at that time my father and mother, without them ever saying anything to my brother and me about it, were avoiding marital relationships. I suppose this was because my mother was afraid of another pregnancy, since mine had been difficult, and contraception was not then much practiced. Since we had only two bedrooms my father slept with my brother, and I with my mother. There was nothing abusive about the situation, but it reflected my mother's anxious state. She also suffered for a year or so with a persistent ulcer on one leg and worried that a harmless lump on her head was cancerous, yet for long would not see a doctor about it.

What affected me most was that it became a pattern of our daily life that my father would be late for supper because he had been playing golf or pool. He never drank and there was never really any doubt about where he was or what he was doing, as my mother ascertained by frequent telephone calls to the golf clubhouse or the pool hall. But if he was late in coming home she always became very anxious, and I shared this exaggerated anxiety with which she seemed unable to cope. At the time I had horrible nightmares, especially of faces looking into the dining room windows out of which we used to peer anxiously into the night to see when Dad was coming home to supper. I became a very anxious child.

Thus I was thrown into panic at school one day at a celestial phenomenon at which both our teachers and the other children merely marveled, the brief appearance of great haloes and "sun dogs" arching the whole sky (I know now they were caused by ice clouds in the stratosphere). I thought it presaged a tornado and demanded that I be allowed to go home. But in half-an-hour the phenomenon disappeared, leaving the sky cloudless. I believe that children need a sense of security more even than they need love, since often they do not yet really understand love, while they do recognize their helplessness.

Yet my childhood sadness does not mean that I did not have many happy moments. Our Christmases and birthdays were joyous, since my father was always very generous with gifts (though he was angry once at my ingratitude because I was loudly disappointed that he had not got me exactly what I wanted). But we always had many toys, especially tinkertoys, construction sets, railroad toys, and painting sets, all of which my parents thought were educational.

Embarrassment overwhelmed me when I was not picked for the school chorus because I did not sing in tune. Neither of my parents was musical but my father bought me a small violin and I took lessons. While I have always loved music, I found myself absolutely without musical talent and spent the required practice time getting drinks of water or inventing other distractions to avoid real work, so the lessons came to nothing. My teacher was a rather strange, embittered man, unmarried, with a bad facial scar, who also played violin in the local cinema where otherwise silent "flickers" were shown. He wanted to hold a little concert with his pupils at which I was to play Gounod's "Ave Maria," but since I could never manage to keep time with his accompaniment, or indeed keep in tune, this never came off, and I dropped further study. Yet my conversations about music with this teacher and my father's purchase of Red Seal Victor records of classical music, Mozart and Verdi, performed by John McCormack, Caruso, Rosa Ponselle, introduced me to a lifelong pleasure only ended recently by my growing deafness.

Religion

Although my father was raised in the Christian Church and my mother in the Methodist Church and although Neodesha and Black-well are in the Bible Belt, after their marriage my parents did not attend any church. My father's favorite book was Darwin's *The Origin of Species*, and he and Mother both felt that the Biblical religion of their youth had been exposed as false by the theory of evolution. They saw the world through H. G. Wells' *Outline of History*, which Mother read aloud to us all. They felt that the religion they had known was for the ignorant and emotionally overwrought and disdained the fundamentalist Protestantism in which they had been raised.

My parent's negative view of religion was confirmed for me also by the example of some neighbors who were enthusiastic "Nazarenes," a charismatic splinter from the Methodists. The daughter of that family, wondrously voluminous, yet called "Dot," was a singing evangelist who vigorously strummed a guitar as she ran through her repertoire of updated hymns such as "Flying to Heaven on the Heavenly Airplane" and "Calling Heaven on the Heavenly Telephone." One of my aunts had told me that at a camp tent revival she herself once heard a hymn, "There Ain't No Flies on Jesus!"

There were not less than thirteen Protestant churches in Blackwell. Only one block north from our house was the Presbyterian Church and a block west the Nazarene Church. On prayer meeting nights at the Nazarenes, when the Spirit was moving, their Pentecostal services could be heard all over the neighborhood. We called them "Holy Rollers" and I was told that in their ecstasies they often used to throw hymnals at each other. When in the fifth grade I read Sinclair Lewis' *Babbitt* and *Elmer Gantry* I thoroughly sympathized with the novelist's scorn of American religion. When my Aunt Viv heard that I was reading such books, she exclaimed, "He's ruined!" No doubt I was.

Nevertheless my unchurched parents also sent my brother and me to Sunday school at the Methodist and Presbyterian Churches as an easily available supplement to the good education they were so determined we should have, but explicitly warned us that it would be up to us when we were grown to choose whatever religion we preferred or none at all. From seven to ten years old I attended whatever Sunday School was handy. After that I never went. I was never baptized nor more than an occasional attendant at the adult services (never at the Lord's Supper which was held infrequently) and hence heard little preaching. At the Presbyterian Church Sunday School I rather liked the hymns, especially the poetical, strange ones, with lines like "Rock of Ages Cleft for Me" or "Holy, Holy, Holy, Lord God Almighty" which to me didn't make much sense and yet were awesome. In summer Bible school I made a carved wooden paper knife and I also received as a prize for memorizing Bible passages on a string of paper cutouts symbolizing texts such as the Beatitudes and the Twenty-Third Psalm. I liked these texts as "literature" which is what my Mother said the Bible was.

Thus my acquaintance with Christianity was not altogether negative. Mother wanted us to be acquainted with Christian traditions and although she did not know enough about other religions to teach us about them, we read from Bullfinch's *Mythology* about Greek, Roman, and Germanic myths. Other favorite books were the folklore of the Brothers Grimm, Andrew Lang's *Green, Blue*, and *Yellow Fairy Books*, and for modern day mythology the *Oz* Books, all of which I devoured.

My mother treated Christianity also as mythical, but at Christmas and Easter she read us the relevant passages of the Bible and showed us pictures by great artists in magazine reproductions illustrating the stories. As a senior in high school I read Virgil's *Aeneid* in Latin (with a translation as a "pony") and Homer's *Iliad* and *Odyssey* in Pope's translation (in college some of the *Iliad* in Greek). One of my fellow students' parents complained to the high school superintendent that the Latin teacher was teaching paganism because Virgil's picture of the underworld did not agree with the Baptist idea of hell.

I took my unsuccessful violin lessons in the basement of the Methodist church. I loved to linger in the main auditorium looking at the stained glass windows that, though of little artistic merit, were radiant in the morning light. My impression of Methodism was that it made much of hymn singing, led by unctuous laymen with bawling voices. As I have already noted, I heard few sermons, but once in the summer Bible School the pastor came and explained to us the doctrine of "vicarious atonement," that somebody had to pay God back for our defying His authority and breaking His laws, so Jesus, God's son, paid this price on the Cross for us sinners. This seemed very logical to me and I remember explaining it—I have always been given to explaining things to others whom I regard as less well informed than myself—to another boy my age who did not seem much interested, but did not believe it myself.

Yet looking back on this time I believe I may have had some kind of inchoate faith in Jesus, although when I related this incident to Mother she did not seem to approve of my preaching. "Yes," she said, "Jesus was a good man." She did, however, teach my brother and me to say night prayers, "Now I lay me down to sleep, I pray the Lord my soul to keep." For her, this was just part of a proper education.

Chapter 2 - Insecurity

High School

As I got to my high school years, however, I was searching for some deeper security. Today the enlightened put down religion by saying that believers are "just looking for security" as if that were a weakness. Sociobiologists also argue that religion originated in animal anxiety. Of course that might mean that science also originated in the sniffing of bushes by dogs. Fulsome praise is bestowed on atheists courageous enough to "live with ambiguity and risk." Yet moderns seem to me engaged in a frantic search for the security of money, of good health, of psychiatric peace of mind. Without our feet on a secure rock nothing we humans attain in this life can be called true happiness since it is indeed ambiguous and always gravely at risk. We may try to live in the now, but the good now floats on the bad now and dread poisons the happy present. I am not ashamed of seeking fundamental security, as I did as a child, provided that it is not self-delusion. To deny that this is possible is to despair too soon.

One neurotic way I sought security was systematically to try to deny my fears. In those times of anxious waiting for Dad to come home and at other times when one of us was sick, I used to try to take a nap so as not to have to think about my fears. But the very effort to sleep kept me awake or nightmares woke me again. Later I developed some strange rituals to calm anxiety, for example, I had a habit of looking in turn at the four corners of the ceiling of any room I was in. Why that made me less anxious I don't know. My mother complained at this odd ritual and I tried to conceal it.

When I was 12 or 13 I also spent an inordinate amount of time walking up and down in the garden back of our house bouncing a golf ball on the cement walk while I engaged in a kind of meditation about the cosmos. These musings were oddly metaphysical and, believe it or not, concerned the problem of the One and the Many. They settled on a conclusion, not unlike the Buddhist doctrine of the Void, that everything we experience is simply a superficial aspect of an ultimate One that is beyond all naming and of which we are just parts. Later, when in high school I read about Spinoza in Will Durant's *The Story of Philosophy* I recognized the similarity of this so-called "God-intoxicated" thinker's views—and those of Einstein who declared himself a Spinozist—to my own vague musings.

One day in the high school library I read Plato's dialogue, the *Phaedrus*. Its sublime description of the ascent of the soul by love to the vision of the One and Good awakened in me an intuition that the One transcending the Many is not a Void, but is the True and Good and Beautiful. Wise Plato! What I owe him! At the time this insight that I had gained from Plato only seemed poetry rather than real truth, but it remained with me as a taste for the transcendent that made me discontent with lesser joy.

In those days no one seemed to question that a bleakly non-denominational Protestant ethos ought to dominate the Blackwell public schools. The teachers had to sign contracts by which they promised not to dance, drink, smoke, or play cards, and to attend some church regularly. I discovered to my amazement, however, that actually my one-eyed Latin teacher, Miss K., smoked and entertained men in her apartment and that a pious English teacher Miss J. was dating one of her students. Every day school started with a brief Bible reading, King James Version, and weekly there was a non-denominational "chapel service" at which various Protestant pastors preached somewhat innocuous sermons.

Once on such an occasion Pastor T. of the Christian Church took time to talk with me. When he found that I listened regularly on Saturday afternoons to the Metropolitan Opera radio broadcasts he invited me to his home to hear his records of Wagner's *Parsifal*. I eagerly went to listen and a real friendship seemed in the making until someone told me that at a "revival" service, Pastor T., for all the theological liberalism he had showed in our private conversations, had publicly applauded the attacks on biblical historical-criticism by the presiding evangelist who was a fundamentalist. Then I decided Pastor T. was a hypocrite and visited him no more. A redheaded, freckled, bullying, Baptist schoolmate, recently "reborn," also tried to save my soul and I laughed indignantly at his well-meant but intrusive efforts.

My contact in Blackwell with the Catholic Church was minimal. Few Catholics lived in our town, mainly Poles who worked at the smelter. Their priest came from Tonkawa, some ten miles away, to say Mass occasionally at a poor little white frame church "back of the tracks" with a cross on top, a feature then absent from all the Protestant churches as too papist. The Ku Klux Klan in Blackwell carried on a campaign to make the town "100% American" and to get Catholics fired from their jobs. But one girl I admired was Catholic and she gave me some Catholic literature. I was curious about it simply because it was counter to the prevailing Protestantism. I also was deeply moved at hearing at school the girls' glee club practice a number prescribed for a statewide singing contest at which they were soon to perform. It was Arcadelt's lovely, polyphonic *Ave Maria*. The budding girls in their white dresses, their sweet voices, and the fact that it was in Latin, which I took so much pride in studying, all deeply imprinted this angelic image in my heart. So I thought of the Catholic religion as somehow older and richer (but of course utterly more superstitious) than Protestantism.

On the other hand I felt then and, for all my ecumenism, still feel repelled by the wordiness and bleakness of so much Protestant worship, and the few samples of aggressive evangelism that I ran into. I found many Protestant ministers and unctuous laymen somehow grotesque, like the characters in Flannery O'Connor's stories that I read later. It was all part of the crudity, drabness, and general cultural impoverishment of Blackwell that I more and more resented the older I got.

I believe it was in my sophomore year in high school that I wrote an essay on "Pericles" which won a history prize. It confidently concluded:[9]

> The zenith of Greek culture is called Pericles' age and "Periclean" is an adjective which indicates the finest of Greek attributes. John Stuart Mill in contrasting the Calvinist with the Greek conception of life says: "It may be better to be a John Knox than an Alcibiades, but it is better to be a Pericles than either; nor would Pericles, if we had one in these days, be without anything good which belonged to John Knox."

Morality

My parents were never severe with us or rigid about moral matters, but I absorbed not a few of my mother's inhibitions. I have related how at about four or five I briefly became conscious of myself as a person. I do not remember at what point this self-consciousness became a genuine moral consciousness, anything more than an animal sense of shame or approval.

The great medieval theologian St. Thomas Aquinas held that in a child's very first truly human act, possible perhaps at about six or seven years of age, the child implicitly chooses as its ultimate goal or highest priority in life either what its intelligent conscience sees as its really highest good, or instead foolishly chooses some good whose attraction is immediate but which the child's reason warns is of lesser value. If we do in fact choose the highest good of which we know, then, as Aquinas argues,[10] we are implicitly choosing God the truly highest Good, although we may be ignorant of who or what God is. God created us good and hence by nature we tend to make this good and reasonable choice, but original sin and the sins of the entire historical world into which we are born pressure us to a foolish choice as our self-centered, autonomous good. Hence, for the child in its first act to choose wisely, Aquinas says, is possible only by God's grace won for all humanity by Jesus Christ. To put it more simply, the first human act of a child may seem trivial but it starts the child in the right direction or the wrong one. Only God can move it onto the right path.

The Catholic doctrine of original sin does not attribute the whole present burden of human failure simply to the two First Parents, but also to the accumulating defects of all their descendants which cripples each of us from the moment of our conception and throughout our lives. But our ancestors also transmitted to us the original blessings of creation and even of grace; however weakened they may now be by the effects of sin. I have already described something of the effects of original sin in the failings of my dear parents, and suggested that this was in turn a reflection of the failings of my grandparents. So on back to the very beginning of human history perhaps 200,000 years ago, the accumulated failings of the human family have shortchanged every child coming into this world of the fullness of the heritage God had intended for each of us in our journey to him. At this time I knew little or nothing of that theological explanation for what I was experiencing very vividly. My father's failing to help me become self-confidently male and my mother's infecting me with anxiety, panic, and denial of what I feared, and the excessive dependency on her that she encouraged had made me very timid. I was ashamed of being a sissy and yet too afraid to take the risks that would have helped me out of this condition. Above all the eclipse of God in my parents' lives by the inadequacy of their Protestant faith to meet Darwinism cut me off from a Christian heritage.

Yet there were so many positive things in my parents' love for me and in the rich cultural heritage I was acquiring through literature, art and nature that it is now evident to me that God's grace was already drawing me toward him. While I do not clearly recall

what my early state of conscience was, there are many events in my
memory which seem to signify that early on I chose as my goal in
life not the highest of the good things known to me but my own very
limited self. I guess I anxiously and timidly accepted the narcissism
that marks my whole temperament.

My ambition to be a writer, a poet, that I began to feel even
before high school, certainly showed that the glory of God radiating
in my parents' love, in the beauty of nature, art and literature to
which I was sensitive was moving me toward God. Yet this movement was deflected by my fears and by my choice to write poetry
that was no more than self-expression. That is why so much of my
poetry took on a decadent, self-pitying tone. While my parents were
good people and their intellectual and moral values were high, reflecting their Christian background and their reading of classical
literature, yet they did little to prepare me for the problems of pu-
berty.

As I have already recounted, in my first years at school the girls
thought I was "cute" and because of my fear of sports I often played
with them at "recess," as play time was called at school. As I grew I
was attracted to certain girls I thought pretty and somehow I was
especially drawn to girls with nice names such as "Ione" and "Myr-
na." But by junior high I began to find that they preferred the more
aggressive and athletic boys. I began to suffer from jealousy and an
even greater feeling of inferiority. I tried to be what kids today call
"cool" in the presence of girls, but it didn't seem to work.

At that time a boy was not likely to discuss such matters with
his parents and schools then did not provide counselors. I was
essentially very much alone in confronting my sexuality. Today,
every writer of a memoir is determined to spare his audience nothing with regards to his or her sex life. Whether it is a confession or
mere braggadocio it has to be explicit and disgustingly detailed. I
too feel compelled to be explicit on this point for several reasons,
but mainly because I feel that after Freud and Jung a discussion of
one's religious development cannot escape this scrutiny.

What I have to narrate about my "sex life" at various points in
this memoir may not be very interesting. Some may think me dishonest. Since one of the chief features of my personality is narcissism, it is evident that I feel a considerable compulsion to look at
myself in the mirror of these pages. This narcissism urges me to
self-exposure and to that extent I cannot feel that what I will put

down is entirely objective and yet I will make an effort to be flatly honest. Only if I manage to be honest, will I feel that I have a right in our times and culture to write about other matters with genuine self-revelation. I will not, however, wallow in details, but only state the essential facts.

During my adolescence my parents never talked to me about sexuality, but they gave me a book entitled, *What Every Boy Should Know*. I read it avidly but didn't quite know what it was talking about. I was very curious, but somehow afraid to ask my parents what it meant. Then a schoolmate one day dramatized in gesture what he called "jacking off" and when I got home I tried it and was amazed at the results. Thus from about the age of twelve until my conversion to Catholicism I became addicted to masturbation and experimented with its various forms. I also constantly indulged in a great variety of not very well informed sexual fantasies. At first I was frightened about all this and tried to limit the times I indulged, but found myself more and more unable to restrain myself. My parents inquired why I was spending so much time in the bathroom. After that I found less noticeable occasions for my activities. By college I accepted it not as something to be proud of or publicized, but as a normal part of life and I engaged in it almost every day. I did not think of it in a religious context.

Those psychologists and misguided theologians who today say that masturbation does no harm and is a normal way that children learn about their sexuality are, in my experience as a confessor and my opinion as a moralist and theologian, wretchedly mistaken. The wisdom of Judaism and of the Christian Church has always rightly taught that such behavior, far from teaching us why God created us to be sexual, addicts victims to a depersonalized search for satisfaction in sex objects rather than opening them to the personal relations of fruitful, married love. It builds a compulsive barrier, difficult to break through, to genuine sexual fulfillment. Recently an important expert in addictive behavior told me that from his extensive clinical experience he suspected that masturbation is the most common way that the so-called "addictive personality" that later manifests itself in chemical and other dependencies is produced. This easy way of coping with life's frustrations by its subsequent feelings of shame generates the addictive cycle. Hence I believe that to resist or overcome self-abuse is a special test of true manhood. It is also my opinion that the oppression of women which feminists lament is largely the result of the way males by their addiction to masturbation learn in adolescence to regard woman as mere objects. While it is not helpful in counseling adolescents to overemphasize their responsibility and guilt, rather than arouse their courage to overcome such harmful habits as the use of drugs, masturbation, and promiscuous sex; nevertheless, they should be shown unambiguously why these are harmful and to be valiantly resisted.

I was particularly curious about my now dead brother Richard's dating when he was in high school. In fact he was involved in a "fast" crowd of students. After too much Prohibition drinking, one night on a date my brother crashed the already obsolescent family car. In the summer of 1931 after enrolling in Oklahoma A&M in Stillwater for a B.Sc. degree in oil geology, without my parents knowledge he married Helen Marie Beal, a telephone operator in Blackwell, and kept it secret until he had finished college. My parents were deeply disappointed at his lack of trust in them and wished he could have married a girl with a college education, but they patiently accepted Helen as his own choice as later they were to accept my ordination to the priesthood as my choice.

My moral problems, however, did not concern only sex. I was shocked sometimes at myself to find how angry I could be with others, how stubborn or ungrateful with my parents, how I could cheat occasionally in school, or how selfish and self-centered I could be. But undoubtedly my worst fault in those days was cowardice. While I have already related how rightfully proud I was of myself once when by my own efforts and after repeated trials I learned to walk on stilts, my general way of coping with difficulties was to avoid them. More than anything else it was this giving in to fears that prevented me from learning to relate well to other boys of my own age and to take part in their sports.

My guide, as for many of my generation, to a better self-understanding became Sigmund Freud's *The Interpretation of Dreams* and his *Introductory Lectures to Psychoanalysis* that caught my eye in the library when I was in the fifth or sixth grade. I did not know at first who Freud was, but his theories shaped my thinking in a very fundamental way and I tried, but not with much success, to find out about myself through my dreams. Today the unscientific character of Freud's theories and his dishonesty in reporting his clinical experiences are shockingly exposed, but I then took them as "cutting-edge" discoveries.

The preoccupation with my own body that Freudianism encouraged was also reflected in my artistic efforts stimulated by reading a book on art history. In my fantasy the typical figure became a Greek pastoral scene of a naked youth playing on a flute. Although I did many drawings of nude women, the male physique in Greek sculpture became a preoccupation. My adolescence was very bookish, with a rich fantasy life, a great interest in music and art (at which I dabbled) and in high school an involved relation that I will soon describe with a girl who shared my interest in literature. The rest of my interest in girls tended to be from the sideline where I felt very awkward and inadequate because I was no good in sports and was shy about typical high school activities.

A lot of my life was turned inward and was very autoerotic, accompanied with much anxiety and guilt of a very vague sort. I was not troubled about "morals" as such, not having had any particular standards to refer to, since my reading convinced me that for an educated person conventional morality is obsolete. Rather my anxiety was about a general sense of the perils of the world and my incapacity to cope with practical situations or to achieve any acceptance by my peers. I also had spells of hypochondria. In the fifth grade I began to have trouble reading the blackboard and after I was tortured with this for some time my parents sent me to an optician. He found me to be quite myopic and I had to put on glasses. The myopia continued to progress and there were periodic crises when I had to have a change of glasses and each time wondered if I was going blind.

Poetry

From the earliest years I was fascinated by symbolism. I had an invisible, beloved playmate named "Prune" whom I imagined as small, black, and wrinkled, and on whom I blamed many of my own mistakes. I played with dolls to a later age than is usual with boys and especially with a stuffed bear who even in my high school years sat on my bed. I was fascinated by the account in Louise May Alcott's novel *Little Men* (her sequel to the more famous *Little Women* which I also read many times) of how a bright young boy and his sister together performed a sacrifice of a doll "to propitiate the gods" and I tried to imitate them. I have already mentioned my interest in mythology, which I studied avidly, as I did astrology, and every sort of intricate symbolism and magical rite that I could read about.

I also loved the theater (although in Blackwell I had little opportunity to experience it) and the movies. I was chosen in a grade
school play to emerge from a giant bottle as the Wizard of Milk to
encourage everyone to drink plenty. When I read that Goethe as a
boy had a toy theater, I made one from a packing box in which dolls
were actors and I lighted it with small Christmas tree lights. How
magical the red and blue light seemed to me! Later in high school I
designed scenery for plays, of which my masterpiece was the scenery and costumes for Gilbert and Sullivan's *The Mikado.* Thus the
realm of the symbolic by which I had entrance to a wider world than
Blackwell enchanted me. That is why, I believe, my meager contact
with Catholicism and its sacramentalism led me to a favorable view
of the Catholic Church. I saw Catholics as an exotic oppressed minority, and I was for all oppressed minorities, especially Negroes,
Jews, and Catholics, because I felt the people among whom I lived
were ignorant, cruel, bullying bigots.

My parents had left it up to my brother and me to choose our
own religion and our goal in life. Every life is a journey and a journey needs a goal. To be an adventure that goal must be a promise
whose fulfillment is a mystery. I have had two very different goals in
the adventure of my life. The first, whose outlines emerged only
slowly until I was twenty-three, was to be a poet. The second was to
be a Christian, a Dominican, and a priest. The second need not have
erased the first, but it has left little time or energy to practice it. The
great challenge now, however, in this memoir is to make my life interesting to the reader. That is the task of a poet, to reveal within
the humdrum the mystery of an adventure. So at last, while remaining, as I pray God I will, on the road to being a good priest, living for
others and not just for myself, I am returning here to the poetic,
narrative task that I first chose. Perhaps in trying to find the poetry
in my prosaic life, I will see my path as priest more clearly to the
end and, I pray, give patient readers some sense of the mystery that
works in the lives of every one of us wandering creatures.

I had been slow to learn the alphabet and I really did not understand what we were doing in the first grade as we learned to recognize words and read simple sentences. My mother continued to read
to me, often at bedtime. One night while she was reading a story, I
looked at the book and discovered to my amazement that I could
read the story all by myself. From then on books became the bigger
part of my life.

What was really remarkable about my parents was that in spite of their meager education they were great readers and strongly encouraged us to read. My father purchased a children's encyclopedia, *A Wonder Book* and then the eleventh edition of the *Encyclopedia Britannica* and the complete set of the *Harvard Classics*. Our family frequently consulted the encyclopedias to settle "arguments" and I browsed them avidly for all kinds of random information. This was long before television. We had a radio, but almost every evening my mother read aloud (and she read very well) from the *Harvard Classics* or some other very serious piece of literature. After I went to college she was still reading in bed to my father such works as Sigrid Undset's *Kristin Lavransdatter*.

This contributed to my bookish isolation, but it also opened to me the whole range of culture. Blackwell was about as much a cultural center as Sinclair Lewis's Gopher Prairie. But the public library, presided over by an uneducated lady, Mrs. P., the town gossip who became my friend and who encouraged my greedy reading, was amazingly well stocked. It was said that Mrs. P. was an easy victim of traveling booksellers who unloaded expensive items on her. Whether this was true or not, she bought many good books. For example she had a fine edition of John Ruskin's *Modern Painters* which I perused with delight, and many other works on the arts and literature.

In junior high school my English teacher, Miss Eva Young, on whom I had a "crush," introduced us to George Eliot's *Silas Marner*, and soon I began to read all of Eliot, who, for all her grim Victorian moralism, became my favorite novelist. Miss Young made *Silas Marner*, so often a bore to teenagers, an interesting story and showed me how to appreciate the novelist's craft. Compared with what many students get today, Blackwell High School then had a very solid curriculum. I had four years of English, ancient and modern history, physics, chemistry, and four years of Latin. Our Latin teacher, Miss K., unlike the attractive blonde Miss Young, was a stringy lady, with only one good eye, a sharp wit, and for Blackwell, as I have mentioned before, unconventional ideas and behavior. Until their recent deaths I exchanged Christmas cards every year with these two dear teachers.

By the time I was twelve or so my time out of school was spent reading or in attempts at "art." I learned to make little statues in clay and to make soap carvings. I learned a great deal about sculpture from a book by someone named Powers on the history of Greek art, and when I was about twelve I did a small statute of Pallas Athena. When I took it to school, one of my teachers said to another in my hearing, "He's a genius!" I began to think so myself. My efforts at painting and modeling were crude and unoriginal, only a bit better than my attempts at the violin, but I was learning a real feeling for good art. Our school provided very little help, but my parents were able to afford a few lessons in oil painting from a very nice lady who used to touch up my efforts between lessons without saying anything about it, although of course I recognized what she was doing and resented it. To really advance in these arts I would have needed better instruction. The only "real" paintings I saw before I went to college were in a hotel in a tiny place in northeastern Oklahoma called Kaw City that housed the collection of an oil-rich lady.[11] She had been sometimes victimized, I fear, by less than conscientious art dealers. But her collection did include, besides an enormous, technically impressive painting of "Jesus Preaching to the Crowds" by some mid-nineteenth century German painter, a number of landscapes by Thomas Moran (1837-1926) and two or three very fine landscapes by Ralph A. Blakelock (1847-1919),[12] as well as a wonderfully sleek peasant girl by the French academic painter William-Adolphe Bougereau (1825-1905). I stood entranced. I also went to the movies weekly and so I knew the great film stars of those days and was enchanted with Norma Shearer, Greta Garbo, Helen Hays, Bette Davis, Charles Laughton, Lon Chaney, and Cary Grant. Today as I see these old timers on the TV late movie I am again enthralled.

As a sophomore in high school I really discovered poetry and with it an appreciation of the wonder of words, of style in writing and I began to write poetry myself. Here I had more talent and was able from my reading to get better instruction. My first real appreciation of what poetry can do came when I memorized Keats' haunting "Ode to a Nightingale." I have only heard that bird on records, but I think our southern mockingbird far surpasses it in the variety of his song. A magical moment for me was lying in bed on a moonlit summer night listening to one of these virtuosos in the mulberry hedge behind our house running through his repertoire and then hearing the calls echoed by another mockingbird in the distance and then echoed by another still further on. To me the world began to seem like a succession of vivid impressions, such as in this poem

that emerged from finding wild plums one evening during a drive in
the countryside bordering the outskirts of my little town.

WILD PLUMS

Down the canyon the dark is seeping,
through the wild plumes it's tartly creeping
down among the lilacs weeping
under the leaves of the sycamore tree

Lights up and across the Marie Hotel
lights coming up above on the hill
a gulf of light around the Sunken Bell
under the sputtering neon Three.

The jet-winged beetle clips the dusk,
the corn silk whitens in the husk,
and the snapdragon clings to a bee.

See how the corners glimmer in the smoke.
O star, how the fireflies glitter!
As the car starting backfires, the spark!
Down in the yuccas the green moths flitter,
the nightjar booms in the trembling sky,
up to their lofty house the martins fly.
The car grinds in and in they crowd
up around in a long black cloud.
The dew drips out of the lily,
flitter and glitter down in the lily
on summer nights it bangs so loud,
glimmer over the lily,
Over the lily, O Star!

The light goes curving down around the long glass bar
wine, women, song,
(but really beer not wine)
look at how the glasses shine
down the long glass bar.

Orange and fire in the west grow pale
and the fish in the creek and the mossy snail

drowse under ripples silverly,
juice dripping purple sweet from the mulberry tree.

To You Bottoms Up and So to Me

Unto thee, O maiden,
wild plum blossoms,
my long sweet song of even,
my long sweet song
sang the mocking bird to the evening star,
Venus glowing in the west afar,
even to me, someday.

I also memorized the "Ode to the Grecian Urn" and much of "St. Agnes Eve," and of course FitzGerald's *Rubaiyat* of Omar Khayyam. Oscar Wilde's *Salomé* also me gave me a taste for decadence. I had learned to type and I began turning out a good deal of verse. Before this I had no clear sense of a goal in life except to enjoy myself in the color, sound, taste, smell of the world and my activities of reading, playacting, and efforts at painting and sculpture.

My troubled energies now focused on the ambition to be a writer, especially a poet, and to become an English teacher so that I could write. By my senior year in high school I was getting acquainted with experimentalism and modernism in literature and with cubism and abstractionism in modern art. I was particularly impressed by what I read of Amy Lowell and the promotion of "imagism" deriving from her passion for Keats and Alexander Pope and also by the works of T. S. Eliot. I had only scorn for conventional types of poetry.

My own poetry was not very experimental, but when in my senior year in high school I began to write a novel it was not only in prose, but also, like this memoir, partly in poetry. In it I managed to express the question of sexual identity that was troubling me, largely I now believe because of the fixation of my psychological development in masturbation. The novel was about the experiences of three high school students, Steve, Carla, and a third boy whose name I do not remember now, no doubt because he was myself, so I will call him Winston. Winston is in love with Carla, but he knows she is in love with Steve, who is the school hero because he is the champion wrestler (this gave me an opportunity to describe his fine physique to which I felt so inferior, as I had also praised Carla's beauty). Just before the novel ends Steve is killed in a motor accident. This had in fact recently happened to a popular high school student, the brother of Miss Young. I attended his funeral, my second experience of death after that of my grandmother, and closer to home because he was of my own age). A question is left at the novel's end, will Winston now get Carla?

This simple story was elaborated with much description of Oklahoma scenery and small-town life and its climax was a fantastic account of a Halloween incident in which the "weirdness" felt by Winston in his ambiguous position in the triangle was surrealistically dramatized. Later I will recount the criticism of Gertrude Stein when Thornton Wilder showed her the manuscript of this novel. When I later entered the novitiate I destroyed the manuscript as too expressive of my life before baptism. A poem that reflects the theme of the novel, my loneliness in Blackwell, was later published:

A DANCE LAST NIGHT NEXT DOOR

> When they call all night coming and leaving
> with sharp closing of car doors and shouts
> and unseen dispersals, I hear them
> as I sit alone or lie near sleep
> between flatness and dreaming, I can tell
> they stand there by the lilacs.
> Two fellows swearing, drinking, noising.
> At the gateway a fellow with a girl—low talking,
> when she laughed it was lovely,
> lovely as the way she must be standing
> curved in the dark, leaning against the gatepost,
> the whole bunch of them milling bunched
> with a concourse of swift sounds on the pebbles—
> all their calling.
> In here shines the moon, shines low,
> straight through the room and up against the door
> ajar and windy.

Ruth

My shyness and sense of inferiority held me back from dating, but I did form one important friendship with a girl. I became the valedictorian of the high school senior class, but for three years my rival had been a girl whom I will call Ruth. She came from a very poor family and was decidedly homely, with thick ankles, a heavy figure, and a coarse face. Beauty was paramount in my romantic thinking. Moreover, I was a snob. My parents, in spite of their lack of formal education and the fact that my father's employment and income put us well below the elite of Blackwell society, looked down on manual workers (except for farmers who owned land) as "common." They would never have been less than polite to such people, but they thought our standards of life were higher and should be maintained. That is why my parents had been so saddened by my brother's clandestine marriage to a girl who was a telephone operator and from a laboring family. I have wondered if my mother ever realized that it was her own refusal to enter into ordinary social relations that failed to facilitate my brother's meeting girls who would have been more acceptable to her.

Ruth and I formed a close friendship based on our common interest in writing. Although she had some talent, she soon acknowledged what we considered my superiority at poetry. She herself had tried to free herself from her situation of poverty by getting a job at the local newspaper and moving into an apartment. There I visited her every week and we spent hours of conversation and discussion mostly about my writing, very little about hers. When I look back on it, I wonder that my long visits in her apartment without a chaperone did not cause scandal in that small town. But it never went so far as even a kiss. For me she was just too little like my notion of feminine beauty and in any case I would have been too fearful and naive to make any advances, though we read very romantic stuff together. I avoided being seen in public with her and she asked me once or twice why I never took her anywhere. To this timid inquiry I made lying excuses.

Later, when I was in college, Ruth wrote me she had moved to another newspaper job in Oklahoma City, that she had an affair with a crude fellow, a friend of her poor family, that she had a botched abortion and almost died. After that I ceased communication with her and later heard she had died in middle age. Looking back I confess the cruelty and self-centeredness of my treatment of her. I made other tentative efforts to get a girl friend of whom I could be proud, but the fact that I had not learned to drive my Dad's car, and that I didn't know how to dance frustrated all that. All I could do was talk and I didn't have the knack of the kind of conversation current among teenagers then.

I knew that some of the other fellows were "sexually active," as we say today. The "Sexual Revolution" took place not after World War II but in the wake of World War I, as is evident from the famous song of the period "How Can You Keep Them Down on the Farm, After They've Seen Paree?" Among the best-sellers of the day were *The Vanishing Virgin* and Judge Lindsay's *Companionate Marriage*, which was later called "trial marriage," and now frankly "cohabitation." The main factor in this revolution, I believe, was that with the 1920s family automobiles became common so that now young people no longer met each other at home under the surveillance of their parents. In the auto they could easily escape them to go to the movies, perhaps in another town, to a dance hall, or to park and "pet" in a secluded spot. My novel described some of this but I never got very far in engaging in such experiments. I heard the boys discussing condoms and in our high school teenage pregnancies occurred but were very rare and never, it seemed, happened to really nice girls.

I had two other good friends, Loyd M., who also liked books but of whom I have little other recollection, and a closer friend, Irvin Frankel, a Jewish boy from one of the very few Jewish families in Blackwell. Our town prided itself on being "lily-white" since in those days the only African-Americans were the family of a man who was a protected federal employee in the post office. There were not even many Native Americans in town, although only a few miles distant there were Indian reservations, surviving from the days when all of Oklahoma was assigned to the displaced "Five Civilized Tribes." Irvin was a smart and friendly lad, rather immature looking, whose father ran a clothing store that failed in the Depression. My Dad remarked, "He is the only Jew I ever heard of who failed in business!" After graduating from high school Irvin got an appointment to Annapolis and returned for a summer visit to be admired in his naval uniform. After that I never saw him again and I believe he was killed in World War II. We were good friends and had much in common, but again I felt somewhat ashamed that my best friend was only tolerated in Blackwell society. Ruth, Irvin, and I were rivals to be valedictorian of our senior class. I beat them both, although Irvin graduated at 15, while I was already 18. I should note, however, that both my parents taught us that racial prejudice was ignorant and stupid. I had many arguments with Ruth about that, because although in my eyes her family was "white-trash," she shared their belief in white supremacy.

By the time I finished high school, as a result of my reading I was an atheist. In fact my atheism, as I suspect is the case with most declared atheists, was actually a kind of Spinozan pantheism in which God and Nature were simply aspects of one reality, the result of my early meditations about the One and the Many, and based on scientific materialism. Yet I still had my Platonic bent toward transcendentalism. Morally, however, I was a determinist and believed that our unconscious mind and social circumstances make our actions inevitable. I liked to say to myself *che sarà, sarà,* "What will be, will be," and to resign myself to a sort of Stoic passivity to the events that made me anxious, a good example of an illusory security. Mine was essentially a passive attitude toward life and experience, a tendency to receive impressions without the courage to respond to them by significant actions. Even my ambition to be a poet that was my deepest goal was not something I strove for with a driving ambition. I wrote only because I felt like it and it was the activity of which I was most proud. Along with the two poems already quoted the following three of lyrics will give an idea of what I was trying to do in the Oklahoma imagery then familiar to me.

CYNTHY DINE

The sphinx moths whir
sunk in the lilies
down in the field hollow.
Like still water
the cottonwood's sound.

Here in Dine's garden
dim lily stems rubbing together
gathered together.
A white hand among the lilies
breaks them,
gathering
stalk and stalk.
A girl breaking lily stems gathering big lilies.
It is shadowy here.

Tall by the fence there she stands looking
against the long sky bright still, looking
by the fence where tall sunflowers
hang against the long west
so still.
Throws back her head, her hair shadow falls
on her white collar. A voice calls
down at the house. She is tall,
touching the hairy sunflowers, looks up
to them. Mother calls,
"Cynthy! Cynthy!"
and Cynthy goes, brushing through grasses,
stumbles on a stone, runs down the dark yard
and, the door opening, light falls behind her
through the picket fence.

Black sunflowers hang against the west,
tall against the cool yellow west.

A DREAM BEFORE SLEEPING

She came slowly out
from the black, level, burned-out west,
carrying a child, its head on her breast,
her feet bare, her head bent.
Walking slowly she came, slowly she went.
The child did not wake.

I leaned sleepily against a crumbling clod
and thought of God
and the way the ripe grain is a sea,
rippling, brightened perpetually
in the dry wind,
until I slept
and all that night no other came,
though the moon
was unwavering bright,
a flame stillborn.

THE CURLICUE HOUSE

Near the edge of the town of Stancher the white house,
remember the frame one with its elms and the lilacs,
a farm house before there was a town,
now where the fields were,
beyond there the lights of an oil well and its chug-chug,
that house, remember?

Jigsaw curlicues,
scrolls and flutes
spools

that house, that shines whitely, lowly,
whitely long between the boles
of the elms

jigsawed shadows
soft scrollings, deeper flutes
silver spools

The brick wall here has sunken little graves of shadow.
The iron fence invisibly pit-pats the trailing hand
with its close even railing, the gates ajar.
Low talk of evening, perpetual slouching on the veranda,
hidden glow of pipes,
down here the sickly, lively glows of many lightning bugs
shining, gathering denser deeper here in the dampness of
the lilacs,
glimmering, wreathed entwining on this dark gentle spray
flick, sway.
There is laughing where the kids are running.
her white small dress.
They're catching the bugs, the glows
to bottle them in fruit jars
for lanterns, at the bottom of the jars
the layer of spent, desperate, sickly stars,
laughing and grabbing at the flicking shower disappearing,
Joe and May.
Way beyond, you keep hearing

deeper than the locusts' screech
the oil wells.
chug-chug,
you do not hear what the men pipe-smoking
on the veranda say,
Joe and May.

The white house in moonlight with the black elms.
Remember?

Transition

In my senior year of high school the problem of my further education became critical, though in those days there was not so much early planning for college as now. My brother had worked at various odd jobs during his high school years. Overdependent as I was, I had never done so, and had saved no money. It was the time of the Great Depression and since the smelter was closed down, Dad was supporting us by working as a night watchman at its silent buildings. It looked like I might not be able to go to college at all, or at the best to the University of Oklahoma at Norman where the tuition was then nominal. I began inquiring about the possibility of getting a loan (there were no government student loans available then), when someone pointed out to me that the University of Chicago gave scholarships nationally on a competitive basis. I had never heard of the University of Chicago.

The following is a notice in the local paper that I suspect was the work of my reporter friend Ruth. She more than generously sums up my high school career and my good fortune.

Winston Ashley, son of Mr. and Mrs. A. B. Ashley, 1202 West Oklahoma, who graduated from Blackwell high school with a scholastic average of 96.6 out of a possible 97, the highest ever attained by any student enrolled in the school is preparing to leave about Sept 21 [1933] to enter Chicago University. Ashley won one of the 30 scholarships annually offered by this institution in competitive examination with students all over the United States. Out of a selected list, he chose the subjects, Latin, English and history, for his examination and received the scholarship upon the merit of his rating in three objective tests covering the subject.

His instruction in these courses was received at the local high school and consisted of four years of English, four years of Latin and two years of ancient, medieval and American history. When a sophomore Ashley won first place at Norman in a competitive examination upon ancient and medieval history among students all over the state. He also was valedictorian of the class of 1933 graduating from the local high school.

In addition to his scholastic achievements, Ashley has given valuable assistance in painting the scenery for various junior high and high school dramatic projects. He designed and painted all the costumes for the opera, "Machado," [sic!] launched last year by the high school glee club, besides arranging the sets and acting as property manager. He also played important roles in the junior and senior plays of the last two years.

Ashley has expressed his intention of specializing in the subjects of science and literature at the university. "I am expecting to promptly slide into the role of a complete nonentity at Chicago," he says. "It'll probably be just one big mass of people, with no emphasis at all upon the individual."

That last sentence correctly expressed my fears. After all, I had been away from home overnight only once in my life when I went to Norman to get a history prize (I still have the little medal) and I had never been in a city larger than Tulsa or Wichita. Even on the morning I left home on the train I was hesitating and required the gentle urging of my parents. Mother said, "Winston, if you get lost, ask a policeman."

Chapter 3 - Grey Towers: Blue Lake

The University of Chicago

The train trip to Wild Onion Place (Ojibwa she-kag-ong), that is, Chicago, in October, 1933, was for me hours of fitful sleep by coach, stopping, starting again and again and then lights flashing by. I awoke to daylight in Peoria. Then came the slow, halting passage through the great Wild Onion City into the old Twelfth Street Station with bums sleeping on benches. The taxi turned onto the Outer Drive with its tattered rags of autumn foliage, a gray-blue Lake Michigan beyond. There on the lakeside where Meig's Field is today loomed the World's Fair, which opened in 1932 to commemorate the great Exhibition of 1892 which itself commemorated Columbus' voyage of 1492. The taxi sped on until it turned in at 57th Street along the sunken, grassy mall of the Midway, once the lagoon of that same Columbian Exposition, bordered on the north side by a romantic facade of gray pseudo-gothic towers.

Columbus was no more astonished at the New World than I was with the University of Chicago! The only university campus that I had ever entered was that of the University of Oklahoma at Norman. I was soon to learn (since I had come without any idea of what I was coming to) that the University of Chicago, in spite of its lack of the credentials of age and academic tradition, was then rated among the four or five best schools in the United States. Founded in the same year as the Columbian Exposition, it was the product of the millions of John D. Rockefeller and the brains of a Baptist professor of Hebrew, William Rainer Harper, it's first president. It was primarily a graduate school with the best faculty Harper could purchase with Rockefeller's money.

The taxi left me off at the south side of the Midway before the Judson-Burton student residence, the latest in English Gothic, suggesting I was really at Oxford or Cambridge. My room in Burton with gothic windows was neat but small. We were soon summoned to an orientation session whose sole message was "You are on your own, provided you don't get into the newspapers."

The first months were so exciting that I found it hard to eat and lost ten pounds. Burton Hall was a new building mainly for undergraduate residents. Since Prohibition had just ended, every Saturday night the restrooms stank with the vomit of drunken youths. In my fright I looked to attach myself to some more sophisticated student as a guide to this new world. My first friend was a Jewish fellow from Tulsa, Oklahoma, who was really as feckless as myself and who had painful flat feet, but he was a kindly soul who reminded me of my old friend Irwin. I even attended a Yom Kippur service with him at the Hyde Park Synagogue. We also went to the World's Fair, viewing it all stretching along the lake from the Sky Ride suspended between two lofty towers to the garish pavilion where Sally Rand, the famous fan dancer performed. Then, back at the campus, classes began and everything grew even stranger. My life became a four-skein tangle of threads that in recalling I must untangle into the academic, aesthetic, political, and religious, trusting that the reader will pardon me for some confusing anticipations of events, since in fact I was myself more than confused.

Academic Entanglements

The famous New Plan for the bachelor's degree instituted by Robert Maynard Hutchins (1899-1977), former Dean of the Yale Law School soon after he had become president at Chicago, was then in full force. According to this Plan all undergraduates were required to take what today would be called a "core" of four survey courses in the Physical, Biological, and Social Sciences, and in the Humanities. Moreover no class attendance was required, and one could pass all undergraduate courses whenever one chose to take comprehensive exams prepared by a special faculty committee. One student I knew managed to earn his B.A. in a single year.

I attended lectures regularly my first year, some given by outstanding members of the faculty such as Arthur Compton, the Nobel Laureate who discovered cosmic rays, Frank Knight in economics, Anton J. Carlson in physiology, and Ferdinand Scheville in history. The students around me were very well prepared, from fine prep schools. I was humiliated to be required to take a remedial course in English composition, the very subject I thought I regarded as my best. By the end of the year, however, I had done well on my first comprehensive and was listed in the first twenty-five of my class. Eventually I was elected to Phi Beta Kappa and also to an honorary club Kappa Alpha intended to help faculty and students get better acquainted with each other, though it seldom met! At the one meeting I remember I read some of my poetry while the faculty members patiently—not commenting—listened, even when my poem ended with an obscene word.

In my sophomore year, 1934-35, flushed with this academic success, I decided not to bother with class and to devote myself to reading to take the comprehensives. This worked well enough, except for the required languages in which I passed reading exams, but never acquired much proficiency, especially in German, to the detriment of my later scholarship. That same year I moved out of rowdy Burton Hall into Hitchcock Hall, a quiet senior residence on the northwest corner of the campus. My gothic windows there overlooked the handball courts across the street where eventually eight years later on a fatal December 2, 1942 the first self-sustaining nuclear reaction took place that led to the atomic bomb. Then for a year and a half (1935-36) I lived in the Beta Theta Pi Fraternity house on Woodlawn Avenue after which I resigned from the fraternity and moved to the Socialist Coop (that I will describe later) for half a year. Having by then completed my comprehensive exams for the B.A., I skipped the degree to save the $25 graduation fee, so that I never officially got the B.A. but went right on to my M.A. that I received in my fourth year on December 21, 1937. I then worked desultorily as a graduate assistant for two years, living for one year with two other friends on Harper Avenue in an apartment and for one year in a house set up for graduate students on Woodlawn Ave. By that time I had become a Catholic and decided in 1939 to finish my Ph.D. in Political Science at Notre Dame in the spring of 1941.

The University of Chicago in the period just before World War II was a very exciting venue because of the activities of its brilliant young president, Robert Maynard Hutchins (1899-1977) and his philosopher friend Mortimer Jerome Adler (1902-2001). They were battling to reform education by a return to the "Great Books of Western Civilization" in order to replace a curriculum centered on "facts" with one centered on "ideas," as the contest was caricatured by the student paper *The Maroon*. Hutchins' and Adler's innovative classicism confronted the anti-traditional, pragmatism of John Dewey which still dominated the University where Dewey, before going to Columbia, had taught and founded the experimental School of Education. Some fifty years later (1987) the Adler-Hutchins classicism was to be eloquently defended by another University of Chicago professor, Allan Bloom in a best-selling book, *The Closing of the American Mind*, with a foreword by the noted novelist Saul Bellow.[13] Bloom, however, no longer put the same stress on the typically Catholic thought of St. Thomas Aquinas that Hutchins and Adler had done. The index of his book cites Aquinas only once and then only to show that great books are profitably studied even in translation.

Robert Maynard Hutchins was the son of a Presbyterian minister, William James Hutchins who had been a student of William Rainey Harper and president of Oberlin, famous as a center of evangelical reform in the United States promoting such causes as abolition, woman's emancipation, and Prohibition. "Bob" was only thirty years old when in 1929 he became president of the University of Chicago, which was then itself only thirty-seven years old. In spite of his eminently Protestant background he personally was not, it seems, a convinced Christian. Yet he and his friend Mortimer Jerome Adler, a non-religious Jew, had come to believe that Aristotle and his Catholic commentator St. Thomas Aquinas were central to the classical tradition of the "Great Books." Hence Hutchins and Adler looked to a Roman Catholic saint and theologian for guiding principles for education in the face of Dewey's relativism and pragmatism, which they thought had undermined high intellectual standards in American culture.

Disappointed by the outraged resistance of the university faculty to their projects for reform, Hutchins and Adler, along with some like-minded friends, Arthur Rubin, Stringfellow Barr, and Scott Buchanan, had gathered around them some other young scholars. They hoped to prepare them to be a faculty for a small liberal arts college that would fully realize their ideas. It was to become the renewed St. John's College in Annapolis. Ultimately Hutchins resigned in 1952 to found the Center for the Study of Democratic Institutions in Santa Barbara, CA, financed by the Fund for the Republic, an offshoot of the Ford Foundation. Adler also resigned to develop his Center for Philosophical Research in Chicago and to plan the *New Encyclopedia Britannica* and the *Synopticon* that reflect his efforts to promote the "great ideas." An excellent account of Hutchins and Adler's educational ideas and the attempt to implement them has been written by a noted historian, member of the University faculty, and my classmate and fraternity brother, William H. McNeill, in his *Hutchins' University: A Memoir of the University of Chicago, 1929-1950*.[14]

I first heard Mortimer Adler lecture in my freshman year. He asked the odd question, "Have There Been Any New Ideas in the Last Five Hundred Years?" This lecture was one of the most important incidents of my life. I was imbued, as almost all young

Americans of intellectual pretensions were in those days, with the Myth of Progress in thought as well as in machines. Surely the newest in thought was the truest, just as the newest detergent is "improved"! Adler laughed at this myth and claimed that he had found only three really illuminating new ideas in the last five hundred years: Spinoza's notion of reality as "modes" of God, Freud's notion of the Unconscious, and (as I recall) Marx's notion of "surplus value." What struck me was not whether these were the only good new ideas, but that old, old ideas may still be valuable, though today often obscured by intellectual fads and unexamined prejudices. That opened wide to me the treasures of tradition without closing to me the door to future search for wisdom.

This new idea that old ideas can be valuable motivated me to apply and get accepted as a participant throughout my sophomore and junior years in the Great Books Seminar conducted by Hutchins and Adler. Unlike my other courses, I attended this seminar faithfully although it had its painful moments. Of the twenty or so students in each quarter not a few dropped out, embarrassed by the Socratic method exclusively and vigorously pursued by Adler and Hutchins. This method allowed students to express their opinions, as most professors allowed them to do, but it also held them responsible to defend those opinions with solid reasons, a much less common demand.

Adler's popular work, *How to Read a Book*,[15] gives a good idea of his and Hutchins' way of dealing with a classic text. The first question was commonly, "What kind of a book is this?" and the next was "In a sentence, what is the author claiming?" and then, "What reasons does he give for what he claims?" Since each week in the seminar we read a different "great book" we naturally did not go very deep. For most of these classics we never got much beyond the identification of the genre and a first formulation of the book's principal thesis. Our very first book to read was the Bible. I heard one sophisticated Jewish student say he had never looked inside the Bible before. As a native of the Bible Belt, I had, of course, some acquaintance with that "Great Book," but what startled me was that we were now asked, "Is this the Word of God?" I had supposed that in a great university like Chicago it would be taken for granted that the Bible was great, ancient literature, but that no modern person could possibly think it was anything more than great, ancient literature. Adler was not asking us to answer his question yes or no, but only to recognize that the Bible claimed to be the Word of God, and had to be read in the light of that claim if it were to make sense. Again Adler had showed me that merely accepting current opinions, even from academics of reputation, without asking on what grounds they might rest, is not thinking.

Later, I attended an "open house" at the home of the Baptist Dean of the Rockefeller Chapel, at which Adler gave a short talk, the theme of which was that "religion" was about "revelation" or it was nothing at all. He left as soon as he had given his talk, and the wife of the very "liberal" Dean expressed great indignation at what to her seemed Adler's preposterous thesis.

Hutchins, in spite of his presidential duties, was regularly present at the seminar, but occasionally some other faculty member would substitute for him. This substitute was most often the philosopher and medievalist Richard P. McKeon (1900-1985),[16] a quiet, enigmatic professor, with a pipe that required constant attention and a teaching style even more Socratic than that of Adler and Hutchins. They had brought McKeon to the University and it was rumored they later regretted this appointment because McKeon, by his historical erudition, soon gained acceptance from members of the philosophy department who were antagonistic to Hutchins and Adler. McKeon, son of Catholic father and a Jewish mother, was a reserved, super-subtle, and to me a bit sinister person, who seemed unwilling to commit himself to any specific position or program, let alone a religious affiliation. He had studied at the Sorbonne under Étienne Gilson the noted historian of medieval philosophy and proponent of Thomism. He published little; but profound learning and a studied, dense ambiguity marked what he did publish.

At least it was clear that McKeon was much concerned—as Adler later in his Center for Philosophical Research was to become—with the strange fact that philosophers in their search for truth always seem to talk at cross-purposes. They caricature each other's positions, never having a true dialogue or meeting of minds. McKeon saw the prime example of this dilemma in the great Aristotle's severe criticisms of his own master, Plato. These criticisms, McKeon argued, although acute, somehow always miss their mark.

McKeon called Plato a "holist" because in the course of dialectic each of his terms—"justice" for instance—gradually expand to include all reality. On the contrary, he called Aristotle a "merist" (from Greek *meris*, part) because the Stagirite's method was always to focus on a precisely defined aporia, or problem permitting of a definite but very limited solution. Later McKeon came to add to these methods the "atomistic" method of Democritus, who reduced everything to its simplest elements, and the "encyclopedic" method of Cicero who simply collected opinions on every topic without definitive evaluation. Once these methodologies were recognized and identified, McKeon maintained, sense could be made out of the history of philosophy. Thus for McKeon—as far as I could make out—all the classic philosophers were equally true and equally false. Hence he seemed to me to be producing disciples who skillfully engaged in endless dialectic, a game of distinguishing "terms," without ever committing themselves to any proposition as simply true or false. My judgment, however, was very superficial, since I began a course with him on Plato's *Republic*, but after McKeon took two weeks to expound the first paragraph, I gave up and withdrew. I was told by those more persistent that as they proceeded (naturally they never finished) McKeon seemed to be elegantly demonstrating that the whole thought of the dialogue was contained in germ in that first paragraph.

In one of his two autobiographies Adler says that it was McKeon who introduced him to Aquinas by telling him where he could find the English Dominican Fathers' translation of the *Summa Theologiae*. He also reveals that he broke with McKeon over McKeon's extreme relativism according to which "All philosophical system are equally valid, but incommensurable." Adler had himself defended a similar relativism in his first book *Dialectic*[17] but soon came to reject it. Adler also had a rather emotional break with Scott Buchanan (1895-1968)[18] over these differences. Stringfellow Barr (1897-1982),[19] who was an Episcopalian, was more on Adler's side. I remember an exciting meeting in a beer hall when I, a mere student hanger-on, got to hear these sages exchange ideas as they planned the future St. John's, arguing brilliantly and wittily with each other.

One fellow student was Martin Gardner, later a well-known editor for *Scientific American* and author of the delightful *Annnotated Alice* in Wonderland[20] and many other ingenious works. I am grateful for his recollections of those days that I received in letters from him in the 1980s. He wrote that he once tried to find out if McKeon believed in God, but nobody knew if he did or not. His second wife, however, seems to have been a Jewish convert to Catholicism, and it is certain that McKeon before his death became quiet friendly to Catholics. Gardner also wrote me that McKeon spoke well of me as a former student. McKeon was the director of the doctoral dissertation of my friend the distinguished and combatively orthodox Catholic philosopher and moralist, Germain Grisez.[21]

In the Great Books Seminar McKeon's skill in leading a student to pursue a point to its logical conclusion was marvelously demonstrated. One evening a burly but very bright science professor's son, who unconsciously always role-played Thrasymachus, Plato's crass pragmatist and positivist, objected to what he regarded as all the sentimental talk about "love" in a Platonic dialogue that was our reading assignment. McKeon, softly questioning this brash young man, finally led him to admit that the reason the moon goes around the earth is really because it is in love with our homely planet.

Hutchins expressed his own educational views in his *The Higher Learning in America* and *No Friendly Voice*.[22] I can add little to the very ample descriptions of his life and character in Harry S. Ashmore, *Unseasonable Truths: The Life of Robert Maynard Hutchins*[23]; Mary Ann Dzuback, *Robert M. Hutchins: Portrait of an Educator*,[24] and Milton Mayer, *Robert Maynard Hutchins: A Memoir*.[25] In my own recollection Hutchins usually during these seminars sat quietly while Adler pursued the dialectic; but now and then when he saw that the discussion was not getting anywhere, he would intervene with his own sharp questioning. One evening he was summoned from class and the rumor went about that it was a call from the White House asking him to be the Democratic nominee for the Presidency. Nothing came of that, but it illustrates his national prominence at the time. We were all utterly in awe of him, and he seemed rather aloof from us as students, but always very courteous.

I cannot do better than to quote a fine and by no means exaggerated description by the sociologist Prof. Edward Shils, "Robert Maynard Hutchins," which appeared in *The American Scholar*.[26]

Robert Maynard Hutchins was the most handsome man I have ever seen, a man of natural elegance in bearing and manners. It is not just that he was tall and graceful in form and movement, extremely well proportioned in his figure, and with fine strong and regular facial features. He had the most illuminated and enchanting smile, both elevated and kindly at the same time. His voice was a dry, clear monotone; it carried a slight overtone of the speaker's distaste or distrust of his audience. His voice did not distract from the matter which his words treated; it was a perfect vehicle for his lucid, almost geometrical thoughts. He always spoke in sentences which were short and perfectly formed; he never rambled and byways did not tempt him from his theme. When he wrote, he did so in the most economical way. When he replied to questions or criticisms, he never fumbled or evaded, he always had a clear and succinct reply.

On the other hand, Shils did not like Adler and says of him, "In alliance with Hutchins, Mortimer Adler was a person of strong intelligence inclined toward schematic constructions and of an expository skill as pleasing in the ear as a machine gun."[27] Edward Levi, whom Hutchins had made Dean of the Law School and who was later to become one of his successors as president, said of Hutchins in an address at the Memorial Service, June 8, 1977.[28]

He was a learning president, and many of his ideas changed as a result of his experience or his own intensive continuing education. He was steadfast in the values he was for, and firm in the inequities he opposed. The influence of what he termed the "parsonage" or his missionary past was "ineradicable." This included most importantly a faith in the independent mind. The preoccupation of the University should be with the intellectual virtues. The University ought to be devoted to the intellectual love of God which is the pursuit of truth for its own sake. The free and independent exercise of the intellect was the means by which society would be improved...In an effort to restate the aims of the University and the means to that end, he criticized the confusion of science with information, ideas with facts, and knowledge with miscellaneous data. In a University dedicated to research, he thought it particularly important to question the collection of unrelated insignificant information, even though this was sometimes called independent investigation. His was the first strong voice to criticize the inordinate length of the formal course of instruction through higher education, and to insist upon a greater communality, among students and faculty alike, required for liberal education and impossible under the elective system. He thought a university seriously committed to education ought to do a good teaching job for its own students. He was very concerned about faculty appointments and believed a President should take a major part in shaping the course of the University.

That is to say that a university president ought to have the power to shake up the faculty and prevent it from becoming inbred, complacent, and full of dead wood. Hutchins later admitted his efforts had not always been very politic, as on the occasion when he was invited to a faculty banquet at which the fatuous toastmaster said, "President Hutchins accepted our invitation only on condition he not be called on for a speech. Nevertheless, I am sure he will honor us with a few words." Whereupon Hutchins rising, said in his dry voice, "As was agreed, I do indeed decline to give a speech, but I will summarize what the other speakers have said this evening." Whereupon he gave a devastatingly witty summary of the faculty speakers' vapidities and inconsequences.

Hutchins' wit was very different from Adler's aggressive logic. Indeed, no two men could be less alike in personality and appearance than Adler and Hutchins, yet their synergy was remarkable. They had become acquainted when Hutchins was Dean of the Law School at Yale and Adler was teaching at Columbia. Hutchins was interested in the logic of legal evidence and had heard that Adler had studied the question. Actually this was not so, and Adler had to bone up on the subject hurriedly, but Hutchins found him very helpful. Hutchins was a young man who had come up in academe so quickly that he was quite aware he had much to learn and he was constantly broadening the scope of his studies. He found Adler a plenteous source of information and philosophical analysis.

The accusation, made by some of the faculty, that Hutchins and Adler because of their favorable view of Catholic thinkers had "fascist" tendencies was absurd. If anything, from my present perspective, he and Adler were too firmly believers in Enlightenment rationality and freedom of speech. Hutchins was later to establish the Center for the Study of Democratic Institutions, and Adler together with the Thomist, Fr. Walter Farrell, OP, to try to demonstrate philosophically that democracy is the best form of government. Hutchins was, however, very much aware of how difficult it is to promote rational discourse in a modern democracy dominated by irrational public media.

In 1940 Adler gave a speech "God and the Professor's" which got much publicity. James T. Farrell, the novelist in *The Partisan Review*, called him "a provincial Torquemada without an Inquisition." Shils, in the article already quoted, tells us that H. L. Mencken then wrote Farrell:[29]

Thanks very much for the chance to see your blast against Mortimer J. Adler. You describe him precisely. I hear confidentially that Holy Church is full of hopes that he will submit to baptism anon. If the ceremony is public I'll certainly attend. I invite you herewith to come along in my private plane. I assure you there will be plenty of stimulants aboard.

Shils names certain especially bitter opponents of Hutchins and Adler in the social science department, of which he was a member, and writes,[30]

I was beginning to hear rumors that Hutchins was seeking to impose scholastic philosophy on the University of Chicago, that he wished to suppress the social sciences, that he wished to put down science and reduce scientific study to the study of classical scientific writings of antiquity and early modern times. It was said that Hutchins wished to replace the study of the modern world by the study of the classics of antiquity and the Middle Ages and that he wished to replace research by ratiocination. It was also said that in addition to giving the armchair precedence over the laboratory bench or the research seminar, Hutchins, though not himself Catholic, was also attempting to promote Roman Catholicism.

In fact it was not until many years later that Adler accepted baptism in the Episcopal Church and shortly before his death at the age of ninety-nine was confirmed in the Catholic Church.

Adler, whom I came to know much better personally than Hutchins, although always on a professor-student and not on a friendly basis, entirely lacked Hutchins' finesse. For his own self-portrait one can see his two memoirs, *Philosopher at Large: An Intellectual Autobiography 1902-1976*[31] and *A Second Look in the Rearview Mirror: Further Autobiographical Reflections of A Philosopher at Large.*[32]

Undoubtedly an element of anti-Semitism entered into the opposition to Mortimer, because as I knew him he typified many of the traits of a New York Jewish intellectual who loved nothing better than a knockdown argument. While his logic was Aristotelian rather than rabbinical, it was wielded with all the determination of a Talmudist distinguishing a jot from a tittle. One of the best things of my childhood was arguing with my father, so I loved Adler for his logic. Yet I do not believe in Cartesian "clear and distinct ideas." No human idea, even those of mathematics is entirely clear or distinct, but the right use of logic is the only way to make ideas more clear and distinct and thus to focus with higher resolution on the realities they signify.

One of Mortimer's lectures was repeatedly interrupted by a lady who to his trenchant replies finally cried out, "Professor Adler, that's not fair! You are using logic against me!" While I think Adler did sometimes abuse logic by setting up rigid dichotomies contrary to the evidence, I loved him and still love him for his logic and for his courage in exposing academic fraud.

Adler had a famous and, it must be admitted, rather silly debate with Anton J. Carlson (1875-1956), a famous professor of physiology who firmly believed that Adler was an enemy of modern science. Carlson himself was a rigid empiricist and positivist, famous for his constant query, "What is the evidence?" When in 1950 Pius XII declared that the Blessed Virgin Mary had been assumed bodily into heaven Carlson criticized this doctrine at length on the grounds that at the temperature of outer space the Virgin would have been again killed. According to a well-known legend, when Carlson's daughter had twins he demanded that only one be baptized and the other kept as a control.

Prof. Carlson loved a bit of theater in his classes, and when he lectured to us in the Biology Survey he insisted that he himself be the subject of many of the experiments. His first experiment required the drawing of a few cc's of blood, and he warned us in advance that some students always fainted at the sight. He then rolled up his own sleeve and with great drama had an assistant insert a syringe and draw some blood from his brawny arm, at which point, sure enough, a student tried to run out of the lecture amphitheater and fainted on the stairs! The Adler vs. Carlson debate, advertised by *The Maroon* as "The Battle Between Facts and Ideas," drew a huge and amused student crowd. Yet Adler had nothing against facts; what he attacked was bad reasoning about the facts.

Personally Adler was a rather stylishly dressed, short, excitable man, whom you might suppose to be a lawyer. In fact when Hutchins failed to get the philosophy department to accept Adler, he obtained for him a temporary appointment to the Psychology Department, and finally settled him in the Law School. Janet Kalven,[33]

Adler's brilliant graduate assistant, years later summed up her debt to him and Hutchins in a letter to Martin Gardner which he kindly shared with me:

> The thirties were a time of extraordinary intellectual ferment at Chicago, in large measure due to Hutchins and Adler. Their stance ran counter to the prevailing campus culture and was propaedeutic so far as Catholicism was concerned. From them I learned to question the received wisdom of the semanticists, psychologists, sociologists, cultural relativists; to respect the intellectual rigor of the Greeks and the medievals; to suspect the reductionism of the physical and biological sciences; to read a text in its own terms, define a concept, and analyze an argument. I cut my intellectual teeth so to speak on all the big questions: the nature of language, knowledge, truth; the nature of man (I was not a feminist then), of society, of justice, the existence of God. The Hutchins-Adler training was a necessary but not sufficient condition for conversion. It made Catholicism intellectually respectable, but it did not make anyone become a Catholic. A much more powerful and intimate witness is necessary, I think, to enable people to act as contrary to our upbringing and education as our little group did.

There were other currents of thought at the University at that time with which I had some contact but which made little impression on me, such as the process philosophy of Charles Hartshorne (1897-2000),[34] the logical positivism of Rudolf Carnap, and in the Divinity School the Neo-Orthodoxy of Barth and Tillich. For a month or so I attended a course in aesthetics from Hartshorne, a very odd little man with wisps of hair waving from his otherwise bald skull. His hobby was ornithology, and with owlish eyes he illustrated in his lectures his passionate conviction that animals also are aesthetes by imitating birdcalls. I remember also that he tried to sensitize us to beauty by bringing colored bath towels to class. His reluctance to confine intelligence to the human species extended even further down the scale of being. At a seminar I heard him admonish Carnap for seeming to deny free will to atoms. I confess that I really understood little about such modern philosophical problems, but since they seemed to fall far short of the common sense of Thomist philosophy as I was becoming acquainted with it, I saw no reason to give much time to what appeared to me very extravagant speculations.

I had come to the University intending to major in English on the supposition that eventually I would teach it in some college. I was now beginning to see how broad and deep the world of books and of reality could be. In my sophomore year I won the Alfred Whital Stern contest "Toward a Higher Ethics and Integrity" (generous people were hoping to build student "values" even then) with an essay called "The Aesthetic Motive for Right Conduct" in which I raised the question:

> Why should I be good? Is there anything left to give me a glow of satisfaction when I am good and a warning discomfort when I am bad? The things that satisfied my family seem not satisfactory to me; God is such a shadowy First Cause of Something, science merely a way of making the world a bigger and less intelligible muddle, neither Aunt Ella's "Respectability" nor Uncle John's "Democracy" seem very attractive inducements to a good life.

And I concluded:

> Perhaps you will still say, "But is the question really answered? You began by asking, 'Why be good?' Where's the answer?" Here it is again: Because the beautiful seems to me to be desired and sought rather than the ugly, I should desire the life that is whole, harmonious and radiant in preference to the incomplete, the muddled, and the dull.

Today I realize all too well that though beauty is a sign of the good, it is not identical with it, and an ethic based on the aesthetic easily becomes very ugly indeed.

After a few courses in English literature I got myself accepted in an interdepartmental Committee for Studies in Comparative Literature. Though I was taking Greek, French, and German, I was too lazy and too timid in speaking ever to become really competent in any of these languages. Yet, once I began to read Aquinas' clear, easy Latin in his *Summa Theologiae*, free of classical rhetoric, I became more competent in that language. In my M.A. thesis, however, I used Greek, Latin, and French, since it was titled: "A Criticism of Three

Plays: the *Crowned Hippolytus* of Euripides, the *Hippolytus* or *Phaedra* of Seneca, and the *Phaedre* of Racine." I came to the conclusion that:

> Euripides' *Hippolytus* is seen to be a tragedy of plot somewhat complicated by certain genuine rhetorical exigencies. Seneca's *Phaedra* has only a unity of means and is not really poetic but pseudo-rhetorical. Racine's *Phaedre* is a tragedy of character, or, a pathetic drama whose unity consists in the object it describes, which is, however, internal to the play. All three are admirable works of their kinds since all the details in each are ordered by the unifying principles, but as works of poetry certainly Euripides' is the best kind, and Seneca's the worst.

In some detail I sought the unifying principle of each work and tried to relate its parts to the whole. In particular I praised Racine's subtle psychology that I related to what I knew of Freud. I made no attempt to view the plays sociologically as reflecting the culture of the times in which they were written, except for some remarks about how Racine's work anticipates modernity by its "Ah, the pity of it all!" thematic. Nor did I attempt any deconstructionist reading between the lines.

On rereading this piece of criticism now I feel some pride for a piece of work for which I would give a student an A (particularly today when if you give a graduate student less than A or B+ you are liable to a lawsuit). It is well written, except for some patches of purple prose, and applies the Aristotelian Poetics with the skill and critical insight that I had learned from a very excellent instructor, literary historian, and critic, Ronald S. Crane (1886-1967).[35] He was editor of the *Philological Quarterly* and author of *The Idea of the Humanities and Other Essays Critical and Historical*.[36] His approach to criticism was influenced by McKeon, as appears in his *Critics and Criticism: Ancient and Modern*[37] in which the Aristotelian uses of the four causes of a literary work are examined. Crane, who often praised Fielding's *Tom Jones* to us as a literary model, was the leader of the "Chicago School" of criticism that promoted a particular version of critical "Formalism." It concentrated on the structure of a literary work (its form and matter) rather than on the author's self-expression, sources, and authorial intention (historical approach) or on audience response and political effects (the rhetorical approach). This formalist way of reading a literary text in its own terms along with Adler's logical approach to philosophical and scientific texts has stuck with me as a theologian, especially in biblical exegesis.

What is divinely inspired in the Biblical text is what the text itself says, not how it came to be, or what it means to various audiences. Thus I was pleased when recently in biblical studies emphasis shifted from a preoccupation with the historical-critical approach to biblical texts in their literary and rhetorical structure. I favor this approach especially if it is combined with "canon criticism" which treats the Bible as the work of a single Divine Author who writes through the instrumentality of many human authors each reflecting a particular personality, culture, and historical context. Today I remain of the opinion that any literary criticism that neglects formal analysis, whatever other insights it may bring to bear in understanding a text, misses a specifically aesthetic understanding of a work.

The reading list of plays which I submitted for my M.A. degree included all the surviving Greek and Roman classical plays, 16 medieval plays, 93 Renaissance plays to 1700, and almost 200 plays and films after 1700 to Eugene O'Neill. It was an international list, but I read most of it in translation. I now can't imagine how I managed to read so much and can't remember a thing about most of these plays that I then swallowed so omnivorously. But I was especially taken with the Greek plays, Shakespeare, Calderon, Racine, and Moliere, Sheridan, the German Hebbel, Synge, O'Casey, Ibsen, and Chekov. I also listed a good deal of criticism including A.J. Bradley and J. Dover Wilson on Shakespeare, critics Crane liked, and also Coleridge and John Ruskin whose Modern Painters I have mentioned reading in high school.

Crane praised the breadth of my reading, but delayed my reception of the M.A. for a quarter to teach me greater care in scholarship, since in my pretentious dissertation I had repeatedly misspelled the name of Euripides! The delay made little difference to me, since by that time I had decided, because of my political activism which I will next narrate, not to go on to a Ph.D. in literature but to switch to political science, a change that the flexible policies of Hutchins' university made possible.

In the meanwhile I had become involved in a project of one of my English professors Norman Maclean, known for his semi-autobiographical novella, *A River Runs Through It*[38] from which a fine film was made recently. He was a thin, intense young teacher, very popular with the students. At that time the Greek letter fraternities on the campus were in decline. Norm was an alumnus of the local Lambda Rho Chapter of the national fraternity Beta Theta Pi. He and another alumnus of the fraternity, D., had decided to try to save the chapter of the Beta's, which seemed to be in its death throes, with only a few boozy members. D. was a very sophisticated, cultured man about town, an amateur violinist and well acquainted with Chicago artistic, musical, and theatrical circles, whom rumor pegged as "gay" (the term then was "a fairy"), perhaps because of his hanging around the locker rooms of university athletes. Norm's and D.'s idea, influenced by the Adler-Hutchins intellectualism was to have the Chapter pledge a select group of students known not for their athletic or social gifts but for their academic merits and to make membership financially possible for them.

Neither my finances (my parents, suffering from the Depression, could give me only a very modest allowance) or my interests would have ever have made me seek fraternity life, but in this situation I was pledged along with some ten or so excellent students. One of these was Bob L. whom we elected as President and whose early death I will describe later. Robert Brumbaugh, a very young product of the University's experimental high school, was to become a distinguished philosopher and expert on Greek philosophy.[39] William McNeill, already mentioned, became a noted historian, known especially for his world history, *The Rise of the West: A History of the Human Community*.[40] F. B. became an air pilot in World War II and then a biologist working for Armour's. He was a big, shy, humorous guy, who always seemed skeptical of my enthusiasms, but whom I admired greatly for his dependability and honesty. W. K. later ruined his health by severely dieting to escape the draft, got a doctorate in philosophy, and then became a resident philosopher with Dow Chemical Company as a personal-relations counselor to their staff of Ph.D.'s. Gene Davis was a young man of great charm, for sometime known in Chicago for his jazz band. Another was T. S. who entered the U. S. diplomatic service. It is typical of that time that no Jewish student, however "intellectual," was invited to join, such as another friend of mine, Herbert Simon, later Nobel Laureate in Economics and a leader in the field of artificial intelligence, etc.[41] It was certainly a group of bright and promising young men, disciples of Adler and Hutchins' intellectual idealism. Our new group was pledged to the fraternity May 20, 1935.

Of these fraternity brothers the two who influenced me most were Quentin, "Bud," Ogren[42] and Leo Shields with both of whom I had become friendly at the end of my freshman year. Bud was a tall, gangling, and wonderfully extroverted fellow of Scandinavian ancestry, whose father I learned had been several times Socialist candidate for mayor of Milwaukee. Bud was a familiar sight on the campus, because he was earning his living as a salesman distributing free gum and cigarette samples to students at various campus busy spots. He was a lively, laughing young guy and, as I soon realized, a born political activist. He eventually became a prominent professor of law at Loyola University in Los Angeles.

Leo Shields was more interested in the cultural matters that meant so much to me and had also joined the Adler-Hutchins seminar. Because of my insecurity about practical matters, I have always tended to seek someone who will give me assurance about going places and doing things, and I found this in Leo, who was a courageous, independent person. He was my age, from Salt Lake City, but not a Mormon, indeed from an Irish Catholic family to which the noted Civil War general, James Shields, had belonged. Thin, with a loping walk, pointed nose, prominent ears and large dark eyes Leo always reminded me of some kind of antelope.

While very open to and sympathetic with my ideas and concerns, Leo was more analytic and independent in his own thinking than I was, so that I often looked to him for confirmation of my ideas and attitudes. We went everywhere together. I supposed today such a close and persistent friendship would be viewed with suspicion or promptly labeled as gay, but there was nothing erotic about it, it was based on common and complementary interests, at first purely intellectual ones, then on politics, and finally and profoundly on religion.

Life with Bud and Leo and the others in Lambda Rho Chapter of Beta Theta Pi was a great stimulus to me intellectually and it was also a psychological help. I will discuss this more fully in the section on my religious development. We lived in the fraternity house, however, only a year and a half, and then Bud, Leo and I resigned from Beta Theta Pi in protest against the refusal of the house to pledge a Jewish candidate. My next move was to live for a semester with Leo (Bud moved elsewhere) in the Socialist Co-op that I will describe in the section on my political activities. It was, however, during this time that I was reading most avidly for my M.A. I often studied all night, ate breakfast at 5 A.M., and then slept to noon. Rent at the Co-op was minimal, but it was a great problem for me to pay my tuition, since the scholarships that had continued during my undergraduate and M. A. studies had run their course. Indeed I got into some trouble with the University over the repayment of loans. Rescue came when Adler invited Bud, Leo, and me to be graduate assistants for two years to do research for a book he was writing, as I will explain later in Chapter 5. The first year we lived on Harper Avenue in an old, smelly apartment where weekly a man came through the halls calling "Exterminator! Exterminator!" and squirting something on the baseboards. It was called Coutich Castle after a former owner who was said to have a great affection for literary people and was very tolerant of their failure to pay the rent. Vachel Lindsay and other writers down on their luck took advantage of his hospitality.

For a while we had a fourth companion in the apartment named Hippocrates Apostle, one of the scholars Adler was grooming for St. John's in Annapolis. He was a dark, thin, beak-nosed mathematician, later a teacher at Harvard and finally at Grinnell College in Iowa who published excellent translations of Aristotle's major works with the label "Peripatetic Press". All day long he did nothing but read Aristotle in Greek, his long index finger following the text line by line, and was little interested in anything else but the Stagirite. When it was his turn to cook, he always served pork chops.

Then during the second year that we were Adler's graduate assistants, Leo and I (but not Ogren) lived with a number of other of Adler's protégés in a residence for them that he had leased to save money, located on Woodlawn Avenue near the campus. One of the denizens was a very young student, Aaron Bell, a bit of a prodigy, something of a pianist and a poet, and a rather juvenile personality. Not long ago I received a phone call from him whom I had not heard of in years. He said he was in the States from Helsinki where he was teaching English, especially to members of the Parliament who needed that language to attend international meetings. They wanted especially to get acquainted with technical terms in different disciplines that might be met at such meetings. Aaron was going around the United States to interview and tape-record former friends who were specialists in various academic fields so as to provide examples of such technical language. He asked if I would do a tape on theology, since he knew few theologians. Of course I consented.

During my interview he told me what had happened to him academically at the University of Chicago. After I left there, he continued to work for his doctorate in political science under Prof. Quincy Wright, well known for his book on just war theory.[43] To Wright's great pleasure, Aaron proposed to write a book on the topic of "Just War in the Speeches of Ten Selected Presidents of the United States." His analysis of the just war theory led him to conclude that it is a very complex concept involving no less than 30 different elements (here I noted McKeon's influence on one of his students). This produced a conceptual grid of 10 x 30 or 300 items that required 300 sections in the thesis. As these sections were developed one by one, the dissertation swelled to such a volume that Aaron had to carry it to his director in a suitcase. He began to plead with Wright to let him cut it down to one president and thirty elements, or ten presidents and one element of a just war, but his mentor kept exclaiming, "Oh, no Aaron, that is the beauty of your dissertation!" Finally Wright died in 1970 and Aaron survived with no degree and no job. Wandering through Europe he found a Finnish wife and settled down in Helsinki to teach English.

I have always associated Aaron's academic tragicomic story with one I read in the newspapers about a mathematician who worked for years on a dissertation, only a few pages long (math dissertations are usually very brief) with which he could never satisfy his director. Finally, however, he finished it and got his degree. But the next day he walked into the director's office and shot him— deservedly—dead. To be fair to dissertation directors like myself, we are some times faced with the impossible. I once had a student who insistently wanted to write "On Heidegger's Concept of How Nothing Nothings Itself." And a dear colleague of mine Ralph Powell (2001) did a thesis for the University of Louvain on "Truth or Absolute Nothing" and dedicated it to a certain professor, "who," he wrote in his foreword, "has been thinking about nothing all his life."

Chapter 4 - Creativity

Aesthetic Polyphonics

During all this time in Chicago I was writing a good deal of poetry, but especially in summer vacation when I was back in Blackwell and could be at my typewriter every day. Much of it took the form of long odes, perhaps recalling my high school love of Keats. The first of these was written in Blackwell before going back to school in Chicago.

A CHANGE OF SEASONS

Summer on fire plunged into cold autumn wind
and tempered
begins to flash and to take the edge of steel.
The shining air is filled with the sparks,
white and sulfur butterflies,
kildees' wings turning and darting,
leaves still green but no longer dusty, no longer languid,
small grasshoppers, dragonflies large and small.

The heat in the cold, steel burning in water,
hisses and roars with the wind over the sun
in the kildees' shrieking.
My eyes and ears freshen,
but through my heart goes now the honed steel.

What is so true among things seen and heard
as that the seasons take their turns,
as that the wind and leaves and fires
live only in procession,
bringing desire that burns
and leaving no possession?
This is the truth of the pledging of summer and fall
that it will be forgotten in the winter's squall.
This is the truth of the flowers' wedding:
the fruit will ripen as the leaves are shedding.

Why is the heart divided by the fact of change?
Why is the mind pierced by the point of time?
Blood appears on the edge of seasons.

Life is severed by the equinoctial blade.
It is not summer's going, the sweating body, the limp mind,
nor fall's coming, bright and ordinary, clear good weather,
nor a vacation's tedious passing, nor old work's return,
nor the beauty which always makes my soul and body ache
and divide against each other like earth and firmament
to form a new world and some new creation.

It is not the newness and not oldness,
but their meeting, the cold new water,
hardening the hot and ancient metal,
summer's fullness made ominous by fall's fresh air,
the sweet grape souring to bitter wine,
the shattered flower condensing into fertile seed,
and feeling frosting into memory.

Why then should the heart feel wounded?
Why is not my heart hardened and my blood chilled?
Newness is here the newness of passing,
the newness of living waters turned to stone,
the newness of seeing through the suntanned flesh
the whiter bone.

Back in Chicago during the school years the University was in many ways a beautiful place to be living. I delighted in its faux-gothic buildings and their gargoyles, the broad grassy lawns, the elms, the majesty of Rockefeller Chapel (though the Chapel's neutral windows made it seem gray and empty). I was even more taken with the parks that surrounded the University. On the West was Washington Park with its striking Fountain of Time by George Gray Barnard with the motto, "Time flies, you say. No Time stays, we go," with hooded Time standing impassive before a great concrete wave of humanity rising from birth, cresting, and falling into death. This park, however, manifested the racial tensions of the City. On its west side was African-American "Bronzetown," and one night as I walked its paths I was terrified when I was chased out of the park by a gang of black youths for invading their turf.

Much more attractive to me, therefore, was Jackson Park on the east, with its relics of the Columbian Exposition of 1892: the golden statue of the Republic by Daniel Chester French, and the fascinating, long classical building which is now the Museum of Science and Industry with its copy of the Caryatid Porch of the Erechtheum on the Acropolis. Between the wings of that building is a remarkable echo that we used to test in the silence of the night. Most wonderful just beyond was the beach along Lake Michigan and the Lake itself whose color varied with the weather from dull gray to green to deepest blue. The Chicago Loop was not especially attractive except for its theaters and I seldom went north to Lincoln Park or the famous Lakefront on the North Side. But my fraternity brother, Tom Stauffer, who was an architectural buff, gradually made me aware of the many historic buildings of Chicago, especially those of Richardson and Louis Sullivan. Moreover at the University was the famous Robie House of Sullivan's pupil, Frank Lloyd Wright. Tom was somewhat of a mentor of mine, since he knew much of Chicago. During the war he worked in the diplomatic service, got sacked because unjustly suspected of being a security risk and had to make out with odd jobs of teaching the rest of his life in California.

Another friend of mine was a Bill Cobb, an amiable, streetwise New Yorker, brother of Natalie Bodanska, an opera singer with a brief career at the Metropolitan, the wife of William Gorman, one of Adler's friends. Gorman, who was helping to put Bill through college, later became a member of Adler's Center for Philosophical Research and an editor of *The New Encyclopedia Britannica*. I loved Bill Cobb. His warm humanness made him very endearing if sometimes very irritating to his friends. As we walked along the Lake Michigan beach one night, he suddenly cried out in alarm, "What's that?" "Why it's the full moon rising," As only one raised in Manhattan's canyons could have exclaimed, he blurted out, "Oh—I thought the moon of 1871was up there high in the sky!" On another occasion I complained to him that he seldom let me reply to his questions, but immediately, without taking a breath, told me what I was going to answer. He indignantly explained, "If you had always talked on the New York subway where in the roar you can't hear anybody, you would understand why I am used to answering my own questions." I am afraid today's so much touted "dialogue" is just a Manhattan subway conversation.

Another vivid sensuous memory of mine is a great fire in the Chicago Stockyards. Everyone knows that early in Chicago's history there was a Great Fire of 1871 that destroyed most of it. But not many realize that the Chicago of the stockyards of which Carl Sandburg sang also perished in flames. When I first went to Chicago the stockyards still covered many blocks and when the wind was from the northwest its powerful smell reached many blocks south to the University. It now seems incredible that a great city would have permitted in its very midst blocks of wooden pens, with their lowing and bellowing cattle, their straw and manure, their bloody packing houses, and their overpowering stench.

One afternoon in my sophomore year when I lived at Hitchcock Hall I looked out my window and saw a great pillar of black smoke to the northwest. The radio blared that the stockyards were burning and I made haste to a streetcar that took me to the stockyard's edge. I stayed there until after dark watching the huge flames and the efforts of the fire trucks to keep it from spreading out of its boundaries. The wooden stockades were charred embers, as were the bovine corpses within them, but the foul smell had been replaced by the perfume of a steak on the grill. The stockyards were never again fully rebuilt. Today most cattle from south and west are shipped to feeding lots widely distributed in rural areas and the meat shipped in refrigeration to packinghouses.   When once I drove by one of these feeding lots in West Texas, the aroma of old Chicago overwhelmed me.

Once I had taken a tour through one of the slaughterhouses in the Yards. At one place I saw the kosher preparation of meat with a bearded rabbi scrutinizing the process to insure that the Law of Moses was strictly obeyed. At another place we saw a line of pigs and a man who grabbed each pig's left hind leg and hooked it to a chain that pulled it aloft into an elevated, moving row of kickers and squealers. An inspector watching the row move by him, only rejected an occasional odd hog, while the passable ones entered a great vat of boiling water and came out dead, to be chopped to pieces by burly men with long, slashing knives. Next we were herded into a ramp to go into another room where other processes were being performed. As we walked along that ramp, not able to see what was ahead, I had the horrid image that when I turned the corner someone might suddenly grab me by the leg and before anyone knew it I would be hoist for the slaughter. What if the inspector found me a passable pig?

These scenes of real life were eye-filling of themselves, but I was also being taught to use my eyes by the works of great artists. The Art Institute on Michigan Avenue was of easy access from the Illinois Central interurban train and I spent many hours there where the whole history of art is accessible. Among my favorite pictures were Quenten Matsys,' "Man with a Pink," the El Greco "Assumption," the Rembrandt (is it authentic?) "Girl at an Open Half-Door," the Cezanne "L'Estaque," the Seurat "A Sunday Afternoon on the Island of La Grande Jatte," a precise Juan Gris collage, Picasso's baffling "The Girl Before a Mirror." As I gazed at them I remembered my first sight of real art in the hotel in Kaw City related in Chapter 1. From Bouguereau to Picasso! On the University campus was also the small but select Breasted Oriental Institute Museum. I remember standing before a statue of the stern god of wisdom, Ptah, and rather self-consciously composing a prayer to this god, fancying myself a pagan. Especially moving to me (beside the friendly mummy encased there) were the reliefs from Persepolis which somehow combined Greek suavity with Mesopotamian power.

It was not expensive for students to attend the Chicago Symphony either downtown on Michigan Avenue or when they played at the University itself. From the highest balcony of Sullivan's magnificent Auditorium Theater (in the building that now houses Roosevelt University) under the golden arches of the ceiling I saw both the San Carlo Opera Company and the Ballet Russe de Monte Carlo in dazzling performances. These were still depression days and the sets and costumes were sometimes worse for the wear. My first live opera was *Aida* performed by the somewhat frayed San Carlo Company in the Auditorium. The enslaved Nubian princess was hefty, and, when she came to sing *Ritorna Vincitor*, to conceal the preparations for the next scene the stage hands lowered an immense painted backdrop behind her. It depicted a high stone wall and rising beyond it the three great pyramids, an obelisk, and the Sphinx, plus a few lofty palm trees. This magnificent view seemed convincing until in her passionate declamation of the aria, the bawling diva waved her arms, struck the backdrop and the Egyptian wall, pyramids, obelisk, Sphinx and palms billowed with the music!

As for ballet I had the joy of seeing Leonide Massine and the long-legged Alexandra Danileva in colorful performances of "The Fire Bird," "Petroucka," "The Three-Cornered Hat," and others. When at the Lyric Theater I heard Kirsten Flagstad and Lauritz Melchior in "Tristan und Isolde," the monumental duo in splendid voice made the Lyric vibrate with continuous melody that lasted nearly forever. In Act III at the middle of the stage the barrel-like Melchior repeatedly swooned under a bearskin on his bed of pain. Again and again he ponderously aroused himself again at the piping of

Kurwenal to toss off the bearskin hopefully, only to sink back each time in mountainous, melodic disappointment.

There were concerts too, of which I especially recall a magnificent performance by the aging Feodor Chaliapin which began with the announcement that he had changed the printed program, with the result that his vocal announcements of each song were of no help to me. I did recognize "The Volga Boatman" in which the great Russian bass gave an unforgettable exhibition of vocal control, beginning in the faintest, most distant whisper and gradually swelling the melody almost to a shout and then fading it away again into a distance echo. Indeed I have never heard another singer who could so vary the quality of sound as he did in this concert.

I also enjoyed memorable evenings in the theater: Helen Hays in Anderson's "Mary Queen of Scots," Nazimova in "Ghosts" and "Hedda Gabler," The D'Oyly Carte's "Mikado" and "Iolanthe," the Abbey Theater's "Juno and the Paycock" and "The Plough and the Stars." I well remember how charming Katherine Cornell was in Shaw's "Candida" and how unconvincing in his "Joan of Arc" in which she made her first entrance in armor with her arms akimbo and her legs boyishly spread. Those were thrilling evenings in rather musty, shabby Chicago theaters. At the University I also heard poetry recitals by Carl Sandburg with guitar and Lincolnesque shawl and Edna St. Vincent Millay in a medieval green gown. I found her singsong delivery and languishing, seductive manner cloying, yet her poetry had much music.

My musical tastes were improved by my association with Ellis Kohs[44] whom I had got to know well in my freshman year at Burton Hall. Ellis was to become a successful classical composer, for many years teaching composition at the University of Southern California at Los Angeles and writing books on music theory. His *First Symphony* was commissioned by Pierre Monteux and performed January 3, 1952 by the San Francisco Symphony. In the program notes for it he said, "Above all, I see my music as my modest thanks to the life forces for having provided me with a 'voice' to 'sing my song.'" Ellis was hardly your typical college freshman. He was a non-observant Jew from New York, the only son of a professor whose wife died when Ellis was small and who always remained very close to his son. Ellis himself was of medium height, thin-faced, with somewhat curly hair, and was at seventeen already a confirmed bachelor. He carried a carefully furled umbrella, planned his day methodically, and had in his closet equipment for every emergency, from needle and thread to sore throat lozenges. He spoke in considered, precisely formulated phrases, with little chuckles. Before playing the piano, he carefully heated his hands in warm water. In the University orchestra he played the timpani. He cherished a framed cover of *The New Yorker* that showed a percussionist anxiously waiting with raised hand to strike his one note in a long symphony on a triangle while over him hovered the Muse of music, Calliope, whispering inspiration in his ear.

Ellis took me once to an orchestra rehearsal at which I was to play the triangle for him, but since I tinkled at the wrong moment that was the second (remember Gounod's "Ave Maria"!) and final try of my musical career. A small group of us, including Ellis, used to read plays together and one night it was O'Neill's "Emperor Jones". We must have driven the others in Hitchcock Court crazy, because for nearly two hours Ellis kept up the sinister drum beats which in that play come all night from the jungle presaging revolt against Jones.

Though I was no performer, Ellis raised my musical taste from Verdi and Wagner to Bach, Haydn, and Mozart. I have since renewed my love of Verdi, but, in spite of Wagner's great dramatic imagination, I now dislike his music even more. I also heard a lecture by Arnold Schönberg that introduced me to modernism in music, though his talk and demonstration of what he called with heavy German accent, "the absolute perception of musical space" (or was it "the perception of absolute musical space"?) left me blank.

Another friend who at nineteen was also a confirmed bachelor was Ralph T. from Quincy, IL, of Lutheran background but himself an agnostic. I once visited his family there and was taken across the Mississippi to see the Mark Twain places in Hannibal, Missouri. Ralph always wanted me to buy chocolate milk shakes at Walgreens drugstores in Chicago, because he said he knew for a fact that Walgreens advertised its low price for milkshakes to attract customers to their stores although at that price they lost money. Ralph wanted revenge for the squeeze that this great chain of stores placed on his father's small local drugstore. Ralph was a very grim looking young man who quickly abandoned chemistry for mathematics and became a mathematical engineer. But he loved music and we went to many concerts and theater events together. I had occasional correspondence with him over the years, but, living in an eastern city, he was set upon in his lonely old age by muggers and never recovered from the beating they gave him.

At the same time I listened to so much classical music I sometimes went with friends to hear jazz "jam sessions" (this was before "rock") and experimented with their rhythms in the following poem, which also expresses puzzlement with how such interests could fit in with Marxist concepts about "the revolutionary masses." My raising in Blackwell, as I noted in Chapter 1, had never permitted any real contact with African-Americans, and there were few at the University at that time, so this music and its performers were for me very exotic. It was written while I was living with Bud Ogren and Leo Shields in Coutich Castle.

JAZZ

By jazz I write tonight, after eating peanut butter and honey,
since we three students have to live only on borrowed
    money.

Jazz or swing is what we hear tonight.

I have seen a little basement room aglow
with nostrils flaring, lips that wildly blow
and hidden in the cigarette haze a swinging light
as the blue-black men swang
with a brown slap and a blue twang,
like a sobbing child,
and the trumpet dirty wild,
with a high moan in monotone
backed by a pursuing saxophone.

Now in such a room by radio are we,
thousands in the little room with just us three
and all the blood drop serum drops hormones
to swing through our vitals with trombones
and the wild, dirty clarinet.
(the clarinet's lips are wet,
the drummer's forehead wet with sweat).
That is what this music is, everybody swings
and there is only rhythm where there were things,

substances dissolving in the flux and flow,
jamming through the cigarettes soft afterglow.
Are these blacks just the oppressed classes
forced to make music for the bourgeoisie?
Or is their music the clarion of the masses?
      Then what havoc we will see!
      What a wild party there will be!
It is the blood beat that marks the time,
it is the heart beat that makes it rhyme.
In the clapping hands the pulses beat
and sets us in motion from head to feet
and feels so sweet throughout our veins,
swells, dilates in our swinging brains.
I beat, I beat, in red desire,
get hot and burst in syncopated fire.

Do the masses in the dark, beat with repressed desire
like the wonder
of approaching thunder?
"Want bread and easy time,
want not the least but the sublime,
want to have a say in every way every day
about things, everything—
freedom to speak out, shout out, have our say
until the mocking words we mutter
and the hammering notes we play
bring down the walls of Jericho!"
To this time they swing and swing—mutter
"Want honey and my own money
and more peanut butter."

Hear the blue-black players,
the never no-sayers,
through the blue marijuana
haze toot toot the tooter,
feel the doped pulse flutter
singers hoot, croon, stutter,
in syncopated rhythm raise
the heat of the beat.

We three students sit inside our room in a bookish maze,
working on philosophy and Marx, with a leaflet to write
and a poster to make for a meeting tomorrow night.
Oh, on the radio
a clarinet swinging!

Masses swing on down
with blood and brain,
dancing in the little room so narrow,
while we three dance only in our minds and marrow,
trying to discern the meaning of the music:
Is it the waking cry of revolution
the clarion of resolution?
Or just the moan
of blue despair?

Forever on the pulsing air the lone
singer hovers on a dirty, wild, high monotone.

As this poem perhaps indicates, with all this aesthetic input of
art, theater, and music, I did not lack stimulus to write poetry. In my
sophomore year I won the Fiske Poetry Contest and made my acquaintance with Thornton Wilder (1897-1975),[45] already a distinguished writer with his best-selling novel *The Bridge of San Luis Rey*.
He had been a boyhood friend of Robert Hutchins who had invited
him to teach writing at the University. I never took any of his courses, although he was known for his generosity in helping students
who were genuinely interested in writing. One night he knocked on
my door and with great sensitivity and tact explained that he was
one of the judges of the contest. The judges had chosen my poem as
best (I don't have a copy of it any more) but there was a problem
about it. It seems that it contained several obscene words (some
words were still obscene in those days) that the judges didn't mind
but which they felt might distress the elderly lady donor of the
prize. Would I consider it an insult to my artistic integrity if these
were censored before the poem was showed to her? Indeed, since it
meant $50, my artistic integrity did not stand in the way.

Wilder, who in appearance and manner seemed to me a typical
youngish professor of some Ivy League school, did me another great
favor by reading a portfolio of my poems that also contained some

examples of my drawings. He told me gently but frankly that he did not find my drawings very interesting and showed me the work of another protégé of his who had done a number of drawings of teeth on which were engraved various designs: daggers, hearts, question marks. I myself did not find these very interesting either. However, Wilder found some promise in my poems, especially because I was so prolific.

Wilder kindly spoke about my work to another of my teachers Norman Maclean and this was probably why Maclean included me in the group he was preparing to renew the Beta Theta Pi chapter, as I have already narrated. Maclean invited me to dinner with his wife and Morton Zabel, the editor of *Poetry: A Magazine of Verse*, and thus got me my first serious publication, a group of poems titled "A Sheaf of Flutes," slight lyrics about nothing in particular, including the these two.

WHEN WE HAVE BEEN AND HAVE RETURNED

When we have been and have returned,
(long journeys lit by flame, filament, and moon,
on wheel and foot and wing and wire)
have been and have returned
and lie remembering our journeying,

and dark and light around us fall,
shadow and shade and glimmer and flare
and the pallor of colors drained through glass,
around us falling the light and the dark,
we lie remembering our journeying—

then curtain me from change and time,
from dawns and settings and all farewells,
from rain from wind from sound from blood.
Oh curtain me from change from time from change from
time
we have returned from journeying.

THEY THAT SAW YOU TOLD ME

You were such a one as that one
that they saw under water,

clearer than sea water,
bright white and clear,
sea-born and foam-nurtured.

You were such a one as that one
that they saw toward evening
paler than that an evening
that was cold and pale,
street-meshed, city-blinded.

Such a one as that one
that was hidden in flute-silence,
Such a one as that one that was lost in the light,
Such a one as that very one
that moved with a lightness
and slept under silence,
and lived among crowds.

During this dinner at the Macleans, for the first time in my experience, a maid served us the food. Beforehand Norm had plied us
with cocktails (a child of Prohibition, these were my very first) and I
was rather light-headed. How terrified I was when the maid proffered me a dish of asparagus and I had to move some slippery
spears from the dish to my plate with the serving spoons! I succeeded, but only in a sweat. While I later published in various student
and radical magazines, I never again published poems in a major
journal. Yet I kept writing, at first short lyrics like the one just quoted from a *Sheaf of Flutes* or with a little more local atmosphere like
this:

AT A COLLEGE PARTY

How all these people long for joy and peace
in trivial conversation, beer, food, noise!
If for a moment all this noise might cease
and stillness would embrace these girls and boys.

Then we might hear the song of joy that sings
in the heart's fountain as it leaps and burns
past the dim branches and the shades of things,
past the brick walls until it breaks and turns

dropping again in quiet spray and light
over the chatter, branches, walls
until the very beer with newer foam is bright
and in the hungry noise a ringing quiet falls.

It was probably Wilder who got President Hutchins to invite Gertrude Stein (1874-1946) to give a lecture series at the university, later published as *Lectures in America*,[46] at the same time as was performed her opera with music by Virgil Thompson, *Two Saints in Four Acts*. Her *Autobiography of Alice B. Toklas*,[47] her lifelong companion, had recently been published and the newspapers were filled with silly parodies of her experimental writing and accounts of how she had helped Ernest Hemingway with his own blunt style. I eagerly read those of her works that I could get hold of, especially *Making of Americans* and her poems *Tender Buttons* and *Lucy Church Amiably*, and I attended the well-performed opera. These pieces were pleasant puzzles. Much of the scenery of the opera was made out of colored cellophane and the saints wandered around the stage singing mellifluously.

Stein's lectures were not held in a regular classroom but in a carpeted lounge where we sat on the floor at her feet. The shadowy, black-haired Toklas, dressed in the style of Paris 1910, hovered in the background, while Stein with her cropped hair and her Buddha-like mask spoke in an even, hypnotic voice. She did not like disagreement with her oracular remarks, as is illustrated by a famous dialogue she had with Mortimer Adler which ended by her rapping him on the head with her fist and exclaiming, "You are a young man that likes to argue!"

Her lectures on literary composition were mainly about grammar and punctuation. She anathematized adjectives, canonized nouns and verbs. She declared that true poetry is nouns, since nouns name things, and poetry is naming things. She also disliked commas or indeed any punctuation except periods. Periods, she said, make things stop, and that is sometime necessary (after *Tristan and Isolde* I agreed with that). She emphasized the importance of using syntactical movement rather than adjectival coloring to carry the burden of poetic expression. When my friend Leo asked her what she thought of the poetry of Gerard Manley Hopkins of which he was fond, she said she never heard of him, and when shown one of his famous sonnets, said, "Too much description, too many adjectives." She did not speak to me about my novel (the one I described in Chapter 1), which Wilder showed her, but when he returned it to me, he told me her opinion: "She said this is one of the two most remarkable things she has read since coming to America; however, tell him to leave out the fleshy stuff." By "fleshy stuff" I am sure she meant the highly adjectival descriptions I had in the novel of the physical beauty of my heroine and hero.

I learned that the other "remarkable" bit of writing she referred to was by a strange hanger-on at the University who lived in great poverty on 52nd Street. I visited him and his girlfriend there and read one of his short-stories which were indeed quite striking. But I never heard of him again and do not remember his name, or know whether he ever became a success. He was a person whose own miseries seem to have given him remarkable insight into people. During that visit, he spoke of a young student we both knew who was in trouble and about whom I expressed contempt for his behavior, "But you don't understand him. You are a person who is very conscious. This guy is unconscious." Yes, perhaps I am too conscious.

At the end of the course I showed Stein a poem, *My Grandmother's Stairs*, in which I tried to follow her dictum, "Don't describe. Write what you are becoming." She thought this poem, which unfortunately I have lost, showed I was beginning to understand what she meant. I felt enormously encouraged. Another poem published in Martin Gardener's magazine *Comment* resembles in style this lost poem.

WHISTLING BOY

Here on the breakwater whistles the foam
and I stand whistling in monotone.
Neither gull nor sail
no driftwood no cloud,
water alone.
I'm whistling real loud.

Sad, sad is the level waste. Sad is the even colored sky,
as far as the eastward eye can see spreading out
away from me
in the light green sea;

but I
am not sad.
I feel proud
because I can whistle like foam
real loud.

Now a boat is showing a flash of sail
way out. Watch it brighten, watch it fail
and now shine clearly and now shoot near
and now dart by and disappear.

Here against my feet subsides the foam
and I stand again alone, again alone.
Neither flash nor sound,
no wind no face.
Water against stone
can leave no trace.

Sad is the waste, sad is the even, even sky.
As far as I ever see, though I try staring to see,
is the sea
and I
am proud,
and I
am proud
because the foam whistles loud like me.

A second poem is too long, but it also represents my efforts to
follow the instruction of Gertrude Stein on making the poem give
experiential expression to the thing described and it has a certain
cubistic quality. It evidently represents my loneliness and sexual
turmoil at the time.

THE CITY, WOMEN, MEN, LIVING

THE CITY:
    A city is rooms,
    a city is streets,
    somewhere in their squares my heart beats,
    my mind blooms,
    my mind has streets,

empty and crowded rooms.
Somewhere within its dark a light repeats,
the square lights everywhere in the square glooms,
everywhere, but here and there at night a window
blooms
square and here by day and there a shadow looms
of wall and wall along each street,
square where sun and shadow meet as wall and wall.
By night and day set square in streets
containing stairs and rooms
where men and women meet and man meets woman
woman man,
human to human now completes
or in a square a woman blooms
in my vacant mental glooms.
So neat that in this street
men meet
women in dark rooms,
human,
somewhere between the streets.

AND WOMEN:
A woman is a dream.
Deep within the darkening round is hid the soul.
within the gleam
that is the dream
within the whole,
she weeping moves so smoothly deeply to control.
Lift up the veil and wound within prevails the subtle
soul,
moving with a soothing sweep around the darkest
goal.
A golden veil veiling with its subtle gleams
beyond and deepening beyond into the revealing
veil,
sleeping within into the truth and dream
within the rounded hole
of death she lives and makes death live
until death living teams with life

sleeping with her, swollen,
while round and around her stream
to die, to live
within a deeper hole
all whole,
live within her moving dream.

AND MEN:

A man is running,
a man is a spark
up over the covering of the dark
upward turning
blank and stark
burning
over and under through to the mark,
leaning in and down and through the yearning,
down and drawing back the bitter and the better
learning
through, across the past and present spurning,
of this and those discovering the sparks
through and above the drawing starkly this from
those
with the clear blankness free of ugly marks
light sunlight running
to be thirsty with the thirst of thirsting
clear more clear demark
sunning dark and darkening sun
under cover from the blankness running
upward and over as a spark
thirst thirsting
turning running
thirsts
the burning of the dark.

AND MEN AND WOMEN:

We are not you,
We are one,
not micks or black or jap or jew
this will be true
beneath the sun
over and above you

as below back and forth as we have done
now then but now we never then somehow knew
if then as now beneath above from what was it
somehow grew
the irish american and the jew, a few
above
but more and never really one
as here beneath we burdened back and forth and
back
and piled the burden higher one by one
above beneath you and you and you,
not rising in power, no power rose,
power and plenty, all the fun
of you not one drew or spun
and underneath it grew
then and now not half begun
irish american jap or jew in power
under you
somehow with us is one.

AND LIVING:

A city is a man in the street,
a city is a woman in a room,
here we against you dividing in the under gloom
meet, bloom, repeat,
until the living are here the dead there in the tomb.
Against each and against all back and forth
the shadows beat
joining this to those and turning in the dark
demark, delete
gathering into together dream and spark complete.
The light burning from the gloom of the square
everywhere wall grows anew from wall
and web unraveled grows one upon the loom.
Street runs into street
where this against that and that to this
ends forever and again resume.
The squared city is in bloom,
power into power, street into street
in my mind and in my room.

Man to woman,
the city is blooming in each street,
human,
the city is a tomb, fun, birth, walls,
this room.

Stein also attended the Hutchins-Adler Great Books seminar one evening, but it was an evening when I was absent. Her presence on the campus, however, did not please the English department who thought her a publicity-seeking fraud. Several of us who were attending her lectures were asked to meet with some of the English faculty to explain why we were so interested in her. It happened that one night in the dining hall several us got to daring each other to do outrageous things. Someone dared Leo Shields and another fellow to hitchhike to Europe. Believe it or not they actually started the next day and got as far as somewhere in Ohio, when the cold weather made them decide to come back to school. I was only dared to have my head shaven, which I did. The English faculty thought I had done this to show my admiration for Stein and did not seem to believe my explanation that my crew-cut had nothing to do with her cropped hair.

Reading and Writing

At this time I was also reading James Joyce's *Ulysses* and T.S. Eliot's *Four Quartets*. Such experimentalism (today we would say modernist) writing fascinated me, but the many journalistic parodies of Stein warned me that imitating other people's experiments is a bad idea. I recently heard of a Catholic bishop who in a sermon joyfully announced that the Pope was soon to canonize Gertrude (he meant Edith) Stein!

I published poems in student magazines including the *Soapbox* which I myself edited. When I showed Wilder some of the poetry I was publishing in the student magazines and that expressed my political views, he very kindly but seriously told me that I would have to choose between politics and poetry. I did not know at the time that some Marxist critics had savaged his *The Bridge of San Luis Rey*[48] for its pseudo-mystical tone and its irrelevance to social revolution. He was at that time working on his *Heaven's My Destination*[49] whose hero is a Bible salesman. He then went on to write the enormously popular play *Our Town*.

Wilder was probably right about me. My political poems were
windily rhetorical and in my activism I wrote less and less. Poetry
cannot of itself create a worldview and a value-system; it can only
express these once they are philosophically proposed. Many of us at
the university were searching for a real basis for our lives. Thus, in
his correspondence with me in 1982, Martin Gardner mentioned his
autobiography *The Whys of a Philosophical Scrivener.*[50] He wrote
that after being a Protestant fundamentalist in Tulsa, OK, as a boy,
he then took up Karl Barth and his Neo-Orthodoxy just then coming
into vogue at the Divinity School of the University, but finally
dropped Christianity. He says, however, that today his views resemble those of Jesus more than those of many Episcopalian priests he
knows, and characterizes himself as now a fideist close in view to
the Spanish philosopher Miguel de Unamuno (1864-1936). He dis-
cusses Adler's views and Aquinas' proofs of the existence of God,
but is not satisfied with them. Was I satisfied?

It was also about this time that I made the acquaintance of
novelist-to-be Saul Bellow (1915-2005)[51] of the class of 1939, the
later Nobel laureate. He was a romantic looking young man with
especially striking large dark eyes and was for a time a fellow traveler of the Young Socialists. I did not know him well. In the 50s
when I was a priest I was at the University in the cafeteria of its
International House and at an adjoining table a stranger greeted me
warmly by "Hello! Winston!" The stranger had a rather haggard and
lined face but I recognized Saul by those dark eyes and we had coffee together. His novels, of course, speak much of New York, but the
philosophical cast by which they are distinguished reflects his University of Chicago years.

In reaction to these various literary influences I experimented
a good deal with long odes such as the following written in 1936
which reflects my Marxism, the Spanish civil war, my poetic experiments, and my growing preference for music of the classic period
over the romantic style which had earlier pleased me:

ODE ON LISTENING TO MOZART
*during the Counterrevolution in Spain
and on the 145th anniversary of his death (1936)*
I

One who alone stares at the moon in a city crowd
among city lights

in the center of brass violence
when the very air is cloven on these shattering nights
as the celestial squadrons take their flights,
he alone can breathe deep breath
in all our worlds declared at war,
only this one listener to silence.

What has he seen between the wires
among the walls along the cliffs
the one man midmost in a history
to listen, listen to the mystery?
What has anyone heard at once when always the firing
fades and echoes
and in all the crevices of hearing the gunfire sifts?
Has no one smiled and sighed at the perfect jointure there
inside
of mystery in history?

History is the shattered story of all the people
in those shattered streets,
bombings, lights, outcries, courage in defeats.
History crowds by.
Mystery is that moon, that silence, that singularity of the
seer
who listens, the internal moon and silence in one hearer.
Mystery is in his eye, his ear.

II

The singular mind has a single eye, wide and deep
since hearing only wakens the mind out of a deaf sleep,
yet no one has seen clearly the moon reflected
in a screaming face,
no painters have seen
nor paintings been
the mystery of sight that finds in history
the ultimate radiance in a black place.
The eye has not found itself much gazing space
in the glittering armies, blazing towns, the fathomless
graves,
nor has such seeing ever been.

III

Among the wheels
of frosted carriages, one Wolfgang heard
the ladies' satins rustle,
then suddenly the twang in parting of the temporal seals
of polished conversation,
of the wheeling and dealing, the squeaks, the squeals
of manners, morals, high policies, war strategies
of nations and of sighing lovers and the sound
of ladies satin gowned

and heard whenever he felt like hearing
alone at once and loud
the forms of silence
the wit of silence,
singularity contented in itself inside the foggy jointures
of the vibrant time, graceful and proud
temperate formation promising, performing all it promised
with all the wit of silence.

Amadeus, lover of God or beloved of Him,
thou listener to infinity's clear space
where radiance again repeats again past all wearying,
singular listener, thou alone
art the repeater without prejudice
of all those sounds that were ever heard,
adding to that totality no personal word,
claiming for self no property on tone,
single listener, thou alone.

IV

He was the single one, he of all the crowd the only one
though he repeated only
and hated being lonely,
since in all their manners he was like all others in all
that was being said or done:
in the shape of his wig and the lily-woven, lily-spun
of his coat with silk facings and his flounced cravat
and the satin lining of his hat,

the wit of his talk, the swagger of his walk,
since he hated being lonely.

What? What is this mob that fills all corridors and crawls
with a hard groaning
and repetitive moaning
into sheltering subways out of the blacked-out moonlight
that splits and screaming
falls with a blank thunder through all Hispania's white walls
with blind brightness down out of the invisible violence
of the planes' repetitive droning?

Silence succeeds the missile, all have heard its solitary
sound
and now not one so deaf as not to feel that silence
shaking like witless laughter in the ground,
the wit of silence after.
Mystery has become a commonplace in every ear this year.
History is not a change of wig or coat
now that we all, all can hear
the changeless form of violence.

V

The single will has a single mind wide and deep
and all art can only waken it from sensory sleep,
yet not one has seen our future like the full harvest moon,
no painter nor poet aloud,
no single prophet cries in the desert of the crowd

Mystery with history.
no one joins them now by an impersonal, timeless tune
singularly discovered, not one not one. Soon?
No poet or painter from the silent mob,
only a quiet tear, a silent sob.
No painter or poet aloud.
yet when the shells shriek like witless laughter
to the hollow silence after,
our Amadeus is the listening throng,
the chaotic, desperate crowd
hearing the first, prophetic clarion notes
of their victory song.

I never did much with the standard poetic forms. But I did attempt the following sonnet in which I tried to express my sense that I must not let myself be carried away by poetic fantasy but must face the world realistically and critically as Marx claimed to do, distinguishing fact from fiction. Today we would call this attitude "the hermeneutic of suspicion."

SEPARATION

This feeling is like crystal or Damascus steel,
a sword against, a mirror for the world,
reflecting all things naked, hairy, real:
the hypocrite host behind the banners furled
in sacred peace, the black child in the womb
of its creamy mother, the curse within the palm,
your hand smooth along my side, the stinking tomb
and maggots in the nose that toned a psalm,
a flaming, leaping word whose mighty hilt
fits in the fingers of my holy wrath,
singing to cleave the massy helm of guilt
or dig toeholds to make a mountain path.
crystal and steel tempered in cold despair,
it lies between us, that were once a pair.

Yet I was still much taken with the paradox of the beauty of spring in the grimy city of Chicago, with its parks, buildings and statutes often in a classic style.

FOUNTAIN OF DELIGHT

I found the spring to be
a white girl shaking down her hair
to make a beacon for a hovering god,
her flowering feet upon the breathing sod,
he trembling aloft in the Olympian cold.
Passion was their spring,
and lover's pain the breeze
stirring new foaming
in the wine-dark seas.

Here in this net of blocks and pipes and walks,
these thousands again watch the spring in the smoky parks
and every numbered street has an unnumbered crowd
wandering through freshening music and still rawer noise
to find somewhere some face that almost smiles.
A desolation with anticipations is this spring,
crowds of aloneness, since in a city love is trouble.
At least again now on parkways the fountains bubble.

Yet always spring is holy spring,
a woman sits here near the wall alone
in this neglected and abandoned place,
and on her lap a stillborn burden,
wounded, a stilled mouth in a still face,
in this cold city with its blinded crowds,
the fair maiden with her dying god.

All passion, all desolation is this spring, ruddy and white,
All lover's pain and emptied loneliness and hope unsaid,
the mother of all life with her sole child dead,
our sea of grief, our fountain of delight.

You are such a one as that one
that they heard was dying,
that lay somewhere dying,
that was lately dead,
short-lived and better at rest
at last.

Yes, you were such a one.

Some of my poems were published in Martin Gardner's magazine of which I was an associate editor, *Comment: University of Chicago Literary and Critical Magazine* such as,

WHEN THE CLAPPERS OF BELLS

When the clappers of bells clap the muffling air
and the loft pigeons scatter down the loft stair
and in the street feet scratch the misted ice

or a car grinding to rest honks twice,

when the shadow of a smoke stack cuts starlight
and under a tin roof creaking there shows the white,
the steel white shadow of a frosted drain
and below the iced edge of a broken pane,

when up the steps come counted footsteps
and the bell rings faintly from the curtained depths
of the house, a face seen faintly through window-steam,
and this is an old dream,

when the face and the voice and the noise and the peace,
when all the colors come, when they cease.
gossip and names and hoarse laughter and the old hurt
come in waves, are remembered, hushed—spurt

into the clear burning of you, quench into me.
When all that is the world and its beaten love and its woven
death,
rise in me and die away and come again like breath,
each like the last, unasked and unnecessary,

then even as my breathing, it all comes as words
and there is rhyming where were faces, shadows,
and the bell-waked birds.

These poems do not seem to me now especially to reflect Ronald
Cranes' teaching about Aristotle's dictum that a poem is mimesis, a
representation of an action with a beginning, middle, and end. I am
afraid I had nothing much to say except to express impressions and
feelings, since I did not want to return to the autobiography of my
novel. I was trying to emphasize the music of verse, much neglected
in contemporary poetry, but without the Victorian vagueness of
Tennyson or Swinburne. I was influenced both by imagism and T.S.
Eliot. I was looking for a vocabulary that was very simple but emotionally charged. Much of my imagery was derived from the openness of the Oklahoma landscape on the one hand and on the other of
the closed-inness of the city.

Chapter 5 - Political Dialectics

The Draft

My high school years had been darkened by the Great Depression. The approach and outbreak of World War II darkened my university years. When the Vietnam crisis and the 60s came, it all seemed to me déjà vu. In high school I was a pacifist but not much interested in politics. Then in my freshman year while still at Burton Hall my second friend, after the Jewish boy from Tulsa, was a very strange person. He was very odd, ugly, poorly shaven, as pug-nosed as the old statues of Socrates. This was the young moccasin shod reformer, Lewis A. Dexter,[52] son of a Unitarian minister in Boston. Lewis, although not Jewish, had gone to an Ethical Culture School and to Bennington College and was the incarnation of the Bostonian determination to do good. He instructed me how our patriarchy had been long preceded by matriarchy. At Bennington he had cross-dressed with his girl friend to learn firsthand the hardships caused by sexual stereotypes. They had also engaged in an experimental boxing match to see if men were really stronger than women and she had knocked him out. To save money from his allowance to promote the peace efforts of the Cosmos Club of the Carnegie Foundation, Lewis was at that time living on a diet of apples and molasses, which he claimed supply all nutrients and vitamins necessary for vigorous health.

When many years later I read Lewis' obituary in a Baltimore paper it noted that he had been a lecturer at more than thirty colleges and universities and that his best known book was coauthored with Raymund Bauer and Ithiel Pool, *American Business and Public Policy*.[53] Ithiel Pool was also a sociologist and college friend whom I will later describe. One day Lewis portentously told me that the American Student Union, recently founded on campus to oppose the draft, was to hold a meeting at which, he knowingly predicted, there would be an attempt at a takeover by the Young Communist League. Out of curiosity I attended this meeting with him. A crowd of about 100 students engaged in a frantic debate centered on whether the pacifist "Oxford Oath" against the draft should be modified to read, "I swear that I will not take part in any imperialist war." This would, as the Communists wanted, exempt from the oath a war to defend the Soviet Union against Hitler. When the resolution to insert "imperialist" into the Oath passed, Lewis dramatically tore up his membership card in the ASU, scattered its fragments about him, and marched out, with me tagging behind.

I was amazed and fascinated by these political skirmishes. My father, as I have said, was a Republican who much disliked the tactics of the unions at the places where he had worked, especially a union in which my maternal uncle was an activist. But he also rejected the Ku Klux Clan in our town and any form of racism. Our next door neighbor was a ranking member in the Klan, and our family once, out of curiosity, attended a cross-burning in an open field, with the result that we were all picking cactus spines out of our legs for a week afterwards. Yet my mother had no interest in politics and neither did I, although I was influenced by what I read of the New Deal, and was antiracist. I was also pacifist, having no taste for the aggressive sports or physical risk.

After Dexter's dramatic protest, on my own I attended a few Young Communist League meetings whose program impressed me more than Dexter's Boston liberalism, because they seemed a radical organization with solidarity, rather than simply an isolated do-gooder like he was. When a march against the draft was held on campus as a Peace Rally, May Day 1934, I joined the march and swore not to serve in any imperialist war. I also took part that year in the May Day March into the Chicago Loop that ended at the famous Haymarket Square where in 1886 the police had martyred labor radicals. We marched with red banners flying dramatically in the wind. I felt part then of a promising worldwide movement for justice and peace.

It was at one of these meetings that I first met Quentin "Bud" Ogren, whom I have described before as a fraternity brother. He impressed me as an enthusiastic but sane, practical person, who was also very knowledgeable about politics, because his father was a politician. When he found I was attending Young Communist meetings and saw how politically naive I was, he undertook to explain the international situation. He related how for a while the Comintern followed a policy of attacking the socialists as a greater danger to the proletariat even than the fascists. Recently, however, the Movement had awakened to its mortal danger from Hitler and had made a 180 degree switch to the "Popular Front" policy of forming coalitions not only with Socialists but with liberals like the American Democrats. To do this they had to disguise their radicalism by working through fellow travelers willing to front for them. Ogren himself believed that the true Marxists were the Trotskyites who in opposition to Stalin's Russian nationalism were still fighting for world revolution. His view was verified for me by the Moscow Trials which had just begun, in which Stalin was exterminating most of the first generation of the Russian revolution in the interest of his own nationalist policies.

Thus better informed, I deserted the YCL for the YPSL (Yipsels) or Young Peoples' Socialist League to which Ogren belonged and which was in the process of being co-opted by the Trotskyites. Not long after in 1936 I attended a national meeting of the Socialist Party in Chicago at which the Trotskyites attempted to take over the Party itself. When they failed they split to form the openly Trotskyite Socialist Workers Party. I enthusiastically became a "card-carrying" (the card was red) member of the SWP. All of these events involved arcane debates about Marxist exegesis, dialectics, and "theory" whose scholastic intricacies fascinated me almost as much as the medieval scholasticism to which Adler and Hutchins had introduced me. What impressed me most, however, was that this struggle over "theory" was hooked up to a struggle over "praxis." The academic circles in which I moved were content to talk and talk without any life commitment, while the Marxists groups, in spite of their sometimes ridiculous futility, strove to put their theories into action. They were struggling to make sense out of the tremendous world movements of the Great Depression, the rise of Fascism, and the Second World War of the century, events that touched the life of my generation and my personal experience. Meanwhile the Academy went blindly on giving degrees and doing research, much of it financed by the war machine.

I belonged to a Trotskyite cell of the Socialist Workers Party whose leader in Chicago was named Herb Passin.[54] The members of the Young Communist League had been ordered by their Party, in accordance with the line adopted internationally by the Communist Party to defend the Moscow Trials, to ostracize Trotskyite deviants and to get other students to do so. We were to be treated as secret agents of Hitler, just as the victims of the notorious Moscow Trials in false, forced confessions were declaring themselves to have been. This did not much bother the members of our cell, which included, besides Ogren, Leo Shields, and myself, Ithiel de Sola Pool, Marty Lieberman, two or three women who accepted subordinate roles, and George Reedy Jr. Reedy was later to be the press secretary of Lyndon Johnson and author of a fine book *The Twilight of the Presi-*

dency.[55] A student publication characterized George as one "who covers his brains with a bush which is expected to flower any month now" (beards were uncommon at that time) and me as "Winston Ashley, inveterate dabbler in all extremes."

Another member was a Christopher S. who later, as I have been told, during the Pacific War sold all he had and bought a boat to sail his family to safety on an ocean island, which turned out to be Okinawa! The leader of the Young Communist League was a Frank Meyer who later became a bitter and vocal Neo-Conservative often quoted in the press.[56] My life became a round of political meetings punctuated by reading for my Master's degree. During the time that I lived at the Socialist Co-op, I used to spend the afternoon at the library, many evenings at meetings, then working far into the night at my books. I would have breakfast at 4:40 or 5 in the morning at some all-night restaurant on 63rd street under the 'L', before sleeping all morning.

I don't think we Trotskyites ever accomplished much either for good or ill, but we met weekly and were assigned various tasks like passing out pamphlets or picketing where strikes were in progress or attending student or other meetings to proclaim our views, but it occupied much of my time. We did, however, with no effect, petition President Hutchins to increase the meager representations of black students at the University.

A poem I wrote at this time expresses my effort to find community beyond loneliness through identification with the "masses."

THE CITY IS A FURNACE FORGING MANY INTO ONE

Dense autumn heat breathes from these walls, steel, brick, stone,
with a torrential gush of feet.
Millions pour forth and I can feel the hot current
of blood against bone.
In the soft smoke I hear the noisy sleet.

In a spreading mesh of structures and bodies there seems one life
involving all its organs in internal strife.
It seems as if the elevator and the lifted arm,
the drawbridge and knee, the stop light and the eye,

the breasts so warm, the building in momentary sun
within the membrane of water, the tissue of sky were one
harsh roaring life that swirls
in streetcar, wind, and factory girls.

Heat breathes. I feel its quivering rush.
I see across the evening's mouth the steel-mills blush.
One life here and in this cheek, yet when they turn
to speak to her or him, to know, to clasp,
I find only the slow, hard beat, the shapeless rasp and burn
of this impersonal living thunder
this vital soulless wonder
all one and yet without feature, word, limit, or skin.
Behold there seems to it no without no within,
only the breath of many mouths, the heat
of one pair of endlessly reduplicated feet.

There is nothing like this life but fire
that in amorphous splendor seems a limitless desire,
able to absorb in one great radiance every dark
atom, every shred, then in a beaming shower rise and glare
with one red featureless visage of the skies devouring the
air,
falling back in unmarked coils of lust
to evanesce in slightest dust,
all one, within a thousand sparks and tongues and curls,
spreading forever with no shape but torrents, and in swirls
living without any self identity or name
but that of living and intimate inner flame.

So this serpent life engulfs me, smothers me.
I am lost in it, within or without I do not know,
only I begin to beat with its beat glow with its glow.
I perceive in the steel the slow fire of the rust
in the stone, the crumbling in the heat, I sense
in the river's flow the current of the crowd in that uproar,
the inarticulate echo from cellular offices floor to floor
and in each cell of the brain the nerve and wire,
one current of atomic fire.

Dry autumn smothers under the night and cold and beneath

the insulation of the sleet
the featureless city's single glare and moan
one current of heat, heat, light, pain, sweat, pleasure,
thought, hate,
one current of feet, hands, girders, tracks, pain, sweet
pleasure
one agony of heat
a furnace within frail crumbling walls of stone, of bone.

Tonight in the cold through city winter clouds shines wide
the moon
and my remembrance of personal despair. Ah, over soon
these hands may lift from the furnace, flame
over the breaking wave, our flame
quivering like a voice
knowing, ah, rejoice!
that now not hands in my incestuous hand wilts in cold
wishing prayer,
but handclasps and fists singing and knowing burn in this
winter's air.

Trip to New York

Recollections of a trip to New York belong in this political context. I had never been to New York City, nor had Leo Shields. Hence
one spring quarter we seized on an invitation from a boarder at the
fraternity to drive there with him on a holiday. This driver was a
wild fellow who was just getting over the binge of the night before
and drove on erratically in his sports car with the top down. He had
another passenger with him in the front while Leo and I rode in
what was then called the "rumble seat." Just before leaving we both
had picked up our laundry for the trip in thin cardboard boxes at
the Chinaman's (no Laundromats in those days) and had to stick
these boxes under our legs in the very tight rumble seat. Naturally,
in the course of the trip we trampled all over our clean shirts. In one
town the police stopped us for speeding and took us into the station
for questioning because they thought we had stolen the car. I was
very scared they would also inspect my small bag and find a couple
of Communist books I was taking along, but they quickly let us go.
The driver, although he was a native New Yorker, got caught in

downtown Manhattan traffic and drove us around in circles. How exciting that forest of towers and rushing crowds on the street seemed! New York makes Chicago look the small town it is, not in size surely, but in character.

Leo and I had been invited by our Trotskyite comrade Ithiel de Sola Pool to stay at his parents' home on Central Park West, though we only saw the house servants and his mother briefly on her way out to vacation. Ithiel's father was the rabbi of the very old Sephardic Synagogue, a beautiful, silent, holy place, next to the de Sola Pool's residence which was large, empty and gloomy. It was very hot in New York, and I remember getting cold borsch with sour cream at an automat; a kind of food and dispenser new to me. We wandered blissfully about the city in the heat, Central Park, the Metropolitan Museum, the Staten Island Ferry. The Twin Towers did not then pierce the heavens, but we viewed the great city from atop the Chrysler Building.

Ithiel is a beautiful biblical name of one of the Benjaminites who returned from the Exile to Jerusalem (Neh 11:7) and so much history was summed up in this thin, aristocratic, elegant young man who was so ardent a revolutionist. The Sephardic Jews were expelled from Spain to North Africa by Isabella and Ferdinand and were among the earliest Jews in the United States. In later life Ithiel became a distinguished sociologist. Though he was not a religious Jew, it surprised me that he was attracted to Communism. After I had entered the Dominican Order, Ithiel needed a security clearance for some government-funded research he was doing. Consequently, I was interviewed by a man from the FBI making a security check. I supposed he would ask me about Ithiel's radical activities, but oddly it was not about him that the FBI agent inquired but about his parents. They were suspect, apparently, because his mother was a prominent member of Hadassah, the very respectable Jewish women's organization!

The reason my name was in FBI files was that for a year or so I was editor of a journal of the Young Socialist League magazine, *Soapbox*. After the war I was several times questioned in the Dominican monastery to which I had by that time gone (see Chapter 6) about various other graduates of the University who were undergoing security checks for government jobs. My policy was simply to answer the questions truthfully, but I was always amazed at how ignorant these FBI agents seemed to be of the real facts about Communism, as also appeared to be the notorious Senator McCarthy whose televised investigations I watched. He was exposing Communism without any real understanding either of its aims or its tactics. From what I saw—of course my experience was very limited—Communism did make real inroads only in a few unions, such as the Electrical Workers and Longshoremen's unions and the Trotskyites among the Teamsters. Furthermore, from the first I believed in the guilt of Alger Hiss. Some liberals who thought that Communism was the wave of the future doubted his guilt, but Whitaker Chambers' (1901-1961)[57] testimony seemed to me then, as it does now, entirely plausible.

Nevertheless, I do not believe that Marxism was ever a real threat in this country, as it truly was in some European and other countries. Its number of supporters here was always small, and its political tactics easily exposed and unacceptable to American culture. Yet the media often inflated this feeble and confused movement into a monster menace. Thus in 1935 the founder of the Walgreens drugstore chain was alarmed when his niece, Lucille, a student at the University, told him that in one of her classes they were required to read *The Communist Manifesto*. The *Chicago Tribune* enlarged this homely incident into a front-page story about the "How Red is the University of Chicago?" that eventually led to an investigation by the state legislature centering especially on the views of Frederick L. Schuman, an assistant professor of political science. Hutchins' took the investigation very calmly and quite properly defended his faculty. Eventually he even persuaded Charles Walgreen to give the University $550,000.

Indeed only a couple of the faculties were Marxist in their opinions and no evidence ever appeared of any deep political involvement on their part. The university officials were well aware that the radical students, although annoying, were an insignificant minority. According to William McNeill, in his Hutchins' University previously cited, in 1932 blacks and Asians were only 2% of the University, though Jewish students, from whom most of the activists were drawn, were about 26%. The reason for the predominance of Jewish radicals (of course only a very small section of the Jewish students) was that a number who had been expelled from New York universities as the result of anti-draft demonstrations had sought refuge at the University of Chicago. But I would estimate that the American Student Union, concerned mainly to oppose the draft, had only about 350 members, with probably only half of them active. Of these

40-80 were Communists, of whom 50 to 25 were active. We Trotskyites were certainly not more than 25.

Knowing our Marxist political interests Mortimer Adler proposed that Ogren, Shields, and I become his graduate research assistants for a book he was writing with the working title of *Summa Contra Marxistes* in which he hoped to build a bridge between Thomism and Marxism. We combed Marxists texts for him and especially the official Soviet *Textbook of Marxist Philosophy* recently translated (1937), but Adler's book never appeared. Later with Leo O. Kelso he published, *The New Capitalists: A Proposal to Free Economic Growth from the Slavery of Savings*.[58] While we were doing research on this for Adler and I was beginning my studies for the Doctorate which I had now decided to do no longer in literature as my Master's had been but in political theory Leo and I lived in a house where Adler was supporting several other of his protégés including Aaron Bell, about whom I wrote earlier. Without this generous help from Adler, to whom I am forever grateful, I might never have been able to continue my studies.

One of the ideas of Marxism that most appealed to me was that it was based on the inevitability of the dialectics of history. Today this seems to me the source of all Marx's errors. He borrowed it from Hegel and the Enlightenment myth of inevitable progress and its appeal arises from the fact that it is a rationalized (Hegel) or secularized (Marx) substitute for the Christian concept of Divine Providence and Predestination. Since, however, it is either atheistic (Marx) or pantheistic (Hegel) and knows nothing of a God who freely created the world, it is self-contradictory.

At the time I became a Catholic in 1938, an event to be described in the next chapter, I was still a Trotskyite, yet saw no great inconsistency in these two allegiances. I had never thought atheism was essential to the social theories of Marx and I thought the social doctrine of the Church with its rejection of laissez faire capitalism might be reconciled with Marxist economics. But as soon as the Socialist Workers Party heard of my conversion they expelled me. As I became better acquainted with Catholic social doctrine and of modern economic theory the fallacies of Marx became obvious to me. Yet I continued to believe and still do believe that social justice requires very profound changes in the capitalist economic system that now dominates the world and reflects the dominance of secular humanism. While the saying that "Young radicals become old conservatives" has its truth, now that I am old I would rather say that since "radical" means "rooted," youthful radicalism is a striving, though often badly informed, to put down deep roots. Unfortunately the roots of Marx's thought are as shallow as those of Adam Smith's. Neither, alas, is a "tree planted near the streams of water, that yields its fruit in due season (Psalm 1:3)."

My pondering on the meaning of history was expressed in a poem:

HOW SLOWLY HISTORY SOMETIMES MOVES

A long stretch of water where the barges move,
bordered by trains following their double groove,
above it complex bridges lift and then descend,
above them many fumes and poisonous gases blend;
a stretch of water green and slow,
below,
ceases never in its flow.

The crowds of thousands in the factory streets,
where the neon whistle puffs and bleats
and the gray sun on huge windows glares
as the streetcars passing ring up fares,
the crowds of thousands stop at either verge,
surge
as the light changes, meet and rub and merge.

This year and the immediate years just on ahead
are days and nights of stench and fire moving so slow
that the factory waters and the thousands hardly know
between which banks, through which channels they must go
between two competing kinds of crazy clamor,
the capitalist demagogue or the sickle and hammer,
But there is a gradient that pulls the water
in polluted eddies downward to the Gulf.
Inevitably
the stream grows heavier, violent, full.
The last stretches of water where the barges move
slides sullenly along in a wandering
yet certain, certain
groove.

Chapter 6 - Opening to God

Meeting the Catholic Church

The central event of my university life was at hand, but I was unaware of its approach. I came to the University not merely an agnostic, but I would have said, if asked, an atheist. After all my parents had the idea that we should choose our own religion when we grew up, and I was now, in a way, grown up. I have recounted how my mother gave me Bible stories to read and taught me some good night prayers to say and how at about ten I went to summer Bible school, got a prize for memorizing Bible verses, and explained the Protestant doctrine of vicarious atonement to another boy. I had never been baptized, however, nor had I ever gone regularly to church. When in junior high school a Baptist friend tried to evangelize me I was insulted. I have already related how in high school I was disillusioned when a friendly Protestant minister who let me play his opera records dissimulated his belief in evolution to his congregation. I have also recounted the nameless fears and anxieties from which I suffered as a child, and my later metaphysical ponderings and attraction to Buddhism and the philosophies of Plato and Spinoza. But along with this went my voracious reading of all kinds of modern liberal and scientific thought that assured me that modern intellectuals rightly regard religion as obsolete. I accepted all this until Adler and Hutchins convinced me that modernity at least is not the final word.

In the University I was not a "searcher after truth." I simply was stimulated by many different ideas. As I have already noted, I found special intellectual satisfaction in the thought of Aristotle and St. Thomas with its clarity and comprehensive systematization. But on the other hand I was deeply moved by Marxist thinking that seemed to explain the historical events which were the context of my life, the Depression and the War.

In Chicago I sometimes visited Catholic churches with Leo Shields and was both attracted by their architecture and liturgy, so much richer than the Protestant churches and church services I knew in Blackwell, and repelled by what in Marxist terms I interpreted as their financial exploitation of the credulous poor. Thus, I was shocked by the fact that on Sundays at the entrance to St.

Thomas the Apostle Church, near the campus, with its beautiful architecture, art, and liturgy, ushers demanded a dime (yes, a dime!) as "pew rent." As a Marxist I believed that the Church always sides with the upper classes and oppresses the poor and that Franco's attack on the Spanish Republic and his alliance with Mussolini and Hitler proved this.

Nevertheless at this time I did experiment a bit with religion in that one Lent I did some fasting and attended Catholic Holy Week services, which I regarded as a striking drama in which I participated emotionally just as I would have done in watching a play. I also argued a good deal with Leo about religion. Later he said that he always felt that he lost the arguments, but this did not seem to have shaken his faith, as he attended Sunday Mass regularly and indeed often daily.

More fundamental was the fact that I became intellectually convinced of God's existence through what I was reading in St. Thomas' *Summa Theologiae* about his famous Five Ways of proving God's existence. At that time Adler too was convinced of the validity of these proofs, although, for philosophical reasons that I then and now consider mistaken, he later decided that these proofs were only probable. Similar arguments also led to the conviction that the human soul must survive bodily death. Thomistic philosophy proposes a proof that the material cosmos is not self-explanatory but manifests that it is the effect of a non-material First Cause, which is intelligent, and creatively free. It also leads to the conclusion that the human ability not only to perform animal activities as a body but also to think abstractly and hence to be free and "creative" manifests that its soul is non-material. This spiritual cause transcends its bodily organs and hence is not liable to bodily death. Unlike the First Cause, however, the human soul although spiritual and immortal is created and is a caused cause dependent on the First Cause for its existence and entire activity.

I am not sure, but I think this realization that there must be a God and that our souls are immortal occurred between my sophomore and junior year. What I remember distinctly was that I announced to Leo one spring that I was not convinced by these proofs, and then during the summer when I had time to ponder them, came to the conclusion that they were inescapably true. Some years later after I was a Catholic and was living in the Dominican Priory in River Forest, I attended a lecture given at Rosary College by the eminent authority on the thought of St. Thomas Aquinas, Professor Étienne Gilson. Gilson was extremely impressive, elegantly dressed and mannered, and perhaps the most eloquent lecturer I have ever heard. But in the course of his lecture he asserted flatly that, although Aquinas' Five Proofs are certainly philosophically valid, no one is ever convinced of them who is not already a believer. This thesis was important to Gilson's notion of a "Christian Philosophy" and his ardent support of Thomism as he interpreted it. In the discussion period I got up and protested that I, before I had faith, had been an atheist who was convinced of the truth of Aquinas' proofs. Gilson seemed irritated by this counter-factual and brushed it off. I was told that later he said of me something very close to Gertrude Stein's rebuke to Adler, "You are a young man that likes to argue!"

No doubt Gilson could have replied to my objection that God's grace was already working on me, and of course it was, but at that time I was certainly not a believer but someone convinced only by rational argument. Since then, I have realized that in a technical sense I did not then have a very adequate grasp of the Aristotelian-Thomistic arguments, but I am also convinced that we often intuitively grasp, though imperfectly, the truth of an argument in its essentials, long before we understand it perfectly. What I saw was that although modern scientific explanations may be very true, they are never complete. Science can only explain events by the action of some changing entity, but such changing entities exist and act only because they are being actualized by some other changing entity. Such a chain of material causation cannot be circular nor can it be infinite but must have a first cause, since without a first cause an infinite chain of agents and recipients would be merely potential and unable to produce the final observed effect.[59] The First Cause cannot itself be changing and material, since if it were such it would again require another cause to actualize it. Thus the causes of our changing material world always presuppose the existence and action of some unchanging and non-material cause or perhaps causes. As I think the foregoing narrative, and especially my poetry, shows, I had (and, today I have even more), an acute sense of the vivid reality of this tangible, colorful, noisily musical world and hence of its utter changing temporality, so real, yet so unnecessary. Unfortunately today Christian writers largely depend on the "Design Argument" to refute atheism. This is a combination of Aquinas' Fourth and Fifth Ways which are valid, but which Aquinas points out are less evident than the First Way and presuppose it. Moreover they defend it not on the basis of simple and evident facts of experience but on advanced modern hypotheses that are open to dispute. Instead the First Way depends only on the fact of motion which if denied destroys the whole of natural science!

Aquinas also notes that there are only two serious arguments for atheism: that the world is self-explanatory and that a good God could not permit the evils of this world. The first of these arguments today takes the form of saying that science can give such good explanations of the world, that the old recourse to gods or a God is unnecessary. But in those days I was learning enough about modern science, in which, beginning with my father's influence, I have always taken a keen interest, to know that the kind of explanations that science gives, although true and useful, stop at causes which are still only caused causes, and thus in no way contradict Aquinas' proofs. The only way to escape these proofs is that taken by Hume, namely to deny causality altogether and this dead-ends first in positivism and finally in absolute skepticism. Kant thought he found the way out of this dead-end by considering the principle of causality to be a feature of our human thinking projected on the data of the senses, but this is just a more subtle form of skepticism. As for Kant's claim that the classic proofs beg the question because they suppose the definition of God as the most being possible, which is what we are trying to prove, this is a confusion between a merely nominal definition of God and a real one. While the proofs make use of a nominal definition of "God" this does not occur in the premises of the argument but in the conclusion to identify the First Cause that has been demonstrated to be what we ordinarily mean by the term "God."

The other argument against God's existence from the evil in the world depends on the analogy taken from human experience that a good person does no evil and seeks to prevent it when possible. Thus if there were an all-powerful God, He would neither cause nor permit evil to occur. But this overlooks the fact that good persons do in fact sometimes permit evil to occur that they could prevent, namely, when they permit an evil to occasion a greater good. This happens in two cases: First, in the case of merely physical evils, because in the material order the existence of one good thing is usually contrary to the existence of other good things, good persons can sacrifice the existence of a lesser good to a greater good. Thus we can weed a garden yet weeds are vitally beautiful in their own way. Second, in the case of spiritual or moral goods, there is no such contrariety of one good to another, but because of human freedom, a good parent or good teacher can permit a student to make a mistake in order to learn to do better. As a teacher I have felt uncomfortable about that, yet knew it was best for the student, and hence for me too. Thus there is no contradiction in an absolutely good God causing physical evils or permitting (not causing) spiritual evil, i.e. sin, for a greater good. Of course we do not always know what this greater good is to be, as we do not know how a great drama will play out, but our ignorance is no contradiction to the wisdom and goodness of God who is a greater dramatist than Shakespeare. Would we like to be players in a game without excitement?

Deaths

Besides the gloomy world events of Depression and War, at this time several student tragedies affected me. One friend developed tuberculosis and had to leave school. Another did not return the next fall and I heard that during the summer he had suffered a psychotic attack, then that he had died from shock therapy, not the rather mild electroshock now used, but a much more violent insulin shock. Still another acquaintance, a very young student, was diagnosed with cancer of the esophagus and I attended his very sad Jewish funeral.

These were awesome events, but somehow did not touch me personally in a deep way, because none of the victims were really close friends. The real tragedy for me was the sudden death of Robert L., the president of my fraternity. Norman Maclean was helping Bob through college and that is why, although Bob was not really an intellectual, he was included in the select group that was to renew the Lambda Rho Chapter. He was a businesslike, neatly dressed young man, with bright eyes, a ruddy complexion, and a self-con-fident gentlemanly manner, the only son of a widowed mother, seemingly on his way to be a business success in the world. For some reason that I could not fathom, Bob, so different than myself, admired me for my intellectuality, and often praised me. As I have related, from my childhood I was used to mockery, not praise from other boys. Indeed I now had other good friends, especially Leo, but Leo was another self, while Bob was the type of person I could never be. Thus I felt deeply about his friendship.

In the spring of my first year in the fraternity Bob was in the hospital a week for an appendectomy (hospital stays were longer then). When it was time for him to return it was decided that since the fraternity house had no elevator he would stay for a few days in the apartment of Maclean and his wife. Then we had a shocking phone call saying that on his way to the apartment in a taxi Bob developed a terrible chest pain, struggled to breathe, and within half an hour at the apartment expired, exclaiming, "Don't let me die! Don't let me die." A blood clot had entered his circulation and lodged in one lung.

In a daze I walked with another fraternity brother that night along Lake Michigan. Maclean asked me to go with another brother to the funeral in Minneapolis. He said, "Do you believe in an afterlife so that you can comfort his family?" We both said we did not, but we went anyway. When we reached Bob's home, to this other fellow's embarrassment, when Bob's mother began talking about what a fine son he had been, I broke down and left the room. I lingered over Bob's open coffin wanting, but not daring, to kiss his dead hand. Yet the day after the funeral when a friend of the family took the two of us on a drive into the country for a picnic (the weather was gray and chilly and the plains of Minnesota like tundra) I enjoyed the lunch and was quite myself again. I did not really grieve over Bob. Life was too full at that time to waste time in brooding, but the loss of someone who really liked me was always there. I think it was that sense of loss that made the triumvirate friendship with Bud and Leo grow still deeper.

One reason I had little time for grief was that I was elected president of the fraternity chapter to succeed Bob. This was the kind of acceptance by my peers of which I had never even dreamed. It really did not entail much responsibility, but in my college world it had prestige. One duty it did burden me with was conducting an open house at the fraternity with drinks and dance, which meant I would have to have a date.

In my sophomore year, 1934-35 as a result of a questionnaire sent to all of us undergraduates (at this time this was about the only effort the University made to show concern for its undergrads) I was sent to see a counselor. It was a funny session. He asked me if I was taking proper exercise. I answered that in my freshman year I tried to learn to swim in the field house, but got so much water up my nose trying to learn the butterfly crawl that I quit. He advised me to try handball, which I never did. This counselor then asked me if I was dating. I said no. He advised me to do so. Since I didn't go to class often, I only knew the women in my Marxist circle who were either already paired up or unattractive. He then inquired about how I was doing academically. When I explained about Adler being my mentor, he looked alarmed and assured me that if I accepted Aristotelian logic and especially the principle of contradiction, I would go crazy! Since I was convinced that people who do not accept that principle are already crazy, his advice did me little good. I know now that this counselor was under the influence of the anti-Aristotelian inventor of General Semantics Count Korzybski,[60] a disciple of Carnap and the logical positivism of the Vienna Circle. The Count had not been able to get a University appointment and so lived on its fringe with a group of disciples. He taught that "Fido," his typical dog, used Aristotelian logic and hence was unable to recognize that our ideas do not precisely mirror external reality. To remedy this error in thinking Korzybski invented a device which he called a "Semantic Rosary" which enabled the victim of "animalistic thinking" to visualize the difference between our meager static mental concepts and the complex vibrant reality to which they refer.

At least I took the counselor's advice in trying to get a date. I finally asked an attractive girl I had met at a lecture and to my surprise she accepted. Since, however, I had never learned to dance, she was chagrined (as I learned she told another girl) that at the party I quickly left her to her own devises and hardly saw her again at the party until it was time to escort her back to the women's residence. That was about the extent of my dating.

Drinking

I got further with the other major aspect of fraternity life: drinking. This was just after 3.2 beer was legalized and soon Prohibition was abolished. Saloons sprang up everywhere, and a favorite student place was Mike Hanley's Bar on 52nd Street that was said to have the longest mirror bar in Chicago, or was it The Longest Mirror Bar in the Whole World? Certainly through the smoke it seemed to stretch on forever. My first real drinking experiences were with a song that challenged one member of the gang to "Down the hatch!" I found I could down the hatch pretty well, but it did not so easily stay down. One night on my way home to the frat house with two or three brothers, one suggested we stop at another frat house, because he wanted to talk to a friend. This friend turned out to be no other than Jay Berwanger, the first Heisman Trophy winner in 1935, and the last great football hero of the University before in 1939 Hutchins took it out of the Big Ten. The great Berwanger was reading in bed, and his friend sat down on the foot of the bed to talk and so did I. Suddenly I gave a violent belch and the popcorn I had taken along with the beer spewed all over the bed covers. While Jay behaved like a gentleman, I staggered home in disgrace.

I then took to drinking gin by the shot with a little water. Why I chose such a tasteless potion I don't know. One night Mr. Hanley came to my table and in fatherly manner suggested I try something else, but I only laughed. Weekend binges became common with me and in this I had the support of some of the older members of the Chapter who had brought the fraternity to its low state before the Maclean renewal. Since a couple of my maternal uncles were alcoholics, I have no doubt that I was fast entering on their boozy road. Some of my fraternity brothers and other acquaintances of the period were alcoholics and one friend from New York, who claimed to be a descendant of an ancient British family, never ceased to astonish me by his sophisticated cynicism and his constant drinking. Drugs, however, never seemed to have been part of the scene in those days, and I was never tempted to try them.

As ultimately illusory as it is, the widespread notion in the 60s that chemicals could give you "spiritual" experiences, seems to me to have a certain truth. As I was to argue later in an essay,[61] the lowering of the psychological inhibitor that Freud called the Censor has a twofold effect. This permits the biological drives (Freud's Id) to rise into explicit consciousness, but it can also permit the super-conscious, which Freud did not recognize, but that St. Thomas Aquinas calls "intuition" (*intellectus* or the *ratio superior*) and the mystics the "point of the soul" (*apex mentis*) to come into consciousness. Thus spiritual insight may arise in an intense way that is ordinarily inhibited for the sake of rational, practical life (Freud's Ego). Probably this is why many religions use chanting, dancing, and other trance inducing techniques to enhance meditation. Thus in chemical experiences people sometimes do become aware of their spiritual yearnings.

I recall once coming back to the fraternity quite drunk and passing St. Thomas Apostle Church that I had visited with Leo and where later I was to be baptized, and woozily clinging to its wrought iron gate, singing a maudlin song. Something was stirring in me I had not been aware of before, and in this poem, needing a rhyme, I rightly called it "grace."

TOO MUCH DRUNK

I am drunk tonight
and in the close oblivion that liquor brings,
the heart yearns for infinity, throbs, sings.

All ye pent up on the narrow whirl of drugs,
bounded by walls and telephone slugs,
what do you know of the rest of reality
or all that is above and below mere men.
Oh beyond the whirl remember the dark against the light
and how infinitely white
is the virgin moon.

Now soon, soon, very soon
we must sink down, down into troubled dreams,
we must struggle to find the "is" in the "seems"
but now we dance and drunkenly cry for joy
in whatever alcoholic mixture we employ.
Yet as the spirit of the grain makes place
for the shout and the lewd embrace
so can the spirit within flesh make way
for grace.

Sweet moon,
we shall be drunk, we drunks, we pray thee soon
with a diviner drink
that rings and peals and drowns
the very body in its circling sounds.

One evening, at the suggestion of a fraternity brother who was a Chicagoan used to its nightlife, after getting drunk we took a taxi to the Near North Side and went to a brothel. Due to my intoxication it was a confused and not very satisfactory experience. Afterwards I was afraid of venereal disease but did not contract it, yet did not go again. The gloom of the area in which the brothel was located haunted me a bit and is one of the published poems called *A Sheaf of Flutes* from which I have already quoted:

CLARK STREET

Clark Street, Clark Street where are you going?
I am lost now in the river in its way and its flowing.
We are going bent under dark and the vagueness of beer—
here, no there, not there, no here
where whither here are we, O Clark Street going?

Here Clark Street they have left open the window
and a hand lies light on the sooty sill.
We are going, and between wheels it is a kind of stillness
of patience, of dimmer profligacy—
yes they have left open one window.

Clark, clark, clark, have we forgotten
going all night with the way of the dark
flowing oh going
O Clark, not forgetting
the light at the corner with the broken globe.

On another occasion, almost by accident, I and two other fellows, one a guest at the fraternity, had a sort of slumber-party at which the conversation turned sexual and we indulged in mutual masturbation. Since I was, as I have explained, a chronic masturbator, to me this did not seem strange and was more satisfactory than lonely self-abuse. It was in no way an expression of love but simply a matter of gratification and I did not regard it as in any way a cause for guilt or remorse. Once afterwards I engaged in it again with another older fellow when we were both drunk. I also made some furtive overtures for similar experiences on three other occasions but nothing came of them. In my inexperience it never occurred to me to engage in any other kind of same-sex activities.

After Bud Ogren, Leo, and I moved to Coutich Castle in 1937 we had occasional parties, and I remember as guests two pairs who were openly gay. In my freshman year one of the resident faculty was notoriously gay, often making overtures to students. I also had one language professor who I learned was gay. Such situations, like drunkenness were looked on as a bit decadent, but "homophobia" was not a feature of the University culture. The sexual revolution was already in place, it simply was not as blatant or controversial as now. In summers in Blackwell, I became friends with two bachelor friends, older than I, one a librarian and another a music teacher. I used to visit the latter's house to gossip and talk about music, literature, and religion. They were rather devout (at least very liturgical) Episcopalians. I learned there was gossip about the musician because he had adopted a boy whose parents had deserted him. Today they would have been labeled "gay" and perhaps they were. Once on a trip to Oklahoma City with the librarian, we stopped at an apartment of a friend whose effeminate behavior was remarkable. Yet, since neither ever spoke of such matters to me or made any advances, I really thought nothing of it.

As to my own sexual orientation, I never thought of myself as "gay" and always supposed that at some time I would fall in love and marry. I was just not ready for all that yet. I had always felt, because others called me a "sissy" due to my bookishness and unfamiliarity with sports, that I was not very competitive as a male. I liked to play with dolls rather late and was interested in female clothing and once experimented with a girl cousin's negligee. On the other hand from the first grade of school I had infatuations with certain little girl playmates and was jealous of other boys whom they seemed to favor. This continued to be a constant pattern in my life through high school. As I have related in Chapter 2, the novel praised by Gertrude Stein that I began to compose as a high school senior had as its theme the three-way struggle of a boy like myself. He struggles with his love for a girl and at the same time his great admiration for an athletic boy of whom he is also was jealous. My fantasies really turned about my autoerotic love for my own body and hence for that of males whom I envied and my desire for the kind of relation with girls that I thought they enjoyed and I didn't. Too timid to engage in sports, I was unable to attract the admiration of girls in high school. This continued into college where my friendships were almost wholly confined to males. The situation at the University of Chicago at that time did not have many women students and the social opportunities for meeting them required considerable initiative. I did make a few tentative overtures, such as the fraternity date already narrated, but nothing came of them. My friendship with Leo, although so constant and intimate, had nothing of the romantic. My brief friendship with Bob L., especially at his death, did have a real tenderness, because I was so moved by his praise of me that was such a new experience in my life. But after my same-sex experiences homosexual fantasies increased and have disturbed me since throughout my life along with heterosexual ones. Yet I have never really fallen in love with any male.

Nevertheless my guess is that if I had not become a Christian, my drinking habits and some of the people I associated with would have turned me to the way of the gay culture into which many literary and artistic people have moved. At that time it was only beginning to form.

Confusion

My moral life was thus becoming disorganized. Though I felt little sense of guilt, I was experiencing the fragility of life in the death of friends my own age, the threatening approach of World War II, and my own sense of being carried along by impulses and experiences that were risky and out of control. The following letter illustrates my state of mind in late 1938 at Coutich Castle. It was intended to be a kind of preface to a collection of poems to be called *Live Fight Know Delight* (a project never finished) and was written after a considerable lapse of my correspondence with Ruth.

Dear Friend Ruth,

You are very wise, so here is something for you to read. My head is so full of beautiful schemes that I picture as like the x-ray photographs of the neat little skeletons of kittens still in the envelope of their mother's womb. Skeletons are inside all beautiful skins but it is difficult to breed offspring beginning with the bones. For a while, therefore, I intend to write something which begins merely with a fertile germ and lives and grows by accident and time. Still it must not be either formless or haphazard or unintelligible. We will see how it can be free of these deficiencies.

The germ—and may it prove fertile!—is a desire that you should know me again and the way I am living. There is no way to go back, really, and relate and explain. Instead I shall let you read what I read in my mind in moments by myself or with others when we are not talking. It is not to be about me though. I want it to be about the way things are as I perceive and feel and understand them daily when I am trying to perceive what is there and feel it rightly and understand it thoroughly.

What I want above all is to learn to write privately without putting down a single private word or phrase. Then you, without straining after the bad personal confusions or tempering your critical wisdom by the good personal sympathies of the first and early days, will be able to understand everything I put down perfectly if only you read it well. I know at first I cannot do this, but I shall begin. See if you cannot feel that everything that I say is what ought to be felt, and to perceive that I am only perceiving what is. If I understand thoroughly what is, then you will understand what I write thoroughly. Therefore, let me tell you those facts about the times and places and movements which are all the particular facts to be understood now.

I am a graduate student with an M. A. degree at the University of Chicago. I am twenty-two and live in an apartment in an old building where many literary bohemians have lived. My two roommates are named Leo and Bud or Quentin. Leo is a Catholic from Salt Lake where I spent Christmas vacation. Strangely enough he is a good Trotskyite revolutionist too. Bud is a Comrade also who got me into the Movement as I got Leo. He is a very good speaker, Swedish, tall, and glad-handed. Leo is Irish and thin and dark. All three of us are living on fellowships while we work on a philosophic work which may be important. It is a clarification of Marxist theory in the light of the Aristotelian tradition and disciplines. We are all very interested in the philosophy of St. Thomas Aquinas, but Bud and I have no religions. I believe in God. He believes the existence of God can be demonstrated, and so do I. We are writing the book for Dr. Adler, a Jew interested in Thomism and Truth and convinced that a revolution is at hand. We however are working for the proletarian revolution as members of the Socialist Workers' Party. We like it and feel sure it is worth doing all our lives. It is strange too that we touch the perennial stream of philosophy here. The campus is divided in three parts about us. The empiricists, skeptics, sophists who believe in social reform generally with whom the communist students are now merely an active section; the McKeonites who are Aristotelians but believe all philosophies are true properly understood, these are professional philosophers; and finally the Thomists who concern themselves with the ethical and political consequences of Aristotelian metaphysics.

We Trotskyites are pariahs. The Communists, I have known them for so long, will not speak to us. Most of us have no philosophy but Marxism but a few now see Marxism through the clear intellectual light of Thomism. We all have the problem of learning how to act as Marxist revolutionaries with the proletariat who know the difference between a boss and a worker without knowing philosophy. All these schisms and controversies are funny. The question is as serious as Pilate's and mostly asked as falsely. We must answer the question the right way. We must act rightly. We must make the right revolution in the best way: the way on the left. To find that way much of our time is spent in meetings and some of it in agitation and organization.

The whole radical movement in the approaching crisis of a World War, in the present horrors of Germany and Italy, of Spain and China, in the blind name-mouthing apostasy of the USSR, has again receded into the backwash of opportunism. The Communists as the Socialists before them are ready to support their nationalisms. We are still Marxists trying to be Bolshevists as well. In our apartment I have painted two murals, one called Theory, one called Practice. Over our mantle are the portraits of Marx, Lenin, and Trotsky. Our party is called the Socialist Workers Party and is a section of the Fourth International.

Leo and Bud and I do pretty much the same things, study philosophy and do our Party Work. Leo goes to Mass every morning at 6:30. Bud has a job distributing Beechnut Gum samples. He is the best sampler in any college in the United States. He is in love but not doing well [he and Paula, a Jewish, lovely, bright, ample, and very lively girl whom he later married; both eventually became Catholics]. I am not in love and neither is Leo. We have many friends of many kinds. I write and am worried about this religion business. Marx saw how superstition held workers back from taking what they had made and he explained there is a physical world of changing matter. I am sure of this too. But God made it, as you used to tell me. What we want to do is to understand things thoroughly and act rightly. I want delight too, that is happiness. Leo says it is beatitude and so says St. Thomas. We all want happiness and are trying to get it.

Now these are all the facts of the matter. Don't bother to untangle names or worry about believing. Read just what I have written. I shall write it everyday if I keep to my intention and plans. I shall send installments every once in a while for you to read first of all.

Comradely yours,

Winston.

The book just mentioned was to be, as I wrote in a draft, a general portrait of all of us when we look inward, all of us that is who are "modern intellectuals." Now the modern intellectual appears to me to be a person under a spell, an enchantment cast upon him by some obscure force which he recognizes to exist but addresses by many names: commercialism, solipsism, sexism, capitalism, communism, materialism, idealism, Americanism, escapism. This book is about that spell. Our hero about to enter college is very uncertain as to what he shall do, where he shall go, and how. Having no one to turn to he stands still a moment and asks himself what he should do. A voice from somewhere, probably from somewhere within, suddenly answers him with great vehemence and clearness, "LIVE FIGHT KNOW DELIGHT." He recognizes in these four imperatives his answer.

When in the letter to Ruth I wrote "I am worried about this religious business" I was referring to something that was happening among a number of Jewish disciples of Adler and Hutchins who were entering the Catholic Church. This was not, however, through Adler's and Hutchins' direct influence, but through that of certain members of the team of professors he had brought to the University to prepare them to be the faculty of St. John's College in Annapolis. Among these future faculty members were three Jews (none of whom in fact ended at St. John's) who had recently become Catholics. The most influential was Herbert Schwartz, the most charismatic of the three and the direct source of the conversion of some twenty non-religious Jewish students. Another was Kenneth "Bud" Simon, a psychiatrist who was to become Fr. Raphael, a Trappist monk at Gethsemane Abbey whose story is told in his memoir *The Glory of My People*.[62] The third was Herbert Ratner, M.D., for long the Public Health Officer of Oak Park, IL, and editor of the journal *Child and Family*.[63] He was deeply interested in the Aristotelian tradition based on respect for nature and its teleology and especially in a great physician in that tradition William Harvey, the discoverer of the circulation of the blood.

Herbert Ratner became a much honored member of his profession, especially by his advocacy of natural birth and breast feeding before that movement was popular and for his controversial criticism of the way the polio vaccine was distributed without adequate testing. His admiration of the Church's opposition to contraception was a chief factor in his conversion. Herbert was to be a lifelong friend until his death in 1997. He was a very humanly warm person with whom I could always find a supportive conversation. I remember one evening when he had visited me, our conversation got so interesting that when he had to leave I walked him back to his apartment where he and his wife Dorothy, herself a physician and part Native American, were living. When we got there Herbert offered to walk me home again and so we kept up our lively talk till finally he left me where I had started!

Martin Gardner in correspondence with me also gives credit to the influence of William Gorman in the University. I have already mentioned Gorman as the brother-in-law of William Cobb and future editor of the *Encyclopedia Britannica* who was a "native" Catholic. Among these converts who I knew well, besides Herbert Ratner and Kenneth "Bud" Simon, were Janet Kalven, Peggy Stern, and Alice Zucker. Janet Kalven,[64] whom I mentioned earlier, was one of the twenty students in the first Hutchins-Adler Great Books seminar and became Adler's secretary. Her brother Harry, never a convert, became a noted professor of law at the University. After graduating Janet taught for ten years in the Chicago Great Books program and then joined the avant-garde Catholic religious community from the Netherlands, called "The Grail." She eventually became the administrator of the Grails' Center in Loveland, Ohio and a feminist activist. No one who knew Janet could ever disparage female intelligence.

Herbert Spencer Schwartz (he seldom used the middle name) was one of the most intense persons I have ever known, with piercing eyes and a sharp, confrontational directness in speech that was very disturbing. He was a New York Jew from a non-religious background. His mother ordered all her children, "You must be geniuses!" He was a gifted pianist and seemed destined for a concert career, but at Columbia where he received his doctorate he became a philosopher. There he studied under Richard McKeon, but like Adler, ran into difficulties with John Dewey over his dissertation on *An*

Aristotelian Analysis of the Elements, Principles and Causes of the Art of Music.[65] For a time, discouraged by opposition to his philosophical efforts, along with his Jewish friends, Herbert Ratner and Kenneth "Bud" Simon (1909-2006)[66] he studied medicine at the University of Michigan. Schwartz was above all a person who insisted on following ideas to their ultimate conclusions in practice and his study of Thomism led him, and Ratner and Simon too, into the Catholic Church in spite of all obstacles. For him the obstacles were not few, first of all his scandalized Jewish family, then the fact that his first marriage had previously collapsed and he had married a second time to a Protestant, Charleen, whom he also converted to Catholicism. Hence it was necessary for them to live as brother and sister until, after considerable delay, the Chicago Chancery obtained nullifications of their previous invalid marriages.

After their Catholic marriage the Schwartzes again lived together in a residence at the University provided by the Dominican Fathers as an informal center for Catholic students. This was occasioned by Cardinal Stritch's refusal to permit a formal Newman Center at the University lest it attract Catholic students away from the Chicago Catholic universities of Loyola and De Paul and other Catholic colleges in the area. This house became a place where Schwartz attracted Catholic and non-Catholic students for heated discussions. In these discussions, following a strictly Socratic method, Herbert exposed the sophistry of the dialectical play of ideas in which they were being trained in the University, and confronted them squarely with the existential decisions of truth and its consequences. A rather gross, but not untypical example of his approach was when he once engaged a prominent agnostic professor in a lengthy debate over the logical validity of the philosophical proofs for the existence of God. When Schwartz saw the lack of seriousness on the agnostic's part, he said abruptly, "Professor, when did you last masturbate?"

Schwartz' strange subsequent life which still remains to be written, can only be given a thumbnail sketch here. He published little but changed many lives. Since the philosophy department at Chicago would not take him, he taught in the music department. I attended some lectures of his musical theory course based principally on Mozart's *Jupiter Symphony* which he Socratically analyzed in minute structural detail, but which led—I was told by those who stayed to the end— to the theology of the Trinity. He taught only briefly at the renowned St. John's College in Annapolis since he fundamentally disagreed with the Great Books which he thought too sophistic. He wanted to teach at a Catholic school and did so briefly at Georgetown University, during which time he, as a member of the Dominican Third Order, became a powerful influence on the faculty and students at the Dominican House of Studies in Washington. This outside pressure on a tightly-knit, Irish dominated Dominican community, suspicious of lay theologians, led to such internal division that finally the religious superiors placed the community under the vow of obedience to have no further contact with him. Similar problems and a similar result later occurred in the Dominican Sisters Community of Adrian, MI because of his influence there.

Schwartz then departed to Laval University in Canada, under the sponsorship of the noted Thomist scholar, Charles De Koninck (1906-1965)[67] who had once been a Dominican novice in the Dominican New York Province, but had been refused religious profession in the Order because of an undiagnosed infection of the inner ear which had caused him to be judged a hypochondriac. At Laval Herbert developed his view, influenced by Freudian depth psychology that the underlying reason for modern secularism was the failure of modern fatherhood to provide loving, forgiving, and wise governance. Hence the remedy was spiritual direction by a true Father. He also taught sometime at the Jesuit Xavier University in Cincinnati, gathering the usual group of disciples, but sharply criticizing the Jesuit approach to truth as mere rhetoric, as he had criticized the Dominicans for mere rationalism. A group seeking his spiritual counsel soon surrounded Herbert wherever he went.

If one asks why a layman in the Catholic Church would assume this role of spiritual direction, it should be explained that Herbert wanted very much to be a priest. At one time he persuaded his wife to enter a Dominican cloister as a nun so that he might be ordained. Charleen tried this for a few weeks; then decided it was a mistake, and Herbert had to return to her. At that time they had no children, so they adopted one, but soon Charleen conceived and they had two of their own. Charleen began to practice as a lay psychotherapist. Then Herbert began to have doubts about the canonical validity of the nullification of their previous marriages and hence of their own marriage. He requested an investigation of the question by the Cincinnati Chancery, which concluded that indeed the Chicago marriage court had been in error. Thus it became necessary for Charleen and Herbert to separate again. This time Herbert again entered the Trappists, only to be told after some months by the

Abbot that his vocation was elsewhere (no doubt because a monastery can take only one abbot at a time). He then lived for some time in Mexico as the spiritual director of the Archbishop of Mexico City, to whom the Abbot of Gethsemane had recommended him. After some time in Mexico he visited Greenwich Village in New York and began to gather a new group of laypersons around him, which was eventually moved to Newburgh, N.Y. and received the local bishop's recognition. Schwartz was, as it were, its lay-abbot until his death.

Herbert Schwartz, God rest him!, remains a mystery to me. His orthodoxy and profound faith cannot be questioned by anyone who knew him. His seeming drive to dominate everyone he met is another matter, but he believed it was what they needed since his dominion was in lieu of an earthly father and above all of the Divine Father of whom his followers had been deprived. Someone who knew him well in his later years said that the real effect of his direction was not to make his disciples dependent on himself but on each other in a Christian community, and this may well be true.[68] My relation to him was only an indirect one. He was never my spiritual director, but was for me a striking example of the courageous submission to truth. When I was ready to be baptized, I asked him, as one of the few adult Catholics I then knew, to be my godfather and Charleen to be my godmother. He refused on the grounds that I had not yet renounced my Marxism, but Charleen accepted. Charleen, after she and Herbert had finally separated, told me that she did not herself consider Herbert a very successful father to their children. But then "A prophet is not without honor except in his native place and among his own kin and in his own house" (Mk 6:4).

The effect that this band of Schwartzian converts at the University (Leo too was a frequent visitor at the Schwartz's) had on me was simply to make me aware that to be or not to be a Catholic was an urgent practical question. It had to be in view of the perspectives opened by Hutchins and Adler and my reading of St. Thomas Aquinas with his clear posing of fundamental questions and his systematic effort to find reasonable answers, free of rhetoric or sophistic evasions. As I have already related, this had led me to admit that objective reason removes the objections to the evidence for the existence of God and hence that evidence must in all honesty be accepted. I was also learning more about the history and actuality of the Catholic Church and its comparison to the other world religions. Since Buddhism had attracted me in high school I was always curious about the world religions and wanted to know more about them, and about mystical experiences, which seemed to me closely connected to intense esthetic experiences.

"Experiences"

For example I was deeply impressed by an experience I had one night while studying in my freshman year, somewhat like the experience I had in high school, as I related in Chapter 1, on reading Plato's *Phaedrus*. I put down my book and became conscious of the silence about me in the room and the faint sounds from the city's noise outside in the night, the glimpse of light and reflections in the windows. I became intensely aware of myself present to myself in this single moment and that I was other than anything else but myself. I have had such experiences on other occasions too, especially in the presence of the night sky, a beautiful scene, or a beautiful object, or in the realization of the inevitability of death.

The essay of Jacques Maritain, "Natural Mysticism" in his book of essays, *Redeeming the Time*[69] seems to explain very well such experiences in terms of Thomistic epistemology. In any act of intellectual knowledge one is directly aware in that very act (*in actu signato*) of some object that is normally a material object (a cat, a rock, the sun), but one is also indirectly aware (*in actu exercitu*) of the fact that one is knowing the object. I know the cat and also know that I am knowing the cat. This indirect knowledge of my own knowing act is "self-consciousness" and is ordinarily implicit, vaguely present at the background of one's mind, like an horizon or context. I can objectify this vague self-consciousness by turning my attention to it, as Descartes did when he argued *Cogito ergo sum*; but although my self-consciousness tells me I exist, what I am remains utterly obscure. I know myself as a conscious existent, nothing more. Yet as knower I know I am not any of the things that I know. This amounts to saying that since all the world that I know directly is the material world, I as knower am somehow not material; I am somehow a spiritual being known to exist as knower but that is all.

Maritain, therefore, asks what must happen when someone practices yoga meditation or other forms of intense concentration in which one's whole psychic energy is concentrated on that intuition of oneself as an existing non-material knower, suppressing as far as possible the concepts or images of any material object. What if I think of a flower, and then mentally remove its petals one by one until nothing remains? The result must be an extremely concentrated, intense, but completely negative, awareness of one's existent spirituality. Such an experience may lead to the conviction that God exists, because as I become aware of the reality of a spiritual realm transcending the material, I at the same time realize my limitations, and hence that there must be a Supreme Spirit on whom I depend. On the other hand, Maritain points out, this can be a dangerous experience, because its negativity may produce the illusion that I am identical with God. I have read somewhere that one of the things that drove Edgar Allan Poe, a man of intense esthetic experiences, to drink, was the terrifying feeling that he was God. That I have never felt! But I have often felt that I was terrifyingly alone in the cosmos, alien to everything material, and isolated from communication with other spiritual persons, who themselves must exist in this same isolation, an isolation in a universe without evident meaning.

ALONE

By billions
super-galaxies, galaxies, stars,
our sun with its planets, and earth
explode the void
leaving me
alone.

Billions of neurons
wave in my brain
but where within
do they imprison
me?

Big the exploding heavens,
small the whirling earth,
complex, complex the woven brain,
simple am I.
Somewhere in the void,
dwindles this point.

The reason that intense aesthetic experiences can also produce such moments of natural mysticism, is that beauty consists, as Maritain also says, quoting Aquinas, is "the splendor of form," or relation of fit between the known and the knower. Hence an intense aware-

ness of the resonance of the object in the knower can produce a
sudden self-awareness of the knower's self. My awareness of a sun-
lit landscape in its beauty, its conformity to my capacity to be aware
of it, suddenly makes me aware that I am the pure observer ("aesthetic distance") for something so marvelous in its real order that I
must be even more marvelous in my spiritual existence. I well believe others who say they have such natural mystical experiences in
sexual intercourse, in the transcendence of the limits of the bodily
self in an act of total self-giving. Certainly that is the claim of much
poetry, but it is also obvious that the sheer material mechanism of
sex often gets in the way. No doubt that this is why in all religions
asceticism has been considered a necessary discipline in the search
for such experiences, and why for many the least material of the esthetic arts, music and poetry, have been used to promote it. Maritain, however, insists that while this natural mysticism can be an
instrument, as in the liturgy, for Christian mysticism, it can never
attain of itself to the supernatural order of the mysticism of such
Christian saints as Sts. Paul, Teresa of Avila, or John of the Cross.
This supernatural mysticism is attainable only by the Holy Spirit's
gift of faith in the revealed Word of God. Thus the current search for
a "God spot" in the brain[70] cannot explain much, just as the use of
LSD produced few real mystics.

Surgery

One of the most important events in my own spiritual journey,
which I was not then at all aware was a journey, happened in the
autumn of 1937. During the previous spring while I was at the Socialist Co-op and the following summer vacation back in Blackwell, I
had abdominal pains that seemed to indicate appendicitis, but
which my doctor decided were only indigestion. Then when I was
back in Chicago and attending a matinee by a noted German male
dancer, I got a terrific pain that did not go away but worsened
toward evening. I called my doctor who said it really sounded like
an appendix attack and told me to come immediately to the University Hospital. I went alone in a taxi since it was very late for my
roommates to accompany me. One might suppose that I was thinking in terror of what happened there to my friend Bob, but I do not
recollect that I was thinking much of anything except my acute pain.

When the taxi arrived at the hospital, the driver could not cash
the twenty-dollar bill that was all I had, so that he had to come in

with me to get cash at the admitting desk. But the sleepy admission clerk said he could not cash money for someone not yet a patient. The taxi driver, no bureaucrat, said that since I couldn't very well get away he would come back the next day for his money. In spite of my protests that I was probably about to rupture, I was required to sit down and fill out a long questionnaire with my medical history. The moment I painfully finished the situation changed radically. The hospital orderlies rolled out a wheelchair and insisted that since I was now a patient I could no longer walk and must be wheeled to the operating room in short order. When now many years afterwards I write or lecture on medical-ethics, my outrage at such bureaucratic stupidity wells up in me again.

The week's stay that was then required after most major surgery seemed endless to me, but also was a time of interesting experiences. For example, I remember someone saying "Breathe deep" as he put the mask over my face and the way the room seemed to expand and contract and the sounds rise higher and then—nothing. How puzzled I was when I first came out of the anesthetic and saw the apparatus for supplying fluids intravenously hovering in the air above me! I did not know at that time that this was a routine procedure. One day during convalescence I was wheeled down to a class of medical students so that a physician could discourse on appendectomy with a patient present. Again a class came to see me and several of them refracted my eyes! I asked what this had to do with my appendix and was told that since I was very myopic my eyes were easy to refract so it was a good opportunity for them to practice.

But the really significant experience was reading the excellent book of Edmund G. Gardner on Dante[71] which by chance I had brought with me and which has long quotations from that supreme poet. I had never gotten further than the *Inferno* and here I tasted *Purgatory* and *Paradise*. While I already believed rationally that there was a God and eternal life ahead, I had not drawn the conclusion that, whatever one thought all this might mean, certainly it meant at least that one ought to pray. So in my hospital bed I began to pray, using the bedtime prayers I had learned from Mother as a child, and the "Our Father." This seemed natural enough and I thought little of what the consequences of this might be for my life. It was simply that it made sense that if there is a God one needs to pray to Him in the midst of actual pain and passing pleasure.

I returned from the hospital and very soon was invited by Leo to go with him to his home in Salt Lake City for the Christmas holidays. He had hitchhiked to Detroit and for $200 bought a second hand car, a real marvel of 1920s vintage, a Franklin Air-cooled. In this antique chariot we started that winter of 1938 toward Salt Lake City. In Iowa the car broke down and had to be repaired while we stayed overnight in a very strange hotel. We drove across Nebraska at night. I remember the sandy flats of the North Platte River glimmering with traces of snow. Next day we came to Cheyenne, started up the Rockies, at that point across the Continental Divide. Here with a vast white and blue landscape about us and with the snow blowing hard across the highway, the car stopped dead—"altitude block" in the carburetor, Leo said. In the blowing, blinding snow he got out to pour gasoline (fortunately we had a couple of cans with us) into the antique mechanism, but found that, since he had no funnel, the high wind blew the gasoline away from the orifice. He had to make a funnel out of a map, finally succeeded, and up and away over the Divide!

Leo had to do all the driving since I had yet no license (at home my father or brother were always using our auto). On we went across Montana into the night, when on a high ridge a tire blew out and Leo (again, because of my recent surgery, I couldn't help) found that the old jack in the car would not go under the back axle. He tried to dig a hole to put it in, but the ground was frozen into stone. Nothing would do but drive on the rim with the bad tire flapping and the rim ringing on the icy road. No help was in sight for miles until suddenly as we came up a hill there at the top was—believe it or not—a blazing neon sign flashing NORTH POLE. Splitting with laughter we found it really was an overnight truck stop with a garage.

The holiday in Salt Lake City, with its grand circle of snowy mountains around its desert lake, was delightful and among other joys we heard the great choir of the Mormon Tabernacle sing Handel's *The Messiah*. Years later I went through the Mormon Visitors' Center in Salt Lake with its exhibits that vividly tell the Mormon Story. Still later when I visited the Catholic National Shrine of the Immaculate Conception in Washington, DC, I wondered why we Catholics do not tell our own authentic Christian Story in its integral truth to the thousands of visitors at the Shrine as well as the Mormons do their half-truths. The Shrine should not only be an expression of Catholic devotion to Our Lady but also, for that very reason, a catechesis of the Church's teachings. Fortunately now the John Paul II Cultural Center near the Shrine can better meet this need. Our trip home from Salt Lake was in the same antique auto but without major incident and Leo and my friendship was sealed by this great adventure. Yet, like the National Shrine, Leo made no attempt to evangelize me. His own faith was simply taken for granted between us.

Returning to Chicago from Salt Lake I wrote this poem:

RETURNING TO CHICAGO AFTER A TRIP WEST

Unfurled banners of industrial enterprise
flap in the rain,
in the smoke of factories weighted with water
pushed by the wind
which rolls out from the city, through the suburbs
into the countryside
where the bare trees, slick limbs are sooted
and the dead bark smirched, the white houses stained.

Remember Iowa richly rolling,
Nebraska's prairies high and dry.
Remember Montana lifted mountainous, white to the sky.
These thoughts of scenery are consoling
here in Illinois which Chicago so befouls
and the blizzard, stinking, howls.

Why then did Iowa seem dreary?
Why Nebraska lonely, Wyoming dead,
why was I weary,
gazing at the Continental watershed?

There is only one thing in Chicago: people,
millions.
They are all just alike too,
more than I ever knew,
you and you and you,
whether very many together or a few.

People gathered together
in a wide spot level
that tonight
is wet, cold, dark,
where in certain places they gather,
whisper, dance, and drink,
even think,
elsewhere they are at home in little places
to listen to their radios,
or doze, or go to bed,
make love or stiffly join the dead.

Even if they work at night
after their shift of victory or defeat,
tonight all will somehow get to bed,
maybe on the street.

Listening

During this period, once I felt better after the surgery, I was on the whole quite happy and certainly quite busy. I was secure in my scholarships and academic progress. I had close friendships with Leo and Bud and many other friendships. I was dedicated to World Revolution and constantly writing. Yet somehow my feet were not on bed rock, a situation expressed in the following poem that expresses an erotic fancy for no one in particular and everyone in general.

TRANSMUTATION

I am not hot with fever-fed desire.
Yet, when I hear your voice about my name,
swift, wild, and varying as flame,
I am the fire.

Nor am I sentiment's soft, tearful daughter.
But, Love, at your hand's touch, the fingers, palm—
helpless, meek, pale, the seas's dead calm,
I am but water.

However free or prideful in free birth,

hearing your feet go by, their measured tones—
mothering and old and bound, roots, stones,
I am the earth.

Love, Love, how missed, how failed, how sinned,
I, that am subdued by your firm mouth's caress,
empty, and faint, wandering, thin, bodiless,
I am but wind.

Yes, my life, just, it seemed, getting under way, was somehow nothing but wind, in Aristotelian terms "All accidents and no substance." Then everything changed. I was born again and life finally and really began. In 1942, sitting in church in the presence of Jesus in the Tabernacle to thank him for my conversion, I decided to record the crucial event as I then remembered it.

While preparing for the fourth anniversary of my conversion, in order to put it down before memory and gratitude grow weaker, the greatest grace I ever received from the Precious Blood through the intercession of the Blessed Virgin, I want to write as well as I can exactly what I remember without adding or interpreting.

It happened in the afternoon—I imagine close to 3 o'clock or maybe a little afterwards. I was alone in the apartment which I shared with my 2 friends. I believe I was reading or sorting papers and my mind was wandering over a number of topics. I think I was in a good mood as I had been most of that rather self-satisfied year. As my mind wandered on it came quite accidentally it seemed to a topic about which I had thought little recently, namely the Catholic Church. I had come to the conclusion which I had frequently expressed some months before that while the system of Catholicism was self-consistent it could neither be proved or disproved on natural grounds, that the only convincing evidence for it would be historical and those [data] in fact on which it depended were involved in endless probabilities, and that God would not expect anyone to stand or fall on such uncertainties. Therefore the Catholic Faith must be illusory.

Because I believed in God I sometimes prayed even asking for light but without any moral movement of the will. I knew that theoretically one should prepare oneself morally for Faith but I seemed content enough with my life in spite of certain strong revulsions and problems which I had suffered the year previously. All the features of struggle, however, were in abeyance and had not been occupying me much. I had been writing poems nightly during this period and they show my emotional occupations to have been largely with desiring some mystical participation in the Revolution, considerably pondering over the paradoxes between the grand undertaking at which the Revolution aimed and its rather miserable beginnings, and a general tendency to find emotional uplift in the sort of poetry written when very tired which plays on the mystery of the present.

As I remember the sequence of ideas which passed through my mind at this moment it was somewhat as follows. Here you have thought how logical Catholicism is for a long time, but that there never could be anything which would make one sure of it and since it is all of a piece it either is to be all held as perfectly certain or not at all. But if it were true and knowable what could make me certain of it? A miracle. Yes, if one experienced a miracle personally one could be certain, at least if it were also something internal, that is a miracle in one's own being. Do you expect a vision or some great external experience especially for you? Then I was overwhelmed—I must say overwhelmed because as I recall it was here my emotions were aroused—with the thought "What right have you to expect any such thing? God who is perfect and infinitely above man, above you, is not in anyway obligated to reveal supernatural truths to you. If the Catholic Church is true He may in justice and power never allow you to know it." When I thought this I was overcome not with fear, as I remember, but with a very intense feeling of humiliation and nothingness.

Now during this time I had in my imagination in the ordinary way a distinct impression of the Sacred Wound in the side of Our Blessed Lord. When this came to my mind I cannot remember whether before, during, or after these thoughts, since, like imaginations, it remained in conscience more or less independent of my real thinking. I believe, however, that it was this imagination which perhaps set me off on my train of thoughts. Perhaps it was something in my reading or day dreaming which led to it. I had previously felt some strong attraction to the idea of Jesus having been thrust through the heart and knew something of its theological significance. The image was very vivid and the contrast of the white flesh and wound impressed me. In any case the presence of this image seemed to me as it were the motive or the center of the deep humiliation which I felt. Intellectually I felt completely abased or subjected by the thought of my helplessness. Emotionally I clung as it were to the wound. Whether I felt sorrow for having caused it was not clear to me, but it made me feel deeply contrite and abased. As soon as I made the judgment, "You can do nothing for yourself, but God can help you if he will. You are foolish to expect a miracle," possessed by this feeling I resolved to do whatever He wanted me to do, and it was plain to me that it would be honest and sensible to begin instructions and see if the Church itself could solve my difficulties, I must give her the chance to convince me.

While saying this to myself I remember I still sat where I was on the low divan and that my emotions brought tears to my eyes. It seemed to me as if something amazing was happening to me and I was doing nothing but submit. Then the thought occurred to me, "Perhaps here while you rejected a demand for a miracle God has given you a vision." I immediately analyzed the mental impression I had to see if it was something extraordinary, but it was certain the image was only entirely in the imagination and in itself no wise different than ordinary rather vivid stray pictures often had in daydreaming. I remember resolving as it were with a sort of effort never to allow myself to be fooled into believing something miraculous had occurred. I got up and walked around the apartment thinking very fast, I realized that if I delayed I might let my resolution to take instructions slip, so I resolved to go and meet my Catholic friend [Leo] and ask him to arrange for them [the instructions] immediately. I was very clear-headed and the blowing snow about me as I walked to see him was impressed vividly on my memory. I kept saying, "Remember this is a great moment in your life." I was so eager to go that I put off committing a sin [masturbation] habitual with me, and though I was [so] hardened as not to realize it [masturbation] was mortal until told so several weeks later and though [for] years before I had been unable to give it up in spite of some struggle, I never committed it again [this, thank God, is still true]. On my way I kept saying, "How shall I tell him [Leo]? I mustn't say, 'I have made up mind to' [take instructions] or 'I have decided' because that might offend God by pride. I must say, 'Something has made me decide to.' I began to take instructions and although my decision had not been to believe all the Church taught, nevertheless I did and without any real difficulties.

Since that moment of my conversion, by what (considering how long that habit had been with me) can only be a miracle of grace, I have never masturbated again. Nor have I even internally fully consented to any other sexual satisfaction, although temptations have been constant, sometimes rather violent, and continue occasionally even now at 93! Of course for many years I had regular nocturnal pollutions, but I do not know that I have ever deliberately consented to their pleasure. Not only in this but in all my life I have been deeply concerned to remain constantly united to God. Later as I studied apologetics I came to see that the "miracle" which Vatican I taught is accessible to all at all times is the One, Holy, Catholic, and Apostolic Church[72] which, as I have recounted, I had well encountered by that time, in sharp contrast to Secularist and Marxist atheism, as well as my earlier Pantheism and Idealism.

Yet since Shields thought that Marx's atheism was not essential to his political thought which could be revised to be a consistent anti-capitalist, anti-fascist, anti-war Christian politics and I agreed with him, my decision to be baptized was for me not a struggle between my political and my religious convictions. They seemed at the time quite consistent with each other. An interview in a school paper, *Today*, Mid-April, 1946, when I was a seminarian, describes me as "A young man of medium height, with dark wavy hair and cheerful smile" and the interviewer quotes me as saying,

"I never did join the Communist Party. I was a member of the Young People's Socialist League which was the Trotskyite socialist group on the campus. I belonged to the organization for three year and in 1936 I edited their Soapbox". His interest in social reform led him to join the League of Nations Association (sic) in an era when isolationism was as fashionable as Nylons are today. "It seemed that things were in a bad way," said Brother Benedict [my religious name]. "Marxism gave a logical answer to the problems. The religious implications of Marxism were of no interest to me then." The thing which interested him most at the time for which Marxism had an answer were the labor problem, anti-Semitism, and war."

"These were questions which demanded answers. I was struck by the idealism and discipline of the socialists on campus. Every moment of time during the day was taken up by the movement. What you did and said, the clothing you wore, even the restaurants you ate in, were dictated from above." As a member of the Young People's Socialist League he took part in student demonstrations and other activities dictated by the party line. Selling newspapers was only one of these chores. I [the interviewer] asked him what opinion he had of the Catholic Church during the period. He said he thought then that the Church possessed a logical system but that it was a reactionary organization. Brother Benedict's first impression of the social encyclicals was that they were admirable in principle but impractical [because of their rejection of a necessarily violent revolution]. He confessed that he had not understood them very well in the beginning, that even now each rereading is a revelation of new social wisdom for him. The constant changes in the socialist party line bothered him because he realized that some fixed moral standards are necessary. In a discussion on the subject with one of his friends, Ashley asked him how he justified his frequent changes of opinion. The reply is classic, "I have one single ethical principle," the friend [I believe it was Frank Meyer, then head of the Young Communist League, as already men-tioned later an anti-communist] said, "that is unwavering loyalty to the Third International."

"This changing of the party line which made it necessary to defend today what you had attacked the day before, finally led to a certain cynicism among the radical leaders on campus. Nevertheless, having no other program, they followed the party line." To Ashley there appeared to be no conflict between the philosophies of Aristotle and Marx. A course in the study of St. Thomas intervened. While taking the course he realized the validity of St. Thomas' arguments for the existence of God and of the human soul. Having arrived at this position Winston Ashley felt that he had to examine the Catholic Church's claim to have a complete system for man's salvation, backed by centuries of experience. "After I studied the church and understood what it taught," he said, "I believed in it." He received his instructions from the Dominicans, during the spring of 1938 he was received into the Church."

Last Year in Chicago

After my baptism I immediately began to go to early morning Mass with Leo in the beautiful, artistically modern St. Thomas the Apostle Catholic Church near the University of Chicago campus. Through Herbert Schwartz, Leo had arranged for my instructions in the Catholic Faith by a Dominican priest. In 1216 a Spaniard, St. Dominic de Guzman, founded the Dominican Order, officially the Order of Preachers, with the approval of Pope Honorius III, "to preach for the salvation of souls." Dominicans are often mislabeled "monks" but are actually friars (*fratres*, brothers), often called the "Blackfriars" because of the black cloak they wear over their white habit, a combination considered photogenic by directors of medieval and renaissance movies who like to picture them as stake-burning Inquisitors.

Monks, belonging to orders that in the Church go back to at least the third century, are committed to live a contemplative life in a local monastery under a spiritual father or abbot. Friars such as Dominicans or Franciscans did not exist before the thirteenth century and were originally "mendicants," that is, they owned no property except, in the case of the Dominicans, their residence and church, but lived by begging. Yet friars, like monks, live a contemplative life devoted to daily liturgical worship, but they also engage in an active evangelical ministry and hence belong to international communities so as to be freely sent to wherever their ministry requires.

The neglect by many medieval bishops because of their secular involvements to carry out their essential ministry of preaching effectively, led St. Dominic, with papal encouragement, to found his Order to supplement their efforts. For that reason, unlike St. Francis, he insisted that the constant study of Scripture and related subjects was to be an essential part of his friars' worship of God. Hence, learned Dominicans, along with the later Society of Jesus (Jesuits) have been leading educators in the Church.

In the United States the Order was founded in 1806 by a young man from Maryland, Dominic Fenwick, who had studied in Belgium at a school taught by Dominicans exiled from England by the Reformation. At the time I became a Catholic, the Order had three provinces in the United States centered in New York, Chicago, and Oakland, CA. The House of Studies for the New York Province is in Washington, DC; that of the Oakland Province in Oakland; and that of the Chicago Province was formerly in the Chicago suburb of River Forest, where I went for my catechesis as a prospective Catholic. Later a New Orleans Province was divided from the territories of the New York and Chicago Provinces.

Father Sylvester Considine (d. 1973) was a Professor of Scripture, who had studied at the famous Dominican École Biblique in Jerusalem under Fr. M.-J. Lagrange (1855-1938) the great biblicist who was largely responsible for the adoption of the modern critical-historical method of biblical interpretation in the Catholic Church. Fr. Considine was the translator of the *Book of Revelation* for the first edition of what is now the *New American Bible*. At that time I went to him in River Forest for catechetical instruction he was an elderly, loveable, but eccentric priest who instructed me by bringing along a copy of Aquinas' *Summa Theologiae*. Since Adler had already made me familiar with that work in a cursory sort of way our sessions went quickly.

What I had read before in the *Summa* out of curiosity now all seemed utterly believable to me. I remember that the only real difficulties I raised to Fr. Considine were about the *Book of Job* and the problem of evil which as a Bible scholar he well answered. Later he was to teach me Hebrew, I am afraid without much effect. In Scripture class he had some trick questions that had two possible answers that were both right, but if you gave one, he would insist on the other, so you were always wrong. One of these was, "How many books are there in the Canon?" If you answered, "73," Fr. Considine would say "No, No, 71!" because Jeremiah, Lamentations, and Baruch were often counted as one book by the Church Fathers. But if you answered "71," he would say, "No, no, 73." When I was a young priest, I was once awakened from my siesta by a very worried lady on the phone. Her non-Catholic husband refused to send their daughter to a Catholic school and in public school her daughter was taught that there were 66 books in the Bible. Since the catechism her mother was teaching her privately said 73, her daughter was upset and seemed to be losing her faith. "What is the right number?" the lady anxiously demanded. Of course I knew about the Protestant rejection of seven Old Testament books, but for the life of me I couldn't remember whether "73" was the Catholic number. I grabbed my Bible, hurriedly counted 73, then wondering if I had counted right, counted again and this time got 72! Since the lady was waiting on the other end of the line and I was so confused in my count, I was forced to knock on Fr. Considine's door to get the correct reply, "Didn't I teach you? Depending on how you count, 71 or 73."

As I look back on the time of my instructions, I realize more clearly than ever that a sign accessible to natural human knowledge had already been given to me that was sufficient to demand from me a supernatural act of faith in the Word of God precisely as the Word of God. As I have already mentioned it is the teaching of Vatican I and II; this sign is the Catholic Church as I had come to know it in its miraculous existence today, in its apostolicity, catholicity, unity, and holiness in our confused, despairing, and sinful world. What had been lacking on my part was the submission of the will which grace had now given me, wholly undeserving as I was then and am now. I marvel now, looking back, how simple it all was!

Since my parents had never had me baptized, I was baptized unconditionally on Palm Sunday, April 10, 1938, at St. Thomas Apostle Church near the University by another Dominican priest, Fr. John A. Driscoll, OP. Leo Shields and Charleen Schwartz were my godparents. I was present at Dr. Herbert Ratner's baptism at St. Vincent Ferrer Church in River Forest.

Because of my conversion I was summarily expelled from the Socialist Workers Party. During the following year when Leo and I moved to the Adler house on Woodlawn and when we were still working on Adler's *Contra Marxistes* project, and while I was studying economics for my Ph.D. comprehensives in political science, I came to see the fallacies of Marxism and so did Leo, although we continued to be liberals in social matters. We were in opposition to Franco, pacifists yet supporters of collective security against fascism, and in favor of the more radical actions of the New Deal.

Reflecting on my Marxist period, I see it as immature, yet I believe it greatly helped toward my conversion to the Gospel, because it freed me from the grip of that dialectical suspension of judgment to which so many of the Adler-Hutchins coterie succumbed. Within the year after my baptism, when I had become better informed on the social teachings of the Church, I repudiated my Marxism. Leo also gradually withdrew from it. Along with Dr. Herbert Ratner, I was confirmed at St. Rose of Lima parish where a bishop was visiting, since in those days, confirmation was given only by bishops and not usually along with adult baptism.

An early experience as a member of the Church that seems to me especially significant concerns the two statues of Our Lady and St. Joseph in St. Thomas the Apostle Church. At first it was before the statue of St. Joseph that I liked to pray. The place of Mary in my life was to emerge only after I entered the novitiate. I found in Joseph that embodiment of God's fatherly love that, as I have written, I had felt was imperfect in my own dear father, while I had never doubted my mother's love.

My study towards the doctorate in political science continued. Then almost a year after my baptism and after the midnight Christmas Mass, which I had attended alone, I was having a snack by myself at a restaurant near the Church, when, with "a strange warming of the heart" as the founder of Methodism, John Wesley, once described such spiritual experiences, it came over me that I must as a Catholic "go all the way" (that is how I thought of it) and become a religious, a Dominican. That was the only religious order with which I was then familiar. My thought was not of being a priest, although I assumed that this was entailed by my being a Dominican, but just to give my whole life and whatever hopes I had of writing or teaching to the service of God. Like my submission to instructions and baptism, this vocation to religious life was peaceful and final. I consulted my Dominican confessor about entering the novitiate immediately, but was advised by my confessor, the saintly Fr. Timothy Sparks (d. 2001), I was too much a neophyte as a Catholic and should wait until I had finished my doctorate.

I had, of course, also started going to sacramental confession. In one of my first confessions I was troubled whether my faith was really genuine. All that had happened seemed so mysterious. The confessor just reassured me that my confusion was quite natural and that I was doing well as a Catholic. It was not until sometime later, as I will explain later, that such temptations again arose. In fact I was still a neophyte. I remember being terrified that I had committed a mortal sin and arousing a poor priest from his afternoon siesta to hear my confession because I had unthinkingly told a small lie to escape some embarrassment. At that time I supposed every lie must be a mortal sin.

What shook me up even more was an incident, trivial in itself, that happened during the summer after my baptism. Instead of returning to Blackwell as usual, I had gone for a month with Bud Ogren to a house on a little lake near Clear Lake, WI. It was a pleasant time and at last I learned to swim (not very well), though in the process I almost drowned and was saved by Bud. The town was a Seventh-day Adventist colony and we had to get used to doing our shopping on Friday afternoon. The only other young people there were some high school girls living by the lake. Foolishly, we college men in lieu of any older girls had dates with them one evening, and after a couple of beers I kissed one of these teenagers who had got a little tipsy. That night I was tortured by the idea that I had scandalized her and had internally consented to impure desires. Next morning I hurried to confession, but the priest was puzzled as to just exactly what I had done. Afterwards I realized that in fact it was not a serious sin, but the pain of the incident contributed to my distrust of my own motives. Yet I found confession, as I do now, a wonderful psychological as well as spiritual catharsis (they are not the same thing). It is Jesus himself, as well as the Church of which I am a member, who forgives me. I know he understands me much better than I do myself, yet forgives me not only for my infidelity to him but the harm I have done others and myself. This does not mean that I will not always be freed of the consequences of the evil I do, but whatever punishment I deserve will be for my good, not my destruction.

That year Leo and I spent at the house on Woodlawn with the other Adler protégés finishing our Marxist project and getting ready for Ph.D. comprehensives. Bud Ogren did not live with us because he had become engaged to his future wife Paula, a plump but beautiful and brilliant Jewish girl. They were eventually also to become Catholics but this was after I left Chicago. During this year I also took a course from Herbert Schwartz with a group of his disciples in which we read much of the first volume of the formidable Latin textbook of Joseph Gredt (1863-1910),[73] *Elementa Philosophiae Aristotelico-Thomisticae.* The class met after early morning Mass before regular University classes in the same seminar room in which I had studied with Hutchins and Adler, and its sessions introduced me to a technical, step-by-step kind of study that I lacked before. An amusing feature of these sessions was that my godmother Charleen Schwartz also attended and greatly irritated her husband, Herbert, by asking about every topic, "How does this apply to angels?" A heated domestic scrimmage would follow, while the rest of us sat back in embarrassment. Then class would resume its slow, rigorous analytic pace.

Two priests were of much help to me: the young curate at St. Thomas the Apostle, who patiently heard my frequent confessions and a Jesuit priest, Fr. George H. Dunne, who was working on his doctorate at the University. In lieu of a Newman Center at the University, which Cardinal Stritch, as I have before explained, would not permit, Fr. Dunne had become the unofficial Catholic chaplain for the students. He has written a lively autobiography that touches on this period.[74] But I got special help by joining the Dominican Third Order Chapter which met in the small weekday St. Vincent Ferrer Chapel at St. Thomas. It had stained glass windows of the Dominican saints because the pastor, Monsignor Thomas Vincent Shannon, had been for a time a Dominican novice in Kentucky and remained a member of the Dominican Laity.

Dominican Laity

In the Middle Ages there were many groups of pious lay people, both women and men, who formed groups in their parishes to engage in special prayers and acts of penance for their advance in holiness and their service of others. When the Franciscan and Dominican Orders were founded, the Church encouraged these groups to affiliate to one or other of these orders of Friars in order to obtain orthodox spiritual guidance and to be protected from the spiritual enthusiasms and fads then current, even as today. Since Vatican II, when it seems that nobody is content to be second or third in anything, these lay groups have taken the name "Dominican Laity" rather than the old "Third Order," after the Second Order of Dominican cloistered nuns and the First Order of priests and cooperator brothers. These lay Dominicans do not live in community but form a "Chapter" that meets periodically to recite the liturgical Hours (at that time the *Little Office of the Blessed Virgin*). They do not take vows, but, after a novitiate of study, make a promise to fulfill the obligations of prayer, reception of the sacraments, and some form of service. Since I could not yet enter the First Order, I now entered the Third Order Chapter at St. Thomas the Apostle.

In her article "The Chapter of St. Thomas,"[75] Johanna Doniat, TOP, says that the famous Bishop of Peoria, John Lancaster Spalding (d.1916) was the first Catholic prelate to speak publicly at the University of Chicago. A Brownson Club was founded there by a student, Edward M. Kerwin, but lapsed in 1922. In 1923 Jerome T. Kerwin (no relative of Edward M.) came from Dartmouth to teach political science and became the first prior of the Dominican Third

Order there. This Chapter was initiated in St. Vincent Ferrer Chapel on the Feast of St. Vincent, April 4, 1937. Monsignor Shannon, Fr. Timothy Sparks (who had been teaching some of the members ecclesiastical Latin), Fr. Peter O'Brien (d. 1971) (the first Provincial of the Chicago Province, a moral theologian), Fr. R. E. Vahey, O.P of the New York Province, and the Dominican Sisters of Sinsinawa, WI, from the parish school were present.

The chapter included Charlene Schwartz, Otto Bird (later professor at Notre Dame), Johanna Doniat and H. Eugene Patrick who were teachers at Chicago schools), Janet Kalven, Charles N. R. McCoy (later an important writer on political theory),[76] Herbert Schwartz (first sub-prior) and Jerome A. Kerwin (prior). Their chaplain was Fr. Alexis Driscoll, OP who had baptized me. Professor Kerwin finally induced Cardinal Stritch in 1938 to permit the opening of a former fraternity house (it was next door to the Beta house where I had lived) as De Sales House with a Calvert Club (named after a Maryland Catholic signer of the Declaration of Independence) as an equivalent of a Newman Center (it still flourishes) and the meetings of the Third Order were moved there.

This chapter also was able to have retreats at Childerly, a ten-acre estate loaned to the Calvert Club by Mrs. Frank R. Lilly, who in 1941 gave it to the Catholic students of the University to be administered by Professor Kerwin and Johanna Doniat. Doniat writes[77] that this chapter produced many vocations to the priesthood and religious life of both women and men.

There are seven university professors and a number of public school teachers. Some have become devoted parents. In other scholarly pursuits there are Dominican tertiaries of the chapter of St. Thomas in the publishing field, in commercial chemistry, in music, a naturalist at the National Museum in Washington, DC, in the state department in Washington, and in the personnel departments of various organizations throughout the country.

Later records name a number of more priests and sisters, including Fr. Albert Moraczewski, OP, founder of what is now the National Catholic Bioethics Center.[78] I am very grateful to have been one of these Dominican Tertiaries whose members immensely strengthened my Christian and Dominican priestly vocation.

The retreat center, Childerly, was also inspiring. Mrs. Lilly, a stately granddame, and wife of Frank Lilly the eminent biologist and founder of the famous Marine Laboratory at Woods Hole on Cape Cod, was a convert from the Episcopal Church, and this group of white frame buildings on a fine plot of land with an orchard near Libertyville, not far out of Chicago, were named "Childerly," I believe, because it was originally for orphans. Everything in it has the name of a saint and the small exquisite chapel and the garden around it has works of art, especially of St. Francis of Assisi, Mrs. Lilly's favorite saint.[79] We were given a list to identify the flowers in the garden by their medieval names, all referring to the Blessed Virgin Mary.

The liturgies at Childerly already anticipated some of the changes of Vatican II and remain with me as holy (if a bit too "precious") memories. Miss Doniat, an art teacher in the public schools of Chicago, old-fashioned and somehow European in dress, was the kindly, ever enthusiastic, and very prudent angel of the place, who was always cautioning us to be careful not to set the frame buildings on fire. One of my recollections is of a conference given by someone on Christological heresies, during which a strange looking bearded priest at the back of the room stood up and said, "I want you to know that I am a Nestorian." Years later when I was teaching in Washington, Fr. Dan Cassidy, OP, who is a biologist, took me on a delightful day's trip to Woods Hole—on the way we stopped to marvel at the grand old mansions at Newport— and by the ocean there I saw another garden the Lilly's had made, with a bell tower, garden, and statues, all with holy names, so much like Childerly!

In this remaining time at the University of Chicago after my conversion I continued to write poetry in which theological themes and biblical imagery began to appear, as in the following which can be compared to the *Ode on Listening to Mozart* that was written during the Spanish War with its Marxist references, quoted in Chapter 4. Perhaps I should note that "Epicurean swerve" refers to the belief of the ancient Epicureans that nothing exists but changeless atoms that, as they fall through the void, tend to swerve, and thus jostling each other and sticking together accidentally and temporarily form the various objects of our experience, including our own bodily selves.

ODE TO MOZART

In him was breathed
the Epicurean swerve of art:
now then, then again, universe on universe
ingeniously to pattern
from the chance patter of the atomic rain of sound.
Worlds like birds dissolving;
over chaotic fear
the shadows of doves.
Before the vocal words of temporal loves resolving again
leave peace profoundly
emptying the heart,
silence through all the brain,
the Epicurean void of silence...

Now, before the atomic jostle again, again returns
contemporal walls of wire,
these records, radio, fissioning
at once revisioning time
in a then not so staccato flow
came in a deluge through his formal garden
where first among tresseled ferns, lace, fountains rococo,
he breathed a vital tempo into moments
fluttering pigeon-like to rest
on the marble space
of a classic forehead, face, breast,
burning their surfaces to rose with the pure beat
of pulsing blood
before that fountain falling from some fatal urn
turned an erasing flood.

Now, now he will create for us again our garden,
patterned from cleansing, absolving rain,
Eden in afternoon, all leaves alive,
the serpent not yet whispering,
our eyes still open in a light that showed an earth
as stainless as a cloudless sky,
we for all time safe to die
still virgin...still free...

O fruitful beauty still all honesty!

After our swerving fall through the dark, random void,
beauty now atomized to wavering fires
of shattering desires disharmonized,
deployed like sterile chaff, like serpent-cankered leaf
sucked down the ashy vortex of the deathless grief
of the knowledge of good, of evil without reprieve,
Now in this moment by his tempering breath
set once again in tune,
find we for helpmate
an immaculate Eve
waking by the living tree.

But when, so tuneful, his fresh rain has stopped,
has it cleansed?
waking, jangled, in flesh the spirit clutches again
the raucous void,
driven it turns
in renewing clashes, shattering loves.
behind us at the garden wall, closed in separation,
burns hissing in the tears of rain,
the angel guardian's sword.

Oh, but that moment, music ceasing, in that silence
just before the reawakening of breath,
before our inward clamor thrusts us forth again into fear,
are not our fragments of flesh, shreds of spirit
pausing to listen?
For this moment again, shall we not hear...

What in his beggared room, bedded in distracted pages,
he heard, sick among soiled laces, chaos returning,
fever filled with singing faces finishing
its resolving burning,
what he heard
composing without rest the self-requiem that he
who finished all by the fine resolvent chord
could not finish...

Was it between the sigh of one Kyrie and the sigh of the

Christe
that he heard and marked a rest and rested,
his mind shroud-invested by the cold altar linen
of his own tune's perfection,
his heart laid in state between the strong, spaced flames
of his own measures,
and then heard still other silence
emptier than that of Epicurus,
more void than all the temple of time
in which his music hovers,
(again for us again)
deeper than all contingent creation
whether by man or god,
heard over it
hovering,
(heart, brain, ear cleansed at least by his own music)
heard the whisper of the Original Breath, the Creating Bird
whispering to him (poor dying sinner)
the Uncreated Word?

Preaching

My poetic energies, such as they were, however, now began to be absorbed by evangelistic impulses which were more overpowering than my Marxist commitments had been and which therefore more dominated my imagination. An important experience summer experience of this time resulted from the fact that my hometown of Blackwell, which had never had a resident priest, recently had received a pastor, Fr. Stephen Leven (1905-1983), who soon was joined by a young assistant, Fr. Charles Buswell (1913-). Both became bishops, Leven of San Angelo, TX, and Buswell of Puebla, NM. Fr. Leven was a native Oklahoman from Newark, a tiny village near Blackwell, and a graduate of the University of Louvain. He immediately began the construction of a neat brick church in a good location in Blackwell to replace the poor frame building on the edge of town that had previously symbolized the marginal status of the few Catholics there.

Fr. Leven, who was a lively, outgoing, active, down-to-earth pastor, in London had visited the Catholic Evidence Guild and had witnessed in Hyde Park the "street preaching" initiated there by the famous English Dominican Fr. Vincent McNabb and carried on by the apologist Frank Sheed and others. Leven saw that this kind of preaching could be an effective means of reaching bigoted Oklahomans. His method was to take a truck equipped with a loudspeaker, park at a street corner in one of those small, stark Oklahoma towns, play a few hymns familiar to Protestants, then mount a portable pulpit and introduce himself. Some lay person he had recruited gave a preliminary talk on the story of a Catholic saint or some Catholic devotion about which non-Catholics might be curious. Fr. Leven's own sermon would be a very direct apologetic or catechetical presentation, often on "What is Confession?" or "Are Catholics Idolaters?" or "Do Catholics Believe in the Bible?" He told me that while training with the Catholic Evidence Guild for this open-air preaching he had been tested by friends who role-played as hecklers. Their hardest question, he said, was always, "Why are Catholic Bibles so expensive?" He asked me when I was still a laymen on summer vacation after my conversion to give some of these little preliminary talks. I felt great thus to be, as it were, part of St. Dominic's preaching band. My talk that Fr. Leven liked best was on Bl. (now St.) Martin de Porres and how he cared even for God's rats. Another of the summer experiences I had with Fr. Leven in Blackwell was helping him and two sweet Benedictine Sisters from their motherhouse in Guthrie, OK to run a brief catechetical summer school. I discovered I was no match for the Sisters in dealing with children.

During the school year of 1938-39, as the *Contra Marxistes* project came to an end, both Leo Shields and I found ourselves wondering how we could get new scholarships to last us till our doctorates in political science were finished. The fact that we had been graduate assistants of Adler did not recommend us to the Political Science Department. Although Leo had attended some classes in the Department, I had never attended any, aiming simply on the basis of my reading to take the comprehensive exams, as was then possible at the University of Chicago, as I have mentioned before. Furthermore, now a Catholic, I wanted to do a dissertation on some topic in Catholic social theory. This might have been possible with Jerome Kerwin, the department chairman, who was a Catholic, but he was already too committed. Kerwin, however, solved this problem for us when he informed us that the University of Notre Dame (which was still very largely an undergraduate school) was trying to upgrade its graduate school with new graduate departments, and was thus starting one in political science and had graduate scholarships available. The new department was to be headed by Prof. Waldemar Gurian, a specialist in Marxism and Prof. Frederick A. Hermens a leader of the German Center Party, both of whom were opponents of the Nazis who had fled to Notre Dame. Leo and I duly applied, were fortunate to receive scholarships as graduate assistants, and in 1939 went to live in South Bend.

Thus I left the University of Chicago after the many cherished experiences I have described, yet, to tell the truth, I did not leave regretfully. That university's intellectualism I admired, but its academic competitiveness, its indifference to its students, its dialectical game-playing, and its utter secularism left me cold. My stay at the University had given me the opportunity to know some great intellectuals and in a very random way to acquire a broad culture, in particular through Hutchins and Adler to get to know something of Aristotle and Aquinas. I was still, however, without the tools or the discipline and methodology to make much further progress in my studies. I am profoundly grateful to the University of Chicago but I have no love for it, only gratitude and nostalgia for Hutchins, Adler, and Schwartz as teachers, and for the other friends I made there.

Chapter 7 - Golden Dome

Notre Dame

In contrast to the competitive, impersonal, utterly secularist atmosphere of the University of Chicago, my two years under the Golden Dome of Notre Dame (1938-1940) were idyllic: the beautiful campus, the totally Catholic atmosphere, the enjoyable work on my dissertation, the friends I made, all seemed so peaceful, yet inspiring. At that time there were no resident halls for graduate students, so Leo and I found a large room for two in a private home in the northern outskirts of South Bend. South Bend seemed a boring town, but it was only a ten-minute walk to the Notre Dame campus on a shady avenue along a cemetery and a golf course. Since then many new buildings have gone up there, but the older central part has been well preserved.

I have never been so cold, however, as on that walk past the cemetery in mid-winter amidst the heavy snows that the west wind picks up over Lake Michigan and to the east of the lake dumps on Notre Dame. As I trudged to school I used to recite from memory the *Little Office of the Blessed Virgin* as required by the Third Order. With a convert's fervor I recited it in Latin, nothing else would do for me, and gradually the Latin got so jumbled up that it became somewhat meaningless, but I kept at it.

These were the days when Fr. John O'Hara, CSC, who later became Bishop of Philadelphia and a Cardinal, was president of Notre Dame. He was deeply concerned that the students live a sacramental life. Every residence hall had a beautiful chapel where Mass was said daily and certain chapels had a confessor available around the clock. One had only to press a button and a priest emerged to hear your confession or to give you Holy Communion. All students were required to be at morning role call in the chapel and were urged though not required to stay for Mass. Before each holiday the student bulletin was filled with gentle reminders to "be in the state of grace before you go home. There are many accidents on our highways." It was noted that Fr. O'Hara himself was always available in his room to hear confessions even far into the night. The presence of Jesus in the Blessed Sacrament in the many residence chapels led me to write the following poem.

NOTRE DAME DORMITORY

In the midst of young men sleeping
three young men still wake,
marking the time on the sills of stone
by the falling flake by flake,
three young men and two of them alone.

Alone one leans his strong body on his bed, kneeling,
for a long while praying,
forgetting time, remembering his friends in his appealing,
remembering his girl, the dead, his work, his game,
lost in a flood of names said in that Name,
alone, yet living
in the one Giver, by the one Giving.

Another lies long athwart his bed, tired, turning
in the uneasy darkness himself uneasy,
remembering his dubious friends, deceptive learning,
remembering that girl, and death, hate, shame,
drowned in a spew of names staining that Name.
With him dying lies one dead,
the Great Loser at his side turning in bed.

The Third is not alone and yet alone, alone
in the smallest room locked in, unseen, unspeaking,
sighing for friends inside the gold and stone,
sighing for hearts, the dead, for love, a sigh of flame,
calling to them to call upon His Name,
giving the first his prayer and peace and cheer,
giving the other one his fear.

One is alone now in the peace of an obedient will,
one lies unseen with some bedfellow burning with chill,
One is Love alone and yet around them both
keeps timeless troth.

Three men are awake now while time and the snow fall
and all the rest are asleep in that darkened hall.

Mass in the college church, an impressive Victorian Gothic, steepled edifice was solemn and on Sundays massively attended. Back of and below the church, which is set on a hill overlooking St. Mary's Lake, is the Grotto, a reproduction of Lourdes with a statue of the Immaculate Conception. Here not only faculty and students but many visitors could be seen praying in the silence, and on evenings in May, a crowd of students went from the dining halls to the Grotto to recite the Rosary. All this piety was very naturally and unaffectedly mingled with the athletic, football cult for which Notre Dame is famous. On the day of the first football game I saw all the players together at morning Mass, but was startled to see them at the end of Mass one by one come up to the sanctuary railing, each one to awkwardly present his weak spot, a shoulder, an arm, or a knee to be blessed by a priest with a relic!

Student discipline was firmly maintained and undergraduates were restricted to the campus and a well-defined "safe" area of South Bend. Campus police kept vigilance on the rest of the city and rounded up those students found out of limits. Only at the end of the Spring Semester on Alumnus weekend were the limits forgotten and the city's bars crowded.

The campus, with its Lake St. Mary and Lake St. Joseph, its fine old trees, grassy quads, and the oddly Victorian but memorable main building with its Golden Dome topped by the statue of Notre Dame, had an embracing graciousness like a real alma mater. I am happy that the great subsequent growth and expanding buildings have not destroyed the beauty of that central campus. When I studied there Notre Dame was still a relatively small school and its present academic stature was only developing. Under the leadership of former President Theodore M. Hesburgh, CSC, Notre Dame has greatly expanded, enriched its endowment, and developed its graduate school, while retaining something of the athletic prowess that has given it popular acclaim. How well it has retained or improved its Catholic communal atmosphere I cannot judge, and have heard different opinions. As it was then it was not academically a great school. In comparison to the broad intellectualism of the medieval Dominican tradition in which I had been initiated at Chicago, the remnants of the rather narrow nineteenth century French tradition of piety given Notre Dame by the intrepid pioneer who founded it in 1842, Fr. Edward Sorin, CSC, did not seem to me very attractive. But it was unmistakably, whole-heartedly, a Catholic school, which as a convert was exactly what I wanted.

President O'Hara not only reinforced the piety of the school, but seized on the World War II situation to bring distinguished Europeans to the campus. In addition to the political philosopher Waldemar Gurian, my dissertation director, the political scientist F. A. Hermens already mentioned, Gilbert Chesterton, Shane Leslie, Christopher Hollis, Desmond Fitzgerald, Charles DuBos, Arnold Lunn, Étienne Gilson and Jacques Maritain all lectured there; and in a second wave, the Thomist philosopher Yves Simon (1903-1961)[80] the physicist and the mathematician Karl Menger and others were added to the permanent faculty.

Refugee Professors

My studies were principally with Waldemar Gurian, Yves Simon, and F. A. Hermens. I also took what was for me an important course on the social doctrine of the Church Fathers from a Holy Cross priest, Fr. Francis J. Boland whose interest was chiefly in proving that the Church Fathers were not socialists. Yet under his tutelage I read St. Augustine's *The City of God* and reread the *Confessions* which I had first read in the Great Books Seminar. These great works are a complete education. Although I am a Thomist, I admit that St. Augustine is the greatest of all Catholic theologians. Since he worked with an idealist epistemology derived from Plato rather than with Aristotle's realism he was unable to achieve the marvelous balance and critical solidity of Aquinas. But it was Augustine who with undaunted intellectual courage faced up to the most fundamental and difficult question for a Christian theologian: sin and grace. Where Augustine goes beyond Aquinas is in attacking the problem of history and here we Thomists must still strive to assimilate this African's teaching better.

Yet I learned most from Yves Simon.[81] Simon was originally a medical student and as he lectured we used to glimpse medical drawings on the back of some of his notes. He was the best teacher I have ever had. In spite of his accent, his English was excellent, and he strove always to improve it. When he would ask the class for the correct pronunciation of some word he found difficult, he usually got several different answers and with great drama would throw up his hands in exasperation at the inconsistency of English, especially American English, and say, "Mon Dieu, what a language!" He once praised the great Thomistic commentator Jean Poinsot (John of St. Thomas) for repeating a point over and over in different terms because in this way a teacher can reach a variety of minds. Yves insisted that every lecture should have a single main point, since a student cannot grasp more than one idea at a time. His lectures followed his own advice. He always stressed a single point that he would approach from various angles, often adding interesting material from current philosophy. It was from him that I first heard of existentialism and phenomenology and European political controversies.

Simon had a severely crippled leg that had given his whole frame a twist. He told us that this bad leg had caused him once to fall on an icy pavement. "As I lay there in great pain and unable to get up," he told us dramatically, "it was then that I at last attained a truly metaphysical intuition of Being, and realized the utter contingency of all that is not God!" He was blond with rather pale, protruding eyes, and dressed oddly, often wearing a blue suit with a lumberjack shirt, a mismatched tie, and suspenders. Yet once in a very fatherly and tactful way he advised me to dress more professionally if I hoped to get a teaching appointment! Simon was thoroughly Catholic, thoroughly Thomist, and truly philosophic. It was from him that I began to learn a solidly critical approach to Aquinas. In particular I have always thought Simon's political thought was superior to that of Jacques Maritain of whom Simon acknowledged himself to be only a disciple. He showed me that Thomism can be an up-to-date intellectual perspective that can confront any contemporary problem in a constructive, not merely a defensive way.

I recall also an incident involving Simon that casts some light on the history of Hutchins and Adler at the University of Chicago. Once Leo and I drove with Yves to Chicago and stopped for a visit at the home of Prof. John Ulric Nef, a noted economic historian. He was a friend of Yves and also of Adler, who happened also to be present. Nef was sympathetic to Catholics and had been instrumental in bringing Maritain to lecture at the University. Although a man of great culture, Nef once admitted to me that he had little concrete knowledge of the Catholic faith and asked me for a book explaining the Catholic Church's doctrines, to which with my usual lack of tact replied that he had best read the Baltimore Catechism! Indeed I have found great ignorance of such matters among academics.

A lively and witty conversation at Nef's house was going on famously, when suddenly his wife, the daughter of the former star social scientist of the University, George Mead, entered the room with an armful of lilacs. It was spring and she had just come from the country. She exclaimed about the beauty of the weather then noticed that Mortimer Adler was among the company and to Simon's horror, but to the entertainment of the rest of us, she turned on Adler and said "You killed my dear father! Because of you he died of a broken heart!" In fact when Hutchins brought Adler to Chicago and met faculty resistance, Mead in defense of academic freedom resigned the post he had long held so brilliantly, and soon after died. Our visit was soon politely terminated, but I for the first time realized how fierce and bloody the battle had been.

Later Simon received an appointment at the University of Chicago but continued to commute from Notre Dame until spinal cancer made it impossible for him to teach. I visited him at his home in South Bend at that time. He was much himself, but was suffering severely and complaining how reluctant his physician was to let him have him sufficient morphine. I heard that a little later he insisted on delivering a scheduled lecture at Notre Dame on his mentor Maritain. Although he had to be wheeled onto the stage, they say he spoke brilliantly for over an hour and as they wheeled him off said, "For the first time in months I was free from pain." Like Aquinas who endured an operation without anesthetic by concentrating on ideas for his writing, in teaching Simon had forgotten his suffering body.

Waldemar Gurian was an entirely different personality.[82] A Russian Jew who had been raised in Germany as a Catholic and in spite of his almost paranoid skepticism was, I believe, sincerely Catholic in faith. He was an obese person with wispy hair on a balding head who often sweated profusely as he talked and, though diabetic, was constantly sipping (non-diet) Cokes. He died in middle age in 1954. Thomas Stritch, class of '34, in an article "The Foreign Legion of Father O'Hara" in the *Notre Dame Alumnus* writes,

> Gurian was massive in most respects: in body, in erudition, in personality, in impact, in persistence. As Christopher Hollis once wrote, "Gurian was as unyielding in conversation as a man can be. I never knew him to shift his ground because of anything that anybody else said to him." That was so, and his opinions, political and otherwise were often mistaken. But he brought to a detached and largely indifferent campus a sense of the twin evils of Hitlerism and Bolshevism.

I am not so sure about Gurian's opinions being "often mistaken." Rather they were amplified by his fears. He was indeed the classical grumpy professor, with a turned down lower lip. He had quickly understood the Hitler menace and warned his friends to leave Germany at once, as he did. Consequently, as the Hitler Wehrmacht blitz-krieged Europe Gurian seemed to take ever grimmer pleasure in his role of a Cassandra. Each day he came to class with a frightening grin on his face, saying, "Have you read the papers? Have you heard the radio?" and then went on still more grimly with his lecture.

Gurian's erudition was indeed both massive and precise and one could see him in the library near the new book shelf rapidly leafing through book after book, finding the significant contribution of each. I had two excellent courses from him (contrary to my ways at Chicago I dutifully attended classes at Notre Dame), one in Plato's *Republic* in which his approach was quite different from McKeon's, not a play of ideas and terms, but a constant comparison with the political realities of Plato's day and our own. The other was on Thomas Hobbes, and here Gurian frequently chuckled to himself over the crass realism and materialism of Hobbes' politics.

In later correspondence a classmate wrote me how he had once been commissioned to teach Dr. Gurian to drive.

"Now, just back out of the parking space, Dr.Gurian." Now we see the mighty brain of Gurian at work. "Now, ven I turn se veel zis vay ce car vill go zat vay? Yess? How do I know it iss in revairse?"

Doctoral Dissertation

Gurian, as I mentioned, was my dissertation director, although I got much help from Simon too. My topic of research was *The Theory of Natural Slavery according to Aristotle and St. Thomas Aquinas*.[83] I chose this somewhat odd topic (but aren't all dissertation topics odd?) because Gurian had made me aware what a blot this apparent defense of slavery appeared to be on the reputation of these two great favorites of mine. As I approached its completion, however, he began to panic. "What if *Time Magazine* got hold of this?" he anxiously said to me. "Would they say that I am now defending slavery?" As a result I had to write a conclusion to make the reader absolutely sure that no one could possibly think that either I (or Gurian) was in favor of slavery.

What I really argued is that the reality of "slavery," i.e. the use of persons not for the common good but for the individual good of the more powerful, by whatever name it is called, remains a permanent problem in all societies, which any realistic political theory must face. Aristotle did not accept the slavery of his society without questioning it. He seems to have seen the same dilemma that Marx saw, that all human beings are by nature free and yet a great part of them are "everywhere in chains" because of what seems an economic necessity, namely, that any liberally educated class of free citizens need some leisure from manual work and hence, it would seem, must be economically supported by an unfree, uneducated class. Such a class cannot really participate in a free government.

Aristotle predicted that if machines could be invented to do the work of slaves, then all members of a society could be liberally educated, and thus free. Aquinas, however, believed that the cause of this inveterate injustice in the world is original sin that has plunged humanity into poverty and war in which the losers became the slaves of the conquerors. Therefore the remedy cannot be machines alone but must be the virtue of justice. This issue in political theory and in political reality is no wise obsolete; although this exploitation is no longer named "slavery" and, covered up by democratic slogans, it continues even in our rich United States where only about half the "citizens" actually vote. This undeniable evil is what "liberation theology" is all about.

Leo Shields wrote his excellent but neglected dissertation on *The History and Meaning of the Term 'Social Justice'* [84] under Prof. F. A. Hermens, a very formal, polite, but kind German Herr Professor, formerly important in the Center Party of Germany, whose constant theme in teaching was that the Hitler disaster was the result of the false understanding of democracy which led the Weimar Republic to adopt electoral proportionalism.[85] This multiparty system, supposedly more democratic than a two-party system, permitted extremist minority groups like the Nazis to get into the legislature where they could discredit genuinely democratic government by constantly interrupting legislative procedures. Thus the Nazis were able to take over with the support of a popular majority disillusioned with an impotent democracy and crying for governmental action in the midst of social chaos. Hermens predicted disaster for other countries adopting proportional representation and multiparties. The situation today in Israel can be taken as another confirmation of his prophecy.

Leo's work, however, was not on this theme, but on how to understand the concept of "social justice" which so often appears in the Church's social encyclicals. He concluded that it is not some new virtue but is primarily what Aquinas called "legal justice," defined, not as its name might suggest by "legality," but as the responsibility of citizens and government to serve the common good rather than private interests. Secondarily, "social justice" is Aquinas' "distributive justice" by which the benefits of the common good are given to individuals according to their individual needs.

Both Leo and I were much interested at this time in the hot controversy which arose over Jacques Maritain's book, *The Person and the Common Good*,[86] in which he tried on Thomistic principles to refute totalitarian political theories like those of the Nazis and Communists by claiming that a member of a society is subordinate to its common good as an individual with a material body, but not as a person with a spiritual soul, since the dignity of persons transcends all earthly societies. Maritain claimed St. Thomas' authority for this distinction, because Aquinas holds that, while pure spirits are formally individuated and hence each specifically different, human beings are formally of a single species and are individuated only by their materiality. Charles De Koninck, of Laval University, vigorously attacked this theory as neither Thomistic nor an adequate answer to totalitarianism in his *La primauté du bien commun*.[87] Maritain did not reply, but a Dominican at Laval, Fr. I. Th. Eschmann, OP, came to his rescue with an essay *In Defense of Jacques Maritain*[88] to which De Koninck replied with an exhaustive exegetical study, *In Defense of St. Thomas Aquinas*.[89] He showed that for Aquinas the human persons as such are subordinated to the common good, because their own greatest personal goods are participations in the common good. In fact each individual human person has a twofold personal good: private goods accorded by the right of private property and common goods shared with others. The former are largely material goods, which we need to own in private since two persons cannot eat the same piece of the pie. The latter are primarily spiritual goods since my share in virtues and truth does not exclude you from sharing in them too. In fact virtue and truth are not easily achieved without a common effort and participation. Thus the error of the totalitarian state is not that it subordinates the good of persons to the good of the state, nor that it demands that when necessary citizens sacrifice their private goods to the common good. The error of totalitarianism is that its goal is the aggrandizement of material goods, wealth and military power which involve the sacrifice of personal rights to tyrants, rather than the sharing of spiritual goods which will liberate all.

Leo and I were convinced by De Koninck's exegesis of Aquinas and his substantial arguments. Yves Simon, although he loyally defended Maritain, later directed a dissertation which in effect accepted De Koninck's position. To me this position is a fundamental importance for politics, since its sets the goal of society not in wealth and material power, but in education to virtue and the pursuit of truth. What needs to be added, however, is the "principle of subsidiarity" without which the just distribution of the common good and the contribution of all members of a society to that common good, i.e., legal and distributive (social) justice, cannot be established. Thus for Leo and me Marxism was finally exorcised by the realization that it is essentially totalitarian because of its materialism. Thus we had formerly been very much mistaken to think that one can separate Marx's social theory from his atheism, since for Marx the aim of human social life is the same as that of laissez faire capitalism, a material not a spiritual common good.

I might add that this controversy was an example of the excessive and uncritical loyalty of certain of Maritain's disciples. Another was the attacks some waged on my friend Dr. Herbert Ratner when he dared to criticize both Maritain and Mortimer Adler for the untenable notion which Adler developed in his *Problems for Thomists: The Problem of Species*,[90] that the human mind is not capable of defining any species of living thing except the human species. I am convinced of Maritain's Christian sanctity as well as his creativity as a Thomist, but I differ from him on this notion which he used to divorce natural science from natural philosophy, as well as on his theory on the classification and foundation of the sciences which has, in my opinion frustrated the development of Thomistic philosophy.[91]

Apostolate of Like-to-Like

An important influence on both Leo and me was our membership at Notre Dame in the Young Catholic Students movement, under the direction of the zealous and wise Fr. Louis Putz CSC This was a movement initiated by the famous Belgian Canon Cardijn (1882-1967)[92] along with his better known Young Catholic Workers on the principle "the apostolate of like by like," aimed at the evangelization of the milieu. We were organized in small cells, like Communist cells, which met regularly, but our activities were based on St. Thomas Aquinas' teaching that prudent decisions have three steps: Observe, Judge, Act. Thus we would read a passage of the Gospels, discuss how it applied to the circumstances of our daily lives and our milieu (Observe); decide how we could make our lives and those with whom we lived more in conformity with the Gospel (Judge); and then, before the next meeting, try to carry out our decision in practice (Act). The aim was not to make a political revolution but to transform it as a Christian leaven. This view of the special role Catholic laity in the Church seems to be superior to the current emphasis on "lay ministry" as a substitute for the role of priests.

Our undertakings were generally modest. For example, one week we decided that each of us would sit down with some seemingly lonely student in the dining hall and engage him in an ordinary, friendly conversation. But we also undertook bigger projects such as urging the University Administration to begin admitting black students. It is shameful to recall that at that time Notre Dame was fearful that the admission of blacks would result in the exit of its southern undergraduates, who formed a significant part of the student body. Our efforts had some good influence on student opinion, but the Administration did not have the courage to take the final step to full integration until in World War II the Armed Services came to the university and required it.

Among the new friends I made at Notre Dame I will mention especially Henry Rago, a charming Chicago Italian and accomplished poet, who in 1955 became editor of *Poetry: A Magazine of Verse*, but in 1969 died in middle age.[93] He kept my interest in poetry alive during these years of transition, although I was not then writing very much, being too occupied with my dissertation. But I did produce a few poems at Notre Dame, such as the one last quoted, and the following,

THE HOLY AVERAGE

In deep chasms of the valley—rocks deep violets, green weeds
quicken in dew.
The pinnacles of peaks show broken surfaces of stone,
show crystals, ices, spar,

under the cliffs of the world the ocean
over the worlds and out of the clouds the summit star.

In deep abysses of the spirit the warm memory, frozen will
of angels shines pure thought,
in flames of love complexly wrought
out of space and sight in aeviternity,
dancing before the eternity of Light.

In deep streets of stone, walls, empty faces,
emptying hands wander and touch.
In high rooms of steel, drawn-out nerves and flesh
tremble, await.
Under the city the sewer, subway, main and wire,
over the city the smoke
and from that smoke rises a sooty spire.

In the depth of earth and of angel and of mere man
here is the depth of emptiedness,
who has touched violets, violet nothingness,
who has loved human, suffering shallowness.
Have you known angels in sudden inspirations?
In the complexities history wrought are there not
on the heights of earth and spirit and mere man
pinnacles of yearning?
Who does not strain on the hill upheave the breast?
Who does not stretched hands to a lover empty armed?
Have you sung by twilight with cherubic mouths
for sky, the beloved, or all the rest?

Here in the midmost crouches one
who sees not either death nor sun,
forgetful of both chasm and cliff,
neither homeless in the garbage,
nor dining with wine.
Who has met neither devil nor the morning star?
Who is this middle, average one?
The man in the street, at the movies,
asleep in a suburb or driving his car?

Your sins are enough for the chasm,
your faith enough for the summit,
ordinary man, ordinary woman, ordinary human,
God and you alone are common.

THE ANGEL AND THE INTROVERT

An angel visited a weeping man crouched in the snow.
The man huddled, rocking to and fro,
his tears freezing and his breath all steam.

"This is the real world, man, not your dream,"
The angel said bending his splendid head,
waving his wings of flame.
"Here is the world of plain, real things:
Around you fields, then hills, then town,
over it all this snow comes down
so all is hidden, all is white.
Look, O man, see how all is right.
Yet inside you all is troubled, smoke, and wrath,
lions and ladies snare your every path.
Inside lie dead friends with faces soft and green,
and Envy wandering through a pastoral scene.
There in your inmost the black hole of hell
where you sit knowing yourself too well,
smelling a faded rose.
Man, man look up, in honest fact it snows."
This the angel said,
his hands of flame lifting my hanging head.

Yes, I saw the hillocks all pure white,
the curvature of boughs, the bright
traces and the gray places, sky and snowy spaces,
common, pure, still.
Seeing how everything
was right,
I wiped my eyes upon his gentle, flaming wing.

This poem came from seeing the sun rise over the empty fields
around the campus.

WATCHING MERCURY AND VENUS WHILE HOPING FOR HEAVEN

Black woods, open sky, twilight low,
filling pure emptiness with a pure glow,
and then the planets
Mercury and Venus
nearest to earth, to Sun
 hanging low,
both with their own still purer glow
and so I know

how it is that the soul longs at the end to die,
to melt through all sensual radiance as the sky
washes out fire in the dew of afterlight
and pale, featureless, embraces night.
How then in that great blankness must the heart
(bright Mercury closely follows Venus, yet apart)
look after life and (Venus-like) the mind,
(blue-white, still only a star and blind)
gaze on into the wood so black, so low
of all my hopes, clear in that pure afterglow.

But Mercury and Venus pass the Sun at last and rise
to pulse above him in the morning skies.
Remember then how at first they seem
isolate, afloat in that great space and empty gleam
and then (as the heart itself gets free from lesser love
in the first pulse of Love Supreme)
Mercury is lost in the bright edge of day,
(as in the space of the Spirit we forget our way),
so Venus over the now golden wood so far below
fades in the emergent fullness of dawn's glow.

The dense woods and the clouded sky and no
single star, then through the emptiness
the restless wind must come, must go;
even to midnight
when the heart,
the mind can find no splendor,

only leaves in the wood, in the wind must blow
to and fro.

Another poem reflects my thinking from the perspective of the
idyllic Christian life at Notre Dame concerning the gritty confusion
of Chicago as I remembered it.

BUT HERE IT IS THE WAY WE ARE

Days of extensive ethereal immensities,
nights of elaborated intricate journeyings,
twilights of tranced gazings down into,
these seem to me
what we should be.

By day we ought to stand upon the undivided plains,
or float unanchored on the unfenced sea,
or quiver suspended in the smooth, the seamless air.
and with cycloramic stare
possess each moment and approve.

We should by night without map or clue
trace out the deep-bored tunnel and the branching mine,
or mount in tendriled wires and launch ourselves on waves,
that circumscribe the earth and beach against the moon
at our commanding whisper.

By twilight then along the empty shore
in multitudes quietly walking or a few
running together, we should all stare out upon
the falling sun and following stars,
enjoying much that universal view.

But here it is, the way we are, the way we are.

Days of half-hearted streets, the enclosing walls, the work,
nights of tired nebulae and quarreling to music,
twilights on buses sleepy morning and fagged evening,
reading in the papers of new rapes, and inconclusive wars.

Let the days come and the nights follow,

let the twilights close in the sides of the jostling bus,
here we are, going and coming from work, here we really
are.

I should especially note that in spite of the many religious and
esthetic experiences I was then enjoying at Notre Dame, I was now
trying to avoid that vague pantheistic mysticism in which I indulged
in my Marxist days and evident in some of the poems written then,
such as in the sonnet "Separation" already quoted in Chapter 4.

AGAINST FALSE MYSTICISM

The stupor of cold sleet in smoke pervades
and stuns.
Dead minds in dark asylums call
for suns,
Shades of mad winter all
howl for a jungle South
with mad eyes over a wild mouth.

So in the chill bombardment of defeat
and doubt,
the bitten glutton in these hard veins
of gout
growls, squeaks, hourly complains
for some hot-savoring salvation
spiced hot with vaguest exaltation.

Come sleet, come cold, come failings of the blood,
come factual death,
rather than petals in a dream,
rather than dreamy breath,
rather than the milk of babes, warm and creamy.
rather would I freeze clean through
than seek your mystic dissolution in the dew.

Another literary friend I made at this time was Charles Daugherty, a youth with an infectious chuckle who later became an English professor at St. Louis University and with whom I shared many
amiable and spirited discussions. We have kept in contact over the

years. A different friendship was with Albert Plotkin, one of the few Jews then at Notre Dame, who became a Rabbi in Phoenix, Arizona[94] and who did me the honor years later of referring to me as his best friend in that school where he must have felt rather isolated. I also enjoyed a few evenings that I spent with Gurian and other professors at a neighborhood bar where the discussion was mainly about the war.

I remember also the very pastoral Fr. John A O'Brien, a well known apologist and polemicist, who upon noticing that I seemed lonely, offered to get me dates with girls at St. Mary's. When I explained that I intended to become a Dominican he did not insist. When he died it was announced that he had saved the money earned by his writing in order to leave Notre Dame a magnificent bequest of a million and a half dollars. He had been for a long time in campus ministry at the University of Illinois, Urbana-Champaign, where he caused consternation by writing articles in which he questioned whether anybody was actually in hell. He was also one of the first priests to promote what we now call Natural Family Planning about which some Catholic moralists then still had doubts. While at Notre Dame I returned to the University of Chicago to take my comprehensives for a Ph.D. in Political Science and passed all these exams except the one for which I had studied hardest, the section on economics. But I retook it satisfactorily the next quarter. Consequently, for some time I thought of also doing a dissertation for the University of Chicago and getting a second doctorate more prestigious than the one from Notre Dame, but after I entered the Dominicans I gave up that idea. Yet to this day I have had nightmares in which I did in fact return to get that Chicago Ph.D.

In May, 1941, I completed my Notre Dame dissertation and was confident in defending it before a board that included a professor whose courses I had not taken, a specialist in American government. But after my defense, to my chagrin the board kept me waiting outside the room for over an hour while they deliberated and I became more and more uneasy. Finally, they summoned me in and told me that they would have to meet again the next day, when they finally did approve me. Gurian told me that what had happened was that the professor of American government adamantly refused to approve my dissertation. He only yielded at last to pressure by the other members of the board who did not want a scandal over a rejection of the first Ph.D. candidate in their new graduate program. Since as a graduate assistant I had taught courses at Notre Dame in

American government and since, in my own opinion, I found no great difficulty in answering the questions on that section of the written comprehensives, I felt that Gurian was right in saying that it was more the dissenting professor's' pique at my ignoring his courses than my faulty performance. No doubt, however, my own contempt for academic formalities was finally my near undoing. Leo, more prudent than I, sailed through his exams without incident and with mutual congratulations we received our Ph.D.'s in political science together.

It had been a happy two years. It is true that the spiritual problem that I will discuss in the next chapter was beginning to show up— my tendency to scrupulosity. I had obtained permission from a confessor to go to confession daily, which was really not a good idea. My concerns were mainly about sexual fantasies, lying (mainly by way of excuse), and rash judgments of others. I have learned as a confessor, temptations usually trouble the scrupulous because, though their common sense tells them that these are not serious sins, yet their fear of self-deception continues to torment them. What for me was really dangerous was that I also began to worry about temptations against faith. Unfortunately none of my confessors ever took the time really to discuss this problem with me. Nor did they seem to understand that scrupulosity often originates in a psychological condition of excessive anxiety reactions in a victim that make it difficult for the scrupulizer to make decisions. From what I have related about my background and childhood it should be evident why I was predisposed to this condition. In pastorally helping scrupulous penitents in later years I found that they need medical and psychological help to reduce their anxiety level. My confessors, however, simply told me I should ignore such scruples and reassured me that I had not lost my union with God, the one thing that was my deepest fear.

Yet none of this in any way shook my happy anticipation of entering the Dominican novitiate. Leo had told me that he too was going to become a Dominican, but not in the Chicago province where I was going. He intended to enter the Western Province in Oakland, CA, where he would be closer to his widowed mother and also his brother Francis. I knew Francis from the time he briefly attended the University of Chicago and I still correspond with him. Leo's decision seemed perfectly natural to me, since I had long ago accepted the fact that we would have to go separate ways after graduation. But then, rather late in the Spring of 1941, Leo announced that he had changed his mind about entering religious life. He never explained to me why. Even at Chicago he had engaged in a certain amount of dating, and it may be that he was again thinking of marriage. In any case this new decision deeply troubled me. If Leo, the native Catholic in whose faith I had so much trusted, felt that religious life was not right for him, how could I be sure that it was right for me? This was resolved for me when I told Fr. Timothy Sparks about it and he simply asked, "Are you Leo, or Winston?" I have never again had any doubts about my vocation, although, as I will relate later, when my father died I was seriously concerned whether I had a right to take solemn vows and leave my widowed mother alone.

Chapter 8 - Entering the Cloister

Entrance to the Novitiate

I arrived at River Forest from Blackwell with my pastor, Fr. Stephen Leven, to enter the Dominican novitiate on July 25, 1941. The Priory and House of Studies of St. Thomas Aquinas was in River Forest, proximate to the Village of Oak Park. It is now owned by Dominican University. These are residential suburbs known for their fine houses, some built by the great architect, Frank Lloyd Wright, who originally had his studio in Oak Park. It is said that Wright had offered to design the Priory, but was rejected in favor of Wilfred E. Anthony of the modernized Gothic school of Bertram Goodhue. Anthony had designed the splendid Dominican Church St. Vincent Ferrer's in New York. Goodhue himself had designed the Rockefeller Chapel at the University of Chicago and the handsome Lutheran Church at Concordia Lutheran Teacher's College directly across the street from the Priory.

The Priory is a fine English Gothic building and during the many years I was to live there I always took great pleasure in its beauty, although its practical deficiencies were all too evident. It is said when the plans were sent to Rome for approval the authorities there wrote back "Are your Friars angels?" referring to the minimal provision for toilets. As a result of the Great Depression, however, Anthony's design was never completed. What is now the lofty chapel he had intended to be the refectory, which itself had to be located for years in the dingy basement. The ground was so swampy that according to legend one of the big machines used in the construction sunk out of sight where an underground creek ran underneath the building and filled a kind of cistern. River Forest was at that time almost entirely Protestant and the residents would not permit the friars to put bells in their tower, in spite of the fact that the chimes of the Lutheran Church rang out gloriously.

Later the neighborhood became a respectable cover for a number of well-to-do Italian gangster families who were, of course, at least nominally Catholic. To his great embarrassment the pastor of the nearby Dominican Church of St. Vincent Ferrer had to baptize, marry and bury the gangsters' offspring, often with much unwelcome comment from the media. One morning in River Forest the police found a bullet-ridden body slumped in a car, but the Catholicity of the exterminators was graciously demonstrated by their leaving the body in the car not on the Priory property but next door on the parking lot of Concordia Lutheran Church.

Later in the 60s a new south wing was built on the Priory to house refectory, library, and meeting rooms. The result comes far short of Anthony's projected cloisters of which nothing remains but the "ghost door" visible from the exterior and now leading only to a suicide leap. The building had extensive well-landscaped grounds providing playing fields for Fenwick High School in Oak Park taught by the Friars. Recently this former House of Studies has become part of Dominican University (formerly Rosary College) operated by the Dominican Sisters of Sinsinawa, WI. Part of the extensive grounds has been sold for residences and part to the Village of River Forest for a public park, while the front portion has been newly landscaped.

At one point during the changes after Vatican II, as a member of the Provincial Council I voted for the sale of these properties. St. Dominic was exasperated when he saw his friars erecting their first house with more than one story. He foresaw that the ownership of buildings would be an obstacle to the mobility of his band of preachers. Did not Jesus warn a would-be disciple, "Foxes have dens and birds of the sky have nests, but the Son of Man has nowhere to rest his head (Mt 8:20)"? I still believe that Dominic was right, but, attached as I am to today in old age to the comfortable priory in which I live, I well understand why in changing times, many of the brethren find security in a familiar home.

My Blackwell pastor, Fr. Leven, thought the diocesan priesthood would have been a much better bet for me than to be a religious, whom he regarded as drones, but he kindly turned me over to Fr. Peter O'Brien, then Provincial. Fr. O'Brien was a supremely taciturn man, who when elected provincial sent a telegram to a friend which simply read, "In". He informed me that there had been a mistake on the date for the beginning of the novitiate year and that I and two other candidates who had just arrived would have to wait a week. It was the Feast of St. James Major, July 25, but also a commemoration of the third century Spanish saint who was martyred under Diocletian, St. Cucuphas. Somehow the ridiculous name of holy Cucuphas seemed to make him our appropriate heavenly patron! The other two were a Mr. Angers, a young man of French ancestry from Springfield, MA, whose uncle was already a Dominican priest, and Mr. Susi, of Italian ancestry from Louisiana.

Both these new friends were dressed in clerical black, while I, not knowing I was expected to have such a suit, was in a beige summer outfit that made me feel very conspicuous. Mr. Angers, though I came to know him as a joker, looked in black like a funeral director, tall, thin, prominent nose, floppy ears, and a very sober expression, who kept calling me "Brother" (I was more used to "Comrade"). Mr. Susi, who was to leave during studies because philosophy in Latin was not his strong point, was not so much like a funeral director as like a tailor constantly occupied with keeping everything neat, always pressing his garments. He later went on to be a very pastoral Monsignor in his home Diocese of Alexandria, LA.

It happened that the younger Dominicans had been at a camp in Northern Michigan all summer, and the north wing of the building that they normally occupied and where the three of us were temporarily housed was cobwebbed, gloomy, and cavernous. We were politely ordered to hand over any money or cigarettes. Within an hour of arrival I found myself in choir in the main chapel, chanting the Divine Office (today called *The Liturgy of the Hours*) in Latin. The week seemed endless, but soon the other members of the novitiate class began to arrive and we were assigned "religious names." Part of the reception ritual for the novitiate included the declaration, "In the world you were called X, now you will be called Y." Angers chose "Joseph." Susi chose "Thomas Aquinas." Though I felt "Cucuphas" might be more appropriate, I decided on "Benedict" to honor the two Benedictine Sisters who, as I have related, that summer had been so kind to me. "Benedict" was an acceptable name for a Dominican because there were two Dominican popes by that name, the saintly Bl. Benedict XI (1303-1304) and the pastorally good but administratively naive Benedict XIII (1724-1730).

To anticipate, when the next class of novices arrived a year later, I was assigned by the Novice Master, Fr. Nicholas Walsh, to prepare a list of names from which the new friars could chose, and I dutifully spent a long time with the Martyrology picking out the most horrendous names I could find there, such as "Deusdedit," "Quodvultdeus" and "Simplicissimus." Fr. Walsh appreciated my idle humor and showed them the list but mercifully did not limit them to it, although one big bruiser of a novice, whom we immediately nicknamed "Bolly" after a notorious Polish football player, did get the lovely name of Hyacinth, the thirteenth century Dominican who missionized Poland.

In 1941 ours was the second novitiate class in the Province of St. Albert, although there were many other students who had made their novitiates at Old St. Rose in Kentucky, the first priory of the Order in the United States. In 1939 St. Albert's Province (Central or Chicago Province) had been separated from St. Joseph's (the New York or Eastern) Province that was founded in 1805. In 1941 there were 152 priests in the Central Province, 71 clerics and 10 Lay (Co-operator) Brothers. Besides Joseph and Thomas Aquinas, my other companions in the novitiate were (each with a religious middle name): Albert John Marie Coburn, a big fellow from Beaumont who already had some diocesan seminary preparation; Daniel Patrick Brady from Lynn, MA, very much an East Coast Irishman whose older brother was already in the Order; John William Sherman, a horseman from a very wealthy family, and Paul Timothy Froendhoff, both from Dayton, Ohio; Raymond Jude Nogar (d. 1967) and Robert Denis McAuliffe (d. 2007) both from the University of Michigan in Ann Arbor; Joseph Anthony Nadeau from Marquette, MI, the youngest of the class also with an elder brother in the Order; Thomas Clement McAndrew (d. 1986), Chicago, whose sister was a Dominican also; William Bernadine Cronin from Pawtucket, R.I.; Daniel Charles Lombard, and Richard Albert Bradley. Bradley never seemed much interested in our life and soon left. Lombard took simple vows but finally left for health reasons.

Br. Daniel seemed to us a bit hypochondriacal and after he left the Order married a Ph.D. in veterinary medicine. During his couple of years in the Order he had much discomfort with his eyes and when sent to a specialist learned that he suffered from a rare condition—of which that specialist claimed to be the discoverer—in which one eye forms a larger image than does the other. As a result several of the novices and clerics decided to go to the same specialist and almost all were found to suffer from the same rare disorder! Bill Cronin was thought at that time to be too immature and was not permitted to complete the novitiate. He remained a faithful friend who often phoned me to talk over old times and to discuss modern biblical criticism of which he was an avid reader. Before his recent death, he had retired from teaching high school, but told me he after these many years still regretted he was not allowed to become a Dominican priest.

Our class was certainly a very mixed catch of fish! At that time it was usual to admit candidates to the novitiate after only two years of college. Only two of my thirteen brothers, Nogar and McAuliffe had B.A.'s from secular universities or intellectual interests in any way like my own. I did not find that a great problem, however. What really worried me was that the life in those pre-Vatican II days seemed to me less monastically rigorous than I had expected and that the *Rule of St. Augustine* and the *Dominican Constitutions* seemed to demand. Yet, compared with our Dominican life today it was far from lax! Actually by post-Vatican II standards, life in a Dominican House of Studies at that time was strictly confined, rigidly scheduled, and intellectually enclosed in a completely traditional Thomism. Yet I felt dissatisfied and longed to live the Dominican life as it was in the thirteenth century, midnight Office, vegetarianism, woolen underwear, etc.! Yet, as I have already said, at no time in my whole life as a Dominican have I ever wanted "to return to the world." I have always wanted and still want nothing but to live and die a Dominican, since its ideal, if not the actual observance of this ideal, seems to me admirable in every way.

I was later to learn that historically the Order in this country, because of its pioneering circumstances had never attained either the formal rigor of observant European priories or their intellectual dedication, but that after World War I a systematic effort was made to achieve such observance under the leadership of priests who had studied in Europe, especially at the University of St. Thomas (the "Angelicum") in Rome. My opinions about this question of "observance" were, however, to be somewhat modified, as I will later explain.

The Novitiate

At that time the novitiate, the philosophy studium, and the theology studium of the only recently founded Chicago Province were all at River Forest and I was to stay there until a year after ordination. I received the habit of the Order and began the novitiate on August 4, at that time the Feast of St. Dominic. Until ordination we were never permitted to go home, except for a very serious illness or death in the immediate family. Since those having families in the Chicago area could have their families come to the convent for visits and they were even sometimes permitted a home visit for the day, this seemed to those of us whose families lived out of town pretty unfair. We could not leave the grounds without permission of the superior and during the novitiate were only occasionally permitted to go to Oak Park village or downtown. In the summer, however, for the months of June and July all the students (not the novices) went to our camp north of Menominee, MI, on Green Bay, which I will describe later, but even there we kept up most of the religious pattern of life of the River Forest priory.

As I have already noted, our Novice Master was Fr. Nicholas Walsh, a very Irish, very pious, very quiet priest, who handled us very gently, but firmly. Although I believe he had a pretty good estimate of the characters of all twelve of us (two were to leave before the novitiate ended), he seldom interviewed any of us, as do novice masters so frequently now, unless there was some quite special problem. His conception of the task of a novice master was simply to see that the routine was observed, occasionally to correct some noteworthy violation of the rules, and to conduct the "Chapter of Faults" at which he gave us simple but very good and rather brief spiritual conferences. This exercise, now I fear obsolete, was the regular opportunity to confess, not our sins, but our violations of the Rule, before the community. Each friar in turn stood up and admitted his failures in discipline during the week, then made the *venia* or humble full-length prostration and received a correction and penance from the superior. Sometimes these confessions could be a bit routine: favorite ones were, "I broke the night silence," or "I failed to keep custody of the eyes." More creative was the one that a certain classmate regularly confessed, "I committed levity in the chapel!" I am afraid this admission tempted us all to "commit levity."

Fr. Walsh, himself, was not inclined to levity, but he was a fine model of personal discipline and piety. Yet the conception of the Novice Master's duties that he exemplified failed to deal with many psychological problems from which the members of my class suffered, the consequences of which were to appear in later years. Once I went to him and asked if, since it contained nudes, I should keep the art book on Botticelli that I had brought with me to the novitiate. In his modest way he glimpsed quickly at it and then went and consulted the noted Dominican sculptor Fr. McGlynn[95] of the Eastern Province who was temporarily assigned to River Forest, who said not to worry. The incident could have been the occasion for some discussion of my problems of conscience, but Fr. Walsh passed over that in silence. Perhaps the best counsel I got at the time from another aged and wise Father was the traditional saying, "In the novitiate keep your bowels open and your mouth shut!" I did avoid constipation.

Our novitiate was a single floor, the second floor over the class-rooms in the south wing. Our novitiate regime was as follows. We were awakened at 6:00 by the "bellman," a novice chosen for this task (often because he needed to learn to get up early), who knocked on each door and said *Benedicamus Domino* to which we were to answer *Deo gratias*! We dressed in Dominican habit, went to the small chapel on that floor and recited the *Little Office of the Blessed Virgin*, with signs of the cross, "head inclinations," and "pro-found bows" at the proper places. As we finished we would hear the bell ring for the whole building and hastened down to the main chapel where the professed brothers and some of the priests were assembling. Other priests were vesting to say Mass at the many al-tars distributed throughout the house, since concelebration was not then practiced. Some of us, along with the student Brothers, were assigned to be "servers" at these "private" Masses. While they were going on, the Divine Office began in the main chapel, followed by the Community High Mass.

When I first entered, the Office was chanted *recto tono* (on one pitch) and not a great deal of plainchant was used except at High Masses at the main altar, mainly on Sunday. One of my early memo-ries is that when the students returned from camp and filled the choir, they filled it chanting the *Miserere* led by the then Student Master, Fr. George (d. 1959), in a sepulchral bass voice. The liturgy at that time was executed very rapidly, but every single word of it had to be said, and if any novice or student made a mistake in his assigned part, he had to make the *venia*, that is, prostrate himself at length in the middle of the choir until the Prior knocked for him to get up. Even when in recitation with others a friar made a mistake he was to kiss his scapular as if to say, "Pardon me, please!"

After Father Bernard (nicknamed "Hiram") Walker became Stu-dent Master in 1944 he improved the quality of the liturgy very much by insisting on an exact observance of the rubrics, including the use of the plain chant in the traditional chant book called the *Graduale* and *Completorium*, but the psalms, except on very special occasions like the Holy Week *Triduum* were still chanted *recto tono*. Nevertheless, I loved the Office especially the *Psalms*, though my mind often wandered. Nothing is more human than the *Psalms*. In them every emotion is given frank and deep felt expression. Our Lord recited them, even on the Cross since his cry, "My God! My God! Why have you forsaken me?" is the first line of Psalm 22 and I like to imagine that I am saying the psalms with him and sharing his own feelings. Are the psalms that express utter frustration and terror alien to Jesus? He felt them all and often. Are the psalms that cry out in anger and express deep hatred compatible with his gentleness and, as we like to say today, "unconditional" love? Not at all, because what Jesus hates is the injustice and self-righteousness that destroy the ones he loves, including their perpetrators whom he also loves. A God without wrath against evil is not a God of justice and hence not of mercy either. I was not pleased when the Vatican II revision of the Office removed some of the harsher psalms or verses. I have often joked with my students that I am no longer reminded to pray for them in particular as I once did now that we leave out of Psalm 137, one of the most beautiful in the *Psalter,* the horrid verse: "Happy the man who will seize and smash your little ones against the rock!"

At that time, of course, the Office was in Latin, and Matins that originally consisted of three Nocturnes of three psalms and three readings each during the night, five psalms for Lauds (Morning Prayer) at sunrise, three each for Prime, Terce, Sext, and None at intervals during the day, for Vespers five psalms, and for Compline three just before bedtime, but, as I will soon explain, modern circumstances required that some hours be said consecutively. The lay brothers (then not yet called "Cooperator Brothers") were present at the main hours of the Office but only required to recite a certain number of Our Fathers and Hail Marys. In addition to all this we recited an hour of the *Office of the Dead* each week. During the months of May and October every evening after supper Benediction of the Blessed Sacrament was celebrated with the recitation of the litanies of Loretto, the Sacred Heart or St. Joseph, and the Consecration to the Sacred Heart. Before entering the chapel at Matins and at Vespers we recited the *Miserere* for the dead, and one Sunday of the month a Rosary Procession was held, on another a procession in honor of the Holy Name, and on a third a Eucharist Procession with hymns and litanies. In the Novitiate we recited ten of the fifteen mysteries of the Rosary each day and had two periods of spiritual reading. With the whole community we had an half-hour of meditation and said the other five mysteries of the Rosary in common. I was fortunate in learning many of these liturgical ropes through a clerical student one year ahead of me, a member of the first novitiate class in our province, Joseph Innocent Hren, who until recently was still teaching Latin in our Fenwick High School.

This liturgical marathon today looks pretty strenuous and some of the pomp and circumstances it involved now seem very extravagant. When the Master of the Order Emmanuel Suarez made his visitation of the River Forest Priory in about 1946, Fr. Timothy Sparks, well acquainted with Roman ways, was anxious that the Chicago Province make a good impression, but what followed was a comedy of errors. In the evening the Master, himself a matter-of-fact Spaniard, not at all pompous, was met by the community at the front door with acolytes carrying lighted candles and incense. After being duly incensed, he was then escorted in procession by the Prior, Fr. John E. Marr (d.1992) who preceded glumly to the sanctuary where a prie-dieu had been prepared for the Master before the tabernacle, but when Marr turned to assist the Master to kneel, he discovered that he was left alone in the sanctuary because the Master had proceeded directly to his place in choir where Fr. Sparks with a flourish placed a special cushion on His Paternity's kneeler.

The kneeling community observed all this with awe and not a few discrete titters. After prayers, the Master was led to his room, which we called "the Bishop's Room" but which was poorly heated —one visiting bishop, after sleeping there, when he heard the room referred to by that title, said "You must hate bishops". Hence for the Master it had been decided to provide that room with a large electric heater, but this overtaxed the wiring so that when Fr. Suarez first switched on the room lights the fuses blew, leaving him in total darkness. News of this incident further entertained the community.

Fr. Sparks also wanted to make sure that the Master would have a Mass server who spoke Spanish and had arranged for this in our finest private chapel, supplying it with a *bougia* (a special candlestick which the server was to hold while a bishop or other high dignitary said a private Mass). But the Master was an early riser and wandered about the corridors looking for a server until he ran into my classmate, John Marie Coburn, who was then a deacon. John Marie, knowing nothing of the previous arrangements, and not very able in either Spanish or Latin, took Suarez to the first private chapel that was handy, only to find that there was no amice—a linen cloth then worn over a Dominican priest's head and shoulders at Mass. So the flustered John Marie had to look for one in the sacristy. This involved traversing the main Chapel where the whole community was reciting the Divine Office while curiously observing John Marie clop through the choir into the sacristy with which he was not well-acquainted and hear him opening and banging shut various drawers looking for a clean amice. Finally he found it, emerged, and with it in hand clopped again through the choir. Exiting the chapel, in his excitement he caught his heel on a step and plunged (he is Texas big) into the arms of the Master awaiting him at the bottom of the steps!

This was not the end of the humbling incidents that proved we in Illinois were not up to Roman pomp. For several days they kept the often bored community delighted. Just as the more formal the music, the funnier the wrong note, so in monastic life little mistakes are immensely risible. One of the traditional stories about St. Dominic was that when a novice master rebuked his novices for their surreptitious laughter, the Founder, said, "But they have cause to laugh! They have just escaped the devil." In the novitiate, as we fled the world, the flesh, and the devil, we had many reasons to laugh, not only at others, but ourselves in our struggling efforts to "live the life."

Nevertheless, a group of us, when interviewed by Master Suarez through an interpreter, petitioned that the recommendation for a return to strict observance contained in our then Constitutions, namely, perpetual abstinence from meat and recitation of Matins in the middle of the night, be strictly enforced. He listened patiently and then said, "Dear Brothers, we live in the age of electric lights." Perhaps he was thinking of what had happened to the lights in the Bishop's Room.

The Community Mass was celebrated daily and attended by all except the priests who were saying their "private Masses" (some said them early so as to be able to get also to the Community Mass) and the brothers who were serving them. Father Walker insisted it be a sung High Mass always and a Solemn Mass on feast days and Sundays. When the Mass was solemn, a Low Mass preceded it. At this Low Mass we "made our meditation" and went to Holy Communion so that we could then eat breakfast before the Solemn High Mass at which only the laity received Communion.

The "private" Masses of the priests at the altars in private chapels and on the balconies and at the back of the main chapel went on while the Community Mass was said at the main altar. Priests then would have thought it deplorable not to say Mass everyday if it was at all possible, even when traveling, and would go to considerable lengths to find a church where they could celebrate if they were in a strange city. They were not supposed to say Mass without a server

to represent the congregation, if one was available, and it was considered a duty and a privilege for a novice or student to serve Mass,
so that some tried to serve Mass several times a day. In the following poem the "Greater Silence" refers to the silence that was observed from bedtime to breakfast, and the "Lesser Silence" to that
which was to be observed throughout the day between classes and
during meals, though not at recreation periods.

DOMINICAN SERVING MASS
VERY EARLY ON AN AUTUMN MORNING

The green vestments wrinkling with gold
and the smooth white linen,
the window glazed with redeeming sunrise,
the purple night rejected
by gray light,
the strong points of the candles not yet blunted
by gray light—

Here the senses as they awaken prickle with color,
the smell of wax, of wine, wool,
beads rattled against a silent wall, water dripping,
the ache of sleep, the stillness and the damp—
Under my black cloak should be white prayer.

The senses awaking irritated
are as this realm of broken color in the realm of the
Greater Silence,
within dark corridors, rays of sensation in the dull body.
Yet now at the center on the smoothed linen
white bread, deep wine
lie ready.
So in the soul the blank mind is bright and stamped
with the Name and with the Cross.,

The will's the chalice in which self-love's three drops
are lost in Love
and these await the Word,
fruit of long sun and labor, rain and the enriched wind.

My mind furnishes no thought.
Imagination fretted like its sleepy eyes;
its ear tormented by the bell,
the Latin drone presents no blessed Face.
Taste thickened, seeks not even sweetness,
and all appetite looks back to the dark and to death.
Yet mind retains the habitual seal,
the will its graven hollow.

Sleepless God-Manity be Thou by my unthought Thought
within these emptied species of my mind,
the unmoved Love
within the surface of this sparkless wine.

The odd thing about this liturgically intense life was that we were given very little instruction about the liturgy; we simply did it. It was in Latin, of which we had an imperfect knowledge, and which often was said so rapidly as to foil efforts at translation. To maintain the pitch of the *recto tono* was not easy, and the zealous choirmasters kept "raising the tone" as the male voices dropped lower and lower. Sometimes the organist was ordered to hold a finger on one key throughout the Office. Fr. Walker, for all his care for the liturgy, simply emphasized obedience to the rubrics and when asked about their meaning answered in exasperation, "Don't expect the liturgy to make sense." While generally the priests said their private Masses with devotion, some the older priests had said Mass so often that they rattled off the Latin. One Master of Theology in the Priory was once asked how he managed to say a Low Mass in less than fifteen minutes. (Remember that at that time the text of the Mass was considerably longer than at present and the priest was required to recite to himself all of the words in the Missal, even those also said by other ministers). The efficient priest answered, "You have to say the words not only when you are breathing out but also when you are breathing in."

Moreover—and this was the source of a good many other of these liturgical abuses—the length of the Office required that Matins (now the Office of Readings, in the Middle Ages said after midnight) and Lauds (Morning Prayer) be anticipated for the following day. Thus for some years at River Forest, Compline (Night Prayer) was said immediately after lunch so that Matins and Lauds could be said before supper! Lauds and Prime were chanted and then the

Martyrology was read with a set of responding prayers called Pretiosa before morning Mass and breakfast. Sext and Terce were recited before lunch. When I asked the Novice Master why Compline, though it was a night prayer, was recited after lunch, he pointed out that though novices were not permitted a siesta, once professed we would share that privilege with the students and priests. We novices also recited the parallel hours of the Little Office before each of the hours of the Divine Office said by all. At that time deacons and priests were bound to the daily recitation of the whole Office (all seven hours) under pain of mortal sin, and many said the office hurriedly to get it over. I remember seeing one of the deacons sitting on the toilet saying his Office near midnight because the lights in our rooms had to be off at ten o'clock.

Our meals were also liturgical. We lined up outside the refectory, then recited the Psalm beginning *De Profundis* (Ps 130:1) and went in. The tables were arranged along three sides of the refectory, the friars sitting facing into the center with the serving done from the center side of the tables. The priests sat at the higher end of the refectory but were always served last, because once when St. Dominic and his first begging disciples had no food, they were served by angels who set that precedent. In the middle of the rectory was a lectern and a novice or student read during the whole meal while the rest of us ate in silence. The *Rule of St. Augustine*, common for friars, was read once a week and the *Constitutions* of the Sacred Order of Friars Preachers was read section by section during the course of a year. Getting the proper accents on the Latin of the Rule was a problem and one novice began, "InCIpit ReGUla BEati AuGUstini," hitting every accent wrong. Since a priest was appointed to ring the bell and correct every pronunciation, at that meal the bell kept ringing.

On other days the reading was selected by the prior and was quite varied. Sometimes it was a spiritual book, but more often history, biography, or even a travelogue. Many of us remember a life of Cardinal Wolsey titled, *Naked to Mine Enemies*,[96] or an account of climbing Mount Everest,[97] or Hershey's book on the bombing of Hiroshima.[98] Some found it difficult to eat those days.

One of the complaints of my strict observance faction to Master Suarez had been that we had meat every day except Wednesdays and Fridays and in Lent, instead of the perpetual abstinence established by St. Dominic. During Father Walker's regime it was necessary to get a dispensation from the Prior not to observe the Long Lent from the Feast of the Holy Cross (September 14th) until Easter. Many got the dispensation, but quite a few kept the Long Lent. For all my talk about observance, I had to get a dispensation because in the novitiate I developed a duodenal ulcer. In fact a good many students developed stomach ulcers and other probably psychosomatic ailments. Looking back, I think that our regime was excessively monotonous, not so much because of its asceticism, but because it had become so formalistic, overladen with rather meaningless historic accretions and out of joint, as Master Suarez said, with the rhythm of our times. What we needed was not so much an easier life as a better balanced life.

Unfortunately after Vatican II many traditional practices without discussion were simply dropped to obtain greater freedom rather than being rethought so as to retain what in them was really sound asceticism and restore it to its original purpose. We went from blind obedience to outmoded observances to a blind scramble to take it easy. I consider it significant that Vatican II dropped the traditional exhortation to religious "to return to the primitive observance" of their orders for the expression "return to the spirit of the Founder of the Order," along with its "sound traditions."[99] St. Dominic himself adapted the form of religious life to meet the needs of his time, yet kept as many of its "sound traditions" as were compatible with its mission.

At that time the community was divided into "categories": (1) the Priests who had finished their formal studies ("Grave Fathers," called by some young priests "Gravy Fathers"); (2) the recently ordained priests ("Young Dads") who were in their last year of theology; (3) the Professed Clerical Brothers, subdivided into (a) those studying theology; (b) those studying philosophy; (4) the Clerical Novices; (5) the Lay (Cooperator) Brothers not destined for ordination but for the maintenance work of the Priory, who were also divided into (a) Professed Lay Brothers; (b) Lay Brother Novices. These Lay Brothers were very important to our way of life, and although the categories did not permit us Professed Student Brothers to know them well, we often admired the selfless service and example of religious devotion that they gave. I regret that in this memoir I cannot say more about them. Members of these different categories lived in different sections of the Priory with their own group and were not supposed to speak socially to those of another category except on very special occasions. Today with our smaller numbers this kind of separation in community life would be quite impractical.

Each afternoon we were required to take an hour's exercise outdoors, a walk around the property, or play touch football or baseball. Though I was utterly inadequate at these sports, I had to play them any way. Each evening we also had an hour's recreation together in one of the classrooms. A big event was the production of a play that I wrote, beginning with the great line, "News is old!" which was put on for an audience of Fathers who kindly attended but did not seem greatly amused.

As I look back over that novitiate year I can't help but think of the German film *Das Boot* that takes place in a submarine. For me the submarine was that long corridor of the novitiate. Yet it was a time of much prayer, of growing identification with the Order, and of trying to live charitably with a "motley crew" of brothers in faith and vocation. Today out of the ten who completed the novitiate and were professed, one left the Order but not the priesthood, three left the Order and priesthood, and I am now the only one still living. I am not sure why the four who left the Order did so, since after ordination we worked in different places, but from what I have heard alcoholism was the principal factor in two cases and in the other two cases the strain of the changes resulting from Vatican II. The three who left the priesthood married but only one had children. These three were good men and good priests who for some years served the Church well, one as missionary in Bolivia, one as a high school teacher, one as a college teacher, but for them the stresses of the Church in our times finally proved too much. In the case of the two who suffered from alcoholism, in my opinion, the communities in which they lived too long delayed insisting on treatment, and one of the cases, a man of deep spirituality was misunderstood by his superior.

It was especially through the influence of this last mentioned brother, that I developed a greater devotion to Our Lady than I had felt before and with my confessor's permission consecrated myself to her by a private vow in the manner of which I had read in the work *True Devotion to the Blessed Virgin Mary* of St. Louis De Montfort (1673-1716), a great preacher of the Rosary and a Dominican Tertiary.[100] I also with most of my classmates took "Mary" as my middle name in her honor, which, as might be expected, has later been the occasion of irritating jokes by younger brethren.

Chapter 9 - Vows and Holy Orders

Vows

When the novitiate year ended on St. Dominic's Day at Vespers, 1942, I made the following resolutions in preparation for taking "simple" (temporary) vows the next day. They express what is often called the "first fervor" of some one seriously beginning the vowed life, a fervor that can quickly cool.

I resolve to examine my conscience on these points every day at least until with the help of the Blessed Trinity, of Mary, and St. Dominic, I am solemnly professed:

1. Have I been absolutely obedient today to the Rule and my Superiors in so far as I know their commands?

2. Have I tried to perfect my service in choir and at mental prayer?

3. Have I said at least one earnest prayer that God will make use of me to save souls and suffer in reparation for sin?

4. Have I done some kindness, at least a prayer, for one of my brother novices?

5. Have I done some little particular act of devotion to my blessed Mother?

Glory to Jesus in Mary!

Glory to Mary in Jesus!

Glory to God alone!

St. Dominic, pray for us.

[Signed] Brother Benedict Mary, O.P.

I don't know how well I kept these resolutions, but for me they essentially still stand. I lived by these simple vows for three years during which I was in the category of Clerical Student until I took solemn vows *usque ad mortem* (unto death) on August 5, 1945.

Studium

After the novitiate there was a problem about what my further education should be, since I already had a doctorate, but my superiors quickly settled this problem for me. I was to pursue the same course as my classmates, three years in philosophy before solemn profession and three years in theology before ordination in 1948, and a fourth year of theology after ordination. We were all dispensed to be ordained a year before completing theology in order to say Mass as "Young Dads" and thus obtain a stipend for our support, but were not permitted to hear confessions.

In those days the undiscussable reason for this decision that I must repeat my philosophical studies was that only the "solid doctrine of St. Thomas" learned from Dominican professors was trustworthy. The philosophical courses I had already done in two major universities counted for little or nothing. Although I found the courses (in Latin) boring, and most of the professors very narrowly educated and not open to contemporary issues or thinkers, I reveled in the opportunity to do nothing but study for seven long years. I am more profoundly grateful for it today than ever. I worked mainly on Aristotle and Aquinas, but also did a lot of reading in Scripture and comparative religion.

One of my professors whom I had come to know even before entering the Order and whom my friend Leo Shields had also greatly admired was Fr. William Humbert Kane ("Hum" as he was known, d. 1970).[101] Leo was especially impressed by Kane's views on the relation of religion and science. Fr. Kane had done his basic studies at the Dominican House of Studies in Washington, DC, and at the same time had studied medicine at Georgetown University in hopes of going on the missions as a physician, but much to his disappointment had then instead been assigned to teach philosophy, first in Washington then in River Forest. He and his friend in the Order, Fr. Timothy Sparks, were the members of the faculty most concerned to promote the intellectual tradition of the Order in the Chicago Province. Kane not only had scientific training, but during his doctoral studies in Rome had been led by the Spaniard Aniceto Fernandez Alonso, (later, 1962-1974, Master of the Order of Preachers in the crucial years immediately after Vatican II) to a very important insight: the realization that, contrary to the views of most twentieth century Thomists, the metaphysics of Aquinas, if it is not grounded in a sound natural science, lacks a critical foundation.[102] According to Fr. Kane, to attempt to build a Thomistic metaphysics on the Cartesian *Cogito ego sum*, or on the "concept of Being" as did many traditional Thomists, or on some "metaphysical intuition" as Jacques Maritain claimed to do, or even on the "judgment of the act of *esse*" as did Étienne Gilson, simply will not work. All these ways of grounding metaphysics, Kane argued, left it open to the modern charge that it is a mere word game.

In fact all these dubious ways of doing metaphysics into which modern Thomists have fallen rest either on the unexamined modern prejudice that modern science invalidated the Aristotelian philosophy of nature, or on Maritain's unsuccessful attempt to save the philosophy of nature by divorcing it from natural science, and constructing a metaphysics completely independent of it. Kane, on the other hand, maintained that modern Thomists were mistaken in attempting to save metaphysics from attacks by modern empiricist science by isolating metaphysics from the other disciplines and attempting to give it priority in *via inventionis* (the order of discovery) when in fact it presupposes the other sciences, especially natural science. While it is formally independent in having its own evident first principles, as any science must be, it is materially dependent on the lower sciences for all its data over which it simply reflects. When Aristotle called it "First Philosophy" he meant not that it was the prerequisite of the other sciences but their coordinator and critic.

To me Kane's teaching was of the greatest importance since it opened a positive way to relate both philosophy and theology to the achievements of modern science. I was convinced without such a bridge the Christian faith could never be made credible or even understandable to the modern world. As I read works on the modern philosophy of science and those of Aquinas, not merely the *Summa Theologiae* required of all the Dominican students, but his Aristotelian commentaries, and discussed them with Kane, I became thoroughly convinced of this interpretation of Aquinas that remains the core of my philosophical reflections. Many years later it became the central insight of my biggest book, *Theologies of the Body: Humanist and Christian*[103] and the argument of the book *The Way Toward Wisdom* that I have recently completed.[104]

I also learned much from Fr. Sebastian Carlson (d. 1990) who became Regent of Studies. He was not a brilliant mind, but he helped me study the textbook of Fr. Josef Gredt, O.S.B., which, as mentioned in the last chapter, I had begun to read with Herbert Schwartz. The last of the Baroque commentators on Aquinas was the Belgian, Jean Poinsot (John of St. Thomas, 1589-1644), who taught at the Spanish University of Alcala.[105] Gredt in his *Elementa Philosophiae Aristotelico-Thomisticae* summarized Poinsot's great *Cursus Philosophicus* in excellent fashion though very dryly and with no attempt to make it "relevant" or "meaningful" as students today demand. It enabled me, however, to get better hold of the Thomistic tradition. Poinsot's work has the form of scholastic controversy common in the Baroque period, not the careful unfolding of human experience which is to be found in Aristotle and Aquinas' penetrating commentaries on Aristotle's works. The great weakness of Thomism as presented by Jacques Maritain (who was very dependent on Poinsot) and Étienne Gilson (who disparages most of the commentators) or Adler (who worked almost exclusively and in translation from the *Summa Theologiae* which is not a work of philosophy but of *Sacra Doctrina*) is that it does not follow this order of learning or *via inventionis* of Aristotle. Consequently these Neo-Scholastics Thomists, so excellent in many regards, plunge into the middle of things without showing the student from what sources in experience the principles and concepts of Aquinas' thought originate.

I also learned much from Fr. James McDonald. He was nicknamed "*Bene*" because he had two brothers also in the Order who were nicknamed, "*Bonum*" and "*Optimum*". He was rather eccentric in manner, with a dry wit and he loved to play on the flute. While he was a boring lecturer who stuck rigidly to his notes, he was excellent in answering the most complicated questions in moral theology. I am especially grateful to him as a confessor, because he handled my problem of scrupulosity better than anyone else, with sympathy, patience, and good sense. He went to God after suffering for some years from Alzheimer's senility.

My other professors, to whom I certainly also owe gratitude for their hard work and patience, were not, in my opinion very simulating. They, like most teachers I have had in grade school, high school, university, graduate school, or philosophical and theological studies, were competent in their subjects but routine in their teaching, as I fear I have also been. The curriculum for philosophy as we then had it, covered the whole of Gredt, and the history of philosophy, and ended for many of us in an M.A. in philosophy. The program in theology was basically the study of the *Summa Theologiae* of Aquinas through four years, divided into a series of courses on its dogmatic parts, and another series on its moral parts, supplemented by courses in "practical moral theology" (application of Aquinas to confessional practice), church history, canon law, Scripture, and homiletics. The teaching of Scripture at that time was very inadequate, although the professors had been well prepared. This reflected, I believe, the confused state of Catholic biblical scholarship immediately after the struggle in the Church over "modernism." Our courses were conservative, but not fundamentalist.

What I did find useful and what seems to be lacking in seminaries today, was "apologetics" aimed at evangelization, for which we used the works of the Dominican, at that time famous, Reginald Garrigou-Lagrange's[106] De Revelatione in two volumes and Reginald Schultes, De Ecclesia. The concept of a "fundamental theology" was not yet as influential as it is now due to its promotion by Karl Rahner. This approach seems to assume that non-Christians are really believers without knowing it. But how can we know they are really believers, if even they do not know it?

I was stimulated in my studies of Aquinas by two older students who worked hard at getting acquainted with the classical commentators on his works, Cajetan and the John of St. Thomas whom I have already mentioned. Among my fellow students were Fr. Valerian Flynn (d. 1997), who, even as a student, was a rather dry, sardonic person, but very kindly. Later in life he switched from Thomistic studies to the Sacred Scripture, and in Denver became a well-known and much loved teacher of the Bible to laypeople. Charles Corcoran (d. 1984) was a learned eccentric, who became professor of psychology in the River Forest Faculty about whom many stories are told. The image that sticks in my mind is that he never permitted anyone to enter his room, but once when he was away it had to be opened and the shower was found to be stacked to the roof with books. This left us with the mystery of how Charlie, who was always personally very neat and well scrubbed, ever took a bath. Although in the opinion of most students he was not much of a success as a teacher, since he tended to lecture by reading passages from many books, he had a great influence on certain bright students. He became a great friend of Dr. Herbert Ratner, of whom I wrote in the last chapter and who was a great friend of the community of the House of Studies in River Forest. Yet "Corky" refused the Doctor's advice about his health and died suddenly of a heart attack. When he was found dead in his room, it was still crowded with books and—another mystery—an astonishing surprising number of clerical shirts, mostly never worn.

During these days of intense study, I was not writing much poetry, but I did help with a student publication, The Dominican Bulletin for I wrote some short articles whose tiles suggest some of my preoccupations:[107] "The Christmas Star," "Utopia and Myopia," "Meet My Mother, "Materialism," "Pagan-like," "Principle or Compromise."

I also drew a few illustrations for the magazine and completely illustrated a booklet on the Rosary by Fr. William Shea, our homiletics teacher. Fr. Shea was from Memphis, a big man, a fine preacher, who was very macho and very critical of any effeminacy on the part of students. He berated me for using rising rather than firmly falling inflections at the end of sentences. But his dedication of his book was "To Momma from Leo," which we all thought hilarious.

"Doc" Shea also liked to recite with gestures and great vocal unction Francis Thompson's *The Hound of Heaven* and another of Thompson's poems during the eloquent recitation of which he patted an imaginary golden-headed child on the head. Joe Angers used to cause the class a lot of trouble when it came his time to give a practice sermon. When Fr. Shea turned from observing Joe to comment to the class on Joe's performance, Anger's with great solemnity would wiggle his ears, which he could do magnificently. This intriguing gesture we could see but Doc could not and was always puzzled by our half-suppressed grins. He also gave us assignments to improve our vocabularies, every week a list of ten words each to be used in a sentence. We competed to write the most absurd sentences possible. Thus Rod Dooley, of the class below ours, took advantage of the fact that Doc, who was from Memphis, had a fondness for words typical of the South. One of these was the name for the fiber left over after the sugar is extracted from sugarcane: "bagasse." Brother Rod's sentence, directed at one of his classmates, later our Provincial, was "Gilbert Graham has a bagasse." Doc Shea, quite unconscious of the vulgarity, corrected the grammar, "No! No! One does not have a bagasse. One makes, stores, sells, or uses bagasse."

Oddly in those days in our Order of Preachers we did not always give much attention to teaching our friars how to preach very well, although Doc Shea did improve our reading and delivery. One part of his course on how to convert the section of the Summa on prayer into sermons or conferences was quite helpful. Once I was in Memphis for a lecture and stayed at his niece's home, a fine old southern house full of antiques. We exchanged many funny stories about Doc. An anecdote I especially appreciated came from a student whose room was directly above Father Shea's. One morning as the student looked out the window he heard the Doctor below opening his window to admit the morning air and heard him exclaim in his most oratorical tones, "Oh my God! One more day of unmitigated hell!"

There was also the tragicomedy called "Lundi Gras" (the French name of the Monday before Lent begins, celebrated in Louisiana) in an unsuccessful attempt to raise funds for the Province. Held under Doc Shea's management in the mammoth Chicago Stadium, it featured, among other events, a bibulous performance by Pat O'Brien of film fame, and two inadequately clad women acrobats. The great hall was half empty and the half-naked ladies cavorting on their trapezes shocked the pious women friends of the Province who made up much of the audience.

Death in Battle

Not long before I made my solemn vows "unto death," in the midst of our monastic routine, sometimes purgatorial sometimes very funny, I received word of the death in battle of my dear friend Leo Shields. Through the war years we friars, free of the draft but constantly praying for all our fellows of every nation suffering in the war (we did not then know of the Holocaust), were very conscious of its events yet were shut off from them. At that time our Constitutions forbade the reading of newspapers as a waste of a student's time and a source of secularizing influences (today I must confess that I waste far too much time after breakfast reading them). This, however, was another instance of the old time formalism, since in fact we were allowed to listen to the news on the radio, and as the war got more intense, the superiors clipped out the war news and sent it down to be read on our student bulletin board. I remember that I constantly dreamed of warplanes, repeatedly one very vivid and recurring dream of a warplane strafing a car in which I was riding on the Chicago 'L'.

In the last chapter I told how Leo had changed his mind about becoming a Dominican as I was planning to do at the end of our time together at Notre Dame. But his hesitation did not last very long. He had gone from Notre Dame to teach at Holy Cross College in Worchester, MA and there returned to his earlier decision to enter the Dominican novitiate in the Western (Holy Name) Province. Just before his entrance, his number came up in the draft, and the Western Provincial, unlike our Provincial, Peter O'Brien, made no effort at obtaining a deferment for him. So in 1944 Leo departed for a staging area in England from where I received several letters from him. He was bored with the military, but was his usual courageous self. The details of his death were never entirely clear, but he died in Brittany

in the Normandy invasion near Saint-Lô on or just before July 20th,
1944.

REQUIEM AETERNAM

You that from beside me turned to pass
another way along the gloom,
Yours is now the way of the unfolding grass
above the folded bosom of the tomb,
your name, years, military rank in brass.
You are still with me in my room.

Yes, timelessness like marble stone
lays cold on the bosom of the dream!
Yes, time loosens with a broken moan
like the flooding mixture of a stream
across me, floundering alone,
Only time's silence can my grief redeem.

Yes, grief will surely have its day;
then new bands begin to blare,
"Someday—Someday—Someday"
(these are the promises we make
in this windy city by a windy Lake).
Again the streets of glory flare
in great parades with glittering array.

There is with me no singing,
with me neither promise nor breath
that is not the repeated ringing
in my monastic cell
of the passing bell,
for your unbidden death,
ringing its requiem
in my monastic cell...
echoed by the requiem
of my whispered prayer.

Indeed I did not grieve long over Leo's death nor dwell on the
horror that his last days in the D-Day invasion must have been. His

letters had showed me that his faith was strong and I am sure it must have sustained him until he departed this life for a better one in Christ. He was 28. I am sure I owe my conversion and the graces of my subsequent life to his prayers as a true friend and I hope soon to see him again.

During my student days in the Order two clerical student brothers died: Chrysostom Seery (d. 1943) after a prolonged illness during which he took solemn vows, Sylvester Fraher (d. 1944) who was ordained just before dying of cancer, and an African-American Cooperator Brother James Bailey (d. 1944) who died suddenly of a ruptured appendix. The death of young men whom I saw daily had focused my often distracted meditations. My student days, however, were by no means gloomy, although often difficult. Two older students were great help to me, one was Peter Houlihan (d. 1968), later to be a missionary briefly in Japan and then for some time in Bolivia, and Arthur Kinsella (d. 2008), for a while a missionary in Nigerian and now for many years an itinerant preacher here in the United States. Both were very observant and prayerful people.

My favorite story on Arthur is how, when, just after Christmas, he planned to visit some Dominican Sisters, he invited to me be (as our Constitutions required and expressed it) his "sober companion." I was delighted to get out of the house, but the journey was interminable, first on the 'L', then on a rackety streetcar to about 130th Street! I had nothing to do but watch the passage of an endless line of bars along Western Ave, said to be the longest streetcar ride in the world. All the time Arthur, then a deacon, was reading his breviary and meditating in silence. It took so long that we arrived at the Sisters just in time for supper, which, according to the discipline of those days the Sisters could not eat with us, so in a small room Arthur and I ate alone. Then briefly we visited with the Sisters who gave us from their leftover Christmas gifts some stationary and scented bars of soap. Then back to River Forest on a long ride while Arthur again had to finish his prayers.. Since we arrived home after the proper hour we had to make the *venia* to the Student Master, who, however, mercifully gave us no other penance, perhaps because he realized that for me, at least, the day had already been penance enough. The soap and stationary lasted me a long time.

Final Vows at Camp

Except for my confessors, however, I don't believe my grief over Leo's death was very evident to others. I was very busy and indeed happy with my studies. Each summer the Dominican students were sent to a camp that the Order owned on Green Bay north of Menominee, MI. It was an isolated place on the shore of the lake with a fine beach, cut off from the highway by dense woods that were second growth from the forests that had stood there before the lumbering epoch that had leveled the area. In the same bay there were only a couple of farmhouses for families that lived largely by fishing. A few years before I went there, student Brothers had constructed the log-cabin type of buildings of the camp, including the beautiful little chapel among the cedar trees.

At camp we kept up the regular routine of religious life with its full liturgy and we wore the white Dominican habit in chapel and at meals, but the rest of our routine was very different than in River Forest. In the morning until 10 o'clock there were chores, then volleyball on the beach. I was a wretched player, but I tried. After lunch we were free until Vespers to fish, go sailing, or hike, except for special crews that had some days to do the laundry or, on certain days, clean fish. Especially delightful were the cookouts on the beach in the cloudless summer evenings.

I especially remember two of these beach suppers. One time as we assembled we saw that the crew that had gone out sailing were unable to get in for supper because the wind had died. Their little boat could be seen sitting motionless on the glassy horizon. As it got dark, we decided to send out a motorboat to tow them in. We heard it chug-chug out into the night until suddenly the motor stopped. We lit a bonfire on the beach and still later both the sailboat and the motorboat, with their weary crews, paddled in, very hungry.

Another time was a supper right after World War II. Because of the draft our superiors had kept us in the camp as much as possible lest the presence of undrafted young men arouse the indignation of local people. We, like everybody else then, lived on rations with very little meat. Then, as the war was ending, John Marie Coburn's father, like his son, a big, generous Texan, arrived with enough fine steaks for all of us and sweated all afternoon at the outdoor grill to prepare us an unforgettable feast! During that wartime, we did some rather nominal study of languages at camp, so that the local draft board could be told that the camp was a school project, but I especially liked the little building we called the Vostinianum after Père Vosté, a Dominican biblical scholar, who for us was a mythical figure because he was so often quoted to us by our professors who had studied with him in Rome. The Vostinianum had become the study of James Athanasius Weisheipl (d. 1984) who was to become a noted faculty member of the Mediaeval Institute in Toronto. Each afternoon he holed up there with his books in spite of the fact that a mother skunk had made a nest for her brood underneath that building. One afternoon we saw her, as handsome as a Dominican in her black and white, her tail extended and, following its point, her young ones processing in a line behind her as she marched deeper into the woods.

My first summer at camp after a big storm, when a sailboat capsized while tacking a mile out in the lake, I was almost drowned. I had not put on a life jacket and with my not-so-good swimming I would never have made it to shore in that very cold water. But we managed to grab the boat and pull it down and upright again. Our experienced neighbors were always complaining that we Brothers were very reckless about boating on the bay which was relatively shallow and subject to sudden violent storms, but our guardian angels did their job.

From camp we made some delightful trips into the Upper Peninsula, for example to a sacred Indian lake, forty-feet deep, of crystal clear spring water, and then on to the Pictured Rocks Lakeshore on Lake Superior, and to Munising, MI,, facing a wooded island. One evening we drove home through the Hiawatha National Forest when the red sunset gleamed through the birches and cedars. Deer with great eyes came out to stare at us. As it got darker, a low fog, milk white in the full moon, flowed into the woods so that as the car rose over each ridge the valley below was filled with it like a white lake and when we descended into it we drove blind, only to rise above it again at the next ridge. As a child I loved the Longfellow poems of Hiawatha and "Gitche Gumee, the big sea water."

Of course some of the brethren, citified as they were, found camp a bore. One from the inner city of Chicago said that the silence at night was sinister and kept him from sleeping. But I loved it and often dream of it still, especially the fact that in late summer one could see the aurora borealis. One night it formed a pale arch at the very zenith like a shimmering curtain. Occasionally, ever the pedagogue, I used to take a small group out to the end of our long pier to point out and name the summer constellations which most had never before noticed, just as the New Yorker, Bill Cobb (as I have related earlier) had never seen the moon rise.

Many of my recollections of brethren now dead come to me in the context of camp. Thus I remember Martin Hopkins (d. 1980), nicknamed "Stainless Steel" for his deontological rigor and his interest in the doctrine of predestination. Once at camp he offered several of us a box of chocolates, although by our Constitutions it was a fast day, though not under sin but only "fault." Whenever someone succumbed to the proffered chocolates Stainless Steel would exclaim gleefully, "You have failed the test!" True to character in later years he bore his death from cancer with great resolve. I also remember an older student, showing us how to find wine in the icebox for an evening sip. I did not realize he was on the road to alcoholism with which he was to struggle helplessly the rest of his life. More happily I remember how George Unruh and Lewis Shea bypassed the edict of the Student Master, Fr. Walker, against hammering nails into the sailboats. George and Louie announced they would put a mast and a sail in a rowboat in a bucket of sand! This, of course, was hooted down as sure proof that they were hopelessly impractical, until they fitted a wooden frame over a rowboat (no nails) to which they attached guy wires that held the mast firmly in place in the bucket of sand, and sailed merrily out to sea. George left before ordination but became a successful engineer and a good friend to me, who in retirement and until his recent death, studied the Church Fathers, taught catechism, and tutored in Latin and Greek. Lewis Shea has been for many years a very daring and successful missionary in Nigeria, known for living in native style.

Another vivid memory is of Ralph Powell and Hilary Freeman doing the laundry. Ralph, of whom I will have more to say later, earned his doctorate in philosophy at Louvain. Hilary, a small fellow, a converted Jew, and an excellent jazz musician, later studied in Oxford and for many years taught logic. To see them doing laundry out of doors, more involved in philosophical debate than in getting our clothes clean, was to understand the "empirical definition" given by the great Fr. Santiago Ramirez, OP, of the University of Freiburg, Switzerland: "Philosophy is a state of vehement abstraction."

The little rustic chapel was of cedarwood with a pungent smell and its windows had no stained glass but simply the green of the cedar trees outside. Once while the community was having its meditation period seated in the choir, one of the Cooperator Brothers who was not quite right in the head suddenly stood up and gazed with a fixed stare at the ceiling. We thought he was having a vision, or more likely an hallucination, until we saw that his vision was a very real and very big snake in the wooden rafters waving its head and half its body from side to side.

It was in that chapel that our class pronounced its solemn vows *usque ad mortem*, until death, in 1945 in the hands of Fr. Alexis Driscoll who had baptized me. After the ceremony as we stood chatting with friends and relatives in the sunshine outside, someone shouted and pointed to another of our sailboats capsizing in the lake. It was again, quickly righted.

Trials

Three more years of studying theology after solemn vows were like the turning pages in a book, but I still had a big chasm to cross before ordination to the priesthood. My father's health was failing. He had some heart problems, then developed a recurring problem of the inner ear and occasional vertigo, which at 90 I also developed. Finally he was forced to retire early in 1941 and he and my mother decided to return to Neodesha to the very house at 815 Illinois Street in which I had been born to be near my mother's relatives. My mother cared for him as he became quite invalided with circulatory disease. When it became clear that he was in his final illness, I was permitted by my religious superior to go to Neodesha to see him in the hospital. I asked him if he would be willing to be visited by the local priest. He consented and (since his Protestant baptism was probably valid) was baptized conditionally and received the other Catholic sacraments. As he lingered on, I had to return to River Forest and was greatly disturbed because on one visit when I had referred to his baptism he seemed not to have understood what it had been all about. The pastor, however, reassured me that at the time he had certainly understood and my mother later told me that he had loved to hold the Rosary that had been given him and with which he was buried. I had an early morning call in River Forest from my mother that she was with him when he had died quietly, Sunday morning at 4:20. He was 67 and was buried in Neodesha, November 30, 1947, and his obituary listed him as a member of St. Ignatius Catholic Church. I quoted in Chapter 1 the commendatory obituary by the editor of the local paper who had known him when he first worked and played tennis in Neodesha.

My mother's widowhood presented me with a very serious problem. With her agreement, my brother and I decided that it would be best that she live with her sister, Aunt May Adams, also a widow and living in Neodesha, who had invited her to do so. So we sold the family house and most of its furnishings. I think Dick and I had no realization of how attached a woman can be to her own home, but my mother never felt comfortable with her sister just because it was her sister's house, not her own, and Aunt May, a very kind person but very close-mouthed about her feelings, left my mother always in doubt as to whether her own ways were really approved by her sister. The tension, along with my mother's deep grief and loneliness, were injuring her health and she lost much weight. My attempt to comfort her by another visit which I was permitted, turned out badly because I came down with flu and Aunt May stayed in her own room most of the time as if to avoid contagion, thus further distressing my mother.

Thus, the question arose for me whether I should go on to ordination or ask to be "exclaustrated," that is to have canonical permission to live outside the Order so I could care for my mother. While in Neodesha I had the opportunity to talk about this with the husband of one of my cousins, the Rev. Cyril Hicks, a Congregational minister. In a very pastoral and reassuring way, he advised me to continue as I was. He believed, knowing my mother, that it would be even harder on her if she were to feel that she had been the cause of my abandoning the way of life that I had chosen. Moreover, he believed that if the question were raised with my brother, Dick would offer to have her live with him and his wife. This is what happened, but I realized that this still had its problems, since my mother had never been happy with Dick's early marriage to a woman my mother thought neither well educated nor helpful to him in his career. How would it work out with the three of them? I finally took Cyril Hick's advice and I believe it was for the best, though it meant also a big sacrifice on my mother's part. I know she accepted it for my sake, though this solution was by no means ideal. But she later took great satisfaction in my priesthood and I hope this was her compensation.

Struggling

Meanwhile, as ordination approached, the increasing scrupulosity which I have described earlier, was mounting to its climax. The focus of my anguish had shifted from thoughts of rash judgment and against chastity to my fear that I was not making authentic acts of faith. It was in the very same apologetics courses that I have previously praised that I had learned that faith presupposes rational credibility. That is indeed sound doctrine, but to me, reared with my mother's example of excessive anxiety that I described in Chapter 1, this meant that before making an act of faith (and, after all, the whole Christian vowed life is a series of acts of faith), it seemed necessary for me first to make explicit to myself the reasons for the credibility of the faith. In the midst of other activities this required a kind of mental gymnastics that became more and more painful as these motives of credibility became more and more obscured by the complex process of explicitating them.

One ghastly night in our Young Dad's narrow quarters, I knelt by my bed for many minutes, maybe hours, trying to make an act of faith. I never denied the faith, never, thank God, let go of it, but I seemed to have run into a blank wall. In the following days, with the help of my confessors Fr. James McDonald and Fr. Kane, for whose great patience I am deeply grateful, I found a way through this agony to a stable situation. Accepting their diagnosis that it was not my faith but my scrupulosity that was the problem, I resolved that I would just take a moratorium on making explicit acts of faith and go on with my life obviously based, as it was, on faith.

This struggle continued and was especially bad in the days after my ordination. The next step in resolving it was to realize that I was not obliged to explicitate these reasons of credibility, but only to be willing to admit their falsity if evidence ever made this certain, because I had sincerely and with objective certitude at the time accepted the Faith on God's Word at my baptism. This I knew I could not have done without rational credibility, since when I was baptized I knew that faith must be reasonable and objective, not merely subjective and irrational, and I believed it as such.

To this day I am convinced that if the Catholic faith were *per impossible* ever shown to be false or without rational grounds, I would be morally obliged to reject it, even if that meant leaving the priesthood, the Order, and the Church, leaving my life in ruins. Faith is an objective and certain truth grounded formally on the Word of God who cannot deceive or be deceived and attested by signs accessible to human reason. The sufficient sign, for me, was and is, the moral miracle of the Catholic Church, the public fact that, in spite of all the frailties and scandals of its members from top to bottom, including myself, it is one, catholic, apostolic, and holy in a way no merely human institution is or can be.[108] My neurotic difficulty that I had to struggle with, however, was the result of an excessively anxious and self-centered personality, with which I have to live and with the grace of God and the help of the Christian community bring more and more under control.

At this time the fight was painful and exhausting, but, thank God, I had plenty of support and plenty of things to do, and the youthful energy to sustain it. Yet its tensions probably contributed to a physical problem, recurrent duodenal ulcers, which led to a vagotomy or resection of the vagus nerve to diminish acid secretion, in use before the more effective types of present day medication, since its basic cause has more recently been shown to be an infection. This operation, I now know, probably did more harm than good. I also had an operation for inguinal hernia. These neurotic and psychosomatic troubles, however, did me an immense amount of good in purifying my faith, my confidence in God, and remedying the lack of courage which had been one of my greatest faults since childhood. It was my daily cross and I learned to walk, however haltingly, with the Crucified.

No doubt my psychological struggle could have been helped by a psychological counselor and even with tranquilizing medication if that had been possible, but none of my confessors proposed I see a psychotherapist, and I never brought the problem to my religious superiors. Today such helps are easily available to Dominicans but I am afraid that sometimes troubled religious and priests put so much confidence in these human remedies that they neglect the spiritual ones. Psychotherapist and spiritual director need to collaborate, as I have experienced a few times in cooperating with a therapist to help other priests and lay people. From my own experience I believe scrupulosity is not so much the cause as the result of a high anxiety level, with which the victim attempts to deal by a pattern of excessive introspection, reinforcing the anxiety in a vicious circle. This high anxiety level may have many causes: genetic, physiological, neurosis, social insecurity, overwork, etc. Such intense introspection results in a disordering of what Aquinas called the "estimative sense" (*vis cogitativa*), an interior sense that in humans takes the place of instinct in animals and connects our reason with our concrete evaluative experiences. Without its work we cannot apply our abstract moral reasoning to concrete practical situations.

While our intelligence, as a spiritual power, can reflect on itself, so that we know that we know something, the estimative sense, because it is a material faculty in the brain, has only imperfect reflectivity. Therefore, when a person in making a practical judgment attempts to observe his or her own process of judgment, as we do when scrutinizing our conscience or decisions to act, this imperfect reflectivity can be forced beyond its capacity. I cannot see the back of my neck no matter how I twist and turn. Scrupulous persons exhaust themselves trying to examine ever more closely the quality of their decisions, unable to trust the normal processes of prudential judgment. The result is neurasthenia or mental exhaustion and confusion that can ultimately render prudent decision impossible.

At the same time the hapless victims of this situation may intellectually be perfectly aware that what they are is doing is absurd. Thus they are driven to seek the counsel of another person (the confessor, psychotherapist or other confidant) for reassurance. This relief, however, is only temporary, and actually produces a reinforcing cycle of anxiety. Proper therapy has to break this cycle and reeducate the sufferer to other less neurotic ways of reducing anxiety. This neurosis of scrupulosity is rather common and has no necessary connection with religion. The true Catholic doctrine about sin is neither excessively punitive nor pessimistic, and the confessional, when not abused, is a help and not a hindrance to overcoming scrupulosity. Yet certainly some excessively negative types of Catholic spirituality can be harmful. The spirituality I was learning in the Order was not of this pessimistic type and my malady originated not there but in my childhood.

Some readers I am sure will wonder—as I often did—if the problem was that I was trying to believe what I really doubted. This is to miss the point of my problem. It was not that I lacked solid intellectual answers to the difficulties against faith constantly popping into my mind, but that I was exhausted by the anxious drive to examine and reexamine these questions, even in the midst of other tasks. I was unable to be content with having settled any question involving whether I was in the state of grace, like the obsessive person who is never satisfied that they have washed their hands clean enough. Indeed the problem first arose not with regard to faith but with regard to other moral matters, but as it grew reverted to faith as the ultimate basis of all true security.

The two things that helped me most were understanding confessors and especially the practice of meditation before the Blessed

Sacrament. I found that meditation, practiced in an atmosphere of quiet and silence and used not as a time of examination of conscience (which for the scrupulous could be harmful) but as a time of quiet rest before God again and again restored my fevered brain to practical common sense. I am sure there are many kinds of suffering that equal scrupulosity or surpass it, but when it strikes at faith and the total trust in God alone that faith demands, it is indeed a crown of thorns.

FEAR OF DROWNING

Silence and the waves of chanting
of psalms that rage, plead, praise,
through the seasonal fasts and feasts,
the days, the nights, sun or moon
filling the silence before the Mystery veiled
in the gilded tabernacle,
fear overwhelming me
that I had let go, Your hand
stretched out to me like to Peter
sensing his feet were sinking,
panic, terror, plunging
into the chaos of doubt, despair.
drowning, gasping for air.

Yet you were there.
In the dark I could see
the spark of the tabernacle-lamp on its stand,
as through the dark there was your hand reaching out.
Like Thomas I felt the healing wound in your hand
that would heal
my doubt.
Under my feet in the receding waves
I felt
firm the Living Rock.

A poem written later on a snowy January 25, 1958 in River Forest suggests something of this same quiet of soul.

WHAT SILENCE SUFFICES?

On snow, falling snow lays shadows blank as snow.
On my heart's silence music falls silent.

Can a stilled heart listen?
Can a heart be stilled
before it lies on a marble slab or under it?
Can a soul unquickened not be dead?
Where in the ashen snow can hot love rest?
What midnight illumines?
What ice melts fire?

Yet if silence is deaf who can hear?
Self-sound cottons the singer's ear.
Is frost ever flame?
Then whence Prometheus borrowed the pure light
that glows in the globed crystal of the sky?

Give music its tribute of hearing, give your stillness.
Give to light the roomy darkness of your inner eye.
Let time spread its infinite circle,
sun expand its boundless sphere
in your hollowness...
the footprint shadow of self,
let time be quenched in a deep ashen blank.

Soft...
Is there full silence in the snow's soft silence?
Can sleep, can death suffice?
Silence that expects is noisy with alarms,
the broken twig, the rustling, whispering, waiting wind.,
Rigid, the rigid dead fear to move lest they miss
the coming footfall
of the Bridegroom Judge.

Stiller than the cold petal falling is the hidden fruit
ripe and full.
The last note of symphonic thunder leaves a silence
built like a nuptial, kingly, priestly city
with twelve open gates.

After the ultimate trumpet
comes the sentence in one severing, quickening word
that made the first and will make the final dawn
with a trumpet echo opening a world in glory,
precise polyphony,
each thing with its own color,
dividing a rainbow in the light,
each with its own voice, taking its overtone
to that Word
consonant,
fundamental,
sufficing,
more still than stillness.

Ordination

My ordination to the priesthood took place June 4, 1948, in the River Forest chapel with the "laying on of hands" by Archbishop William David O'Brien of Chicago, who had been consecrated by Cardinal Mundelein, in a line of succession going back through Bishop McDonnell of Brooklyn, then through three Archbishops of New York: M.A. Corrigan, John McCloskey, John Dubois of New York; Archbishop Maréchal, of Baltimore, Bishop Cheverus of Boston, and Archbishop John Carroll of Baltimore (1735-1815), the first United States Bishop, himself consecrated by the English Benedictine Bishop Charles Walmsley, O.S.B., who was consecrated in Rome by a Cardinal Frederico Lanti in 1756. I list these bishops because to me it is essential to priestly identity to realize that we have a place in the apostolic succession that goes back to Jesus Christ of whom we are only instruments in His ministry to the world. Although theological questions arise about this view, it was confirmed in Vatican II.[109]

Just as the office which the Lord confided to Peter alone, as first of the apostles, destined to be transmitted to his successors, is a permanent one, so also endures the office, which the apostles received, of shepherding the Church, a charge destined to be exercised without interruption by the sacred order of bishops.

I have mentioned in the last chapter that when I entered the Order, priesthood was not uppermost among my motives. During the study of theology its significance became clearer to me. Only recently in my study of the question of women's ordination have I really developed a more adequate understanding of its symbolic, sacramental nature.

For the motto on my souvenir card customary at ordinations I chose a quote from St. Catherine of Siena's Dialogue in which God said to her:

I have placed you in the midst of your fellows that you may do to them what you cannot do to me, that is to say that you may love your neighbor of free grace without expecting any return from him, and what you do to him I count as done to me.

At my ordination retreat in 1948 on June 4th, the Feast of the Sacred Heart of Jesus, I made certain resolutions, that reflect another passage in the Dialogue in which God says to Catherine, "Remember I am He who is, while you are she who is not." I think in this saying God is telling us to remember that we have nothing but what He has given us, but in the Bible he also tells us that He created us "very good," (Gn 1:31). These resolutions were:

I am nothing.

What is good in me is made by God out of nothing and with all this good I have done nothing of myself except to spoil it, and to be His again whatever I have of myself must be again made nothing.

Mary,

a) the one who knew that she was nothing in whom nothing was done that was not wholly the work of God, for she spoiled nothing of His work.

b) Mary is all love (I don't understand what "love" means).

My Lord and my God,

a) I cannot be healed except through His Humanity, that is by His Church and His Sacraments.

b) To be like Him is to do the Father's will, that is to try to do perfectly the will of the Father not as I imagine it, but as it is manifested evidently.

c) Jesus is all Love (Help me to understand!).

To be a priest for me is to be conformed to the work of Jesus for Mary by doing what the Church and the Order tell me to do, receiving from Him for Mary's sake through the Church all that is necessary to do His will. All this will be love when I have

learned to love. Mary, my Mother, Mother of Fair Love, teach
me!

This remains my prayer.

The day on which I was ordained I was still struggling with the
scruples problem. As I lay prone with the other candidates praying
to the Holy Spirit just before the bishop's imposition of hands I was
tormented by thoughts about whether I had so sinned against faith
that my reception of the sacrament would be invalid, but I struggled
to dismiss such thoughts and succeeded.

My first solemn Mass was to be the following Sunday, June 6,
1948 at St. Joseph's Church in Blackwell and I was accompanied by
Frs. William Kane and Peter J. Houlihan (d. 1968), the latter a good
friend of mine who, as I have already mentioned, was to become a
missionary first in Japan and then in Bolivia. I no longer hand any
relatives in Blackwell, since my father was dead and my mother was
in Neodesha preparing to move to Lake Charles, LA to live with my
brother Dick and his wife Helen. The reason for going to Blackwell
was primarily to please the pastor Fr. Stephen Leven who hoped my
ordination might stimulate vocations in his parish. He had entrusted
the ceremonies to the Polish Felician Sisters whom he had brought
to Blackwell to run the local hospital. I was startled when one of
them told me, as if it were a matter of fact, that "Your bride will
bring up the chalice and paten at the offertory." My "bride"?   She
turned out to be a small girl in white with a wedding veil that Polish
custom required at a First Mass to symbolize the Holy Church. I was
a bit embarrassed but the "Church" was very pretty and very sweet
and so has been to me the Church she symbolized. It was a lovely
Mass but the last I was to see of Blackwell. Recently I was invited
there to our high school reunion, but my schedule made it impossible for me to attend. The picture they sent of my classmates made
me feel like the wicked stepmother in the fairy tale looking with
dismay into her mirror.

My ordination was followed immediately by a second wonderful
event. My mother had written from Neodesha that she was thinking
of becoming a Catholic as I and my father had done. So I went from
Blackwell to Neodesha to get her and we traveled together by train
through Little Rock to Lake Charles, LA. As we got off the train the
June heat almost bowled us over, but in the evening Dick and Helen

took us down for a refreshing boat ride on the lake. It was our first view of the tropical landscape of Louisiana. The lake was hemmed by live oaks with grey Spanish moss hanging from their branches. There were the lavender beds of floating water hyacinths, gossamer dragon flies and painted butterflies skimming over the water out of which jumped fish radiating ripples across the mirroring surface of the water, and finally, not far from our boat, the demonic eyes of an alligator slitting the surface.

My mother had asked me to baptize her (conditionally of course, since she may have been baptized a Methodist as a girl). It was a quiet little ceremony, June 15, 1948, with my brother and his wife present. They had given her as a memento a nice Rosary of quartz beads which was for years my best memento of her. I had scrupulous worries about the validity of her baptism later because this was the first time I had baptized anyone, and the parish priest who assisted me seemed to think I was not doing it properly, so to assist me he grabbed my hand as I poured! I later had to inquire from a theologian whether this invalidated the sacrament (of course he laughed at me), before I ceased to worry about it.

My mother then returned to Neodesha where she went to her first Mass and Holy Communion on June 27th and soon made friends with a Catholic lady of her own age, named Mamie, who was a great help to her. Soon she made up her mind at last to move to Louisiana and live with Dick and Helen. As for me I stayed a while in Blackwell to join Fr. Leven in his street preaching as I had done when still a layman, but now as a priest. He complained, however, that my study of theology seemed to have had a bad effect on my preaching, depriving it of the direct natural quality which he thought it had in my earlier efforts as a layman. When I returned to River Forest I used this experience to write a little article about street-preaching which appeared in the Youth Section of *Our Sunday Visitor*, April 13, 1951. In it I was attempting a popular style and I quote it to prove that, although my work has been so academic, I have always dreamed of being an "itinerant preacher," a favorite phrase among Dominicans today.

Hit 'Em Where They Are

Eighty per cent of all Americans are non-Catholics. How many are so because we have not told them about Jesus Christ as he lives with us in his Church? But have we not discharged our duty when we preach Jesus from the pulpit and in the discussion club, on the radio, and in the Catholic press?

Well, preaching requires two things: first there must be someone who relates the Gospel and the other that there be someone there to listen. Now this is just our problem: the non-Catholics are not there to listen, most of them.

The average American is not a Catholic. Because he is not a Catholic, when a Catholic radio program comes on he does not think it is for him and so he either twirls the dial or goes on with the Sunday sport page. Because he is not a Catholic he is never at church on Sunday to hear our Catholic sermons, or in the discussion clubs to hear our Catholic lay-leaders. Because he is not a Catholic he does not subscribe to the Catholic press nor buy Catholic pamphlets from the church rack. The average American is just not there to listen. He will not come there until he has been attracted.

This vicious circle has hampered the apostolate in this country for a long time, but like most vicious circles in spiritual matters it can be broken by following the example of Our Lord and His Apostles, by going to the average man where he is. "You have not chosen me, but I have chosen you." We must choose the non-Catholic and he the Church. In the very footsteps of the Apostles, American street-preachers are going out to find their listeners, to find them on the street and in the park. In most average American towns the non-Catholic is reluctant under any persuasion to enter a Catholic church, but he is willing to park on the street and listen. In small towns in the summer everyone is out in the evenings trying to find something to do. The sound of a loudspeaker out in the cool is like the street lights to the June bugs. In the city everyone knows how the sidewalk lecturer on patent medicine has only to put up his stand and raise his voice to have a crowd.

Why should the followers of Peter and Paul be any less humble in their methods? Everywhere a speaker and informal crowd standing around, sitting in cars, or on the curbstone means a free discussion, questions impertinent or honest at least frankly asked, and the answer correspondingly open and clear.

To the non-Catholic the Church is a mysterious and dubious thing hidden away behind dark portals or symbolized by unfamiliar cassocks and religious habits. On the street the priest becomes a human being marked only by whatever education and sanctity he may possess, qualities which shine even more clearly in a street discussion. Superstition and bigotry vanish before this open and candid effort to preach the Gospel.

What could be more revealing to a non-Catholic who believes we have no reverence for Jesus than to hear the Catholic Jesus preached on the street? What more confounding to the bigot who believes we give Our Lady divine honors than to hear the simple truth concerning our love for her declared openly on a twentieth century street corner? Street-preaching means the end of traditional American prejudice against Holy Church.

Street-preaching as it has been thriving in Oklahoma and some eastern cities for several years and as it is now starting up throughout the Middle West both in the small towns and in the cities, already is a practical reality. It only remains to make it a permanent institution in every parish. It is an ideal example of cooperation between the clergy and laity. The pastor can and should retain his place as the ordained preacher of the Gospel; the layman aids him in every preparation and joins him in speaking on those subjects where his testimony is most needed. The young people have a special mission in street-preaching because a young man or woman militantly proud of his or her faith is one of the best of all witnesses on the Gospel soapbox. The lay apostle who passes up street-preaching as a method of helping his pastor or as a possibility to be kept before his pastor's eyes, had better remember that there is no use preaching to non-Catholics when the non-Catholics are not there to listen.

I am sorry to say that today, when in summers we are all in air-conditioning watching television, these hopes for direct evangelization by Catholics have not yet been realized, although some, like Scott Hahn of Franciscan University, Steubenville, Ohio, are demonstrating that it can be effective. I would now rewrite my argument in terms of preaching on the Internet, the World Wide Web!

First Year as Priest

That fourth year when we were Young Dad's, that is, priests but still in our last year of theological studies, was very difficult for me. Because we were a separate category in the Priory we were housed in an upper corridor that was dark and narrow. No longer directly under the Student Master, we were guided by a *Magister Spiritus*.

Our Magister had formerly been sent with another priest for graduate studies to the Dominican Pontifical Theological Faculty in Fribourg, Switzerland. When the European War broke out, our provincial, fearing the two might be separated from us while the war lasted, hastily brought them home. Then, so they might continue their studies at a faculty that was both Dominican and Pontifical, sent them to the University of Santo Tomas in Manila! Of course, the Japanese interred them for the duration of the war. No wonder that after this experience our Spiritual Master was a little odd. He was kindly but erratic and his idea of a party for us was either "Spudnuts" (a kind of doughnut), or a whole coconut. Later in Dallas TX he was the priest who, hearing of President Kennedy's assassination, was first to hurry to the hospital to give him the last sacraments.

Each morning, we had to arise very early to drive, often through Chicago's bitter winter weather, to say Mass at one of the parishes or religious convents in Chicago's western suburbs. I often went to the convent of the Sisters of Providence or the house of the Christian Brothers at the huge parish of St. Mel's on Chicago's West Side. At the Sisters I would be admitted in total silence by a ghostly figure and while vesting in the tiny sacristy would hear in the chapel a thin, high voice reading off the "points for meditation" for the day while the Sisters sat in silence in their choir. These "points" belonged to the school of spirituality that our homiletics professor used to call the "O Lord, I am a Worm School."   At the Christian Brothers, unlike at the Sisters, we were given breakfast (always somewhat metallic tasting scrambled eggs, toast, and coffee) in a small room off the Brothers' dining room, where we could hear one of them—we Dominicans at least did not have to suffer this at breakfast—reading in a gruff monotone a book that went something like this: "When Brother Benignus left St. Bernard's in 1889, he was assigned to St. Gertrude's in Milwaukee, where he taught until 1910 and then was reassigned to St Bernard's."   I then drove home through the dawn in the snow to sit in an overheated classroom while we were led *articulatim* (article by article) through St. Thomas Aquinas' magisterial discussion of the virtue of Fortitude, its subjective, integral, and potential parts.

I was completing my studies and writing my unpublished Lectorate dissertation on Contemplation and Society in which I argued that contemplation is essentially not solitary, the Neo-Platonist "the alone to the Alone," but socially shared as it will be in heaven. Then in 1949-50, no longer a "Young Dad" but a member of the category of senior priests I was sent from River Forest to live at the Priory at Fenwick High School in nearby Oak Park, to write my second Ph.D., dissertation, this time in philosophy. A peaceful year (1949-1950) followed, since I had nothing to do but write and occasionally celebrate Mass or hear confessions in suburban parishes. It did get me acquainted, however, with the problems of our Dominican fathers who taught high school. Fenwick (at that time for boys only, now coed) has an excellent record as a college preparatory school, although it has always been an issue whether in serving middle-class families of the western Chicago suburbs to prepare them for secular universities that so many attend, should have such a priority among the works of our Chicago Province. It has also been an issue whether our Fathers were properly prepared to teach religion at that level.

The gap between the medieval *Summa* of St. Thomas in which the Fathers were trained and needs of modern adolescents is not small. We were all required to take some "education" courses during our own student years, so that any of us could be certified to teach at Fenwick, but many of us found these classes boring and ineffective. One Father told me that all he ever got out of them was that in giving exams one should remember, "When you give tests, you must know what you are testing for."

The Fenwick Fathers (who, except for the athletic coaches, then comprised the whole faculty) worked very, very hard. Tuition at Fenwick, which was rather low considering the affluence of some of the parents, went directly into operating the school. Hence, to support the Priory the priests had to hear confessions and celebrate Mass in the suburban parishes, thus in effect having two jobs. Teaching in high school involves not only getting to class and grading papers, but also supervising all manner of extracurricular activities in late afternoons and evenings. Furthermore, the prior of Fenwick insisted that all attend the full liturgical schedule designed for medieval monks. The result was that some more enterprising Fathers quickly got themselves assigned to less taxing jobs than teaching high school. Those who remained were steady, devoted men, who without much stimulus to further intellectual advancement, taught the boys year after year often until they rested in death.

At the beginning of the fall semester, after my first summer of pastoral experience, when I was beginning to teach in the Studium, on September 16, 1951, I defended my second Ph.D. dissertation. The reason that it had been decided that I needed this second doctorate from a Pontifical Faculty of Philosophy was that there might be no question in Rome that I was prepared to teach in such a faculty, since Notre Dame did not have that status, and in any case my first Ph.D. was not in philosophy but political science. At a much later date some have questioned my writing on theological questions, when neither of my doctorates is in theology.

The dissertation dealt with the question, "What aspects of the thinking of Aristotle and Aquinas on natural science were invalidated by the so-called Copernican Revolution and what remain valid today?" This topic of course was a part of the research on which William H. Kane had launched my classmate Raymond Nogar and me. Nogar wrote a parallel dissertation in which he analyzed the epistemological nature of modern science, its emphasis on the quantitative and neglect of the qualitative aspects of physical reality, while I was to analyze the break between medieval science and modern science.

My research covered all of Aristotle's works on natural science, but my material became so bulky that the written dissertation covered only his physics, astronomy, and chemistry. The major parts of the dissertation were later published in *The New Scholasticism*,[110] and in a reprint as *Aristotle's Sluggish Earth: The Problematics of the De Caelo*.[111] This odd title which became a subject of Dominican jokes, pointed to the thesis which I tried to establish that, contrary to the popular notion that Aristotle exalted humanity by making us the center of the universe, he actually believed that the earth was the bottom of the universe as its least noble region. The following is the abstract given to those attending the formal defense:[112]

Aristotle's Special Physical Science: Physics and Chemistry

The attempts of modern Thomists to solve the vital and thorny problem of the relation between "philosophy" and "science" are conditioned by failure to interpret Aristotle's general physical science contained in the *Physics*, *De Generatione et Corruptione*, and *De Anima*, in the light of his attempts to solve the scientific questions contained in his special scientific works.

The present dissertation, after a summary of Aristotle's general physical science, undertakes a detailed analysis of the first two parts of his special physical science, namely his physics and chemistry. The results of a separate study of the final branch, the biology, are summarized.

This analysis reveals not only the falsity of the older criticisms of Aristotle as anti-empirical, but also of the newer charge that he neglects mathematics and controlled experiment. It is shown that these latter methods play a real though small role in his science, not because he is ignorant of their value, but because he perceived that they cannot form the main structure of a strictly physical science. Aristotle saw that their true value lies in their role as indirect and dialectical procedures which prepare and complement genuine physical analysis and proof, but which cannot replace them.

The notorious failures of Aristotle's special science, failures which played so great a role in the complete discrediting of Aristotelianism in the seventeenth century, are shown to flow not from his principles, methods, or viewpoint, but from his hypothesis of the perpetuity of change. This led him to untenable views on the heavenly bodies, the stability of the earth, the system of chemical elements, and the functions of heart and brain.

Aristotle's special physical science thus emerges not only as fully comparable to the hypothetical systems of Newton and of Einstein, but also as methodology superior to them in its rigorous adherence to a strictly physical viewpoint, which includes but subordinates mathematization and controlled experiment to direct qualitative observation and direct analysis of sensible nature. As such it remains a valuable model and outline of physical problem for modern scientists.

Thus my original goal of being a writer, after being replaced by that of being a social revolutionary, was at last replaced with the goal of being a Dominican preacher, whose chief theme in preaching was how to bring the Gospel to a world constructed by a powerful but misconceived modern science. Research in philosophy was to be directed to supporting theology and theology to supporting preaching. With vows taken and priestly ordination received and a Ph.D. in philosophy completed, I hoped I was as ready for that task as, given my gifts and my limitations, I could be.

My first real pastoral experience as a Dominican priest, however, was in the summer of 1949 at our parish, St. Anthony's in New Orleans. The beautiful, Spanish colonial style Church near where Canal Street ends in vast, fantastic cemeteries, was built by Dominicans of the Province of the Holy Rosary in the Philippines. That Province had its novitiate in Spain, but also had houses in Louisiana and Texas where its priests could spend some time learning English before going on to the Islands. At that time, however, they were no longer in St. Anthony's, which had been given over to our Central Province. I was immediately struck by the charming quaintness of the Dominican Sisters who, since air-conditioning then was not common, carried black lace fans to keep cool.

The first pastoral task assigned to me was to attend the meetings of the Rosary and Altar Society and give a little talk. After my pious exhortation, the ladies served cake and coffee (the New Orleans saying is that coffee should be "as sweet as love, black as night, and hot as hell!") and I monitored their vivacious chatter in hopes they were discussing what I had said and taking it to heart. I discovered that their lively debate that June night was about their "theme" gowns for the Mardi Gras the following February. That summer I also taught a course in theology at Xavier University, founded especially "for Indians and Negroes." At that time at St. Anthony's, as in all New Orleans churches, the last few pews where marked off for African Americans and they came to Holy Communion after the whites.

Yet, in spite of the blatant racism that prevailed, I was very fond of New Orleans and of all southern Louisiana. The region, with its meandering bayous and tumbled down mansions and flood-invaded, unpainted houses, seemed well on its way to returning to the swamp, as it almost has done in the Katrina flooding. Yet there were also gorgeous places, like Oak Alley on the Mississippi with its pink columns and double gallery standing at the end of the blue-green foliage of the alley, fourteen live oaks on each side leading down to the levee and the steamboat landing.

Dick, Helen, and Mother, as the oil business demanded, had moved from Lake Charles, first to a tiny place called Bunkie where the existence of two worlds, white and black, side-by-side, was so noticeable, then to Lafayette, a larger, more prosperous town where the natives held themselves socially aloof from the newcomers that the local oil boom had brought in. Whenever I visited my family in Lafayette, my mother and I took many rides through the country, enjoying the picturesque Cajun culture, the remains of ancient Indian settlements at St. Francis, the Evangeline country, Jefferson Island and its salt mine, Avery Island with its tropical gardens and seabirds. These "islands" are actually mounds of salt rising from the swamps that slant down into the Gulf of Mexico. Then I returned to River Forest to begin my assignment, not in the pastoral ministry, but as a teacher of philosophy and theology, as I have been ever since and on that topic I will say no more in this part.

Yes, my descent into the black hole of atheism had been reversed. Reason, under the hard-headed guidance of Mortimer Adler and, still better, of St. Thomas Aquinas had convinced me abstractly of God's existence. And the grace of God had led me to open my mind to His further instruction. I had committed myself to him in baptism, solemn religious vows, and priestly ordination. Yet I know that my journey to union with Him had only begun. Now these many years later as I read the works of the so-called New Atheists their best arguments shatter on the rock of reality as I have experienced it. Why can't they open their minds to see: (1) the universe in continual process of motion and other changes cannot exist and continue in change unless there is an unchanging First Cause, which is intelligent, free, and thus personal, God, otherwise science and all rational thought would be impossible; (2) Am I not bound in conscience to inquire without prejudice whether God has given me signs of a trustworthy guide (and that cannot be atheism) to living in this world of which I am a part and whose condition I share and which I see is wonderful but has somehow got very mixed up? As a Christian, a Dominican, and a Catholic priest I give many thanks!

THANKSGIVING

At least
in Jesus
through his Spirit in thanksgiving
have I lifted the bread, the wine
his Body, his Blood
for and with God's People—
often distracted,
sometimes with tears.

In soul and body grateful,
now with my incarnate God,
I offer my needy humanness,
my wandering recollections
of my unmended sins,
his golden graces
chaliced in his Humanity—
lift them to the Father
that Jesus' Spirit
may renew in me
the image of Adam,
the Only Son created,
and redeemed as the New Adam,
Jesus, God made the Man,
risen from sin, from death.
I, a mendicant vowed to live by begging
and having for advocate
the New Eve, Mary, vessel of the Spirit,
stretch out my hands,
lest the just Father should demand of me
for the talent
oddly invested in me,
a quite unprofitable servant,
his due in justice;
but yielding to her asking
as Mother of all the living,
Jesus, her compliant Son,
will fill my empty cup
with the full measure
of the one thing needed
to satisfy
the Father's justice,
the wine, the Spirit
Love.

2 yrs. old

7 yrs. old

Mother, Bertha

Father & Richard

Wild Flowers

Mess o' fish

8th Grade

HS Grad

U of C "Buzz Cut"

Winston & Leo Shields

At Notre Dame

With Leo & Harry Rosecrans

Part II
Vatican II A Rocky Ridge: Educators and Bishops

Chapter 10 - Vatican II on the Horizon

Catholic Intellectual Inferiority

In ancient times no culture surpassed that of the Greeks in intellectual achievements. Until 1600 CE the Catholic Church revived and advanced these intellectual achievements more than any other institution, before it fell behind with the advance of Protestant Christianity and then of Enlightenment Secularism. Nevertheless the Second Vatican Council (1962-65) in its final document *The Church in the Modern World* (*Gaudium et Spes*) promulgated by Pope Paul VI, Dec. 7, 1965 expressed confidence that it is able to assist the world solve the problems scientific advances have produced since 1600.

Though mankind is stricken with wonder at its own discoveries and its power, it often raises anxious questions about the current trend of the world, about the place and role of man in the universe, about the meaning of its individual and collective strivings, and about the ultimate destiny of reality and of humanity. Hence, giving witness and voice to the faith of the whole people of God gathered together by Christ, this Council can provide no more eloquent proof of its solidarity with, as well as its respect and love for the entire human family with which it is bound up, than by engaging with it in conversation about these various problems. The Council brings to mankind light kindled from the Gospel, and puts at its disposal those saving resources which the Church herself, under the guidance of the Holy Spirit, receives from her Founder.

To me as a convert to Catholicism in 1938 in the period when the revival of Thomism (1880) and the emphasis on social justice (1891) by Leo XIII (Pope from 1878 to 1903) was flourishing, this promise of Vatican II was indeed a "joy and a hope" that has not faded. In the first part of this work, "Atheism Bumps into Reality," I have recounted in detail how my conversion took place through the study of St. Thomas Aquinas and a rethinking of my Marxist views on social justice. Yet the often violent conflict within the Church that has resulted as an aftermath of Vatican II has involved me in many intellectual controversies internal to the Church and also ecumenical in character. These have made it evident to me that the Council was not theologically ready to face head-on certain pressing problems of education, science, and health of the human person that are central to modern culture. I do not claim, of course, to have solved these theologically, but through a long lifetime I have had to debate them, and my religious superiors have asked me to write down my reflections.

In Part I, "Atheism Bumps into God" I spoke of a "poetic empiricism" which seeks to place abstract argument in the context of our concrete experiences as a way of freeing these arguments from prejudice. As in that part I tried to follow that method in arguing against atheism and in favor of the Catholic faith, in this part I will use it in treating of questions of education, science, and human health that I think Vatican II failed to address adequately.

Why these three topics only? The central one is that of modern science whose "wonder and power" *Gaudium et Spes* rightly acknowledged, as in the quotation above, but did not get from theologians the help to address in detail that it needed. The Council rightly said (n. 5):

> Intellectual formation is ever increasingly based on the mathematical and natural sciences and on those dealing with man himself, while in the practical order the technology which stems from these sciences takes on mounting importance. This scientific spirit has a new kind of impact on the cultural sphere and on modes of thought. Technology is now transforming the face of the earth, and is already trying to master outer space. To a certain extent, the human intellect is also broadening its dominion over time: over the past by means of historical knowledge; over the future, by the art of projecting and by planning. Advances in biology, psychology, and the social sciences not only bring men hope of improved self-knowledge; in conjunction with technical methods, they are helping men exert direct influence on the life of social groups. At the same time, the human race is giving steadily increasing thought to forecasting and regulating its own population growth. History itself speeds

along on so rapid a course that an individual person can scarcely keep abreast of it. The destiny of the human community has become all of a piece, where once the various groups of men had a kind of private history of their own. Thus, the human race has passed from a rather static concept of reality to a more dynamic, evolutionary one.

But where did Vatican II discuss the theory of evolution, so central to the current debates about science and religion? As I will relate later I played a small part in the revision of the draft of the *Catechism of the Catholic Church* that in the revision of 1997 was supposed to incorporate the teachings of the Council. For that revision I proposed a statement on evolution, which many bishops had requested, but it never appeared. Thus the topic of *science* will be the central problem I will deal with in this part, but closely related to it is that of *Catholic education* which is going down the drain of secularism principally because it does not know how to deal with the science vs. religion problem. As for *human health*, it is particularly in the field of bioethics, with such issues as abortion and stem cell research, that our Christian views of human values have recently conflicted with our scientific advances in the control and remaking of nature.

The problem of the historical approach to reality, which is also mentioned in the above quotation, could have been included in this book, but I have not done so, because in my opinion on that issue the Church is in a much better position. The theologians advising the bishops on the Council had already been forced to meet the historical attacks on the Church and on Biblical inspiration. In fact my "poetic empiricism" in dealing with the three issues in which I am most interested reflects that advance in historical understanding. Thus I begin with an account of my own experience as a teacher in the Dominican Order (Order of Preachers), noted for its preservation of the wisdom of St. Thomas Aquinas, so central to Catholic intellectual life since Leo XIII (1878 -1903).

Teaching Future Preachers

I began to teach in the Pontifical Faculty of Philosophy of the St. Albert the Great Province of the Dominican Order at River Forest, a suburb of Chicago, in the fall semester of 1951 and continued to do so until after Vatican II in 1969. I was not facile in speaking Latin, so after teaching logic in 1951-1953 I was assigned courses that were regularly taught in English: history of philosophy, which I taught throughout these years, and from 1959 social philosophy, and sometimes the course called "Texts of Aristotle and Aquinas." Since I had the advantage of study at two important universities, the University of Chicago and Notre Dame, I was keenly aware that my Dominican clerical students, most of whom, according to the practice at that time, had completed only two years of college, had a rather narrow education. So I was anxious to open up to them the vast range of learning I conceived necessary for a Dominican preacher, especially the thought of St. Thomas Aquinas so favored by the Catholic Church.

I loved and still love teaching, but I am afraid my method has never been "student-centered." What I believe I am good at is giving lectures that clearly and simply synthesize a lot of material. In spite of my Chicago experience of the Socratic method I never found that the school schedule, crowded as it was, gave enough time to use it. As for the emphasis on student motivation and activity, I felt that was the students' problem, not mine. My job as I saw it was to help these fledgling preachers find their way through a vast and complex tradition and see its current applications.

At this late date I can't say that I was very successful at this undertaking, though I think my reputation as a teacher has always been good. My old pupils often twit me about my struggles to lecture in Latin, as was then required. Fortunately I usually taught history of philosophy for which English was tolerated. Yet when I compare myself, for example, to my Dominican confrere Fr. James A. Weisheipl (d. 1984) who developed a group of very loyal and enthusiastic disciples who now carry on his work,[113] I realize I have not done as well. I am always very happy to see my students again and proud when I hear of their good work, but I have not followed them up or made a special effort to keep in contact. What I got from Chicago was that a professor can give the student some good tips and directives, but learning is something you have to do on your own and put it to your own uses.

My Dominican students were very docile but had a hard time believing that philosophy had anything to do with the theology they realized was necessary for the priestly ministry to people that motivated their vocations. Only an occasional student actually caught fire with the problems of philosophy and wanted to know more. My own approach to the history of philosophy also puzzled some. As an

Aristotelian in epistemology I firmly believed that in learning one goes from a confused whole to its analysis into parts. Then, after a closer examination of the problem, one returns by way of synthesis to relating all these parts once more into the whole. Finally, from this clear understanding of the whole, one returns to the parts. The process continues in an "hermeneutic circle." There is a apt Chinese saying,

> For a scholar at first a tree is a tree, a mountain a mountain, a bird a bird. Then after study it begins to appear that a tree is not just a tree, nor a mountain a mountain, nor a bird a bird; but then again, after many years of study one sees that after all a tree is a tree, a mountain a mountain, a bird a bird.

Consequently, I thought one should first get a notion of the development of human thought as a whole before looking at the parts. Hence, I began my course in the history of philosophy with a brief account of the evolution of the universe and of the human species so as to set the subject in place and time. (Recently I had a horrible nightmare that I was "birthing the universe"). Then I took a look at what we know of the earliest human cultures, the rise of civilization and literacy, and then I gave lectures on Chinese and Indian philosophy (my own knowledge was, however, mainly from standard secondary sources). I tried to put Greek and Roman philosophy in that world context as the kind of critical thought which to date has been chiefly used in the formation of Christian theology. Only then did I move through the standard periods of ancient, medieval, renaissance and modern Western philosophy. I fear most of what I had to say about Chinese and Hindu philosophy did not sink in.

In later years the only recollections of these courses I hear from priests who were then my students is (a) "You started the history of philosophy with the Age of Fishes;" (b) "I remember how you used to talk about the Twelve Worthies of the Bamboo Grove." Even for me those Twelve Worthies are now no more than a pleasant image in a Chinese painting. One student accused me of never having mentioned St. Augustine of whom he never heard until he got to theology. This showed me he had been asleep for most of one semester in which the thought of Augustine was my constant theme. I don't know that I actually inspired many students in the multicultural direction that is now so fashionable and with which I have always heartily agreed.[114] They probably thought it was just a "snow job."

The courses I taught in ethics and social philosophy were more rewarding from the student point of view and gave me an opportunity to use my doctorate in political science. As I became more thoroughly grounded in the ethical doctrine of Aristotle and Aquinas (and the text courses often were expositions of the *Nicomachean Ethics*) I was unconsciously moving into my later specialization in moral theology. Unfortunately I was assigned to teach the "cosmology" course only one or two times, which was, as noted in the last chapter, my real focus of interest.

The teaching of philosophy is a perplexing business, because many students never see the problems that confront the philosopher, or the need for logical consistency in one's thinking. Only when philosophy teachers manage to awaken in a few of their students the puzzlement they themselves have experienced in the face of these apparent contradictions in the various aspects of experience, can learning begin. When I was a student, I heard some of my fellow students laugh at Fr. William Humbert Kane (d. 1970) because he used to say such things in class as "You can't drink your second beer until you have drunk your first," or "If you don't see it, you don't see it" (or as Aristotle is supposed to have said, "He who asks why we admire beautiful people has no eyes"). It is wonderment over such obvious facts that is a philosopher's game, but a very serious game in which the whole universe is at stake.

A GARDEN IN THE BRAIN

In the center of the brain as in a garden,
with a history of earthquakes, tempests, dry mildew,
is the small patch of reason, a monument with graven
words.
You find these patches in the city sometimes,
walled in by sidewalks, sealed by office towers,
sometimes where the city has suffered earthquakes,
tempests, or dry rot.
In such a garden, alive but ancient,
a monument stands forgotten, useless,
yet ever surviving these and all disasters.

This garden allegorizes in every half-curled and porous leaf
the complex, diverse, timeless, changing particularization

of our puzzle of a world.
Of all the pebbles each is turned and spotted diversely.
Of all the grass blades each is burned and yellowed
differently.
The overloaded and rank flowers cannot be comprehended
and the forms of heaped debris remain uninventoried.
The returning and re-sprouting layers of all reality
deposited, collected, reshuffled, disarranged.
Yet the words on the monument though half obliterated
are never altered.
In the center of the monument unread
they were carved deeply.
Whoever carved them in writing cried out,
"This is the truth."

If philosophy is a bit of a mystery, theology, which I was later to
teach deserves much better than did the Soviets that description
Churchill gave of them, "a riddle wrapped in a mystery inside an
enigma."

TRUTH

In the center of the court stands Jesus.
I have seen no one stand so before a puzzled judge
but a rebel who was framed, and he cried out
in full measure denouncing the law
that had declared contradictions without shame.
Here Jesus stands and after saying quietly
the plain truth, is silent.

The many people differing in feature and expressions,
the knots of threads on Pilate's robe,
the maze of Roman law,
all in a net hold this silent witness fast.
What have we caught here, men,
in reason's sweep among the seas of blindness.
"Who is our fish?
Classify this One by genus and by species."

When the categories of creaturely mind
fail to pigeonhole the specimen—
the net is broken.

The fish then hangs by a single thread,
Pilate's weary question,
"What is truth?"

A Widening Range of Education

I had gone through the novitiate, philosophy and theology, and first years of teaching all in River Forest, a suburb of Chicago, because the Priory there was more than adequate to house the whole student community and faculty. But the ending of World War II had brought a huge increase of vocations, GIs returning from that conflict and from the Korean War. Consequently our Provincial at that time, Fr. Edward Hughes (d. 1966), in 1949 moved the novitiate to a lovely new building on a high hill outside of Winona, MN. Eventually, after Vatican II and the decline in vocations it had to be sold and those who purchased it then sold it, to our distress, to the schismatic followers of Archbishop Lefebvre, opponents of Vatican II. In their sectarian fervor they have preserved the Dominican features of the building.

Also, at the request of the Bishops of Iowa, in 1950, Fr. Hughes built a new Priory of St. Rose of Lima in Dubuque, IA. It was to house our students in theology with their faculty so that it could also teach the students for the priesthood of the dioceses of Iowa, who already had their residential seminary, Mount St. Bernard's on an adjacent hill. Thus for some years Dominic candidates for the priesthood made their novitiate in Winona, MI, then took simple vows and studied philosophy for three years in River Forest, IL, and then completed their theological studies in Dubuque. My life as one of their teachers was eventually to be divided between River Forest and Dubuque.

Besides a full program of teaching to Dominican clerics I also did occasional teaching elsewhere. Thus in my second year of teaching I gave a course on "philosophy of art" at the nearby women's school of the Dominican Sisters, Rosary College, now Dominican University, and in 1954 taught a theology course there. From 1956-1961 I was also teaching part time at St. Xavier's College in south side Chicago. For several summers I taught theology in New Orleans at Xavier University to mainly African-Americans (then just "Blacks"), and then in 1950 and 1956 at St. Mary's Dominican College to Sisters. One summer I taught at Mt. Mary's College in Milwaukee, and another at the Catholic University of America, and again at the former Mount St. Mary's in Denver. These summer schools were pleasant experiences that gave me an opportunity to teach a wider audience, including many women students.

To understood the educational atmosphere of this period before Vatican II one must realize that Catholics suffered then from a sense of inferiority about intellectual life unlike today when our schools are compared favorably with secular ones at least for good discipline and for "teaching values." Then, on the one hand we compared ourselves unfavorably to the Catholic Revival in France where many of the European intelligentsia battling anticlericalism were militantly Catholic. On the other hand, we were humbled by a well-known book of Monsignor John Tracy Ellis on American Catholic intellectual life that gave us very low marks.[115] We were an immigrant Church of working class people. Typically Sisters and Brothers with meager preparation operated our parochial schools, and our colleges and universities were staffed by priests equipped only with seminary training or perhaps a degree from a Roman theological school of narrow outlook. Therefore, it was a time of Catholic determination to do better.

Notably among the teaching Sisterhoods there was an important movement led by Sister Mary Emil Penet, I.H.M.[116] She with a Sister companion traveled tirelessly by automobile all over the United States urging the raising of educational standards for Sisters. At that time Sisters working in the parochial schools often began their teaching careers with little more than a high school education and were expected to study summer after summer to get their B.A.'s and full teaching certification. Sister Emil was especially concerned that they should receive good instruction in philosophy and theology, since it was common for Sisters to be required to teach "religion" in addition to their regular subjects. At that time almost a third of the men in our Dominican Chicago Province were engaged in teaching philosophy and especially theology, mainly in Sisters' colleges, because the Jesuits had a near monopoly on men's colleges. Hence we Dominicans were very much in sympathy with Sister Emil's project, but our approach was markedly different than hers, which was strongly influenced by her Jesuit advisers. The difference at this time between the Jesuit and the Dominican perspective in this matter I will explain later.

I also had dreams of reaching students in secular universities, and one of my first efforts after ordination was a series of lectures at the University of Chicago Calvert Club, dealing with science and

religion. I worked hard on my presentations but they failed misera-
bly. My topic did not seem to meet the then current concerns of
Catholic students and my Thomistic approach, critical of the University's secularism, seemed odd and irritating to them. In the years I
had been immured in the House of Studies the Adler-Hutchins
epoch had faded at the University and the tone had become that of
the happy confidence in the superiority and progress of American
culture that so permeated the 1950s.

My Dominican classmate Raymund Nogar (d. 1967) and I made
another such attempt to reach students at a secular university. In
1951 rather brashly we gave a presentation at the University of
Wisconsin on the way the survey course in the social sciences was
being used by some professors to attack the family religion of students and to inculcate moral relativism. This double lecture aroused
considerable controversy and was reported in *The Milwaukee Senti-
nel*, March 19, 1951. I also entered on the pro side into the controversy of the National Forensic Commission of the National Federation of Catholic Students over whether it was advisable to debate
the recognition of Communist China, an issue on which conservatives were adamantly con. Few other opportunities for university
contacts presented themselves and it has always been a big regret
on my part that so much of my ministry has been within the Church
rather than outside it. Priests are not easily received in our culture
and we can only hope that the lay people we teach will pass on the
Gospel to the world.

During these years I also engaged in much occasional lecturing
on my favorite topic, science and religion.[117] These, talks, ephemeral
as their effects may have been, at least kept me moving about, meeting a good many people, learning what they were thinking—
thoughts often very different than those that formed the intellectual
atmosphere of the Studium in River Forest—and helped me better
formulate my own convictions. I have found that every time I teach
a class or give a lecture my theme stimulates new insights, new
facets of the subject in my thinking. Honest thinking can never be
simple repetition; it must be transformation.

Adult Education

I was also much engaged in what is today called "adult education" for Catholics through participating in the work of the Thomist
Association. This Association was largely the result of the work of

Fr. Walter Farrell, O.P (1951), who, although a member of the Chicago Province, upon his return from studies in Europe became Regent of Studies in the New York Province and began a popular lecture series on theology, interrupted only by his service as a chaplain in the Navy in World War II. "Theology" for him simply meant the *Summa Theologiae* of St. Thomas Aquinas, which he praised as "true wisdom." He believed that all adult Catholics who were of college caliber should study theology and acquire this same precious wisdom.

The Thomist Association that he inspired was a lay organization with its own officers and was established in Chicago and in several neighboring cities in Illinois and Wisconsin. It employed Dominican professors, mainly from our Studium faculty, as its lecturers and it also raised funds for scholarships for Dominican clerics who could serve as future lecturers. The talks were given on Sunday mornings, beginning with Mass and a special sermon relating to the topic being studied. After this there was a convivial breakfast and then an hour's lecture, followed by discussion. There were no exams, but a certificate could be earned by three years' participation. The lectures worked consecutively through the materials of the *Summa*. Participants were encouraged to read the *Summa*, or if they found this too difficult, Fr. Farrell's four volume *Companion to the Summa*[118] based on his own lecturing. There was excellent attendance at this various groups for about twenty years (1949-1970) by teachers, professionals, and others simply desirous of growing spiritually.

I mainly served the group in Oshkosh, WI that met in the local Catholic hospital (the antiseptic smell of my bedroom there revives in my memory!). Oshkosh is a lovely town famous for its "overall" work-clothes factory (no small item in the Midwest farmlands). In the local park stands a heroic bronze statue of Chief Oshkosh, the Native American leader after whom the town is named. The Chief is in full regalia including leather riding chaps that look oddly like the famous local product! Oshkosh was also the birthplace of a Dominican confrere whom I have already mentioned, James Athanasius Weisheipl, the only child of parents who were both deaf mutes. As a professor at the Pontifical Mediaeval Institute in Toronto where he taught for many years, he became a noted medievalist and author, among many other publications, of the standard work, *Friar Thomas D'Aquino: His Life, Thought, and Work*.[119]

I would go to Oshkosh by train Saturday night, give the lectures Sunday morning, and return late Sunday afternoon. I would get back to Chicago often late at night and then walk from Union Station through very dark streets to the 'L'. The boarding platform at that point was very high, up long stairs, and at the top I was usually entirely alone. It was a bit scary, but nothing bad ever happened. Today I would never dare such a spot at night, but our cities then seemed much safer than now. The group to whom I lectured were devout Catholics eager to learn about their faith and to communicate it to others. I don't believe we Thomist lecturers—certainly I did not—made much effort to connect the *Summa Theologiae* with the current problems of the laity or the Church, especially the problem of the relation of religion to modern science. To us that was the laity's own task, once they understood theology as the Angelic Doctor had so splendidly presented it.

The Albertus Magnus Lyceum

Yet in my last years at the University of Chicago after my conversion to Catholicism my Catholic friend, Leo Shields, who later died in World War II in the Normandy invasion, told me how impressed he was with some lectures on the relation of religion and science by Fr. William H. Kane, OP. Kane's emphasis on the great importance for theology of a reconciliation of modern science and philosophy was very different from Fr. Walter Farrell's approach to theology which, I believe, raised no problems about the traditional presentation of metaphysics provided by the scholastic manuals. Under Fr. Kane's guidance I spent much of my years in the Studium reading the commentaries of Aquinas on Aristotle's works on natural science. Thus I wrote my second doctoral dissertation on these works in an effort to defend Aristotle's foundational scientific principles in his *Physics* by showing they are not implicated in Aristotle's two major erroneous hypotheses, one about the eternity of the world and the other about the function of the heart, which on the basis of the medical knowledge known to him he supposed was the primary organ of the body rather than the brain. St. Thomas Aquinas, however, had argued that, although faith reveals that the universe is not eternal, the question cannot be settled by reason. As regards the heart and brain, Aquinas knew that later Greek doctors such as Galen considered the heart the primary organ and supposed that this fact supported Aristotle's theory of "delayed hominization" of the embryo and fetus, according to which the human person originates a month or two after conception.

I argued, therefore, that these errors of Aristotle and Aquinas were merely secondary theories that like many plausible scientific hypotheses in time come to be falsified, not the fundamental principles on which Aquinas sought to build an empirical natural science. Galileo and Harvey respectively had questioned these hypotheses, just as Einstein questioned Newton's. That these empirical hypotheses eventually proved false does not, therefore, tell against Aquinas' contention that a sound science of nature can demonstrate the existence of God and human intelligence as non-material realities as so many currently assume.

What then of Aristotle's *Physics* is of service to modern science? Briefly it supplies the following principles that are confused in current science and render it unable to give a realistic interpretation of its mathematical hypotheses so as to sort out the certain truths they contain.

Since all our rational knowledge is derived from the senses and sense objects are known only from their behavior, that is, their motion as it results from their interaction and action on our body, all of natural science describes its objects in terms of their correlative actuality (formal cause) and potentiality (material cause).

These changing bodies that make up the universe are relatively independent substances (that is, have independent existence) and need to be described and classified down to their observed species according to nine general properties (the categories). These are: (a) correlative quantity (they have continuous parts) and quality (differing modifications of these parts); (b), relations (such as equality and inequality of parts, or similarity and dissimilarity in quantity); (c) among these relations are action (efficient causality) and reception, that is, cause and effect; (d), this presupposes contact between these bodies, that is, place, position, and environment; (e) and time of interaction and change.

Thus scientific demonstrations are not a priori but go first from effect to cause and only then logically reverse to produce our understanding of nature in terms of formal, material, and efficient causes. The stability of the universe is explained in terms of uniform change (final causality, natural law, determinism) but also includes chance (indeterminism) and free will.

All material substances exist and are known through their changes, but because in understanding them that we must not violate the Principle of Non-Contradiction, then, it follows that the very fact of their existence and changes must depend on the existence and action of the First Prime Mover that is not itself material but can be known by us analogically through these material effects. Moreover, in studying the behavior of natural substances we can come to some knowledge of the subordinate material prime movers (fundamental forces such as gravity) and also of the fact that there are created prime movers, including the human soul with its intelligence and free will that transcend materiality.

Given these foundational principles, many surprising modern hypotheses, such as indeterminism, the Big Bang, and evolution at least become plausible without contradicting common sense convictions that there is a Creator God and we human beings are made in his image. This opens the way to a supreme rational discipline (metaphysics) that compares and unifies the results of other types of knowledge and makes way for a supreme science of theology based on a reasonable faith in the Christian religion.[120]

In this contention that modern science needs an Aristotelian rather than a materialist or idealist foundation, I had the welcome support, not only of Fr. Kane but also of Fr. Raymond Jude Nogar, a graduate of the University of Michigan and also a convert, whose interests were especially in biology and who had written his own dissertation on the nature of modern science. Jude was a very attractive personality, blonde, lively, a former college gymnast, intellectually keen, and an exciting speaker. From the novitiate on I found him a sensitive and sympathetic friend.

Now that Jude and I were priests, Fr. Kane decided with us to found a special institute, The *Albertus Magnus Lyceum*,[121] to promote dialogue between Catholic philosophers and theologians and the world of modern science. It was named "Lyceum" after Aristotle's own school to indicate our Aristotelian approach, and in honor of Aquinas' great teacher, Albertus Magnus who was traditionally entitled the *Doctor Universalis* and in 1941 declared by Pope Pius XII the "saintly patron of those who cultivate the sciences," who also was chosen as the patron of our Chicago Dominican Province. In founding this Lyceum in 1951, the three of us knelt at Our Lady's altar in the River Forest Chapel and placed it under her protection. At her altar was a statue, actually plaster painted ivory color, no great work of art, yet gracious, and with a large rosary hanging from her folded hands and there I often prayed as I practiced the "True Devotion" of St. Louis de Monfort to Our Lady that I had adopted in the novitiate. My growing interest in the science-religion question did not seem to me contradict my efforts to write poetry that had begun in high school, but rather supported it. The wonder aroused by the beauty of nature and of the human person enhances scientific curiosity. At the same time these seem confounded by the ugliness of the environment that scientific technology has produced.

TO OUR LADY

The moon appears in an emptied space
(for me it is thy wounded face)
glowing by the sun's pure grace.
All emptiness its silver fills,
reflecting in earth's tenuous rills,
and where it burns it stills,
whatever throbs it chills,
and every less lovely light it kills,
a queen conquering on high her place
(For me it is thy humble face).

The city is sealed within dead stone,
(the heart that watches is mine own).
those crowded people, each alone,
all hearts entombed in restless sleep,
shallow as eyelids and as sewers deep,
in broken dreams where verminous vices creep,
lying in hell like bloodless sheep,
or Jonah in his ventral keep,
enclosed as is the mind in bone
(the eyes of free mercy are thine own).

Although the initiative to start the Lyceum was approved by our then prior, Fr. John Marr and our provincial Fr. Edward Hughes, it was without much hope of success. I believe they regarded it simply as a pet idea of "Hum" Kane, whom they thought was far too deep into philosophy to be very practical. As I learned, however, he was a true philosopher in the Aristotelian mode, constantly seeking to root every concept and principle in sense experience. He had a thorough knowledge of Aquinas' commentaries on Aristotle, too much neglected by modern Thomists. Under his tutelage I was also able to study these during my studium years.

His superiors found him somewhat a problem because he was always asking for more time for study and writing when they needed some one to hear confessions at a local parish. Some complained that, although he had spent much time studying a famous Treatise on Obedience by the Baroque Thomist Passerini[122] and although he was certainly obedient, he perversely made his obedience a complicated process for his superiors. Actually his fondness for Passerini was that this great Thomist made clear that a religious gains the merit of obedience by every obedient act of his life, not merely by obeying formal commands of the superior.

In fact, as I learned when I got to know him better, Father Kane suffered greatly not from self-interested motives but because it pained him to see how much the intellectual mission of the Order was sacrificed to what seemed to him much less important concerns. Personally "Hum" Kane was a tall, loping, big-boned man who every day walked around the grounds saying his Rosary and in the chapel made the Stations of the Cross. He was deeply spiritual and taught me much about the spiritual life from St. John of the Cross. His problem about getting enough time for study led, he told me, to a seven year depression. I believe from certain things he told me about his struggles with the fact that his superiors had so little appreciation of what a life of intense study involved that he had experienced the spiritual "nights" that St. John of the Cross describes. He felt that the United States Dominicans were too occupied with parish work. He once told me that for seven years he had felt as if he was "outside his window clinging to the sill by his finger nails about to fall many stories to the ground." Yet he was a down-to-earth sort of person who during Prohibition had used his knowledge of chemistry to brew beer for the other Fathers. He loved golf. I can still hear him say when a nice day came along, "This year, there won't be many more days like this to play golf!" as he hurried to the links.

In view of his absorption in study, his independence of mind, and his unusual personality, I am also sure that to our superiors Kane's Lyceum project seemed pretty far-fetched, considering that none of us had advanced scientific training, except for Kane's medical studies at the Georgetown University when he was in Washington. Moreover the House of Studies in River Forest was remote from any university with a full scientific faculty. Finally, the rest of our Dominican brethren in the Province simply "didn't get it." What was this all about? Why was it important? The project seemed to most unconnected to our traditional preaching and teaching of theology and in the United States our responsibilities for parish ministries. But the three of us thought we had a great idea and should try it. I have never lost faith in that idea.

Indeed I see it today as even more important than ever. Just today I read an article by an eminent Catholic scientist who is working hard to reconcile the Church and modern science. But he argues that there should be no conflict between science and faith since "the business of science is to explain," but "God is not an explanation, he is Love." This kind of confused and sentimental thinking simply will not do.[123] God is indeed Love, but he is also the Creator and First Cause of all things, and therefore their ultimate explanation. The question is not how to keep science and religion from conflict and in dialogue, but to show how scientific explanations and theistic explanations are mutually supportive and complementary. This is what Aristotle and Aquinas tried to do and, in the Lyceum's conviction, did successfully, although in view of the great advances of modern science such solutions always need critical analysis and reformulation.

This is not the place to write a complete report of the Lyceum project, but as I go on with my story I will try to indicate some of its ups and downs and the fruit it still continues to bear long after its official closing in 1969. In 1951 the Lyceum published a brochure explaining our aims and in July of 1952 held a five-week workshop, reported in a published volume, *Science in Synthesis: A Dialectical Approach to the Integration of the Physical and Natural Sciences,*[124] 1953, by the three of us along with Fr. John D. Corcoran, OP, then teaching psychology. Besides the four of us the participants included Fr. William A. Wallace, OP,[125] then studying physics at the Catholic University of America, Dr. Herbert Ratner,[126] my friend from the University of Chicago and a scholar in Aristotelian biology, and Vincent E. Smith,[127] Professor of the Philosophy of Science at Notre Dame, all of whom were permanent members of the Lyceum, as well as some fourteen participants who included physicists, chemists, a mathematician, biologists, a medical doctor, and two psychiatrists. Professionally they were not perhaps a very distinguished lot and were all men who had a summer free and an interest in broadening their thinking. Later we were to be joined by a woman biologist, Sister Adrian M. Hofstetter.[128] Of our Chicago Province Fr. James Athanasius Weisheipl, OP, (d. 1984)[129] who was to become a noted expert on the history of medieval science and Albert Moraczewski,

OP,[130] who was to found the *National Catholic Bioethics Center* and of the Eastern Dominican Province and William A. Wallace, OP, who was to become an expert on the work of Galileo were not members of the Lyceum but associated or were to be associated with it.

Unluckily Fr. Kane's approach was simply to tell the good news of our Aristotelianism to these modern scientifically trained persons as if the truth clearly presented would be evident. Because of our experience in secular universities, Fr. Nogar and I realized this would never work and tried to take what we thought to be a more dialectical approach, although not ending there but aiming at ultimate certitudes. The scientists of course wanted to explain science to us "philosophers" and tended to regard the questions about modern science we were trying to raise as simply uninformed. The permanent members of the Lyceum, however, felt that this summer session was at least a beginning and *Science in Synthesis* formulated our project more clearly.

In 1952 I also took the opportunity to present our ideas in a paper, "Research Into the Final Causes of Physical Things" at the *American Catholic Philosophical Association*[131] in which I argued that for Aristotle final causality is not occult but is observable by seeing how regular, and therefore natural, processes lead to determined results in the stable existence of even inanimate species of things. My argument, however, at once met opposition from those who contended that final causality is a concern of philosophy but not of natural philosophy since science deals only with probabilities and accidental aspects of things while only philosophy deals with certitudes and essences. Hence, they claim, the two disciplines should simply be allowed to go their own ways. Although I had striven in my paper to be clear that we were not proposing the revival of pre-Galilean science, but a critical rethinking of post-Galilean science in light of Aristotle's analysis of such basic concepts as motion, causality, matter, quantity, time, and place, many members of the *American Catholic Philosophical Association* continued to think that "The River Forest School," as we were called, were nostalgic advocates of Aristotle's quintessence and a geocentric cosmos.

We never again, however, had either the money or the time to organize a seminar such as that of our first summer. Instead we had annual meetings of the Lyceum's regular members and encouraged them to write on various aspects of the project and to present papers at the learned societies, especially the annual meeting of the

ACPA. This last venue, however, got us into some difficulties for two reasons: First, our frequent appearances as a group at such meetings to read papers or to intervene in discussions was thought to be bad manners by other Catholic philosophers, who were content always to appear as individuals. We were felt to be a kind of sect trying to force our ideas on others with excessive zeal. Second, what we were proposing ran counter to the views of Jacques Maritain and Étienne Gilson who at that time dominated American Catholic thought.[132]

How great this resistance was became evident to Jude Nogar and me when we were invited by the Philosophy Club of St. Louis University to talk at one of their meetings. We found the Jesuit philosophy faculty, although politely hospitable, very cool to discussion with us. While I am not sure of the reasons for this coolness, I have an educated guess. At that time the philosophy department of St. Louis University, under leadership of the Jesuit Fathers George Klubertanz, S. J., (d. 1972) and Robert Henle, SJ, (d. 2000) was one of the best at any U.S. Catholic university. These two were ardent promoters of Thomist philosophy (of the Gilsonian variety) against the remains of the Suarezian tradition, but they had become alarmed by what they saw as the "theological imperialism" of the Dominicans as represented by a zealous disciple of Walter Farrell, Fr. Thomas Donlan, OP, in his book, *Theology and Education*.[133] Of course, as I have indicated, the thinking of Kane and the Lyceum was quite other than that of Farrell's, but the Jesuits did not know that, just as we did not realize how they were struggling to get more recognition for philosophy in the university curriculum in the face of the relative indifference of the university's Jesuit theologians.

Chapter 11 - A Science Based Curriculum

The St. Xavier Curriculum Project

It did not appear, therefore, how we of the Lyceum were to advance our cause, although a few others joined us, such as Sister Adrian Hofstetter, already mentioned. She is an ardent advocate of many good causes who today continues to work for ecological reform. Hence, we were very happy when Fr. Charles Johnson, OP who taught theology at St. Xavier's College for Women then located on 49th and Cottage Grove Avenue in Chicago, suggested to its administration that the Lyceum members might be of assistance in helping the college develop a liberal arts curriculum for which she had obtained a $170,000 grant—very big for those days—from the Ford Foundation.

What did this research on the curriculum have to do with the science and religion problem? We saw them as intimately related. Historically our educational system goes back to the Greek through the Christian medieval system but has become fragmented by the modern "knowledge explosion" and what C. P. Snow called "The Two Cultures," the "hard sciences" and the "soft humanities."[134] This had arisen after Galileo in the seventeenth century as a result of the mathematization of the natural sciences that placed it into opposition to "philosophy" that was demoted to the "soft sciences." Previously the term "philosophy" was distinguished as systematic thought from "common sense" as unsystematic thought, but included the whole range of systematic disciplines. For Aristotelians all these disciplines, even the logical skills, were ultimately grounded in sense knowledge and hence in natural science. In American education this tradition (which is still retained in our term "Doctor of Philosophy" and in our caps and gowns in academic processions) has been further confused by John Dewey's pragmatism which was closely related to the "theory of unity and praxis" of Marxism, to which I was committed before my conversion to Catholicism. Thus we members of the Albertus Magnus Lyceum viewed the restoration of the curriculum as an important application of our developing view of modern natural science.

This cooperation with St. Xavier's curriculum project thus gave the Lyceum opportunity to work with a college faculty (including its science departments) that was already influenced by the Great Books ideas of the University of Chicago, only a few blocks to the south. St. Xavier's was an old Chicago institution operated by the Religious Sisters of Mercy of the Union but at that time it was on the brink of moving out of what had become a dangerous neighborhood into the suburbs. Its President, Sister Josetta Butler, was one of the most remarkable persons I have ever known.[135] She was born in Chicago, attended St. Anne School and Visitation High School, eceived her B.A. from St. Xavier's and was the first women to get a Ph.D. in chemistry from the University of Illinois. She joined the faculty of St. Xavier in 1939 to teach chemistry, became Dean from 1940 to 1956, from then until 1961 was Executive Vice-President and Dean of Faculty, and finally became President in 1960, enlarging the school from 300 to 1000 students and rebuilding it handsomely on 55 acres at 103rd Street (it eventually has become a co-educational university). Over 500 women got the M.A. in the college's theology program that she initiated. She established scholarships for religious women from Third World countries, and in 1962 went to India to better understand their backgrounds. She also played a major role in the Sisters' Formation Movement and in preparing Mercy Sisters for hospital ministry. Then from 1963-1969 she served as Executive Secretary for the Better World Movement in Washington, DC and as its Secretary General in Rome. Returning to Chicago in 1971 she became for some years Vicar General of the Sisters of Mercy of the Union helping them accommodate to the changes initiated by Vatican II, which she welcomed with enthusiasm. Until her death, February 4, 1995, although often in poor health, she continued a spiritual ministry to retired Sisters.

In the fifties when I worked for her, she was a handsome, ample, motherly lady swathed in the voluminous black of her congregation with a white linen coif stabbing her rosy cheeks and a black veil which was always slipping backward on its leather headband only to be yanked forward into place. She told me that when she was the only woman studying for the doctorate in chemistry and was working in the laboratory one hot summer along with two young men students, after they had shed their shirts to work more comfortably in their undershirts, one turned to her as she labored away in her enveloping black outfit and in sympathy exclaimed, "Sister, can't you take off something?"

Sister Josetta, who had the full support of her Provincial, Mother M. Huberta, was a woman with an open, broad mind, always looking for the good, the true, and the beautiful for her students, with humor, and generosity. When I first met her she was already working to move Xavier's and erect its buildings on a great new campus. She hoped this move would be the occasion to set up a new curriculum for a Catholic education and a model for all the educational work of the Mercy Sisters. It would include the whole range of primary, secondary, and college education, making use of the lower schools that were located near the college campus. Above all this new curriculum was to be animated by a sound and vital Catholic theology.

Sister Josetta appointed as director of her project Prof. Oscar Perlmutter [136] of the faculty, who had studied at the University of Chicago and was imbued with the Hutchins-Adler outlook. This seemed rather bold, since Oscar was not a Catholic but a Jew; but he had a quizzical admiration for these sisters along with an outsider's objectivity about their Catholic way of doing things. In future years he was finally himself to become a Catholic. He was a thoughtful, gentle, and very perceptive man, and he gave to Josetta a cultural breadth not furnished by her American Irish and chemistry-teaching background. Perlmutter had no difficulty getting along with Dominican priests, and in fact, he enjoyed working with us, with all our oddities, and we much admired him.

Thus from 1952 to 1962 the Lyceum and St. Xav's cooperated in the development of a *Plan for the Liberal Education of the Christian Person* as its 1953 report to the Ford Foundation outlined it. This entailed not only designing the curriculum from kindergarten to B.A. graduation and preparing special materials for teachers, but conducting training sessions each summer for the faculties of the three schools engaged in the experiment. This "Institute in Curriculum and Teacher Development," was held at St. Xavier's in the years 1954-1957. Various members of the Lyceum taught in these sessions, but I became the chief liaison as a part-time professor of philosophy at the new St. Xavier's. I am proud to say that it was I who suggested that the main entrance have the inscription, "Wisdom built herself a house with seven pillars" (Prov 9:1). I asked and was granted that seven of the columns at the entrance of the main college building be inscribed with the names of the seven liberal arts of the medieval universities. I think Sister Josetta herself was a good stand-in for Lady Wisdom. She could also cook, and one winter afternoon when a conference had detained me at St. Xavier's late she saw I would miss dinner by the time I got back to River Forest, she sat me down and fried a steak for me!

A Christian Curriculum Grounded in Natural Science

The new curriculum we developed for St. Xavier's was not a Great Books program, although we sought to encourage study of classical works. Its basis as shown in the last chapter was Aristotle and Aquinas' theory of the order of the sciences, a scope wider than the classical seven liberal arts. But central to the curriculum was Bible-based religious education beginning with graduated catechetical instruction through primary and secondary school. The students read Bible stories and heard them in the Liturgy as the teacher developed their doctrinal and practical implications for memorization in succinct formulas as is today recommended in the *Catechism of the Catholic Church*. We believed that in lower education memory plays an important role, but in a sacramental religion such as Catholic Christianity so does the imagination, and that the Holy Bible with its vivid stories and imagery should be the fundamental tradition into which the Catholic student is incorporated. At the college level, then, this catechetical instruction was to be completed by systematic theological study following the theology of Aquinas so highly commended by the popes.[137]

For such a theological orientation, however, a broad liberal education is required following the systematic unfolding of serious reflection on our experience as Aquinas analyzed it. First should come logic, as the *organon* (tool) of learning and communication, and mathematics as the simplest, clearest, and most certain exemplification of logical thinking. Logic is pedagogically the first of the sciences, although epistemologically natural science is first. Aquinas accepted Aristotle's view, opposed as it was to Platonic idealism on the one hand and Stoic materialism on the other, that all our knowledge begins with the senses, but intellectually abstracts from them, that natural science is first in the division of systematic disciplines. Although natural science is constructed logically, logical relations are mind-dependent and hence are understood by analogy from real distinctions analyzed by natural science. The liberal arts, therefore, involve an interplay between logic and natural science, not a separation of the so-called "humanities" from the hard sciences that has developed in education since the 17th century.[138] Thus the study of logic and natural science should begin in the first grade and reach its systematization in high school. For this I wrote and illustrated a text, *The Arts of Learning and Communication*[139] that, with simple illustrations and exercises, provides an introduction to each of the liberal arts, following the more developed system of Aristotle in which "logic" includes all the arts of language and of systematic thinking (grammar, poetics, rhetoric, dialectics, scientific logic).

In this I was influenced by the Adler-Hutchins conviction that the four years in typical United States high school is largely a wasted time. These liberal arts should be learned before college because they equip the student to think, read, speak, and write. The arts of language (the *trivium*) would be taught in the standard English courses and the mathematical ones in math, science, and music courses. Finally in college, these liberal arts would be completed by the study of more advanced literature and mathematics, and by the science, social science, and philosophy courses, all united in the study of systematic theology. Other subjects now standard in college would not be neglected, but would be secondary to this basic pattern aimed at forming a student with an enriched memory, who could also think critically and had a basic knowledge of the whole scope of human learning. We proposed to implement this program with certain innovative teaching procedures: students were to advance individually at their own pace through achievement exams and with the assistance of "teacher's aids" (assistants) and early graduation from high school, "advanced placement" in college was to be encouraged.

Besides *The Arts of Learning and Communication*, other instructional materials were developed and used in draft form. Thus Fr. Denis Zusy, OP (d. 2000) and Sister Olivia Barrett, R.S.M., prepared a four volume text for a required science course in college, using a historical approach, and Sister Dominic Merwick and I prepared catechetical syllabi for primary school religion. In the meantime the brilliant Fr. Francis Cunningham, OP (who died young from cancer in 1963) had edited a four volume *College Theology* that was used in many Catholic colleges. Soon after Fr. Eugene A. Mainelli (with a committee of which I was a member) at Fenwick High School edited a four volume religion series for high schools that also attempted to provide a Bible-based approach.[140] Our hopes were that these models would succeed and be followed by other Catholic schools.

The whole program was put into effect at St. Xav's and seemed to be proving itself, but met two obstacles. The first, of course, was that it took time to develop successful textbook materials. But far more serious (and this seems to be the case with every experimental educational program) was the fact that "Teachers teach as they were taught." The teachers in the St. Xavier schools had come up through an educational system in which most teachers prepared a lesson plan from a current textbook which reflected no integrated view of knowledge and in which everything was compartmentalized and confused by all the vicissitudes of the mighty Western intellectual tradition.

For example, I struggled with a bright high school teacher of English to try to get her over the fallacy perpetuated by modern linguists that grammar is purely a matter of usage and to see that it embodies a deeper logic, which, if it is not communicated to the student, renders the concept of good speaking and writing utterly arbitrary. One college English professor at St. Xavier's was outraged by my claim that poetry is logical. I never meant, of course, that the logic of a poem is identical with the logic of a scientific article, but that both, each in its own very different way, obey the laws of human thought, imagination, emotion, and communication. I also struggled with a college mathematics teacher to convince her that mathematics is difficult for students mainly because its logical structure is never made plain. I tried to persuade her of the falsity of the current notion that the axioms of mathematics are merely human constructions and hence that math is simply a logical game in which "truth" is arbitrary. Since mathematics is the simplest and clearest exemplification of truth, if it too is arbitrary then truth in other fields is also impossible. Without knowing it she was teaching skepticism, as do so many teachers in many school subjects unconsciously teach bad philosophy.

I believe that if Descartes had realized that his reduction of geometry to algebra in fact made it dialectical and approximate rather than strictly probative, the whole surrender of modern philosophy to skepticism and relativism might never have occurred. Even in simple arithmetic we fail to make clear to students that 1 is not a number, thus contradicting the definition of a "number" as "a whole with discrete parts," but instead is the principle of numbers and thus fool students into thinking of a "fraction" like ½ as a part of a number, instead of a ratio between whole numbers. And we fool them even worse by calling 0 a number instead of a notation for "no number." This process of hidden analogy then leads on to speaking of "time" and the degrees of qualities as if they were lines and finally to "set theory" and "infinite" numbers and the fading away of math into logic. All these mathematical devices are entirely legitimate, great rational achievements without which modern science could never have progressed; but when taught without making clear the steps from univocal concepts to stretched out analogies might well leave naïve minds with a thicket of paradoxes and Humean skepticism.

No wonder students find learning difficult when their teachers, who are supposed to be opening the road to truth, erect these road-blocks. Of course some educators glory in these sad results because they too have lost faith in our capacity to know the truth and be set free by it. I thank my friendship with that faithful Aristotelian and Harvard mathematician, Hippocrates Apostle (d. 1990)[141] for opening my myopic eyes to these simple, pure mathematical truths.

My conviction is that while much of what I or anybody else claims is true is in fact only probable or even false, yet you and I know some things that are certainly true and with these as clues we can work slowly to enlarge our genuine certitudes. I believe it is the goal of education to help students find these limited but real certitudes and attain the skills to use them as the criteria for discriminating more extensively between truth and falsehood.

Educational Renewal and Vatican II

The St. Xavier Plan began to work and grow and I believe it might have become thoroughly established and then spread to other schools if it had not been for the great "changes in the Church" that came in the wake of Vatican II and overwhelmed this little project of the Sisters of Mercy. We had heartily welcomed Vatican II when its assembly was announced by Pope John XXIII in January of 1958 because we saw it as a renewal of the Church's intellectual tradition that would free it from modern confusions that had arisen with Descartes' idealism. This renewal Leo XIII initiated in 1879 by his commendation of the thought of St. Thomas Aquinas, but distorted Neo-Scholastic versions of Thomism tended to stifle its efforts to unifying knowledge without destroying the order and autonomy of different types of thought. Thomism became "philosophy" or "metaphysics" isolated from scientific progress instead of its vital source and stimulus as Leo XIII intended. He wrote:[142]

While, therefore, We hold that every word of wisdom, every useful thing by whomsoever discovered or planned, ought to be received with a willing and grateful mind, We exhort you, venerable brethren, in all earnestness to restore the golden wisdom of St. Thomas, and to spread it far and wide for the defense and beauty of the Catholic faith, for the good of society, and for the advantage of all the sciences. The wisdom of St. Thomas, We say; for if anything is taken up with too great subtlety by the Scholastic doctors, or too carelessly stated—if there be anything that ill agrees with the discoveries of a later age, or, in a word, improbable in whatever way—it does not enter Our mind to propose that for imitation to Our age.

During this time of preparation for the Council I wrote a good many articles explaining curricular renewal[143] and in 1961, beginning from the bottom I coauthored with Sister Mary Dominic Merwick, R.S.M., three volumes *The Story of the Kingdom of God*, a draft catechetical text for elementary schools. At the same time I was giving papers at philosophy meetings to provide a more scholarly defense of the Lyceum's view of the relations between science, philosophy, and theology on which the curriculum plan was based.[144] I also wrote articles on the liberal arts in education and on "Finality" for the *New Catholic Encyclopedia*,[145] the editing of whose philosophy articles of which, as well its final rescue from editorial disaster, was the work of a Lyceum member, Fr. William A. Wallace, OP. During this time I also served as chairman of the Midwest section of the *American Catholic Philosophical Association* and as an assistant editor of its journal, *The New Scholasticism*. The only spiritual writing I did during this time was "The Beginner at Mental Prayer,"[146] in which I tried to show how visits to the Blessed Sacrament can develop into contemplative prayer.

In the ecumenical spirit that was to be central to the Council and remembering my debt to Jews at the University of Chicago, I also engaged in efforts to promote better Jewish-Christian relations. I well remember a meeting held at a synagogue in River Forest, located just opposite our House of Studies, whose purpose was to overcome the anti-Semitism aroused by a new Jewish presence in that suburb. On that day the Jewish women in the dialogue were a bit late, and while we were waiting for them, one WASP woman raised the question whether such discussions didn't create problems where none really existed. "There really is no anti-Semitism here," she said. When the Jewish ladies arrived I had the nerve to repeat what the WASP had said. The look on the Judaic faces spoke volumes! Later in the discussion an elderly Jewish woman made a lovely speech about how in spite of religious differences we should all be friends. But when one of the Gentiles said, "How do you feel about intermarriage," the old lady exclaimed, "Oh, that's different!"

The traveling that I did during this period was almost exclusively to conventions and meetings around the country, otherwise my world was between River Forest and St. Xavier's except for my summer teaching already mentioned. In Chicago traveling itself can be an adventure. St. Xavier's is almost an hour ride from River Forest, mainly south down Harlem Ave. The traffic can be outrageous and in winter the road perilous. One winter evening I left Xavier's quite late in the afternoon but did not arrive at River Forest until after 9 P.M. The streets were covered with ice from an afternoon rain and a sharp change of weather. It was a nightmare drive in dark, blowing snow, with all sorts of strange detours necessitated by the traffic stalled on icy, impassable overpasses. Another time driving home in rain I got out to help with an accident by the road (in those days priests were supposed to stop at all accidents to administer the sacraments). Two Hispanic workers living in a small enclave along the street had been walking along the roadside to a nearby tavern and in the fog were sideswiped by a passing car. They lay there in the mud, their necks broken. I gave them conditional absolution as the ambulances drove up, but I was so distraught that I had a hard time remembering the "form" of the sacramental prayers, and kept repeating it. Death was there encountered in the black mud with the lights of the ambulance glancing on the rain.

As I went back and forth in the city to teach or left it to lecture or attend a meeting and then return I was always conscious of the immensity and complexity of Chicago that seemed to mirror the modern world that Vatican II was seeking to reorder. Often from a plane I marveled at how in the night the lights of Chicago spread out in a great grid of amber, green, red, blue and white stars. And as I walked in the Loop I marveled at the variety of people crowding the streets, the stores, on the 'L', in cars and trucks under the 'L'. At the same time I marveled at its many churches in so many styles of architecture and such different neighborhoods in which I knew Jesus was present in the Blessed Sacrament, and I was conscious that in our convent in River Forest we were constantly at prayer, a spiritual presence in this city where good and evil were so entangled.

ODE TO AN ANGEL OVER CHICAGO

Athwart the gray smoke you spread your snowy wings
And, as with easy strokes a swimmer turns his head
sinking his unflinching countenance and steady eyes
into the whirling water with one fast breath,
so quickly do you cleave downward
into the murk of this great city.
A bright hand raised in holy pity.
you give your benediction
to our sinning city.

Where the green waters scrape the stony shore,
where through the bridges' iron the thousands pour
and from the dank sublevel to the highest floor
you whisper softly in the rising roar.

On the isolate winter tundra of some park,
right past the cold statue and the emptying arch,
through mingled leaves, pebbles, and splintered bark
you guide the blinded down the dark.

At entrances where workers meet or scatter,
or in the restaurants glare and clatter,
or where blank faces smile, wince, chatter,
you gather the pieces when the glasses shatter.

In factories where the wheels keep turning
you note the heavy eyelids of the workers, yearning
for sleep, for dreams of vacation and blue skies,
when you for the moment close their weary eyes.

In the center of small rooms where two or one
have forgotten what we all have done,
until the renewal of the unseen sun,
you finish their work still unbegun.

You say the words not graven by steel on stone
and to each hidden in brick and iron
you speak alone.
You mark the way not made by city-planners anywhere

straight between the deep lagoon of death
and the speedway of despair.
You save the unshodden foot from bleeding and the so soft
hand,
and when the dance is ending you finish, flourishing
the last note of the band,
you end the love song of those that will not sing,
the loving of those who will not love nor live,
you give the gifts
we do not have to give.

Regent of Studies

In 1962, the year that Vatican II, after three years of expectant preparation, began, the routine between River Forest and Xavier was disrupted for me by my appointment as *Regent of Studies*, in charge of the Studium in River Forest and Dubuque and all the intellectual activities of the Province. This meant I would again have to restrict my teaching to Dominican students. I have also always felt rather guilty about this appointment. Fr. Sebastian Carlson, OP, had been the previous Regent and in the last period of his term he had decided we ought to try to get secular accreditation for the degrees our Pontifical Faculty offered. Under the provincialate of Fr. John Marr almost a third of the province's priestly personnel was teaching philosophy or theology, chiefly at women's colleges, but also at coeducational DePaul University in Chicago. At this time the degrees given by seminaries generally had no secular accreditation and this was a distinct embarrassment for Dominican priests seeking acceptance in university programs either as students or faculty, not only in secular schools but even in secularly accredited Catholic universities. Thus it would be the task of the next Regent to try to obtain this accreditation, then hardly imagined for a Catholic seminary.

The obvious candidate for Regent was Fr. Bertrand Mahoney (d. 1980), an erudite, loveable, but rather lackadaisical person. By passing what was called the examination *Ad Gradus* he had already qualified for the post-doctoral degree of *Master of Sacred Theology*. The *Ad Gradus* was an oral exam before a faculty board in which the candidate had to defend in the medieval scholastic manner and in Latin 100 thesis in philosophy and theology. To be appointed Regents of Study in the Order a friar was required to pass this exam and could then expect in due time to receive the S.T.M. Thus if Fr. Mahoney had received the appointment he could have expected to receive the degree for which he had labored to qualify.

I am too bookish a person, too impractical, really to be ambitious for an administrative job, yet I was also very much concerned to get my ideas realized. I was especially anxious that the project of the previous Regent, Fr. Sebastian Carlson, to obtain accreditation for our school would succeed and I was fearful that Fr. Mahoney would not push this difficult project through to success. I have always been ashamed of the way I made known these doubts to a number of the faculty since I think it may have influenced the decision to appoint me instead of Bert, since I believe it was for him a great disappointment. Later I will relate something of his long physical suffering and the holy patience and cheerfulness with which he bore it.

My choice in his place of course meant that I would have to abandon St. Xavier just as the Plan there was getting going, but over optimistically I thought that it was firmly planted and thus my worries for the future of our Province seemed the more immediate concern. Yet, unlike Fr. Mahoney, I had not yet passed the *Ad Gradus*. Since my proficiency in speaking Latin left much to be desired and I was given only two weeks to prepare, this requirement was no small embarrassment. But the examining board was very patient during my two hour ordeal and I passed. I did not, however, receive the S.T.M. until somewhat later.

My task as Regent was not simple, although it was on a very small scale compared to the presidency of most schools. First of all it meant a reorganization of our educational structure both in River Forest and Dubuque, since by that time the theological faculty of the school had been moved to St. Rose Priory in Dubuque, as I related in Chapter 10 above. Hence I had to lead the faculty in the "Self-Study" process that the North Central Accrediting Association requires. We decided to take a new name, no longer were we the "College of St. Rose" in Dubuque and "the College of St. Thomas Aquinas" in River Forest, but that of a single corporation, "The Aquinas Institute of Theology and Philosophy" which is now flourishing in St. Louis minus the "and Philosophy."[147]

Dubuque was then headed by a *Lector Primarius* who became Vice-President when I became President. At first, while Fr. Raphael Gillis was *Lector Primarius*, I attempted to supervise his decisions in Dubuque. When, however, Fr. Kevin O'Rourke, a big Irish-American canon lawyer, who was not easily bossed, became *Lector Primarius*, I decided to give him free reign in the theology department at Dubuque, while I gave most of my attention to the philosophy department in River Forest. I remained resident in River Forest, while traveling to Dubuque on occasion to see how things were going. We then had to shape the curriculum for both places, the credit and grading system, the administration and finances and our whole way of running the school more along the conventional lines of an American institution, rather than according to our former European model. Only in this way could we obtain accreditation and insure that our graduates had regular American degrees recognized everywhere.

The Self-Study for accreditation was done with much ado. In writing it I did my best to make it sound as if our small operation was highly sophisticated and I used all the expected educational jargon. Our Studium curriculum was, of course, based on an age-old European scholastic tradition and its terminology had to be translated for the examiners into modern educationese. The very last day the Report was due, since—a symbol of our marginality—we then had no Xerox machine, I had to take it to a copy shop to get it done on time. The examination by the people from North Central went smoothly enough both in River Forest and Dubuque and after a time I was called to a conference of the Association and told that we had been accredited although with a notation that we really were too small and isolated from a university to be conferring the doctorate in philosophy even if we had the status of a Pontifical Faculty, as we did. The telephone call I made to our provincial Fr. Marr to tell him that we were accredited was probably the greatest feeling of success in my whole life. I had been given a job to do, and I (with my guardian angel's vigorous prodding) had done it! Yet later I was to wonder whether this conformity to secular educational standards was entirely compatible with my curricular ideal.

This conformity also requited accreditation by the A.T.S. (Association of Theological Schools in United States and Canada). We were one of the first five Catholic schools to receive accreditation from that very Protestant body. Two recollections of it are vivid in my mind. The first was my anxiety on learning that the Catholic member of the examining team, who would have the job of making our odd school intelligible to the Protestant members, was the notoriously acerbic former Jesuit, the noted Biblical scholar John L.

McKenzie. Little interested in philosophy, he was silent during the River Forest exam, and as we rode on the fast train to Dubuque that evening I was very worried. Fr. Kevin O'Rourke, by then the *Lector Primarius*, took us to dinner, and to my terror began to talk about the trouble we were having with the Archbishop, a matter I will soon discuss. I thought we were finished. Then I perceived O'Rourke's subtle purpose (subtleness is not his ordinary mode). McKenzie, a rebel by temperament, did not at all like bishops, and he immediately got the impression we were fighting authority. From then on the exam went smoothly; on every questionable point he stoutly defended us.

At the annual meeting of the *American Association of Theological Schools* Aquinas and other four Catholic seminaries were the first officially received into membership and we heads of these schools sat on the platform. John Bennett, the noted President of *Union Theological Seminary* in New York, gave a speech about what a historic, ecumenical moment this was. Then when the formal vote to accept was over, the meeting turned to regular business, and the first intervention was from a president of some Protestant seminary who, quite oblivious of the incongruity, plaintively complained that, "Too many seminarians are getting scholarships and then marrying and having babies, costing our schools too much money." He then suggested the Association make a rule that before receiving scholarships all seminarians should promise to practice birth control! This initiated a very hot debate until Bennett in great ecumenical embarrassment rose to say, "Stop! Stop this discussion!"

My efforts at first were directed at trying to "modernize" our philosophy curriculum. By this I by no means intended to abandon our Thomism, instead I tried to recast it in a more authentic Thomist order and content, as we had been developing this in the St. Xavier Plan. The modernizing feature was that I asked each member of the faculty to become a specialist in some important modern philosopher and I added a couple of courses nicknamed "Couth Courses," to make our students less "uncouth" by broadening their knowledge of the liberal arts. These courses were taught by Fr. John Walsh, himself a University of Chicago graduate, who, I am very sorry to say, later left the Order. I also tried to bring in some outsiders to teach or lecture and I myself used to take groups of students to the glorious Chicago Art Institute and lecture them on art history. Fr. Anthony Schillaci, our metaphysics professor (he also was to leave the Order), showed a series of classical films on which he lectured. His talks were very good, but it became something of a joke among the students that in every film (he loved Fellini and Bergman films) he always found a "Christ Figure." The students, not surprisingly, were used to thinking of films simply as entertainment with neither metaphysical nor theological implications.

Yet in spite of these accreditations Aquinas Institute remained for many years a very closed institution: the only lay student who ever earned a M.A. degree from us during this time was a thin, pale, soon to be married, young man, Germain Grisez, who later, after begetting nine children and earning a doctorate in philosophy from the University of Chicago under Richard P. McKeon, became a tiger of a moral theologian, independent in his thought yet thoroughly loyal to the teaching of the Church.[148] Although I have been critical of his proposed revisions of Aquinas' moral theology, I sincerely thank him for major contributions to the post-Vatican II revision of moral theology and especially his leadership in defending Church teaching on marital and pro-life issues.[149]

Under the next Provincial, Fr. Gilbert Graham, in 1963 a new wing was built on to the south end of the River Forest Priory and completed in 1964. As explained earlier, because of the Great Depression the neo-gothic Priory had never been completed. Even our library was confined to one small room. As Fr. Kane ironically commented, we had always eaten in the dank, sunless basement and the reason for a new wing was neither to rise into daylight nor to get an adequate library, but only because the laundry machines in the basement were inadequate. To get room for new laundry machines, we had to move the refectory and to build a wing for a new refectory meant that we now also had a second floor for a library. Thus our priorities seem have been laundry first, food second, and books third!

While this was underway it was necessary temporarily to move the philosophy Studium to Dubuque for one year. When we finally returned Fr. J. B. S., OP, did a fine job in developing the new library in the spacious new wing on the south side of the old building. Thus the little old library room became my office, with beautiful wall-to-wall carpeting. I was so proud of that office with its orange carpet! It later became the office of the *Fra Angelico Art Foundation* run by Fr. Vincent Zarlenga, OP. The two Zarlenga brothers, Angelo and Vincenzio, came to our Province from Italy. Angelo was a sculptor and painter who fulfilled many commissions in Chicago and New

Orleans. After his death in 1986 his brother, a teacher, and a priest of Italian refinement and beautiful manners has carried on his promotion of the arts in the service of the Church, a form of preaching traditional in our Order. Thus it has produced Bl. Fra Angelico (d. 1455), Fra Bartolomeo de la Porta (d. 1517) who influenced Raphael, the noted Spanish artist Juan Mayno (d. 1646), and in the twentieth century the Frenchman Fr. Pierre M. A. Couturier who encouraged modern artists like Matisse to make works of religious inspiration.[150]

As Regent I inherited Fr. Carlson's secretary, Br. Joachim Thiel (d. 2004). It became a community joke that Brother Joachim, a short, stout, puffing, rather gnome-like person, was the real Regent, because he was much more practical than I, and bossed me around fearlessly. Again and again there came a day when he stomped his foot on my orange rug and said, "Sit down! I have got to talk to you! I can only do one thing at a time! Don't give me new things to do when I haven't finished the old things!" Not that he found me any worse to work for than my predecessor Sebastian Carlson. Joachim said that Carlson was always making notes to remind himself of things he had to do and then making other notes to remind himself to look for the previous notes, while in the end (according to Joachim) Joachim had to do it all.

After Br. Joachim, who had helped me so much to get started in my job, finally gave up on me, my next secretary was Br. Hugo Wreisner (d. 2001) who had entered the Order to be a priest, but suffered a seizure that was suspected to be epileptic. At that time epilepsy was an impediment to ordination (no doubt a relic of old popular notions that such seizures looked like demonic possession). Although Hugo, now recently deceased, at this time seemed free of any such problems, our superiors always felt it necessary to get a dispensation from Rome to ordain him, but could never get a physician who would supply Rome's demand for an unequivocal answer. Hugo therefore remained a Cooperator Brother for many years, but was finally after Vatican II ordained a priest. He was a slight, boyish looking fellow, the opposite in appearance of Joachim, and he handled the multiplicity of my demands with aplomb, supplying well for my lack of skill in the administrative manipulation of the people I had to deal with.

Hugo quickly got things in the Studium in order and became a benign political force in the House and Province. I am very grateful to both these Brothers for their patience with me. I also recall the personal support given my efforts by a confrere, Gerald Kroeger (d. 2004), a priest of great cheerfulness, who later served the Province as a campus minister and in other pastoral roles. I have always experienced that, if only I am open to friendship, Jesus, who in sorrow looked for the support of friends, sends me a friend to keep my head above life's stormy waters.

Since I was not only now President of Aquinas, but Regent of Studies for the whole Province, I also had responsibility for all the Province's teachers and had to visit every school in which our Fathers were employed to negotiate their contracts. We Dominicans had convinced many colleges that they should require a full program in theology for all their students. Many of these priests, as a matter of fact, were neither very interested, or gifted, or especially prepared to be teachers, particularly of young women. They did their best using Fr. Farrell's *Companion to the Summa* or Fr. Cunningham's *College Theology*, but I am afraid they largely provided nothing more than a simplified repetition of their own seminary course, rather than a real assimilation of Aquinas' thought reinterpreted in the light of their students' experience—quite contrary to Aquinas' own account of how we learn. In each college I met with the Sister President (in those days such Catholic women's colleges always had women in charge, not laymen as is often now the case) and heard whatever complaints or praise she had of our men. The Sisters asked for the retention or replacement of a Dominican Father as they wished, and we sent one, whomever we might have at hand, without prior interviews!

In these years my health was on the whole good, although I had recurrences of the troubles of my digestive system that had bothered me as a Dominican student. On one trip in 1965 with the Provincial, Fr. Graham, I mentioned some recent digestive trouble and he asked me to come with him when he had his own physical checkup in Boston at a well-known clinic, Baptist General. They found I had gallstones and recommended that I have the operation immediately right there. It was an old building, but excellent care. My chief nurse was a man, a Jamaican black, who was extraordinarily kind to me. While I was still not in good shape the Baptist chaplain breezed into my room and urged me to attend chapel service. Although I told him I was a Roman Catholic priest and in a couple of days would be able to say Mass, he continued to insist that I come to chapel, though I refused. When later in Houston I was teaching students in Clinical

Pastoral Education this was my favorite example of a mistaken attempt at pastoral care.

It took me some time to feel well again and I spent a week or so at Dover, Massachusetts where at that time the Dominican clerics in philosophy for the New York Province lived. Sickness for me has always been a time for more fruitful meditation than I have usually found in "retreats" which seem to me to be too artificial. Yet in these years I also found the long winters in Chicago extremely depressing, as the traffic becomes so difficult and darkness comes so early.

ODE TO SNOW IN DARKNESS

There is nothing I know so strange as snow in darkness
new fallen or frozen, then melting now,
in the black shadow
of a sun-bleak row of houses
or in the blackness of a zero night.
I cannot see it but I know how delicate how light
it falls,
how soft
it lies,
gentle as the Virgin's eyes,
the merciful snow,
the all-forgiving snow.

I know how all things in the dark are strange
how the dead are blind, how in love
the eyes are covered with a mist of heat
how in darkness the sound of feet
and the sound of time and of thunder die away
how faces dwindle in the dark, how hands
in love or deadly hate move there unseen,
also how the rat, the wheel, the wave
move, and in the grave the industrious worm,
all move and turn, how in the dark burn
all the constant fires of destined change
how in the darkness even you, my friend,
are strange,
how warmth is strange, how death is strange,
and unforeseen the snow,
mercifully blank.

Yes, what is so strange as white snow in the dark,
falling and freezing or melting,
or lying so soft,
the final layer of the night
there in the dark so glimmering white?
I cannot see it here in this blank room
yet I know how white
it blows
how bright it falls
how smooth
it lies,
under tropic skies on mountain peaks,
on deserts, graves, on the Atlantic's waves
the barren snow,
the arctic snow.

Yet, in Chicago's sooty night,
in gracious park or city blight,
no transformation I know
can be more strange,
than the way a recent snow
gleaming so virgin white,
unmarred by print or track—
can change
(just as when, decreed by fate,
gentle love turns cruel hate)
to sooted black.

Chapter 12 - Vatican II Polarization

The Ambiguous "Spirit of Vatican II"

There were more serious reasons to be depressed that winter, however, than the ugly snow. By 1968 our Pontifical Faculty of Philosophy in River Forest was faced with declining numbers of incoming novices and the fact that as a result of our accreditation and Vatican II changes, we could no longer receive students into the Order until they had completed their bachelor's degree, instead of, as formerly, with only two years of college. This imperiled our status as a Pontifical Faculty of Philosophy of which at that time we were so proud. One very difficult evening I put this problem to the faculty at a meeting for a decision as to whether we should eventually move philosophy to Dubuque where it had been for a year during the building process in River Forest. It was very hard for the faculty to face this necessary decision. My mentor Fr. Humbert Kane looked gray, panic-stricken, since his life's work had been invested in the Pontifical Faculty.

Fr. Humbert Crilly (d. 1969), one of our younger professors, also looked sick and put his head down in his arms on his desk. The next morning he woke me very early to say that all night he had suffered from chest pains. I drove him immediately to the hospital and found he was having a very serious heart attack. He survived only for a couple of anxious and depressed years.

As I have already related, I had been filled with great joy when John XXIII announced the calling of Vatican II. Ever since my conversion I had been acutely aware how hampered in her mission the Church was (and is) by the burden of certain historical baggage in the face of our rapidly changing and secularizing age and the urgent need for ecumenical unity as a witness to the Gospel. While I was thoroughly convinced, as I have said so often, of the wisdom of the Church's choice of Aquinas as a guide in clarifying modern confusions, I believed even then that Thomism was not well understood or taught, nor had it been brought into a vital relation with modern science and culture. I hoped that we Dominicans would play a major role in the Council and its implementation.

In our Chicago Province the knowledge of what was taking place in the Council from the approval of the *Decree on the Liturgy* in 1963 to that of *The Church in the Modern World* at the end of 1965 was largely dependent on the lively but tendentiously liberal reports of

"Xavier Rynne" in *The New Yorker*.[151] Yet everything in the Council's decrees as they were published delighted me. While at first I did not like the idea of abandoning the Latin liturgy, once it was decided I felt happy about it. It seemed to open the way to a much better appreciation of Catholic worship. I had always been distressed by the difficulty of so many of our Fathers in appreciating the Psalms of the Divine Office that we chanted daily.

Vernacular liturgy certainly made it easier to keep attention on the words of Mass and Office, yet it was sad to find the Gregorian chant and the beauty of many Latin texts fade into memories. Vatican II seemed to me a very solid statement of the Catholic tradition, freed of some of its less happy historical accretions, richly expressed in language full of Christian hope. With the accession of Paul VI, too, we seemed to have a pope much influenced by the Thomism of Jacques Maritain and Yves Congar. I was thrilled to attend the symposium "The Theological Task Confronting the Church Today," held in Chicago at St. Xavier College, March 31-April 3, 1966 when Vatican II had just closed, at which several of the outstanding theologians of the Council, including Karl Rahner, Yves Congar, and Hans Küng spoke. Another read an English translation of Rahner's paper for him, while Rahner himself sat on the stage saying his Rosary.

I also heard Hans Küng lecture to an enormous crowd in the convention center, McCormick Place. He looked charming but his talk was Herr Professor boring and the audience, especially a group of high school students on the front row, got restless, until, very incidentally, Küng remarked that perhaps after all failure to attend Mass was not a mortal sin. At that the high schoolers broke into wild applause.

Yet these winds of change let in by the Council began to unleash unforeseen forces. Vocations to our Province had been in considerable part the fruit of our Fenwick High School in Oak Park and the efforts of teaching Dominican Sisters who in their schools vigorously promoted Dominican vocations. An important contribution had also been made by Fr. Richard Butler, OP, (d. 1988) a good friend of mine, who promoted vocations through well-designed publications and friendly correspondence, and later as a campus minister. He was at one time National President of the Newman Association.

Richard, whom I always found very simpatico, was a tight-lipped, puritanical Bostonian, a very proper native of Salem. While living in Rome he became a friend of the famous philosopher George Santayana, but then to Santayana's displeasure, wrote a book critical of this mentor's sophisticated naturalism.[152] Butler had entered the Order from The Catholic University of America along with his friend Gilbert Graham, who later became our Provincial, and whose personality was in amusing contrast to Richard's. Gilbert had created the lead role, later made famous on Broadway and in film by James Cagney, of George M. Cohan in *Yankee Doodle Dandy*, premiered at Catholic University under the directorship of Gilbert Hartke, OP. Graham was the other convivial type of Bostonian who became a friend of the famous Mayor of Chicago, Richard M. Daley, and of the Speaker of the House of Congress, John McCormick.

Friendship, like romance, is sweet, but can turn sour. Up to this time I had personally known only two Dominican priests, my contemporaries, who had left the priesthood, and this for them meant excommunication unless they returned penitent. One, in the class previous to mine had been assigned a teaching job for which, though very bright, he was not fitted and in his discouragement had taken up gambling. He finally left the priesthood and for some years supported himself by driving a taxi. The other departure was of a priest, who even as a Dominican student was always talking about women, but nobody thought it serious until he deserted priestly and religious life to marry. Although over the years our Province has had to remove some priests involved in child sex abuse and compensate their victims, this was not a major reason for these post-Vatican-II departures.

During my years in the Dominican Order its members have generally seemed to me to be quite well chosen. Yet Fr. Walker as Student Master complained to me, then his assistant, that when after World War II vocations became plentiful, our provincial, Fr. Hughes, repeatedly accepted for profession certain candidates whom he, Walker, could not approve. Walker was afraid that we were taking men "against whom," in his words, "there is nothing negative, but for whom also there is little positive." He felt we had too many Dominicans whose motivation was tepid. In any case with the decision of Paul VI to dispense men from the priesthood and allow them to marry, suddenly an exodus began. For me the greatest sorrow of my life has been to see Dominicans who solemnly vowed their life *usque ad mortem*, "even until death" to the Order and to the Church leave the Order and the priesthood. I would be no moral theologian if I did not realize the complexities of such decisions and the great mistake of passing any judgment on the motives of priests requesting dispensation. Almost all of those who departed seem to have married honorably, cared for their children and wives, and been successful in the professional world, making a good use of the extensive education and discipline they received while in the Order. Some of them have taken up work in the service of the Church.

Most of these ex-Dominican priests whom I still know seem to look back on their days in the Order with gratitude and even nostalgia. Only a very few seem to be bitter. We have occasionally invited them to meet together with us for auld lang syne. Among the very gifted priests whose departure from the priesthood and the Order especially affected me because they were or had been members of our faculty were Michael Faaron and Anthony Shillaci, who were excellent metaphysicians, and the latter expert in the esthetics of film and the media, Daniel Hunter, an enthusiastic promoter of social justice, John Thomas Bonee, a logician, and Augustine Rock, an editor and publisher. Faaron, Rock, and Bonee are now dead; the others have had successful secular careers, but none, in my opinion, have had anything like the influence they would have had as Dominican priests. A far as I know, each made up his own mind and announced his decisions to depart without any real possibility of the rest of us having the opportunity to help them remain with us.

Yet a solemn vow and ordination to the priesthood are in my understanding eternally binding. The Christian Community can in mercy, as Paul VI decided (and apparently John XXIII seriously considered but finally declined not to do), to dispense men from the particular obligations of their vows and the exercise of their priesthood, but in the view of Aquinas (and the Church documents avoid explicitly repudiating his arguments) they remain obliged to God for their self-dedication and somehow will be called by him to account for it. To us the words of Scripture apply, "You are a priest forever, according to the order of Melchisedech" (Heb 5:6, quoting Ps 110: 4).

I would not, however, leave the impression that in this post-Vatican II period with all its questionable experiments, that Dominican priests were no longer devoted to the liturgy. We experimented with it in order to make it more meaningful and less routine. The celebration of the great feasts of the year in religious communities, especially Easter and Christmas, remained and remains rich with wonderful symbols. Throughout the liturgical changes such feasts continued to support our life in River Forest and never for most of us lost their traditional meaning. I personally continued to say the Rosary in which these feasts are constantly renewed, and some of my poems illustrate how the use of one's imagination can feed meditation. Here are two Christmas poems that turn on the Third Joyful Mystery, the Nativity.

THE WISE MEN

The splendor grew on the trembling beard
and shivered on the crown.
With a sigh of pain the old king
knelt down.

It shone upon the ebony brow
gashed with long-healed brands
of sword and fire.
The warrior king
folded his hands.

It blazed across the breathing lips,
flamed in the hair,
it flared across his hazel eyes.
The boy king, bright eyes in his black face,
just stared.

The young king offered his crown
holding it out with a hoarse shout.
The old king proffered his golden cup,
weeping with his years.
The black king frowned as he held up
his scepter like a cross
and said no word,
and shed no tears,
but in the night heard a great wind howl
and in the tree by the gate an owl
moaning at the sudden light.
He heard the bell-toned footfalls of bright
seraphic feet, on the packed courtyard sands,
yet imagined them the rattle of sleet,
and clenched his steel mailed hands.

The splendor fades, the old king shivers with cold
and limps way in darkness with a clinking
of heavy gold.

The radiance fails, scatters. The warrior turns,
in his hard fist the hilt of his sword
freezes and burns.

The night comes. Bitterly and slow
the tall boy king walks blindly
through deep, untraveled snow.

In the windy cattle pen,
between Mary's warming breasts,
the kingly Child nuzzles, yawns
and sleeps again,
as Joseph readies for their flight
into that alien Egyptian night.

ADORATION OF THE CHILD

The desert and the vastness of their expectation
and their increasing age-old sorrow
at each step, and the burning of the soul
approaching an unseen fire,
the trackless desert and their dry desire,
with a weeping dew on their cold lips,
nothing but the journey to fill tomorrow.

None of them slept at night but all dreamed
now that at least it seemed
they should reach the end, see, touch
the goal of all that journey and their watch.
They wandered among the dunes, so far, so on,
led by one so urgent star.

The plain and the quiet beasts, the usual night in view,
when the shepherds woke and gazed,
expecting nothing new,

only the plain, the stirring beasts, the night,
the chilling dew.

This is emptiness and I must wait
when the night is very late
and feel a feeble yet eternal wonder
watching in my heart and mind,
feeling cold, so blind.

The kings, the shepherds
all of them found the babe
cozy in the cave.
Alas!
So sweet, so small
on Mary's breast,
the child who had no home still found no rest.
Discovered, therefore, forced to flee
with Mary, Joseph and the ass
into Egypt hastily,
the greatest, emptiest desert of them all...

Yet here within our void, O Child, O Hidden Light!
We once again discover the fallacy of night!

Departures

How to explain the departures from the priesthood recounted in the last chapter? Why did they follow Vatican II which was supposed to renew the Church? When the seriousness of the situation in our own Chicago Dominican Province became apparent, it was proposed by some friars that a "self-study" of the province be conducted, as had already been done for the secular accreditation of our Studium.. Our provincial, then Fr. Marr consented, although Fr. Peter O'Brien, who had been the first provincial of the province, thought we should not have done this without first asking the Master of the Order for permission. Since I had the experience of directing the accreditation self-study of the Studium, I was put in charge and prepared the lengthy questionnaire, which I asked the well-known former director of the National Public Opinion Research Center, Fr. Andrew Greeley, to criticize. He thought it was a good instrument for what we were attempting to do. The final report of the research was published as *Self-Study of St. Albert's Dominican Province, 1967.*

Later I was criticized by some of our friars for this self-study as having contributed by it to the upheaval in the Province. Undoubtedly it was unsettling to learn certain things about our membership and administration. Since my life was so involved in the situation it revealed, I quote below from the conclusion of the Study the "weaknesses" and "strengths" that it revealed that were fully justified by the research statistics, which, however, I will not here repeat. Our Province has since taken a good many steps to improve these weaknesses, with considerable success in some areas.

What has this study revealed about ourselves?

It seems to show that the principal WEAKNESSES of the Province are:

1. We tend to think too much in terms of ourselves, our limited United States middle-class backgrounds, our Dominican "family" and its problems, instead of thinking in terms of *the needs of the people we serve.* Hence our life and work lack a clear, specific, unifying purpose, which would be to assist the Church today to develop an effective Ministry of the Word.

2. We tend to operate through *organizational structures* no longer adequate to so large a Province carrying on such diversified and specialized work. As a result our communications are poor, the Provincial is overburdened, the local communities are timid about initiative, some sections of the Province feel neglected and individuals suspect they are being used to fill jobs, rather than being helped to develop spiritually and apostolically.

3. We tend to be content with a mediocre communal and personal spiritual life because we have been timid and apathetic about adapting the basic means found in our form of life to our practical circumstances, not in order escape them, but to make them meaningful and effective. These weaknesses seem to lie at the root of the two most serious signs of spiritual sickness that appear in our Province:

- A considerable number of our men feel that they have failed to accomplish anything worthwhile for God or neighbor, and they feel that is partly due to the fact that the community, in spite of its good will, was not able to provide them with help they needed to overcome their own weaknesses.

- A considerable number of our men do not feel strongly their obligation to sacrifice for the community in order that it may be renewed along with the Church.

This study also seems to show the principal STRENGTHS of the Province today are:

1. *Our specific work of preaching,* or the ministry of the Word, far from being obsolete, is very much needed today. Furthermore, the basic features of the Dominican way of life: practice of the evangelical counsels, liturgical prayer, study of God's Word, genuine brotherhood—these remain vital sources of an effective apostolic ministry and can be made truly practical in today's world.

2. *Our theological heritage and spirituality,* from St. Dominic, St. Thomas, St. Catherine, and others are not dead-ends, but lead us into the mainstream of the tradition of the Church, if pursued in the broad spirit of their authors, open to all truth.

3. Our Province already has *houses in most of the important urban centers of mid-America* and is engaged for the most part in apostolic activities which, if properly focused, can be profitable *for the ministry of the Word* and it has already a considerable portion of *well-trained younger men.*

The report then went on to make specific recommendations under the headings of Administration, Community Life, Apostolate, Formation, and Continuous Renewal and Self-Study. Thus the level of dissatisfaction was not high, but it was real. Although only about 9% regretted entering the Order, 25% of the priests rated their classmates as "mediocre or performing below their potential," 11% were in work that "they believe the Order should discontinue," and only 57% thought their "energies and abilities are being fully used." Yet about 75% thought themselves "well-adjusted," "found their work satisfying" and to be "considered by those who know them well to be growing personally and performing effectively." There was evidence of lack of confidence in our leadership and uncertainty about where the province was going. I was especially disturbed to see how the spiritual discipline we had tried to inculcate in the Studium tended to weaken in the ministry. For example only about half of the priests were continuing to make a regular meditation as they had done for their eight years before ordination.

The meetings that were held locally to prepare for the questionnaire and to discuss its results opened the door to a great deal of expression of various kinds of dissatisfaction, and finally led to a meeting in Chicago attended by a large group, predominantly of younger men. The provincial Fr. Gilbert Graham, whose background I described earlier, did not forbid this meeting, but he held aloof from it, and some of the most radically discontented made numerous demands for change. In all this I was sympathetic with the younger and more liberal men, not so much because I agreed with all they had to say—which I didn't—but because I thought they needed to be heard. That meeting finished in deep gloom and confusion. Yet the exodus from our Order was not Fr. Graham's fault and was comparable to that taking place in other religious congregations in the Church in the United States as shown below by the statistics compiled for the Provincial Chapter of 1973 covering the worst period of exodus, 1969-73.

If all the foregoing seems very depressing, I should add that through this whole crisis the province was continuing to do much good work, as is evident from the fact that in 1951 we began a Nigerian Mission which is now an independent Province with a great church in Lagos and a flourishing theological school in Ibadan. Although an attempt to cooperate with the Canadian Dominicans in a Japanese mission did not work out, we also in 1959 founded a Bolivian mission which will soon become an independent province. I will describe my experiences on visiting these two missions later.

In 1969 the Province (omitting our Nigerian and Bolivian missions) had 304 priests and during that time 42 left (8 of these left without dispensations), about 10 a year. At last count in 2004 it has only 198 professed members, U.S. 171 priests and 19 priests in our Bolivian mission, the rest not yet ordained. This year 6 novices made simple profession, but there were only two ordinations to priesthood. Though these figures seem shocking, it must be remembered that in the period of the French Revolution the Order declined by perhaps 90%; while at present the membership of the Order of Preachers worldwide is present in some 83 countries and has increasing vocations. The other three United State provinces are doing much the same.

I am convinced that decline in priestly and religious vocations is not to be blamed so much on Vatican II as principally on the general social changes in Europe and United States and especially in the latter on the fact that during this period so many Catholics, formerly of recent immigrant and working class background moved into the middle class with wide occupational options. The great exodus from priesthood soon after the Council, which has now declined, has usually been explained as due to the emotional immaturity of the young men raised in the confines of seminaries in an excessively cerebral manner. Already at the time of World War II, a Master of the Order, Father Gillet wrote an encyclical warning of the dangers of what he called "hothouse formation."

Yet in my opinion emotional immaturity was not the main factor but rather the increasing secularism of our times. These priests had been raised in our secularizing culture and they quickly reverted to a secularized world when Vatican II exposed the Order's counter-cultural life, to which they had been only superficially conformed. The effect of this renewed contact with secularism was violent because the change was violent and only time can uncover a successful *modus vivendi.* Could this change have been less painfully negotiated? I believe it could have been if we in leadership positions had been able to anticipate its coming and could have engaged in discussion better to discriminate what was to be changed from what was to be maintained. In the case of our Order in the United States there were obstacles to this discriminating change.

First of all, the rigidity of areas of responsibility and of "categories" of personnel that I described in the last chapter prevented us from cooperating to meet the challenges of the Council. Thus as Regent I was in charge of the academic formation of young men yet was forbidden to intervene in their religious formation because it was under the exclusive jurisdiction of the Student Master. We almost never sat down together to talk about what was happening. The Provincial too became isolated from other officials. One of the best changes came about when "formation" was entrusted to a "formation team" which included all who were responsible for any phase of the process.

Second, American Dominicans were intellectually isolated from the theological discussions going on in Europe and which fed into the Council. We were Thomists who knew little of the anti-scholastic, patristic, phenomenological, existential trends, etc., of European Catholicism. When we met them, we did not comprehend them and often unconsciously succumbed to their more negative pressures.

I must add, however, that there were efforts made to be more open to contemporary thought. The Albertus Magnus Lyceum had anticipated this need and among the Lyceum founders, Fr. Jude Nogar, was especially sensitive to it, as his widely-read book *The Lord of the Absurd*,[153] which deals with existentialism and atheism, testifies. In the philosophy faculty in River Forest, I asked each of the professors to specialize in some modern author, and in the theological faculty in Dubuque similar efforts were made by Christopher Kiesling (d. 1986) with his work on Tillich, Thomas O'Meara with his studies on Schelling, Paul Tillich and Karl Rahner,[154] Ralph Powell on Heidegger,[155] John Sullivan with his The *Prophets of the West* on the philosophy of history,[156] as well as his work on the philosophy of language with Mortimer Adler's Center for Philosophical research in Chicago, and Donald Goergen with his works on Teilhard de Chardin and Christology.[157] Among my students Edward Cleary has written important works on religious sociology[158] and Richard Woods[159] on religious psychology and spirituality. The faculty of Aquinas also turned attention to patristic studies, as in Sullivan's The *Image of God in St. Augustine* [160] and Francis Cunningham's *The Indwelling of the Trinity*.[161] This last work is a major contribution to American theology that unhappily has received little attention. Our province can also be proud of the many works on spirituality by Jordan Aumann.[162] Also later, Fr. Benedict Viviano,[163] formerly of the École Biblique in Jerusalem and now of the University of Friburg, Switzerland became a distinguished Scripture scholar.

Yet the unhappy consequence of this transition from an excessive conservatism to the open "spirit of Vatican II" was that during the 60s and 70s we American Dominicans, and the Central Province in particular, simply let go of a great many features of our Dominican heritage indiscriminately and without due reflection. One morning we would wake up and find that some traditional practice had just disappeared. To take a characteristic example, one of the most cherished Dominican traditions is devotion to the Holy Rosary of the Blessed Virgin Mary practiced in the Order and preached to the people at least since the fifteenth century. Our Constitutions, even as revised after the Council, require each of us to recite a third of the Rosary every day and formerly this recitation was in common. Some loved it; others found it a tedious but accepted exercise. The Self-Study had revealed that once out of the Studium, not a few neglected it. One day it was announced in River Forest without preliminary study or discussion in the community and without any reason given, that from now on recitation of the Rosary would be "in private" which for many seemed to mean that it was now obsolete. A couple of years later a young priest came to me and in some embarrassment asked for a book that would give him the names of the "mysteries" of the Rosary. Soon after his ordination he had returned home to attend a funeral and at the wake had been asked to lead the customary Rosary and was greatly embarrassed to admit he did not know how!

In our communal recital of the Office of the Hours, that—thank God!—was retained, the praying with the body by bows and gestures for which St. Dominic was celebrated as illustrated in his *Nine Ways of Prayer* were much reduced. In the same way it became less usual to wear the Dominican habit, then even clerical dress, and many other symbolic practices declined or became obsolete, although some have now been restored—again, thank God—especially in the novitiate and studentate. The New York and Oakland Provinces better conserved many of these traditions than did the Chicago Province. No doubt we Middle Westerners dropped some of these practices for good reasons, but I am afraid we dropped others for little, wrong, or no reason at all.

More serious was the notion, hardly justified in the Vatican documents, but somehow thought to be according to its "Spirit," that the liturgy was now to become "creative," freed of the rubrics and open to the invention of the celebrant. If some of the creations had not been so comic, one might weep over the liturgical extravagances we indulged in. Once Fr Hum Kane muttered under his breath to me as we went in procession to celebrate the Eucharist not in the chapel but in the refectory, "Whom the gods would destroy, they first make mad!" In fact it seemed that in those days Mass was said in almost every room of the Priory except the chapel. And when it was said in the chapel, there might be dancing and, yes, balloons! Fr.

Matthew Fox,[164] later so publicized for his "creation-centered theology" and his "rave Masses" and who after his dismissal from the Order styles himself a "non-denominational priest," outraged the community by playing as Vespers service, evening prayer, an interminable recording of Mahler's *Das Lied von der Erde*. Others also engaged in no less arbitrary and annoying tinkerings with the liturgy. An anthropologist once attended a Dominican Eucharist, at which I also was present, held in the chapel of the Dominican Sisters of Adrian, MI, in which the opening processional hymns was "Prepare Ye the Way of the Lord" from *Godspell* and there was dancing and general whooping it up. He said to me, "You people are higher than some groups I have seen who were on drugs."

These creative efforts were, I admit, never without reverence and real piety and some were actually quite beautiful and devotional experiences but they were too often purely personal rather than appropriate to the public and traditional character of real liturgy. I have since heard conservative Catholics denounce such unrubrical manipulations of the liturgy as gross disobedience to Church law bordering on heresy. In fact at that time we sincerely thought we were conforming to Vatican II and subsequent documents that seemed to encourage variation and experimentation in liturgical practice.

I myself, with my artistic interests, went along with these experiments, although I was often not at all comfortable with the results. I engaged in a few experiments of my own. For example, Hugo Wreisner, my secretary and then a Cooperator Brother, became an enthusiast for the simplicity of Japanese art and arranged in his cell what the Japanese call a tokanoma, a little bench with a carefully chosen flower-vase or a scroll. Hugo studied the Tea Ceremony which, as he learned, had been formalized long ago by a Japanese gentleman who was a Catholic. He suggested that we might sometimes have Mass in his cell in the manner of this ceremony with its emphasis on simplicity and humility, seated on mats, and for the chalice a simple Japanese ceramic tea bowl. These were quiet, meditative Eucharists which, I must admit, were refreshing after the noise and clamor of some of our guitar Masses in the Chapel.

Another instance of my own "creativity," was when I was asked by one of our Dominican ex-priests, living in New Mexico, to baptize his infant son. This priest had left the Order and married a former Sister civilly because he felt mandatory celibacy for priests was unjust. I told them that with the permission of their local pastor I would baptize their child but could not offer them Holy Communion. The ceremony, however, was not to be in a church but in a private home which, in the style of the southwest, was built around a swimming pool. I celebrated the Eucharist at the pool's edge. When time for baptism came, I removed my vestment and habit, and in swimming trunks entered the pool and baptized the child by immersion, then dried myself and resumed my vestments. My idea at the time was the importance of baptism by immersion as a more complete symbol than by simple pouring. What impression this odd performance made on the laity that were in attendance I don't know. Considering my scrupulous concern for sacramental validity, my openness to liturgical experimentation was paradoxical. The contrast between priestly vestments and swimming trunks—it was a sign of the times.

Another set of incidents typifies this for me. While still Regent, but for the sake of a little change of pace, I accepted a request from the seminary of the archdiocese of Chicago, St. Mary's of the Lake in Mundelein, IL, to teach for a semester. At one time St. Mary's had an all Jesuit faculty, but then this too was changing. I stayed with what was left of the Jesuit community there, and enjoyed their hospitality while noting how different a Jesuit community is from a Dominican one. The Jesuits seemed much more a group of disciplined individuals than a family.

The Dominance of Psychology

One day at the seminary I had a discussion with one student about mandatory celibacy and he expressed surprise that I favored it. "Our professors," he said "tell us that by the time we are ordained, celibacy will be optional." In fact, not long afterwards several of the younger faculty of the Seminary, selected to be spiritual directors for the students, left and married. What was dominating formation was current psychology, especially, I believe, the writings of the priest psychologist, Eugene Kennedy, who dwelt constantly on the theme of the emotional immaturity of priests.[165] He himself eventually married. From his writings many were drawing, perhaps mistakenly, the inference that genital sexual experience is necessary for full emotional maturity.

The comic aspect of all this psychological emphasis became clear to me once when my Prior, Fr. Francis Shaw (d. 1990), came to pick me up to return to River Forest for the weekend, as I regularly did that semester. He found me in the Bishop's Residence, built by Cardinal Mundelein at the seminary on its extensive campus center- ing on a lake north of Chicago. The Cardinal's dream was that this institution would be not only his seminary but a great university. On the shore of the lake he built a large Georgian style residence where he held official functions. In its interior was a grand recep- tion room patterned after those traditional in Rome for Cardinals. It was oval, with dark red damask walls and gilt framings with golden cherubs winging from the ceiling. At one end was a gilded chair like a throne and the floor had a rich oriental rug. At the end opposite the throne were glass doors.

I asked Fr. Shaw to take a peep into this grand throne room. What he saw was that the throne had been pushed into a corner; the oriental rug rolled back, and seated in a circle on the bare floor was the seminary faculty in informal garb. In the center of the circle were two men wrestling. I said to Fr. Shaw, "That is the Rector and the Academic Dean of the Seminary." What was going on was a "group-dynamic" session being held for the faculty that weekend with two psychologists as facilitators. I had participated in previous sessions, and was able to explain to my Prior that in the self- revelations encouraged by the facilitators tensions between Rector and Dean had surfaced and the two were trying to resolve their feel- ings of rivalry by this physical struggle. Under our feet we felt Cardinal Mundelein rolling over in his grave! Yet he is reported to have said that he wanted his seminary to be a "West Point for Priests," so, since today psychology has penetrated even the mili- tary, perhaps he would have looked on this more tolerantly than from the ceiling the golden cherubs seemed to do.

Chapter 13 - Psychology and Sexuality

Science and Sexuality

The question of the psychological maturity of priests, if it was not the major cause of priests leaving, was still a central question for discussion at this time. As Thomists we had understood how much a priest needs such maturity, but we thought of it in terms of the moral virtues that imbue the human passions for pleasure and aggression with temperance (moderation) and fortitude (courage). We believed that these are supernaturally given in baptism to every Christian, but to operate fully require constant practice under the control of reason, both our own reason and that of the community in which we live. Modern psychology actually says much the same thing but without acknowledging its supernatural dimensions. Certainly I was not unaware of modern psychology since in high school I had read Freud's *The Interpretation of Dreams* and was always interested in such phenomena and in my own subjectivity.

In the sixties a brilliant younger member of our theological faculty in Dubuque, Fr. D., who taught moral theology asked for a sabbatical year at the Menninger Clinic in Topeka, KS, a world famous center of modern psychotherapy,[166] and I readily arranged this, since I believed that moral theology should make full use of modern psychology. Fr. Kane had told me that he had sensed when he taught Fr. D. that although he got high marks, he was not really understanding Aquinas because he was unable to break out of the mindset he had acquired as a science major in college. I did not realize how serious a problem this was for Fr. D, nor did I know that this young priest himself had a deep psychological problem from family conflicts that also involved his sexual identity. Hence the clinical acuity and sophistication he met at Menninger's quite overwhelmed him, and he seems to have made little effort to interpret what he was learning in Thomistic or theological terms. I later heard that for him Thomism compared with Freud was "a bunch of crap." It is only in recent years the value of Freudianism has come under scrutiny as dubiously scientific.

On D.'s return from Menninger's his influence over the students became very powerful and he gave them a great deal of counseling time, eventually to the great discomfort of Fr. T., the Student Master, a piously conservative priest, for whom the "changes" were unintelligible. He, therefore, tried to resign, but Fr. Graham, the provincial, retained him because he thought him a stabilizing presence. In fact the stress of this situation eventually led T. to leave the Order and the priesthood. After his wife's death he has returned to the priesthood but not to the Order. He had always been rigidly faithful to attendance at the liturgy, but is reported to have said, "When they [Vatican II] changed the Office, I lost that, and when they began concelebration I lost my Mass. So what is there left for me?"

I began to hear rumors that this priest trained at Menninger's no longer considered masturbation to be a sin. I am afraid that I too timidly asked Fr. D. whether this was what he was teaching, and believed his rather equivocal denial. On a visitation by Fr. Aniceto Fernández (1962-1974, d. 1981), then Master of the Order, he remarked to me that Fr. D. seemed to have rather "advanced" ideas, but told me not to remove him from his teaching in the Studium, but to "keep an eye on him." Unfortunately my residence in River Forest, and my policy of leaving the theology program to its own officials, made this difficult, and I now very much regret that I did not look into the whole matter more realistically. As for Fr D., I will later report the tragic outcome of his story.

One reason for my failure to understand fully the danger of Fr. D.'s influence was that I had found one of his projects very helpful for our faculty. He had suggested that our faculty, or at least all who were willing, should attend a four-day seminar in 1965 at Menninger's similar to the ones the Clinic regularly offered to business executives. All but two or three of the faculty joined in the trip and it was, we all thought, a very successful experience. The lectures on interpersonal relations in organizations were very expert, and our opening dynamic session, which certainly now seems commonplace, was for us a "revelatory moment." The psychologist asked our faculty to discuss whatever problems that we were experiencing in our dealings with students. As this went on, the faculty divided into our usual two factions who differed in their diagnoses of what was wrong with our students. As we argued, the psychologist brought us to a halt and asked each of us to describe the "feelings" we were experiencing. It turned out of course that what underlay the various rational arguments we were opposing to each other, was really not what was wrong with the students at all but what we faculty thought was wrong with each other. That was, I believe, a true insight and has had a deep influence in the subsequent history of our province. Although St. Thomas Aquinas provided us with a very profound analysis of human emotions and their influence in our lives, we Dominicans have traditionally been, I think, unduly rationalistic. In our efforts to attain intellectual clarity and precision, we have suppressed the perception of our own emotional life in its subjectivity.

Turn to the Subject

Indeed, I believe, it is this greater appreciation of the subjective aspects of human knowing that has been the major contribution of modernity to classical thought. In human cognition the subjective aspect of knowledge is secondary to the objective aspect, but it is perilous to neglect it. Aquinas clearly recognized its existence, since he said, "Whatever is received is received according to the mode of the recipient," but gave it only cursory attention. From Descartes on, "the turn to the subject" became the focus of modern philosophy, unfortunately to the neglect of the primacy of objective truth that was handed over to the "hard" sciences of nature.[167] It is a feature of post-modernity that this distinction between the hard and soft sciences is breaking down, but again unfortunately not in such a way as to lead to their proper balance but only to a still further exaggeration of the role of subjectivity, with a resultant increase of irrationalism, relativism, and skepticism. Unfortunately Dominican Thomists have largely ignored the positive aspects of this "turn to the subject" in philosophy, although Jacques Maritain made some interesting forays into it. A modern revision of Thomism will have to incorporate these topics, without losing Aquinas' realistic epistemology as, I am afraid, so-called Transcendental Thomists have done only by succumbing to Kantian idealism.[168] I think there is a good basis in Aquinas' own thought for assimilating these modern insights, but the task is complex. For myself I have found music, friendship, and prayer as ways to let feelings rise to the surface and be refined.

MUSIC AND SILENCE

Pauses in music have nothing to say,
nothing at all,
yet say well
all there is to say.

I tell all in song.

Now you know.
I reveal all through silence
and in silence you know
I cannot lie...
Reply
then only in music
or in silence.

You comment on my tune by your silence.
Its quality is true applause.
I would criticize your silence by my music,
yet I pause...
Have I heard... really?

Let me question by a melody that will not rest
until by silent smiling you have guessed
the end of melody,
silent friend,
is stiller silence.

Yet the attention to the subjective side of human knowing needs to be fitted into the proof, earlier mentioned that the human soul is a non-material prime mover, that unlike a pure spirit is dependent on a body to supply its intelligence and free will with the data of the senses. This means that "psychology," a term not invented as the name of a discipline until the sixteenth century is, in fact, a borderline research, the bodily aspect of which is the ultimate achievement of natural science and the spiritual aspect of it an area pertaining to metaphysics and to theology.[169]

Reconciliation

In the wake of Vatican II we seemed to live in continual turmoil and increasing polarization between conservatives and liberals, yet our Province was very fortunate in having a succession of peace-making provincials. Fr. Collins, a large, comfortable, conservative friar, whose name, "Clement," reflected his mercy and forbearance to progressive projects with which he did not himself agree. He was a real healer, though his own poor health did not permit him to push forward. Fr. Gerard Cleator is a charismatic, whose simple and direct style of preaching so evidently based on personal experience I always found personally very helpful, did much to encourage growth in spirituality. A Texan, Fr. Damian Fandal was elected by a conservative majority, weary of what they regarded as the reluctance of the two previous provincials to retrench on Vatican II innovations. Yet, very much the southern gentleman and a person of great charm and humor, he took a very middle-of-the-road approach. It was he who ultimately decided that Aquinas Institute should move from Dubuque. During his time in office, however, as he was preparing to visit the Nigerian mission, he suffered brain damage from an aneurysm that could have proved fatal. He recovered well, but suffered some loss of short-term memory and after returning to the University of Dallas where he had been Dean, died in 1994. His successors, first Fr. Donald Goergen, Fr. Edward Ruane, and Fr. Mascari, all three former professors of theology, have proved very able administrators, although Fr. Goergen had to deal with the notorious and painful case of Fr. Matthew Fox, whose name has already been mentioned, but concerning whom I will write later.

In regards to my own needs and concerns I have always found my superiors very considerate of my concerns and, in my opinion on the whole our province has been fortunate in its provincials. My experience has shown me both the strength and weakness of the elective system St. Dominic set up. Although it is well known that the New York Province suffered for some time from the political manipulations of one provincial in his concern to retain his the office term after term; this has been an exception in the United States. The weakness, however, is our Dominican democracy is that majorities tend to elect fine men but ones who "will not rock the boat," known more for their kindliness than their vision.

At this time it was not only Dominicans who were theologically liberal that felt they must leave, but also some conservatives came the same conclusion. One said, "I took vows to the Order as it was traditionally. Since that Order is gone, I no longer feel bound by them." Perhaps more typical was a state of confusion. Thus Fr. R. when he decided to leave, said to me, "My problem is that my mind is liberal, and my feelings conservative."

This Fr. R., had worked very hard to build up our library but by nature was an interior decorator. He had made the friendship of a Jewish couple who ran a furniture store. They offered to help their friend, Fr. R., raise some needed funds for the library by holding an art exhibit and sale, a method common in Chicago synagogues. When I heard of this project I had visions of horrible furniture-store kitsch, which might disgrace the school. I insisted on seeing the paintings in advance and this made it necessary for R. and myself to go to New York to the wholesalers where his advisers had suggested he obtain the works for the exhibit. I will never forget the enormous rooms of that New York store with rows and rows of paintings and other objets d'art, produced wholesale by hack artists. We were shown landscapes with Alps and cottages done with a palette knife and "painterly" brush strokes, and were assured by the salesman that they had these masterpieces in several predominant colors to match any color-scheme desired, a blue, pink or purple Alps, with snow on the cottage or without. I accepted only what I found not too appalling, but, alas! the exhibit as a fundraiser was indeed too appalling. Catholics came and looked but found the prices of a real "hand-painted" painting too high. They were used to cheap reproductions. Toward the end of the sale our furniture-store couple frantically lowered the prices, but we still made no sales.

I should add that Fr. R. was always much concerned about keeping the library well-cleaned. Once he was taken by a friend on a vacation to England. When he returned I asked him what he had seen that impressed him most. "Westminster Abbey," he replied. Since I my self had been rather displeased by its clutter of monuments, I asked him what about it had impressed him, and he answered, "How well they keep all those monuments dusted."

When Fr. Gilbert Graham, whom I have already described, was elected provincial and I was elected member of the four man *Diffinitorium* or executive committee of the provincial chapter, Graham proposed that the whole River Forest building be renovated since the plumbing was in bad condition. We chose as a new Student Master Fr. M., a former missionary from Bolivia, because we wanted a very well-balanced "regular guy" to replace the former Student Master whom some had regarded as a "spiritual creep." Unfortunately, Fr. M. who was indeed a "regular guy" had also on the missions developed radical ideas about religious life and tried to go even further than the rest of us had gone in dropping traditional forms. Meeting resistance, he finally resigned and married.

The Sexual Celibate

What do I myself think of priestly celibacy? The recent scandal concerning sexual abuse of minors is the worst part of the problem, but the violation of priestly celibacy by adult relations heterosexual and homosexual has also risen again and again in the Church although priestly celibacy goes back to Jesus himself and St. Paul. Of course celibacy, is not optional for those who choose the consecrated life based on the vows of celibacy, poverty, and obedience. Yet somehow soon after Vatican II the notion got around that religious, as well as diocesan priests, were suffering injustice because they were not allowed to marry. As I have mentioned, the psychological notion that "maturity" could not be obtained without sexual relationships was very seductive. Fr. Donald Goergen, later, as I have mentioned, an able Provincial of our province, wrote a very popular book, *The Sexual Celibate*[170] which attempted to deal with this problem by distinguishing "sexuality" from "genitality." Don argued that "sexual" relationships need not be "genital" because we are sexual beings all of whose relationships are colored by our sexuality. I felt that this way of discussing the question was somewhat naïve, since it seemed to defend celibacy by saying that it was no sacrifice. On visitation by the then Master of the Order I told him that I was worried about the influence this book was having and he had it reviewed by a couple of theologians who did not agree with my fears. Yet celibacy is a great sacrifice as any priest who reaches middle life cannot fail to experience when he sees the beauty of Christian family life and finds himself alone. Of course Don, a very spiritual and contemplative priest never intended to deny this but I still think it would have been better to be very clear on this point: those who vow themselves to religious or priestly celibacy should face this sacrifice, and if they choose to make it, do so unambiguously and realistically. I am afraid that a failure to emphasize this in priestly education during the 60s to 80s has played an important part the recent crisis over sexual abuse by priests, because this failure led to a situation in which, as one bishop has remarked about his own downfall, "At that time we were experimenting."

Such theories in so far as they were saying that a male celibate is still a male with feelings who also needs non-genital friendships with persons of either sex do not contradict Dominican spirituality. The friendship of Bl. Jordan of Saxony and Bl. Diana d'Angelo; or between St. Catherine of Siena and Bl. Raymund of Capua are famous in the history of our Order. Yet unfortunately a good deal of this talk after the Council was dangerously ambiguous and some priests found that these friendships soon became what was later called in pop psychological jargon "codependency" and ultimately genital.

BAREFOOT JOURNEYING

In my years as a confessor of seminarians our practice was to tell a brother who confessed masturbation that if he had not been free from this sin for a year before taking final vows, he should leave the Order. In general I know that during their eight student years, when hormones must have been at their most raging, almost all seminarians achieved this absolute chastity and indeed the great majority practiced it from the time of their simple vows. My hearing of priestly confessions, of course, was not so extensive, but I, at least, did not often encounter a priest with a real problem of being true to his vows. In middle life, however, the problems of celibacy sometimes revive and I know that at this time the notion that masturbation is not a serious sin spread among some confessors encouraged by the views of Fr. Charles Curran, then a professor at the Catholic University of America.[171]

Among such theologians the notion that homosexual relations are not necessarily sinful was not far behind. In my opinion, although I cannot prove it, it was a lapse into this kind of ambiguity about the meaning of celibacy that was a major cause of the abandonment of religious and priestly life. In fact the teaching of the Catholic Church has never been the least ambiguous on this score even in those times and places that practical laxity was tolerated. Religious and priestly vows mean exactly what they say, no orgasm or mental consent to such fantasies or any relationship that occasions such internal or external activities. We cannot close our ears to the words of the compassionate Lord,

> Everyone who looks at a woman with lust has already committed adultery with her in his heart. If your right eye causes you to sin, tear it out and throw it away. It is better for you to lose one of your members than to have your whole body thrown into Gehenna," (Mt 5:28-29).

I believe this ambiguity about chastity arose because older religious simply could not imagine that honest and decent men would engage in genital sexuality without admitting that it was seriously contrary to their vows. Yet I believe that quite a few otherwise honest and decent priests were led into temptation by this doublespeak atmosphere which seemed to have psychological and even theological warrant. I am convinced that celibacy can be lived faithfully by all who take vows if the religious community and the

Church maintain unambiguous support of such fidelity and the practice of the spiritual disciplines. Yet history tells us that, when doubts about moral standards spread in a community, individuals quickly rationalize their lapses and their attitudes and bad example spreads through the community, with the grossest hypocrisy as a result. *Corruptio optimi pessima*, the corruption of the best is the worst.

Mandatory celibacy for all priests is as old as the Church, but historians dispute about when it was made mandatory and the Church has been repeatedly forced to renew its mandatory character. The Eastern Church after 600 A.D. relaxed it for all but bishops, while today the Roman Catholic Church has dispensed from it for married Protestant clergy converted to the Church and married permanent deacons. In the early Church, certainly from 300 on, although the call to ordained priesthood was often to already married men, they were then required to abstain from sexual activity.[172]

"Return to the Spirit of the Founder"

Along with these difficulties that followed Vatican II was the great event of the revision of our Dominican Constitutions in conformity to the Council's urging for religious orders to "return to the spirit of the founder" rather than as previous Councils had urged "return to strict observance." I have already related how the River Forest Community and Faculty of Philosophy had to move to Dubuque while the new wing was being added to the River Forest Priory. When we returned in 1967, the renovated priory was already being prepared for the international General Chapter of the Order of 1968 that was to deal with this historic revision of the Constitutions of the Order.[173] This took place during the last two and for me exceptionally difficult years of my term as Regent and school President.

During the General Chapter the studentate was again disrupted by the need to make room for the capitulars and the students were moved into the former Bishop Quarter School (an unusual Catholic school run by the Adrian Dominican Sisters on a military plan!). I moved with the students and one day running downstairs wearing my Dominican habit—I was still very proper about that—to answer the doorbell I caught my foot in the Rosary (that is part of that garb) and badly sprained one knee, so that it pained me during most of the year.

Fr. Benjamin Russell who was then Student Master was concerned (and I heartily agreed with him) that our students should become more social minded. Since this was the time of civil rights demonstrations that sometimes included block burnings in Chicago, interest in social justice was high. I had arranged that in summers some students might have ministry experiences in the inner city. Fr. Russell himself took a group of students down to see the anti-Vietnam protests outside the Democratic Convention and several were beaten by Mayor Daly's cops. Benjamin was later to be both a successful pastor and an effective teacher and administrator at Aquinas Institute in St. Louis.

Not long after that when I came home from Xavier one day, I was excitedly told, "Come look at the TV! Chicago is on fire again!" and I saw that whole blocks on the West Side were going up in smoke. My political interests had been in abeyance for a long time, since I was so occupied with other matters. Moreover, I was moving in an all white world, except when I had occasion to move about the city out of my usual routes and came to recognize again how much of Chicago was African-American. On the Chicago 'L' I often thought how handsome many of the young African-Americans were and how out of place they seemed in Chicago's snowy winters. I had taught blacks one summer in New Orleans, but I did not really know many of them personally until I went to live in Houston and in St. Louis.

BLACK IS BEAUTIFUL

With dark faces they trudge in the snow
to wait at the bus stop in a dark row.

Once under blossoms purple and white they stood,
listening to bright parrots in a dense wood.

Now by the corner they shiver and wait,
asking each other why the bus is late.

Dark gleaming backs in the waterfall,
ugly coats hunched by the ugly wall,

Their color was not made for this bitter cold
but the garden of Paradise green and gold.

The social "conscientization" of our Dominican students which I attempted at this time was not really a success, because our very middle-class clerics were so shocked by their new realization of our country's social problems that they left the seminary. Some of those who exited are now still engaged in social work. What I did not know was that with this new freedom of movement some of our students were also visiting gay bars and other dubious inner-city hangouts on the excuse that they needed to see "real" life. In 1968 the Dominican Students in the Province of Paris are said to have locked their prior out of the priory and hung red flags from the windows. Our Dominican students never went that far, but we certainly did feel the winds of the notorious 60s blowing through our monastic windows.

The Dominican Constitutions that were to be revised had been first written in the General Chapters of 1221 and 1222 and bear the mark of the organizing genius of St. Dominic. They had remained intact for 700 years but had become encrusted with later and now obsolete legislation and were further deformed by the attempt to harmonize them with the Code of Canon Law as revised in 1917. Vatican II, however, called on all the religious Orders to review their constitutions. Questionnaires were sent out to all our provinces for suggestions how to revise ours. Fortunately modern research, especially that done by Fr. M.-H. Vicaire, OP, author of the standard biography of St. Dominic,[174] had put us on solid historical ground. The revised Constitutions produced by the extraordinary Chapter of River Forest in 1968 are in my opinion a masterpiece.[175] The "Fundamental Constitution" with which it begins states the basic principles of our Order that cannot be changed, and the rest states the application of these principles to modern situations. It centers our life about four pillars: the preaching mission, community life, prayer, and study. Study should deepen prayer, be shared among the community, and enrich the preaching mission.

The actual conduct of the Chapter, as observed by me from outside, had many comic moments. The delegates from many nations were culturally diverse and at various stages of post-Vatican II change. The very first problem that arose concerned the seating in our refectory. Fr. Shaw our Prior, went to Fr. Aniceto Fernández, the white-haired, serene Master of the Order, and made clear to him that the traditional seating at table and service according to "order of religion from time of reception of the habit" was now totally impractical for us. Instead the capitulars would have to serve themselves cafeteria style. Fr. Fernández, a man of great prudence and humility, agreed and set the tone at the next meal by himself going first in the cafeteria-line to the astonishment of many of the more conservative capitulars. Business was conducted not in Latin as formerly but with simultaneous translation. Secret voting was no longer by dropping black or white beans in a ballot box but by pushing a button. Some of the learned delegates had trouble pushing the button they intended!

Meanwhile, the students who continued to have classes in the Priory, although living at Bishop Quarters School had to go back and forth in their new found freedom. At this time there was controversy in the media over whether seminarians in order "to attain psychological maturity" should continue to date girls. Getting wind of this some of our students, themselves only a couple of years or so out of high school, had been making friends with the senior girls at nearby Trinity High School run by Dominican Sisters. Some of these teenaged girls would show up in the public halls at the Priory after school to see their friends. What the capitulars thought of the frequent presence of these girls in our Priory corridors I never learned. At last the Priory returned to normal, but even then normal was strange since it was at that very time that the experimental liturgies reached their height of creativity.

Perhaps the best illustration of the permissiveness of that time was the fact that my secretary, Hugo Wreisner, who was an exceptionally talented pianist and singer of popular ballads, and who, as I have explained, for reasons of health could not then be ordained a priest, therefore obtained permission from his good friend, our Prior, to work as a singer in a "piano bar" in a well-known Chicago hotel. He there carried on a "ministry" to well-soaked patrons who often confided their life stories to him. Later Hugo left the Order because he could not find a community to live in, but later returned, after making a living for himself for some time with his minstrelsy, and finally was permitted to be ordained. His innocence in all this was patent. He wanted nothing except to be a Dominican, but somehow the Order did not know what to do with him.

Seminary Renewal

Thus after the Albertus Magnus Lyceum's attempt to develop a curriculum of studies that would overcome the modern separation of hardheaded science and the softheaded humanities and then apply it practically to Catholic theological studies in a way that would meet secular certification, I became involved in a wider educational scene. In the wake of Vatican II a worldwide movement was going on to renew seminaries that were receiving criticism from every side and a *Midwest Association of Catholic Seminaries* was formed of which I was elected the first chairman. Its purpose was to promote the exchange of ideas among the hard-pressed seminaries, religious and diocesan, and it was centered in Chicago. It facilitated the accreditation of seminaries by the ecumenical *Association of Theological Schools* that I have already described. I was also a member of the Board of the fifteen schools in the *Chicago Theological Association*. In the Chicago area one of our big projects was to form a cluster of Catholic seminaries centered on the University of Chicago.

The Passionist Fathers were the initiators of this idea that eventually resulted in the *Chicago Theological Union*,[176] which, as I will explain later, Aquinas Institute ultimately decided not to join. The original project was more ambitious than what was actually achieved, since it was hoped that this union would include the prestigious Divinity School of the University of Chicago, thus giving the Union both an ecumenical character and a university affiliation. We also hoped that the Archdiocesan Seminary, St. Mary's of the Lake, would join. If it had done so the Divinity School of the University of Chicago might very well have capitulated. But Cardinal Cody was suspicious of the whole deal, although the property of St. Thomas the Apostle—the church of my baptism near the university—was available and the sale to developers of the huge and remote property of St. Mary's of the Lake would have helped greatly with diocesan finances.

The Cardinal's method of escaping the necessity of moving the seminary (against what, I suspect, was his own will) was characteristically adroit. Those were the days when students had to be consulted on all matters concerning their formation lest they cry out to high heaven at this breach of injustice. Though the faculty of the seminary had approved the move, the Cardinal, with scrupulous attention to democratic due process, insisted on a vote by the seminarians. They, more concerned about the uncertainties such a move would raise for them in their remaining years at the institution than for the future interests of the archdiocese, promptly voted "No" and let the Cardinal off the hook.

The Dean of the University Divinity School at a ceremony for the dedication of the new Lutheran seminary, built on the edge of the University with great hope of a formal relation to the University, made it very clear that, since the University remembered only too well its difficulties with its affiliated Protestant seminaries that it had no interest in any future Catholic unions. I still believe that this was a great opportunity lost for all concerned.

This involvement in midwest seminaries led to my being invited to participate in a committee of the National Catholic Bishops Conference (NCCB), whose able and kindly executive secretary was Fr. T. William Coyle, C.S.S.R., to prepare the first edition of *The Program for Priestly Formation for the United States*.[177] The first shock I had in working on this priestly formation program was how many bishops, despite the fact that the future of their dioceses depends on the preparation of future priests, tend to leave this matter largely to the rectors of their seminaries. Now that there are many fewer seminaries available, the bishops tend to send their priestly candidates to those schools whose discipline resembles what they themselves received. Sometimes they intervene when it comes to their attention that dissenting views are presently being taught their students, but otherwise they still seem to be too busy to pay much attention to what the students are actually learning.

This was amusingly illustrated for me when one bishop asked me for counsel on an impending accreditation visit of his seminary. I told him that the visitation team would certainly question him about the reasons for his appointment of a priest as his liaison with the seminary rector instead of dealing directly himself with the rector. The real reason, embarrassing to admit, was that the bishop found direct contact with this rector, who was a religious not a diocesan priest, too irritating. His Excellency therefore asked me to draft the response he might give to explain this awkward situation, and I did so as diplomatically as I could. I had already pointed out to the accrediting commission that it was an improper "conflict of interest" for me, a part-time faulty member, to also serve on the visitating team, but to save money on transportation they insisted on this arrangement. When the bishop and the administration of the seminary met with the visiting team, the anticipated question came up and the bishop promptly read his prepared reply. Then unfortunately the head visitor probed a bit further and asked the bishop about some detail of this reply. The bishop, a blunt, utterly frank man, turned to me and said, "Benny, you explain that point, you wrote it."

Of course a bishop ought not micromanage the educational processes of a school, but it seems to me he ought to take the time to have a very concrete idea of what his clerics are learning. Bishops should make known to seminaries in more detail than the present "Program of Formation" provides what they believe their future coworkers will need to know in order to meet the pastoral needs of the diocese. Seminary rectors or faculties do not always understand such issues. True, the modern bishop is an exceedingly overworked person; besides his liturgical and preaching responsibilities, in most dioceses he is CEO of an elaborate variety of services, for which he must also find money. In addition to all these duties, he probably serves on committees of the NCCB and hence is constantly traveling to meetings or preparing for them. Today there are many opportunities for bishops to keep abreast of theological developments through workshops conducted by leading theologians and other specialists. All this takes time and has contributed to the apparent negligence of bishops in sex abuse of children and young people by priests that has recently caused such scandal. Yet what is more important for bishops if they are to avoid such scandals and other tragic failures in ministry than recruiting and properly preparing future priests?

In serving on this curriculum committee I was concerned especially with the philosophy requirements, a section much revised in a subsequent edition. Looking back on this I have my regrets. I was familiar with the strong three-year program which our Dominican students then received, but I recognized it was too narrowly scholastic and to be in keeping with Vatican II directives needed to be more open to current thought and more closely integrated with the theology curriculum. I felt that diocesan seminary programs had always been somewhat weak even in scholastic philosophy, let alone in current thought, but that some middle course would have to be found in view of the given length of the seminary program. Thus I was very open to various compromises, and felt that the seminaries could be trusted to work out their own programs if they were provided broad guidelines. I have since realized that this hope was much too optimistic.

Today I would fight for the development of a detailed syllabus that would increase the chances of a cleric receiving the fundamentals of the Catholic philosophical tradition and an appreciation of its relations, positive and negative, to secular philosophies, as well as helping them to be open to the thought of other than western cultures. I would give special attention to a close integration between philosophy and the theological courses, since too often students fail to grasp the relevance of what they learn in philosophy to their pastoral work. Hence the seminary teacher of philosophy should consistently and constantly demonstrate how philosophy and especially natural science assists in understanding theological texts and applying revealed doctrines to current situations and controversies.

As I have indicated, the location of the philosophy faculty in River Forest had now become problematic. Our house council in 1968 urged that the River Forest properties be sold and the philosophy wing of Aquinas Institute be moved to Dubuque with the theology wing. Negotiations for the sale of the land and building began with the Lutheran Concordia Teachers' College, which was just across the street from us and with which we had some ecumenical cooperation. The reaction to this proposal in the Province was, however, very negative, and the faculty of Fenwick High School, which depended on the property for its athletic playing fields, strongly objected and proposed that instead they close their St. Dominic's Priory at the school (thus giving them more office space there) and move into the House of Studies which received the new name, Priory of St. Dominic and St. Thomas Aquinas. I had voted for the sale of properties. In the euphoria of Vatican II I believed that the ownership of large properties has always hindered the flexibility of the Order in changing the focus of its ministry to meet changing times, and therefore was contrary to the "spirit of the founder." St. Dominic was very angry when he saw the first priory with a second story being built. I am still of this mind, although I admit that such ownership is an important factor in giving stability, visibility, and continuity to a religious community and St. Dominic's Priory continued for some years to function as a conference center. Fortunately, today in 2002 a sale of these properties to nearby Dominican University (formerly Rosary College), which is now a flourishing co-educa-tional institution sponsored by the Sinsinawa Dominican Sisters, has been successfully completed. The athletic fields will be leased to Fenwick High School.

A major feature of these years when I was Regent of Studies and the Vatican II changes were beginning was the frequent travel by plane demanded by my necessary participation in many meetings all over the country and abroad. An experience that characterizes our age is spending many wearisome hours in airports in all the uncertainties of weathers and schedules. I wonder who all those

people are and where they are going and why. One of my poems was
the result of seeing such a stranger.

CHINAMAN AT THE AIRPORT

His large blank face between the heavy shoulders
shows he is not uneasy at the sun's rising.

In the hovering glory he sits silent
looking more than ever like an idol smiling
in the golden descent through layers of morning,
his face glowing yellow he waits calmly,
his hands laid humbly together and his eyes
without staring expect some oddity,
ready for awe.

He then turned eyes earthward
and beheld on the ground a shadow
racing and increasing, converging to the plane,
the plane's shadow blue and glittering
on the thawing snow of the long runway.
The shadow nearing, his slit eyes following.

"The shadow of myself proves
that behind me a sun is waiting,
the shadow of myself approaching means
that almost I am again on earth,
firm, the dizziness of height is passing
and my destiny at last is here."

He from the East is no more bewildered,
 seeing now this West in broad daylight.
China was big enough and old enough
to have made room for every explanation
of all things.

In New York he is interested most
by that small child
who saw him at the gate and cried.
"Why do you cry, small boy?"

"Because you don't look like
my papa!"

China can explain all things, but no easy explanation
can really answer that question:
"Why do you cry, small boy?"

Mother

While my work required not only many tiresome meetings in
the United States but also abroad, I found times of relaxation. First,
but not always so relaxing, were my visits to my mother living with
my brother and his wife. By 1952, my brother was still following the
oil business, but he and his wife had moved from Lake Charles to
Bellaire, a suburb of Houston. Houston was booming as a result of
oil and also of the availability of air-conditioning that made its semitropical climate livable, but the downtown area was still small-town.
By 1958 my brother and his wife had moved again, this time to
Lafayette in western Louisiana, a town where, my brother said the
natives never really accepted the newcomer oil people.

Happily, in this new home my mother enjoyed easy access to the
parish Church that had a very lively pastor, a former Newman chaplain and later a bishop, who unfortunately became alcoholic, but
who at the time we knew him was a kindly "live wire." One of his
stories I recall was how he once thought he had an inspiration on
how to teach his school children the liturgical meaning of the Ember
Days, originally set aside to bless the fields. Since he could not visit
every home to bless the gardens, he asked the children to bring to
Mass on an Ember Day a shoebox of dirt from their backyards so he
could bless all the gardens at once. Now imagine the beautiful new
church he had just built filled with kids, each with a brimming shoebox of dirt spilling out over everything!

On my visits to my mother in Lafayette I enjoyed that small
town and our drives into the surrounding country, with its extensive rice and sugar cane fields. I have not saved my mother's weekly
letters to me, but by chance after her death I found one in her very
clear hand to my aunt Vivian Kammerer, that for some reason my
mother never mailed. I quote it here in order to show what her life
in Lafayette was like and give some firsthand impression of her personality:

Dear Viv,

I thought about you and Neodesha on Memorial day and wondered if any of the other relatives were in to see you. Harriet [a
niece, daughter of another aunt] sent me a card some days ago
telling about being locked in the cemetery. I surely appreciate
her writing to me and you also, for I know you both have a great
deal on your minds.

We had a sprinkle of rain Memorial day, but only sprinkles are
what we have nowadays. I would like to see a nice rain again
and not a tornado, or flood. The electrical storms have been bad
here this spring. Just a few days ago a little girl was killed by
lightning while wading in a ditch. I think I have told you that the
streets in many of the subdivisions are blacktopped and ditches
are on both sides along the front yards and no sidewalks. Water
stands in the ditches most of the time and the children play in
the dirty water a good deal and especially if it rains they put on
bathing suits and stay outdoors.

I am always reminded of Chink [my Dad]. During a thunder
storm he would never allow the boys to take a bath and one
evening especially, Dick was so mad because he was going out
that evening and was late, waiting to get dressed, on account of
the lightning.

Helen [Dick's wife] is mad this morning. While she was away
yesterday the new neighbors back of us were searching for the
stakes that mark the boundary lines of their yard and they
practically dug out a shrub on the corner of our backyard. The
surveyors drove metal pegs in the ground on all four corners of
the lots, so everyone would know the boundaries of their yards.
I suppose the new people are thinking of having their back yard
fenced. They have two small children.

They had their troubles moving. The painters who were to
decorate the inside of the house painted the rooms the wrong
colors and had to do the work all over again, which delayed
their moving. The moving van was a day late unloading the
furniture, and the city men, owing to the holiday, delayed turning on the water, etc. The neighbors seem rather fussy besides. I
probably will never know them.

Owing to union rules, Dick had a holiday Friday and he and
Helen mowed the yard. The grass was so badly injured during
the winter that the yard was bare, so they spread a commercial

fertilizer on it and it was surely good for the weeds. The lawn mower was completely exhausted and so were they. Saturday they went fishing to get rested. They happened on a school of fish and caught over 50, but could only keep 25 according to the law on size. They came home about 2 o'clock [in the afternoon] on account of a rain shower.

The neighbors keep the fish for them because we do not have a deep freeze. To get rid of the accumulation of fish, the neighbors gave a fish fry Sunday evening. I didn't go, but cooked my own supper, a fancy dish of sliced potatoes and onions boiled together, and watched television shows that Dick and Helen don't like.

Winston is over in Hammond, Louisiana, this week. That is in the eastern part of the state and we will not see him, but he may telephone (I hope). He may be sent to Washington, DC next week. I don't like so much traveling for him.

I received a letter from Mamie Krudwig [the Catholic woman who befriended Mother in Neodesha after she became a Catholic]. She said she was going to Colorado to visit the next day. She and you are the ones to get about.

Helen took me to the doctor last week and he said I am as usual. My cough is about the same, but the asthma is bothering more. It must be something in the air. The people in New Orleans are worse. They have so much trouble all the time, the doctors say it might be dust from loading and unloading the grain from the huge elevators there.

Our television is given over to giving interviews with movie stars the last few days. Betty Davis and Joan Crawford and others are in Baton Rouge making a movie. The governor gave a reception for them and the citizens are going wild. It is all very interesting and so amazing what can be done now to keep people looking young. I read that a method has been discovered to make people look 10 years younger.

Did you get to visit Harry? [my uncle, a Christian Science "reader" in Wichita, but in bad health]. I hope you did, or will. Although I know it is a hard trip for you all, I hope you can go.

My love to you all,
Bert

Sisters in Habits

Among the more memorable places I visited was Annapolis, MD, with its colonial buildings and several times I went to Atlantic City for meetings of the *American Catholic Educational Association*. Atlantic City meant Sisters then still in all kinds of habits walking up and down the boardwalk, the ocean gulls screeching above them and old Jewish people from New York lying on deck chairs wrapped up to their eyes in blankets "to take the sun." I also flew to Denver and the Rockies and in 1958 to Albuquerque, New Mexico, where I first saw the southwestern desert and drove to the top of Mt. Sandía ("Watermelon," so named because at sunset it looks like a pink slice of melon) and out to the west to Acoma Pueblo on top of a mesa, its antiquity contradicted by a TV antenna on every adobe house.

Again in 1961 I was in Washington, DC, to lecture on philosophy in a summer program at The Catholic University of America and to see Mount Vernon with its magnificent view over the wide, gleaming Potomac. I was in Washington again the next year to attend a workshop given by the Jewish Anti-Defamation Society on the anti-Semitic influence of Christian religion textbooks. All expenses were paid at the Mayflower Hotel where we had steak for breakfast, lunch, and dinner. In 1963 I visited St. Louis or rather Clayton, MO as a consultant on theological education to the Danforth Foundation. The staff of the Foundation at that time seemed all to be graduates of Yale Divinity and after dinner one played the piano and the others sang old Protestant hymns, while the Catholic Bishop of Albany, also a member of the committee, reciprocated with musical comedy numbers from his college days. The beauty of his tenor made me wonder about the validity of his episcopal consecration, but since I have met one or two other bishops that could also sing.

I walked the Gettysburg battlefield with its countless monuments in companionship with two Dominican historians, Frs. James Weisheipl and Fred Hinnebusch, who insisted on reading the inscriptions on every monument. In 1964 as my mother's letter had requested, I went to Wichita, KS to see my Uncle Harry, the Christian Science reader who was dying pretty much alone, and then proceeded to Denver, Santa Fe, and Taos. Next I went with Fr. Richard Butler, OP (whose criticism of George Santayana I mentioned before), to Salem, MA, his home town and visited the House of Seven Gables, and later also Plymouth, Concord, and Boston, where on Beacon Hill I saw houses of the first families marked by their windows whose glass, imported in those early years from England, had been stained purple by the heat of a shipboard fire. Later that year I gave a workshop on the liberal arts in Asheville, NC, and saw the wonderful Biltmore Estate and the Blue Ridge Mountains with their rhododendrons in massive bloom. We also drove to the historic festival of the Indians at Cherokee, of special interest to me because my home town, Blackwell, OK, is in the Cherokee Strip to which many of these Native Americans were cruelly transported on the Trail of Tears. I also gave a workshop for diocesan priests at Conception Abbey, MO, a depressing affair because some of the priests were unhappy about having to attend and the weather was dismal. Another workshop for priests and religious teachers that I gave in Salina, KS, went much more happily.

In 1965 I visited Toronto, the University of Dallas at Irving, TX, founded by conservative Catholic laymen; the interesting art school of Cranston at Bloomfield Hills, MI, which had a marvelous antique Italian Paschal Candlestick carved with all of salvation history; and in 1966 I lectured in London, Ontario. The Dominican chaplain, a Canadian himself and a former student of mine invited me there and he took me to an English tea at the home of a grand dame who owned the biggest brewery in Canada.

Interesting trips that I can't quite date were a retreat I gave at St. Leo's Abbey, Dade City, FL, where I enjoyed the beautiful orange groves growing in sand. I visited the fascinating early Catholic region of Kentucky where the Dominican Order, Fathers, Brothers, and Sisters began in the United States at St. Rose, and went on to nearby Bardstown with its old Cathedral, and then to nearby Gethsemane Abbey where, when I was still at Notre Dame, I had once made a retreat along with Thomas Merton, at that time a layman preparing to enter as a monk. On that trip I also visited the motherhouses of the Sisters of Charity of Nazareth and the Sisters of Loretto, both founded in the early days.

Oil Business

Shortly before my first trip to Rome I got some bad news from my family. My brother had supposed when he went to work for the Sun Oil Company in Lafayette that his employment was safe for the rest of his life, although he had given up hope of further advance in the company. The oil business in the United States in those years, however, underwent a remarkable transformation. The major oil pools so far discovered in United States territory (other than Alaska) were reaching depletion and these companies began to find it cheaper to buy oil abroad in South America and elsewhere than to explore for it. Oil exploration is a risky business since about 90% of the wells drilled turn out to be dry. As a result of this situation all the oil companies began to downsize their geological departments at the same time and few positions as geologists remained available. Moreover, for even these few positions young geologists fresh out of school and up-to-date on new technology were preferred. Field experience, which formerly was considered very important in this type of work, now counted for nothing. Thus my brother, faced with this midlife disaster, was forced to retire from his profession but without a sufficient pension to support his wife and my mother.

Dick decided, therefore, to take what savings he had and buy a motel on Lake Greeson, a lake owned by the Federal Government, about fifty miles west of Hot Springs, AK, in the tiny village of Daisy. Fishing had always been the favorite recreation of Dick and Helen and in former years they had spent their vacations at this five room motel in the Arkansas backwoods amid the western foothills of the Ozarks. My mother had to move with them, although she silently disapproved of what she thought an unwise decision and one that took her away from the possibility of Sunday Mass which she had faithfully attended ever since her conversion. Dick and Helen, without additional help, ran the little motel, with all its backbreaking daily work of cleaning and readying the rooms. Moreover, the tourist traffic at this remote resort was seasonal and never heavy and hence none too profitable. Nevertheless, in what free time they had, Dick and Helen were able to fish on a very lovely, well-stocked expanse of water between high pine-covered ridges, peaceful when not too disturbed by the tourists' motorboats and the water-skiers.

They had a few friendly neighbors, especially a strange native woman named Jody, a real hillbilly, and a prominent member of the little Free Will Baptist Church which had just undergone a schism over the Sunday School books sent them by their national headquarters. Jody who was at best semiliterate opposed the use of these books for theological reasons; why I was never able to ascertain. Another neighbor was a Catholic woman and her husband invalided by emphysema. She was a sweet old lady who showed the greatest respect to me as a priest, even though I did not wear clericals while visiting there. Yet another elderly couple, Frank and Lily, spent almost all their time fishing on the lake. She was a simple little woman of no education, while he was a remarkably intelligent old man who had traveled and read a good deal, and was a delightful conversationalist.

I remember also visiting a retired couple who had built a little cottage in the woods with a large picture window opening onto their backyard with a bird-pool. We sat for an hour watching all kinds of birds come and go, as the couple also evidently spent much of their days. Almost all the inhabitants in the area were older people living on "welfare."

My mother, accustomed as she had been to small town living, nevertheless found this all very primitive. Since Helen still excluded her from any share in domestic activity, Mother spent most of the day in her little room reading, emerging only in the evenings to watch TV with Dick and Helen who were exhausted from the day's work and whose choice in programs was not to her taste. My visits at Christmas and summer vacation were a consolation to her, especially because I read to her, and because each day we celebrated Mass in my motel room. For me too this was a very intimate experience of faith. The rest of the year she was unable to attend Mass at all, although a priest from a larger town visited her a few times. She complained little of the situation, and found some interest in the odd hillbilly neighbors who were kind to her. I tried to share with her the travels I was enjoying during the year with weekly letters and pictures and after her death I found that she had made a big scrapbook of the pictures. She read a good deal, since there was a mobile library van that stopped at Daisy. Most remarkable of all she decided to pass the time by copying by hand the entire Bible! Apparently, however, she did not save this manuscript, since I could not find it among her things after her death. For her it was simply a way to concentrate on the text. Her daily praying of the Rosary was her greatest consolation.

MARY PONDERS

Alone, she thinks of Him alone
as round and around Him
this total universe expands
dark, light, chaotic or designed,
its brief time no more
than a few booming billion
light-years moving out of sight

never to stop
not much more, I think,
than it had taken
of all her tears
a single tear to drop
when in her womb
he had needed
so little room.

Chapter 14 - Expanding Horizons

The City of the Keys

Certainly my most memorable trip was my first one to Europe in 1966 for a meeting of Regents of Study in Rome. Flying out of New York at six in the evening I was surprised how long the plane traveled up the North American coast before launching out on the comparatively short distance to Europe. At that time transatlantic planes often made a stop in the dead of night at Gander, Newfoundland for refueling. Gander reminded me of Leo Shields and my stop at the sign of the NORTH POLE, which I have recounted. Then in the early morning I woke from uneasy sleep to see the coast of France; then on down, with a glimpse of the Alps, to Rome, places I had read about all my life. The bus from Leonardo da Vinci into Rome showed me some earth-colored Italian farmhouses with their red tile roofs. The first sight of Rome was St. Paul Outside the Walls, and then we entered by the Pyramid of Cestus and the taxi took me up the Aventine to Santa Sabina, our Dominican headquarters. It is a fifth century basilica, one of the best-preserved churches in Rome, with wooden doors on one of which is the oldest known carving of the Crucifixion. At one time the convent of this church was the residence of St. Dominic, whose cell is preserved there, and of St. Thomas Aquinas. Both must have preached in that Church.

My business at Santa Sabina was to attend a meeting of the Regents of the provinces of the Order to prepare a statement on our intellectual mission after the Council. Vincent de Couesnongle (d. 1992), soon to be elected Master of the Order to succeed Aniceto Fernández, chaired the meeting. During the siesta times each day I made my own tour of ancient Rome and saw many of its wonders. Rome is a great place for walking tours since in almost every block one discovers something historic or artistic, even if it is only a few stones of a ruin overgrown with grass, housing two or three stray cats.

Returning from Rome (which a couple of years later I revisited on similar business when I was able to do even more sightseeing) I visited several of our houses of study. I went by bus to Assisi and to Florence and decided that Florence should be the place for me to retire. Then I flew on over the Alps to Geneva and then to Friburg, where the Dominicans have the faculty of theology by contract with the government. Dominicans got this contract as a result of the

Swiss Government's law, only recently repealed, against Jesuit faculties and that is also why Hans Küng, himself Swiss and a diocesan priest, had to go to Germany to teach. From there I went to Amsterdam and to Nijmegen to the Dutch Dominican house of studies and just over the boarder to the German house of studies at Walberberg. I then flew to London where I stayed in a hotel in Piccadilly Circus and by chance attended at the Royal Haymarket Theater a performance of Richard Sheridan's *The Rivals*, with Mrs. Malaprop played by Margaret Rutherford—near retirement and a bit forgetful; she is quoted of her performance in this part as saying, "I added a few malapropisms of my own"—and Sir Anthony Absolute by Ralph Richardson. What a delight! Then I flew to Dublin with a side trip to the Irish Dominican novitiate in Tallaght.

In Dublin I stayed at St. Savior's. The hospitality was remarkable, since they shined my shoes and left them by my door with an evening newspaper and tumbler of whiskey by my bedside. One evening Fr. Paul Bowe who had taught in River Forest, took me to dinner in a fine restaurant with more good whiskey and drove me to some of the sites in Joyce's *Ulysses*. My last dinner in the Dublin Priory was a bit whimsical. The Prior made a little speech at the beginning of dinner saying how grateful they were for Dubuque's care of Irish friars sent to study there, and ended by saying, "We want to celebrate this occasion, but I am sure Father will understand that we must maintain our ancient austerities." These "austerities" consisted of a seven course dinner served on separate plates (something I had never experienced before) but in strict silence in the traditional Dominican manner, although, since there was no reading, a couple of the Fathers got out their newspapers and read to themselves! After dinner, however, we all met in another room for cigars and after-dinner drinks with hearty, witty Irish conversation.

The only other dinner I ever attended that quite came up to that was after our Provincial, Fr. Graham, was taken by his friend Senator John McCormack one afternoon to introduce our Master General Fernández to President Lyndon Johnson. The President had expressed a desire to meet him because Lucy Banes Johnson, his daughter, had recently become a Catholic. That evening we were invited to a dinner at the Spanish Embassy where the Master was to receive a medal of honor. After we had been served more than one cocktail, we sat down to a very formal dinner (no ladies present, out of respect to the clergy), with liveried waiters, and a special wine with every course, then cigars and brandy. As we were getting our coats we were served a gin and tonic for the road. If that is what embassy dinners are like in Washington, no wonder Congress is in such a stupor.

Elegy

The saddest event of these years, besides the departure of priests, was the loss of Fr. Jude Nogar (d.1967), cofounder of the *Albertus Magnus Lyceum*, whose friendship I so much valued and who was so important a member of our faculty. He had influenced many of our students especially as a teacher of preaching, due not only to his personal eloquence but also to his careful study of rhetoric as a liberal art. Thus he initiated in our province a new interest in preaching which now belatedly is flourishing in the Doctorate of Ministry in Preaching conferred by Aquinas Institute in St. Louis. Nogar, as has already been mentioned, had notable success with his book *The Wisdom of Evolution* that was translated into French and Spanish and which anticipated in its theological position the recent address of John Paul II to the Pontifical Academy of the Sciences. Modern science is tending with New-Darwinian evolution and Big-Bang cosmology to slip from a study of the laws of nature into a universal history. As such it hardly gets beyond an explanation of our world in terms of sheer chance. Can't we do better?

Tragically, Jude's health failed early. On two or three occasions when celebrating Mass in a local parish he fainted, and it was thought he was suffering a heart attack. This made him more and more anxious about saying Mass publicly. Thus with a doctor's prescriptions he began taking tranquilizers, a very popular mode of treatment at the time, to control his increasingly hypochondriacal worries about his health. Apparently he was overdosing himself and began to exhibit syndromes such as a masklike facial expression. His behavior then became more and more reclusive until he was finally sent to a psychiatrist in whom, however, he had no confidence so that the therapy failed. Jude ran up huge long-distance telephone bills, calling people he had met on his lecture tours, and engaging in long rambling talks that utterly puzzled and troubled those he called. He no longer came to meals, but ate in the kitchen late at night. Finally, he was found in the night on the stairs, with food he was taking from the kitchen to his room, dead of a heart attack. As I look back on this I am confident from another case that I have known that the origin of his difficulties was what today is recognized as "anxiety attacks" which were as mysterious to him as to us and which his physicians never diagnosed or treated properly.

During his gradual decline Jude published a brilliant but somewhat irrationalist—now we would say "postmodern"—book based on very successful public lectures, *The Lord of the Absurd*. As I mentioned earlier, it answered existentialist atheism in a very original way. His withdrawal from much communication with us had been especially painful to me, because of our former close friendship, but I felt helpless about it, although I gave him every support I could. I am happy to say that one of the good "changes in the Church" is that religious communities are much more sensitive and open today about psychological and chemical dependency problems than they formerly were and much quicker to insist on adequate psychiatric counseling. Formerly, such matters were regarded as so confidential that nothing was done about them until it was too late.

Jude's contribution to the Studium and to the Lyceum was very significant. He was undoubtedly the most original and brilliant of its members and for me a more sympathetic friend than any I have had since. It was awful for me to see him withdraw himself from that friendship into his drug-dependent isolation, but many today experience that same tragedy. The following elegy is dedicated to his memory.

ELEGY

You, from beside me, turned to pass
another way along the gloom,
and lie now under the unfolding grass
above the enfolding bosom of a tomb,
a narrow plot that none trespass...
yet you are still with me in this room.

Yes, all eternity like massive stone
lays the foundation of our dream!
But time unloosens with a broken moan
like the flooded mixture of a stream
across me, floundering alone,
I mourn, grimace, let go a dream.

But grief will surely have its day
and then new bands begin to blare,

"Someday—Someday—Someday,"
(such are the promises we make
in this windy city by a windy Lake),.
again the streets of glory flare
in great parades with glittering array.

There is with me no singing,
no promise waiting to fulfill,
that is not the repeated ringing,
of your passing bell
here in my monastic cell.

There is no timely singing
but only prayerful, living breath
for your untimely, how untimely!
death.

More on My Own

For me spiritually this was a time in which I was still constantly struggling with my scrupulosity problem, but also one of great activity and growing self-confidence. I was the President of a school with a certain degree of power and public recognition. The tragic deaths of Nogar and of another of our young faculty members, Humbert Crilly (d. 1969), from heart attacks, and the need to close River Forest, were very difficult, but did not prevent my busyness and interest in my work. Vatican II and our Order's revisions of its Constitutions gave me great hope that once the inevitable travail of a new epoch in the Church ran its course, things would soon settle down. Yet it was at this time that the bright young nephew of Father Kane, Fr. J. E. returned to Dubuque where he was prior, after spending his sabbatical at Union Seminary in New York, and announced at the Christmas party that he was leaving the Order and the priesthood because he was convinced that in 25 years religious orders would have ceased to exist in the Church. Sadly we all had to keep struggling on.

My own interior life, during when the priesthood was being so questioned, was certainly centered on the Lord Jesus, and I never had any doubts about my vocation, but I was far from transparent to His light. He told us to be "like a lamp that gives light to all in the house" (Mt 5:15) but as long as one is opaque to oneself how can the light shine through?

THE WITHOUT AND THE WITHIN

Where is the center of my Me?
Where is my enclosing skin?
Where about me is my without?
Where in me is my within?

Freud says I am a Cartesian surface desperately smoothed
under which blank sheet a frantic chaos heaves,
the fountain of the deep, the idiotic Id .
Fathomless within is the primeval dark,
stories under stories mined in dreams.
There, there is my real Me, a Titan blinded,
dripping with old gore, yet burning
with the force that makes the world unfold.

Jung says that deep within
the Anima unfolds like a butterfly.
The Mad Aunt confined in the antic,
is the very Cinderella who awaits
the Prince with the sparkling slipper.

To me it seems that what they call the depths
is the outer darkness only.
I am a sphere whose surface is not skin but blood,
the ancient flood whose multiplying life
sprang forth from the great ocean of the lifeless world.
Ice cold at first around me
it flows now in a tropical current,
channeled in fine tubes strung on the rocky coastline
of the bones, tissues, muscles, viscera,
all living the physiological rhythm,
caverns for its flow.
It is the thirsty flood dissolving all,
the fiery lava flood that flows on, out
to produce new islands.

Within this mingling ocean floats a magic net,

the fine gauze of the skin, the reticule of nerves,
knotted eye and ear, in tongue and nose,
spread dense in the hands, about the face,
wide and loose around and around.
Through it the outer world swims in,
the inner world swims out
in glittering words and hungry deeds.

Within the net a great creation rises,
first the outer sphere of night
lit by the swimming moon and stars,
the dream world of memory and imagining,
the sphere of fear
and all desires fed on the blood,
a world of storm,
or strange enchanted calms.
Now we are sailing within
beyond the atoll of all creeping life
up to the island of the day.

Here is the world of Me,
a world within ruled by the law
of reason and the power of will,
a multiplex world in which a thousand citizens
sing like an orchestra, having its parts,
while into this city flow the treasures of the sea
drawn up in nets, cast shining on the land
to die and be digested and to live once more
no longer slime and scale nor even blood,
but the pure wine of life,
a wine that flows in rivulets of light,
each drop drying in pearls and diamonds.

Yet the world of reason is only a city built about
an inner garden, deeper than any cave,
so far within the world
that it is the source from which the world expands.
The great ocean is only the last reach of the tide
that left its fountain.
Here only spreads the tree of life,

here only is the wedding
of the within with the without,
here, deep within.

Or rather is this garden
a high mountain top, the summit of existence
whose vast volcanic cone spreads out and down
into the ocean's abyss?

This garden centers in the tree of life or in an altar
or a wedding ring or any other sign you may suggest
that speaks of inner holiness. Here are wed
the reason transformed from king to priest,
to reverent intellect and loving will.

Yet what can wed these two opposing powers
that struggle in the mutually destructive
war of the sexes?
Truth strikes at Love in bitter hate
and Eve bites at Adam
as if he were the apple,
with a serpent's teeth, venomous with madness.
The schizophrenia and alienation
that can thus divide the outer world
into battling torrents by so high a wall
as that dividing Truth from Love,
Justice from Mercy.

Yet may not the Spirit hovering on the waters here descend
to transform Truth to Love and Love to Truth?
Remember how the angel
came into the inner room and spoke to her
who was all love and pure obedience,
so that from on high
Truth put on the living robe of our humanity?

In me may He descend, deep then within, and make Me one.
Unifying the most high thorugh the most low
comes peace within, like the creative word that runs out
forth
to all the ends of the earth to transform the without,

to open the gates to let the inner light shine forth,
from depth to surface
speaking clear and plain,
without fear—here.

Attachment to Chicago

Thus I was busy without, but not very clear within. Since my term as Regent expired at this time so that I did not have to be transferred with the philosophy studium to Dubuque, I decided a change would be good for me and I looked forward to a new assignment. Living in Chicago I was once taken to see the Chicago waterworks connected with the famous pseudo-gothic Water Tower that stands on Michigan Avenue in the heart of the North Side. It survived the Great Chicago Fire and when Oscar Wilde came to the city his hosts proudly took him to see the Tower as their finest bit of architecture. Even Wilde could not think of anything very witty to say about it. Inside it when I visited it was a great wheel that once had something important to do with the city's water system. Watching it turn gave me a sense of inevitability of time and change in my own life. Thus the world travels and going to and from meetings and the circle of administration and teaching in the school-years gave me a deep sense of the temporal nature of the physical reality that science studies and the still deeper timeless, spiritual, metaphysical power that this endless flow analogically implies beyond our conception.

TIME AND OLD WATERWORKS

Clocks are wheels and in their insides
are wheels within wheels.
The time they measure is a wheel,
the hours and minutes wheel round, round,
the stars too wheel as does my mind.

At the old Chicago waterworks,
we saw a wheel that pumps water
out of the Lake,
all night that wheel turns
making a steady breeze
so that near it one can feel warm air

with a cool eddy under it.

It stopped one night, no one could bathe,
for no water ran in the pipes and conduits
and there was no whir in the engine room.
The great wheel's rim that we had seen
as an even blur of brass
then showed its surface smooth but marred
and the spokes seemed like crucified arms
inside this brassy band,
so in the engine room there was no breeze.

If it was not for time, then how could the water
be sent through the pipes and conduits
tunneling through miles of stone?
How could we bathe, cleaning away the past
in the so necessary oblivion of that Lethe?
These were my circling thoughts.

But then the workmen at the wheel
made it go round and round once more.
We heard water gushing and a workman said
"Overtime! It's time to go on home to bed."
Then I learned that time's that kind of wheel,
not made to lift Lethe's oblivion for the dirty past,
but to make us work to keep it going,
to keep time wheeling ever round and round.

Soft breeze and cool eddy, how it turns, its whir
is as constant as its brass rim in a smooth blur.
Are we the squirrels that turn this mighty wheel?

Move to Houston

A change of career at midlife (I was now 54) is at once a new lease on living and a profound reminder of death ahead. With my term as President of Aquinas Institute of Philosophy and Theology completed, my religious superiors gave me permission to work elsewhere for a while. Then Fr. Albert Moraczewski, OP, invited me to join him at the *Institute of Religion and Human Development*[178] in the Texas Medical Center in Houston. Albert, a native of Chicago whose father was Polish and his mother French was, like myself, a graduate of the University of Chicago from which he received a doctorate in pharmacology. He had been a coworker with me in the Albertus Magnus Lyceum and we had in common the Lyceum's purpose to study the relation of natural science to philosophy and theology.

Albert is a friar with a methodological scientific mind and a compassionate heart, although he claims that in his biochemical researches he has guillotined many thousands of rats! Many people have depended on him and brought their troubles to him and I have always found his sympathetic ways a great consolation in my own life. As I reflect on the matter, I note how important my mother, Ruth, Irwin, Leo, Jude, and Albert have been in my life as persons who were sympatico, others with whom I could feel a harmony of feeling. What gifts of God such persons are! His invitation eased my "midlife crisis" in which one suddenly feels insecure, since the daily tasks that support our usual lives, suddenly fall away and one has a sense of falling, which I once expressed in the following poem.

ODE TO PANIC

The small moth fell on the polished table, fluttered
    and died.
    I heard the falling measures of its death
    along my hand I felt the air it made
    like passing breath
    strive and subside.
Everywhere around was death,
heat without breath.
heat without breathing in the uneven midnight sky.
I felt the midnight, the midnight die.

    Grey moth dusted green,
    what had it touched or met or seen
    that caught it, crushed it, let it fall...

    There was nothing there,
    but a faint shadow on a white wall.

The great plane crashed against the mountain,
    screamed, and flared.

Across my face I felt its plunging heat.
I saw the entire twilight twist in one bright sheet.
The chasm glared.
Everyone is blind with death.
Heat without breath.
Heat without breathing in the opened morning sky,
I saw the darkness flare, flare and die.

Great plane steadily spread.
What had it marked, pursued, or fled
that had pressed or led it on?..

In the noon of knowing I crashed, and fluttering
    screamed and died,
    I the poor failure plunging into death
    gasping for darkness, gasping for breath.
I shuddered, cried.
    Everywhere within was death.
    The heat of my own breath
    fogging the cold window as we fell
    fell through the flaming sky.
I, dead, I felt I ... I might not die.

Poor living thing poor mind.
What could explode, singe, blind,
dangle me, caress me, let me fall...?

There was nothing there nothing there at all,
but my faint shadow on my mind's white wall.

Ecumenism

The new situation I was going into soon fascinated me. Christianity, at least in a Protestant version, is a strong force in the public life of Texas, and when this Texas Medical Center, an enormous complex of hospitals including a branch of the University of Texas Medical School and Baylor School of Medicine, was established, one of its components became the *Institute for Religion* in 1955 housed in a handsome building in the very center of the campus. It was supported financially by many of the Protestant seminaries in Texas in order to provide their students with what is called Clinical Pastoral Education (CPE). Its President was a Methodist, Dr. Thompson L.

Shannon who wanted to open it also to Catholic seminarians and broaden its program. To express this hope he added "and Human Development" to the Institute's title until 2002 when it has become the *Institute for Religion and Health.*

When I started to work there, Dr. Shannon, in view of this expansion, had recently added to the faculty a group of teachers and supervisors in family therapy and also the Presbyterian theologian Rev. Kenneth Vaux and, as a Catholic, Fr. Moraczewski OP, who had been for some years working at the nearby Baylor College of Medicine doing research on tranquilizing drugs. It was on his advice that Shannon also appointed me as a Catholic theologian to the staff. Kenneth Vaux, later at the University of Illinois, Chicago branch, was a young, tall, energetic, very kind minister, who was also serving as a chaplain at Rice University. He had studied under Joseph Fletcher (d. 1991),[179] the medical ethicist and noted proponent of "situation ethics." Ken made me feel very welcome at this new work, but his theological views did seem to me rather vague. Officially my title was "Research Professor" and I was not required to teach but only to participate in the other activities of the Center that gave workshops of various sorts on medical ethical and pastoral problems. But I was also able to teach one course a semester at the diocesan seminary, St. Mary's, a lovely spot in the piney woods of suburban Houston.

Thus I was working in two different milieus and found it convenient to wear my clerical garb at St. Mary's and a contemporary secular suit and tie at the Institute. Contemporary clothes had for a while become the customary thing for religious priests, including my Dominican confreres in most schools, even in Catholic ones, but I returned to clericals after I left Houston. I am of the opinion that priests or religious should normally declare their consecration by their style of life, including clerical dress. The post-Vatican II notion that by dressing like lay persons priests and religious men and women would be renouncing clerical privileges and would be better able to communicate with those they serve does not seem to have been confirmed by experience. Of course Jesus and the Apostles wore no special garb, but their manner of life as itinerant preachers made them conspicuous; while most priests and religious today because of their professional education and work are inconspicuously blended into middle class society, giving no countercultural witness to the Gospel's presence in the world. A failed experiment should be admitted to be such and abandoned.

This appointment in the Texas Medical Center put me at last in an atmosphere of modern science and technology where I could have exchanges with persons at the forefront of modern biological and psychological progress. Therefore, I soon began work on a book that would address the question "Can we create ourselves?" raised by the capacity of modern medicine to reconstruct the human body by transplants and genetic recombination. Since the concept of "human nature" as a given since we are created by God in his own image, is so fundamental to Christian theology and to classical philosophy, it seemed to me that this question brings the Lyceum's science and religion problem into sharp focus. Hence it was still in pursuit of the goal for which we founded the Albertus Magnus Lyceum that I shifted my field from my previous interests in philosophy and education to that of moral theology and medical ethics. To do research on medical ethics took a great deal of retooling on my part, but the Institute was a splendid place to begin it. Hence I also began work on a book, which became *Theologies of the Body: Humanists and Christian* that was not to be completed until 1978 in a different setting as I will describe later.

Departure of My Mentor

Thus the concerns of the Lyceum were still very much with me and this made the death in 1970 of Fr. William "Hum" Kane, the original inspirer of that project, for me especially sad. In the last years of my work as President of Aquinas Institute when I was preoccupied with the changes that we were having to make in the education of our Dominican students, Hum seemed more and more withdrawn from me. I realized that he saw these changes as the destruction of all that he and Fr. Timothy Sparks had labored for in trying to raise the intellectual level of our Dominican Province. I believe he was profoundly disappointed in me, though he kept silent. In 1969, the year I left River Forest for Houston, I heard that he was ill. In spite of, or because of, his medical training, he had always believed in staying away from doctors. He had been complaining about intestinal troubles that kept him awake at night. When finally he was forced to see a physician it was found that he had inoperable colon cancer. I went to see him in the hospital in Chicago and found him very wasted and with a frightening brightness in his eyes. Our conversation was, alas, very formal and I never saw him again, and he died in 1970. As I said in the proceeding chapter his view of Thomism has been the basis of all my writing. He was also a deeply spiritual influence on me, although my background and temperament were so unlike his.

Hum and I, at a better time, had not only discussed philosophical questions, but also much about spirituality. He was deeply read in John of the Cross and the other spiritual classics. While he was never very self-revealing I learned from his deep understanding of spiritual matters that he had gone through very great interior sufferings and was advanced in the mystical life. Certainly it was evident that, for all his love of golf, he lead a very ascetic life and never relaxed his intense routine of prayer.

At one period in his life, in the early sixties, he became the spiritual director of a remarkable woman, a professor of biology in one of the Chicago universities. I met her a few times and found her a brilliant person, but never came to know her well. Hum, however, told me that she had all the gifts of St. Catherine of Siena and that she was preparing to found a religious institute of a very new type, especially for professional women like herself, and in fact she and a couple of disciples did form a community to follow a rule she had written. At this point Fr. Kane was assigned to a brief period of teaching in Rome and he told me that her letters to him greatly troubled him, since she seemed unwilling any longer to accept his guidance, had been deserted by her companions, and was moving in directions he did not understand. When he returned he found that she had left Chicago to teach in Louisiana. Not long after she left the Church and was found murdered at a lonely spot on a levee in New Orleans! A professor at the university where she was teaching was a suspect but the murder was never solved. Hum only said to me after this shocking event that so profoundly grieved him, was "Pride is a terrible, terrible thing." Thus I had only a glimpse into the inner life of Fr. Kane, and I think most of those who lived with him tended to think him as stubborn and eccentric. I hope that when I meet Hum in heaven, as by the mercy of God and Hum's prayers I hope to do, I will be able to tell him that I have always tried to be true to the deep insights, both spiritual and philosophical, that I received from him. His death and the suffering around me in the Medical Center provided many a meditation.

ODE TO THE HEALER
God did not make death...the creatures of the world are
wholesome ...there is no destructive drug among them (Wis 1:14).

Today I feel not well, a shivering,
a slight fever...soon I am imagining
the many around me mauled by pain,
or, like me, dreading it will come again
with secret, stunning paw and mangling maw,
the ancient beast that on its belly—creeps,
the insidious old worm that seeps,
uncoiling from the fathomless deeps
of nights while life outdoes its stay
and sleeps...then ebbs away.

We all, though symptom free, are terminal
with a dire plague, genetic and incurable
by pill or potion, drowning us in an ocean
of oblivion, in a careening flood
of dissolution, freezing the blood,
smothering the laboring breath
in the primordial chaos, dust and slime,
out of which we came, naked, without name...
now again return...the clock ticking the time,
the unpredictable time of not uncertain death.

Why are we,
save Mary and Mary's Son,
one and all, everyone
sharers in that first steep fall?

Spying the fruit of the ambiguous tree,
Eve bit into ashes, then offered it free
to Adam charmed with her beauty
and her sweet, smiling generosity.
In you, Father, primal head of all humanity,
having, still more than Mother Eve, responsibility
for all the families through all the years to be
in you, our Father, we too ate the bitter core.
You, Mother deceitful, fooled Father, evermore
infused the serpent's venom into your vast brood,

we who receive the gift of your flesh and blood
in which the fatal virus breeds along with life,
our ambiguous gift from Adam and his lovely wife,
which we too employ to spread the poison
mutating ever more virulent, on and on,
even as the herbs God gave to make us whole
we brew to vitiate our body and our soul.

Yet in the face of the serpent's lie
and Mother Eve's and Father Adam's folly
let us in faith the holy truth declare
that there is healing in the vital air
of the Word, cleansing in the water,
an herb was made for every ill;
there is a Healer with the holy skill,
to cleanse contagion and to kill
the lying dragon and our destined death,
to foster life, yet prune with steel.
Here is Mary's Son whose virgin heel
crushed the deceiving serpent's head.
He, for us bitten, sheds the blood
that in its life-renewing flood
washes us clean as Mary, virgin pure.
It is for certain death the certain cure.
For faith, more true than lying death,
eternal life is simply sure.

St. Mark's Priory at Rice University

Rice University is adjacent to the Texas Medical Center and on
its borders the Diocese of Galveston-Houston has established a
Newman Center for students attending Rice, itself a first rate but
very secularized university. This Center was housed in three remodeled houses, one for the Center itself, and two for St. Mark's
Dominican Priory, a residence for the Dominicans who were chap-
lains for the Newman Centers at Rice and the University of Houston.
It was here that I lived in a community of ten priests, a new experience for me, since as a Dominican I had for twenty years lived in the
large, formal priories of River Forest and Dubuque. This was a time
when there was much talk among Dominicans about the need to
break up these large priories and return to a more intimate frater-

nal style of life. But even with ten members led by a very understanding Fr. Albert Moraczewski as Prior, I found that "small communities" are also not free of constant problems.

Two of the members of the priory at that time were alcoholics. Two other members constantly talked about the need for greater community "togetherness," but one was in the process of leaving the priesthood, the other kept a pet monkey whose contribution to community life was purely negative. This smelly imp used to get out of his cage, tear up the furniture and any newspaper or magazines lying about, and suddenly jump from the fireplace mantel onto my head or lap. Other friars were too busy with their work to come to community meetings and I complained about how much time such meetings took from my study and writing.

The other enthusiast for "togetherness" at St. Mark's community was the same Fr. D. who, as I narrated in Chapter 13, had been responsible for our faculty going to the workshop at Menninger's. He had come to Houston from Dubuque to work in the Medical Center but, disappointed with our lack of "community" soon left the Order and priesthood to become a marriage counselor. He was successful at this, but "came out of the closet," left the Church, and after some years finally died of AIDS, not notifying any of us that he was near death. After much therapy, he had never been able to resolve his own psychological problems or the relation between his psychological knowledge and his faith. When I knew him he was a very intelligent, emotionally intense, and very kind and sympathetic person, who found me much too cerebral to be able to share his thinking and concerns. I think he knew I probably would not agree on many points with him, and I did not know how to make him trust me. May God have mercy on us both! Only one other death of a member of our Province to my knowledge has been the result of AIDS, and that was of a clerical student who had contracted it before entering the Order. Other tragic deaths of Dominicans I have known haunt me, two who were killed in airplane accidents, two killed in automobile accidents, and still sadder, a former student of mine who with "the changes" took up a long-haired style of life and a ministry to street-persons, and was finally killed by one of them. Again, may God have mercy on us all!

Later another younger Dominican lived with us who later asked the Provincial to assign him to study medicine. When he had earned his M.D., he left the priesthood to become a brain surgeon in Alaska. At that time we often financed young religious through their doc-

torates who then promptly left us. It was a generation very concerned about social justice, but who seemed entirely oblivious to the
injustice of committing themselves for life to a religious Order that
paid for their education and then promptly deserting the community, like, as someone at the time said, "rats leaving a sinking ship."

Modern circumstances of pastoral mission certainly often make
it necessary for religious today to live in smaller communities,
sometimes even alone, but in my opinion this need should not be
accepted as normal, since only in communities of considerable size
can all the benefits of communal life be achieved. Of course it is also
true that in larger communities special efforts must be made so that
individuals do not withdraw from communication into isolation, like
boarders in a hotel. Nevertheless, at St. Mark's, with the aid of a psychologist "facilitator, "Buzz" O'Connell, of the staff of the local Veterans' Hospital, we did at last manage to develop a good community
spirit, get the alcoholics into AA, cage the monkey outside in the
yard, find closure to our grief over Fr. D., and keep up regular prayer
in common and our various pastoral jobs.

In this Priory our liturgy was reduced to Morning and Evening
Prayer read in English without music and celebrated rather infor-
mally in the living room of one of our two houses. In the other house
in the small meditation chapel where the Blessed Sacrament was
reserved a community Eucharist was celebrated once a week. I continued to say Mass privately each day in that same chapel, to make
my half hour meditation and recite one third of the Rosary. I have
clung to this minimal discipline of prayer in my scattered and not
very consistent life because without it I would certainly have been
spiritually at sea or shipwrecked. We had community meetings every other week. We had a cook and housemaid who prepared our
dinner five days a week. The African-American cook, who sometimes served dinner dressed up to go out to a dance afterwards,
once quite seriously threatened to shoot any of us if we gave any
information on her income to the IRS, since that might lead to an
investigation of her "live-in boy friend" who like many of the Afro-
Americans in Houston managed to avoid most taxes. On weekends
we either each fixed something for himself or went out together to a
restaurant of the hearty Texas style. Reading at meals was long forgotten. We each had friends whom we visited occasionally, had a
three-week vacation, and sometimes went to a movie or to the
beach in Galveston together.

Galveston is about an hour's drive from Houston and a visit there was always a great pleasure. It is a quaint city with old houses, palms, old buildings, some former cotton warehouses, and a 1880s mansion magnificent in its variety of carved and polished wood-work with a grand staircase. The Bishop of Galveston-Houston had purchased it as a residence, but since he had his chancery in Houston, had converted it to a student center. Galveston is connected to the mainland by a causeway and is surrounded by a high seawall erected after the disastrous hurricane of 1900 in which thousands were drowned. I have always had an urge to experience a hurricane, although recently the New Orleans devastation by Hurricane Katrina has made me think otherwise. While I lived in Houston, a big one came into Galveston Bay, but in the hours before the storm the police blocked people from entering the city for surfing. Though the Gulf waters are generally tepid, the beach is magnificent, except for nasty gobs of petroleum from the oil tankers in the harbor. I did bathe in the surf, but for me it is generally enough pleasure simply to gaze at the ocean waves coming in from the long horizon.

A Pleasant Time

I greatly enjoyed residing at St. Mark's with my Dominican con-freres and working in the Texas Medical Center. The Priory was just across the street from Rice University that has attractive buildings of a rather unusual design and a dense grove of live oaks like those in Louisiana. Among these trees I enjoyed my daily walks, usually in the warm evenings, though this was sometimes disturbed in season by flocks of thousands of starlings settling in the tress and making a demonic racket. The university library was accessible to me and I spent much time there. Across the street in another direction was a very modern Protestant church surrounded by garden with cacti, yuccas, and palms. Not far away were the Houston Art Museum and the Houston Museum of Modern Art. Near it was a beautiful foun-tain and beyond it a park of pine trees where outdoor symphony concerts were held. The trees and plants were semitropical and wonderfully lush.

Those of us at St. Mark's also enjoyed unusual places to eat, like a restaurant on the ship canal where there was Greek music and the Greek sailors from oceangoing ships used to come and dance like Zorba. Friends also occasionally invited me to lunch at the Petrole-um Club overlooking the city. These good meals and the fine houses I saw when driving to the Seminary through the River Oaks section of the city made me acutely conscious of the extravagant wealth that surrounded me in Houston. Although much of the population of that ever-expanding city is from outside Texas, yet when I met a real native I experienced the warmth of manner and broad dialectic indigenous to that extraordinary state. Soon after I arrived there, still not ready to don the usual Texas boots, I tried to buy a pair of regular shoes at a large department store. The clerk looked in puzzlement at my rather small size 7 and said with embarrassment, "Father, I'm very sorry, but you may have to try the boys' department. We just don't have that size feet in Texas!"

Chapter 15 - Theology of the Body

Sutures

The Texas Medical Center was an extremely busy place with many hospitals. Its famous emergency room at Ben Taub Hospital was jammed on Saturday nights with victims of shootings and stabbings. It had a remarkably compassionate rehabilitation center, a mental health research center, a fine medical school, and, most famously, Dr. DeBakey and Dr Denton Cooley the great heart surgeons. Sitting in a Methodist hospital looking down through a glass bubble I watched DeBakey do open heart surgery, not a transplant but a valve implant. I looked down on the patient's blood pumping through tubes kept vibrating to prevent clotting, while his heart, with its fibrous white interior, lay open as a new valve was neatly stitched in. My three years in this milieu made me vividly aware of the ethics of health care, its enormous economic and political complexity, and the depths of human suffering that modern technology augments even as it heals.

HEART TRANSPLANT

Crushed in the sick mob of the poor
I stretch my contagious hands to touch you, Jesus alive!
Against your healing hands my breath is foul.
Bend, breathe life
again into my slime!

In a white room
green doctors excise a pale, bruised heart,
sew in a dead man's red, hot heart,
shock it to beat and to keep its beat
until the dying body of the still living, too far gone
        rejects...
Doomed life retains the strength to kill.

In a ghetto
before a dying church
a statue of the Sacred Heart spreads wide its arms
its lifeless marble leached by slimy rain.
The temple's granite walls crumble to let
in creeping, crawling things.

O Heart, you come again
to cut open our bodies, to thrust in your hand,
to tear out this dead lump, to drop it back in the mud,
to stitch into my shocked body your healing life,
your Heart, You
live in dying Me.

Too far gone?
Will my corruption, gasping to live,
        reject?

The activities of the Institute for Religion also fascinated me as I heard the reports of the CPE students and watched the family therapy sessions through a one-way window. I have already recounted what a revelation the visit to the Menninger Clinic had been to our Aquinas Institute of Theology faculty and now I was able to see in a very concrete way how modern psychotherapy can benefit Christian ministry. Clinical Pastoral Education is a training program invented by a Protestant clergyman who was a victim of mental illness and thus knew how inept clergy often are in dealing with the mentally and emotionally disturbed. The method of CPE is to combine lectures on pastoral counseling with daily clinical experiences of pastoral responsibility for a hospital ward. Each student visits the patients on an assigned ward, keeping a written record of the interview, and then goes over this "verbatim" with a supervisor. Students also meet weekly in a group to recount their experiences and difficulties and to carry on a critical interchange. The goal of this training is to help clerical and lay ministers come to a better sense of their identity, strengths, and weaknesses as pastoral counselors in order to be more sensitive to the needs of those they serve. Just recently one of our Dominican students engaged in this summer program told me that in a session with his woman supervisor, she said critically, "You never cry!" and when he tried to answer this criticism, she burst into tears!
While the psychotherapeutical level of CPE in the Texas Medical Center was high, the program lacked an in-depth theological component. The students, both Protestant and Catholic, had very diverse theological orientations and preparation. I remember a session in which a Protestant patient was interviewed who had com-

mitted a heinous crime only a week after being "reborn" in baptism. The students asked him many questions about his family background and his feelings, but none mentioned the fact of his conversion and baptism. The supervisor asked why this was, and a student answered, "I didn't think it proper to inquire about people's religious beliefs." I hope that I was able to contribute something to this local program by lectures on the relation of sacramental ministry to psychological therapy. For many of the Protestant students this was something quite new, for the Catholic students something that they were coming to think was "pre-Vatican II."

Indeed it became clear to me that the relation between the theory and practice of counseling based on modern psychotherapy and that based on traditional pastoral counseling or spiritual direction is complex and not very well understood. In the post Vatican II period not a few priests and ministers on encountering psychotherapy and finding how much it has to say about our human attitudes and behavior, yet often lacking in their personal self-understanding, have lost confidence in the religious view of life. They have come to translate religious categories into purely psychological ones, and some have abandoned Christian faith altogether.

Since before I became a Catholic, indeed from my high school years, I had been a Freudian and after becoming a Catholic had always endeavored to relate the psychology of St. Thomas Aquinas to modern psychology, I was not unduly disturbed by these new psychological insights, but I did come to realize that the pastoral counseling of the Church has often been too moralistic and negligent of the psychological and physiological complexity of moral life. Thomism presents an anthropology in which the rationality and objectivity of the mature human person is taken as the paradigm and the model is Jesus Christ, the New Adam, healthy and whole. This is, I believe good theology, since health is the norm in the light of which disease must be understood, not the other way round. Yet in a fallen world in which we must minister to the spiritually, psychologically, sociologically, and physically sick, it is necessary to give full weight to human subjectivity. Such reflections contributed to my research and work on *The Theologies of the Body* with which I was then struggling.

In particular I began to see from the demonstrations of family therapy which I witnessed at the Institute how important is the notion of a dynamic system, and especially of the family system, in understanding human behavior. Psychological behavior is not just the function of an individual psyche but of the dynamics of the group in which the individual lives. For example, to talk about the "sexual orientation" of an individual does not explain much unless we study individuals in the context of their families, then in the wider society of heterosexual persons, or in a gay or lesbian community.

Other than my work on *Theologies of the Body* I did not have time for much writing, but I did publish a few articles while in Houston. Relating directly to my work was ""Roman Catholic Medical Ethics" in Sylvester D. Thorn, *The Faith of Your Patients: A Handbook of Religious Attitudes Toward Medical Practices*;"[180] but I was still thinking about reform in education as in my article, "The Discipline of Theology in Seminary and University,"[181] and always about religious life as in three other articles, "Religious Orders and Social Involvement;"[182] "Toward an American Theology of Contemplation;"[183] and "Retirement or Vigil."[184] I also wrote brief popular articles on "The Meaning of the Virgin Birth,"[185] in reply to an attack on Raymond Brown's treatment of the subject and on "The Sacred in Art," (participation in a television program for national Canadian television, printed in *artscanada*.[186]

The Peak of the Human Soul

In a more philosophical mode, I developed two of the themes essential to my argument in *Theologies of the Body*. The first was "A Psychological Model with a Spiritual Dimension"[187] in which I applied what I was learning in the Institute about current psychology to argue that the psychoanalytical attribution by Freud of human creativity to the unconscious Id, or by Jung to a collective unconscious, is inadequate, since it attributes the cause of the most free activity of the human psyche to its least free level. Yet it is also clear that creativity cannot be reduced to the Ego, i.e. to everyday rationality.

I believe the solution to this dilemma should be sought in the notion of a Super-Conscious (not to be confused with the Freudian Super-Ego which is part of the Id). This was recognized in medieval thought and the writings of mystics who distinguished the *ratio superior* or *intellectus* from the *ratio* or discursive reason. Jacques Maritain has called this "creative intuition."[188] This part of the psyche is "unconscious" only in the sense that it is not easily expressed in words. Maritain terms such knowledge "pre-conceptual," but since every act of the intelligence forms concepts, it would be better to call it a "pre-verbalized" or "inchoate" concept. When I write poetry or really pray I am using intuition rather than argumentative reasoning. Modern education with its emphasis on "how to do it" and Neo-Scholastic education with its emphasis on "deduction" both tended to stifle intuition, but Aquinas, for all his careful syllogizing, insists that the essence of intelligence is intuition rather than argumentation. I have also retained my interest in dreams in which sometimes certainly a kind of poetic creativity takes place. I would not attribute this to the Id, however, but to the fact that our spiritual intelligence is not wholly inhibited in sleep but often operates though imperfectly. This is why the poetics of dreams is always fragmentary, as in these two poems of mine:

TWO TROUBLED DREAMS

I: CHRYSANTHEMUM

In a big city, in a dream,
I try to give directions
to an alien woman,
Japanese,
to an address unknown, or rather
permutated, scrambled, unremembered,
partially remembered:
5 Thousand or 15 Hundred 50
Parkway
East or North?

Sinister forces
on the right, behind,
around the corner, behind the streetlight's dazzle
diverted, perverted,
evaded us
and faced us in a glimpse
at every turning.
What she unclearly says,
so shyly,
I further still confuse.

And before hotels, in shops

as the streets blacken and the smog pervades,
the information given
gets entangled
or she,
permutates, scrambles it,
15 Thousand 15
Southwest Darkway
or Downward Highway?

Never, never
did I remember
nor did I dare to tell her
who, what, sure not where
we sought—
5 thousand, 5 hundred, naught, naught!

At some last turning
I escaped
her
turning into my hotel
or jogging to my shop
(where?).
Over my evading shoulder I still saw
her standing alien, lone,
small, female,
Jap,
under the white
chrysanthemum
of a lamp
in the big, empty...
the black city.

II: AFTER FLU

After fever, achy, dull,
Through my window,
I find you, crystal morning, cool
and a red leaf drifting down
across my window

Fever dreams are about machines.
I dreamt of computers,
woke in a shiver.

Sleeping again,
in my dream
I heard two cars crash
I heard a scream
I am the driver,
the dreamer,
I am the screamer,
I am the scream!
Red ambulance lights flash
across my window...

Today they say it was no dream,
    the crash occurred, it really did
    yet I was not wakened,
weary with fever, through it all
    I kept snoring.
    No, I never screamed.

Toward earth the red leaf slips.
Crystal the silence of the wakened world.
"What is the really real?" Thus metaphysicians query.
This window's vague rectangle
expands into the empty blue
    beyond the reach of any sound, of any counting?

Or my brain-computer printing out
the disconnected windings of a dream
    in fever?
The night crash in which two drivers
(neither or both were me)
died screaming?

Crystal, God's morning's stillness....
Through the window glass
the crashing of the drifting leaves
    is minimal.

Evolution Evolving

In a second article "Causality and Evolution,"[189] I asked (granted that biological evolution is a fact as I had always believed from my father's enthusiasm for Darwin's *The Origin of Species*), "How can evolutionary theories be reconciled with the principle of causality according to which a more highly ordered effect cannot result from a less ordered cause?" I showed that neo-Darwinian evolution locates this causation principally in a sequence of changes of the environment that select those mutations that are best adapted for survival. But this sequence of changes in the environment is itself explained by the conjunction of many factors that are not governed as a unified complex by any general natural law. Thus modern evolutionary theory explains the origin of new species only by a sequence of merely chance events, i. e., it is an explanation by history not by natural law. We must conclude, therefore, that modern science requires the existence of higher causes that are not part of the physical cosmos. This fact need not and should not deter the scientist from his pursuit of explanation by secondary causes. Thus prayer for healing is in no way contradictory to the full employment of medical procedures, since what one prays for is that these procedures, which of course sometimes fail, will in fact succeed.

Therefore, I suggested that since science ought not immediately to explain reality by God as first cause, it ought to posit the existence of many finite kinds of intelligences as part of the cosmic order and as relatively first causes in the many lines of causality evident in the universe, just as Aristotle did. I would add here that though today scientists are attempting to reduce all forces in the universe to unity, they do so only by returning to the Big Bang and even if this succeeds it will only establish that there is one generic kind of force in the universe, not one specific line of causality. Thus evolution provides a philosophical proof of the existence of angels, a notion not easily accepted, I regret, by the "modern mind." The recent fad for books about "angels" and the sci-fi fantasies about Martians and other aliens from outer space shows that the popular mind in an intuitive way grasps a truth to which scientists seem blinded: namely, that the scientific method as now practiced explains much but at no point gets to the bottom of the mystery of the actual course of human and cosmic history. This argument, of course, was an elabo-

ration and application of the proofs of the existence God I had
learned from St. Thomas Aquinas before my conversion.[190]

New Experiences

While I was working on these themes of evolution and of human
creativity, I was being stimulated by a multitude of new experiences. Three of these stand out in my memories of these Houston years.
One was an internal battle that went on in the Institute between its
President and the three marriage counselors whom he had brought
to the Institute in view of his vision of broadening it from a CPE
training school to a center for the study of religion and human development.

These counselors who were, I believe, highly competent but suffering from disillusionment with the Christian religious tradition
and had only a secondary interest in the religious mission of the Institute. They felt betrayed because Dr. Shannon was unable to fulfill
some of the promises he had made to them for advancing their own
clinical practice when he had invited them to the Institute. This was
because he was having difficulty in raising funds because the
churches that had previously supported the CPE program for the
training of their clergy were less enthusiastic about Shannon's
broader, ecumenical project. I never doubted Shannon's integrity,
but I am afraid that I allowed myself to be manipulated by this
group of marriage counselors as they tried to put pressures on
Shannon that made his life very difficult. I had no other intention
than to save the Institute in what appeared to me a major crisis, but
the fact that the counselors eventually deserted the Institute and set
up their own counseling center was disappointing. It was another
proof of the tension between a primary trust in Christian faith and
in modern secular technology.

The Black Chapel

A second major experience at the Institute for Religion and Human Development came about when its President Dr. Shannon
pulled the Institute through its financial crisis mentioned in the last
chapters by finding for a time a new major sponsor, and a very interesting and generous one. John and Dominique De Menil were two
very prominent but rather exotic Houstonians, reported to be worth
over two hundred million dollars derived from the great Schlum-
berger Corporation. Dominique's Belgian father had invented a
method of detecting the presence of petroleum in geological

formations by sonic waves. I had often heard my brother talk about its very effective use in exploration for oil in the fields of Oklahoma and Texas. John De Menil was a native Catholic and Dominique, a professor of art history, a convert who had been instructed by Fr. Marie-Alain Couturier, OP,[191] a well known artist and editor of *Ars Sacré* and promoter of modern art in the Catholic Church, for example, the famous Matisse chapel in Vence, France.

Fr. Albert Moraczewski was acquainted with the De Menils and through him they met Dr. Shannon and decided to sponsor the Institute. In this way I came to make their acquaintance and visit their home in the fashionable River Oaks district of Houston. They had given generous support to the art museums of Houston, but their most remarkable gifts had been to the University of St. Thomas. This school, with its Center of Thomistic Studies, is sponsored by the Basilian Fathers, known also for their Mediaeval Institute in Toronto that Étienne Gilson had headed and where my friend and colleague Fr. James A. Weisheipl, one of the members of the Lyceum, was a noted professor. The De Menils made it possible for the University to have Philip Johnson, one of the best known architects in the United States, design many of the school buildings. They enriched these buildings with many handsome works of art from their extensive collections.

Finally, the De Menils proposed to furnish the University with a chapel also designed by Johnson, but the Basilians—legend has it—were critical of Johnson's stark, octagonal design, and noted that it contained no space for toilets. For this reason or some other the De Menils concluded that the Basilians did not really appreciate art and terminated their benefactions. Johnson also repudiated the chapel, because of changes the De Menils made in its design. After this dispute they purchased land adjacent to the University on which they erected the chapel. It is now famous as the Rothko Chapel from the mural paintings by Mark Rothko[192] and is faced with a reflecting pool over which looms the striking inverted "Broken Obelisk" of Barnett Newman.[193] Adjacent to this is now the Menil Museum,[194] a unique building designed by Renzo Piano surrounded by a whole section of small rental houses, all painted in "Dominique gray."

The De Menils owned a collection of over 15,000 works of art, with an emphasis on African and surrealist art. I was invited to lunch at their residence, which is a low modernistic building set back in a semitropical garden which seems to invade the house, since there are also many tropical plants within a glassed-in area. I was overwhelmed to be surrounded in this domestic setting by modern art, from a huge Warhol Campbell's Soup Can in the kitchen to a Picasso over the fire place, with odd touches everywhere, such as a black-on-black Warhol that on closer inspection turned out to be a portrait of an electric chair, and what I remember as a strange, large seventeenth century colonial Spanish architectural painting that anticipated surrealism. I was also given a glimpse of a storage room containing hundreds of items of Cycladic Greek and African sculpture—John De Menil had written a work on African art.

I must confess that during the three or four times I was in their house I fantasized that one day they might hand me, a mendicant friar, at least a small Picasso, a second-class African mask, or a minor work of Max Ernst (I would even have accepted a little Warhol). The dream never came true, but I have a debt of gratitude to the De Menils since I believe they must have paid my salary at the Institute for a couple of years. Indeed, even my slight acquaintance with two such remarkable people was itself a fine gift.

The De Menils' sponsorship of the Institute also meant that they sent their decorator to brighten its offices. The motif again was somewhat tropical with potted plants and grass mats, while the paintings from the De Menil collection were mainly somber and sinister Magrittes.[195] Whether they thought that Magritte's surrealism was appropriate for an institute devoted largely to family therapy and pastoral counseling, I am not sure. Anyway I enjoyed the gloomy Magrittes.

The most memorable experience this contact brought me was the day when the Rothko paintings were installed in the chapel named for them. Texas sunlight is harsh and it then filled the stark, octagonal windowless brick building through its glass ceiling, since moderated by canvas awnings. The twelve panels over ten feet high were brought in their packing cases and I eagerly watched their uncovering. I had seen a number of Rothko's color-field works in New York, and was expecting brilliant hazy reds, blues, and yellows. Instead all the panels seem to be flat black! When they were raised in place in a quieter light it became evident that this black was toned by subtle red and purple washes. Yet, as one steps in from a blazing Texas day, the total effect of the walls is a space of empty night.

In this Rothko Chapel one often remembers that Rothko soon after completing the panels, along with his wife, committed suicide. I think much more significant is his reported saying that he had taken his inspiration from a famous Catholic chapel in Italy, but that for him all traditional symbolism had become emptied of meaning, so that it was necessary to find a new, non-iconic, way of expressing the human spiritual search. I have seen many people, sitting in meditation in the chapel, especially young people who like to assume what they think of as yoga or Buddhist postures as they gaze out into the void of Rothko's art. In a way I think the chapel is absurd, yet its absurdity is truly and artistically expressive of the spiritual desert of our time and hence worthy of nameless meditation.

So is the Barnett Newman upended obelisk before the chapel. The De Menils had first offered this work to the city of Houston as a public monument to Martin Luther King, Jr. When the city fathers rejected this offer because of the inscription to King, John De Menil is said to have proposed to locate it facing Houston City Hall with the offending inscription replaced by a biblical quotation. When asked what this biblical verse would be, he said, "Father, forgive them for they know not what they do."

The Rothko Chapel was intended to be ecumenical in the broadest sense. Soon after the paintings were installed I was asked to celebrate a Mass for an ecumenical group one evening, the first Mass to be offered in the chapel. I thought it would be effective to have the temporary altar set in the center of the darkened octagon with only a central light over the altar and instead of the customary altar candles to have ones on the floor before each painting in some high black iron candlesticks that were at hand. After these were set up John De Menil happened to enter the chapel and was horrified, exclaiming that Rothko would have never have permitted this. Just why I never found out, but I embarrassedly removed them. The De Menils' starkly odd taste is beyond my criticism. Dominique De Menil also once discussed with me a project of an exhibition of popular Hispanic religious art and I wrote up a theological schema for it, but I don't believe anything ever came of this. She was a woman who was elegantly gentle in manner and yet unpretentious, very serious, and quiet.

Certainly this was not an experience I had expected in Texas. It agrees with John De Menil's answer to the remark of a New York friend who asked him, "Why do live in Houston? It's a cultural desert!" De Menil simply said, "But it is in a desert that miracles happen." Those who visit Houston today know that it is culturally quite enriched, and much of this is the result of the magnanimous influence of the De Menils. Yet it remains a paradox that the De Menil taste, so subtle and so eccentric, should flourish in, of all places, boisterous, in-your-face Texas.

John Paul II and Theology of the Body

Through all this I kept working on *Theologies of the Body*, trying to become a moral theologian who could bring modern medicine, modern psychotherapy, and yes modern art which has much to say about modern bodily existence, into some kind of synthesis. At that time I do not believe I was aware that Pope John Paul II was also developing a remarkable "theology of the body." Must we, like Mark Rothko, conclude that modern culture is a windowless room opening on to the void with a wordless question? The Pope came to this question especially through his profound reflections on human sexuality. My poor efforts, however, arose from my rejection of the Marxist view that we can create ourselves. We ought not to confuse human "creativity" that always works constructively by imitating nature and bending it to human, freely chosen purposes, with God's creation out of nothing not for his own advantage but purely for the goodness of what is created. Yet in the fine arts there is an analogy to this creation for the sake of the work itself.

Thus it was fortunate that I was able to continue a this time of artistic events that enriched my thinking. While I did not go to the theater or concerts often, I did hear the Houston Symphony and opera a few times and saw a good production there of Tennessee Williams's, *The Rose Tattoo,* and on a visit to Minneapolis a remarkable production of *The Tempest* in the Guthrie Theater. Williams' plays like those of O'Neill's seem to me to be suffocatingly sentimental and typical of the false "compassion" bred by the secular transformation of that noble virtue into self-pity. Another experience was the pleasure of being included in a Canadian TV symposium, "The Sacred in Art," already mentioned, in which I commented on the difficulty of artists like Rothko and others to adapt modern abstract and surrealistic styles, designed to express the artist's totally autonomous "creative" freedom, to express instead the "sacred," focused on the artist's submission to inspiration by a higher truly creative power.

Daisy

I also had esthetic experiences in the varied landscapes through which I traveled when I went from Houston to visit my mother, brother, and his wife living in Daisy, Arkansas as I explained in the last chapter. To reach Daisy I drove each time from Houston through East Texas and through the astonishingly ugly town of Texarkana, but before and after in delightful contrast the country was very beautiful Many people think of Texas as a brown prairie like Dallas or Midland, but in fact this huge state encloses a rich repertory of landscapes. East Texas is rolling wooded hills with pine and hardwood forests. On the way north from Houston is Lufkin where in the piney woods there is a cloistered monastery of Dominican nuns founded by a nun with whom remarkable phenomena were associated. Some believe that she was possessed, and I talked with a priest who personally had witnessed her levitate and knew of her immediately fulfilled prophesy of the great oil explosion at Texas City. I might add that another priest in Houston told me of another woman he was counseling who also had extraordinary mystical gifts. I mention these reports not because I could verify them, but to illustrate that the Marian apparitions which are now being reported in such numbers are simply a continuation of phenomena which are always a part of Catholic experience in the midst of our prosaic life.

In Daisy, my mother and I were able to take a few drives by auto through the surrounding country which was rugged and picturesque and visit the diamond mine (advertised as the only one in the United States) at Murfreesboro, where for a small fee one can dig a diamond for oneself. We tried it, without luck. The first year I was in Houston I drove to Daisy and then for a meeting on to St. Louis through the heart of the Ozarks, which are geologically an ancient extension westward of the Alleghenies, along a winding, mountain road of great beauty. Another scenic memory of driving from Daisy to Houston at the end of a Christmas holiday visit is especially vivid. The night before there had been snow and an ice storm. For some fifty miles through the pine forests the road through the hills was shining glass so that I had to drive with exceeding caution, but the trees were beautifully filigreed as the ice-coated clusters of pine needles shone in the rising morning light.

THE BIG YET LITTLE BANG

The universe is a sea of light
ultra red and ultra violet
positive, negative
vibrating in all directions
mirroring, focusing emotions,
reflecting, condensing thoughts
expanding from a point
too bright for color,
ever entropically darkening
chilled to zero;
yet these quickening minutes
my heart thumps thump,
air pulled in and then let go
so that at a spiritual point
I choose my fate.

Chapter 16 - Practical Ecumenism

Dubuque

During the three years, 1969-1972, when I was enjoying this pleasant interim in Houston and shifting my interests from philosophy to bioethics, yet always in view of the science-religion problem, I was called to Dubuque. Our Central Dominican Province had decided that the decline in vocations following Vatican II made it finally necessary to close the philosophy studium in River Forest and move the whole of Aquinas Institute to Dubuque as it had been during the time, described in the last chapter, when River Forest was being renovated. Fr. O'Rourke who had succeeded me as President of Aquinas Institute in Dubuque ended his term in 1972. His successor was Fr. Cletus Wessels, a native Iowan and a man of delightful personality, a dear friend of mine and very generally liked. He was himself philosophically and theologically a Thomist, but nevertheless very taken with the "spirit of Vatican II" which he understood to mean not only the ecumenism Fr. O'Rourke had promoted but also an openness to new psychological and sociological ideas. Thus in religious life he favored experimentation with "small communities" and tried living with only a Cooperator Brother, Vincent Dirienzo, in an apartment outside the Priory. Br. Vincent whose work is maintenance is a notably cheerful and flexible person. Though not highly educated, Vincent never seemed to find talking with intellectually oriented priests a problem and was an excellent companion. Fr. Wessels attended workshops on futurism, on methods of adult education, and on psychological testing of the faculty, etc. These novelties were unsettling to a faculty and community already troubled by rapid changes and reinforced the lingering influence of the Menninger experience and of Fr. D. whose departure from the Order and priesthood I have narrated. The Prior during these years in Dubuque was Reginald Masterson, a tall thin priest, whose older brother was also a Dominican priest. Reginald was a man of enthusiasms and high ideals, who had suffered from tuberculosis before entering the Order and seemed rather fragile. It was said of him that one day he was theologically conservative and the next liberal, but never anything less than intense.

As my three years in Houston drew to an end, I received word from my Provincial that Fr. Wessels, as President of Aquinas Institute of Theology ("and Philosophy" had by now been dropped from its title), needed me in Dubuque as professor of moral theology, since no permanent replacement had been found for the aforesaid Fr. D., who had held this position for some years, with the dubious results already mentioned. Since I have always loved teaching Dominican students I found no difficulty in leaving my Houston post, stimulating though it was.

Fr. Moraczewski, as a member of the former Lyceum, had helped me to see medical ethics as an important field where science and theology might be brought together. This three years in a great medical center had taught me much which I was trying to incorporate in *Theologies of the Body* on which I was to continue to work for some years in Dubuque. It seldom snows in semitropical Houston and never did it snow during my years working there, but when on the February morning that I drove for the last time to the airport it was through slush and with snowflakes on the windshield. It was still dark when I left that interlude of my life behind.

I quickly grew to love Dubuque, a quaint old town with friendly people on a high bluff among lovely hills along the broad Mississippi. Sometimes, however, driving down the steep streets from the heights to the flats of downtown in the long winters could be like skiing. Dubuque has retained at Fourth Street one of the old cable cars or "lifts" which at one time made it possible to ascend to the top of the bluffs that mark the west side of the Mississippi floodplain. It is an inexpensive and modest thrill to ascend and descend in this cable car like the angels on Jacob's ladder. Dubuque also has an antique shot tower where round lead shot for the Civil War was produced by dropping gobs of molten metal from the top of the tower into a pool of water sizzling at the bottom. The French trader Julian Dubuque chose the location of the town because of the lead mines in the region. Under our property at St. Rose Priory there were such abandoned and long unexplored mines. The myth of the "old lady from Dubuque wearing tennis shoes" who is supposed to personify provincialism merely shows that the town is a style setter since now everyone wears his or her Reeboks and Nikes to the opera.

Dubuque is a largely Catholic town, with Lutherans numbering second. One sign of its Catholicism which I first noted was the number of houses that had shrines to the Blessed Virgin Mary in their yards or gardens. These were often created out of old bathtubs set on end and half-sunk into the ground to make a nice niche for

Mary's statute and surrounded with shrubs and flowers. Dubuque
winters, however, are severe.

WINTER FOG

Ugly,
ugliest day of the year, patched with dead snow
       dead grass, dirty earth.
       (How can the holy earth be dirty?)
swell and fall under the scattering houses of
       "Historic Old Dubuque."
with dullard window-eyes in the blank glare
       of a sun trying and failing
       to push way
       the uglifying fog.

Yes, yes, the spring will push away
       this last late fog of winter.
Yes, yes, but I have lost that simple faith in spring
       and stand so hopeless
protected only by this dirty glass
       from winter air,
       myself
       needing repair.

This day is a void between lost winter,
       faintly promised spring,
Meaningless
       yet revealing here in me
       an ugly gap.

O holy earth, down in your hidden roots
       the sap
       begins to rise, green, yellow,
       flowers—
              sun—
                    light—

Here in chill facticity
without rebuke,

historic old Dubuque.

In that town the future had both a prayerful and humorous quality. One of the Chicago-bred friars remarked, "If you have cancer and only six months to live, come here to Dubuque and it will seem like six years." The poem just quoted I can compare to an older winter poem written in Chicago in my Marxist days where the note of hope was in a revolution produced by the proletariat "men of steady will" that would bring human solidarity.

SNOWBOUND

The snow closes each street, thickens on the wind.
My thoughts are narrowed too.

A train moves through a silent distance,
no walls are felt, nor the great wheels,
internal meshes of pipelines
and of wires connecting
places unseen.

A train whistles in farther, farther distance until muted.
Other people are out there too
not known
to me.

People of steady will, men wondering
that other men knowing other men knowing well
common causes, usually
working together, do not turn and speak.

Here in the snow no one could hear me if I called,
by impalpable impenetrable white coldness walled.

Not known, unseen.

Views

The view from my corner window in St. Rose Priory overlooked a pleasant golf course with the towers of two Catholic schools, Loras College for men and Clarke College for women, in the distance. On the west were the buildings of Mount St. Bernard Seminary and the former Good Shepherds Convent for "Magdalens" that was composed of a pre-Civil War house and a rabbit warren of buildings added on by the nuns. We Dominicans occupied that labyrinthine convent for a year or so while St. Rose was being built, a very large structure that could house 250 persons, with a vast chapel and refectory, and an ample auditorium and library. While a very practical building, it was in the stark, redbrick style of the 1950s that inspired the name of the "Coca-Cola Factory" by which some called it. Moreover its location was odd. As a native remarked, "Only Dominicans would have build not on the top of a hill but in a hole!"

I lived at St. Rose under two excellent priors. Fr. Matthew Hynous is a canon lawyer, who has served our province selflessly in many tasks. He is from the Bohemian suburb of Chicago, Berwyn, whose citizens are known for their frugal ways and their mushroom hunting. In spite of his skeptical caution, he somehow always let me do what I pleased. Fr. John Taylor proved a remarkable administrator and I will speak further of this later. As a post-Vatican II prior he knew how to combine a democratic style with decisiveness.

Although the very conservative and pious Archbishop and the presbyterate of Dubuque tended to treat us as alien intruders with whom they hardly knew what to do, we were very popular in the town, and our Masses on Sundays and holidays were crowded. I believe our preaching and liturgy were outstanding, although we were still given to some dubiously "creative" liturgies which might well have displeased the more conservative. I myself found the liturgies at that time among some of the most spiritually rewarding of my life. In this poem I refer to the fact that the liturgical colors of the penitential seasons of Advent and Lent are violet, except that on the third Sunday of each season they brighten into rose since on those Sundays the liturgy rejoices (*Gaudete! Laetare!*) in anticipation of the great feasts to come.

VIOLET AND ROSE

> For Advent vestments violet and rose.
> Violet and rose for Lent.
> > Violet for sorrow of waiting.
> > Rose for anticipating
> > out of sepulchral violet

the Sun's renewal.
Christmas morn, the tree of splendor.
Where eagles gather, Judgment dawns.
From the rose wounds in feet, hands, heart—
    through His flesh the Splendor.

Yet now the violet tedium—
O Lord, how long, how long?
Silent confusion.
Fragments of ruins.
How heavy the stone
for my weak strength.

Joy in the heart's sorrow.
Prudence! Vigilance! You bridesmaids,
vested in violet
broidered in rose!
In silence your vigilant song,
"O Lord, how long, how long?"

Moral Theology Renewed

I rejoiced in teaching moral theology at Aquinas, and also in the program for permanent deacons for the Archdiocese with classes at Waterloo, a very boring two hours' drive away. Later I even briefly tried to popularize this material by writing a column on "Moral Directives" for *The Christian Family Weekly*, September 1978 to August 1979. In a newspaper interview to the local paper in 1973 at the time I said,

The field of moral theology is critical for Christians at the present time. Catholic have always had a well-developed traditional system of ethics and it is important that students be thoroughly acquainted with this tradition. These traditions, however, were formed when society and institutions were very stable. We are now in a period of great change and technological advance, with many new problems arising which require us to rethink our traditional system. What is needed is an ethical outlook which lays stress not so much on rules of behavior as on practical ways of achieving fundamental Christian values in society and in our personal lives.

This statement reflected the fact that at this time there was much discussion among theologians about the necessity of the revision of moral theology promoted by Vatican II. One of the proposals for such a revision was called "proportionalism," a theory I will discuss at some length in the next chapter. Thus I was faced with studying such new proposals and making some difficult decisions about their merits. To do this it was necessary for me to study a still deeper question that underlies the debate about proportionalism and from which the Vatican II demand for a revision of moral theology has arisen, namely, "What makes a human action moral or immoral?" or as a student once asked me, "Father, what makes good better than bad?"

My work on bioethical questions in Houston had already made it painfully clear to me that disagreements about such questions arise from deeper and more general differences about how moral decisions should be made. Thus I became preoccupied with more theoretical questions than the concrete practical problems such as are met in hospitals. While these arguments sometimes seem like a post-Vatican II political battle in the Church between "conservatives" and "liberals," it actually has very deep historical roots. One notion of morality is that a human act is good or bad, moral or immoral, depending on whether it conforms to some moral law or norm, such as the Ten Commandments carved by God on stone, that has been legislated by a higher authority, whether this is public opinion, the government, the church, or God. This view is called deontological or duty ethics (the Greek for duty is *deontos*). In competition with duty ethics has always been means-ends or teleological (from Greek *telos*, goal) according to which a human act is good if it is an effective means to the ultimate goal for which we all strive, true happiness; but it is bad if it blocks the way to this happiness.

These two views are not as such contradictory. Sometimes, of course, as when God commanded Abraham to sacrifice his son Isaac, we have to obey even when we do not understand why God commands what may seem wrong. Yet we obey because we are sure that God knows what is best for us and this is why he commands it. God, therefore, is primarily a teleologist and only secondarily a deontologist.

The Mosaic Law called for a dutiful obedience to many ritual regulations whose purpose in the course of time became obscure. Hence the whole rabbinical tradition is legalistic and rabbis are not priests but canon lawyers. The biblical Prophets, on the other hand, never ceased warning the people that what God asks of them is not simply a legalistic, external obedience, but a change of heart. It must be a sincere commitment to the true goal of life that God has set before them, "Choose life", not death!" (Dt 30:19). The Wisdom writers reinforce this prophetic teaching by showing from human experience that good behavior leads to happiness, bad behavior to misery.

Jesus said (Mt 22: 36-40) "Love God and your neighbor as yourself for this is the law and the prophets." Thus Christian morality is above all a "Way" to union with God and neighbor, a "narrow way that leads to life," (Mt 7;13). It demands that every step we take be in view of our true goal. At the same time it confirms the moral laws (though not the ritual and judicial laws that were given only to the Jews) of the Old Testament as sound guides on this way.

In the history of the Church these two aspects of morality, the deontological and the teleological, have continued to be taught and sometimes to compete with each other. Generally, however, the Fathers of the Church and the writers of the early Middle Ages emphasized the teleology of the New Testament. In the High Middle Ages the university theologians, and most of all St. Thomas Aquinas, found that Aristotle's systematic and strongly teleological ethics was a valuable philosophical support to this New Testament, teleological approach. In the Late Middle Ages, however, beginning with Duns Scotus and in a still more radical form in the Nominalism of William of Ockham, skepticism (not unlike that of the rabbis) arose about the power of human thought to understand God's mysterious laws. Hence, the emphasis shifted toward a deontological approach to moral theology that was voluntaristic (of the will) and legalistic rather than, as it had been previously, sapiential (of wisdom) and teleological.

With the Protestant Reformation this Nominalist, voluntaristic deontology was pushed to the extreme. Luther had been raised in Nominalism and conceived God's Law as so holy that sinful man cannot hope to obey it. Instead Jesus has fulfilled that impossible Law in our place ("vicarious atonement") and wiped the books clean. Of course, the Catholic teaching had always taught that we cannot fulfill God's laws except by the transforming grace of Christ, but also had taught that grace frees us to seek him freely with our whole hearts. Calvin, on the contrary, so strongly emphasized the sovereignty of God that he thought it impious to seek out God's reasons for his laws. Later the leading philosopher of the Enlightenment, Immanuel Kant, who had been raised a Lutheran, reinterpreted this "divine command ethics" by replacing external law (heteronomy) with moral self-legislation by the individual's use of reason (autonomy). Hence, to escape the subjectivism and moral relativism to which Kant foresaw this emphasis on moral autonomy might lead, he argued that for persons of good will human reason provides a set of transcultural moral categories accessible to all rational beings. Kant had difficulty, however, in showing how these formal, transcendental, abstract norms can be given concrete, categorical content.

One might have thought that Catholic theologians, therefore, would have reacted to Protestant and Kantian deontologism by returning to Aquinas and Augustine. In fact, however, embarrassed by Protestant accusations of moral laxity, Catholic moralists, under Jesuit leadership, produced manuals of moral theology to guide confessors that stressed a dutiful obedience to moral norms without much effort to show a teleological justification of these norms. When in the nineteenth century Catholic theologians were pressured by the great success of Kant's radical, idealist deontologism, they sometimes retreated in confusion. Only when Leo XIII revived Thomism in 1879 did Catholic moral theologians begin to revise ethics in a teleological direction. After Vatican II both conservatives and liberals have supported a teleological revision of moral theology, but have often sharply disagreed about exactly what form this revision should take. In what follows I will try as briefly as I can to discuss the chief controversies in which I have been involved and will typify each of them by saying something of the personalities of those with whom I have had dialogue, if indeed it was a dialogue, as I hope it was, rather than a polemic.

Second Term As Regent of Studies

As I moved to Dubuque not only did I find that I was to teach moral theology, but that I was again to be Regent of Studies for the Central Province, though the duties of office had now been changed. Previously the Regent of Studies for the Province was also the President of Aquinas Institute. Now the regency was separated from the presidency, occupied by Fr. Wessels. This left to me as Regent little more to do than act as an academic counselor for Dominican students. Yet I did have one special project in mind for which I obtained the President Wessels' approval. After Vatican II it was realized throughout the Order that the isolation of our houses of study from the university world had cut off Dominican formation from modernity. This isolation, so different from the prominence of Dominicans in the medieval universities, was the result of the secularization of those universities by the Enlightenment. No one deplored this isolation more than I, since it had always been my dream to see our studium located at the University of Chicago! But how would that be possible without a physical relocation? In fact many of the Dominican provinces have in recent years reduced their houses of study to student residencies and sent the young friars to the theology departments of universities. But, as pointed out by Vincent de Couesnongle, our Master of the Order during much of this period, this has resulted in a loss of our unique Dominican intellectual identity. More practically, it has led some provincials, always under pressure to find recruits for various jobs, to think that since there is no longer need to prepare a studium faculty that they no longer need to send friars for higher studies.

To solve this dilemma, my idea was to send our students to universities with a theological faculty while maintaining a small group of Dominican professors living in the student residence who would conduct continuing seminars in which these students would critically reflect in the light of the Dominican tradition on what they were learning elsewhere. I thought that this was the truly Dominican ideal, exemplified by St. Albert and St. Thomas, openness to truth wherever it is to be found, a critical, countercultural openness. I realized that Dubuque, lacking a major university, was not an ideal place to do this, but at least, as Fr. O'Rourke had seen, Dubuque supplied the ecumenical opportunity to study in the cross-currents of the Catholic, Lutheran, and Presbyterian faculties where many of the trends of modernity were in evidence. Moreover, I hoped to experiment with organizing such a seminar, which if it worked, might then be used in case, as I already suspected, we would soon have to leave Dubuque and seek a university center.

My experiment, however, did not work. It was undertaken at a time when the decline in vocations had reached bottom, so that our Dominican students were few and disorganized by the Vatican II transition. To them an additional required seminar without formal credit was not something they could take seriously and I was unable to inspire them to any understanding of its necessity for their Dominican ministry. Moreover, although I tried to explain my goals to the faculty, they remained passive to the project and seemed to me to do little to support it before the students. I still believe in this model for Dominican education, but it would have to have full faculty support and be built into the required curriculum.

I was most troubled by the decline in solid instruction in Thomism among our Dominican students who were on the whole much more concerned about modern psychology and certain theological fads. The problem, I believe, was that our Dominican professors, who in the past had been, as I have explained, to my mind much too narrowly Thomist, were now desperately trying to catch up with Vatican II theology and had difficulty in synthesizing what they were learning with their own Thomistic training. The ideas of the Lyceum that might have given a clue to such a synthesis had chiefly influenced our philosophy professors in River Forest, but had never had much influence on our Dubuque theological faculty.

The emphasis in the school administration seemed to be "futurism," the prediction of short-run and long-run trends in society and education, an enthusiasm of Fr. Wessels. The preoccupation with psychological analysis that had begun with the trip to the Menninger Clinic also continued. Thus in 1978 the faculty were all asked to take the Myers-Briggs Personality Self-Assessment based on Jung's theory of the Introversion-Extraversion distinction and his theory of four—Sensing, Intuition, Feeling, Thinking—dimensions of the human personality. The psychologist who administered the tests gave me the following feedback:

You tend to be an extrovert who uses intuition as your favorite process of perceiving, and feeling as your favorite process of judging, who tends to face the outside world primarily in this judging manner. Occupationally you tend to the esthetic situation where there are many opportunities for self-expression, but you also tend strongly to the investigative or scientific. You get along well in an academic setting with academic types. This is congruent with your occupational preferences. You have little inclination to the "realistic" or "conventional" occupations, some inclination to the enterprising and social (extraversion) and most to the esthetic and investigative."

We were each required to comment on our analysis and I wrote:

This all corresponds pretty well with my personal perception of myself and confirms my feeling that the common idea in the community that I am primarily rational and philosophic is not very accurate, since the esthetic is more important to me. I also was confirmed in my feeling that pastoral counseling is not my inclination. On the side of things I need to improve the following: (a) More development of sensing (in sense of awareness of facts and situation) and perception as auxiliary modes of dealing with situations. (b) I need to enjoy and take satisfaction in present accomplishments more, and live with less regrets or future anxieties, and with less punitive feelings because of past failures.

This last point was based on the fact that I had rated very low on "time competency" (living in the present) and on ability to accept weaknesses, while on other points I was in the normal range. I didn't know what to make of the revelation that according this test, the work at which I might best hope to succeed was "Policeman"! How does law-enforcement fit my teleological ethics?

I recounted in the last chapter what brought Aquinas Institute of Theology to Dubuque as St. Rose Priory, but I did not explain how it became ecumenical. The bishops of Iowa housed their seminarians in the nearby Mt. St. Bernard's on a hill opposite St. Rose. Originally the intention was to send them to classes at St. Rose along with the Dominican students but this proved impractical because the diocesan clerics were prepared by only two years of philosophy in English compared to our Dominicans' three in Latin. Consequently, the final arrangement was that the Dominican faculty after teaching our Dominican students had then to repeat their classes to the diocesan clerics at St. Bernard's. Furthermore, there was a tension between the three diocesan priests in charge of St. Bernard's: the Rector, his assistant, and the spiritual director. Our Dominican professors were forbidden to interfere in any way with the diocesan students' personal formation, yet were required to vote on their eligibility for priesthood.

Fr. Raphael Gillis (d. 1979), a tall, gaunt Dominican, who when he lectured seemed to be boxing our ears, but who was a man of great principle and integrity, was the first *Lector Primarius* of theology in Dubuque. He was constantly exasperated by the difference in perspective between us Dominicans and the diocesan clergy. This irritation was aggravated by the very meager financial contribution the bishops made to the maintenance of the St. Rose community in compensation for the work of the faculty, considering that it included some thirteen professors with doctorates.

This tension came to a crisis when the so-called "Vatican II spirit" filtered into Mt. St. Bernard from other diocesan seminaries and the Dubuque seminarians sent out letters to the priests of the diocese calling for help against what they claimed was the Rector's tyranny. Actually the Rector was a timid soul who dared not even grant a school holiday without consulting the Bishops' Board of the seminary. Legend has it that when he was asked to liberalize the seminary "rule" he gave permission to the students to smoke, but only in their rooms and provided they used ashtrays of a type carefully described in his gracious dispensation.

The Archbishop, a kind but also very timid and cautious prelate, requested Fr. Kevin O'Rourke, then Vice-President of Aquinas (I was still President but living in River Forest) to quietly remove two members of our faculty, who had been reported by certain students as encouraging their rebellion. These two (one was the troubled and troubling Fr. D.) but the another the prudent and brilliant Fr. O. were prominent members of the faculty who denied any interference more than to express sympathy with the students' unhappiness. Our faculty as a whole supported the accused and even threatened resignation if they were dismissed. We explained to the Archbishop that our Institute would risk its accreditation if we violated academic freedom by dismissing these professors without due process, so that a formal hearing of the charges would be necessary. The Archbishop took the position that if he were to agree to such an investigation he would be violating the confidence of the students who had informed him of the situation. The matter rested until a year later when the Board of Bishops, without further discussion with us, announced that they were closing Mt. St. Bernard so as to save money on its maintenance and to be free to send their seminarians to various other schools. This sudden definitive action without consultation and, as we understood it, out of line of with our contract, seemed to us unfair, but we did not oppose it.

Ecumenical Efforts

In the meantime, Fr. O'Rourke had wisely formed an academic association with the School of Religion at Iowa University in Iowa City and with the two Dubuque seminaries, the Lutheran Wartburg Seminary of what was then the American Lutheran Church (now merged with the Evangelical Lutheran Church in America) and the Presbyterian Seminary of the University of Dubuque. Since by this time our Dominican student body was in serious decline, we found it possible to offer office and residence space to the Presbyterians who were in need of a new building at the University of Dubuque. Since Wartburg was not far away in that small city, this effected a very intimate union of schools of Catholic, Lutheran, and Reformed tradition and one that proved to be what some educators have told us was the most practical ecumenical venture of this type in the United States.

Our Dominican community had to make a considerable adjustment in its life to accommodate this new situation. We had also arranged with the Franciscan Fathers of the Assumption (a community of Polish origin) to send their students to us, so that St. Rose now consisted of a Franciscan wing, a Presbyterian wing, and a Dominican wing, together with a common refectory, library, auditorium and lounge, and a front section with Dominican and Presbyterian faculty and administrative offices. The main chapel continued to be used for Catholic liturgy and a section of the building was remodeled as a chapel for the Presbyterians. The common refectory gave much opportunity for the Presbyterians and Catholics to eat together and get well acquainted.

On the whole this was a most pleasant and profitable experience for us all. The faculty profited most because we had frequent meetings and discussions both about academic business and about theological topics. The students, I regret to say, profited less, because both the Catholics and the Protestant students were hesitant to take full advantage of the possibilities of cross-registration. To the Catholics the Lutheran atmosphere of the classes seemed depressing, while the Presbyterian seemed provincial and rural. I never heard the Protestant students expressing their reactions very openly. Nevertheless we enjoyed a general friendliness and politeness on all sides and this close association did not lead to doctrinal indifferentism, as some initially feared.

I used to joke that our main ecumenical achievement in Dubuque was that at the early faculty gatherings when the Presbyterians were asked what they wanted to drink, the reply was usually a hesitant, "Well—perhaps a little dry sherry," but by the time we left Dubuque they were reaching for the bourbon to pour themselves a hearty slug, just as we Dominicans did. Actually we Catholics learned much from this cordial relationship and I hope the

Protestants learned more than a heartier attitude toward a convivial drink.

What did I personally learn from our ecumenical situation in
Dubuque? My contact in Blackwell with Protestant clergy as a youth
in Blackwell had given me a rather low view of Protestant intellectuality, but here I met intellectual equals or superiors. Next I
learned a deep respect for the Christian character and piety of my
Protestant colleagues and their warm humanity. I had no reason to
distrust their *fides quo*, i. e., the good will with which they accepted
the Gospel as they had heard it. The ecumenical problem, of course,
is the *fides quod*, i. e., the recognition of what the content of the Gospel really is. As regards this content too there was—praise God!— a
broad area of agreement, yet certain suspicions on both sides colored that agreement.

My confrere, Fr. Ralph Powell (d. 2001) who set the highest priority on ecumenism of anyone I know, especially enjoyed this constant ecumenical interchange. Among the friends Ralph and I made
are the two from the Presbyterian faculty with whom for some time
we kept contact: Donald Bloesch and Richard Drummond. Bloesch,
a Protestant systematician of note and author of many publications,[196] with great humility often consulted me to get certain points
of Roman Catholic teaching straight, but I always felt he could not
quite free himself of the conviction that Catholics are at heart
Pelagians. Of course we are, as are Protestants, since Pelagian self-
righteousness taints us all, but the teaching of the Catholic Church
rests unambiguously on the saying of Jesus, "Without me, you can
do nothing," (Jn 15:5). Dominicans loyal to St. Thomas Aquinas have
always made that saying the basis of their preaching and teaching
against every trend to qualify that "nothing," while at the same time
we have defended human freedom, since we are most free when we
are most dependent on Christ who came to set us free. "If the Son
frees you, then you will be truly free," (Jn 8:36,). Richard H. Drummond, for many years a missionary to Japan, is a man of great,
catholic heart, open to all that is good and true, and his works on
Buddhism and Christianity are an important ecumenical contribution.[197] Our experience with the Lutherans was similar. They made
wonderful, pious, and very learned colleagues, but I always felt that
for them every theological assertion had to fit into the opposition
between Law vs. Gospel or it was suspect. Are my categories as a

Catholic theologian this rigid?   May the Holy Spirit to whom we pray in the Latin hymn, heed our prayer:

Flecte quod est rigidum,   Flex the rigid,
fove quod est frigidum,   Warm the cold,
rege quod est devium.   Make the crooked straight.

While the three schools were able to set up a team-taught course on the Bible that worked very well (it would not have been so easy if any had held to Biblical literalism), however we never managed to do so in the field of church history, which seemed so ideal for team-teaching. The reason was that while our Dominican faulty and the Presbyterian faculty agreed to divide the time of the two required courses into approximately chronologically equal periods, the Lutheran faculty could never bring themselves to give less than an entire semester (half the time) to the sixteenth century.

Also with two very ecumenical-minded professors I team-taught a course on Christian Ethics. At the beginning of the course we decided we would each give a lecture on the general characteristics of ethical teaching in each of our traditions. In my lecture I emphasized that for Catholics the moral life is a journey toward God, a growth in spiritual likeness to Christ. My partner questioned the metaphor of "journey," and the talk of "spiritual growth." Why had I not rather emphasized "forgiveness"? As for the Presbyterian, he confessed that while he had much to say about twentieth century Christian ethics, he was not well acquainted with the history of the Reformed tradition in ethics, and asked me if I could recommend a good book on the ethical teachings of Calvin! Both professors were puzzled what I meant by the term "moral theology" rather than the term "Christian ethics" to which they were accustomed.

Such experiences showed me that ecumenical theological efforts must be especially directed to certain key concepts that must be clarified before we are sure that we understand each other and even to the metaphors by which we express these concepts. Thus the metaphor of a "journey" fits the Catholic conception of grace as a process of growth and transformation involving the cooperative efforts of the traveler. But this sits uncomfortably with Protestants for whom "grace" is rather an act of forgiveness pronounced by God, like a lenient judge in a courtroom letting a prisoner go free. There is truth in both metaphors but like all metaphors they are ambiguous.

I also became convinced that it is highly profitable, perhaps more profitable than theological discussions, to share with each other our actual life of prayer and spiritual struggle. Here I think we are closer together already than in our doctrinal understandings and formulations. The three schools shared quite a good deal of common worship that was truly edifying.

A particular problem arose from the fact that both Lutherans and Presbyterians frequently attended our Eucharists, which they found lively and beautiful. Could they also go to Holy Communion? The Presbyterians generally realized that their Reformed Eucharistic doctrine made this inappropriate, but many of the Lutherans wished to receive since they fully accepted the Real Presence of Christ, although they were not committed to what they considered the non-biblical notion of "transubstantiation." Catholic canon law allows the local bishop to permit participation in Holy Communion by baptized but non-Catholic persons who believe in the Real Presence, provided that they are unable to attend Eucharistic services in their own churches. We hoped that in view of the fact that the Protestant practice was to hold such services less frequently and thus that the students in their seminaries found our Masses much more available than their own Eucharists that the Archbishop might judge that this law applied to them. He, however, did not see this as possible and asked us to announce occasionally at the Masses that the official teaching of the Catholic Church generally permits only Catholics to receive Holy Communion at Catholic Eucharists. We complied, but did not turn away those Protestants who still came up to communion, as in fact we knew many did. This, I believe, is generally the pastoral practice of American priests.

Some theologians argue that since the Eucharist is not only a sign but a cause of Christian unity, we ought to permit open communion at least for the baptized so as to further ecumenical unity. This seems to me to exaggerate the *ex opere operato* (the efficacy of the sacrament in itself) to the neglect of the *ex opere operantis* (the proper disposition of the recipient of the sacrament), a fault of which we have often been accused by Protestants. In other words, a policy of open communion neglects the fact that the sacrament does not confer grace unless it is received with a true act of faith in the sacrament. While no doubt Protestants receiving Catholic communion do receive the grace of an act of faith in Christ, as in any reverent, prayerful act, yet it is not clear that, due to our lack of unity in the content of the Gospel, they receive the specific sacramental grace that effects ecumenical unity.

In the case of the Reformed tradition, which, following Zwingli, does not teach the Real Presence, this seems especially clear. For Lutherans whose belief in the Real Presence signifies the union of the individual communicant with the forgiving Christ, but not the communion of the whole Church under the Catholic bishops, successors of the apostles, and the Pope, successor of St. Peter, it is still not evident that the specific sacramental grace of ecclesial unity is received. No doubt the sincerely intended reception of Catholic Holy Communion, as we shared it in Dubuque, was spiritually profitable to us all and psychologically brought us all closer together in a common act of prayer but that it overcame our lack of unity as the Church Catholic is doubtful.

Moreover, I fear that if such a practice became official it would probably lead to a general decline in the understanding of the Eucharist by Catholics, which sadly is already somewhat attenuated, because they would gradually cease to understand it as an act of Catholic unity. Instead they would begin to see it in a Protestant fashion either with the Reformed as merely symbolic, or with the Lutherans as an act of individual piety. I knew a Sister who said she had received Communion at a Lutheran liturgy and, when I asked why she had done so, said, "I didn't want to offend them." The question of the validity of the consecration of the Eucharist by a minister, who, according to Catholic doctrine, had not been validly ordained, never seemed to have entered her mind.

In brief, for me our ecumenical experience in Dubuque showed that very practical cooperation is possible between Catholic and Protestant (and I would guess Orthodox) seminaries and that it does not usually put the faith or Catholic identity of the students at risk if its purpose and limits are fully explained. Moreover, it increased my empathy and insight into the problems of ecumenism. This was sobering, yet gave an impetus to hope and work toward Christian unty.

My Mother's Death

Not long after my return to Dubuque I received a call from my sister-in-law Helen in Daisy that my mother had suffered a stroke and was lying unconscious in a hospital in neighboring town of Murfreesboro. I hastened there and found her completely comatose. The doctor told me that her condition was probably irreversible and

it also might be difficult to maintain her on intravenous feeding in-
definitely and that I must be ready to decide at what point this medical intervention was to stop.[198] After several days I had to leave her
in the care of my brother Dick and his wife Helen and return to
Dubuque. Mother lingered a month without regaining consciousness before being again anointed and dying peacefully. Thus I experienced how painful bioethical dilemmas can be.

I have read that one's own chance of a fatal illness in the year after the death of a parent is doubled. Certainly its effect is a profound, inexpressible event. Yet I too was at peace. Mother had
repeatedly told me she was ready to die, although once after saying
that she said, "But I still want to live." I know that she had a simple
and absolute confidence in God and I believe that she and my good
father are with Him. My remaining concern, other than for my own
salvation, was my brother and his wife.

Since there was no Catholic Church within miles, Mother's funeral was held in the little Free Will Baptist Church in Daisy. I celebrated the Mass and we buried her in the old Daisy cemetery. The
friendly locals came to the funeral, but I am sure they thought the
whole proceedings very strange. Often when traveling and seeing
some beautiful or historic sight, I find myself thinking about how I
am going to share it with my Mother in talk or by letter as I always
did, then realize how much her joy in my experiences had been essential to my joy in them. As the Psalmist says, it is often at night
that we think of the past and wonder how to understand it and especially our relations to the dead. In Dubuque the winter nights
were long and the snow deep, but unlike in Chicago, blankly white.

ODE TO THE DEAD OF NIGHT

There is a time they call the dead of night.
    It comes once more upon the clock's footfalls
    along the halls and fills the cube of these four walls
while all outside is smoothly blue, bluely white
    with day old snow.

    Near dead, I also seem, what with the long cold
    and lying awake watching dark thoughts unfold.

The night certainly is dead. It has that stare,

its face is smoothing with that faint glare
    that mourners know.
The hands of passed time are folded up. Upon the stair
the mourning cold creaks, I hear it panting with its climb.
The night is dead. Ah, lay it out
on a morgue slab, shroud it close about
so still and naked on the marble, rigid and chill.

    I know I am alive because the pain
    leaves me a little and comes back again.

Here in the cold I think of the hot wave
    that in the summer edges the long light beach
    I think of the green worm in the yellow peach,
the red bird in the sun. Then of Dad and Mother
    lying under the distant snows
that fall again, again, then, thawed, the water flows.
    I think Dad wanted me to succeed as an author
    not end a priest, poor and obscure.
    Mother wanted a daughter
    after my only brother...
but little of their dreams was laid on me.
    Used in life to many a disappointment,
    they heard my choice and made no comment.
How could I doubt their love for me,
all that I took so thanklessly?
    Dreaming I feel its certainty;
    waking, in their long absence
    feel their humble presence,
    warm in the cold.

I hear, waking later long past the dead of night,
    a little noise begins again,
    traffic, streets iced, goes slow,
as into my unconscious my memories sink
Outside my window in the rising light
    the snow
    begins, now pink,
    to glow.

Chapter 17 - Consultant to Bishops

In Process

During these years in Dubuque I did a good deal of traveling, lecturing and giving workshops such as one I gave in 1976 on "Theological Trends" at the Franciscan Center, Lake Geneva, IL. Certainly the most memorable of these for me was in August of 1980 when I participated in a Theological Consultation for Bishops at the Cardinal Spellman Retreat House, in Riverdale, the Bronx, in which the other presenters included such noted theologians as Hans Urs von Balthasar; the Jesuits John Connery, Avery Dulles, and John Mahoney; Walter Kasper, John P. Meier, Jerome D. Quinn, Wilhelm Ernst and the philosopher Kenneth Schmitz with whom I was later to teach in Washington, DC at the John Paul II Cultural Center.

I also did a fair amount of publishing and continued my seemingly endless work on my *Theologies of the Body*. Two articles, "Change and Process"[199] and "Aquinas and Process Theology,"[200] especially helped my progress on this larger work. These articles dealing with an evolutionary view of the world were partly occasioned by the great popularity of Teilhard de Chardin's work at that time and the fact that while in Houston I had assisted a younger Dominican, Donald Goergen, later to become a Provincial of the Central Province, with his doctoral dissertation devoted to Teilhard. I have often wondered if by chance I once met Teilhard himself, since I remember an encounter at about the right date at Rosary College in River Forest with an interesting French priest whose name I did not ask but who was on his way home from China.

I have been seriously interested in process philosophy, but as an Aristotelian Thomist it has always seemed to me a kind of Neo-Platonism that does not take change seriously enough. Whiteheadian "process" is the predetermined explicitation of what already exists implicitly in the mind of a God who is not the free Creator since, for Whitehead to be really God, He is necessitated to create. The influence of Leibniz's idealism and Bergson's dubious evolutionism on Whitehead is all too evident. My interest in these authors but disagreement with them led me to argue in *Theologies of the Body* for a "radical process philosophy" but of an Aristotelian type.

Aristotle, it is true, did not reduce all reality to "process" since he maintained that the primary existents are at least relatively stable substances. Yet, unlike Plato and the Neo-Platonic tradition, Aristotle maintained that (a) process (change) is real and not the mere adulteration of being by non-being; and that (b) all material substances in our earthly region are subject to substantial changes that reduce them to pure potency. Aquinas pushed this position to its logical conclusion, namely, that even the heavenly bodies and the spiritual intelligences that move them are contingent, since in all but God existence is really distinct from essence.

Therefore, all created things exist only in real process. On the contrary, for Whitehead even God exists only in process, and since this universal process is thereby necessary not contingent, it ceases to be real change. Instead it becomes what the Neo-Platonist Plotinus called "the moving shadow of eternity," a kind of "dream of God" as it is also in Hindu philosophy. Thus Aquinas, following the logic of Aristotelianism, clearly distinguishes the reality of creaturely change from God's eternity and then relates them as effect to cause by God's free creative act, thereby defending the reality of a processive creation.

Since for Aquinas the universe is related to God but God is not related to the universe, process philosophers frequently raise the objection that this means that for Aquinas God must not be immanent to the world. This is a complete misunderstanding, due to equivocation on different medieval and modern uses of the term "relation." What Aquinas really meant was that God creates the world freely and is not dependent on it for his own life, but for that very same reason God is intimately present to the world by his power, knowledge, and love. "God is more intimate to me," as Aquinas quotes Augustine, "than I am to myself." When one needs another in order to know that other and to love that other, one's own thoughts of self and self-love compete, at least to a degree, with one's knowledge and love of the other. Since God's self-knowledge and self-love are satisfied by his own total truth and goodness, He is absolutely free of any concern to satisfy any need of his own and therefore able to know and love us wholly for ourselves. If we ourselves advance in holiness in imitation of God our own knowing and loving of others takes on something of this divine freedom. We learn to seek little and give much.

LOVE WITHOUT NEED

Because You do not need me
you can love me as I am,
so that only by your loving
I am what I truly am and, yes, can be
and all the harm I did myself
and those you love like you love me
in forgiving me you also healed,
so that in you I am again
what your love made me to be,
and even more like You,
loving all you love yet needing
none but You who love me
just for myself,
and all the more when I am
myself truly.

Collaboration

My major publication of this period was the result of my Houston medical experience and was coauthored with Fr Kevin O'Rourke.[201] When Fr. O'Rourke, my successor as President of Aquinas finished his term he moved to St. Louis as a Vice-President of the Catholic Hospital (now Health) Association, the CHA, a voluntary association of most Catholic health care facilities and publisher of the magazine *Hospital* (now *Health Progress*). Its offices were at that time located in the Medical School of St. Louis University, a Jesuit sponsored institution, since the first President of the Association had been a Jesuit. The CHA recognized its own need for sound research in medical ethics to guide its work. Therefore, in 1972 it gave the seed money to found the *Pope John XXIII Medical-Moral Research and Education Center* first chartered in St. Louis, MO. Soon after I left Houston, Fr. Albert Moraczewski had also left the *Institute for Religion and Human Development* in Houston to become in 1973 the first president of this Pope John XXIII Center in St. Louis. It was later moved to Braintree, MA, and is now the *National Catholic Bioethics Center* in Philadelphia.[202] Fr. Moraczewski and I thought of it as in some respects a continuation of the efforts of the Albertus Magnus Lyceum and of our work in Houston to effect a better interchange between the Catholic tradition of philosophy and theology and modern science and technology.

Bioethics and Bishops

This NCBC also provides consultation on bioethics for individual bishops, Catholic hospitals, and others, and publishes a bulletin, *Ethics and Medics* and a journal, *The National Catholic Bioethics Center Quarterly*. Perhaps the Center's most important work has been a four-day workshop it has conducted for sixteen years in Dallas for Catholic bishops. The bishops have the ultimate responsibility for overseeing the ethical standards of Catholic health care facilities in their dioceses, although they often have little power to enforce these standards. These workshops proved an important occasion for theological discussion among the bishops and have given me much valuable insight into the working of the Catholic Church in the United States. The recent crisis over child sex abuse by clergy has lessened public trust in bishops, but I know from my participation in these workshops how seriously the bishops take their responsibilities in these matters. What the public does not realize and the media fails to make clear is the moral complexity of the decisions bishops are often called on to make, pulled this way and that way, as they are, by different tendencies among the faithful.

Because I was a regular speaker at the Dallas workshop I became known to many bishops. Since these workshops are designed for frank interchange among the bishops and hence are not public, I have many times urged the Center also to invite speakers who dissent from official Church teaching. I think this would assure the bishops that they are getting the whole picture and would give defenders of Church teachings the opportunity to answer them directly before the bishops. I believe that in such a setting, free from the pressures of the public media, and in the honest and charitable atmosphere that these workshops maintain "the truth will prevail." The administration of the Center has feared, however, that the necessary announcement in advance of such dissenting speakers would deter some more conservative bishops from attending. In fact two cautious attempts at having such speakers resulted in one case in the dissenter avoiding anything controversial, and in the other of a campaign of protest by certain zealous pro-life activist laity to get the Knights of Columbus to withdraw their financial support. Fortunately, the then Grand Knight, Virgil C. Dechant, courageously resisted this.

The first of the Center's annual (later biannual) workshops for bishops, with some two hundred attending from the United States, Canada, Mexico, and the Caribbean, was held in Dallas in 1980. Bishops have told me that my talks were helpful in relating medical questions to moral principles in terms with which they are familiar from their theological study. I have found the United States bishops quite free in discussion, always very kind, and pastorally well informed. They are not looking for trouble by adopting an inquisitorial attitude toward theologians. But, since they are seldom learned theologians themselves but only hardworking pastors beset with criticisms from both right and left, they are glad to find theological advisers whom they can understand and can trust to be consistent with papal teaching. In particular a book was needed to explain the Ethical and Religious Directives promulgated by the National Conference of Catholic Bishops in 1971. It also needed to be ample enough to serve as a reference for Catholic health care facilities, yet also be suitable as a textbook for physicians, nurses, and administrators and college students in courses on the subject.

Fr. Kevin O'Rourke, whom I have already frequently mentioned, while working with CHA, saw the great need of such a book. He had been educated at the Dominican Fenwick High School and Notre Dame and got his doctorate in canon law but later took up moral theology and bioethics and, as mentioned above, was at one time a vice-president of the Catholic Health Association. He then taught medical ethics at the Medical School of St. Louis University where he became internationally known as an expert in bioethics. He was also the founder and sometime director of the Department of Health Care Ethics at that School which grants the doctorate in bioethics. Until his death in 2012, he taught at Loyola's Neiswanger Institute in Chicago. Although thoroughly orthodox as a Catholic, he was a very independent minded person, but was also noted for his ability for teamwork and for a very practical but principled approach to moral issues. Kevin was not a man to avoid combat. When young he was nicknamed "Oxey" because of his solid, athletic build and for many years he daily exercised daily by running several miles and annually took part in a marathon. In middle life, unfortunately, he overdid this and had a brain hemorrhage that for over a week left him with constant exhausting hiccups. Since then he has been amazingly active in his work and travel but with difficulties that requires great courage.

Busy as Kevin was with administrative duties, he asked me to serve as coauthor and editor of the work, but its sound basis in clinical and teaching experience and its decisive theological judgment are to be principally credited to him. Moreover, without his practical drive I feel I would never have been able to stick to a task that was not altogether congenial to my main interests, which have been more theoretical. This was for me a mammoth job and required much reading and research on unfamiliar topics, as well as spending time, especially in summers, in St. Louis where library resources were available and where we could consult with medical specialists. Especially wearisome was correcting all the "sexist" language that seemed to invest our drafts. This concern with the gender of pronouns on which publishers now insist has, in my opinion, really done less for gender equality than caricature it by forcing writers, male and female, to use plurals when singulars would be more vivid English.

Thus under Fr. O'Rourke's lead and coauthorship, my most successful publication, *Health Care Ethics: A Theological Approach*[203] written originally on commission from the Catholic Hospital Association, was finally completed in 1978. It has also been made available in a shortened textbook edition, *Ethics of Health Care.*[204] The popularity of the first work through five editions seems due to the fact it gives full credit to the Church's teachings on this complex subject. This has been especially needed at a time when other books, even those written by Catholics, either avoided doctrinal issues or dissented from church tradition on important points in the direction of a proportionalist methodology. In writing this book Fr. O'Rourke and I found that one of the central problems of medical ethics is the difficulty that our technological culture has in dealing with the inevitability of suffering in life.

In the following poem I wanted to emphasize that it is only in this life that we freely choose our destiny and freely accept the suffering necessary to achieve heaven. In purgatory we will have to suffer, but our heaven will be already assured. In hell we could suffer forever against our unchangeable, selfish will.

PURGATORY

God's purgatory is for heaven.
    Souls are there drawn upward
    through still lakes of ice and vortices of fire

        toward a peace of pure desire.
Their eyes never deviate,
with hands folded in fixed decision
     in healing agony
     they wait in prayer.

Another process urges us to hell,
      here we spin downward through the circling crowds
      of rage, mobs in flight
         into the confusing clamor of the night.
Our eyes never deviate,
our hands harden in fixed decision
     in willful savagery
     in futile hate.

For we have given up choosing anything but a button to touch
      (our subconscious does that better too),
now that we have machines to guide, to lead, to speak,
      to wait, to watch, there is not much for us to do.
Since we can no longer lift our rubber arms in prayer,
we leave that far behind with hope and unpolluted air.

Now we shall amuse ourselves with thoughts
      shining like aeroplanes in the sun
      prepared to bomb whatever we see run
      and who can care
      at last that we have far outsoared
      terror,
      even despair.

But since in purgatory no soul bleeds
    and as long as something can be given
    the free will must be fixed
    empowered by the gratuities of heaven,
then as long as skin withers only to be shed,
we must keep running as we strive
    with anxious hands bruised but alive
    generously scarred.

Then, then indeed must our purgatory be here and now

for I see not one giving and bleeding, only many dead
broken under the pulseless red
feet of machines run by ones with safe pale skin
who choicelessly push one button
to kill dead men methodically
free of hate, even of sin.

Oh, only One really alive
could
melt this hell-bound purgatory
even
into heaven
with his blood!

Subsidiarity

During this time I continued as a Senior Fellow of Pope John Center and was appointed by the Archbishop a member of the Dubuque Archdiocesan Medical-Morals Committee, 1975-79. The chief event of this Committee during my time of service was a lively discussion with the administration of one of the member hospitals over the question of "medically indicated" sterilizations. The administration claimed that if in hardship cases it were to forbid such operations, the largely non-Catholic medical staff would resign and start their own facility and this would make it necessary to close the only Catholic hospital in the area.

At the time I felt it especially important that Catholic institutions, following the principle of subsidiarity, should take moral responsibility for making their own informed decisions about hard moral situations, rather than always turning to local bishops who frequently find it difficult to become sufficiently informed about such complex cases. Consequently, as the theologian on the committee, I confined myself to explaining as well as I could the traditional principles of ethical "material cooperation." The result was that the administration decided to permit such operations in certain "medically indicated" cases.

When I explained what had happened to the Archbishop, who as I have already noted, was very conservative theologically, he approved with the proviso that the hospital's ethics committee study each case individually. At the end of each year they were to report to him on the number of surgeries and the reasons for them. A year or so later the administration of the same hospital went a step further by asking that at the request of the patient and physician in "medically-indicated" cases that also involved a Caesarian delivery, the permission be given routinely without previous referral to the ethics committee. I then perceived that the physicians would probably continue to push ethical limits until sterilization became a routine permission, and I advised that this further concession not be granted. The question was still under advisement at the time I left Dubuque. My present opinion, however, is that Catholic hospitals should not submit to this kind of threat from physicians.

I recount this experience because it strengthened my convictions about the respective role of laity and episcopacy in such moral dilemmas. The principle of subsidiarity is certainly valid and therefore we should resist the pre-Vatican tendency for the laity to abdicate responsibility for difficult moral decisions. They should not be encouraged to pass this responsibility to centralized authority that cannot easily be adequately informed of the details of particular ambiguous situations. Nevertheless vigilant episcopal oversight over Catholic institutions must be maintained, else these Church sponsored institutions will quickly become secularized. Sterilization is a ready source of money for physicians and hospitals and the pressure to permit it in some cases has been the chief source of ethical conflict in Catholic health care facilities.

Sometimes the norm against contraceptive sterilization has been not very honestly evaded by resort to so-called "uterine isolation" on the excuse that this is therapy for a pathological condition of the uterus. It fact it has no therapeutic effect but is performed to avoid future risks of pregnancy and its possible dangers and hence is really contraceptive sterilization. I met similar problems when in 1976 I was appointed to the Board of Theological Consultants for the Mercy Health Care Corporation and attended many of its meetings in Farmington Hills, MI outside Detroit.

I published another book in Dubuque at the request of the Archdiocesan Department of Religious Education (for which I was a consultant, 1976-1979) to guide teachers in the Catholic schools of the diocese in raising social consciousness, *Thy Kingdom Come! An Overview of Catholic Social Doctrine.*[205] It systematically arranges the principal conclusions of papal documents on social justice issued up to that time. Of course it is now out of date, but working on it enabled me to review the whole range of the Church's social doctrine and stirred up my old interest in social ethics that had become somewhat dormant. Yet in truth I have never lost a passionate interest in political questions. On a visit to Houston in 1974, I was asked by a newspaper reporter what I thought about the very popular film at that time, *The Exorcist*, and I answered as I would today:

> The [current] indifference to human misery in the cutback of the poverty program has a demonic character to it. The works of devils is much more evident today in the national and social pride that leads the United States and other great powers to neglect the poor, seek the maximum of wealth and domination, engage in lying, deceit and fraud, than it is in strange incidents of possession. Watergate is a clearer expression of the demonic than the events pictured in the movie *The Exorcist*.

Pro-Life

I was following Watergate on TV and was depressed by the Nixon era and the dominance of the Republican administration by business interests. Yet I caused some local scandal in Dubuque among pro-life Catholics because I spoke against voting on a "one-issue" basis, which forced one to vote Republican. I even took part in a demonstration at the Dubuque airport when Edward Kennedy arrived there to speak in order to offset the pro-life demonstration against him. I did so because at the time I thought that on the whole he was the more worthy candidate, although on the basis of his record I emphatically no longer think so. I certainly believe in what Cardinal Joseph Bernadin (d. 1996) called "A Consistent Ethic of Life" and cannot agree that opposition to abortion is the only issue the voter must take into consideration because, as it is argued, "Life is the supreme value outweighing all others." President Reagan seems to have been sincere in his anti-abortion position and should be commended for his opposition against federal funding for abortion. Yet he made no serious use of his office to change public opinion on the matter through education; and his position on other matters of human rights was deplorable. The pro-life talk even of most other Republican candidates has seemed to me purely political, resulting in no effective action.

Scandalously many of our Catholic politicians, like Mario Cuomo, have waffled by saying that they privately oppose abortion while publicly favoring pro-choice. This is an indefensible position for a Catholic. The right of an unborn child to life cannot be a merely private matter. In the Iowa campaign already mentioned, I obtained a meeting with the Democratic senatorial candidate who though not a Catholic had won his seat mainly with Catholic votes. I urged him that if he could not take a pro-life stand, then at least he ought to recognize Catholic pro-life opposition respectfully. He should make clear in his speeches that while in view of the division of public opinion he judged that it was not politically possible to abolish abortion, yet he understood the pro-life concern and would do what he could to educate the public on alternatives to abortion.

I still believe that this is generally the right stand for a Catholic politician on this question in our divided country. Until public opinion has been educated to favor efforts to reduce the number of abortions, laws against it cannot pass and even if they were passed would not be effectively enforced. What Catholics must make clear to the public is that no matter what one thinks about the so-called "right of a woman to choose," it is an outrage, comparable to the Holocaust, that since Roe v. Wade millions of infant lives have been destroyed in the United States. It must be made easier for women to refuse abortion. I believe with the Catholic Church that direct abortion can never be morally right, but even, as pro-choice advocates maintain, if it could sometimes be justified in hardship cases, these hardship cases are few compared to the present widespread practice. My faith tells me that, as Lincoln said in his Second Inaugural Address about slavery, by the just wrath of Almighty God this country will someday have to pay a frightful price for this crime, as have Germany and Russia for their similar crimes against humanity. Indeed we have probably already murdered more human beings than either Hitler or Stalin.

Of course, I understand that many pro-choice people sincerely are unconvinced that the existence of a human person begins at conception defined as fertilization of the ovum. They have the ethical responsibility, however, to examine the solid biological evidence on which this question and the question of whether cloning is also destructive of innocent human life, must be decided. To avoid considering this evidence as the Supreme Court Justice did in Roe v. Wade can no more be justified than can the opinions of racists and anti-Semites who retain their prejudices without reference to objective biological facts.

I discussed this problem in the first of the workshops for Catholic Bishops held in Dallas by the Pope John Center in, "Pro-Life Evangelization,"[206] and in the articles "The Religious Heritage of the

Stewardship of Life: Perspective of a Moralist,"[207] and "Ethical Assumptions in the Abortion Debate."[208] During this time I also dealt with pro-life problems in writing on questions of sexual ethics in "From Humanæ Vitæ to Human Sexuality,"[209] and "A Child's Right to His Own Parents: A Look at Two Value Systems."[210]

A more scholarly piece of research on this topic was my article, "A Critique of the Theory of Delayed Hominization."[211] In this article I argued that the appeal being made by some Catholic moralists to the authority of St. Thomas Aquinas (oddly since otherwise these same moralists largely ignore his other moral views) in support of the theory of delayed hominization and hence to attack the Church's absolute ban on abortion neglected both a correct understanding of Aquinas' own arguments and the presently known biological data. In fact, when Aquinas' principles are applied to modern biological data much more adequate than was available to him, they lead to the conclusion that human life begins at conception. I also taped for video five lectures on "Problems in Medical Ethics" commissioned by the Department of Health Affairs, Diocese of Lansing, MI, 1978. More original was a paper I did as a result of previous discussions I had participated in at the Institute for Mental Research, 1972 in the Texas Medical Center, "Ethics of Experimenting with Persons."[212]

Dominican Degree

In the midst of these activities I received encouragement in a way I had not expected. Earlier I recounted how I took the examination *Ad Gradus* as the necessary prerequisite for my first appointment as Regent of Studies in River Forest and explained that this was the first step before being honored with the degree of Master of Theology. The Dominican Order from its earliest days was permitted by the Popes to grant the degree of Master of Sacred Theology, the highest degree in this field in the medieval universities, to candidates in the Order who had attained some distinction in the teaching of theology. In the course of time this had become a much sought after honor because it had been loaded with privileges, above all lifetime membership in the provincial council and provincial chapters. This political privilege was laudably intended to make sure that the intellectual tradition of the Order was honored in all provincial decisions, but it had become an abuse, since it led to this degree being awarded to candidates who were more political than learned. After Vatican II in 1968 when the General Chapter of River Forest made the general revision of our Constitutions, these privileges were abolished and it was decreed that while provinces could still propose candidates for the degree to the Master of the Order, they must also be approved by an international committee of the Order on the basis of the candidates' publications.

Before this reform of the S.T.M., when I was a member of the *Diffinitorium* (executive committee) after our Provincial chapter of 1965 I had voted with the majority that our Province should refrain from nominating any member of our Province for this distinction because of its political abuse. Hence I was embarrassed when our Provincial Chapter of 1978 nominated me for this honor. It was, however, out of the question to refuse it (even if I had not been pleased at the honor, which to tell the truth I very much was), since the other nominee was my old friend of Albertus Magnus Lyceum days Fr. James A. Weisheipl, OP. He was by then professor at the Pontifical Mediaeval Institute of Toronto and I certainly thought he deserved to be so honored for his distinguished work, especially because I knew that in Canada he felt somewhat forgotten by his Chicago brethren.

I later became a member of the International Committee that now reviews such nominations and I have had the pleasure of proposing to our Chapter for this honor the names of Frs. Kevin O'Rourke and of Jordan Aumann (d. 2007), author of many important publications on spirituality.[213] Since the degree now has no special privileges except the acknowledgement of scholarly efforts, I think it should continue to be awarded to encourage such endeavors, which some friars seem to value little. It is said that when in a vision Jesus from the crucifix said to St. Thomas Aquinas, "You have written well of me Thomas. What reward do you ask?" Thomas replied, "Only yourself, Lord." That ought to be every Dominican's personal attitude, yet I think it should also be the attitude of Dominican communities to be ready to give appropriate honor to every member for his or her work.

Fr. James Athanasius Weisheipl received the S.T.M. in 1979 in an impressive ceremony in Toronto before the faculty of the Mediaeval Institute. I was present and he was also present at my ceremony in the River Forest chapel. I have worn the biretta and ring conferred with the degree at a few academic events but not otherwise. The ring conferred on me was inscribed at my request with the motto, Magister unum Christus ("You have but one teacher, the Christ" Mt 23:10). "Athy" was to die in 1984 from a heart attack. I found out how bad his health had become when he visited to Dubuque to arrange for a collection of his books that he had stored there to be donated to the Center for Thomistic Studies in Houston and I saw how debilitating his emphysema was. Entirely devoted to study, he never took proper care of his health and suffered from chemical addictions although constantly at work as a professor at the Pontifical Institute of Mediæval Studies Toronto. He left unfinished a work on St. Albert the Great which would have matched his well known book, already mentioned above, *Friar Thomas d'Aquino*. He, however, left a legacy of loyal disciples who carry on his work in various universities.

Dominican Tradition of Spirituality

As for my own writing, I could not help thinking more about the changes in religious life and in particular about what should be retained from Dominican tradition in order to be true to "the spirit of the founder" as Vatican II urged. My research and reflections on this topic were expressed in several articles: "Models for Dominican Relationships,"[214] "A Guide to St. Catherine's Dialogue,"[215] "Three Strands in the Thought of Eckhart the Scholastic Theologian,"[216] "What Do We Pray in the Lord's Prayer?"[217] and especially 19 audio cassettes on *The History of Dominican Spirituality* which eventually became my book, *The Dominicans* (1990). In this research I learned how important Meister Eckhart (1260-1328) has been in the tradition of the Order and both the Catholic and the Protestant Churches, since through his disciples John Tauler (c. 1300-1361) and Henry Suso (1300-1366) he influenced both Luther and the great Spanish Carmelite mystics. Eckhart's introverted type of theology stands in sharp contrast to the apostolic Thomistic spirituality of St. Catherine of Siena and her followers. I also contributed an article, "St. Albert the Great and the Classification of Sciences" to a remarkable volume edited by Fr. James Weisheipl, OP, *St. Albert and the Sciences: Commemorative Essays*[218] which reflected my continuing Lyceum interests.

The activities described in the last chapter were, however, incidental to my main task as Regent of Studies for our U.S. Central Dominican Province in promoting the education of our Dominican students. In 1974 Fr. Aniceto Fernández, Master of the Order, appointed me to the Permanent Commission for Promotion of Studies, and Fr. Vincent de Couesnongle (Fernández' successor but then his Associate for the Intellectual Life) called a meeting of the Commission for the same year to discuss the *Ratio Studiorum* or syllabus for academic formation for future Dominican priests. As a result of the meeting I helped to write "Serving the Word: A Syllabus of Study for Ministry in the Order of Preachers," which was presented to the General Chapter of 1977.

I felt deeply moved at this privilege remembering that the first such *Ratio Studiorum* was the work of St. Albert the Great, St. Thomas Aquinas, and Peter of Tarantaise, the future Pope Innocent V. This experience also led me to write an article for a more general audience, "Philosophy and Priesthood"[219] on the problems we had so long discussed in the 60s in the committee for which I was a theological consultant in preparing the Program of Priestly Formation which the U.S. National Conference of Catholic Bishops approved in 1970.

Rome and Mexico

This second trip to Rome with a brief residence again at Santa Sabina could not, of course, be as memorable as the first. The only time for sightseeing (Fr. De Couesnongle was a chairman enthusiastic for regular work) was during the siesta period when so many Roman churches and other sites for tourists are closed. Nevertheless, I had a wonderful time wandering around Rome and seeing things I had missed before.

A more novel experience for me was a trip to Mexico, primarily to an institute at Cuernavaca to promote intercultural understanding conducted by the remarkable Msgr. Ivan Illich (d. 2002).[220] Since some of our students were being prepared for Hispanic ministry I felt I should get some notion of what this might involve. My plane landed a little late in Mexico City and to my alarm I found that the hotel room I had reserved was already taken, but the desk clerk kindly found me another hotel, though it was a faded, musty place.

The next day I walked down to the great plaza surrounded by the Cathedral and government buildings. This was between Christmas and New Year's, but it was a lovely evening with the full moon just rising over the great plaza. The remains of the Pyramid of the Sun under the Cathedral had then not yet been excavated, but I felt them there under the great colonial church that is sinking into the ground. I wandered over to one of the government buildings opposite the cathedral to see the Marxist murals of Diego Rivera with their depictions of fanatical friars oppressing the Indians.

The bus ride to Cuernavaca with the volcano Popocatepetl on the horizon, was a too-thrilling adventure because the driver of our little bus kept playing games with another bus on the road, speeding ahead of it and then falling back. The city itself, the summer retreat of the great Conquistador Cortez was charmingly picturesque with its promenade around the city square and its delicious weather. Ivan Illich was an intense priest with bright, darting eyes. He said that since he was a cosmopolitan who had no native culture or language, Thomism was his home. Indeed he was theologically essentially conservative, yet politically radical in his penetrating criticism of American colonialism and consumerist culture.

For me, however, the event of this time in Cuernavaca was a liturgical change of mind toward favoring enculturation. During all our liturgical experiments my own tastes had remained strictly gothic, Gregorian chant, etc. What I experienced there in Mexico were the possibilities of a liturgy expressed in local folk-culture. I remember unforgettably a Eucharist held one late afternoon in a dimly lighted room with a large open door overlooking a balcony. The candles were set in irregular niches in the wall of the room that had a ceiling of exposed dark wooden beams and rough, white plastered walls. We concelebrants were vested in fabrics that had a Native-American weave and were seated on wooden benches in a semicircle before the altar silhouetted against the open door to the balcony and the sunset. This door also gave a view of the purple bougainvillea blossoms that hung profusely on the balcony railings. In the distance were snowcapped volcano peaks, glowing pink.

After the Mass we sat for a long time on the balcony while Illich kept pouring wine in our glasses, and a mariachi band serenaded us under the brilliant stars. During my years in River Forest I had always felt such an incongruity between our beautiful medieval liturgy and our tasteless student recreation with the radio and movies and popular music of the commercial variety. Here I seemed to experience a situation in which religious and recreational culture were harmonious, and the spirit was not vulgar and commercial, but simply and beautifully human.

I had a couple more days in Mexico City before returning and this gave me the opportunity to visit the marvelous Anthropological Museum and also north of the city the great Pyramids of the Sun and the Moon. Then we stopped at a colonial monastery of the Augustinian Friars where in each of the cells there was a little window seat where a friar could say his prayers looking out at the purple mountains. I had, of course, seen pictures and some pieces of pre-Columbian art in museums, but I had always supposed that Aztec and Mayan art was "barbaric," much inferior to Egyptian and Greek art. I was overwhelmed by the grandeur, sophistication, and also humor, of what I now saw. I still don't know just what to think of the pagan spirit behind it, but I cannot forget its splendor.

An opportunity to deepen this experience of Hispanic America which opened entirely new vistas for me was the invitation in 1976 from Fr. De Couesnongle, now Master of the Order, to attend a meeting of the Regents of Latin America held in the Dominican Priory in Bogotá, Columbia. Before going there I decided to visit our Province's missions in Cochabamba and Santa Cruz, Bolivia. I was thrilled as we stopped briefly in Panama City at night to see for the first time the Southern Cross blazing apocalyptically in the black sky. Next day Cochabamba proved to be a delightful place halfway up the mountains with a pleasant Dominican priory. That very evening the cook who cared for the Fathers was getting married and I was taken—in the back of a truck—to the wedding dance at the little home of the bride. Since I neither dance or speak Spanish or Quechua, I could only sit out under the vines on the sideline exchanging smiles with the old Indian folks who sat there and drinking their powerful native beverage. I found this potion rather alarming, but sipped it anyway, while the young people danced, delightfully waving handkerchiefs. The climate of Cochabamba was balmy and the night star-studded.

The history of our Central Province's missions in Bolivia is at once painful and splendid. The first Dominicans, contemporaries and, at a later time, students of mine, were invited there in 1957 to set up a seminary for the native diocesan clergy. This had not succeeded because of the scarcity of vocations. Then two remarkable experiments were started, one was IBEAS (*Instituto Boliviano de Estudio y Accion Social*), the other the charismatic movement. IBEAS was an institute to train Catholic lay leaders for a country with almost no middle-class, torn by social strife, and with a very active Communist party. For a time IBEAS gave promise, according to the evaluation of Msgr. Ivan Illich, of being one of the most successful missionary efforts in Latin America, since the priests took the role of animators and educators, while the activity was in the hands of the laity. A switch in government to the left, however, ended its existence, because unknowingly the Dominicans had accepted some funding from the United States that turned out to be ultimately from the CIA, though given through a front agency. This disaster was demoralizing to our Dominicans who had worked so hard to build IBEAS and resulted in two or three of these discouraged missionaries leaving the priesthood.

In the meantime, things took a different direction. The charismatic movement was beginning to have its influence in Catholic circles. Two friars, Chrysostom Geraets (d. 2001) and Daniel Roach, had been students of mine and in the 60s when they were teaching college we had collaborated on a project to provide a textbook on Catholic social doctrine that was never wholly completed. Later they were sent together to Bolivia where, influenced by a brother of Chrys, a Benedictine monk who was a charismatic, they introduced charismatic prayer meetings in Santa Cruz. They found themselves endowed with charismatic gifts and Chrys had a prophetic enlightenment telling him to proclaim that "Christ will appear on the streets of Santa Cruz!" He later told me that at that time he had not learned to confirm such inspirations through the charismatic community and had at first interpreted these words too literally. But in fact this charismatic movement did grow most remarkably and still provides a vital presence of Christ among the people of the city.

On Good Friday I attended a service with a huge congregation in Chrys' and Dan's open air church. It lasted many hours in which the regular liturgy was expanded by popular singing, giving of "testimonies," and preaching. The foot-washing was performed by calling on anyone in the congregation who felt moved to do so to come forward, receive a basin of water and a towel, and wash the feet of someone in the congregation. Many did so throughout the church and I was moved to do so also, washing the feet of a stranger who permitted it with great humility and embraced me with tears.

It was also moving to see that the two, Dan and Chrys, lived a life of poverty from hand to mouth like that of St. Dominic. Their clothing and daily food was provided by small gifts brought into them in their little hut, built on the grounds of La Mansion, the student center. Their whole time was given to prayer, catechetical meetings there and on the radio, and to the services in the open-air church. The people who attended these services came from the entire range of Bolivian society.

Yet some of the other Dominicans did not favor charismatic life. They thought the mission should be more occupied, as IBEAS had been, with political and social reform. The charismatics, on the other hand, claimed that they too preached a great deal on social topics, especially against the widespread corruption due to the drug trade, and that their wide popular support gave them a protection against the politicians, the lack of which had been fatal to IBEAS. This split between the liberation theology and the charismatic movement troubles Catholic missionary activity in Latin America to this day. And there are also Dominicans, like the German Dominican missionaries in Bolivia who continue to give their efforts to building traditional type parishes.

I, with a Dominican companion, flew to Bogotá, Columbia by way of La Paz, Bolivia, which is perched 10,000 feet in the frightful Andes, bare, black crags piercing the sky. Taking a short walk in the airport I grew weak with the altitude. Bogotá is a strange juxtaposition of the colonial old and the skyscraper new. The Dominican priory is a large handsome building with tropical plants in the cloister that was at that time defended by a fierce dog named Bravo who was let out at night into the cloister so that I did not dare walk outside. A high wall surrounded the priory grounds and I understood why when I saw that nearby on the mountainside were squatters living in tin-roofed shacks. Descending toward town we saw a fine residential section but with walls around the houses, wrought iron gates, and security guards.

When I went downtown in modern Bogotá with a confrere to a money exchange, he stationed me outside to keep an eye out for suspicious looking characters, because he said robbers often watch people coming out of exchanges, follow them down the street, and at a convenient moment mug them at knifepoint. Later I was sitting on a bus near the rear exit bracing myself with my hand on a bar that protected the seat from those going out the door. Suddenly I felt someone grab the stretch-band of my wristwatch, pull it right off my hand and jump out the bus exit. The door closed, the bus started off, and my watch was gone! I didn't even get a look at the robber. Then I noticed that on many corners in the city there were men selling watches. I hope the adroit thief got a good price for mine.

In this city where the poor are very evident my visit to the gold museum in the National Bank shines out. After I had marveled at the many fantastic little works of art in pure gold made by native craftsmen ancient and modern exhibited there in the Bank's museum, I followed a crowd into a carefully guarded, unlighted bank vault. When we were all inside, the great door was closed, leaving us in total darkness. Then suddenly the lights were turned on and with a unison gasp we all saw that the walls were glass cases filled in solid array with countless gold objects all ablaze! I also cannot forget the gigantic white marble statue of Christ that stands on a mountain rising directly out of the city park. As I returned to the United States I realized how ignorant I am of this whole southern world, its poverty, its riches, it past, its possible future.

Travels with My Brother and His Death

The most deeply affecting experiences of this time, however, were in relation to my brother Dick. My brother was six years older than I and we had never had much in common. After I was ordained and my mother went to live with him and his wife Helen, I had visited them every year, but had few conversations with him alone. In 1973 Helen, who like Dick was a chain-smoker of cigarettes, died of lung cancer after a painful year of radiation therapy. My brother was then entirely alone. He sold the motel, bought a trailer and moved it to a lot in the woods near Lake Greeson. I knew he was very miserable. His life had been in many ways sad. Although he and his wife loved each other deeply and shared their love of fishing, they had few other recreations and no children. They had thought of adopting a child but never came to a decision. I have already described his loss of his job as a geologist and the difficulties of running the Daisy Motel.

While I lived in Dubuque, he, without great enthusiasm, accepted my idea that we pass our vacations together and so we made two long motor trips in his pickup truck. Traveling in a pickup might not seem much fun, but in fact it was quite comfortable. It was roomy and its elevated seat gave a good view of the many wonderful landscapes through which we passed. We did no camping, but slept at inexpensive motels on the road. On the first trip I met him at Oklahoma City and we journeyed through western Oklahoma and Dodge City, KS, to Denver. There we stayed at the Dominican parish and went on through the Rockies to Salt Lake City then through the Uinta Mountains of Utah, visiting the amazing Dinosaur Museum. I wanted to go on to California, but Dick was ready to turn back. He had read that as you go west and north in the U.S.A. coffee gets weaker, and by this time the coffee in the motels, compared to the Louisiana coffee he liked, was watery indeed. We then went further south through the Petrified Forest and on to Arkansas.

On a second trip he drove up to Dubuque and we then went north through Minnesota (Dick wanted to see the so-called Kensington Viking Runestone)[221] to Lake Superior and around its north shore with its deep forests and clear lakes, stopping at a uranium mine and at a field where one could pick up stones with large amethyst crystals. Again I wanted to go back through Chicago, but he did not want to see so large a city. As a geologist what really interested him were rock formations. The landscape riches of the United States and Canada are inexhaustible and I found great pleasure in it all, just driving day after day. He did not talk a lot, we could not find many agreeable topics of conversation, since I found his redneck political opinions hard to take and he seemed little interested in things I liked to talk about. We had a few hard moments but on the whole these were fine trips for which I was very grateful and which, I hoped, helped him in his loneliness.

Something unusual had happened to me about a year before this. I had attended the International Congress of Medieval Studies, a remarkable annual meeting of over two thousand scholars interested in all aspects of the Middle Ages held annually at Western Michigan University in Kalamazoo, MI. Driving back I took the opportunity to visit Notre Dame and walking about the campus stopped for a few moments of prayer at the Grotto. While praying there I was filled with a sense that death was coming soon, my own death I supposed, having not so long ago experienced my mother's death. The impression stayed with me for some time and led me to pray often about it, but since nothing happened it began to fade away. I now believe that it was to prepare me for my brother Richard's death that was to be something more difficult for me to meet than my mother's death had been, since I knew she was so well prepared spiritually for it, and I was afraid he was not.

Not long after the last of these trips Dick had a routine physical checkup and was told by the physician that like his wife, he had inoperable lung cancer, although with great difficulty he had stopped smoking entirely after her illness began. He didn't say much about it. It was just a fact to be endured. He began radiation treatments and each time I phoned told me how sick these treatments made him, but he nevertheless seemed to manage pretty well. An alarming episode occurred on one of my visits when he told me in a rage about the trouble he was having with an annoying woman neighbor and said that if she provoked him into a quarrel again he was going to shoot her. I was in a dilemma about how seriously I should take this and whether I ought to warn the woman, but finally I decided that Dick was probably just talking, since he had always had more sense than to do that and had never engaged in violence, while if I gave the neighbor warning, it might produce a still worse situation, with great trouble for Dick. I still don't know if my decision was right, but in any case, nothing further did happen.

Finally, when from our phone conversations I thought he was still in pretty good shape, I received a call from a neighbor that Dick had been found with a broken leg on the floor of his trailer where he had lain for almost a day. I flew down to Hot Springs, rented a car and drove to Daisy and then sent for an ambulance that took him to the hospital in Hot Springs. The hospital staff made him comfortable and I stayed there for almost two weeks. Hot Springs, Arkansas is a one-time fashionable spa, now faded except for a racing season when the old, luxury hotels are filled. It has a raised promenade overlooking the bathhouses on the side of the mountain ridge from whose base the hot waters flow. It was strange living there, saying Mass in the hospital chapel, and spending much of each day with my brother who was slowly declining. I wanted very much to talk to him about his spiritual state. His acquaintance with religion from youth had been almost entirely with Southern Baptists and other fundamentalist Protestants and he was convinced they were all ignorant hypocrites. He was himself an essentially honest person, whose life had been frustrating and embittering, and he seemed completely cynical and unable to see any meaning in it. Each time I tried to raise the subject with him he turned me off. Since the doctors did not know how long it might take, I had at last to return to Dubuque for my teaching, but decided to write him a letter about the Faith. I quote it in full because it says so much about my own outlook,

April 24, 1980

Dear Dick,

I am writing you because I feel very helpless at this time which must be very hard for you with your illness not going so well. I hope that you will not be exasperated by what I am trying to say, because I certainly do not want to add to your burdens. Yet I feel that I cannot just let you face the crisis of possible death without talking with you about what it means to both of us. Up to now I haven't said much, because I know you don't like unnecessary fuss.

I have admired the courageous way you have faced this, as Helen also did, and I hope that I will be able to do so when I have to. You have always seemed to me to be a strong person, and I always marveled how you and Helen met all your troubles in life with little complaint and much hard work. Yet I sincerely wish that at this time you could also draw some strength from a faith in a future life. You said once that you do believe in God, and so I suppose that you have some religion of your own which you don't talk about, although lately you have probably had to think even more about it. I know that you have always been turned off by "religious" people whom you have found to be so often dishonest and untrustworthy. That very fact shows me that you have a high ideal of what religion ought to do for people (and which it often does not do, I admit), namely, make them honest and trustworthy in their dealings with others. But I want to explain to you, as honestly as I can, what my own convictions are about life and death.

1. God created the world. Although science has shown that everything has come to be through evolution, there still must be a God who is the cause of evolution itself. He is a wise God and a loving God to have made this world.

2. The evil in the world, which we experience every day of our lives—the wars, the corruption, the injustices, the sicknesses— were not caused by God but by human wickedness and stupidity. God gave us free will, so that we could do either good or evil, but we have done evil and made the world a pretty miserable place. Why then hasn't the good God put an end to all this? God is like a good father who allows His children to bear the consequences of their own actions, so that we can learn from our mistakes and grow up.

3. Yet God has not just abandoned us. He is going to give us a future life beyond death, after our time of trial is over, in which He will see that the wicked are punished and the good rewarded for every least good they have done. This future life is something we cannot imagine, but in it we will be reunited with those we have loved in this life and we will at last understand all the things that puzzled us here. That this hope for a future life is not just an illusion is clear from the fact that many of the best and

wisest through the ages have been convinced of it and science has never disproved it. We human beings are more than animals, because, unlike the animals, we have an intelligence and free will which make us want to live after death, and God would not have given us this inborn desire just to frustrate it.

4. In order that we might keep our hope alive in a dark world, God through the ages has sent great religious leaders who founded the different religions of the world which have kept the human race from sinking into barbarism. All of these great religions contain some truth and they have led men of every country to a better life, but only in Jesus, His Son, has God clearly manifested Himself to us. Jesus showed by His life of courage, of truthfulness, of concern and sacrifice for every human being and by his death of sacrifice, that God is in fact love, mercy, and forgiveness, as well as a God of justice. "God so loved the world that he gave his only Son, that whoever believes in him may not die but may have eternal life," (John 3:16).

5. We know that the Biblical account of Jesus' life and teaching is not a myth, because He founded a Church which for two thousand years has been guided by the Spirit of Jesus in preserving His memory and witnessing to its conviction that He rose from death and is still alive today with God. This Christian Church has often failed in many ways, and being made up of human beings has shown all the human weaknesses. It has been divided by internal squabbles and it has compromised with the world's evils. Nevertheless, in spite of these human failures, this Church, which is centered in the Catholic Church, has been able to outlast every human empire and survive every internal division. Today it continues all over the world—it includes one-fifth of the human race—to tell the story of Jesus to show what God is really like.

6. Jesus did not teach that only members of His Church organization will be saved or that the rest of the world will be damned. Rather He showed that God in His mercy will save all those who put their trust in God, as they know Him, and do the best they can in their life. The purpose of the Church is not to condemn those who are not members of the Church, but to offer comfort, hope, and strength to all who are sorry for whatever harm they may have done in their life, and who want to have a greater hope and confidence in a future life. The "Gospel" means "Good News" for us, not condemnation.

You see then, Dick that why I am writing you is just to let you know that my prayer for you is that you will find hope in God at this hard time in your life, and that you will be convinced that death is not the end for us. God is a loving God who never rejects anyone who puts his trust in Him. He is a God who is wise and knows how to bring out all things right in the end. I believe that what is important is not whether you are a Catholic (although it was a great joy to me that Dad and Mother became Catholics), but that in this time of sickness, you will find confidence in God (however you understand Him) to make up to you for whatever you have had to suffer in this life and to repair whatever harm you may have done in your life and which you regret (we all have failed in many ways). Prayer to God helps us to find Him and to realize that He really is there. For me the best prayer in the world is the Lord's Prayer which I learned as a child.

This is what I have often wanted to say to you, but perhaps you have already been thinking it yourself. Anyway this will let you know that I love you, even if I seldom say so, and that is why I have wanted to share with you my confidence that God will take care of you, even at this time when the future is so cloudy. I look forward to be with you and Helen and Dad and Mother when this life has turned into eternal life.

I will be in Denver giving some talks until May lst. I can be reached there at [phone numbers]. From May 1st to 4th I will be at a convention at Western Michigan University, Kalamazoo [phone number].

Love,
Wint

Whether he read it I don't know, since he never said anything about it to me. Eventually he grew so ill that I again went to Hot Springs and brought him by chartered airplane back to Dubuque. It was a strange ride in the small four-seater plane since it was a morning after a heavy rainstorm and the sky was very threatening. By that time Dick was no longer mentally very clear and he kept talking about "the birds" which he seemed to think were diving about the plane. I put him in Mercy Center Hospital in Dubuque where he lingered for a couple of weeks. There I asked him if he was willing to be baptized and he seemed to understand and, thank God, said "Yes," that and nothing more, and I baptized him. He fell into unconsciousness and was anointed by the hospital chaplain. A couple of days later I was awakened in the early morning by a call saying Dick had just died, age 71, June 23, 1980. His funeral was held in the chapel of St. Rose Priory and he is buried in the Dubuque Catholic cemetery. I have visited his grave only once, as also my Dad's grave in Neodesha, and my mother's in Daisy, Arkansas. Our family never had much piety about graves.

This marked for me the end of any family except the Dominican Order. I had never known my paternal relatives, and of the maternal ones I had only some cousins in Kansas and Texas with whom I had only occasional correspondence. In a way I felt it a relief no longer to worry about them since I knew gratefully that Dad, Mother, and Dick had died in the Lord. I had also had one opportunity to speak with Helen before her death about the Baptist faith in which she had been raised. She never attended church during the time I knew her and yet to my surprise she at least still maintained faith in God and told me that she prayed.

During these years my own health was good, but I began to feel some signs of aging, and worried about myself, especially when it was discovered I had colon polyps that had to be removed, a mild case of infectious hepatitis incurred somehow on a trip, and recurrent prostatitis. As I began to feel middle aged and my ties of family relationships were severed one by one, Aquinas Institute in which so much of my life was tied up, was also coming loose from its moorings. As I will explain in the next chapter we were faced with the necessity of moving our priory and school again this time from Dubuque.

DEATH AND TAXES

The Lord of Life and Death
to a greedy collector of taxes
said quietly, "Come follow me,."
Without drawing another breath
Matthew followed
to preach the Word till death.

The Lord of Life and Death
to me, a greedy word collector,
reader, talker, writer,

whispers, gently, regularly as breath,
"Come follow me."

Who pays the tax?
The poor, never the rich,
I have ideas but lack
the facts, I itch
with thoughts
but cannot scratch,
am subtly futile,
all answers but no questions,
but a surfeit of suggestions.

Yet within my noisy talk
I hear your silent call,
"Leave all!"
The solid truths that I invent are hollow,
when, when will I shut up and follow?

Matthew left his coins
wrung from the poor,
shining in heaps upon his table.
But am I able to leave these lofty words
that at minimum, untaxed expense
in the library's dusty, silent nooks,
I squeeze from dead
and sometimes deadly books
that I have never really read,
lay down my pen and then,
not one word of defense,
enter the wordless light?

Matthew followed Life
even unto death.
Can I wordless follow
Life's death relentless call
even past life into that life
where only one Word is spoken
because He has said it all?

Other Dominican Brothers

During this same time there were other deaths at Dubuque which touched me personally, such as the death of Bertrand Mahoney, who died Dec. 16, 1980. He failed to appear one morning at breakfast and a student brother was sent to his room to see if he was ill. The brother, white-face, returned to the refectory where we were eating and announced that Bert was unconscious. I hurried to Bert's room, just opposite my own, and found that he had been dead for some time, but, since I was not sure when he had died, I anointed him and many of the community who had gathered sang the *Salve Regina*. I preached at his funeral Mass. Everyone in our community loved Bert. A native of Chattanooga, he too had graduated from Notre Dame, and as a student was known for his fiery temper, but this had been moderated by years of suffering as a diabetic that finally made him an amputee in a wheelchair. Surgery for colon cancer was successful but left him with a colostomy. He was much too independent to permit much nursing by us and we did not know for some time that he had developed a serious bed sore.

This trauma, when finally discovered, made it necessary for him to be nursed for months at the Villa in Dubuque, the retirement convent for Dominican Sisters, who gave him the tenderest, expert care until he could return to us. One of my memories was seeing him saying Mass seated in his chair in a circle of superannuated Sisters in all states of physical and mental decay.

Bert liked to have a drink, but so little was left of him that even a little alcohol made him a bit reckless and a few times he shocked our straight-laced Presbyterians with his jokes and profane outbursts. But he was unfailing kind to us all, and became a marvel of humorous patience and humility, working for some years as the school's business manager. When this became too much for him he was simply content to answer the phone for us all. We all look back to Bert with laughter and love.

I should also mention two of our Cooperator Brothers associated in my mind with Dubuque. After Vatican II some of our brothers who did not seek ordination went on with studies and took up professional ministries, notably Edward Van Merrienboer who from being a bookbinder for us became a professor of the Church's social doctrine and for some years the Assistant for the Apostolic Life of the Master of the Order, traveling all over the world. Some Cooperator Brothers were content to maintain our priories by their manual skills, yet they were each unique personalities that contributed much to community life. For example, Brother Martin Hartung (d. 1990) had been a farmer living near Dubuque. After his entrance into the Order he was in charge of maintaining automobiles and the grounds of St. Rose, but also spent some time on the Bolivian missions. He never hesitated to express his disgust with the impracticality of some of the more "intellectual" Fathers, myself included, but his down-to-earth views were always worth hearing. Marty rigorously saved his allowance so he could use it on vacations when he traveled to the most distant parts of the world, his luggage consisting of a large paper bag. We received postcards from him on his trips from Tierra del Fuego and from Iceland.

Brother Ambrose Jura, on the other hand, was not in vows, but was an "oblate." He had been a waiter in Austria, who somehow our Province inherited from the House of Studies in Washington when Fr. Bertrand Walker, who had been prior there, returned to River Forest. Ambrose was a kind of ghost in the house, never quite sane; he dutifully set the tables every day, and then retired to his room to smoke, so that it became impossible for others to enter that room because of its dense smell of tobacco. Fr. Joseph Gillespie, who had an adjacent room, told me that a couple of nights after Ambrose's death he was awakened by the unmistakable sound of Ambrose shuffling along the corridor to his room just as Joe had so often heard him do. So convinced was Joe that it was Ambrose shuffling along, that he ran out into the corridor only to see the door of the elevator just closing. He ran down to the next floor and saw the door open... but the elevator was empty.

My work did not give me much occasion at this time to administer the sacraments, except for Mass and an occasional confession, but I had the consolation of baptizing Paul Pearson, a fine musician, and Randy Smith, students at the Mediaeval Institute in Toronto who had been influenced in coming to the faith by Fr. James A. Weisheipl, OP, who sent them to me for final instructions and the sacraments. Our chapel was not a regular place for baptisms and confirmations, but with the Archbishop's permission I baptized them there in a beautiful celebration. I hoped Paul might become a Dominican but he has become an Oratorian priest in Toronto, while Randy has completed a doctorate at Notre Dame and now teaches in the Center for Thomistic Studies at, the University of St. Thomas, Houston.

Learning, Ever Learning

I began this work with the assertion that Vatican II needs to be completed by enriching theology with the findings of modern natural science, but that this will be possible only after a critical examination of the empirical foundations of natural science, as Aristotle and Aquinas strove to do in their own times. I have treated this in terms of my own experiences in trying to do this beginning with the work of the Albertus Magnus Lyceum, then with long contact with these problems, especially as regards (a) Catholic education and (b) bioethics and the right to life. As a consultant to the Committee on Doctrine and Practice of the National Conference of Bishops I had the opportunity to see these issues as they arise in the pastoral work of the Church. As a teacher in many situations I have been reinforced in these convictions. I have narrated these experiences is in its many homely, humorous, and aesthetic contexts with the hope that those who think that at best only a "dialogue" is possible between science and religion will wake up.

SINGULARITY ETERNAL

Lord, more single
than the "Singularity"
when with the Bang
the angels sang
your plenitude in solitude,
Community Triune,
exceeding, completing,
"All Possible Worlds"
even the "Probability"
and inevitability
of "Quantum Quivers"
so busily employed
in the "Expanding
Void,"
thus well beyond all "Evolution"
You, O Lord,
already have arrived
and "Fittingly Survived,"
entirely un-Entangled"
in any dubious hypothesis

over which our curious scientists
have rangled
then by some little fact
 been forced to shift
and take another tack
because not their verbosity
but their very curiosity
is your creative gift.

Yes, Lord in your creation
you are revealed,
as in a diamond
light is a rainbow
vibrant, yet still,
Three-Personed
in Power, Truth, Love,
Wisdom, Freedom, Will
light not blinding,
nor concealing
but revealing,
undividing, uniting
ever delighting,
a full and spotless Moon
of endless peace
a brighter, gentler Sun
renewing
ever, ever One,
far more single
than the Singularity
current science guesses
yet the simple facts suppresses,
nor an infinity of possibles
nor numbered uncountables
but the Actual, the Real
the Threefold, Holy,
wholly One.

Novice, 1942

Student at camp

In Choir at RF

Some Novices 1942

Ordination 1948

Ten Years Ordained

Street Preaching

At a First Mass Dinner

AI Faculty in Dubuque

AI in St. Louis

In Ibadan, Nigeria

Part III:
Barefoot in a Quiet Valley:
A Spirituality of Aging

My soul yearns for you in the night,
yes, my spirit within me keeps vigil for you (Isaiah 16;9)

Chapter 18 - Vigilant Spirituality

Experience and Spirituality

Today even the Naturalists who deny that anything but matter exists claim on the Internet to have a "spirituality." They say:[222] The spiritual experience—the experience of meaning, connection and joy, often informed by philosophy or religion—is, from a naturalistic perspective, a state of the physical person, not evidence for a higher realm or non-material existence. Nevertheless, this understanding of spirituality doesn't lessen the attraction of such an experience, or its value for the naturalist. We naturally crave such feelings and so will seek the means to achieve them consistent with our philosophy.

In truth "spirituality" in its proper sense is not just a matter of "feelings," yet feelings do play an important role in spirituality as is evident from the classics of Christian spirituality such as the writings of Meister Eckhart and of St. John of the Cross. For that reason I have chosen in this book to write in concrete autobiographical terms as a priest of the Order of Preachers (Dominicans) about the spiritual experience of aging since I was 65 to my present age of 95. Precisely because I am a priest and a religious of a famously theological Order and because, even at this point, I seem only a beginner spiritually, my reflections may be of some help to any Christian seeking spiritual growth. The theme that will be central to this account will be one which I wrote about some years before my actual retirement, the suggestion that old age should be a *vigil*, a term which in the Catholic liturgy is a time of prayer on the evening of some great feast, for example, the Easter vigil.[223] I became officially a professor emeritus in 1983 and listed by our Dominican province as in "limited service." But in this work I will count 1980 when I was 65 since in the U. S. for those born before 1938 this is still officially the age of retirement and also the year when I began my residence in St. Louis as the year when for me this vigil began. Just this year in

June 2010 I have moved to my religious order's Central Provincial Headquarters and retirement center at St. Pius Priory in downtown Chicago where the parishioners are mainly Mexicans.

As I reflect on this last period of my life as a vigil I note that it has seven simple features each of which I will each treat in the following chapters. These are:

1. We must take time for mature friendship and appreciate their great value.
2. We old folks must reflect on the limitations of our personal experience.
3. We can lean more from others that we can ever learn by ourselves.
4. We must now use our greater leisure time for contemplation.
5. "The Spirit itself bears witness with our spirit that we are children of God."
6. We must fix our minds and hearts on Jesus, God made Man.
7. We must pass beyond our physical needs by the theological virtue of hope.

So in this chapter I will show how with retirement one begins to take time for mature friendships and appreciate their great value." As it says in Proverbs 18:24, "Some friends bring ruin on us, but a true friend is more loyal than a brother." But let me first summarize very briefly my previous active life narrated in the two first parts of this autobiography.

I was born in 1915 in the little town of Neodesha, KS, and through high school raised in the only slightly larger town of Blackwell, OK. My father was an accountant with only a high school education and my mother had only an eight grade education, but they raised me and my six-year-older brother, Richard, on the Harvard Classics. They were Protestants who did not go to Church, because Darwin had disillusioned them with the Bible. Hence they did not have my brother or me baptized.

In 1933 I matriculated at the University of Chicago, where through the influence of the noted Jewish philosopher Mortimer Adler I was introduced to the thought of St. Thomas Aquinas and came into contact with the Catholic Church. As a result I passed through Marxism, popular as the result of the Second World War to Christian faith. I was baptized in 1938 and a year later requested entrance into the Dominican Order, but was advised to finish my doctorate in political science at the University of Notre Dame, which I completed in 1941 and entered the Dominican novitiate in the Province of St. Albert the Great, River Forest, IL and received priestly ordination in 1948.

From then on I first taught mainly Dominican friars philosophy and later moral theology and bioethics until I became emeritus in 1983. But I was also was the first President of Aquinas Institute of Theology, first in River Forest, then in Dubuque, IA (it is now in St. Louis) as well as teaching at other institutions and acting as a consultant in moral theology to the Committee on Doctrine of the National Catholic Bishops Conference and as a Senior Fellow of what is now the National Catholic Bioethics Center. During that time I also authored a number of articles and books, especially on the relation of science and religion.

Moving to St. Louis with Aquinas Institute

How did Aquinas Institute of Theology, with which my life has been intertwined, come to move to St. Louis, a city that we had always been told was Jesuit territory? Downriver from Dubuque, St. Louis is where the Mississippi reflects the soaring Gateway Arch, "Gateway to the West." This was the departure point of the Lewis and Clark Expedition that opened up almost two-thirds of the present United States to settlement. From the neighboring village of Florissant, Jesuit missionaries, like Father DeSmet, SJ, carried the Gospel all the way to the Rockies.

In its simplicity the St. Louis Arch, designed by the Finnish architect Eero Saarinen, is one of the noblest monuments I know and is linked in my visual imagination with the white marble obelisk of the Washington Monument at the end of the Mall in our nation's capital. The simple geometry of these two images, one pure white on the green Mall, the other stainless steel by the brown Mississippi, mark in my memory the happy days in St. Louis and Washington, DC and finally my return to Chicago that this book is to narrate.

Although in Dubuque our ecumenical cooperation with the Lutheran and Presbyterian seminaries located there was improving every year, the number of our Dominican students had been declining and the town was becoming still more isolated. By 1979 Dubuque was in an economic crisis. Formerly one could reach there easily from Chicago, either by a fast train, the Hiawatha, or by Ozark Airlines. But now the Hiawatha was discontinued, Ozark was sold to

TWA (now American), and only commuter planes were available. The chief industry in the town had been the Dubuque Packing Plant which temporarily closed to squeeze out its union, but never again opened. Eventually a dog racing track took its place as the town's chief industry.

Aquinas Institute was preparing to endure these trials when negotiations for a merger of Lutheran synods began that eventually resulted in the formation of the rather liberal Evangelical Lutheran Church in America. Hence Wartburg Seminary was informed to prepare itself for a possible merger with the Lutheran Seminary in Chicago. Since Wartburg was the stronger of the two Protestant schools, Aquinas was also threatened, and our faculty began to plan to meet the emergency. Ultimately Wartburg seminary (which is fronted by a huge bronze statue of Dr. Luther pointing to the Bible and saying, "Here I stand. I cannot do otherwise. So help me, God!") stayed put after all, but our machinery for a move was already in motion.

The Aquinas faculty proposed to our Provincial Council that we set up an extension of Aquinas at another location, probably in Chicago. Then if we were forced to move, we could expand this extension into the main school. But the Council decided that since our situation was so precarious it would be more practical to decide at once on a future location at some large university. Thus we began to look for a place we could relocate in two years. The exploration and negotiations were protracted and Fr. Thomas McGonigle, OP, who had recently been appointed to succeed Fr. Cletus Wessels as President of Aquinas, was faced with the painful task of administering a school in transition. It was no easy decision for us, since we had come to love our Lutheran and Presbyterian friends.

The first possibility was for our Central Province to consolidate our shrinking resources with the houses of study of the other two U.S. Dominican provinces. The Eastern and Western Provinces, however, while eager to receive our students, could not imagine closing their own schools in Washington and Berkeley, let alone face the dreary possibility of meeting in the drab Middle West. A referendum of the friars of our own Chicago Province no less patriotically insisted that we keep our own studium.

Fr. McGonigle favored going to Berkeley, but not only was this very far away but many were suspicious of the "lotus land" of San Francisco as a place to form celibate friars. Our next possibility was to join the Jesuits at the University of Chicago where they were co-operating with nearby Chicago Lutheran. Another possibility was to join the Chicago Theological Union whose formation I had promoted when I was chairman of the Midwest Association of Theological Schools. Again these choices closed when the Jesuits, dwindling in numbers, consolidated all their seminaries in Boston and Berkeley and when we discovered that if we joined CTU we would retain little control of our own students' Dominican education. Next, negotiations with the theology department of Chicago's Loyola University seemed promising until we saw this too might mean not cooperation but absorption.

Since I had been the first president of Aquinas Institute, all this doubt about its future deeply troubled me. In all these meetings, my own proposal was to send our students to a major university and then to supplement their university courses with a seminar in our own residence. I thought that such a seminar, conducted by a committee of Dominican philosophers and theologians, would submit what the students were learning in the university to critical reflection in the light of our Dominican tradition. This dream of mine, however, was not given serious consideration by our Provincial Council.

Finally, when we were beginning to despair, unexpectedly we received an invitation from the Jesuits of St. Louis University to consider their campus as a site for our school. By this agreement our faculty and accreditation would remain independent of the University, but it would provide Aquinas Institute with library and cross-registration privileges. We would continue to confer our own degrees provided they did not compete with those of the University's theology department.

Available for our lease was the old Law School Building, conveniently adjacent to the library, which the University agreed to maintain and renovate for our needs. This was a rather ugly redbrick building in the style of the 1920s with gothic limestone trim and had for some time been occupied only by squirrels who gnawed themselves through the window sills into the old law library. It was later remodeled but never had elevators. A Benedictine student, later Abbot Thomas Frerking of St. Louis Abbey, who is crippled form polio, when he was a student with us had to crawl up our stairs to class!

As for a residence for our students, to be named St. Dominic's Priory, it was arranged that they, with some senior Dominicans, would live in an old hotel already renovated as "Jesuit Hall." The Dominican student community would have two floors of this building in which the Jesuit community was occupying the upper floors. We also would have the old ballroom remodeled as our chapel, its black and white tiled floor seeming to anticipate Dominican occupancy. For me, however, in spite of the color provided by two small stained glass windows preserved from our Dubuque priory, this chapel seems rather drab and the Blessed Sacrament somewhat "marginalized." Yet Morning and Evening Prayer there are liturgically better than anything we had previously known in our Province, thanks to the excellent work of Frs. Frank Quinn and David Wright, both musicians and liturgical scholars.

The Dominicans at Jesuit Hall also share with the Jesuits the sunny cafeteria, but enjoy a handsome recreation room of their own. We are most grateful to the Jesuits for this hospitality to our school and St. Dominic's community and for their generous care and remodeling of both buildings. It has been a mutually beneficial cooperation that shows that an honest "multi-culturalism" is possible in the Church. On the Jesuits' part this was a very generous offer, though promoted, I believe, by disappointment over losing their own theologate when the U. S. Jesuit theologates were consolidated in Boston and Berkeley.

As a I write, our students are about to move out of Jesuit Hall into a renovated Sisters' Academy on the edge of the campus. I did not favor that decision because it may mean that more Dominicans will have to staff the building, rather than to engage directly in our preaching mission. St. Dominic wept when he saw the first two storied priory of his new Order, not in joy but in fear that his men would settle down like monks rather than keep free like beggars!

Within the Catholic fold there are many "spiritualities" that reflect the experience of particular founders of religious orders. Chief among these are those of the Benedictine monks, the Franciscan and Dominican Friars, and, since the Protestant Reformation, the Society of Jesus or Jesuits who have set the pattern for many other religious congregations.

Between the Dominicans and the Franciscans there have been many unfortunately bitter theological disputes and even more so between the Dominicans and the Jesuits. A recent study by a Jewish historian on the Galileo case[224] of the Dominican versus Jesuit controversies located the sore-spot in their debates in the fact that St.

Dominic based his work on what St. Thomas Aquinas called the dictum, "Contemplate and then share with others what you have contemplated." On the other hand the founder of the Jesuits, St. Ignatius Loyola instituted an active order that did not stress liturgical and studious contemplation, but "spiritual exercises" by which a Jesuit is taught a "discernment of spirits" in active life and ministry.[225] This lead to the bitterly fought battles of OPs with SJs over grace and free will, probabilism and probabiliorism, The Dominicans emphasis on the *vita contemplativa* and metaphysical consistency in theology hardened into a "dogmatic Thomism," in sharp contrast to Jesuit emphasis on the *vita activa* directed to the rhetorically effective presentation of Church doctrine to a changing culture perhaps better served by a "pragmatic Thomism." Thus the Jesuits, sensing a theoretical defeat such as they had suffered in the grace controversy, strategically reversed their position favorable to Galileo, thus resulting in the condemnation of his still unproven, but eventually substantiated views.

There are many other old jokes comparing the diverse spirit of religious Orders, the gist of which is usually that Benedictines are common sense, Franciscans pious, Jesuits practical, and Dominicans abstracted. The story I tell is that my novice master, when any other Order was mentioned, always assured us that some Dominican had really founded or reformed it. For the Jesuits he said, "Well you know they would never have survived if a Dominican confessor had not helped St. Ignatius recover from scrupulosity!" To which I add, "And they never have had any scruples since." My other lame joke on this subject is that I often warn people, "See, the End Times must be close at hand. The Prophet Isaiah said that then 'The wolf and the lamb will graze together' and this is fulfilled now that the Jesuits and Dominicans in Jesuit Hall eat together in peace!" If they then ask, "Which is the wolf and which is the lamb?" I point out that the Dominican habit is white, while Jesuits wear clerical black.

As a matter of fact, however, due not only to the generosity of Jesuits but to their practicality, our cooperation in St. Louis has worked very well. But at first some lay faculty suspected that the university administration, engaged in economic downsizing, were hiring us as cheap clerical labor to take their jobs! In fact these fears were mistaken and the cooperation has proved beneficial to all concerned. Eventually, an association has been formed between the University's theological department, the archdiocesan Kenrick Seminary, and Aquinas Institute. Unhappily, nearby Seminex, a Lutheran seminary that had split from Concordia Seminary, as a result of fundamentalist attacks on its faculty, soon joined Chicago Lutheran, so that Aquinas has never fully regained the ecumenism it enjoyed in Dubuque. Concordia and Covenant seminaries though friendly to AI are cool to ecumenism. When I first met a member of the Covenant faculty, he asked, "Why do you use OP after your name? For us that means Orthodox Presbyterian." Although a colleague of mine Fr. Joseph Gillespie, OP, has often taught at The United Church's Eden Seminary and found its faculty and students curious about "Catholic spirituality," it is rather too distant both in location and in theology to facilitate ecumenical cooperation.

Thus my old age began in this new situation of contrasting spiritualities and intellectual traditions. I think this is the first aspect of any good spirituality of aging, to begin to reflect on the limitations of one's experience.

Life in a New Priory

It was in the summer of 1981 that we closed St. Rose Priory in Dubuque. Its building was later purchased by a conservative Bible college that has removed the statues of saints and built a gymnasium. We did not get a good price but we were very lucky to save ourselves the cost of prolonged upkeep and happy that it is preserved in pious Christian hands. We had already moved our whole community to St. Louis, except for a few faculty members who decided to take the opportunity to teach elsewhere. Already in 1967 Fr. Francis McNutt, OP, had moved there to edit a journal on preaching for the Christian Preaching Conference. He soon established the Thomas Merton House on McPherson Ave. as a center for the charismatic movement in which he had become a prominent leader. Then Fr. Albert Moraczewski, OP, came from Dallas in 1973 to St. Louis to be President of the Pope John Center for Bioethics. In the next year Fr. Kevin O'Rourke came as Vice-President of the Catholic Hospital Association, but in 1980 became founder and Director of the Center for Bioethics at St. Louis University School of Medicine, winning the respect of the closed fraternity of the MDs by his straight forwardness and hard work.

With Fr. Moraczewski and Fr. Neal McDermott, OP, chaplain for the students at St. Louis University, O'Rourke had already renovated an old house in the Central West End, at 97 Waterman Place. This has become a second Dominican priory in St. Louis, a residence for five to eight friars, most of them members of the Aquinas faculty, with the name of "St. Louis Bertrand Priory" in honor of Luis Beltrán, OP, a sixteenth century Spanish missionary to Central America. I was one of the original seven there along with Fr. Ralph Powell, a famous character of our Province who was a year older than me in age but three years younger in the Order.

Ralph was born of a prominent Washington, DC family and "in the world" (as it used to be said in our reception of the Dominican habit) was named Austin. He studied under Jesuit teachers whom, he said, were in his eyes "all thirty feet tall." When he went to study at the University of Louvain, where he earned the doctorate in philosophy under the influence of Transcendental Thomist teachers, he became a philosophical idealist, firmly convinced that he was "concreating the world with God." In his studious isolation he began to think he was telepathic and by the power of thought could guide the flight of birds he saw from his window. He only abandoned this extreme idealism under strong pressure from his mother and brothers. Briefly he had taught at St. Michael's College, Canada, and then at Georgetown University. Yet, as he often said to me, he always remained more European than American and was much influenced by European scholars, notably Dr. Goetz Briefs,[226] a notable figure in the Christian Democratic reconstruction of Germany and of Europe after World War II.

In Washington, along with his younger brother DeSales, Ralph became a disciple of the remarkable Herbert Schwartz,[227] a Jew converted to Catholicism whom they had met there at the Dominican House of Studies. Largely through Herbert's influence, Austin, after considerable hesitation, decided to enter the Dominican Order and took the religious name "Ralph." He told me that when, years afterwards he was teaching in Rome, Schwartz came there to seek a dispensation from marriage so that he might become a priest and timidly asked Ralph's intercession. Ralph thought that it was his too enthusiastic advocacy of Herbert to the wary Vatican officials that led them to deny this dispensation!

He applied first to the New York Province but was refused admission because of the lengthy letter he wrote them conscientiously enumerating all his faults and failings. Our Chicago Province, then new and eager for applicants, took the risk of accepting him. We came to take pride in his uniqueness. As he used to reply to conventional inquiries about how he was doing, "Far better than I deserve!" Ralph taught for many years both in River Forest and Dubuque, but also for a time at the Angelicum (the Dominican University of St. Thomas) in Rome. There he published a work in anticipation of Vatican II arguing that the civil state is bound only by the natural law. Hence even if the majority of its citizens are Catholic it has no obligation or right to give a special status to the Catholic Church and must acknowledge and defend the rights of conscience for all. A Dominican official of the Holy Office warned that the orthodoxy of this view was suspect, but nevertheless the Vatican press published the work. Ralph expected to remain in Rome the rest of his life, but was soon reassigned to teach at Dubuque.

When in Dubuque the ecumenical association with the Lutherans and Presbyterians came about, Ralph spent much of his time with them and was fascinated by their conversation. From then on the interest closest to his heart was ecumenism. He believed that the Catholic Church must radically reform itself to be free of everything that is secondary, especially everything acquired from the time of the Constantinian Establishment, so that it can speak to Protestants in purely biblical terms.

Both when in River Forest and Dubuque Ralph lived with Dominican students he was looked on with wonder because of his eccentric studiousness and ascetic behavior, almost like that of an alien from outer space, and hence was nicknamed "Doc." Yet his confreres loved him for his great generosity and humility, even when these were expressed in odd forms of diet, dress, and manner. Ralph's petitions during the offertory at Mass often startled us by their references to political and personal events that were on his mind only. A famous one, relating to a former student of his in whom his great hopes had been disappointed, was, "Let us pray for the greatest metaphysician our Province has ever produced, who has left the Order and the priesthood, only to fall into ill-health and dire poverty, supported by his wife who works as a go-go dancer!" We found it difficult to proceed with that liturgy!

The day Ralph and I drove from Dubuque to live in St. Louis, just as we were five minutes away from St. Rose, he suddenly said to me, "Let's go back!" I said in surprise, "Why? Did you leave something behind?" "No," he answered, laughing wildly, "But you know all the years I lived in St. Rose Priory I hardly saw any of its rooms except the chapel, the library, the refectory, and my cell. Shouldn't I go back now and take a look at the rest of the building before it is too late?" I did not turn back, but I must also note that driving to St. Louis, on a perfectly plain route, we still managed to get lost, and arrived late for our first evening there. My continuous dialogue with Ralph had a way of getting lost in a maze of such humorous sidetracks.

The renovated residence for St. Louis Bertrand Priory where we seven lived had been built in 1904 for a bachelor and his two spinster sisters, only a couple of blocks from Forest Park, where the World's Fair was in progress. It is a red brick house with white columns on the porch and some of the nice interior detailing for which the old houses of St. Louis are noted. We remodeled it to provide rooms for eight Dominicans, with a guest room. It has a large tree-shaded back yard, with squirrels, rabbits, many birds, and for a while a mother raccoon who lived with her brood in a chimney. One of those "private" streets closed at one end, typical of St. Louis, it is quiet, tree-lined, with flowerbeds, and flowering trees in spring. The resident families, mainly professional people, are racially mixed.

I quickly learned to love St. Louis, though it is a city suffering suburban flight, with a devastated North Side that begins just two blocks north of Waterman Place and entraps many black citizens without employment. Yet the city is a poets' city, once the home of T.S. Eliot, Tennessee Williams, and Marianne Moore. The lyric poet, Sara Teasdale, who died in 1933, lived only a block from our Priory on another private street whose elaborate gateway features a naked green nymph sometimes provided by pranksters with a modest brassiere. In our priory we cultivated the "togetherness" and "sharing" so much the ideal of religious life today. Our perhaps overly comfortable, middle-class life facilitates this, though we daily kept up the recitation of the liturgical Hours and community Eucharist in our small chapel and were conscientious about the vows we have taken to, "have all things in common."

St. Louis has excellent cultural opportunities, a first-rate symphony and much other music, even a brief opera season, good libraries, a fine Art Museum, theater, and extensive parks. I often walk in Forest Park, yet, ever a small-town boy, I miss the hills and fields of Dubuque. But living in a community of brothers can provide some very fine times of mutual enjoyment. Thus a second feature of the spirituality of aging should be in taking time for mature friendships and appreciating their deep value.

MUSIC WITH WINE

As a signet of an emerald in a work of gold,
so is the melody of music with pleasant and moderate wine.
(Sirach 32:5-6).

From earth, its deeper waters, its stored sun,
life rises into vine, leafs green, swells purple,
and crushed to blood, runs fire,
yet finally
    clears to a molten jewel.

        Here it is in crystal.
        Bind a family, a people with its pledge.
        Bind us to God by its oblation.

        Friends, together
        lift a glass, this wine
        grown in a particular earth,
        the one we all have frequented,
        its places, things, and sounds,
        its limits measured
        by our walks together...!

From human clay, its font of tears, its prisoned moon,
the tide of life spreads from a heart,
that beats, sings in the throat,
is measured in a form and numbered,
hammered and bent into a golden circle,
hallowed into a cup
that holds dark wine,
enough at least for two.

        Try this song:
        "Bind family, nation, globe in one great choir;
        Bind us and God in one antiphony!"

But we two
sing an old tune learned one remembered day,
the very one we spent alone together,

its hours, seasons, generation measured
by much talking, more silence...

Good friends, good wine.
poured in due measure like a signet emerald.
An old tune once more, once more repeated,
never to be broken...
let it be the ring
set with a loyal jewel
all aglow
to enshrine
our convivial rainbow
in the wine.

But "togetherness" at times can also be wounding.

TRAUMA

Feeling misunderstood
by those one thought
might understand,
Reacting with emotions,
more than I expected
to the point of tears,
I hid them in a days' depression,
angered that the cause of truth
was treated as peculiarly personal,
a self-interested imposition
of a too often heard opinion.

It made me understand, my Lord,
just a little, yet more truly
how it seemed to you
when, Truth Eternal,
they all misunderstood
even those ones you surely had expected
if they did not understand
at least might feel
that what you spoke
was who you truly are.

The years from 1981-1988 were the most peaceful of my life. Although in 1980 I had become only an Emeritus Professor of the Aquinas Institute faculty, I made the ten-minute drive to Aquinas at the SLU ("Sloo") campus each weekday to teach courses in moral theology and Dominican spirituality. Now that clerical students were few, and others clerics hard to recruit, the then President of Aquinas, Fr. John (Jack) Taylor, favored the interests of Sisters and laity preparing for various types of lay ministry. Jack, who lived at St. Louis Bertrand's, was an excellent administrator, but seemed to grow increasingly uncomfortable with his own priesthood, with the so-called "post-Vatican II retrenchment." John Paul II's refusal to ordain women, it seemed to him, flatly contradicted his own libertarian, egalitarian ecclesiology. Not long after the completion of his presidential term and a couple more years working for an ecumenical organization, he left the priesthood and married. We were all deeply saddened since he had for so many years been an excellent prior in Dubuque, a hardworking president, and a cooperative confrere.

Thus my students at Aquinas were in minor part Dominican men preparing for priesthood and in major part Sisters and laity. It was depressing to count so few young Dominican men and to note the aging of the Dominican Sisters, no longer picturesquely medieval in their garb. Because most of the students lacked the philosophical preparation formerly expected of Dominican clerics, they found the rigorously scholastic approach of Thomism unappealing. My own knowledge of Thomism seemed less and less relevant to their "felt needs." As now a teacher of peripheral subjects, I used to pass Fr. Joseph Gillespie's classroom and hear the fascinated student laughter as he taught his pastoral theology course on "Grief and Depression." He is a hardworking, very popular and friendly person who has spent many hours in personal and family counseling. A man of wide interests, he always gives me a sympathetic hearing, although he is not greatly interested in the theoretical questions that intrigue me. He has a robust, native, Irish Catholic faith, and since he entered the Order at the most radical phase of Vatican II changes, takes change for granted and is skeptical of rigid ideological tendencies. As an unselfish prior and a business manager for us, he always sounded a cheerful note in our community chorus.

Our greatest sorrow at St. Louis Bertrand Priory was the death from bronchial cancer of Fr. Christopher Kiesling, beloved as sacramental theologian and editor of our magazine *Spirituality Today*. His condition had been discovered in Dubuque but surgery seemed to deal with it successfully. From the time Chris's cancer reoccurred in St. Louis until his death, when it was agreed, following his expressed wishes, to withdraw further treatment, our community truly shared with him the whole dying process. His reception of the Sacrament of Anointing of the Sick at our community Mass is a sacred memory for us all and a model for our own dying. We are especially grateful to Sister Joan Delaplane, OP, for the special help, like a true sister, she gave him and us through this ordeal. To care for his own elderly mother Chris had moved her from Chicago to St. Louis. She survived him for some years, and Joan and others of our community, especially Ralph Powell visited her regularly in her nursing home. Later Walter Ingling (d. 1992), a pastoral psychologist and pleasant confrere joined our community. He was, however, also to die in midlife soon after being assigned to another Priory.

During these years of teaching at Aquinas I also gave lectures in a variety of places but I will mention only a few to give some sense of what today it means for a theologian to be an "itinerant preacher" in Dominic's footsteps. One tries to shed a Christian and Catholic light on many current topics, in many places, "in season and out of season." How many lonely hours I have spent in an airport crowd waiting for my plane! How many nights in motels, hotels, college dormitories, rectory bedrooms, at a convention, or conducting a workshop! And some of my Dominican brothers are much greater travelers than I, busy not only with lectures, workshops, conventions, meetings, but with baptisms, weddings, funerals, often in Latin America, Australia, Japan, India, Africa. We do not trudge on foot as Dominic did, say early biographers, walking barefoot or on clogs, but at least we wait weary in airports wondering why the plane is overdue and whether the snack provided will be more than coffee and peanuts.

As a professor emeritus with less teaching hours than other faculty members I also did a certain amount of special tutoring. One attempt, which ended abruptly, related to the Charismatic Movement, which I had first met in Dubuque. I will not easily forget a Eucharist held there by a meeting of charismatics. After the communion a kind of musical murmur of "tongues" began spontaneously in the whole assembly and continued for some time like a gentle ocean wave of praise and then subsided into meditative silence. In St. Louis this movement flourished under the leadership of Fr. Francis

McNutt, OP, who, as I have already mentioned, had founded a preaching center in St. Louis called Merton House that became also a center for charismatics. When St. Louis Bertrand Priory was founded we had hoped he would join us there, but soon afterwards he left the Order and the priesthood and married, to the great dismay of the movement in which he had been so prominent.

Yet Merton House continued to operate under two brothers, Jesuit priests, and a woman who was a convert to Catholicism. She eventually married one of the two, but all three have continued a ministry of charismatic healing in the Church. She wanted a guide in reading St. Thomas Aquinas' *Summa Theologiae* and I was struck by her quick intelligence. We progressed famously until we came to a passage which showed that the Angelic Doctor really believed that God permits some people to damn themselves to an eternal hell! How could this ever be reconciled with her idea of a loving, unconditionally accepting God? She politely found excuse to terminate the tutoring.

On another occasion when I was away from St. Louis I spoke on the subject of "Is AIDS a Punishment from God?" and a priest vehemently objected and declared, "A loving God would never punish anyone!" I wondered how he understood and preached on the many passages about God's wrath even in the New Testament and read in the liturgy. A loving and merciful God still has to punish sin for the same reason that a loving parent punishes a child's misbehavior or our courts punish crime. If wrongdoing is not punished the wrongdoer is not likely to desist, and even if he or she does not, others are not deterred from copying the wrongdoing, or finally the moral standards in the community (in the child's case, in the family) are not upheld and the victims of the wrongdoing cry out for justice. The one who punishes in justice punishes in love of the wrongdoer, the victims, and the community of both. If the wrongdoer refuses to accept the efforts of the community and the grace of God, who never ceases to offer us his grace as long we live, then nothing remains for him or her after death but that eternal self-exclusion from the community of those who love God and each other. To try to deduce from God's absolute goodness, as Origen did, and as some theologians such as Hans Urs von Balthasar today seem inclined to do, that none of us will ever use our God given freedom to choose this final exclusion is a logical fallacy, and a theology that eliminates the cosmic drama for the sake of making us comfortable is hardly worth the effort.

Another much happier tutoring experience occurred when I was asked to assist a student who was also interested in studying texts of St. Thomas. When he came to see me I beheld a polio victim, a Benedictine monk walking with difficulty on two canes. When I asked about his previous studies, expecting at most some college or seminary courses, he replied, "Undergraduate work at Harvard, a D.Phil. from Oxford, and some teaching at Notre Dame." He knew a great deal of patristic theology from Oxford, but not much about the medievals. Awed to have so advanced a student, I asked him to read some sections of the *Summa* in Latin and come each time with written questions on puzzling points. Thus began for me a delightful series of dialogues in which Thomas Frerking and I shared the wisdom of Aquinas. That is the contemplative life! Not much later his superiors decided he should be ordained. He became Principal of the Abbey School and soon Abbot, leaving him, as Pope St. Gregory complained, little time for contemplation. Thus a third aspect of a spirituality of aging is to learn that in instructing others one can learn more them than one could ever learn by oneself.

Engaging in Philosophical and Theological Controversies

Though this was a peaceful time, I began again to be involved, as I had before and have described in the second part of this autobiography, in theological controversies. Is an autobiography a good place to discuss what are sometimes rather arcane theological disputes? Well, surely an account of one's spiritual life ought to reveal the inner as well as the outer life of the subject. Much of my inner life is not poetry, nor contemplation, but inner dialogue about philosophical and theological controversies. In the following poem I refer to the terminology of St. Augustine followed by St. Thomas Aquinas who speaks of the natural knowledge of the angels as "twilight knowledge" in comparison to their supernatural beatific vision as "morning knowledge."

DISPUTATION

Even on a point,
the finest point of the finest needle
in quantum leaps the lively quarks
from virtual existence

glide, bubbling into reality
and to quantum time
keep dancing—
or so they—
the quizzical scientists,
say.

In an older game
young schoolmen learned their trade
in battles theological, debating
"How many angels possibly can dance
on a needle's point?"
Knowing full well that such a "point"
being still matter, extended, yet conjoint
is wider than any merely mathematical and hypothetical
or point of singularity
burning in clarity
and also that no angel, however lowly
in the high spiritual hierarchy
is bound by space or even by time
but in spiritual freedom
lives in thought and willing only.

Yes, the angels dance upon a pint
but all their dancing is in thinking
upon a point of truth,
questioning and questing yes or no.
And as they dance—
the Angelic Doctor argues—
in the dusk of twilight knowing
their dance becomes a war of truths
partial and conflicted
that can find its ultimate resolution
only in the peaceful symphony
of dawning morning knowledge
in the One Truth,
the infinite plenitude,
all doubts satisfying,
of one perfect Word
sung by His Spirit

in the concordant light
of eternal silence
of a song complete,
a circling dance unending
around its Triune
Center.

Theologically we battle
in a time, cacophonous, chaotic.
caught in a dusk where rays of dawn
can only bubble up
quanta of truth
out of our dimly virtual void.

O Lord of cosmic celebration,
may our cacophony of words
reset to charity's melodious hymn
at last deploy
to beat for floating feet
a lovely, lively dance,
voices diversely unison,
each sounding one sweet,
necessary note
that one and all enjoy.

Thus, from now on in this memoir theological controversies will crowd my personal narrative. The context will especially be my work as a consultant to the Committee on Doctrine of the National Conference of Catholic Bishops and their dealing with the necessary but painfully difficult problems of revising moral theology after Vatican II.

It is often a feature of old age, especially for those professionally educated, that people consult you, hoping you have learned something in all the years you have been around. When I was still President of Aquinas in River Forest, I participated in the work of a committee to prepare the 1970 document *The Program of Priestly Formation*. After 1980 my talks at the annual Pope John Center workshop for bishops in Dallas also made me known to many bishops as a theological consultant. Hence when Msgr. Richard Malone, formerly a Vatican curial official, became secretary for the Committee on Doctrine of the National Catholic Conference of Bishops

(NCCB), he occasionally called on me for an opinion, mainly on moral questions, and I later served regularly during the terms of Frs. Michael Buckley, S. J. and Michael Walsh as executive secretaries of the Committee, both leaning toward more liberal positions and the more conservative Augustine DiNoia, OP, when I still lived in St. Louis and then later in Washington.

The first controversy, however, into which I was drawn as a consultant to bishops concerned dogmatic rather than moral issues. Fr. Richard McBrien is a big, breezy, Irish personality who, when I had occasionally heard him lecture, impressed me very favorably. It was rumored that he had been appointed chairman of Notre Dame's theology department to break up a Protestant clique whose domination of the department had resulted from post-Vatican II ecumenical euphoria. The leader was the brilliant, theologically militant Stanley Hauerwas, who, under McBrien's chairmanship, soon departed for Duke University. Hauerwas had generated a theological trend still influential at Notre Dame in the person of his doctoral student Fr. Michael Baxter, CSC. It interests me as an alumnus of Notre Dame that Fr. Baxter by his admiration for Dorothy Day and the Catholic Worker movement seems to renew the spirit of the Young Catholic Students Movement to which I once belonged at Notre Dame. That Movement fostered a countercultural attitude opposing the accommodationism of American education to bourgeois values.

On the contrary, Richard McBrien's at that time widely syndicated column seemed to aim at enculturating Catholicism in American culture in defiance of "Roman entrenchment," for example, by his arguments against mandatory clerical celibacy. His major work is *Catholicism*,[228] a title that seems to promise a coolly objective account of what the Catholic Church stands for without, of course, ignoring the diversity within its official unity. Though it lacked the imprimatur by the local bishop, it became widely used for collegiate and adult education as a reliable presentation of post-Vatican II theology. After reading this book for the Committee on Doctrine at Msgr. Malone's request, I gave my frank opinion that while *Catholicism* was pedagogically effective, it too often confused the Catholic faith with the personal theology of Karl Rahner.[229] Older textbooks also erred in confusing the Catholic faith with Aquinas' theology, but this at least was long tested and canonically approved in the Church, an approval not yet given to Rahner's thought, in spite of its distinction and wide influence in the Vatican II Church. Karl Rahner's theology is based on an interpretation of Thomism, proposed by Joseph Maréchal, SJ, termed "Transcendental" because it claims to find in St. Thomas' thought an *a priori* element which can provide common ground with the Cartesian "turn to the subject" which initiated modern philosophy and especially with its climax in the idealism of Immanuel Kant. It is more that doubtful that this claim can be textually verified.[230]

Though I have learned much from Rahner's investigations of particular historical issues, his idealist epistemology causes him in his more systematic works to retrench from the progressive features of Aquinas' thought.[231] Aquinas broke through the tradition of Platonic idealism in the Greek Fathers and St. Augustine, and on which too much of Christian theology has been constructed, and replaced it with a realistic Aristotelian epistemology which roots the objective certitude of human knowledge not in some *a priori* element in human thinking, but in the publicly verifiable observation of the sensible world. It is this realist epistemology that is the true common ground between Thomism and contemporary thought. It alone can furnish a way to construct a theology in which modern science, the realism of the Bible, and classical philosophy can communicate. If this is to be achieved, however, modern science itself also needs to be freed of Kantianism. Rahner wrote much about spirituality, much of it excellent, yet because of this philosophical transcendentalism it tends to depart from the empirical foundation which St. Thomas attempted to give to all of theology and hence to spirituality and on which I felt I could build more securely.

I have tried to express the foregoing in the following poem. I originally in high school intended to be a poet and, as will be evident in this book, I find poetry, even if it descends to doggerel, can often better express the analogies required by spiritual events better than abstract prose.

VIGIL

On the edge of sunrise
as hopelessly they prayed
the women saw open
the black tomb where,
they were so sure
Life
now dead, was laid.

How fast you ran,
Mary of Magdala,
as if all seven devils
possessed you,
like Eve, again,
to fetch the witless
Keeper of the Keys
and the young Beloved,
so that when they left again
(the one confused, the other hopeful)
instead of this unhelpful pair
she saw two dazzling,
puzzling angels seated
yet hopeless still kept on her vigil
weeping among the garden tombs
where never a flower blooms
until sudden as the sun
edged up she heard
the Gardner's steps.

Let us keep vigil, friends
in the dark garden on dawn's edge
till, like that once sinful Mary,
now an Eve by love redeemed,
against the rising sun we see
out of that hopeless prison
the new Adam,
now forever risen.

Chapter 19 - Science Supports Religion

Disappointment

As noted in a previous chapter, one of the feature of a spirituality of aging is that as Jesus said to some learned Scribes who argued with him (Mt.22:29)"You are misled because you do not know the scriptures or the power of God.," Thus we old folks must reflect on the limitations of our personal experience.

My many years of teaching had been in Thomistic philosophy and theology. Now, in spite of my primary engagement in theology, during this period of my I began to realize I was keeping vigil for death; yet I had kept up my interest in modern science and now I hoped to be able to give more time to it and how it enriches these scholastic disciplines. Any incarnational spirituality has to deal not only with spirituality but with its relation to our material bodies and the world of which they are part. I regret to say, and it is only my opinion, that our Dominican Order after Vatican II has not made a consistent, effective effort to promote our great heritage of the thought of St. Thomas Aquinas on the human person, soul and body in the material universe.

Although our Chicago Province had established the Albertus Magnus Lyceum in 1950 to study this question and this project continued with considerable success until 1969. it had ended with the move of the Aquinas Institute to Dubuque. Some who regretted its closing held a meeting on "The Future of Thomism" in River Forest in 1988, but this proved, in my opinion, quite sterile. Paralyzed by Maritain and Gilson's "existential" Thomism and then blown away by the Heideggerian, Wittgensteinian winds which Vatican II unintentionally let in when it "opened the windows," Dominican philosophers and theologians generally are, I am afraid, "without a clue." Thus it seems that in the United States today more is being done for Thomism by laypersons than by Dominicans.

I must add, however, that conservative Catholic intellectuals, who laud St. Thomas Aquinas, are also often too engaged in deploring liberal trends to respond to more positive efforts to develop Thomistic thought in relation to modern knowledge. Thus when I gave a keynote address at an annual convention of the Fellowship of Catholic Scholars (which I found too negativist to join) on "The Church's Message to Artists and Scientists,"[232] I met with no sympathetic response. I must add that the unpublished paper "Theological Method Today" which I delivered as part of the Bishops' and Scientists Dialogue of the NCCB, 1987, also found no support from the other theologians present. By writing in eight popular columns, "Science and Religion", for *The National Catholic Register* in 1987, I kept trying to speak to the general public for a much more positive, productive view of the relation between science and religion.

A better understanding of modern science leads directly to an improvement in anthropology—our understanding of human nature and its distinction from changing cultural developments. This in turn strengthens the foundations of a moral theology which respects human nature and the natural moral law. Hence I wrote a paper on "An Integrated View of the Christian Person"[233] and another on "Theology and the Mind-Body Problem."[234] On the latter topic I argued against the widespread belief that computers can be made to think since thought is merely the activity of the brain. To bring together bits of "information" in any material complex they must be transmitted from one point to another, as we see in a computer's circuitry or the brain's still more intricate neural networks. In an extended entity, however, it is impossible to make all points coincide at a single point. Self-consciousness, on the contrary, requires that I not only possess some information but that I know that I possess it. I not only know something, but I know that I know it, and indeed, that I know that I know that I know it. The mind totally reflects on itself as if it existed at a point, or rather outside all spatial location and hence transcends the activity of the brain in which information always exists at spatial location.

My former college classmate and Nobel laureate, Herbert Simon (d. 2002)[235] was very confident that it will be possible to invent machines that "think." We should not, however, confuse thought with a language, which is, after all, something material, a sequence of sounds or letters or other sensible symbols. A computer manipulates material symbols that can be made to approximate the patterns of thought but remain meaningless until a human mind interprets them. As we know with ordinary language, the expression of thought in language is ambiguous and requires to be specified by a thinking human being. Thus our brains are, in this life, necessary instruments for our thinking, and computers are highly useful but not necessary to aid our thinking, but my brain does not think self-consciously, any more than my word-processing computer is thinking as I write with it.

Thus a Thomistic epistemology insists that while intellectual thought depends on sense knowledge and is therefore, like science, empirically realistic; it is not materialistic, since the spirituality of the human intelligence can be shown empirically from the observable differences between concrete animal "intelligence" which deals only with images and human intelligence which uses images to arrive at abstract concepts and can therefore express itself in invented, syntactic languages quite unlike animal signaling.

Writing on these topics supported the themes treated in my already published *Theologies of the Body: Humanist and Christian*[236] on which I also gave a course at the Institute for Thomistic Studies of the University of St. Thomas in Houston and there in 1987 delivered an Annual Aquinas Address on, "St. Thomas and the Theology of the Body."[237] I elaborated the same theme in an article "Constructing and Reconstructing the Human Body."[238] A better anthropology that combines Thomist psychology with modern psychology will enables us to revise moral theology of which spirituality is a part. Therefore a fifth note of a spirituality of aging is an increasing appreciation of what St. Paul meant in Romans 8:16, "The Spirit itself bears witness with our spirit that we are children of God."

Renewing Moral Theology

In the early Church Christian moralists followed the prophets and Jesus in preaching not just external obedience to the Law, but its motivation by love. Aided by Greek philosophy, they developed a teleological (ends-means) concept of morality: an act is good if it is a good means to the supreme goal of human life, union with God and neighbor. It was for such a life-journey that God designed human nature, and heals and transforms it by Christ's grace. Moral laws or norms must be obeyed, but not because God is the Almighty but because he is all loving and all wise. Because he loves us he guides us toward his kingdom in which we will joyfully share his eternal life. Hence moral teaching aims first to form human character by the virtues, and chiefly by the virtue of prudence by which norms can be intelligently applied to actual situations for the right motives.

This teleological moral theology came to its fullest development in the High Middle Ages, but then in late Middle Ages the nominalist William of Ockham (1188-1347) proposed an ethics based on the principle that an all powerful God is free to legislate as he wills for reasons we often cannot discover; hence to be moral is to obey his laws without questioning them. Ockham even said hypothetically that if God will us to hate him we would be bound to do so!. This voluntarism was favored by the growth of centralized monarchy, Reformation fideism, Catholic concern to refute Protestant accusations of laxism by encouraging frequent confession, and the suspicion of teleological thinking with which Immanuel Kant infected modern science. Protestant ethics originated in Luther's nominalist, voluntaristic education and Catholics even now are not yet wholly free of voluntarism.

Vatican II, aided by the nineteenth century Thomistic revival, has promoted a general effort by Catholic moralists to retrieve a teleological moral theory emphasizing character formation, virtue, and prudence and a greater New Testament concern for motivation through love. Consequently many controversies have arisen in moral theology over questions of moral decisions in conflict situations and the relation of individual conscience to the teaching authority of the college of bishops headed by the successor of St. Peter.

Thus, even before Vatican II, it was generally realized among Catholic moralists that a revision of the voluntaristic and legalistic moral theology of the post-Tridentine manuals is imperative. Some of these attempts, however, have been open to serious criticism. In several short articles I wrote against legalism and in favor of a natural law ethics, i.e. a teleological ethics: "Why is Breaking God's Law a Sin?"[239] "What is the Natural Law?"[240] and "Moral Inconsistency and Fruitful Public Debate."[241] In "The Scriptural Basis of Moral Theology"[242] I argued against the current notion that biblical ethics is so time-conditioned that it gives us little more than abstract values, while actual concrete decisions must be guided more by reason than revelation. Though "natural law" is a Stoic not a Christian term, the equivalent "order of creation" and the teleological metaphor of life as a journey to the Promised Land or the Kingdom are thoroughly biblical.

Related to this problem about the use of the Bible in the revision of moral theology is the trend to treat "human experience" as a third source of revelation on a par with the Bible and Tradition, which can easily lead to rejecting whatever in Bible and Tradition does not seem to square with our contemporary "experience." I developed this criticism in "A Response to John P. Boyle's, 'The American Experience in Theology"[243] at a convention of the Catholic Theological Society of America.

The very notion of "spirituality" as a field distinct form moral theology goes back only to the sixteenth century. This separation came about as a result of the rise of the false mysticism[244] such as that of the Quietists, such as the French Madame Guyon (1648-1717) who proposed a theory of "pure love of God" that re-duced Christianity to a yoga-like trance, indifferent to one's own or one's neighbors salvation. This was condemned by the Church and theologians, notably by Jesuits who proposed a counter theory of "two vocations," one the extraordinary mystical way of being a Christian and the other the ordinary way of being a Christian by the practice of the commandments. Eventually this two-vocation theory was attacked by the Dominicans, the Spaniard Juan Arintero (d. 1928), now a candidate for beatification, and the Frenchman Re-ginald Garrigou-Lagrange (d. 1964), who in magisterial works argued that all Christians are called to attain contemplative prayer, since this is only the flowering of the Gifts of the Holy Spirit given to all in baptism.

Although few theologians would now defend the two-vocation theory, its influence lingers in seminary curricula and in theological terminology. Yet it should be obvious that all Christians are called to the perfect exercise of all the virtues, including that of contempla-tive prayer, although perhaps only a minority attain it before death, the rest only by passing through Purgatory in the next life.

Thomist theologians are also often criticized for neglecting his-tory and its effect on moral thinking. It is true that Aquinas' theolo-gy uses the Aristotelian model of a "science" which deals with universals only and not with "history" which deals with individuals. Nevertheless, for Aristotle and Aquinas all knowledge is derived from sensible individuals and seeks universal "scientific" principles only to understand individuals, which alone exist. Therefore, I as an Aristotelian Thomist find no great difficulty in adopting the modern historical orientation in theology. I often discuss issues of historical development as when in a Dallas workshop for bishops, in "The De-velopment of Doctrine about Sin, Conversion, and the Following of Christ," I argued that moral theology must be founded not on ab-stract, ideal values but on the example of the historical Jesus, a first century Jew.[245] Thus a sixth feature of the spirituality of aging is the fixing of mind and heart on Jesus, God made Man.

CARPENTER

Creator of a world now broken
busy at your sweaty work,
at the rough bench
you measure, saw, and nail
lest chaos should again prevail,
practicing some day
to die by bloody nail
in hands, in streaming feet
on that tree of wood
beam of evil, beam of good,
its fruit ripened now so sweet,
life that can never fail,
  your carpentry complete.

Proportionalism and the Revision of Moral Theology

Because "spirituality" cannot be separated form moral theology and because human physical and mental illness are rooted in original sin, medical ethics, now secularized as "bioethics," has always been important in Catholic spirituality. Jesus was a physical as well as a spiritual healer and the two kinds of illness are inseparable. In writing *Health Care Ethics: A Theological Approach*,[246] Fr. Kevin O'Rourke and I have had to deal with what was certainly the most influential attempt in this whole post-Vatican II period to revise moral theology, namely, "Proportionalism."

Proportionalism is a theory not about the goal or goals of human life but about moral decisions, that is, about what means to choose to attain these goals. It was first proposed by a noted Jesuit professor of moral theology at the Roman Gregorian University, Josef Fuchs, SJ (d. 2005).[247] Well known for his expositions of Aquinas' views on natural law, he was asked to serve on the papal commission on population control that in its "majority report" urged Pope Paul VI to declare that in certain circumstances and to strengthen a marriage, contraception is justified. Paul VI finally rejected this view in *Humanae Vitae.* Fuchs then, without directly opposing the papal declaration, in a trenchant 1971 essay, "The Absoluteness of Moral Norms,"[248] defended his new theory of moral decision on which the majority of the commission's advice seems to have been based. Thus Fuchs' theory became not only the chief theoretical support for dissent from papal teaching on contraception, but for a more radical revision of all Catholic moral theory and practice, replacing the complex older theory of moral decision by a single "principle of proportionate reason."

This new theory received able support from Fuchs' fellow Jesuits Peter Knauer and Bruno Schüller and also from the Louvain moralist, Louis Janssens. Finally these views were popularized in the United States through another Jesuit, Richard A. McCormick (d. 2000),[249] in his instructive "Notes on Moral Theology" in the leading American Catholic journal *Theological Studies*. For some years these notes were for United States priests considered the most reliable source of information on progressive trends in the Church. For me personally, it was Fr. McCormick who best typified and defended proportionalism. I knew him especially from our three year participation in the official Catholic-Methodist dialogue on death and dying (to be described later) that contributed much ecumenically to my vigil meditations. He was a tall, bluff, Irish type who always presented his views very clearly and persuasively. He came from a medical family and was always excellently informed on bioethical questions so that he was frequently invited to be the representative Catholic theologian on government and other commissions dealing with bioethical controversies.

Fr. McCormick based his arguments for proportionalism on the principle attributed to Aquinas that the morality of a human is specified by its object, circumstances, and intention (motive). Proportionalism, he contended, supported this Thomistic view but improved the presentation commonly given to it that exaggerated the role of the object.. The object of an act, McCormick pointed out, takes its moral character from the intention or motive for which it is performed and to separate the object abstractly considered from its concrete circumstances ignores practical reality. Therefore, he argued, moral decisions are rightly made only if we take all three factors together and weigh the positive and negative values they entail. If it then appears that the positive values of the act outweigh the negative ones, then in view of this preponderance of positive values the act should be judged morally good, even if some abstract general norm forbade it.

When the opponents of this theory objected that this seemed to approve "doing evil for good to come from it" or "the end justifies the means," McCormick answered that the weighing of values concerned "pre-moral values" not moral values as such, since it was only when this evaluation had established the preponderance of good values or bad that the act was considered precisely as a moral rather than a merely physical act.

My own and many others' objections to this seemingly plausible theory of moral decisions were as follows. First, it confuses Aquinas' real position on the specification of the moral act. Aquinas held that a physical act is morally specified primarily and essentially by its relation as a means to the true final end of human life or more immediately as a means to some of the other natural goals that are measured and unified by that supreme goal. That essential specification can be secondarily and accidentally modified by circumstances. These circumstances can render an essentially good act bad, as for example, the normal and good act of eating can become bad on a religious fast day, or they can make it even better, as eating to celebrate a religious feast, or they can make an immoral act somewhat less bad, as eating only a small snack on a fast day. Since, however, circumstances are not the essential determination of the morality of an act they cannot make an essentially bad act into an essentially good act. This is true even of a "good intention."

This becomes clear if we note that "intention" has three quite different ethical meanings: (1) The intention of the ultimate end, which Aquinas holds is involved in every free human act, since it motivates our entire way in life. (2) The intention of the particular act that is being considered as a means to that goal and about which we must make a decision; this finality is precisely what makes the act a moral and not merely a physical action, since it is the measuring of the means by the end for which it is to be performed. (3) Other possible intentions good or bad that are purely circumstantial and hence can only *qualify* the morality of the act but cannot make an essentially bad act essentially good. McCormick, in my view, tended to confuse the third sense of intention with the other two.

Therefore the fundamental error of proportionalism is that it leads to a denial that any acts are essentially (intrinsically) evil by reason of their moral object in all circumstances. Thus it is a denial of the validity of "absolute" (exceptionless) moral norms. It was for this reason that later in 1993 John Paul II in his encyclical *The Splendor of Truth* condemned any ethical system that denies that there are some absolute, exceptionless, concrete negative moral norms forbidding intrinsically evil acts and in another encyclical *The Gospel of Truth* 1995 declared that the Bible and Catholic tradition make clear that the direct killing of innocent human beings, including abortion, is intrinsically evil. Thus it is basic to spiritual development that first of all one resolutely avoids the dark realm of intrinsically evil acts that exclude one from the way that leads to God, our only true happiness.

After these encyclicals were issued some proportionalists have dissented on the grounds that John Paul II has misrepresented or misunderstood their position. For example, they claim that they admit some absolute norms, although only ones that are "formal" rather than concrete, such as "Never choose an act whose negative values exceed its positive values" or "Love your neighbor as yourself" provided that the term "love" is simply abstract. They also claim that they too say that "murder" is wrong; because the term connotes that there are no excusing circumstances for the killing. It is clear, however, that Catholics must admit that some kinds of *concrete* acts are intrinsically evil.

As someone who thinks in the Dominican tradition, I cannot help but see in proportionalism, proposed under the very nose of the Pope at a Roman university noted for its orthodoxy, a revival of the great controversy that raged in the Catholic Church from the sixteenth through the eighteenth centuries over the competing theories of conscience: "rigorism," "probabilorism," "probabilism," and "laxism." This controversy, never definitely settled by the popes, is intelligible only in the context of the deontological, voluntaristic type of late medieval theology. The question under debate was whether conscientious Catholics seeking to obey the moral law but who are puzzled by finding that theologians do not agree on what that moral law forbids, may then in good conscience choose to follow that one of the opinions that they themselves find more lenient. The popes have always vigorously condemned laxism, but permitted debates between probabiliorists who hold that the more probable of the opinions ought to be followed, and probabilists who said that any solidly probable opinion might be followed if supported by one great authority in theology or by four or five lesser lights, the "standard authors." Dominicans and Franciscans were traditionally probabiliorists, but many Jesuits, moved by pastoral pragmatism, opted for probabilism. This probabilism, though only tolerated by the popes, became widely accepted in practice. At the end of the eighteenth century papal recommendation of the moral manual of St. Alphonsus Liguori (1696-1787) founder of the Redemptorist and a moderate probabilist, seemed pragmatically to settle the controversy.

Obviously in a teleological ethics it is foolish to choose any road to our true goal in life other than the one more likely (*probabilior*) to get us there. In a deontological ethics, on the contrary, it is quite reasonable to suppose that if a wise legislator had intended to oblige his subjects to a law in its stricter interpretation, he would have made this clear in the law itself. In this legalistic, probabilistic tradition long favored by most Jesuit moralists, it is understandable that a proportionalist theory such as Fuchs' is congenial, though many older Jesuits were quick to repudiate its more radical implications.[250]

Thus proportionalism became for many moral theologians the paradigm of forward looking post-Vatican ethics and it was generally taught in American seminaries and thus formed a whole generation of Catholic priests. But probabilists never denied that some kinds of acts by there very nature are intrinsically evil and always forbidden. Thus McCormick's own teacher Fr. John Connery, SJ, who preceded me as a theological adviser for the Committee on Doctrine rejected proportionalism on the probabilist grounds that its requires a comprehensive notion of the values of an act and its possible consequences that render the theory both impractical and arbitrary and can lead to scrupulosity!

Logically, however, it was never clear why on deontological grounds a probabilist might not find exceptions for any law, since if a law binds only by reason of the will of the legislator, why cannot the one who makes such a law, sometimes, if he will, dispense from it? Only a teleologist can logically maintain that some acts, whatever their circumstances, can never be made good, even by God, because they contradict the inherent teleology of human nature. Thus teleologists maintain that forced sex (rape) is always wrong because it contradicts the purpose of sex intrinsic to human nature, namely to give oneself to another freely. Thus my opposition to proportionalism was rooted not just in my Dominican tradition, but in my fundamental personal conviction that Catholic philosophers and theologians have a grave responsibility to overcome the disastrous anti-teleological (anti-natural) understanding of natural science. It is this erroneous interpretation of the achievements of modern science that has placed science in opposition to Christian faith. Like nominalism of old, it has caused our modern culture to despair of grounding ethics in teleological human nature and thus handed it over to moral relativism. Thus proportionalism, in spite of the claims of McCormick and others, is in reality not a teleological ethic at all (John Paul II calls it "teleologism") but a radical form of a legalistic deontological ethics that ingeniously seeks loopholes in the moral law. Its arbitrary character is illustrated by the fact that although McCormick never accepted abortion, Daniel McGuire of Marquette University, another proportionalist, accepted abortion provided its motivation and circumstances were appropriate.[251]

For these reasons, in our *Health Care Ethics* Fr. O'Rourke and I criticized proportionalist theory, as I also did in an article, "Ethical Decisions: Why Exceptionless Norms?"[252] Also in a review article on Germain Grisez's, *The Way of the Lord Jesus*,[253] I praised his arguments against proportionalism and his courage in writing after Vatican II a complete treatise on moral theology as comprehensive as the classical manuals. With all these controversies about Christian morality rife, little wonder so many Catholics, were disturbed by the media's simplistic accounts of these theological wars, are very confused and confounded. Many Catholics have only a legalistic understanding of morality. Thus they seize on the old legalist maxim "A doubtful law does not oblige" and conclude that if noted theologians and bishops cannot agree on moral norms, they themselves are free "to follow their own conscience," i.e. do what they please. Unfortunately they do not have many opportunities to hear both sides of theological questions objectively presented or in a manner understandable to them.

The celibate clergy are accused, often by advocates of liberation theology, of a morbid preoccupation with problems about sexuality, instead of the more important issues of social justice. When once at a workshop for priests I was so accused, I replied, "If I am talking too much about sex, why do you only ask me questions about sex?" We celibate clergy must be concerned about sex because we deal pastorally with people for whom sex is a major problem. No wonder, since God created humanity with physical pleasure as a support for the proper satisfaction of our physical needs, but after original sin the desire for physical pleasure that pertains to our nature as animals has become inordinately powerful while our spiritual appetites have been weakened.[254] Yet although old age lessens this excessive urge for food, drink, sex, and comfort, it remains, I must admit without bragging, true for myself. The Bible in its wonderful account of David, whom it calls "a man after God's own heart" (1 Sam 13:14), yet who murdered his faithful captain Uriah to take his wife Bathsheba, then repented, and in his old age took the young girl Abishag to nurse him (1 Kg 1:1-4) as he kept vigil before he died happy after seeing his son Solomon enthroned.

I was often asked by bishops, troubled by current theological debates, for a synthesis of Church teaching on sexuality and marriage, and tried to meet this need in several essays: "The Use of Moral Theology by the Church,"[255] "Pastoral Problems in Sexual Morality,"[256] and "The Family in Church and Society."[257] Later in 1990 I tried to show how the Church's teaching on sexuality might be communicated in Catholic high schools in an unpublished address to the Secondary Education Association of the Archdiocese of Boston, October 27, 1990, "Education in Chastity."

My most substantial effort in this field, however, had been in 1981 "A Theological Overview on Recent Research on Sex and Gender" written as an introduction to a research report of the Pope John Center, *Sex and Gender*.[258] In this book Albert Moraczewski, then director of the Center, made a bold attempt to collect accurate up-to-date information on what the scientific sexologists have been able to establish. One of the editors, Mark Schwartz was on the staff of the well known Masters and Johnson Center for sex therapy in St. Louis and obtained a number of leading sexologists to present papers for discussion by a group of Catholic theologians. These were excellent papers but when the theologians raised ethical questions the sexologists got very uncomfortable, while the Director of the Pope John Center in St. Louis (now the National Catholic Bioethics Center in Boston) at that time also got anxious about what the board of bishops might think if the Center published the sexologists' papers. The result was that Albert's study, which was intended to be ongoing, never got further than one volume.

I also participated in a number of workshops that from a pastoral point of view dealt with sexual issues for the Pope John Center, most memorably with Fr. Moraczewski in the Archdiocese of Los Angeles in September of 1986. Cardinal Roger Mahoney, then only recently installed as Archbishop of Los Angeles, summoned all his priests to a workshop on sexual morality. This was short notice for priests not used to such events, and they did not come in a receptive mood. They complained bitterly to Archbishop Mahoney that the first talk by Fr. Albert on the biology of sex was too elementary. Actually it was no mere "birds-and-bees" sex talk but, as Fr. Albert has found from long experience, it is usually necessary to inform any audience of basic scientific facts about which even priests often have inaccurate ideas. There were many hostile questions from the floor. After my own talk stating the Church's basic positions, one pastor arose and began by declaring pointedly, "I am a compassionate priest." They found the official Catholic teaching on sexual morality, "a hard saying" (Jn 6:61), which (perhaps especially in the paradise of California) it is.

To placate Archbishop Mahoney's alarm at this reaction from his priests, we called in Professor John Haas of the Josephinum seminary, a former Anglican priest and father of nine, who was later in 1997 to become head of the National Catholic Bioethics Center. As a father of a large family, his defense of the Church's stand on sexual morality always has special force, and on this occasion he helped save the other sessions of the workshop. I learned from this not very pleasant experience that the hardest audience to whom to preach Christian morality is often the clergy who themselves ought to preach it. The topics on which I spoke and wrote most frequently were bioethical. As a Senior Fellow of the Pope John Center I continued to work as a consultant to bishops and others and with the tireless Kevin O'Rourke on the successive editions of our *Health Care Ethics;; A Catholic Analysis*, 1977, 1993, 1997. 1993, 2006.

I was unexpectedly confronted with a practical application of the theology of human sexuality when Fr. Albert Moraczewski roped me into my most unusual pastoral endeavor in St. Louis, though it lasted only a year. A layman had asked Albert to be spiritual director for a "Courage" group, but his presidency of the Pope John Center made this impossible for him to do. Courage is a national organization founded by Fr. John Harvey, OSFS, made up of support groups for homosexual persons.[259] The reason that the Church has spoken of homosexual orientation as a "disorder" (a term greatly resented by some as "insensitive") is because the Bible, as well as evolutionary theory, understands human sexuality as ordered to family life. Consequently a homosexual orientation is an obstacle to a fruitful sexual union and hence "disordered." The term, like the term "disabled," ought not to be understood as in anyway depreciating from the personal dignity of the disabled person. Thus as disabled persons today often seek support groups to help them deal with the problems their disability raises, so Courage is for homosexually oriented persons who, if they are unable responsibly to marry, seek support in living as celibates as their baptismal commitment demands.

I am convinced after considerable study of the scientific data on this question, that sexual orientation, though it has genetic roots, is partly learned. Normally in the familial network children learn to be heterosexual from the loving relationship of their parents, not just cognitively but also affectively. This process is so complex that at critical phases it can fail, and thus sexual orientation can become ambiguous or misdirected. The most plausible, but not yet scientifically verified psychological theory of the process, is that of Elizabeth Moberley[260] who believes that when young persons for some reason fail to achieve acceptance by their gender-peers, their sense of inadequacy may cause them to become fixated on same-sex others who seem to them models of their own gender to which they feel they cannot attain. If this fixation becomes eroticized, such persons fall in love with those who personify what they obsessively long to be. One reason this theory seems plausible to me is that it fits with a certain ambiguity of my own orientation that led me into a couple of misadventures before my conversion. A consoling part of my vigil is to recall that after my baptism this has never got me into trouble. The defect in my family, as I look back on those remote times, was that while my father had given much attention to my older brother, for some reason when I came along some six years later he tended to neglect me and gave me little support in activities that ordinarily help a boy attain comfortable masculine identity. I was often regarded as a "sissy." My father did, however, give me some very helpful attention in my reading and intellectual discussions.

In any case the Gay Rights Movement makes a gross simplification when they divide the human species into "gays," and "straights," with some "bisexuals" in between. In fact sexual orientation is a spectrum heavily concentrated at the heterosexual limit and with not more than 2% (not the 10% often cited from the unreliable Kinsey Report) at the exclusively homosexual limit. This is what is to be expected if in fact heterosexuality is normal development, and the various degrees of chance sexual variation developmental defects. Hence, to stereotype "gays" and "lesbians" by the social construct of the "gay life style" is like using "disabled" as a definite pigeonhole, when in fact even most normal people have some disablements.

It is disputed whether exclusive homosexuality can be overcome, especially after adolescence, but it is wrong to encourage persons to label themselves definitively homosexual, "come out of the closet," and adopt the "gay life style," rather than to continue to seek heterosexual maturity to whatever degree possible. Homosexuality is a serious disablement that is an obstacle to living a successful married life and having a family. Denial of disabilities helps no one. Rather, like alcoholics, drug-addicts, persons with sexual compulsions, etc., homosexuals need community support to face the realities of their disablement and to find how to manage it so as to live as normally as possible.

Most absurd of all is the argument that some writers have used: "God made some people homosexual, so he can't condemn them for acting homosexually." If homosexuality is a disability, as I have argued, it is not God's fault, but the fault of disordered families and disordered society into which they themselves were born that has distorted the child's psychosexual development. We do not know how to prevent or remedy it because we have failed to do the necessary research to understand the causes of this disorder. Paradoxically such research is blocked by the Gay Movement's systematic promotion of denial and by the American Association of Psychiatrists' well meaning but entirely nonscientific disclaimer that it is a psychological disorder, a disclaimer intended to discourage "stigmatizing the victim." No person should be stigmatized for any disability he or she has not deliberately incurred. Those responsible for their own disabilities, if they achieve virtue through their struggle, deserve our great admiration and praise.

Until better treatment for this disability is found, the teaching of the Catholic Church that homosexual persons, along with others who cannot enter into a successful marriage, are morally required to live the celibate life is the only advice that realistically accords with the known facts. Some argue that such celibacy is impossible without a special charism such as that given Catholic priests and vowed religious. They forget that all the graces needed to keep the moral law according to one's own situation in life are available to every Christian. But this also means that the community, especially a Christian community, has a serious obligation to support disabled people who are striving to live well in spite of their disability. Hence as a Church we are all obliged to provide special support and care for persons with such disorders and to teach compassion and respect for them, neither encouraging the denial of their disability or condoning the immoral actions which may be occasioned by their disorder, but helping them form chaste friendships.

I expressed these very politically incorrect ideas in an essay "Compassion and the Homosexual" in *The Church and Homosexuality*,[261] a collection of essays promoting the position of "Dignity" a support group which dissents from Church guidance and promotes "responsible relationships." In this collection of essays, the one by Archbishop Quinn of San Francisco and the one by me are the only defenses of the Church's position.

My brief year's experience with this Courage group seemed to confirm my studies. The men involved came to Courage largely because they had grown disgusted with the gay life style (one man had been tempted to adopt it but had not). Most had tried "Dignity" groups that they reported tended to serve only as "a dating service" for Catholic gays. What I heard repeatedly was how difficult it is for homosexuals, even those living as celibates, to find a social life outside the gay community. They often feel out of place among married couples, who sometimes rudely inquire why they do not marry. This leaves them nowhere to find friends except back in the same gay lifestyle they are trying to escape. Parishes need to make special provision for social events for singles, and preaching should occasionally touch on the proper attitudes toward single persons whom no one should judge to be homosexual just because they are single or even because they have a same-sex companion.

At our Courage meetings I gave a short talk on various aspects of the Christian life. Then we had an hour of group discussion and a concluding Mass, preceded by an opportunity for confession. Too much of the time of the discussions, I felt, was spent by the members in expressing self-pity, rather than in positive, constructive communication. Moreover, a leader of the group was later to discover he had already contracted AIDS, from which he eventually died. Nevertheless, I was to learn that through this group some of the members made genuine, nonsexual friendships, which gave them real strength in their efforts to live according to their Catholic consciences.

I believe that if we had continued longer on this road the group would have become increasingly constructive. Unfortunately, in 1984 other prior obligations made it necessary for me to ask the Archbishop to appoint a diocesan priest in my place. The number of Courage groups is, however, increasing throughout the United

States and Canada. They hold annual national meetings, and publish helpful literature. I would hope that they would also sponsor research on the problem and support the training of good psychotherapists.

COURAGE

Can any of us say we suffer from no "disorder"
kneeling as we do on the very border
    of heaven and hell
since Eve so lovingly offered Adam the forbidden fruit
    and in turn, lest it be wasted
        he lovingly took and tasted
that luscious apple the snake had pointed out
    to beauteous Eve
        to see
and pluck from that strange tree,
    quietly suggesting,
      "O Woman, you are so fair
I rate you God's equal or his better,"
and quickly pondering she held it
    then with a little frown
    in her white hand
       and
with one decisive bite of her white teeth
turned the whole universe upside down?

That sweet apple so surprisingly bitter
caught on this very border
    of heaven and hell
    all must chew,
    yes me, yes you,
man or woman or strangely in between
    must take, eat and then
    deep in the belly feel the ache
    common to all caught on that border,
    of our deep disorder.

Chapter 20 - The Is and The Ought

The Pontifical John Paul II Institute in Washington

I noted in Chapter 18 that an important feature of a spirituality of aging must be that as we keep vigil we begin to better realize that we can learn more from others that we can ever learn by ourselves. As Isaiah 29:24 says, "Those who err in spirit shall acquire understanding, and those who find fault shall receive instruction." Of course I knew that before, but now I see how even the little I have learned was my personal discovery. Hence we must never get locked up in our own minds. That is truly dementia. Fortunately in 1988 a new vista was opened to me.

After a year working with Courage I had to ask Archbishop May to be relieved of this task because these years in St. Louis, although they were by now for me a vigil, were a very busy time. Besides my teaching, writing, and consultancy work I made some appearances on local TV on medical ethical issues, participated in the 1984 Pro-Life March in Washington, joined in the provincial assemblies which my Order held in River Forest every three years, and I attended meetings of the St. Louis Priests' Senate on which I served for three years as the representative of the religious priests of the archdiocese. I also engaged in preparatory meetings for a diocesan synod, and preached "appeals" in small Missouri towns for our Nigerian and Bolivian missions.

During the years in St. Louis when I began to be more and more occupied with consultancy for bishops, I thought I would teach there for the rest of my years, but in 1988 I was invited to teach in Washington, DC. My consultancy continued and was even intensified by my residing at the Dominican House of Studies next door to the splendid new building of the national headquarters of the NCCB. John Paul II has given priority in his pontificate to the work of renewing the Christian family as the basis of church and state. In this the Pope is not, as some think, retreating from Vatican II. In its most progressive document, *The Church in the Modern World*, the Council gave major emphasis to the need to restore family life and in 1980 the Synod representative of the whole college of bishops confirmed this emphasis.

Therefore, at the Lateran University, attached to his cathedral church and, unlike the Church's other Roman schools, his direct responsibility, Pope John Paul II in 1982 established the "Pontifical

John Paul II Institute for Studies in Marriage and Family" to confer a theological licentiate and doctorate, and in 1988 set up a branch for the United States in Washington, DC. Perhaps it was the shocking rate of divorce among Catholics and the high number of marriage annulments that are granted in our country that suggested to John Paul that we especially need such an institute. Thanking the Knights of Columbus, for financing the cleaning of the facade of St. Peter's, the pope said, "You have restored the face of the Church, now restore the family!" The Knights gladly accepted this mission and selected a prominent Knight, now Grand Knight, Dr. Carl Anderson, a canon and civil lawyer. Carl is a keenly intelligent, taciturn lawyer, a convert to the Church and a family man, who had previously been a consultant on family issues to President Ronald Regan. While his political stance differed from mine, I always found him courteous, charming, and unfailingly concerned for my welfare as an older person, from out of town and out of the "loop."

Through the wise counsel of Fr. Romanus Cessario, OP, of the Pontifical Faculty of Theology at the Dominican House of Studies in Washington, Anderson contracted to locate the Institute in that same building, with its advantages of a fine theological library and a site adjacent to The Catholic University of America. Anderson and Cessario invited me to a planning meeting and when they saw how enthusiastic I was for the project asked me if I would accept appointment as Senior Professor, in fact, for the opening year of the Institute, its only full time teacher. I accepted only for the year beginning in the autumn of 1988, but then continued there until 1992. Happy as I was at St. Louis Bertrand Priory and getting more tired every day, I felt it truly a call from God to be a coworker, as it were, with the successor of St. Peter in a very important undertaking.

Many today, especially American theologians, think John Paul II was a reactionary who attempted to reverse the reforms of Vatican II. Yet he was certainly one of the most philosophical of popes, with pastoral, prophetic vision of the future of a Church that can inspire the young and the poor and give wise guidance to intellectuals. His was the hard task of maintaining unity in a church seriously polarized by globalization and rapid cultural change. He strove heroically in conformity to Vatican II, to promote necessary changes in the Church to make its mission more effective in a changed world while remaining true in its witness to the Gospel. Jesus said, "Every scribe instructed in the kingdom of heaven is like the head of household who brings from his storeroom both the new and the old," (Mt

13:52) and as my friend Augustine DiNoia, OP, has wisely said, "*Aggiornemento* (updating) must be combined with *resourcement* (recovery of the sources)."

Later in a visit to Rome, when I was introduced to John Paul II as one who had helped inaugurate the Institute in America, he said to me, "Thank you." These simple words were for me the climax of my life and oil for my vigil lamp. This was confirmed when on retiring from the Institute, through the great kindness of Washington's Cardinal James Hickey, I received the medal *Pro Ecclesia et Pontifice*.

The faculty of the Institute (JP II as the students nicknamed it) began its work in the uncomfortable atmosphere of post-Vatican II polarization and in an odd milieu in which its Pontifical Faculty of Theology looked across the street at the less than friendly Pontifical Faculty of Theology of The Catholic University of America, and side-by-side with the competing Pontifical Faculty of the House of Studies. I often wondered why the Cardinal Chancellor of the University and the Vatican did not intervene to demand some type of cooperation among the three pontifical faculties. I am glad to report that recently Catholic University and JP II have agreed to official cooperation.

Although the JP II is dedicated to "thinking with the Pope" on the restoration of the family in light of Vatican II teaching, within the limits of orthodoxy it has a spectrum of theological opinion. Especially influential in the Institute is the theology of Hans Urs von Balthasar (after I left, the editor of the journal *Communio*, Prof. David Schindler joined the faculty) and of other contemporary Catholic theologians who have broken with neo-scholasticism, often favoring a more patristic approach. At the start I was the only representative of a classical Thomism, but found this breadth of thought, which builds on the Church's tradition rather than undermining it, thoroughly congenial. The variety of views at the Institute was enriched by a number of part-time colleagues such Paul C. Vitz, a professor of psychology at New York University, whom I found especially stimulating, John M. Hass then of St. Charles Borromeo Seminary in Philadelphia, already mentioned, John Finnis, the quiet, precisely reasoning analytic philosopher from Cambridge, Robin M. Maas, an expert in spirituality from the Methodist Wesley Theological Seminary in Washington, and from the parent Institute in Rome its President Carlo Caffara and Professor Stanislaw Grygiel, a personal friend of John Paul II.

I especially found much in common with another member of the JP II faculty, the biblical scholar Fr. Francis Martin, a thin, quiet, former Trappist monk and leader of the charismatic Mother of God Community in Gaithersburg, MD. When I visited this community, I was deeply impressed with its stability for over twenty years and its remarkable union of adult theological education with charismatic inspiration. I have heard it later suffered from the domination by a clique, a problem to which charismatic communities seem especially liable, but that healing has taken place through the pastoral care of the Cardinal Archbishop. I think the JP II students found Fr. Martin, for whom this crisis was a difficult trial, a very demanding but very profitable teacher, because he expounds the latest subtleties in hermeneutic theory, while also going beyond a merely histori- cal-critical approach to a richer theological exegesis. His book *The Feminist Question*[262] has influenced my own thinking about the fem- inist views that so strongly affect theological schools today.

Another faculty member was the Puerto Rican Monsignor Lo- renzo Albacete, at that time Cardinal Hickey's theologian, who was used to shuttling back and forth between Washington and the Vati- can, a large man, rather negligent in dress, hyperbolically eloquent, very knowledgeable and always witty. I had first met him when he spoke on a Pope John Center program. The introducer had, as so often happens, outdone himself in listing the speaker's merits. Moreover, he did so in such a way that the audience could not help but anticipate that they would be hearing a lecture that would be theologically very right wing. The Monsignor, looking very formida- ble as if about to fulfill this anticipation, began to speak with seem- ing dead seriousness, "I thank so-and-so for his gracious introduc- tion, but I regret he failed to mention that I drafted the papal encyc- lical against birth control and prepared the brief for the CDF against Hans Küng, Charles Curran, and Edward Schillebeeckx, and I deeply deplore inclusive language." It took us a full minute to realize he was laughing at what he saw to be our suspicions of his theological stance.

Closest to me in my Thomistic orientation was William E. May, at that time still a senior professor of moral theology of Catholic University where he had been a forthright critic of the controversial Fr. Charles Curran. But May, whom I have known for many years from the time when he was an editor at the Bruce Publishing Com- pany in Milwaukee, has adopted Germain Grisez' revision of Thom- ist moral theory which I will discuss later. Bill is a much valued friend, a kindly, chunky, hobbling moralist, vastly read in his field, a happy family man, and a fair critic. While we see eye-to-eye on most moral issues, our difference on the question of the hierarchy of moral ends has been, I believe, the cause of our uncomfortable disagreement on one much controverted issue. On this topic we battled in a public but friendly debate in which I read a paper "The Family's Response to the Care of the Permanently Unconscious" at a symposium in 1991 on the "Future of Health Care", sponsored by the John Paul II Institute and Providence Hospital, Washington, DC. We also debated that difficult topic before a committee of bishops. On a recent trip to Washington he also asked me to present my views before one of his classes.

My partner Kevin O'Rourke and I have long disagreed with May and his partner Germain Grisez over how to apply the Church's teaching in the 1980 "Declaration on Euthanasia" of the Congregation of the Doctrine of the Faith. Kevin and I have always contended that artificial hydration and nutrition can be judged to be part of the care that in the terms of the "Declaration" is "extraordinary" or "disproportionate" and hence that such care is not obligatory for permanently unconscious patients even when they are medically "stable." May and Grisez, at one time they had favored this same view, but then changed their minds and now along with a good many pro-life activists hold that hydration and nutrition even when artificial are to be considered "ordinary" care, unless they cause an excessive burden to the patient or when the patient is actually dying.

After the debate had gone on for some time a draft document prepared by the Pro-life Committee of the NCCB under the chairmanship of James T. McHugh, Bishop of Camden, NJ supported this latter view. John Boyle and I, as consultants to the Committee on Doctrine of the NCCB which reviewed this draft, had prevailed in arguing that pro-ife statements, if they chose to take the more strict view, should leave open the question of the legitimacy of the less strict opinion we favored, since the Holy See, although it has taken counsel on the question had not yet spoken decisively on the issue. Since then the Congregation for the Doctrine of the Faith has answered questions from the NCCB that support the stricter view for reasons I will later explain.

Pondering Grisez' Revision of Moral Theology

Our disagreement on the care of the dying, however, raised for me a deeper question about the radical revision of moral theology that Grisez and his colleagues were proposing. Many "conservative" Catholics were beginning to favor this theory as a barrier against the influence of proportionalism favored by many "liberal" Catholics. While I wanted to praise the orthodoxy of the former as vastly preferable to the dissent of the latter, I also vastly preferred the unrevised views of St. Thomas Aquinas to either, although, of course, I granted then and still grant, that Aquinas' general principles must be applied to the better empirical data about human nature and behavior that is sometimes provided by modern biology, psychology, and sociology.

Germain Grisez and his followers seemed to me to have obscured the fundamental structure of the moral theology of St. Thomas Aquinas by replacing his view that the first principle by which every moral decision ought to be determined is the single supreme good of life. For this supreme goal they substituted some eight "incommensurate goods." By "incommensurate" was meant that these are not measured by any single supreme goal and cannot be hierarchically ranked. Yet these diverse goods must somehow be harmonized to constitute "integral human fulfillment."

Grisez is a layman philosopher and later a theologian, a former student at Aquinas Institute of Theology in River Forest. After receiving his M. A. there, he earned his doctorate in philosophy at the University of Chicago under Richard P. McKeon. With his pioneering book *Contraception and the Natural Law* (1964) Germain defended the Church's traditional position on this topic, when many others dissented or were silent. In fact, he has told me that he assisted Fr. John Ford, SJ, a member of the anti-contraception minority on the Birth Control Commission, in his efforts to oppose the unsuccessful attempt of the majority of the Commission to persuade Paul VI to modify the Church's traditional position.

As I noted in the preceding chapter, in 1984 I reviewed the first volume of Germain's immense textbook on moral theology, *The Way of the Lord Jesus, "Christian Moral Principles."*[263] I commended it as the most important American contribution to the post-Vatican II revision of moral theology. While some are turned off by Germain's aggressiveness in controversy, for me this is entirely excusable, since his arguments are always objective, not personal, and clearly and frankly expounded. Moreover, considering the harsh attacks he has suffered over the years by disgruntled dissenters from Church teaching, his defensiveness is quite understandable. Grisez now holds an endowed chair at Mount St. Mary's Seminary in Emmitsburg, MD and has won over to his revision of Thomistic moral theory two eminent ethicians who were my colleagues when, as I related in the last chapter, I taught at the Pontifical Institute for Studies on Marriage and Family, Washington, DC, William E. May and John Finnis, a visiting lecturer from Oxford, as well as Joseph M, Boyle, Jr. of St, Michael's College, the University of Toronto. While this sturdy school of thought led by Grisez is generally considered conservative, in fact it proposes a quite original revision of the moral theory of St. Thomas Aquinas. I have discussed this system in some detail in a 1994 essay "What is the End of the Human Person: The Vision of God and Integral Human Fulfillment."[264] Again at a symposium on the work of this school held at Princeton University I discussed, "The Biblical Basis of Grisez's Revision of Moral Theology."[265] My dissatisfaction with his system can be summed up in four points.

First, Grisez attempts to construct an ethics independent of an anthropology of human nature. He considers moral theology "dialectical" rather than, as does Aquinas, a "science" in the Aristotelian sense of a discipline that is strictly demonstrative.[266] Nevertheless, Grisez seems to regard philosophical ethics as a true science since he strongly insists that, like a true science, it must rest on evident first principles. Hence he argues that if ethics as a science depended on the science of anthropology, this would entail what G.E. Moore, one of the fathers of Analytic Philosophy, called the "naturalistic fallacy" of deducing "ought" statements from "is" statements, that is, imperative propositions from indicative ones. Pondering this point led me to compose the following poem.

IS AND OUGHT

After sunset by a creek
gleaming between black banks
under some leaning boughs
of great black leaves
a silver sliver of moon.
The coolness promises an early autumn.
Such are the present facts.

It is a fallacy, they claim,
to pass from facts to oughts,
deriving soft evaluations
from hard assertions.
To pass, then, from truths to love.

Yet is that fine moon hard fact
or duty's stern command?
I ought to stay a moment here to stare
astonished and afraid.
I must not turn away.
Its tender light
makes it imperative
for me to love
here, now.

Thus what Grisez neglects is Aquinas' claim that although the sciences are formally distinct and independent, nevertheless for Aquinas there is also an "order of the sciences." Since our human knowledge is dependent on our senses, we move from truths more evident to us yet less evident in themselves to truths more evident in themselves but less evident to us. Consequently, the principles of ethics do not become critically (scientifically) evident to us until we have first learned in the lower science of anthropology to identify those needs innate to human nature. It is these innate needs that are to be indicatively stated that determine the goals that furnish ethics with its evident first principles that must be imperatively stated.

Second, having rejected any necessity for ethics to identify anthropologically the goals that are its first principles, Grisez then pro-poses eight incommensurate goods that constitute "integral human fulfillment." At the theological level he attempts to correlate these eight goals with the eight Beatitudes of the Sermon on the Mount. Actually his biblical grounding of his philosophical theory is quite weak, since he makes little attempt to deal with current biblical scholarship.

Third, Grisez claims, contrary to Aquinas, that these goods are "incommensurate," that is, they are not, as classical teleological ethics and Aquinas held, subordinated to a *summum bonum* or supreme good. Grisez, of course, does not deny that in the order of grace the ultimate end of human life is the beatific vision of God, but he rejects the arguments of Aristotle and Aquinas which show that even in our

earthly life every human act must intend the supreme good of contemplation. He thinks Aquinas clings to this notion because of the
medieval clericalism that gave insufficient attention to the facts of
lay life. Yet for Aquinas "contemplation" extends to the whole range
of truths that concern the laity just as much as they do the clergy.
Thus Grisez' theory leaves ethical decision without any unity. How
can I ever decide between different goods without measuring them
by some supreme good? Though Grisez realizes this difficulty, he
only answers it by saying that his four substantive goods: physical
health, knowledge of truth and appreciation of the arts, play and
exercise of skills, and marriage are "harmonized" by his four existential ones: self-integration, practical reasonableness or authenticity, justice, and friendship, religion. These four substantive goods are
similar to Aquinas four fundamental needs and the four existential
ones resemble what Aquinas assigns to the work of the virtue of
prudence. But exactly how these four incommensurate existential
goods can unify his four other incommensurate goods in Grisez'
system is as vague as the notion of fundamental option in Rahner's
system, which I will discuss in the next chapter.

Fourth, Grisez gives only a secondary place to Aquinas' virtue
theory because, he claims, it fails to provides middle premises necessary to making concrete moral decisions that his incommensurate
goods do provide. This to me makes clear that Grisez, like Rahner,
has failed to provide us with a genuinely teleological ethics, rather
than a legalistic one. For Aquinas, moral decision can become effective in achieving the goal of true happiness only if we have become
connatural to that goal (which truth, it seems, is the best feature in
Rahner's otherwise obscure system) so that the good tendencies of
human nature can be fully operative in a unified way. It is this consistency and unity of action that the virtues supply. Above all the
virtue of prudence is what makes good moral decision possible even
beyond the guidance that any ethical system can furnish, since it
measures each decision about some means to the true goal or end of
human nature by a clear identification of that single goal.

Beside my disagreement with the influence of these positions of
Grisez on the John Paul II Institute, I have been also somewhat concerned by the influence in the Institute of the thought of Hans Urs
Von Balthasar. The value and orthodoxy of Von Balthasar's theology,
like that of Grisez's is beyond question, but I would prefer a firmer
grounding in the thought of St. Thomas Aquinas, so strongly rec-

ommended by both Vatican II and John Paul II's *Fides et Ratio*. I also was disappointed about one feature of the curriculum that I again and again brought up in faculty meetings but without success. I argued that the faculty should include a specialist in the sociology of the family so that the Institute might take on a more empirical approach. I felt that this was still another example of the difficulty current theology has in integrating modern science into its thinking. Neither Charles Curran nor his polar opposite, Germain Grisez, give adequate attention to the life sciences. Indeed, Curran constantly inveighs against "biologism" and "physicalism" in moral thinking, while Grisez considers ethics as independent of anthropology. This question is also little considered by Von Balthasar. Yet I have a great admiration for the work of the Institute for the Studies in Marriage and Family and advertise its merits among young students of theology whom I meet.

My students at the Institute were a highly varied group, less than half of them clerics, but—a big difference from the students at Aquinas—not many of them Sisters. I found that the motive of many of them in enrolling was not just a concern for marriage and family (although we had surprising number of marriages emerge), but also their distrust of the orthodoxy of most of our Catholic graduate schools. This distrust was partly the result of the fact that a number of them had attended Thomas Aquinas College in Santa Paul, CA or Christendom College in Front Royal, VA, liberal arts schools influenced by Hutchins and Adler's educational ideals as I had been in my youth, but with a conservative Catholic outlook. On the whole I found these students more open and better prepared philosophically and in the liberal arts (I am ashamed to admit) than I had experienced for some years at my beloved Aquinas Institute in St. Louis.

Other JP II students had suffered from poor catechesis or from the random opinions in college or seminary of dissenting theologians without any satisfying synthesis to help them to a mature faith. I tried to set a reassuring tone as I taught the major courses dealing with moral theology and the family but I did not avoid the difficult problems of our contemporary culture and I found the students open to facing these issues objectively.

Sometimes, however, I found that these students had picked up liturgical and devotional practices that seemed to me smacked of dissent to the right, comparable to those of dissent to the left. Thus some students made a point of kneeling before receiving Holy

Communion, of not taking it in the hand, and not receiving the chalice, as if this was somehow more orthodox. Once in class when I called on a student to begin our class with prayer, to my surprise he recited the Prayer to St. Michael, formerly said at the end of Mass, against diabolic attacks on the Church. Their liturgical uses had been officially eliminated even before Vatican II and before most of the class were born. Evidently they had learned it in their conservative colleges, while I had long forgotten it.

Among my students at JP II I would especially mention Fr. Peter Uglietto, a diocesan priest from Boston, teacher at the John XXIII Seminary for "late vocations" who invited me to lecture; Fr. William Virtue, a friend of Fr. Charles Corcoran and Dr. Herbert Ratner of whom I have written in former chapters, an enthusiast for all that is good and true. Mark Latkovic was a student of mine and is now a professor at Sacred Heart Seminary in Detroit, who had the generous idea to write his doctorate dissertation on my work in moral theology. The vivacious Ms. Gloria Falcao (now Mrs. Ennis Dodd) was not only an excellent graduate assistant but she also helped me better understand conservative Catholic viewpoints. To protest the irreverent fripperies sometimes indulged in by Catholics at weddings, she insisted that the processional hymn for her own wedding Mass be "Lift High the Cross"! Finally, I must make special mention of Prof. Mark Johnson, now of Marquette University, at whose expense I enjoyed so many delightful, stimulating, lengthy phone calls.

It was especially rewarding to come to know the Sisters of the Franciscan Congregation of the Blessed Sacrament who were among the few women religious who studied at JP II. I visited their little convent in Baltimore and later their motherhouse in Meriden, CT. This community, an offshoot of the congregation of Sisters we had known at La Crosse near Dubuque, under an outstanding leader has decided to retain the Franciscan habit and many traditional features of religious life, but is at the same time very innovative in its ministry. What could better illustrate the principle of *nova et vetera* than one of these Sisters who travels the globe in full habit as an expert trouble shooter for ailing computers and a guide to their puzzled users? At Meriden I shared in their lovely liturgy with its excellent music. I admired how they have inspired a lay community to gather around them for spiritual growth and the houses they have built for couples, one or both of whom are dying with cancer, but who are still able with nursing help to continue regular living. One of these

Sisters, Paula Jean Miller, a woman of exceptional intelligence and energy, after ministering to women in the Holy Land for some years, studied at JP II, became professor of moral theology at St. Mary's Seminary in Emmitsburg, MD and recently received an appointment at the University of Houston. I am proud of having been the director of her now published doctoral dissertation on St. Bonaventure's theology of the Sacrament of Matrimony.[267] I found especially intriguing the contrast that I had before little appreciated, between the entirely different but complementary conceptions of theology held by Bonaventure and Aquinas. For Bonaventure every topic of theology contains the whole of theology, since every created reality is an image of the Trinity. Thus in explaining Matrimony the great Franciscan Doctor sees marriage as the chief symbol of God's loving relation to his creation, and of Christ to the Church.

During my time of teaching at the John Paul II Institute I developed more adequately my ideas about the family as the foundation of society. This enabled me to refine and focus my thinking about questions of human sexuality, which my earlier pastoral experience with Courage had raised. I began to see that the central issue of today is not *Humanae Vitae*, gay and lesbian rights, feminism, or whether clerical celibacy should be optional, but disagreements about the purpose of the family in God's design for humanity. Why is it that right-wing Catholics are hot for Church teaching on sexuality and cold to its teaching on social justice, while left-wingers reverse these attitudes? In fact the Church subordinates its teaching on sex to its teaching on social justice. That is why it sees contraception and abortion more in the light of their social consequences than in terms of personal fulfillment. Yet, because sexual morality affects the family and the family is the basic institution of society, the Church gives questions of sexual morality great emphasis. Why then does the family get such scanty attention in liberation theology?

I also began to realize I had not adequately treated this issue in my *Theologies of the Body: Humanist and Christian,*[268] written before I was aware of John Paul II's profound thought on "the nuptial meaning of the body." I now understand this "nuptial meaning" to be that the sexual teleology of the human body to committed marital love is the paradigm of all just and charitable human relationships and of the human community. It is also the most revealing of metaphors for the psychological integration of the person in the harmonious relation of body and soul. John Paul II has thus uncovered the

deep truth concealed in Freud's dubious psychological pan-
sexualism.

OPEN DOOR

Whether the shut door will open
            is the question,
and the answer all depends
            on whether
you trust your body or your soul.

But I ask you,
            "Can the body
            trust the soul?"

My money says
            In God We Trust,"
but what price the ticket
            that opens
            the heart's closed door?

The Curran Controversy and the "Right to Dissent"

My various engagements in the controversies over the revision
of moral theology made me acutely aware all the time I was teaching in Washington of the turmoil within Catholic University over
"The Curran Affair" which had been going on for twenty years, but
had reached its climax with Curran's dismissal from the theological
faculty in 1986. It is not surprising that not all theologians interpret
the work of Vatican II in the same way. In my view we should first
listen to the authoritative interpretation given by the popes entrusted with its mandate.

Immediately upon the issuance by Pope Paul VI of his encyclical *Humanae Vitae* (HV, "On the Regulation of Birth") in 1968
Curran and some associates very publicly claimed "the right of responsible dissent" and he later extended this claim to any other
moral question not yet infallibly defined. Since some theologians
who agree with him also maintain that the Church has never infalli-

bly defined any moral norm and perhaps cannot do so, the fact that Curran (unlike Hans Küng) excludes infallible doctrines from this right is not very significant. He also argues that such freedom of dissent serves the Church since it helps the bishops and pope correct their teaching in the light of scholarship and thus promotes a healthy development of doctrine.

Fr. Curran, whom I have known for many years, was a former student in Rome of Bernard Häring. He is a tall man, not especially distinguished in appearance, but very cordial in manner and he has a fine reputation as an articulate and fair teacher. His many publications are informative, but not particularly analytical or systematic. Over the years he has always been very pleasant and friendly to me and I have heard he has very fairly assigned O'Rourke and my *Health Care Ethics* to his students in medical ethics.

I agree with Curran that theologians have a "right of responsible dissent," if "dissent" means critical study of episcopal and papal pronouncements (and I would say even those solemnly defined!) as to their precise authoritative weight, their mutual consistency, their bases in Scripture and Tradition, their recognition of established scientific and historical facts and human experience, etc. This is indeed how theologians serve the Church and assist development of doctrine. My disagreement with dissenters like Curran is over what seems to me their defective understanding of theological responsibility, the criteria for which I would list as follows. (1) Theologians as scholars must first determine whether their dissenting opinion is objectively certain or merely probable. (2) If their thesis is certain (not easy in moral matters), they should seek to help authorities correct the error. (3) If it is only probable, they should make unambiguously clear in public presentations that such merely probable opinions based on scholarship cannot substitute for conciliar or papal teaching which, even when not infallible but only probable, has the superior authority which Christ in the Holy Spirit gave the apostles and their successors to shepherd the Christian community. One may have a strong conviction based on highly probable reasoning that an authoritative Church teaching is wrong, but unless one is objectively certain that it is wrong, one may honestly submit to that judgment of higher authority and is in fact obliged to do so. As I will mention later Fr. O'Rourke and I in the 5th edition of *Health Care Ethics* explicitly state that if our opinion on hydration and nutrition of permanently unconscious persons has been rejected by the Mag-

isterium, as is perhaps now the case, that the magisterial decision is
to be followed.

But what if theologians believe that an error in non-infallible
teaching by the Church will do great moral harm unless they publicly advise the faithful to disregard it? I believe this was what led Curran and others to dissent from HV as soon as it was published. They
greatly feared it would cause an agonizing crisis of conscience for
married couples and perhaps loss of their faith. Yet were Curran
and his supporters objectively certain that HV was wrong? The arguments they offered can hardly claim more than probability. As for
the harm the dissenters sought to prevent, the resultant confusion
among the laity and the decline of sexual morality in our culture favored by contraception raise serious doubts about the prudence of
their public campaign against HV. While I was very convinced, even
after HV, of the wisdom of the Church's teaching on moral matters, I
found these concrete problems often very puzzling.

BALL OF TWINE

Who will untangle
   this great ball of twine our thoughts have wound
      in three millions of years;
         man, woman, children, peoples
            thinking and thinking,
snarls of cogitation meshing in the twisted circuits
   of the brain,
      puzzling wars of dialectical maneuvering
         in uneasy hours of fogged-in mornings,
            afternoons declining, broken sleep.

Empedocles bumped into Wittgenstein,
   twin tadpoles in the muddied waters.
When will truth break through the thaw of dirty ice
   into a clear, sweet stream
where at the brim of the brook, like eyes
   blue flowers widen,
      reflecting God's great sky
         open to light?

The small orb of the brain, the great ball of the earth
   turn with a twist
   and a tangle
   afloat in fog...

As I said, most probably the arguments against HV are only probable, even if they seem to some very probable. But how probable are they really? Long before HV I had pondered this question, much debated in Chicago where the Christian Family Movement which favored the modification of the traditional teaching was centered. The dissenters then and now rely on three main arguments to which, as far as I know, nothing much has been added since 1968: (1) Since many, even most, believing Catholic couples practice contraception, this *sensus fidelium* is the Holy Spirit calling the Church to change; (2) HV is founded on a too "physicalistic" or "biologistic" conception of the natural law; (3) The positive values of contraception used as a means to strengthen marriage outweigh its possible negative effects. Curran especially stressed (2) and added a variation on (3) by his theory that our fallen state justifies a "theology of compromise," as Aquinas' justified the toleration of slavery and war after the fall and even included them under natural law.

None of these reasons, nor all taken together, seemed to me to be certain or even solidly probable. As to argument (1) from the *sensus fidelium*: it is true that the *sensus fidei* (Vatican II's preferred term) or the instinctive faith of the whole Church must ground any authoritative teaching by pope or bishops, this same faith requires these shepherds of the flock to discern the Gospel from mere public opinion. "For all that is in the world, sensual lust, enticement for the eyes, and a pretentious life, is not from the Father but is from the world (Jn 2:16)." As for reason (b), it is not true to say that HV is based on "physicalism" rather than on moral intention. No intention, however good, to do a physical act contrary to human nature can make that act morally good. As for reason (c) and Curran's' theology of compromise, these amount to the theory of proportionalism.

Long before HV, like most priests, I struggled with how to minister in the confessional to married persons. At that time the practice was not to question married penitents who did not confess this sin but to refuse them absolution if they would not promise to desist and to destroy contraceptive devices or drugs in their possession. It was very rare; however, that it was necessary to refuse absolution, since penitents usually accepted the Church's teaching without argument and promised to try harder. As confessors we knew that we too would sin mortally if either we gave absolution to unrepentant contracepters or refused it to those who promised to try to desist.

The only honest argument favoring contraception that ever seemed plausible to me, and which I was still pondering when HV was issued, was that it seemed contradictory for the Church to reject contraception yet approve periodic marital abstinence for the good of the marriage, since in both cases the couple intend to fulfill the unitive purpose of the marital act directly and the procreative purpose indirectly. Hence the fundamental principle on which HV rests, namely, the inseparability of the unitive and procreative meaning of the marital act," seems to be satisfied in both cases. But on reflection I came to see that this argument is really just another form of Curran's intentionalism. Couples who with sufficient reason practice periodic abstinence do not directly intend to sterilize a naturally fertile act, while those who contracept directly intend precisely that. HV does not contradict itself, but contraception contradicts the interrelated unitive and procreative purposes for which God made us sexual.

Why is this perversity of contraception so obscure to the modern mind when Christians in the past, both Catholics and Protestants, thought it obvious? Is this not because our culture is so permeated by Kant's error that the Albertus Lyceum sought to expose? Kant denied we can know teleology in nature and claimed we only impose human meaning on nature. As modernity has advanced it has drawn the further conclusion that such human meaning is not, as Kant thought, necessitated by categories native to all human minds, but can only be arbitrary and subject to culture, so that while in one culture contraception, homosexuality, sadism, and bestiality may appear unnatural, in other times and places they may appear perfectly natural. HV, influenced no doubt by the thought of Aquinas but much more by the Bible, insists that the Creator has endowed nature with a recognizable and intrinsic meaning and purpose. We are stewards of God's creation, cooperators, not autonomous creators.

The Vatican CDF, after years of correspondence with Curran concerning his frequently published dissent from important points of authoritative Church teaching on morals, especially on sexual morality, declared he could no longer be considered a "Catholic theologian," by which the Congregation evidently meant a theologian speaking in the name of the Church by reason of the "canonical mission" given him when the Holy See approved his original appointment to the University's Pontifical Faculty of Theology. The Chancellor of the University, Cardinal James A. Hickey therefore dismissed Fr. Curran from the University and Curran decided to sue for breach of contract.

St. Paul urged the early Christians to settle their disputes within the Church. "Can it be that there is not one among you wise enough to be able to settle a case between brothers? But rather brother goes to court against brother, and that before unbelievers," (1 Cor 8:5-6). It was painful to see, therefore, that Fr. Curran believed it necessary to have recourse against the action of The Catholic University of America in the civil courts. After the CDF had declared that it could no longer be responsible for him as a Catholic theologian, the University, following the due process required by its statutes (which had, however, been modified after the time Curran received his appointment and tenure), removed him from teaching theology, but since he was tenured offered him employment in another department. This he reasonably refused on the grounds that he only had a right to teach in his own field of competency and so he sued.

Curran so acted, I am sure, out of a sincere conviction that he was defending not only academic freedom but the "right to dissent" in the Church. I am equally sure that the CDF's motive was to fulfill its responsibility not to mislead the clergy, laity, and non-Catholic public by permitting a teacher in a Pontifical Faculty of Theology whose appointment had been approved by the Church to "teach in the name of the Church" dissenting opinions as it these were alternatives that could be safely followed in conscience. I myself have heard Catholics, especially clergy, say in effect, "I know the pope says this, but if he lets theologians like Curran say that, then the pope doesn't really mean it. I was taught that when theologians disagree, you could follow a probable opinion. So many theologians agree with Curran that his opinion must be solidly probable."

The dilemma is that Curran did not think he was speaking "in the name of the Church," but simply as an academic responsible to no one but his academic peers. He also argued that when he was appointed he did not receive any document stating that he had a "canonical mission" to speak "in the name of the Church." Also he no longer taught in the Pontifical Faculty as such.

Curran's plea exposes a "paradigm shift" in the self-understanding of the identity of a Catholic university and of Catholic academic theologians that, I believe, threatens the very possibility of such institutions. Formerly, Catholic theology was understood as a discipline whose basic principles were received from the pope and the college of bishops who as Vatican II again declared,[269] have the obligation to proclaim the Gospel in the name of Christ and the Church and therefore to pass judgment on what that authentic Gospel is. This judgment establishes the very principles on which the discipline of theology rests and to dissent from it is like a mathematician dissenting from the axioms of arithmetic or a physicist proclaiming a theory contrary to laboratory evidence. I will return to this thorny issue in the next chapter.

When the case went to court, I was surprised to be asked by the University's lawyers to testify as a theologian of academic experience in regard to the nature of academic freedom and of canonical mission. They asked me to do this because I happened to be in the city but not on the faculty of the University or previously involved in the local battle. I cannot say I was reluctant to consent since the case interested me intensely, but I knew that by doing so I might be making enemies. When I appeared in court as a witness, Curran's lawyers challenged my expertise on the ground that since JP II was a branch of a European university I was not competent to speak about American educational standards. The Jewish judge, however, who in my opinion handled the case with consummate jurisprudence, allowed me to testify subject to his later rulings. I testified that (a) "academic freedom" in all schools necessarily has limits which in religiously affiliated schools are set by the Church which sponsors it and which it serves; (b) at the time Curran received tenure, approval by the Holy See of an appointment to a Pontifical Faculty was understood also to formally confer a canonical mission.

Whether my testimony had any effect at all on the judge I don't know. In the end he decided that he had no jurisdiction in the case except to decide whether a legal contract had been broken, and that although the University had made certain changes in its policies concerning academic freedom after Curran was tenured, such policy changes in schools were normal and within their rights. Hence in invoking its own statutes as they presently read the University had not violated Curran's contract by refusing to assign him to teach theology.

Thus not only on contraception, but on many other questions, especially the new and disturbing issues in medical ethics, the American bishops found themselves caught between what seemed the consensus of "mainstream" theologians and the Church authorities acting on its own traditional standards. Thus the Curran affair and other conflicts between bishops and theologians (they are in fact relatively rare), led to an "Ad Hoc Committee on Cooperation between Theologians and the Church's Teaching Authority" of the Catholic Bishops which was to report to the Catholic Theological Society of America, recommending that CTSA and the Canon Law Society of America develop norms "to guide the resolution of difficulties which may arise between theologians and the magisterium in North America." In 1980 they published such a study, *Cooperation between Theologians and the Ecclesial Magisterium*, edited by Leo J. Donovan, SJ, now President of Georgetown University, which both societies approved in 1983. The NCCB turned over the matter to its Committee on Doctrine, which through a subcommittee began work on what was to become "Doctrinal Responsibilities: Approaches to Promoting Cooperation and resolving Misunderstandings between Bishops and Theologians" adopted on June 17, 1989, which was finalized only after consultation with the Holy See. I took part only in the later stages of this discussion.

In 1985 some bishops requested that this document *Doctrinal Responsibilities* be accompanied by another document that would lay a theological foundation for its norms. I was a consultant of this subcommittee, chaired by Bishop Richard Skelba, auxiliary bishop of Milwaukee, a biblical scholar and an active participant in the Catholic Theological Society of America. I was also a consultant to the full Committee on Doctrine as they went through the long six years of meetings required to produce in 1991 *The Teaching Ministry of the Diocesan Bishop: A Pastoral Reflection*, to supplement *Doctrinal Responsibilities*. In the meantime the Vatican CDF had produced its own document on this topic *The Ecclesial Vocation of the Theologian* (1990). I prepared a commentary on this document, "'The Truth Will Set You Free: A Commentary on the Vatican CDF Instruction on the Ecclesial Role of the Theologian," which the Committee requested *Origins* to publish, but which the editor rejected because it mentioned the Curran case on which he thought too much had already been written. I offered to remove this brief reference to the Curran case, but the article never appeared.

In 1991 I reviewed *My Witness for the Church* by Curran's distinguished teacher, Bernard Häring, CSSR.[270] Häring, though not a proportionalist, was a also dissenter on certain moral cases and presents himself as a martyr of the "Holy Office of the Inquisition." I criticized his attempt to revise moral theology by what seemed to me an uncontrolled use of *epikeia* as a way to find "pastoral" and "compassionate" solutions to hard moral cases such as contraception practiced for health reasons by pleading exceptions to moral principles. "Epikeia" is a typically legalistic concept and refers either to (a) taking exception to a law in a situation which the legislator failed to provide for; or to (b) making by a judge of an exception to the law as it literally reads in order to achieve what the judge believes was the legislator's real purpose. Yet it cannot be used to excuse an intrinsically evil act no matter what the laws may say. Acts that are intrinsically evil first of all injure the doer and it is false compassion to defend them.

CRITICISM

To criticize should be
first listen patiently, sagaciously,
Then, forsooth,
pick out that tiny, shiny, grain of truth.

Chapter 21 - Return to the Creed

Concern for the Catechism of the Catholic Church

In Chapter 18, I noted that another important feature of a spirituality of aging must be to use one's greater leisure time for contemplation, as it says in Psalm 118:18, "Open my eyes to see clearly the wonders of your teachings." Central to the spirituality of the Order of Preachers to which I belong is the dictum "To contemplate and then share its fruits with others," a great saying of St. Thomas Aquinas. Of all my activities in Washington the one that is for me the most cherished is the very small role I played in the revision of the draft of the *Catechism of the Catholic Church.* The great creedal truths stated by this *Catechism* are those on which our contemplation ought to center rather than on learned theological debates.

Before going to Washington I had written a short piece, "The Coming Extraordinary Synod,"[271] for a symposium on the hopes for the unprecedented consultation of bishops by John Paul II held in 1985, in which I said,

> Therefore, what I hope from the Synod, which in two weeks can do no more than call for a new phase in the implementation of the Council is that it will encourage the Pope to give priority to the work of educating clergy and laity in the fundamental truths of the Gospel, doctrinal and moral, as these were stated for our times by Vatican II.

Since that Synod, which disappointed some, had as its main result the production of the *Catechism of the Catholic Church*, essential to Catholic education, my own hope was in principle realized. "If you remain in my word, you will truly be my disciples and you will know the truth, and the truth will set you free," (Jn 8:32). What remains for us is to communicate this liberating heritage to all the members of the Church in a way that they can understand it and put it into practice. It was a Dominican, Fr. Christoph Schönborn, who was appointed by John Paul II to be the Executive Secretary for the Commission of bishops appointed to prepare this new Catechism. This undertaking, first purposed by Cardinal Bernard Law, and requested of John Paul II by the Synod of Bishops seemed to me not a regressive step, as some fearful liberals seem to think, but a very progressive step aiming at stating the faith of the Catholic Church as it was formulated in Vatican II in clearer terms so as to make the work of the Council more accessible to the whole Christian community. I was delighted to be asked by Fr. Schönborn to be one of the many theologians who were to help in the revision of its first draft.

Almost the entire fabric of the *Catechism* is derived from the Vatican II documents. It may not say all the things that some theologians would like, but it does say what the Council said and is open to further developments through dialogue in the Church. Moreover, it provides a firm foundation for such dialogue. It is not simply a document of the CDF, nor of even of Pope John Paul II, but of the universal college of the bishops, since they were fully consulted in its preparation. It does not declare that everything it contains is *de fide*, that is, something that ought to be believed on divine faith as God's own word, but it does contain the essentials of the ordinary and universal teaching of the college of bishops under the successor of St. Peter at this point in history set by Vatican II. Therefore the *Catechism* bears the mark of orthodoxy, even if it does not propose every one of its statements as infallible and irreformable.

After the consultation of all the bishops of the world on the first draft, as well as of many theologians (many of whom made detailed criticisms especially of Part III on Christian Life), all bishops were again asked to send in recommendations (*modi*) on any omissions or additions they might wish to be made. A great many bishops did so, no doubt often after consultation with their own theologians. These recommendations written on individual slips for each number in the *Catechism* were then distributed among many theologians whose task was to classify and consolidate the suggestions, just as was done at Vatican II. I would have liked to have been assigned work on a section of Part III on morals, which was the most controverted part and most closely related to my field, but instead I received a section of Part I on Creation, which because of my concern for the science-religion issue, was also welcome. The slips with their recommendations came in English, French, German, Spanish, Italian, Latin, but for my section national differences were not very evident; nor were their great problems about reducing them to a few main points. Thus a number of bishops were concerned that biblical scholars be consulted on biblical citations, especially those relating to texts which are often too literally interpreted.

I found this a bit amusing. Bishops these days are very well aware that the arguments *ex Scriptura* that they may have learned in their seminary days have been attacked by historical-critical biblical exegesis. Hence bishops often seem to be terrified by the formidable expertise of biblical scholars. It seems to me that if bishops will survey current scholarship they will find that since there is so much disagreement among exegetes, the results of such scholarship, even at its soundest and most enlightening, tend chiefly to be negative. Exegetes can save bishops from resting their understanding of Scripture on an overly literal or ahistorical hermeneutic, but current exegetes contribute less than one might suppose to the positive understanding of the Word of God which it is the bishops' duty to proclaim.

Ultimately the truly theological or doctrinal reading of the Bible, therefore, cannot rest on theories about its documentary sources, or on the seeming conflict of viewpoints exhibited by the different human authors. Rather, as explained in *On Revelation* (*Dei Verbum*) of Vatican II, the Bible must be read in its canonical totality as the inspired Word of God to be interpreted by the light of the Holy Spirit in the Church's Sacred Tradition. The bishops are the divinely authorized and ultimate witnesses of that Tradition, since it was to them that Jesus said, "What you bind on earth shall be bound in heaven," (Mt 16:19; cf. also 18:18, which speaks of the Church, but who in the Church can speak for it as a community but the pope and bishops?).

In consolidating the bishops' criticisms of the *Catechism's* treatment of the doctrine of Creation, I reported that a considerable number of the *modi* asked for statements clarifying the Church's attitude to the modern theory of biological evolution, especially human evolution. Therefore, I made the following suggestions (the numbers are from the draft not the published document):

In #1151 I think there should be a mention of miracles, such as: Although God has created the world to operate according to uniform natural laws these determine history only with probability. Hence history commingles natural law, chance, and freedom, as well as the miraculous signs by which God wills to lead us to faith. All such events remain under the sovereign control of the Creator.

#1167 Add at the end of the first paragraph: The wonderful progress of the natural sciences in our times has enriched our appreciation of God's inexhaustible work. The Church is confident that controversies about the relation of scientific facts and theories to revealed truth can be solved through dialogue between scientists and theologians and further research.

#1171 The material universe as modern science is coming to understand it is vast in space and the result of billions of years of cosmological evolution, culminating in the evolution of a great variety of life forms and ultimately in human persons. Moreover, the matter and energy which constitute it display a wonderfully dynamic microstructure. In the human person the realms of spirit and matter meet, so that the human body is marvelously adapted to its spiritual functions: "Your hands have formed me and fashioned me...With skin and flesh you clothed me, with bones and sinews knit me together. Grace and favor you granted me, and your providence has preserved my spirit," (Job 10, 8, 11-12). This increasing knowledge should not blind us to the Creator, but rather enhance our self-understanding and our thankfulness for the achievements of scientists and technologists as gifts of God. They can say with Solomon, "For he gave me sound knowledge of existing things, that I might know the organization of the universe and the force of its elements, etc. ...for Wisdom the artificer of all, taught me," (Wis 7. 17-22).

I suggest the following replacement #1174-1179 which depend too much on the commentary in the draft on the "work of six days" that many *modi* find not helpful:
#1172 Thus, while we do not look to Scriptures for what the human sciences are called to contribute, we place the findings of science in a perspective which emphasizes: (1) The great variety of created things, each with its special and irreplaceable con- tribution to the order of the world; (2) The interdependence of things, especially our human dependence on our earthly environment and our responsibility for its care; (3) The riches of our world for proper human use and development; (4) The dignity of man, endowed with intelligent life and free will, beyond the powers of animals, plants, and non-living things, and destined for eternal life with God; (5) The goodness and beauty of the world as a whole emerging from the primeval chaos; (6) That all this reflects the wisdom and goodness of the Creator toward us, a pledge of his personal presence to us in the

Incarnate Word, Jesus Christ.

For the "In Brief" to replace the Draft #1181 and #1182 based on the "six days" theme use the following:
#1181 The Biblical faith perspective on the material world and what modern science can tell us about it helps us to understand the wisdom and goodness of God, the order and interdependence of all things in the universe, our human selves, our relation to the world, and our responsibility to study and care for our earthly home and its creatures.

#1182 Our understanding of the material world as God made it and gave it to us to use and care for helps us to understand why the Son of God himself has deigned to enter into that world as a human being to redeem, restore, and bring it to fulfillment and has called and empowered us once again to share in this task.

And in the In Brief #1182 I would add:
3. Controversy between revealed truth and the findings of the natural sciences can be solved by dialogue and further research by theologians and scientists.

#1189. To this paragraph, at the end add:
Although the human body of each individual is mediately created by God through the generative action of the parents, and still more (as modern science has come to believe) through the mediation of evolutionary processes, yet the spiritual soul cannot be produced by any material process but only by the immediate and unique action of the Creator (*Humani Generis*). Thus, every human person is brought into existence in a direct and personal relation to God.

In #1191 there still needs to be a more explicit word about the evolution of the human body asked for by several bishops. I would suggest you add to this:
God also creates the human body of individuals through the instrumentality of the parents, and, if the scientific theories of human origin are verified, has created the physical existence of the whole human species by the instrumentality of lower forms of life. Thus God alone is the creator of human life.

In #1192 I would meet a very common modern objection to
human dignity and satisfy the *modi* of several bishops who wanted
something about man as microcosm by adding the following:
> The immensity of the universe revealed by modern science has
> made many consider humanity "only a speck of dust." They fail
> to realize that the spiritual creation of the angels is far vaster
> and more varied than the material cosmos, and that the human
> person shares in both realms.

#1204. For the first two sentences of this paragraph which
seem very evasive, substitute the following:
> By the gift to humanity of intelligence, enlightened by grace, we
> have the capacity, if we use God's gifts wisely, to overcome each
> of the physical evils to which we are liable. Thus the right use of
> modern science and technology under the direction of Christian
> wisdom can serve to restore a measure of the original physical
> integrity of the body and of the environment intended for us by
> God.

I suppose the reason that so little of this material appears in the
final revision of the *Catechism* in spite of the requests of many bishops is that it includes little that could be explicitly documented from
Vatican II or other existing magisterial documents. On these scientific questions and especially on human evolution no such documents yet existed, except Pius XII's statements in *Humani Generis* on
the direct creation of the human soul and the difficulty of reconciling evolutionary rejection of polygenism with the doctrine of original sin. Since that time I have wondered if John Paul II's recent admission of the Church's mistakes with regard to Galileo and his very
positive allocution on the theory of evolution may have been
prompted by his knowledge that so many bishops had raised this
issue during the consultation on the *Catechism*.[272] In spite of my disappointment on this topic, however, I was very gratified when
Archbishop Schönborn told me that my suggestions on other points,
because so detailed, had been among the most helpful in revising
the draft.

Science and Religion
While in Washington I also participated in an series of colloquia
held for the Committee on Human Values of the NCCB, chaired first

by Cardinal Hickey of Washington and then by Bishop Pierre Du Maine of San Jose, with the purpose of establishing closer communication between the bishops and the scientific community. An especially interesting session was held at Notre Dame with sociobiologist E.O. Wilson, physicist Freeman Dyson, geneticist Jerome Lejeune (d. 1994), and the philosopher of science Ernan McMullin as presenters. Wilson was negative in his attitude to religion as a source of objective truth. Dyson was more open but skeptical of traditional religion. McMullin contended that scientists and theologians should follow their own methods without attempting to harmonize their results. LeJeune, however, said that his faith and Bible reading often suggested insights that proved scientifically fruitful, yet he thought theologians and scientists should not be troubled that at any given moment in the progress of both disciplines their results could not immediately be harmonized. LeJeune's view seemed to me both the most nuanced and the truest.

It was an amusing moment when LeJeune expressed a doubt about Neo-Darwinism (never accepted so definitively by continental European biologists as by the British and Americans), as an entirely satisfactory theory of evolution, and Professor Wilson reproachfully said, "You know, Professor LeJeune, that 95% of biologists would disagree with you!" LeJeune with French finesse smiled and replied, "More's the pity!"

In the discussion I objected to McMullin's position (as I have kept doing ever since we first met at a philosophical conference in the 1950s), because in my opinion, since although he rightly accepts a realist rather than an idealist interpretation of modern science, his position seems to result in a kind of "double truth" theory like that of the Averroists in the Middle Ages. To think, as he and the disciples of Étienne Gilson do, that the Catholic faith is intellectually secure because it is bolstered by a metaphysics that is independent of natural science is an illusion. To admit a realistic interpretation of modern science is to give it some degree of "ontological" truth, how-ever tenuous. Since the truth of sensible experience with which science deals is epistemologically prior to and a necessary condition of metaphysical truth, metaphysics and a metaphysical theology cannot stand without developing positive relationships, not merely McMullin's negative, live-and-let-live relationship with modern science. These positive relations may be tentative and flexible, as LeJeune suggested, but they cannot be neglected and thus theology and science left to go their own ways. I must confess that in some addresses, though not explicitly in his recent Encyclical *Fides et Ratio*, John Paul II sometimes seems to speak in terms of a disjunction between metaphysics and natural science that resembles the one McMullin defends. The contrary point of view I hope will soon become more widely known and appreciated.

One of the most successful of these sessions between bishops and scientists was held in Washington, DC, and included a brief course on genetics, elegantly presented by scientists from the National Foundation for Health. The bishops who participated found this exposition and the possibilities it opened up fascinating. In the discussion I tried to raise the question why scientists are so opposed to using teleological concepts in explaining nature, since it is this "final" causality in nature which for the Catholic tradition is the ground for moral evaluations (natural law). The answer I got was hardly illuminating since it only amounted to saying that scientists were not accustomed to thinking in such terms. In brief, the bishops were open to what the scientists had to say, but the scientists seemed locked up in their own thought world. Yet at the same time these scientists were asking for help in meeting the ethical problems that they recognized are real.

I have experienced this dilemma many times. Once at a meeting called by the Kennedy Foundation at Georgetown University on the ethical problems of artificial reproduction, Dr. Robert G. Edwards, who, with Drs. Patrick Steptoe and Barry Bavister, had shared in the production of the first "test-tube baby," pleaded eloquently with the theologians present for guidance on the difficult ethical questions that such procedures had begun to raise. Responding to this Paul Ramsey (d, 1988), a theologian who pioneered in bioethics with his book, *The Patient as Person*, and who was well known for his devastating critiques of positions he disagreed with, made what for him was an unusually mild response saying that ethical considerations might put some limits on the types of experiments a researcher might want to do. Interrupting this reply, Dr. Edwards sprang to his feet in manifest indignation and said, "This is Galileo all over again!" While the arrogance of theologians is famous, it is well matched by some scientists in the face of criticism or ethical restrictions. The more recent outcry of scientists against President Bush's restrictions on stem cell research in order to prevent killing human embryos is another example of this arrogance.

These conferences kept me philosophically alive and I also gave a paper "Experience as a Theological Resource" as the annual Aquinas Lecture at the University of Dallas (1989) in which I opposed the view of some moral theologians who claim that along with Scripture and tradition, "human experience" is a third "source" of revelation and theology. I pointed out that while Aquinas uses the term *experientia* in an unambiguous way to refer to sense knowledge; it is currently being used ambiguously for any kind of cognition except abstract reasoning.

In 1990 at a conference of the Jacques Maritain Association at Fordham University I had the opportunity to criticize another theological trend, that of Transcendental Thomism of the type proposed by Bernard Lonergan SJ (d. 1984), in a paper, "Thomism and the Transition from the Classical World-View to Historical-Mindedness."[273] Lonergan promoted a very influential distinction between "the classical worldview" and modern "historical consciousness." In fact, however, the "classical worldview" as he described it is only that of Platonism and not that of authentic Aristotelianism, though Lonergan fails to make that clear. Although Platonism dominated much of Christian thought until the thirteenth century, and later colored even much of Neo-Thomism, it does not accurately describe Aristotelian Thomism whose starting point is from the world of change not that of timeless abstractions.

I dwelt on the same theme in another essay on the mathematization of modern natural science, "Astronomy as a Liberal Art."[274] Consequently in "The River Forest School of Natural Philosophy", a paper given at the International Congress of Medieval Studies at Kalamazoo in 1989,[275] I summed up the River Forest interpretation of Thomism in a series of theses, arguing that the decline of Thomism has resulted from the faulty interpretation of Aquinas' thought with regard to natural science and metaphysics. The Existential Thomists, such as Maritain and Gilson, and the Transcendental Thomists, such as Lonergan and Rahner, made this misunderstanding popular, the last pair having the greatest effect on post-Vatican II theology. During this time I also lectured on occasion at the Catholic University of America, Notre Dame, and Stanford Universities, and conducted several workshops on medical ethics for priests across the country in which I kept promoting the Lyceum theses overtly or covertly.

The ideological polarization in the Catholic Church since Vatican II due to the decline of Thomism as a common language, has not sweetened theological dialogue, but has sometimes introduced a comic note. On one occasion at the annual convention of the Catholic Theological Society of America to which most Catholic theologians belong, I was nominated by a conservative faction for a position on the board only to be publicly removed from nomination by the chairman of the meeting who announced sternly that I was ineligible because I had not paid my dues (my oversight). One kindly theologian arose and offered to pay for me! In fact I, like a number of other theologians I know, have not often attended the CTSA conventions in recent years because we have felt "victimized" by its feminist monopolization and unseemly sniping at the Magisterium.

Bioethics Debates

Even when my work at the John Paul II Institute was my primary assignment, I continued to work as a consultant to bishops and others and with the tireless Kevin O'Rourke to revise *Health Care Ethics* for its fourth edition in 1996. In the meantime the Pope John Center in St. Louis (now in Philadelphia) at the invitation of Cardinal Bernard Law, Archbishop of Boston, had left St. Louis in 1985 for Braintree, a suburb of Boston. The Cardinal had previously been the Bishop of Cape Girardeau, MO and chairman of the board of the Center. Thus he generously came to the Center's rescue when a difference between its more conservative ethical approach and the more pragmatic attitude of its original sponsor, the Catholic Health Association had led to difficulties.

I continued to participate in the Center's workshop on medical ethics for the bishops of U.S.A., Canada, Mexico and the Caribbean, sponsored by the Knights of Columbus and held annually beginning in 1980. My first talk for these workshops was on "Pro-Life Evangelization."[276] At the Center's workshops for bishops in Dallas in 1990 I spoke on, "Contemporary Understandings of Personhood,"[277] in 1991 gave the keynote address, "Elements of Catholic Conscience,"[278] and in 1992 argued against the notion "Delayed Hominization: Catholic Theological Perspective."[279] In the last of these talks I refuted, on biological as well as theological grounds, the argument that only at implantation does the human embryo become a human person. In the Center's bulletin *Ethics and Medics*, I published, "Rules and Reasons,"[280] "Is AIDS a Punishment from God?",[281] "Nature as a Basis of Medical Ethics,"[282] and "Moral Inconsistency and Fruitful Public Debate."[283] I also delivered a paper that I never published on "The Human Person and Medical Ethics," at a symposium sponsored by the Pope John Center with the same title at St. Joseph's Hospital, Houston, TX in 1991.

In all these papers my interest was centered on "the dignity of the human person" as the foundation of human rights and moral norms. This emphasis is characteristic of papal documents since Vatican II, as I showed in an as yet unpublished paper, "The Human Person and Medical Ethics."[284] Why is the term "person," which simply means a living organism with intelligence and free will so questioned today as if unborn babies are not persons but only "fetuses" or mere "human beings" without the same human rights as we who happen to be already born? In an article, "A Child's Right to His Own Parents: A Look at Two Value System,"[285] I argued that every child has a natural right to be born into its biological family since that is its natural environment needed for not only for proper physical but also for psychological growth. Certainly it is sometimes necessary to compensate for the lack of this parental environment by adoption. It is wrong, however, deliberately to produce children in the laboratory, not for the child's sake but for that of infertile parents. This is to deliberately produce a child deprived of the natural link to its parents through their marital act of covenanted love. Although this link might seem of little importance, this is refuted by the great interest adopted children show in learning who their natural parents were.

The social effect of this separation of children from their natural link to their parents is just another step in the reduction of the human person to a commodity. This concern led me to write a paper "Genetic Engineering"[286] in which I argued that it is ethical to use genetic recombination to correct genetic defects and even to improve the human body in harmony with its essential nature. But it is not ethical to pass beyond these limits and distort or destroy this nature, a masterpiece of the Creator and his image.

I also began to study the difficult problems at the other end of life and the respect due the dignity of the person who is terminally ill or actually dying. On this topic I wrote "Principles for Moral Decisions about Prolonging Life,"[287] "How the Roman Catholic Position on Euthanasia Developed,"[288] "Financial Burdens and the Obligation of Sustaining Life,"[289] and "Hydration and Nutrition: Ethical Obligations."[290]

Again it seems to me that the division among Catholics on these bioethical issues stems largely from differences in concerns and fears. Those inclining to the pro-choice side are concerned for the mother's freedom; those inclining to the pro-life side are concerned for sacredness of life. Somehow we must keep these two concerns together, since personal freedom cannot be respected if we do not respect human life in all its conditions and situations. These are not merely abstract, theoretical problems but are at the heart of the very existence of our society. For the Christian they must be seen in the perspective of God's love for each of his human creatures, since God's Son was conceived in Mary's womb, but only by her courageous, free consent.

Ecumenical Dialogue

The intellectual debates in which I have participated both in St. Louis and in Washington have gone on mainly within the Catholic community, but I have never lost my interest in ecumenism. For three years I served on a committee of the official Catholic Methodist Dialogue sponsored by the NCCB. Seven Catholic theologians, headed by the Catholic bishop of Fort Worth, TX, and seven Methodist theologians, headed by the Methodist bishop of Houston, TX engaged in this dialogue. The late Fr. Richard McCormick, SJ, was a very helpful participant and joined in our Catholic consensus against suicide and assisted suicide. When asked if he thought there were exceptions to this norm he replied to our surprise, considering his well-known proportionalist position, that he did not, although, he admitted that for him this was more a matter of "gut feeling" than conclusive reasoning. This year (1997) after delivering an excellent lecture on the same subject, he gave a similar answer to an inquiry by Dr. John Haas, head of the Pope John Center, aimed at eliciting his proportionalist convictions. How sound is proportionalism if, put to the test of an issue like suicide, it forces one to make an exception to the principle that no concrete negative moral norm is exceptionless?

For our dialogues we met in various places, each time for a couple of days during which we shared prayer and pleasant, informal fellowship. The Catholics gathered daily for Mass, the Methodists for their own prayers and hymn singing, but we also had common prayers. One of these common liturgies was by one of the women Methodist ministers in a feminist style that left us doubtful just to whom we were praying, God, Nature, or Ourselves. On the whole our Catholic group largely agreed as to what we would like the report to say; but the Methodists were significantly divided. One member, who had been an observer at Vatican II and who was an erudite expert on John Wesley was ready to accept the Catholic suggestions, which after all were traditional to all Christians. But two of the Methodist members were reluctant to oppose suicide in the case of AIDS victims and balked at any mention in the report of a future life or of a relation between death and sin. When I argued that it was necessary in the report to deal somehow with the biblical texts that assert that death is the consequence of original sin, one of them said, "You are more Protestant than we are!"

Some of the Methodists were also puzzled because we Catholics kept referring to the Vatican documents on euthanasia, when their church had no such official stance, and I was asked to make a historical presentation, "How the Roman Catholic Position on Euthanasia Developed" (1987). Eventually we published a joint report, *Holy Living, and Holy Dying* which concerns "death with dignity" issues, but the Methodists then hastened to publish also a separate statement of their own, which to me seemed not quite fair. I don't know why they did this, but perhaps they felt that if an official Catholic document on the subject existed, as they had learned from the dialogue and my paper, they felt their church should also have one. I have never published my paper, but writing it made me more keenly aware of the lack of any adequate history of the development of Catholic moral thought, not only as moral theology, but also as praxis. How necessary this is for an adequate post-Vatican II revision of moral theology! The task is beyond my powers, but remains a topic on which I keep reading.

Thus this was not the most satisfying of my ecumenical experiences, though both Texas bishops, as joint chairpersons, were extremely cordial and helpful. Yet by no means did I conclude from this particular dialogue that ecumenical discussions are futile, but only that ecumenism is a rocky road, and not without its comic stumbling and fumbling, though one that the Holy Spirit at Vatican II certainly urged us to travel. In this case there was a lot of good will on both sides but also a lack of success in finding a common basis in Christian tradition, biblical and ecclesiastical, on which to build. In my ecumenical experiences in Dubuque this had never been a major difficulty; appeals to Scripture, the Creeds, and the Ten Commandments were generally accepted as shared principles.

Bishops

During these years both in St. Louis and Washington so much of my work involved meetings with bishops that I must say a word about how enjoyable I found these occasions. Many were held in Washington, at the old, very crowded and unsuitable building at 1312 Massachusetts Ave, NW, where we stayed at a nearby hotel, and others at various places around the country convenient to the bishops of the committee. The most delightful were at a resort hotel at Gulf Shores, near Pensacola, FL where my room had a balcony that overlooked the beach. I loved the sound of the surf through the night. At a meeting held in San Diego there was a magnificent view of the Pacific, and at St. John's Abbey, Collegeville, MN, a vista of lake and forest. The food and drink were always good, the conversation jovial. Of course one is sometimes awestruck by the majesty of the apostolic office and what are sometimes its mediocre embodiments. But it pertains to the essence of the Gospel that divinity be present in very ordinary, even ridiculous humanity, as I tried to say in a poem:

YOUR EXCELLENCY

As for the mystery of the seven stars which you saw in my right hand, and the seven lamp stands, the seven stars are the angels of the seven churches and the seven lamp stands are the seven churches.
(Rv 1:20)

We see in pomp the bishop, a dull clod
decked out in purple, pointed mitre, odd...
Yet as I put my trust in God
and the Bible's final, unsealed scroll
from which the ultimate thunders roll
from the rent heaven's fiery lips,
the furious Apocalypse,
Your Excellency's an angel
a portentous star,
an unbusheled lamp which beams afar
from the city on the mountain height
the long expected light,
the strange good news
for women as for men,

for Greeks and, yes, for Jews,
faith, hope, love,
God's Word cascading from above
with us to dwell
in the frail mesh
of this blood empurpled flesh
between God's heaven
and the devil's hell.

Can we forgive a star pomposity?
An angel pious platitudes?
Your Excellency excel!

What is my actual impression of the American episcopacy from these meetings of selected groups and the much broader representation at the Dallas meetings? It is no longer true, as it used to be, that the bishops are mainly canon lawyers. On the average they are able and very hard workingmen, not all that different from the average conscientious pastor of a parish. Before their appointment by the Holy See their reputation and record have undergone a careful screening and their fidelity to the Holy See and its teaching has been an essential consideration. This of course may mean that priests of independent mind or special creativity may fall under some suspicion, while the conformists get preference. Nevertheless, as St. Paul said, speaking of those entrusted with the apostolic ministry, "It is required of stewards that they be found trustworthy" (1 Cor 4:1). Therefore, there must be unity in the action of the bishops under the successor of St. Peter. I have found the U.S. bishops always grateful for any service done for them and unfailingly kind to my often wordy drafts or presumptuous advice.

If the U.S. bishops have a general failing it is that they are rather unsure of how to deal with current theology. European hierarchies often have many learned theologians; the U.S. hierarchy has some, but the majority are practical pastors, conscious that their theological studies are rather outdated. Although they have attended updating workshops of various sorts, they still feel uncertain whom to trust theologically. Bishops have frequently told me that they have appreciated my lectures and consultations because they believed to be them to be informed, balanced, and clear. Whether that is the case of course can be disputed by the more liberal, but I do believe that this is the way I have been perceived by many, and why I have been often been called on as a consultant.

The recent scandal in the media concerning the failure of some bishops to protect children from sex-abuse by priests must be of grave concern to all Catholics. In my opinion it had two fundamental causes, besides the prurient anti-Catholicism of the media. The first has been the influence of certain theologians and psychologists whose dissent from Church teaching on sexual morality had wide influence among the clergy during the 1970s and 80s. As bishops are being asked to admit their mistakes, I pray that some of those false prophets will confess theirs. The second is the great complexity of the tasks that face bishops today, especially in large dioceses. In fact the U.S. Bishops have been discussing the problem of sex-abuse by priests for twenty years and had formulated good policies with regard to the matter; yet in certain dioceses these policies were only slowly and poorly applied. Experienced persons whom I respect also believe that a culture of secrecy exists in the hierarchy that leads bishops to hide their problems rather than to face them. This may be true, but I do not think it is at the root of the scandal. No organization wants to advertise its mistakes. The bishops have a responsibility not only to protect the reputation of their priests but to avoid exposing Christians to temptations against faith. Only if the episcopacy is confident of a fair hearing in the press can it responsibly become "transparent," as it is now forced to become by its former failure to face this ugly problem promptly and by united action.

Life in Washington

The Priory of the Immaculate Conception, the House of Studies for St. Joseph's (the Eastern) Province was built in 1903 to be near The Catholic University of America. This event marked the emergence of the Dominican Order in the United States from its obscure origins in the backwoods of Kentucky and Ohio. Leo XIII had urged the U.S. bishops to found the University as the national center for the higher education of the Catholic clergy, and many religious orders built houses of studies near it. In recent years, however, these orders have formed the Washington Theological Union, because they felt that the University's theological department was more concerned for an academic reputation than the preparation of pastoral clergy.

Living in the Washington Dominican House of Studies was a great pleasure for me, although I missed St. Louis Bertrand Priory and remained assigned there, returning each year for Christmas holidays and more at length for summers. The fabric of Immaculate Conception Priory is a rather grim, gray fortress built around a cloister garden in a stark version of Gothic style. I have been told it was copied from Belgian monasteries. The cells are small and bare, with common bathrooms on each floor. Its chapel is Victorian Gothic, dark, ornamented, romantic. The stained glass windows are patterned on paintings by a French Dominican, Hyacinth Besson (d. 1861), a companion of the great preacher Fr. Henri Lacordaire (1802-1861) who refounded the Order that was then on the way to extinction. A large mural of Dominican saints in the style of Fra Angelico covers the sanctuary wall.

This priory keeps up many of the Dominican traditions that I experienced in my early days at River Forest, the celebration of all the Hours of psalmody, the wearing of the habit in the house, and reading at meals. But the friars now sit at small tables, and the reading is somewhat abbreviated. I also was happy to eat and talk with the Dominican students, so open and so frank. I also enjoyed the company of the Fathers though recreation was usually rather late at night and the common room often empty. There are ample grounds for walking that, as I have already mentioned, border the new offices of the National Catholic Conference of Bishops.

Directly across the street from the priory, on the university campus is the National Shrine of the Immaculate Conception with its constant flow of visitors. This huge edifice, many years in building, and dedicated to Our Lady as Patroness of the United States, is of somewhat eclectic architecture that has caused it to be unfavorably compared to the consistently gothic Anglican cathedral. I personally, however, found much pleasure in the Shrine as a place of prayer. Its criticized eclecticism fits the multiculturalism of its many chapels sponsored by different ethnic groups and seems to me appropriately to symbolize the multicultural character of U.S.A. Catholicism. My one regret is that the Shrine does not provide visitors with the sort of catechesis for Catholicism that I saw at the Visitor's Center of the Mormon Temple and Tabernacle in Salt Lake City does for Mormonism. Later this has been partially supplied by the John Paul II Cultural center near the Shrine.

I believe that no task is more important for the Church today than the catechesis of its members. Formerly Catholics absorbed much of their Christian culture simply by living in their parish, but today in our secularizing culture many often have minimal contact with Church life and actually know little about their faith. Until this situation is improved the greater participation of the laity in Church decisions that some call for can never be successfully achieved.

From the outset of my stay in Washington I asked to be called a guest rather than a member of the community, because I did not want to worry about its inner politics; but the hospitality I received was generous and fraternal. I enjoyed several new friendships in Washington besides that of Fr. Cessario already mentioned, of which I will note only a few. Fr. Kurt Pritzel, OP, was then a professor of Greek philosophy at the Catholic University of America and is now Dean of Philosophy. Frs. Michael Cicconi and Matthew Rzechowski, both Dominicans, encouraged and assisted me in my writing on spirituality. Fr. John Vidmar, OP, invited me to come along on the fascinating tours he made with students of the great Civil War battlefields around Washington, Harper's Ferry, Manasses, Antietam, and Fredericksburg. Fr. Dan Cassidy, who is a biologist, took me on an instructive trip to the Biological Research Center at Woods Hole, MA.

These experiences and theological debates, therefore, which would not have been possible for me until I was a professor emeritus, with years behind me, focused my meditations on the Church's teachings, helping to overcome some of my spiritual blindness and drawing my attention deeper to fundamentals. The Parable of the Sower (Mt 13: 3-9) sums up true spirituality;

> And he [Jesus] spoke to them at length in parables, saying: "A sower went out to sow. And as he sowed, some seed fell on the path, and birds came and ate it up. Some fell on rocky ground, where it had little soil. It sprang up at once because the soil was not deep, and when the sun rose it was scorched, and it withered for lack of roots. Some seed fell among thorns, and the thorns grew up and choked it. But some seed fell on rich soil, and produced fruit, a hundred or sixty or thirtyfold. Whoever has ears ought to hear."

The vigil of aging can accomplish this enrichment and cultivation of the soil that is the human personality, if one opens ones ears. I know I am rocky ground, Lord, and the seed of your Word has a

hard time sinking any root in me; but between the cracks it makes
its way slowly but evermore surely. Let the rain of grace, the
warmth of truth, and time ensure its slender passage!

DEBATE

You claim this, I claim that
wrestling on the verbal mat
reasons thin, assertions fat,
concord, discord
sharp, flat,
my quizzical friend, Oh yes, you're floored.

Chapter 22 - Pilgrimage to Calvary

Prayer Life

At the beginning of this book I said that a major feature of any spirituality of aging must be based on the words of St. Paul, Romans 8:16, "The Spirit itself bears witness with our spirit that we are the children of God." A Dominican's work ought to be the overflow of his or her spiritual life of prayer. While our age is intensely preoccupied with sexuality it is also intensely interested in "spirituality"—vague as the usage of that term is—and perhaps the two preoccupations are not so different. Even science fiction has taken on the theosophic air of a "spirituality," in which "spirit" has become again, what it is was for the Stoics, a kind of energy or "life force" pantheistically or panentheistically identified with material nature as a kind of "world Soul."

We are also immersed in the depth psychologies of the Jungian type and the profundities of Hindu and Buddhist gurus and their eclectic popular versions in New Age. This is evidence of another negative feature of Post-Tridentine moral theology which today demands revision, the divorce of "spiritual" from "moral" theology, as if the motivation and goal of moral life were obedience to law rather than holiness, life in the Holy Spirit. Although at this period of teaching in St. Louis I managed to publish only a single article on spirituality, "Catherine of Siena's Principles of Spiritual Direction,"[291] I began researches that would lead later to considerable writing on the subject.

Besides the more formal liturgy that the Washington priory provided, I also experienced an occasional wind of the Spirit blowing from the Charismatic Movement just as I had in St. Louis through contact with Fr. McNutt's center mentioned earlier. Several of the Dominican students in Washington had gone to the charismatic Franciscan University at Steubenville, Ohio. I was invited to participate in a colloquium held there in October, 1989, by another group dissatisfied with the liberal trendiness of the Catholic Theological Society. Franciscan University is a school that has been brought by its President, Michael Scanlon, TOR, to international notice as a community of study where the charismatic gifts of the Holy Spirit are recognized and flourish. For this colloquium I prepared a paper "The Development of the Doctrine on Grace to the Reformation" which remains unpublished since a second part of the survey, to be done by another theologian, was never written.

I stayed at Steubenville in one of the dormitories, and going to my room, I heard in the same elevator a group of students talking animatedly. One exclaimed to the others, "Wow! what a Saturday night!" I thought this was a typical college conversation, until the young man added, "Wow! What a prayer meeting!" Charismatic enthusiasm seems to many Catholics, not to mention outsiders, as emotional silliness and group-delusion. Yet enthusiastic prayer, along with phenomena such as healing and deliverance from demonic powers, were present in the ministry of Jesus and the apostolic Church and has characterized the Catholic Church throughout its history. While the bishops have viewed such manifestations with caution, fearing schismatic or heretical tendencies, and have sought to moderate charismatic enthusiasm, the Church, nevertheless, has always admitted that such phenomena may well be the authentic work of the Holy Spirit.

What I saw at Steubenville was a faculty and student body who in large number attended the Eucharist daily with lively devotion and where the sense of Jesus' presence is central to school life. It contrasts to some Catholic schools where, I regret to say, students meet a priest in clericals on the campus with a blank stare. Hence I regard the charismatic movement first as a response to the need of Christians to pray with their whole persons, as St. Dominic did,[292] and this includes our feelings and our bodily gestures. A Sister came to me once very troubled and said that, because of the sickness of a dear friend, she had decided to make a retreat to pray for her at a Benedictine Abbey near Chicago known for its charismatic prayer meetings. During the meeting she was astonished to find herself "speaking in tongues" and when she returned home she found that sometimes in her private meditations this recurred spontaneously. She was frightened because, as she said, "I am a biology teacher, scientifically trained, and this is so out of character for me, I don't know what to make of it." I suggested to her that perhaps what was happening was that she had been merely too cerebral in her praying and had not learned to pray with her whole being. Now God was calling her to this more holistic kind of prayer and praise.

I myself have not verified the authenticity of the healings, prophecies, deliverances, etc., that charismatics claim, although I have heard some quite convincing accounts. I also once heard a talk by a woman, herself a Ph.D. in psychology, who claimed to have been delivered from demonic possession, the result of being offered as a small child to the devil by her Latin American parents who belonged to a cult. During her possession she had repeatedly mutilated herself. In her autobiographical lecture she appeared quite calm, intelligent, insightful, and rational and her priest and spiritual director confirmed the facts of her self-destructive behavior and recovery after prayers by a charismatic group under his leadership.

My guess is that these manifestations range from genuine actions of the Holy Spirit to various psychological aberrations. That they can all be explained by psychology seems to me unlikely since by scientific standards modern psychological theory is itself not well verified. The reasonable attitude, therefore, is to retain our belief in prayer, make room for holistic prayer in Catholic life, and center our lives in faith, hope, and charity, rather than in an overly curious preoccupation with the paranormal. We should, moreover, always remain open to recognizing the work of God even if it transcends our way of thinking.

I joined in charismatic prayer meetings held by some of the students in the Dominican House of Studies in Washington led by two young Dominican friars who had found their vocations at Steubenville under the influence of Fr. Giles Dimock, OP I did not speak in tongues, but I was deeply moved. Praying together, however, is not always enthusiastic singing and praising, just as it is not only formal liturgy. It is also done in silence. I appreciated that there were opportunities at the House of Studies for silent meditation before the Blessed Sacrament and this was much practiced, as it had been in my early days in the Order. I regret that in my own Province because our liturgists, by rightly encouraging the perception of Eucharist as an act of worship, have unfortunately discouraged devotion to the reserved sacrament by making it unnecessarily inconspicuous.

PRAYING

> There was a candle burning in the center of the room
> where the air was soft and rather dim.
> I knelt awhile,
> thinking of Him.
>
> How wonderful, I thought, is all creation,

how keen with joy, how tempered with despair!
I felt the gentle warmth so radiant in the air.

The universe, I thought, is but a veil now rent by woe,
that the infinite complications of the inner light
might just a little show.

The universe, I mused, is blind with joy and truth revealed,
placed in the quiet heart for keeping
and sealed with searing pain.

The flame was trembling quietly, the light
all round pulsed clear and golden white.
the circling air was golden too,
yet dim.
I knelt a long while,
praying with you
to Him.

This stimulus from the Charismatic Movement, requests from our novitiate in Denver, and from Dominican Sisters at Aquinas for information on the history of Dominican spirituality encouraged the research I had already begun in St. Louis. This prompted me to write some articles on the subject: "Catherine of Siena's Principles of Spiritual Direction" (1981); "Common Life, 900-1200: Factors Which Shaped the Thinking of St. Dominic," (1990, coauthored with David Wright, OP) and several short papers, never published, delivered at meetings of the International Congress of Medieval Studies, Kalamazoo, MI on such topics as, "Dominica Cavalca and his Influence on St. Catherine of Siena," "The Correspondence of Bl. Ossa De'Andreasi," "Savonarola as Prophet," "Dominican Women Prophets," "Dominican Artists," etc.

This research finally resulted in a book *The Dominicans*[293] which, although largely based on secondary sources and not documented in thoroughly scholarly fashion, was intended to be of help especially for Dominican novitiate programs, including those for women. I was unable, however, to find much material on many of the women writers of our Order. This is a field that sadly needs research preferably by Dominican women themselves.

I also had got involved, even when I was in St. Louis and not of my own volition, in the exasperating controversy over the "creation-centered spirituality" of Matthew Fox, then a member of our Province. Matt was a remarkably intense and energetic Dominican who founded and directed (but without any moderation by our Central Province), an institute of spirituality in San Francisco to promote his very popular writings. Though I was once Matt's teacher, his work, I must admit, has had more influence than my own. He did indeed begin with a splendid insight, which he claims to have received from the famous French Dominican, Père M.-D. Chenu (d. 1990), with whom in Paris he also studied: "We cannot make sense of the doctrine of original sin, unless we first make sense of the doctrine of original blessing."

Much of my own thinking and writing sounds that same theme, which in fact all Dominicans get from St. Thomas who emphatically teaches the intrinsic goodness of human nature, body and soul. But in his preaching of our original blessedness Fox suppresses the doctrine of original sin and in a one-sided way, neglectful of sound scholarship, sometimes seemed to identify the doctrine of the goodness of creation with an uncritical acceptance of all the fads of the Age of Aquarius.

Cardinal Ratzinger, head of the Vatican Congregation for the Doctrine of the Faith, Now Pope Benedict XVI, wrote our Provincial about the increasing inquiries about how a Catholic institute could harbor on its faculty a self-professed "witch," namely, Starhawk, a Jewish woman from Brooklyn, hired to teach Native American Spirituality. (Of course in feminist circles the term "witch" can have a positive meaning, but certainly in general usage it is *male sonans*). The Cardinal, following the Vatican policy of referring such complaints within the Church about clergy to the local bishop or religious superior, asked our Provincial to have three of Fox's books read by a committee to which our Provincial appointed me. We were not asked to examine the work of his institute, which we did not visit, but only to examine the books. Our committee of three in its report noted some of the theological imbalances in these books and recommended that in the future Fox should have his drafts read and criticized by other theologians of the Province, not to suppress publication, but to encourage works more representative of our Order and its mission. A Dominican preaches and writes not just under his own name but also under that of the Order that has a responsibility for him. That does not mean that everybody in the Order need agree with what he says and writes but it must be concerned that what he produces is as useful to the Church as possible. I personally have much improved my major publications by submitting them to readers appointed by my provincial. I note that many academic theologians in the prefaces to their works thank colleagues for reading and criticizing their drafts. Thus two of my books were meticulously reviewed by Fr. Victor LaMotte, OP, former editor of the journal *Listening* who made many helpful suggestions and gave me warm fraternal encouragement. I am not sure that anyone else will read my books with such care!

The Cardinal on receiving the report of our committee noted in a letter that it seemed to contradict itself since it commended Fox for his "creativity and hard work" and at the same time charged him ("as Fr. Ashley does") with serious theological faults. Of course that inconsistency was due to our desire to give fraternal support to Matt that might encourage him to enter into more dialogue and accept suggestions to improve his books. Eventually Ratzinger asked Fox to be silent for a year of sobering reflection. Matt accepted this but also raised money from supporters to publish a full-page ad in *The New York Times* declaring that he was being persecuted by "Brother Ratzinger"!

Eventually our Provincial Counsel decided that the Order could not be accountable for Fox since he refused to be accountable to us and with the consent of the Master of the Order dismissed him from the Order. He has left us for the Anglican Church but now calls himself "a non-denominational priest." Much talent, and, for us, a great waste! Like parents we can only ask, "Where did we go wrong?"

As a result of my involvement in this painful affair I was later twice asked to speak at the Franciscan University of Steubenville to groups who were concerned about the influence of Fox's books on the Charismatic Movement. These groups linked Fox's views with those of the New Age movement. He has indeed taken up many of the New Age themes, but as far as I know, has not promoted their central theosophist theory of the transmigration of souls. I criticized his views at two conferences on "New Age Sects": "A Critique of Matthew Fox's The Cosmic Christ and the Notion of Creation-Centered Spirituality" in 1990 and another "Creation-Centered and Redemption-Centered Spirituality," given at conferences on "The New Age Sects," at Franciscan University of Steubenville, 1991, the former unpublished, and the latter published in cassette form.

Spirituality

As I have already indicated, "Spiritual Theology" should not be considered a separate field from moral theology but its culmination. At Aquinas I had taught courses on the Dominican tradition of spirituality and published an article: "Common Life, 900-1200: Factors Which Shaped the Thinking of St. Dominic."[294] My researches in this field led to a book, initiated by the publisher to be part of a series on the different religious orders, but for which only a Benedictine and myself finished our works. This book titled simply *The Dominicans*[295] was intended by me to serve in the formation of Dominican novices. Although Fr. William Hinnebusch's excellent *A Short History of the Dominican Order* as well as his *Dominican Spirituality: Principles and Practice*[296] had been written for this purpose, it seemed to me something which more directly highlighted the principle features of the Dominican tradition, its community life, its preaching mission, its intellectual life, and its spirituality was needed. I had to work largely from secondary sources and I am conscious of many errors in the book, but I hope it has been of some help to those beginning Dominican life.

Vacations

Not all my experiences were work experiences or theological debates. Before I went to Washington my summer vacations during this time were usually spent in St. Louis. Since most of my confreres vacationed with their families, and my own family was now gone, it was pleasant to be able to read and travel around the city without being tied down to any specific task. But I spent one vacation at Sinsinawa, WI. Fr. Samuel Mazzuchelli, an Italian, professed as a Dominican in 1825, at a time when the Order seemed close to extinction, was called to be a missionary to the Indians and came to the United States in 1828 to Old St. Rose in Kentucky. After priestly ordination and missionary activities on Mackinaw [Mackinak] Island and throughout what is now Wisconsin and Iowa, he eventually founded the Dominican Sisters of the Congregation of the Holy Rosary, devoted especially to teaching. Their motherhouse is on The Mound, an isolated hill that overlooks the cornfields in southwest Wisconsin near its junction with Iowa and Illinois, not far from Dubuque. He had hoped also to found a province of priests and brothers of the Order there, forerunner of the present Central Province of St. Albert, but his little group of friars died or deserted him.

Undaunted, Mazzuchelli continued his work with the Sisters and pursued extensive missionary labors throughout Michigan, Iowa, Wisconsin and IL. His cause for beatification is now progressing. The Mound is still a very active motherhouse and its extensive buildings center on the old stone building erected by the founder himself. On a vacation I spent two peaceful weeks in the rectory there and wrote a poem, not about the neat, well tended cemetery of the Sisters, but some almost forgotten graves on the hillside.

AN OLD CEMETERY ON SINSINAWA MOUND

Older already than were so many buried here,
I stop to taste the last red raspberries.

A few unseasonable snowflakes
blow out of the furrows of the clouds
through which the chilly sky shines clear
across the terraced cornfields
and other darker fields new furrowed
which to the sky respond
as do the flakes,
thistle down
blown from dry pods
also responding.
I too respond
to those here
perhaps forgotten.

I could not believe it when I glimpsed
even at this late season
glowing through fallen leaves
two violets in late October!
White grave stones brightened
with orange lichens
(the church has disappeared)
commemorate the long interred, failed hope
of Father Samuel,
who thought to lie here
while they kept his work alive!

Brothers Dominic and Hyacinth

never ordained, lie here,
the failed hope also of a Mr. Baxter
who lost a wife and three small heirs
all within one year.

Most who died here with their hopes
counted fewer years than I can count
as now I watch a flake melt
on a dried raspberry
and another
frost the provocative violets.

Not in time,
our sweet and bitter years
or cycling seasons
did Samuel place his hope,
nor can I dare
to hope for time
for work well done to leave behind.
These failing violets speak
neither of summer now fulfilled
nor spring to come
but Life
eternally alive.

Another vacation was spent at a cabin 8,000 feet up in the Rockies. I drove there with friends by way of Interstate 70 and stopped for the night at a little roadside motel in western Kansas. As I walked outside to see the dusty red sunset I noticed a couple I had seen at an earlier stop, who looked by their clothing and manner vaguely European, oddly walking not on pavement but in a ploughed field. Meeting them later in the motel I said to make conversation, "It's very flat out here isn't it?" Indeed it was flat as a table with hardly a tree for miles under an infinite sky. In a foreign accent they answered, "This is the most remarkable thing we have yet seen in your country." As an Oklahoman I too appreciate the beauty of that "flatness," a visual quality the critic Clement Greenburg praised as the mark of the best modern painting.

The cabin that was our destination, which belongs to the parish of St. Dominic in Denver, is just above the resort village of Nederland at the head of Boulder Creek, CO. Panting, I felt the altitude when I climbed up and down from the cabin to the village. From there we made trips to many other wonderful vistas and Alexander Pope's famous simile in his "Essay on Criticism" for the difficulties of learning the writer's craft came to my mind (I hate to quote its elegance in a chapter where my own ragged free verse may be compared to it!):

> So pleased at first the towering Alps we try,
> Mount o'er the vales, and seem to tread the sky,
> The eternal snows appear already past,
> And the first clouds and mountains seem the last;
> But, those attained, we tremble to survey
> The growing labors of the lengthened way,
> The increasing prospect tires our wandering eyes,
> Hills peep o'er hills, and Alps on Alps arise!

So prairie flatness and mountain grandeur each have their wonder and these wonders by contrast make each more wondrous still. Yet at this time, as I will describe more fully later, I continued to struggle, although not so continuously as formerly, with my scrupulosity. Now I was beginning to be more content to accept the chill mountain air of faith.

MOUNTAIN IN DESERT

> Purple mountain, gray desert.
> Rise star between these rocks!
> Sink eyes within the impenetrable stone
> as I climb up to darkness,
> as I sit down in void.

> Beneath me rests the rock, the void at its rim.
> Above me stars hang on the spiderweb of night.

> I do not trust this rim of the rock.
> I cannot catch at this web of the night.
> Only the void will lift me
> only the dark sustain.
> How vain my fear.
> I am safe up here!

only up here...

The most remarkable vacation I spent while in St. Louis, however, was not anticipated. I had never wanted to go the Holy Land, biblical and historical though it is, because my mental picture, from photographs in Bibles was of a rocky desert devastated by centuries of anguished struggle that must have obliterated the traces of the *heilsgeschichte* enacted there. Yet Kevin O'Rourke had organized a commercial vacation tour to Israel by way of Egypt for a group of friends, mainly in hospital administration, and, to fill out the number, asked me to go along. I have had qualms about vacations of this type fitting my vow of poverty, but my religious superior thought that since I no longer had a family to visit and spent most of my vacations in St. Louis, this was reasonable. As the trip was planned I hoped we might go by way of Greece, but was told that we would only land in Athens for refueling, then go directly to Cairo for three days, and then on to Tel Aviv. As it turned out, though we were not told, the plane blew a tire taking off and it was necessary to take two hours in Athens to change it. Some of us therefore hastily took taxis to the Acropolis. I managed to climb it and in half an hour see all the sights I had dreamed of all my life, then return to the airport in time to fly again. The Parthenon had gleamed startling white against dark blue storm clouds and far glimpses of Homer's "wine-dark sea."

We reached Cairo at sunset, the sky deep red with desert dust. In the sinister twilight we drove by a vast cemetery in which there were thousands of roofless houses of the dead in which homeless people sometimes take shelter. After passing for a long time through this city of some 15 million through badly lighted streets, we came to our very fine hotel and went to bed not knowing exactly where we were. Rising in the morning, I pulled back the curtains and there in the blazing sun across the hotel garden were the three great Pyramids! As a child I used to gaze for hours through my Dad's stereopticon at the photographs of Egypt, the mummy of Ramses II, and the three pyramids all in realistic 3D. Now here they stood! Our hotel had been converted from the vacation home of the nineteenth century Khedive who ruled Egypt under the sovereignty of the Sultan of Turkey. For the sake of his foreign guests he had located his residence at the very edge of the desert.

During our three days in Cairo I climbed up into the inner chamber of the Great Pyramid, at night saw a sound and light show at the Sphinx, and visited the step pyramid at Sakkara. After a short, very uncomfortable camel ride, we also descended into a Third Dynasty official's tomb with walls exquisitely sculpted in low relief with scenes of daily life and of the government tasks he supervised. I especially admired the depiction there in exquisite low relief of humble little donkeys carrying immense loads as shaven-pate peasants striding at their sides urged them on. On our return to Cairo as the bus passed through little villages there were those very same donkeys and those identical peasants still toiling onwards!

Of course I wanted to go up the Nile, but we flew directly to Tel Aviv, where, imitating John Paul II, I knelt and kissed the holy earth, then up the coast to Caesarea Maritima and its Roman ruins, then by Mt. Carmel to Haifa with its crescent bay, then to Acre's gigantic Crusader ruins, and finally east across the olive groves of Galilee to a kibbutz called Hagoshrim, located on a little creek, the River Dan, that flows into the baptismal waters of the Jordan. This was just before the Israelis invaded Lebanon. Hagoshrim is directly below the Golan Heights and in its peaceful farming complex were air raid shelters with Mickey Mouse paintings ready to entertain the children during a threatened bombing. Staying there two nights, we made trips to the lovely springs of Banias and Caesarea Philippi where Jesus named unreliable Simon "The Rock," and then went down to Capharnum. There we visited the spot which, because since it is marked by the foundations of a very early church, archaeologists believe, is the site of the house of that same fisherman, Simon Peter. Finally we sailed across the blue Sea of Galilee to Tiberias and to the Mount of the Beatitudes.

It was on that Mount that our group celebrated our first Mass in Israel, not in the lovely Italian chapel there, but in the open air of its garden, with the Lake of Galilee before us. Until this moment it had all seemed just a nice trip, but here our group began to realize the presence of Jesus, the Word made flesh, in such concrete daily reality. I think we all quietly shed a tear or so. We went on to the supposed site of Cana, to Nazareth, and to Mt. Tabor, the possible scene of the Transfiguration and of the first prediction of the Passion.

THE FOURTH BEATITUDE

Blessed the hungry!
>   Through the labyrinthine supermart,
>   I push my loaded cart,
>   down aisles, aisles, aisles
>   of glorious packages,
>   cans, bottles, jars,
>   cellophaned wrapped meats
>   and even greeting cards
>   whispering love for birthdays,
>   cuddly bunnies for Easter,
>   violet condolences for the dead
>   whose mouths, closed finally,
>   hunger no more.

Not by bread alone
>   nor all my supermarket's plenty
>   am I ever filled,
>   my hunger blessed
>   with honest joy,
>   if still my heart is empty
>   as a glass of soured wine
>   poured in the thirsting dust.

Yet blessed will my hunger be,
>   if that hunger, if that thirst
>   will be to share my bread, give drink;
>   to fill my empty heart
>   with all the fullness
>   the overflowing plenty
>   of the poor now fed,
>   of the thirsty
>   taking at least a sip
>   of joy.

Not by bread alone or rather
not by cellophane wrapped bread,
sliced thin for those who have to diet
after consuming the portions of the poor;

but by the bread of honest work,
honest words,
common life,
summed up
in Jesus' body, Jesus' blood,
the blessing of those who hunger and who thirst
for justice, and in forgiveness make peace.

Since troubles were stirring in Samaria, our route to Jerusalem was along the Jordan, where at the probable site of Jesus' own baptism we stopped to dip hands in the water, then on to the ruins of Jericho, and finally turned west through desert to the Holy City. Our group were pious pilgrims and we sang a hymn and I recited Psalm 122,

I rejoiced when they said to me,
"Let us go up to the house of the Lord."
And now our feet are standing
within your gates Jerusalem.

In the Holy City we stayed at the Americana Colony Hotel, once the harem of some Muslim official. We were awakened each morning by a piously ugly recording of the Islamic call to prayer from a nearby minaret. The Dominican École Biblique was at hand as we took the short walk to the Damascus Gate of the Old City. We spent a week in the Holy City and made a tour along the Dead Sea to Masada. Our guide was an Israeli schoolteacher, who when I asked him about the condition of religion in the country, replied that the great majority like himself found observance of the minutiae of the Torah impractical, but that he had to admit that it was observant Jews who had made Jewish survival possible. He kept apologizing to us when he sensed our shock at the Israelis' treatment of Palestinians, painfully reminiscent of racial discrimination in our own country. He showed strong patriotic pride in taking us to Masada, saying that Jews had no hope except in their army and would commit suicide rather than ever again submit to a Holocaust.

When I asked this guide if we were going to stop at Qumran near the caves where the Dead Sea Scrolls were found, he said that since we were going to see the Shrine of the Book where some of the scrolls are exhibited, this was hardly necessary. To my frustration the rest of our party accepted this reply passively; but I kept nag-

ging. Finally on the return trip, near evening, we did stop to explore
the famous ruins, charmed in particular by the recollection that the
Qumran ascetics were the forerunners of all Christian monks and
friars, and that the Dominican scholars of the École Biblique, Père
Roland De Vaux above all, had played a vital part in the Scrolls' discovery.

We, of course, saw the principal sites in the Old City and had
time to wander about by ourselves without the guide. Often, as I
had anticipated when the trip was first purposed to me, I stopped to
puzzle over some ugly heap of stones, but just a heap of stones can
be a history and a prophecy:

A RUIN

Nothing so reassures me as a ruin:
To know the flowering grass will soon come back.
Through rains and suns
green waves will mount the rubble,
covering the trash, the rotting beams, the broken marble
with fresh oblivion and a healthful silence.

Assurance always, since some trace remains,
visible at least in aerial photos.
the straights and curves laid down by human rule,
promise that those who one time liked this place,
will like it once again,
and stones will grow
with fresh, sharp noise
into a tower
in the ruined wild.

The Holy Sepulchre is a confusing ruin, but almost every day I
visited it and once as a group we were able to celebrate Mass there.
The Catholic altar is located peripherally on the back of the north
wall of the Greek chapel facing the Sepulchre, and the Franciscan
custodian stopped us when we tried to sing a hymn, because the
Greeks were chanting their Office in their own chapel over the wall
from us, while the Armenians were circumambulating the Sepulchre, their discordant chant echoing among the dark pillars. One of
our group came early one morning and saw a Greek Orthodox

custodian enter the Sepulchre and dust everything, only to be followed by a Franciscan who dusted it all over again! It seems that in the Near East a customary right is lost unless it is scrupulously maintained.

When I had first entered the Church of the Holy Sepulchre, I noticed the pilgrims kissing what is called the "Stone of the Anointing" of Jesus' corpse. I had just read in the guidebook that this slab had been placed there only in the nineteenth century. Nevertheless, I knelt and kissed it with the rest. The authenticity of relics and sacred places is not so important for pilgrims such as me as is the concrete, physicality of praying in what might be the place of a holy event or the relic of a holy person. Yet it is also most fortunate that modern archaeology has in fact given high probability to many of the traditional holy places in Israel, the Holy Sepulchre among them. I spent some hours trying to understand in detail that strange building. While some people are shocked by its mutilated condition and the denominational struggles that go on within it, I was prepared for this and found it rather like an honest Christian confession of our mutual offenses that pleads to God for mercy and should inspire us to greater ecumenical efforts.

TOUCH

Aristotle,
named "the man who knows,"
by Dante, poet of poets—
yes, Aristotle claims
that all we know reduces
to certainty
only in touch,
vaguest of all our senses,
yet existential,
contacting the real,
the *Ding an sich*,
in its facticity.

How knowing then was Mary of Magdala
reaching out to hold fast her Risen Lord!
How knowing a fool Thomas was to reach out
to touch the wounds in the Lords'
hands, feet, his opened heart!

"Touch me not, I am not yet
risen to the Father!"
He said to her whose faith
already touched and held him.
"Put your hand into the wounds,
into my feet, my hands, my heart,"
he said to Thomas who did not dare
yet found his heart confessing
his Lord, his God.

I kiss the cold rock of Calvary,
kissed by moist lips of millions,
lovers, doubters, pleading
to touch and hold You risen.
The stone and my cold, dry heart
grows hot
with the drip, drip of blood
from your feet, your hands—,
yes, from your riven heart!

Just as I enjoyed my travels abroad I also greatly enjoyed Washington, DC when I began to teach there, though I hardly had time to
enjoy it fully. It is a beautiful city with its neoclassical buildings and
in springtime its flowering bushes and trees, not only the famous
cherry blossoms, but the azaleas and white and pink dogwood. Its
museums also furnish ample opportunity to see the wonders of the
world. I spent what time I could at the National Gallery of Art and at
the Stickler and Guggenheim Museums, although the Frick (which I
had seen on previous visits to Washington) with its Whistler Pea-
cock Room and oriental art, was closed for restoration during most
of my stay. The range of art of the first quality thus available provides too rich a banquet.

What I especially sought out were works, of whatever period or
country, that seemed to convey the real. I don't mean the mere appearances of the real, but works distinguished for their sense of
tangibility, existentiality, and clarity. That is why impressionism,
now so popular, leaves me cold (except perhaps for Degas if he can
be so labeled). It is too vaguely pretty. Thus I wrote in a poem:

WATER LILIES

Monet's lilies are not mine.
    Cloudy among the clouds
    his float so silent
    in a light unfathomable.

Mine slap the ripples, slippery pads
    opening their ivory blooms
    out of an oily dark.
Only in shallow pools my lilies grow,
    rooted below the slowly wavering fish
    in mud and ooze.
In stillness their aroma rises,
    leaving behind the smell of stagnance.
    In a breeze I see the pads flap,
invert, showing underneaths
    so slimy pale.
I hear the water from the flowers dripping,
    drop on drop
    where the goldfish flop
    and the ripples spread,
    circle in circle,
    circles cutting circles.

When on the circled surface a cloud floats by,
    it drifts as heavy as the rooted flowers,
    noiselessly moving,
    broken by wavelets and is scattered
    among the intransient lotus leaves.

Neither my impressions nor expressions
    look the least
    like artful Monet's dreamy dabs.
For me unskilled,
    in sharp facticity
    my odd lotuses are grossly real,
      yes, yes, so really there—
Real or reflected?
If reflected,

then even the intersecting
circles of doubt
cannot disguise
the glowing facts
that ripple right into
my doubting eyes.

Chapter 23 - Hagia Sophia

More Traveling

I wrote, in Chapter 18, that another feature of a spirituality of aging is that we must fix our minds and hearts on Jesus, God made Man, as it says in *Hebrews* 12:1-2, "Therefore, since we are surrounded by so great a cloud of witnesses, let us rid ourselves of every burden and sin that clings to us and persevere in running the race that lies before us while keeping our eyes fixed on Jesus, the leader and perfecter of faith" In the third century St. Irenaeus of Lyons was troubled by the fact that if Jesus died young, how did he "recapitulate" all of ordinary human experience. Irenaeus found his answer in the facts that Jesus' opponents said (Jn 8:57) "So the Jews said to him [Jesus], "You are not yet fifty years old and you have seen Abraham?" Thus Irenaeus suggested that Jesus was in his forties when he died and thus "recapitulated" old age. Today most scholars think he died at the age of 33, but Jesus may have been born as early as 6 BC and crucified as late as 36 AD , thus dying at age 42 which it his time would have been considered the beginning of old age. In any case in his short ministry he experienced more than most of us do in our lifetime and was constantly aware that death was at hand.

My consultancy meant four and often more meetings each year, not only in Washington, but also at retreat houses, one looking down on the "homes of the stars" on Malibu beach, another run by the Jesuits near San Jose, a third a beach hotel on the Gulf.

As I was finishing my time in Washington in 1992 I accompanied the same group with whom I had gone on pilgrimage to the Holy Land on another pilgrimage to Turkey and Greece, to see some of the places St. Paul had visited. Since earthquakes have destroyed many of these sites, we began not with a Pauline city, but at Istanbul, immensely significant in church history.

In Istanbul our small hotel looked across an alley at Hagia Sophia, the Church of Holy Wisdom. A half block away was the gate to Topkapi Palace, at the end of the peninsula of ancient Constantinople, built by the first Christian Emperor Constantine, and rebuilt by the Sultans of the Ottoman Empire.

I counted eight mosques on the horizon of the city. I preferred the great Mosque of Suleiman to the rather gaudy Blue Mosque facing Hagia Sophia. Not much Christian architecture is left, but there is the Chora, a church glowing with mosaics and frescoes of the Virgin's life, and the Galata Tower with its great view, and nearby the medieval Dominican church, now a mosque, and the only present one, of the Italian Dominicans secluded from Muslim notice, where we said Mass.

The Byzantines and the Ottomans had been only names to me. Now in a shrine in the Topkapi palace I saw Muslim clerics reciting the Qu'ran continuously day and night, and the swords of the Prophet and the first four Caliphs, hairs from the Prophet's beard, and a plaster cast of his foot, a large corn on one toe. An immense museum displays ceramic pieces sent in tribute to the Sultan from the entire East. Oddly the garments of the Ottomans, though jeweled and embroidered, retain the patterns of the nomad horsemen's garb of the Inner Asian steppes whence the Turks came. The ruins of Constantine's circus and the transformation of suave forms of classical art into clumsy, inexpressive imitations, makes one wonder about our own culture's fate.

I spent as much of the week as I could in Hagia Sophia. The Muslim Turks must know it to be their greatest tourist attraction, yet carelessly neglect it. What celestial liturgies must have been celebrated there, the imperial cortege assisting! When the Muslims finally breached the walls that for centuries withstood their siege the Sultan on his horse, planning to turn the church into a mosque, leapt onto the high altar to stop the mob from looting. Of course we also enjoyed the busy bazaar, a trip to a rug factory where we were served hot apple juice, and the cozy mornings with breakfast under a vine-covered arbor.

From Istanbul we went by bus to Gallipoli and the Hellespont by ferry crossover to Troy, and stayed overnight at Izmir, the Smyrna of St. Paul and St. Ignatius of Antioch. Homer told the truth that Troy is on a windy plain, but for all my love of Homer for me Troy was a disappointment. On a hot, hot afternoon with an inadequate guide, the instructive signs were hard to read, and we were all tired. I did think of how Homer told how the old men sitting on the walls watched Helen as she passed by, muttering to each other, "Well, such a woman is worth a war!" Next day Ephesus was better than we expected, with its Pauline sites, marble streets, amphitheater, forum, public ruins of toilets and brothel, and especially its grand library with statues of Episteme (Science) and Sophia (Wisdom), giving a splendid idea of a Roman colonial city. There our guide, a badly crippled Muslim, gave us in good English, which he had learned in London, detailed historical information. At the ruins of the public brothel next to the library he said, "This made it possible for a husband to make a truthful excuse to his wife, `My dear I was at the library.'" Surely St. Paul shook his head in Judaic scorn as he strode by these houses of pagan error and lust to preach to the rabble in the forum.

From Izmir we took a tourist steamer to Athens, a boring day on foggy water, with nothing but glimpses of looming islands. Our Athens hotel was "The Parthenon" almost at the foot of the Acropolis. One fine evening from a nearby hill we watched a beautiful light show at the Parthenon itself. Afterwards on another hill we watched lively Greek folk dancing. After the show I suggested that our group take a shortcut back to the hotel by going out another entrance. I was woefully wrong and we had an hour and a half walk back to our hotel through unknown and for all we knew dangerous streets. My friends recall this moonlit misadventure as if it were our trip's most memorable disaster.

No less memorable for me was another trip to a theological Congress at the Lateran when I drove with Dr. Carl Anderson and Fr. Romanus Cessario from Milan to Bologna, Ravenna, Florence, Siena and then to Rome.

Aging More

I truly enjoyed these years of Dominican work in St. Louis and Washington, since my health continued on the whole good. Of course I was taking pills for gout and high blood pressure, my enlarged prostate was waking me more at night, and my old digestive tract problems still required me to sleep with the head of my bed elevated and to have regular endoscopic exams of both my esophagus and my colon; but on the whole I felt well. Today members of religious orders get excellent medical care, and I felt it not hypochondria to take my complaints to a doctor, since preventive medicine could save the Order a good deal in money and care. Just before going to Washington in 1987 I had written the following:

SEVENTY-THREE

> They come, they go,
> colors of fall
> then of spring,
> leaves small,

leaves large,
then a silent pall
of months of snow.
The circle of years
echo with laughter.

Then, when we hear
that friends have died,
in silent tears
the echoes subside.

Yet, Lord,
an odd, odd thing—
In my autumn
I walk in spring.

Toward the end of my stay at Washington I began to have more evident health problems, a rise in blood pressure, more prostate trouble, "dry eyes," etc., which meant frequent visits to a doctor in Georgetown.

WHITE PURGATORY

 A blank white room:
"The doctor
will be with you shortly."

Waiting amidst apparatus:
the examining couch, a desk, a chair,
charts of the interior of God's temple,
my body prophesies
discovery of fearful things
about its deteriorating state
too late.

Why is it that this short time,
emptied for fear,
even when held bravely in check
with hopeful thoughts,
can be a slowly growing ache,

a blanked out agony?
Pain awakes in places that were cozy.

"Shortly," the nurse has promised,
but how long is "short"?

With all this traveling, teaching, writing, and talking, talking, talking, where was my interior life? As I have already said my scrupulosity was subsiding. I went to confession only every month and made most decisions quickly and definitively. But I was often delinquent in making my annual retreat, and my daily meditation seemed increasingly obscure as noted in another poem.

REFUGE

I know no way
        but the deep way across a sandy floor
        where the crabs slide sidewise
        out of the rippling sun
        into ripples of shadow
        depthwards.

Abyss within abyss,
        I travel,
deep on deep traverse
to the unfathomed bottom
        where burning, boiling
        out of the riven floor
        a lava fountain wells.

Bright steam bubbles break there far above.
But here the roots of islands are constructed
        to be leafed and flowered with corals.

Yes, here,
        here at the bottom
        again I can breath
        the absent air.

After three years at the John Paul II Institute I was ready to return to St. Louis and Aquinas until retirement, but for scheduling reasons I taught one more semester at JP II and then left Washington not realizing I would return to teach there from the fall of 2001 to the spring of 2002.

Life at a Computer

With my reception of the medal *Pro Ecclesia et Pontifice* mentioned in the last chapter, I realized my service in Washington was completed and I returned to my house of assignment in St. Louis. I presumed it was a return to my teaching at Aquinas, which I thought would continue until I dropped. I was feeling quite well, but in fact by then the signs of terminal old age were apparent enough, in 1992 I was seventy-seven. People I have not seen in some time said to me, "Why you don't look any different than when I saw you last time!" Indeed, I don't think I had changed a great deal in appearance for some years. Yet I had an increasing number of physical problems, pretty well controlled medically, but I tired rather easily. I had to have a prostate resection and the biopsy revealed a low-grade cancer but after I had hormone therapy (chemical castration) my tests went down to normal and continued so. My physician assured me that I was likely to die of something else first.

Just before that, returning from the Medieval Congress in Kalamazoo, I had a serious infection in my right eye (probably due to my lack of tears and something that got in my eye on the long drive back and forth) and as a result developed a cataract in that eye and had to have artificial lenses implantation. My sight with glasses was restored to normal, but I had to wear annoying hearing aids. Even more annoying I began to have trouble remembering names. I was mildly diabetic, my skin was too dry and often itched, but I retained a pretty good head of hair, walked normally, and had no trembling. My heart showed some irregularity in beat that could suggest the eventual need for a pacemaker. I often thanked God that the poor old body that was not ever really in too good a shape was holding up not too badly.

As I completed my eighty-second birthday it seemed to me that my time of work could not be very much longer. Perhaps the fact that my prior Fr. Stanley Drongowski and my provincial Edward Ruane at the time asked me to write this memoir was the clearest sign of all to me that a new life lies just beyond the horizon. Stan, a preacher of talent and literary tastes, has had his scrape with death with a dangerous skin cancer that required very painful reconstructive surgery on his face. Ed, formerly a very effective homiletics professor at Aquinas, has great interest in its history, so he wanted my recollections of the Province preserved. Everything changes, but in changing uncovers the unchanging essentials. I still wrote poetry, although I read very little of the many distinguished recent poets. As a boy I greatly loved the echoing song or, rather, songs of the mockingbird, common in Oklahoma, and of poetry. The memory has made me write another poem.

ODE TO THE MOCKINGBIRD

That operatic mockingbird
which more than sixty years ago
I heard in the dark mulberry hedge
under a fine full summer moon—
running through its repertoire,
with encores now and then, until
a little farther on another mocking voice
began to answer,
and in the faintest distance still a third—
Teenaged in Oklahoma,
entranced with poetry and the ecstatic nightingale
which in that English garden for an hour
sang Keats out of his depression.

Neither depressed nor drunk, but lonely,
longing for a voice to answer me
with such sweet mockery, in song,
but not the wordless song of nature
but a voice that would call my name.

Yes, it was a hot summer and a fine full moon.
In the dark hedgerow the purple mulberries
were ripe and sweet.
I hear it in my eighties, on a windy April night
walking among the white blurs of the dogwood
in the dusk,
along the walk some purple iris
(though in Sooner State we called them "flags")
blended with the windy dark,
catching my shoe in dead twigs

swept from the new-leaved trees.

The song repeated then and now
in my deaf ears and a long memory
has called me to this poem
and brings to mind both a long life
and the approach of death
with such a varied melody, so sweet, so mocking
in the midst of the half-hour meditation
I make each day, of which I pray
a third to the Holy Spirit,
by him to the Son,
with the Son to the Father,
each a third of the half hour,
each ten minutes, walking in twilight,
not in the chapel, or my room,
in this St. Louis neighborhood
where Sarah Teasdale and Tom Eliot lived,
a poets' place, with flowering trees.
John Keats heard the vocal spirit
that inspired his ode
in that unvaried voice among the leaves,
unseen, forlorn.

Walking an old man's pace alone
I hear that song as nature's voice,
just as I heard it then
out of the prairie of an Okie June
in the symphony of dry wind and scratchy katydids
in that wide empty space,
but here in a city neighborhood a little sheltered
from the muffled surf of traffic.
Yet now I hear no longer
the mocking voice of poetry and youth
nor a concordance of natural sounds
but the Spirit's voice
calling me with the Son to the Father—

The virtuoso mimicry
not of a literary nightingale

but our own, real mockingbird
that made me truly young
now echoes the voices of the dead
who live again,
not in my memory merely
but in the timeless Word,
the ever-varied Song,
never repeating, never the same
that will call me once and for all
by name,
but only in His Name.

Thank God for the years he has given me in his service! Although to be honest I must confess that I have wasted his gifts in scattered and sporadic efforts and have not always used them with the purest motives. After all it is His work only, carried out by his Holy Spirit, that can and will fulfill his promise. Yet I have taught many of my confreres and have always been an interested, though sometimes alarmed and critical, witness of the development of my Order and my province in it. Long ago I wrote an article on "Retirement or Vigil"[297] (1972); now it applies to myself. In it I said that often in the New Testament we are urged to "Keep awake! The Kingdom of God is at hand!" and in the Early Church this note of watching was celebrated liturgically by night vigils of which our Easter Vigil is the reminder. In the same way the end of life for the Christian is not wasted, but is a vigil.

A good place to keep watch is in a garden. Our Lord watched for his final hour in the garden of Gethsemane. I have always lived in a garden. In Blackwell the open country was close at hand, at the universities of Chicago and Notre Dame, Washington and Houston each campus was a park, in River Forest we were surrounded by extensive monastery grounds, in Dubuque my room overlooked a golf course and a park that had been the grounds of a mental asylum, and here in St. Louis when I lived in St. Louis Bertrand Priory the extensive Forest Park was just at hand, and now in Jesuit Hall there is a little park outside my fifth story window where I looked down on students playing with their dogs. The biblical symbol of the Garden is in this poem:

GARDENS

Three gardens:
    New flowers clothe a virgin Eve
    as from leaf shadows slides the seducing snake,

    Night fog of olive branches veil Jesus a-tremble,
    hearing sly footsteps at the creaking gate,

    Magdalen, demon free, starts at the Gardner's
    shadow
    her swollen eyes in the tomb's shadows blinded by
    dawn.

And the fourth,
    Between twelve trees heavy with healing fruit
    the lucent river smooths below the lustrous gates
    of the Lamb's city.

And thus O Thou, O Thou,
    our wounded Sun,
    low in the dawning skies,
    trampling our aging shadows,
    rise
    upon this ultimate garden,
    virgin new.

Another feature of these my later years had been living in St. Louis Bertrand Priory in a small community of six or seven priests where "togetherness" was intensified. After my return from Washington the eccentric Fr. Ralph Austin Powell, whom I mentioned in Chapter 18, and I were often the only ones in the priory and we prayed and usually ate lunch together. Our ages and intellectual interests made us twins in the eyes of many of the younger men. Ralph did not teach regularly after we came to St. Louis but every day put in many hours of study and writing. In Dubuque he had already found a disciple in John Deely, who was for a time a student in the Order. Together they pondered the difficult works of Martin Heidegger and then moved on to the new field of Semiotics. Deely eventually became head of the philosophy department at Loras College, Dubuque and is now teaching at the Center for Thomistic Studies, the University of St. Thomas in Houston.

In their massive bilingual addition and commentary on the *Tractatus de Signis*[298] of the great Baroque Dominican Thomist, Jean Poinsot (John of St. Thomas, 1589-1644)) Ralph and Deely show that St. Augustine and Poinsot were in fact the fathers of semiotic theory. This work was favorably reviewed in *The New York Times* by the noted semiotician and novelist, Umberto Ecco. Ralph published a number of other articles in semiotic journals, but had little interest in reaching a wide audience. In Chapter 18 mentioned his book on the separation of Church and State. He published two other books that, since he did nothing to promote them, got little attention, with titles that have amused some, such as his Louvain dissertation, *Truth or Absolute Nothing* on the French Catholic idealist philosopher, Jules Lachelier (d. 1918). His principal publication, however, was titled *Freely Chosen Reality.*[299] The last work set out to prove that most modern philosophers now agree with Aquinas' view that "relations" are real and not merely, as Nominalism held, mind-dependent, and also that it is only through these real relations that "substance" is knowable. Therefore, he believed that to make Thomism credible to our contemporaries we must take real relations, not substance, as the point of departure for all philosophical analysis.

Powell was also striving to develop an understanding of modern science somewhat different than that of the rest of us of the River Forest School, that is, of the Albertus Magnus Lyceum. While most of its members, including myself, sought to show that natural philosophy is about changeable substances (*ens mobile*) and as such explicable in terms of the four Aristotelian causes, Powell, without denying our approach, sought rather to consider modern science as it actually is, namely a mathematical physics, whose validity was admitted by Aristotle and Aquinas but considered secondary to a science of *ens mobile*. Powell's key concept was that of a fifth type of causality whose full recognition he attributed to Jean Poinsot, namely "extrinsic formal causality" found in real measurement relations. The mathematical character of modern science requires it to abstract from efficient and final types of Aristotelian causality. Thus, it reduces the other two types of causes to relations of measurement, but this still leaves extrinsic formal causality available for a mathematicized natural science to provide genuinely causal explanations of natural phenomena in their concrete, physical reality. Thus, Powell, maintained, it is not necessary to deny the genuinely causal character of modern scientific explanations, and through these, it is possible to establish the knowability of human nature and hence of the natural moral law. At least that is the best description I can give of this daring and fascinating philosophical proposal.

Like Penelope at her loom, Ralph for twenty years worked on the *magnum opus* that he constantly unraveled and rewove. This work aimed at saving the concept of "natural moral law" on which Thomistic ethical theory is grounded by approaching it not from the concept of a "substantial human nature" as has been traditional among Thomists, but from the real relations of persons to other persons and things. When I was researching for my book, *The Dominicans*, I learned that many Dominican scholars of the past labored long on difficult problems, only to leave their manuscripts in the archives. I, however, have preferred publication to profundity.

Ralph and I certainly came to know each other very well and in fact went to confession to each other as well as almost daily celebrated Mass together. Yet for all this constant companionship, no two persons could be on such different wavelengths and our community was often disturbed by our constant and often heated "dialogue." What we argued about was principally the different ways that we saw the present life of the Church. Ralph regarded himself primarily as a philosopher and me as a theologian, but had difficulty in viewing my thinking as anything but one of pessimistic conservatism. He was often troubled that our confreres and the faculty of Aquinas Institute also seem to regard me as such.

Yet, because of his European orientation and his constant struggle with idealism, not only our personal temperaments but our philosophical and theological outlooks never jibed. His many original insights arouse from his sensitivity to the ways the modern world sees Catholicism as intellectually outmoded and even absurd. With deep faith and constant, contemplative prayer, he struggled always to see the Catholic Church through the eyes of outsiders. Since I myself was once an outsider from Blackwell, OK, this is not at all my way of looking at things. Yet I have greatly profited from such of Ralph's insights, as I have understood them.

Ralph constantly surprised me with what he saw in books and in the world that was so unlike my own perceptions. He cared little for consistency in what he said, preferring to expand the insight of the moment. I was told that once on the last day of class in a philosophy course he had taught, he strode enthusiastically into the room and said to the startled students, "Tear up your notes, Brothers, everything I have said in this course was wrong!" Every day at lunch our fraternal dialogue often exploded, but before sunset he would always ask pardon for any rudeness on his part. If it had not been for his humility and transparent goodness, our disputes would have driven us apart, but instead they forged between us a deeper friendship.

Ralph's central concern for ecumenism led him to take the side of the liberal opinion in its evaluation of Vatican II and its aftermath. Hence he often charged me with being deaf to the liberal faction in the Church. Yet at that same time many of his attitudes were super-traditional, since he wanted to return to what he believed was the simplicity of the early Church. He especially wanted to do away with the Vatican Curia and the designation of the Pope as "Supreme Pontiff," a title of pagan origin.. Moreover, his other intense interest, derived from Goetz Briefs, was in the social doctrine of the Church and in the success of Christian Democracy in Europe in establishing a "corporate" state. He, too optimistically I think, believed that the European Union had for the first time in history overcome poverty and thus shown itself much superior to American democracy with its foolish trust in the free market.

It was Ralph who gave me the clue to understanding modernity, namely, that the real enemy of the Church in our times is the secular humanism of the Enlightenment and that this arose as a punishment from God for the religious wars of the Reformation period. Yet I was constantly exasperated by what seemed to me the wild inconsistency of his thinking and his tendency to erect elaborate theories on very slender data so as to project his hopes for ecumenism on a very complex and discouraging reality. He constantly asked me what I thought of his theories and then we argued endlessly when I tried to point out what I consider to be the hard and not always pleasant facts. He complained, on the contrary not only of my conservatism but that I monopolized the conversation. Typically such an argument ended by him saying, "Well we are different, and isn't that wonderful!"

I would have preferred, however, to find genuine common ground and was not happy with his conviction that I am a conservative defender of the status quo in the Church and could never face change. I am sure that God, who of course has an infinitely greater sense of humor than I have, put us together in our old age for the benefit of us both.

THE BEST DEFENSE IS AN OFFENSE

"You never listen!"
I must admit the truth of what I hear you say...

How can I listen
if I do not say what I hear you say
       just as I think it makes some sense
       and lest I say it quickly before we lose it?

Sometimes I interrupt, always I interrupt.
Sometimes I say what I know you will say before you
       have a chance to say it,
but also I speak before
       I have a chance to think
       because only in saying is thought born live!

Listening is responding.
To hear you is to speak to me
       as you make me alive
       to you
when the horizons of our two worlds
       concenter.

Oh, there is a deaf listening
       that takes in,
       sucks up,
       or echoes like an iron wall!

I would rather interrupt,
       make you fight for your speaking space.

Now at last I am listening...

Somehow all I hear from you seems like
       the dead repetition

of my own dead thoughts.
Are you repeating what you heard from that famous time
          that for once you listened?
I was not inspired that day.

Better we battle,
          loud arguments growing irrational.
          Hours and years
          will they remain to think it over,
find the sense of what you said,
          admit that you were right?

Chapter 24 - Moral Theological Battles

The Revision of the Directives for Catholic Health Care Services

I noted in Chapter 18 that a basic feature of a spirituality of aging is that although our bodies are failing and need medical attention we must in spirit pass beyond too much concern for our physical needs. St. Paul says, "But you are not in the flesh; on the contrary, you are in the spirit, if only the Spirit of God dwells in you,"(Rom 8:9). In 1995, my eye infection and a cataract and prostate operation and then in 1999 heart bypass surgery, as well as diabetes, and in 2010, heart failure hindered some of my work. It was only by the time of that last surgery that, though somewhat weary, I could still travel a good deal.

During these years I continued to go to Washington, DC and other cities as a consultant for the Committee on Doctrine of the NCCB. As I related in the preceding chapter, the concerns of the Committee when I first began to act as a consultant had to do chiefly with the relations between the bishops and theologians. During the period I am now discussing, however, its main problem was the revision of the *Ethical and Religious Directives for Catholic Health Care Facilities* that had been issued in 1971, with some revisions in 1975, by the United States Catholic Conference.[300] Such an ethics code had been preceded as early as 1955 by one proposed by the hospitals themselves through the Catholic Hospital Association.

To decide on whether such a revision was needed in view of changing medical practices, the Committee on Doctrine sought the advice of existing Catholic bioethics centers in the U.S., and a number of other medical ethicists who were actually engaged in counseling hospitals. Almost unanimously they agreed that such a revision was timely. They also made many suggestions as to the form it should take, and asked that it be no longer than just a list of "do not's" but a pastoral document explaining the aims of Catholic health ministry and making explicit the principles on which the concrete directives were based.

Because Jesus was both victim and healer, the Church is always concerned with physical health since it is so intimately related to spiritual health. Even the beauty in the world reminds us that it is a suffering world.

MEDITATION ON A ROSE IN A BOWL

Red rose,
  red, red, redder than any rose dares be,
  you fill the infinite hollow of my eye with an expanding
    blow,
  soft as one petal
  floating down.

Blue sky, white snow,
  so blue you are infinity
  opening
  beyond.

My room a still space,
rose at the center,
sky, snow beyond the one window.

Dying light
  bleeding to death
  in this one drop
  of life.

In the still space
  where my heart once lived,
  Let the rose
  bleed.

To Holy Father Dominic, we brothers daily pray,
  naming him *Rosa patientiae,*
  the "rose of suffering,"
  remembering how each night he scourged himself
  throwing his bleeding body over the mouth of hell
  lest death and the devil
  swallow poor sinners.

The small suffering I have borne
is no more than one, cold drop...
  may the Spirit's love warm it
  red, red,
  redder than this
  fading rose.

The bishops on the Committee on Doctrine as they worked on the revision of the *Directives* wanted not mere "guidelines" such as the Canadian bishops had issued, but precise instructions having authoritative force. During much of this time, Fr. John Boyle of the University of Iowa and I, since we were the two consultants in matters of moral theology, were especially involved in studying medical ethical questions that came before the Committee. Boyle, however, was generally rather reserved in the discussions, because, I believe, he felt his opinions (leaning more to the "liberal" side, as indicated by his book on sterilization[301]) were less acceptable to the majority of the bishops on the committee than were mine. Nevertheless, we were often, but not always, in agreement.

The procedure of the Committee on Doctrine was to work from a draft diligently prepared by two young professors of moral theology chosen by the bishop in charge of the Committee on Health Affairs. It happened that both had received their doctorates from the Gregorian University in Rome under Josef Fuchs, SJ, the main proponent of the theory of proportionalism as a system of ethical decision. This guaranteed that the draft was the work of theologians who were very competent but who certainly could not be considered theologically conservative. It was the general opinion of the Committee (with which I too agreed) that this draft was a very well constructed document, presenting an excellent exposition of the Christian purpose of health care and the broad principles governing it, having a strongly positive and pastoral, rather than legalistic tone.

The difficulties came, of course, in formulating the concrete directives. In the 1975 version of the code there were only 43 such directives and these were clearly and unambiguously stated. The proposed new directives numbered 66 in order to cover the chief points of present practical concern and showed an excellent grasp of current hospital dilemmas. Personally, however, I thought this was too many directives and urged they be somewhat consolidated. The arguments of the drafters on this point, however, prevailed. When the many actual directives were examined, though none were in explicit dissent from the many Church documents on bioethics, not a few were so vaguely stated as to leave room for broad interpretations not consistent with the manifest intent of these Church documents. They seem to open the way for a legalistic, minimalizing casuistry; the very thing the bishops needed to avoid.

Though several of the bishops immediately expressed their dissatisfaction with the ambiguities of the drafted directives, as the Committee reviewed directive after directive, most of the burden of pointing this out in detail fell to me (since Boyle made only occasional interventions) to question this lack of precision. This of course was not very pleasant for the drafters, since they had to defend their document to the bishops point after point against my critical observations. I was happy that the drafters accepted this in a good spirit, but it was a tedious, fractious process. Happily the document in its final, much debated form was found acceptable to the Vatican *Congregation for the Doctrine of the Faith* to whom the Committee sent it for comment.

Why it is so essential to state Catholic teaching on these bioethical questions in as unambiguous language as possible was made clear to me on another occasion. The Vatican inquired of the Committee on Doctrine why some bishops were permitting a procedure called "uterine isolation" in hospitals in their dioceses. Better informed Catholic physicians, including my friend Dr. Herbert Ratner, previously mentioned, had long protested this procedure on the grounds that it is simply a form of contraceptive sterilization condemned by *Humanae Vitae* but under a euphemistic name.

In order to reply to this enquiry of the Holy See, and in view of the difficulty for bishops to stop practices they had, usually on the advice of theologians, already approved, the Committee on Doctrine made a very careful study of the matter. To complete this study the Committee with its consultants interviewed two very prominent Catholic gynecologists who were fine Catholics of high professional probity. Yet, as I listened to their answers to the bishops' questions, I was struck by how little thought these teaching physicians had given to reconciling their professional decisions and their Christian outlook on reality. Their professional thinking and their faith-guided ethical thinking were on two different tracks between which there was no exchange. It was evident that the philosophy and theology these doctors had learned in Catholic schools had done little to overcome in their minds the divorce between science and theology that in this memoir I have so often bewailed.

"Uterine isolation," so euphemistically named, was defended by the argument that if a uterine pathology indicates that a future pregnancy might be dangerous for the patient and if formerly this pathology was usually corrected by a hysterectomy, then the less invasive procedure of tubal ligation is both medically and ethically justified. The weakness of this argument is that although both hysterectomy and tubal ligation sterilize a woman, the pathologies of the uterus that can be remedied by hysterectomy cannot be remedied by a tubal ligation. The real purpose of tubal ligation is not to treat a present pathology but to render future fertile acts of intercourse sterile as a means to prevent a pregnancy. Granted that the woman with a pathological uterus has a good reason to avoid a pregnancy, that good end is obtained by a bad means, namely contraceptive sterilization, and could usually be obtained by an ethically good means, the practice of periodic sexual abstention (Natural Family Planning).

To this criticism the proponents of "uterine isolation," however, reply by noting that Catholic moralists generally justify certain forms of mutilation that are not curative but merely preventive. For example, moralists hold that missionaries may ethically avoid the risk of appendicitis at a place remote from any hospital by having an elective appendectomy before leaving home. This reply, however, fails to consider that while an appendix can be removed without destroying a major human function, the immediate purpose of the tubal ligation is to permanently destroy a woman's ability to conceive and, therefore, is a contraceptive act, not an act to prevent further pathology. Therefore, as a result of this study the Committee on Doctrine replied to Holy See's inquiry that it would attempt to enforce the Church's teaching on this question. Yet their efforts to stop such procedures in Catholic hospitals, I have reason to believe, have not yet been completely successful.

Such pragmatic attempts to evade Church teaching, often concealed by ambiguous language, with which the revision of the *Directives* had to deal, became most evident in regard to the "joint ventures" in which, under the pressure of the great changes in our health care system, Catholic hospitals are now being forced to engage. Moral theologians have always considered the distinction between "formal and material cooperation" one of the most difficult principles to apply in practice. One cooperates *formally* with unethical actions by facilitating them by action, approval, or failure to prevent them when possible. But one cooperates only *materially* when one foresees that one's cooperation with others in ethically good affairs indirectly assists them to promote other unethical projects. For example, a citizen materially cooperates when he dutifully pays taxes to the government to support civic law and order, but foresees that politicians may divert some of these monies to serve their own unethical purposes.

If we could never ethically engage in such materially cooperative endeavors we would have to neglect many of our moral obligations. Therefore, in order to prevent material cooperation from degenerating into formal cooperation we must be sure that (1) the good we seek to accomplish could not be otherwise accomplished; that (2) it will exceed the evil we foresee our partners will do; that (3) we have done what we can to prevent or mitigate this evil; (4) that we in no way directly approve or participate in their evil acts; and finally (5) that our cooperation does not tempt others to do evil.

The CDF has always held that abortion can never be justified on grounds of material cooperation, but it has left the way open for possible toleration of contraceptive sterilization in a joint venture between a Catholic and non-Catholic hospital, provided the traditional criteria of licit material cooperation are observed with "great prudence." Thus the Catholic partner of such a joint venture cannot perform such sterilizations, nor profit from or promote them, or tempt others to perform them ("give scandal"). Because of the complexity in explaining the conditions of legitimate cooperation our committee decided to provide only a brief appendix on the subject that did no more than refer bishops to the "standard authors." When the Vatican CDF reviewed our draft it suggested that it would be more helpful for bishops if we expanded this appendix to summarize these traditional criteria.

Because a national meeting of the NCCB at which this document would be voted on was immediately at hand, this expanded appendix had to be prepared very quickly. Hence, its final version was left to a subcommittee, with unfortunate results, because, as published, this appendix was open to the interpretation that the performance of intrinsically wrong acts (e.g. sterilization) can be justified by "duress." While some older authors seemed to have accepted this view with qualifications, it is very difficult to reconcile it to the basic principle, now affirmed by the encyclical of John Paul II, *The Splendor of Truth* (1993), that nothing can ever justify deliberately participating even under duress in acts that are intrinsically evil, such as are sterilization and abortion, since this really amounts to formal cooperation. The examples given by the older authors mentioned seem to be cases where the duress is such that it removes freedom of choice and hence are only equivocally "cooperation." Acts of surgical sterilization, of course, cannot be performed without deliberate choice. When I learned of this problem, I urged the chairman of the Committee to issue a note of clarification. Fortunately, the Holy See has recently informed the bishops of the ambiguity of this reference to duress and made the correct teaching clear.

I believe that the new Directives provide sound and useful guidance for health care and I am proud to have had some share in their revision, although most of the work in writing this ethical guide was not mine, but that of the drafters and the bishops. Like any document, however, it requires an honest interpretation that does not undermine or evade the consistent teaching of the Church. Such directives must not be treated legalistically as mere positive laws whose obligations are to be interpreted leniently. They rest on the Church's teaching as to what is of help and what is harmful to human dignity. If the healing mission of the Church is to be effective it must really seek to heal the whole person, not only physically but morally, and not make excuses out of expediency for what is known to be harmful to the integrity of the human person and the community.

The real problem, of course, is to enforce these Directives in Catholic hospitals which are often now under the control of a lay board and served by a largely non-Catholic medical staff. Even the Catholic members of the board and administration are often uninformed or misinformed about Church teaching. Hence, I proposed that the Committee include a directive which would explicitly require the administrators of each hospital to meet with the local bishop so that all might mutually agree upon a due process for dealing with such ethical issues, appropriate for local conditions, and that this process be incorporated in the hospital's bylaws. The Committee, however, perhaps afraid of imposing on fellow bishops any further responsibilities than the great load they already bear, felt that my suggested directive went too far. They were satisfied with a statement asserting the bishop's right of doctrinal supervision, but which says nothing about how this is to be implemented or enforced. Therefore, I fear that our Catholic health ministry, like our Catholic universities whose perilous situation was exposed by the Curran affair, is also in grave danger of secularization unless our bishops take more decisive action.

The importance of such action is illustrated by a recent situation in which the Jesuit President of St. Louis University and its lay board, against the express opposition of Archbishop Justin Rigali, decided to sell its teaching hospital to the huge secular, pro-profit hospital corporation called Tenet. Such actions raise a serious question about whether our Catholic educational and hospital ministries in the United States can survive, or will succumb to secularization as have the Protestant institutions once so influential in our country.

Three More Bioethical Debates

Besides my work as a consultant in the revision of the Directives I was especially involved in three other difficult and important bioethics controversies. The first two of these had to do with the beginning of life. One concerned the question, "When Did I Begin?"[302] The other concerned abortion, the most politicized bioethical issue today. The Catholic Church unequivocally declares that abortion, because it is the killing of an innocent person, intends to do what is intrinsically evil and hence cannot be justified by any circumstances or other good intentions. Yet without dissenting from this judgment some Catholic theologians have questioned when human personhood begins and even appealed to the scientifically outmoded opinions of such medieval theologians as St. Thomas Aquinas and Duns Scotus who on the basis of the ancient embryology held theories of "delayed hominization." Hence, the Pope John Center (now the National Catholic Bioethics Center) commissioned a biologist Albert S. Moraczewski, OP, and myself to coauthor a study, "Is the Biological Subject of Human Rights Present From Conception?"[303] which developed research that I had already published in 1976 in an article, "A Critique of the Theory of Delayed Hominization."[304] Albert and I have recently developed this theme still further in another article, "Cloning, Aquinas, and the Embryonic Person."[305]

In these essays Albert and I have tried to show that although Aquinas' criteria for determining the time of the hominization of the embryo are sound, his application of these valid principles to the data then available led him to accept the hypothesis of delayed hominization that has now been falsified by modern embryology. In fact when his principles are applied to modern data, it becomes biologically certain, that the complete human organism is present from the moment that the human ovum is fertilized by the human sperm. On philosophical and theological grounds this biological conclusion can only mean that human ensoulment and personhood begins at conception taken in the sense of fertilization.

We also showed that current biology contradicts the notion favored by Charles Curran, Richard McCormick and others that because it is only at the time of the implantation of the embryo that the formation of identical twins becomes impossible, it is only then that is certain that any individuated organism actually exists. Therefore, since until this organic individuation takes place, human ensoulment is impossible, the pre-embryo (that is the conceptus prior to implantation) cannot be a human person. To the contrary, we argued that the biological data clearly demonstrate that individuation occurs at the fertilization of the ovum and it must be then that a new member of the human species comes into existence. After that this unique human organism requires no further individuation, but simply the maturing differentiation of its functional parts.

Therefore the argument from twinning is fallacious; because the production of the second identical twin presupposes that the first individuated twin already exists and continues to exist otherwise the second could not be cloned from the first. Thus our recently acquired understanding of the cloning process has outmoded all delayed hominization theories. The famous cloned sheep Dolly would never have existed if the mother sheep from which she was cloned had not existed as an individual before her. As I studied this issue, I puzzled more and more about how odd it is that some theologians with total inconsistency enthusiastically promote environmental ecology, yet ignore the harmonious teleology the Creator has built into his creation!

How could the teleology of nature be more dramatically exemplified then in the embryological development of an organism from a single cell to marvelously complex maturity! I am also constantly haunted by the fact that in the United States over a million children a year are exterminated in the womb. Thus our genocide has surpassed that of Hitler! What right then do we have to cry out before God about the few thousand of our countrymen killed by terrorists imitating our rationalized violence?

Hydration and Nutrition

At the other end of life than contraception and abortion is a third bioethical issue debated among Catholic moralists, even those who do not dissent from Church teaching. This issue concerns the problem of the care of patients who have been medically judged to be irreversibly unconscious. They are in what physicians call a "persistent vegetative state" (PVS). This term is misleading, since these are not vegetables but are still living human persons. Moreover, their condition is not just "persistent" but must instead be irreversible. The bishops and consultants on the Committee for Doctrine were of one mind on this issue, but we had to give due consideration to another "safer" opinion maintained by the Pro-Life Committee of the NCCB and by some regional conferences of bishops concerned not to give an inch to the promoters of euthanasia lest they take a mile. Certainly all patients should be given at least "comfort" or "palliative" care, that is, what classical moralists called obligatory "ordinary" care, but in what does that consist? The Vatican CDF instruction On Euthanasia in 1980[306] reformulated the traditional Catholic distinction between "ordinary" and "extraordinary care" of the sick by saying that care is "extraordinary," and therefore not morally obligatory, if the benefit to the patient is less than the burden to the patient and to those who care for them. It is never wise or just to impose moral obligations on anyone, unless these can be well established. The Holy See, although often queried on the subject, has never qualified this teaching except to commend prudence in its application.

My fraternal colleague, Fr. Kevin O'Rourke, who has had firsthand experience with PVS cases and has argued the issue in many publications and concluded that the principle by which "benefit" of any form of medical or nursing care is to be measured is not whether it maintains physical life. Of course, human physical life is something good in itself (*bonum per se*), but in the hierarchy of human goods it is subordinated to higher spiritual goods. Hence, classical Catholic ethics has always maintained that the true principle on which to decide whether a certain mode of care for human persons is beneficial is whether it will enable them to perform at least some specifically human acts that can further that person's journey to the true goal of human life, union with God. From a Christian perspective this is the principle that has always been used to explain why martyrdom, especially that of Jesus on the Cross, is not suicide.

Forms of care that do not meet these standards are not morally obligatory. In fact, they may be morally forbidden as imprudent since they prevent the caretakers from engaging in the fulfillment of other moral obligations, such as the truly beneficial care of others. This conforms to another important principle of medical ethics, namely, that of "triage" by which in a situation of limited resources those who will benefit the most from care should be the first to receive it.

Therefore, it would seem that if it is medically certain that a patient can never again make specifically human acts, only such care as respects the human dignity of the unconscious person remains obligatory, and the process of dying due to the patient's pathology may be permitted to take its natural course. The phrase "such care as respects human dignity" refers not so much to the unconscious patient as to the feelings of the caretakers and means first that it is never permitted to directly kill the patient, and second that good hygiene be observed.[307]

Many pro-life activists, however, argue that physical life is an "incommensurable" benefit that it is intrinsically wrong to violate. They contend that hydration and nutrition, even if these have to be given artificially, is always morally obligatory unless the patient is actually dying or at least finds them disproportionately painful and for those totally unconscious no treatment is burdensome. As for the burden to the caretakers, it is argued that the administration of hydration and nutrition by tubes is a relatively easy procedure and hence is only a light burden for the caretaker. They fear that if physicians are permitted to cease giving hydration and nutrition to any patient except those actually dying the door will be opened to euthanasia. To the contrary it is argued that once persons have been conservatively diagnosed as irreversibly unconscious, artificial means of sustaining their lives are of no benefit to them. To insist that this care be continued places a useless and often very heavy burden on others that will make the arguments for euthanasia seem compelling.

Yet John Paul II not long before his own death in an address to World Federation of Catholic Medical Associations, March 20, 2004, deplored the term "persistent vegetative state" for the condition of persons diagnosed as irreversibly unconscious, and seemed to accept the medical opinion that all such persons may be at least minimally conscious and hence to be kept alive by hydration and nutrition. The United States Bishops, therefore, requested a clarification of this point from the Holy See and received it from the Congregation for the Doctrine of the Faith, September, 2007 approved by Benedict XVI. This reply states "The administration of food and water even by artificial means is, in principle, an ordinary and proportionate means of preserving life," according to the Congregation's response. "It is therefore obligatory to the extent to which, and for as long as, it is shown to accomplish its proper finality, which is the hydration and nourishment of the patient. In this way suffering and death by starvation and dehydration are prevented" and this holds" regardless of the prognosis of recovery of consciousness." In a commentary some exceptions were noted,

> "When stating that the administration of food and water is morally obligatory in principle, the Congregation for the Doctrine of the Faith does not exclude the possibility that, in very remote places or in situations of extreme poverty, the artificial provision of food and water may be physically impossible.... Nor is the possibility excluded that, due to emerging complications, a patient may be unable to assimilate food and liquids, so that their provision becomes altogether useless. Finally, the possibility is not absolutely excluded that, in some rare cases, artificial nourishment and hydration may be excessively burdensome for the patient or may cause significant physical discomfort, for example resulting from complications in the use of the means employed.... These exceptional cases, however, take nothing away from the general ethical criterion, according to which the provision of water and food, even by artificial means, always represents a natural means for preserving life, and is not a therapeutic treatment. Its use should therefore be considered ordinary and proportionate, even when the 'vegetative state' is prolonged."

This answer does not contradict the Congregation's 1980 *Declaration on Euthanasia* on which O'Rourke and I had based our arguments and does not, it is essential to point out, approve the moral theory of Germain Grisez as to "incommensurable goods" but it does reject O'Rourke's and my view that artificial hydration and nutrition are not, as such, "ordinary care" required for all patients. It seems to me that John Paul II's 2004 address was influenced by the growing support for euthanasia and by recent medical opinion that a good many cases that had been diagnosed as PVS were in fact states of minimal consciousness. Is such a declaration infallible? The Congregation for the Doctrine of the Faith in its document *On the Ecclesial Vocation of the Theologian*, n. 24,[308] gives as a fourth degree of magisterial authority the following:

> Finally, in order to serve the People of God as well as possible, in particular, by warning them of dangerous opinions which could

lead to error, the Magisterium can intervene in questions under discussion which involve, in addition to solid principles, certain contingent and conjectural elements. It often only becomes possible with the passage of time to distinguish between what is necessary and what is contingent.

Since, however, magisterial authority is of a higher order than theological reasoning I have honestly (although embarrassedly) accepted the Vatican's judgment on this matter and I cite this debate especially to show how difficult some of these borderline cases in moral theology can be, as with a headache I have often experienced. This question of dying, of course, is more than speculative, since the image of my mortality is ever present and has emerged in several of my poems two of which I cite to show that I am not thinking about the matter in mere abstractions.

AUTUMN

At four I woke to find
  a ghost by my bed,
  the harvest moon
  low in the sky.
Yes, I will die.

This afternoon,
  leaf flames descending
  into this clear pool,
  the birds ascending south,
while melting in the mouth
  the pear flushes,
  or the apple blushes.
On the withering vine
  the grape gushes
  blood-red the wine.
Bluer than blue
  above treetops yellow, red
  (but some green leaves tarry)
  an open sky.

All must die? Must you?

Yes... I too...I too...I too.

FIRESIDE

Grey hill on hill,
        snow reaches a fierce red line
        where the day shuts down.

In this closed room
        by this red fire I brood,
        chill at my back like death.

I doze and spring begins anew,
        quivering green in the delicate wind,
        stars in the grass and petals on the water,

My Lord, nearer than fire on my face
        even than that chill at my back,
        farther than a summer
        that will never flower...

By the fire I brood
        chill
        at my back.

Grey, aging, dozing...
"Ah, would that the Spirit's flame,
(that Spirit who is Love),
as that fire in the grate
grays the log to ashes,
totally, finally, fiercely,
enkindle and
consume me!

Out of the flying sparks
I see
flame-winged
a phoenix rising!

These intricate biomedical problems are rather gloomy topics to be pondering on. I wonder if my gloomy preoccupation made me hard to live within community life where good cheer is so much appreciated.

BEING CHEERFUL

Gently my confessor,
"You once were known as always cheerful,
in aging where has gone your joy?"

Well, well,
now as always, even at ninety,
cold and warmth,
color, music, food and drink,
comfort, sleep,
thinking, company,
talking, reading, laughter.
all these I still enjoy.

But enjoyment's not joy.
Joy is a friend present.
My Lord, best friend,
is present in my waking, sleeping,
in my enjoyments, in my distress,
my disappointment, fear, and anger,
often in questioning,
by night, in days
yet, for faith, there always.

But that presence is silent,
veiled in the Sacrament
that begs for faith,
enforces hope,
with a present love.

Such joy is sorrow,
grief for past forgetting.
fear of future letting go;
care for the critical moment.

One by one the years tarnish,
the sterling silver of our vows.

Yet my young cheer
hid the same sorrows, the old griefs,
and the same Friend was there always
in word, in sacrament, in prayer.
What age unveils
is this mystery of presence in absence,
the immanently transcendent
Presence,
nearer to me than I am
to myself.

In cheerless age
    changing enjoyment
to vigil,
You, You are Joy.

In this period I wrote a number of essays on bioethical topics, often inspired by my work with the Committee on Doctrine. Thus I wrote "What is Moral Theology?",[309] and "The Development of Moral Doctrine: Change and the Unchanging"[310] read at the Bishops' workshop in Dallas in 1995 to show how theological principles do not change but our understanding of them can undergo development. It was for the Center also I that presented "The Documents of Catholic Identity"[311] at that same workshop in 1996 to show the present state of Church teaching on bioethics. Once more in 1997 at that workshop I talked on "The Current Revival of the Sense of Moral Obligation: Autonomy and the Common Good"[312] to analyze the causes of the present state of moral confusion in the United States. Dealing with such entangled problems and my work on the Directives helped me help Fr. O'Rourke in the fourth and fifth and revised editions of our *Health Care Ethics: A Theological Analysis*, as it was taken over by Georgetown University Press.[313] I have also formulated my concept in recent years of this discipline in a brief article "Health Care Ethics" in the *Encyclopedia of U.S. Biomedical Policy*.[314] After these efforts my consultancy for the bishops has been only occasional, including the writing of a commentary on the Committee's document, "On Anencephalic Infants and Their Care" that was printed in the Vatican's *L'Osservatore Romano*.[315]

Ambiguity in Moral Theology

My work on the Ethical and Religious Directives made evident to me how much damage has been done to current Catholic moral theology by the ambiguities and arbitrariness introduced by Proportionalism, as I argued in the preceding chapter. One of the chief the sources of proportionalism seems to have been a famous article, "On the Question of a Formal Existential Ethics,"[316] written by Karl Rahner, SJ, although Rahner never declared himself a pro-portion-alist. Hence in a symposium of the Rahner Society in 1995 I pointed out this obscurity of his ethical thought in a paper, "Funda-mental Option And/Or Commitment to Ultimate End."[317] The other two speakers, Professor Jean Porter and Fr. Timothy O'Connell also concluded that the notion of fundamental option has proved of little practical help in actual moral decision making. Yet they praised Rahner for his emphasis on the "ambiguity of moral decision." But, I ask, what moral theologian was ever unaware of this ambiguity? It was precisely this inevitable ambiguity that the old legalistic casu-istry, today under revision, was all about. Personally, through my painful struggles with scruples, I realize this ambiguity of moral decision most vividly. But this fact of moral ambiguity should not be made an excuse to be content with an impractical obscurity in ethics.

I have had the pastoral experience of counseling people suffer-ing not only from neuroses, like scrupulosity, but from psychoses. The tragedy of these situations is precisely that the victim has lost touch with the concrete reality that Aquinas made his epistemologi-cal basis and brought into his ethics and which enables us to arrive at moral certitude. Moral certitude differs from theoretical certitude in that even when I only have theoretical probability that a certain action is objectively moral, I still can be morally certain that the ac-tion is a prudent one, what I ought to do in the given circumstances in which I must act. I was for several years the spiritual director of a friend, T. C., who was schizophrenic. His sufferings showed me how important it is to keep in touch with reality as it is in its brute fac-ticity and act on such certitudes as one can achieve and not on fan-tasies. God is the Really Real and our world, for all its absurdities, receives its truly real though dependent existence from and in Him.

Hence we primarily know God not in the hidden depths of our subjectivity, but first of all in the facts of his creation and through our own nature as manifested in our public behavior. Once, as I walked in a park near where I was living and was meditating on the problems of another young man I was counseling who was suffering from bipolar disorder, I wrote the following poem.

WALK IN FOREST PARK

December, Christmas chill.
A hundred crows, more maybe
    flap through the trees of the empty park
    startled by a black leathered rider
    and a black horse.
Now come a few joggers, in tight black too a girl,
troubling the space as the crows settle
under the drooping sky
in December dusk, the dead lagoon
pacified by frozen scum.

Visiting me today my manic friend
scattered his thoughts
like scattering crows
(off his lithium again
for fear it's poisoned):
the Baghavad Gita, his divorce,
conversion of the Jews,
the Masons' plotting—

Mania, they say, is just the cover,
the ice-thin surface of depression.
Through my own mind a hundred—more—
black thoughts
flap cawing, scattering.

"The world is mad my masters."

"You have only one Master."
Lord, on the dark cliff over the black sea
where the swine, not a hundred, but legion,
plunge possessed, stretch out your hand

(I see the wound, but need to touch it)
the hand that from black chaos
              shapes our glowing universe
              beyond these sullen clouds,
reshape my scattered mind,
reshape our manic world,
calm down my friend!
calm down my fears!
"Peace to the world!"
at Christmas, peace.

In the dusk, under the lapsed clouds
a gold line of sunset
cuts through black boughs,
in the chilled park.
Peace?
Or the scum of ice?

The sunset line cuts through.
Under the black waves plunge
the demonic porcine legion
of crow thoughts
and cawing fears
(The black rider, the black rider).

Why? From nothing this! Here! Now!

Beyond me in the park four joggers,
Indians reclaiming their wide land?

The sunken sun for no reason here and there
displays the brown oaks, the black-green pines.
No reason I can give for the cold pale sky,
or down in the brown lagoon the stillness
after the four are gone, one after one,
that pads its jogging question after me:
the Indian four. Why not three or five or six?
Why from nothing—me? Why me, here, now?

In all its mysterious facticity I sense

your presence, Father, you who simply are.

Not lithium, Lord, but your own peace!
Lord, quiet our startled minds!
(Yes, my friend pledged
he would take his lithium,
poison or no poison).

      Exiting an emptied park
      quieted, I leave
      the manic crows
      settled for the night.

Thus, although, moral decision is complex and our fundamental commitment to a vocation or goal in life is certainly made deep in our souls at the level of insight rather than of discursive reasoning, it is still an act based on our human experience in the world. Thus it is best explained, as Aquinas explained it, in everyday, realistic language, and not in terms of our obscure subjectivity. That is why, I believe, although the famous method of spiritual direction developed by St. Ignatius Loyola emphasizes the development of an inner, "spiritual sense," he also emphasized the need of a spiritual director and the importance of "thinking with the Church" to correct too great dependence on subjectivity. Rahner, of course, as a Jesuit understood this point very well, yet his philosophical idealism and the obscurity of his notion of "fundamental option" has in fact lead some of his disciples into errors their master would have rejected.

I once had a conversation with a Christian Brother, well known as a lecturer on spirituality and a follower of Rahner. He argued with me that no sin, no matter how "serious," could be a "mortal" sin except the sin of hatred against God. But Aquinas held that one can sin mortally, without hating God, by loving some created good more than God and thus implicitly making it, rather than God, one's goal in life. Therefore John Paul II in *The Splendor of Truth* warned about the ambiguity of the term "fundamental option" and condemned the notion that between venial and mortal sin there can be "serious" sins that are not mortal. A venial sin is like a step backward on the way to God, while a mortal sin takes us altogether off that way by doing something that can never be a means to toward our goal of true happiness. Thus what make a sins "serious" is the same as what makes it "mortal," namely, that it at least implicitly is a commitment to some created good rather than God as our supreme good and ultimate goal.

Rahner was one of the Transcendental Thomists who seek to reconcile Aquinas with Kant by finding in Aquinas' epistemology an *a priori,* idealist element. But Aquinas is a thorough realist for whom our self-knowledge and hence our free commitment to an ultimate goal in life begins with our sense experience. Hence Aquinas, following Aristotle, establishes what the true goal of human living is by an anthropological study of external human behavior and from this infers the needs innate to human nature. These chief needs are four: physical health and security, family, society, and a true understanding of reality. The goods that can satisfy these needs are not just means to happiness but per se goods (ends in themselves) that are integral to our happiness, but they are also hierarchically ranked in order of their importance for our happiness.

Thus the supreme good or ultimate goal of human life is to know the truth about the world, ourselves, and our Creator. As Jesus said, "Know the truth and it will set you free" (Jn 8:32). It is this possession (contemplation) of the truth that distinguishes human beings from animals and makes possible our achievement of lesser goals while directing them to our ultimate goal.

Rahner, however, because he was an epistemological transcendentalist who leaned toward Kantian and Cartesian idealism, sought to establish our ultimate goal not from our sense experience of externally observable human behavior, but instead from our inner self-consciousness, prior to sense experience, of the self as a thinking, willing subject. This is why he replaced the term "ultimate goal" with "fundamental (a priori) option." Whatever the merits of this philosophical position, it results in an exceedingly obscure identification of our supreme good and how it is to be related to our concrete behavioral choices. I reacted unfavorably to Fr. McBrien's *Catholicism* as having a misleading title because it is more a presentation of Rahner's personal theories than the official teaching of the Catholic Church. I am also of the opinion that, although we can certainly learn much from both Descartes, Kant, and Rahner about the subjective aspects of human knowing, they give us little help in constructing a concrete ethics.

Liberation and Feminists Revisions of Moral Theology

Another major but very different effort to revise moral theology after Vatican II has been "liberation theology." Because of my long-time political interests and because I worked so much with Dominican Sisters who had great interest both in social justice and feminism, I had to think a lot about these influential and rapidly developing theories.

I shared the opinion, common at that time, that all of Latin America would soon be socialist. I also wrote the following in a report on this meeting, "OP Studies in Latin America," in our *Dominican Newsletter Forum*, May, 1976:

The most striking thing about Latin America is the outburst of new theological discussion and publication. It is not merely academic, but arises from the effort of theologians to learn from and to give Christian guidance to the rapid social trans-formation. Although at the moment most of these countries are under the tight control of military dictatorships, which many Latin American observers believe are supported by U.S. colonialism, it is probable that the whole South American continent is going to adopt some form of socialism. Almost a third of all Roman Catholics are in these countries, and the Church has to play an active role in this social process. Every-where there is talk of the new "Theology of Liberation," which is an effort to assimilate what is good in the ideas of Karl Marx, just as medieval theologians attempted to assimilate what was good in the pagan philosophers. Some of the first efforts have been rather naive, but the discussions are now taking a much more mature form.

I had written only one lecture on this topic in 1985, "Liberation from What?" delivered in the St. Catherine Symposium at the Dominican House of Studies in Washington. I praised liberation theology for reviving the biblical notion of the Exodus, and "the advocacy of the poor," and for emphasizing the interrelation of moral theory and "praxis." I expressed some suspicions, however, of the utopianism of this trend for its uncritical Marxist and anarchistic political theory. I was grateful when later the CDF published its well-balanced analysis of this trend,[318] and recently when Pope Benedict XVI, who, when head of the CDF had been responsible for this analysis, in his first encyclical, *God is Love*, repeated this teaching.[319]

The support given by many Catholic social activists to the Sandinistas in El Salvador seemed to me, a former Trotskyite, to be as politically naive as the support to fascism given by many Catholics before World War II. *Ecclesia semper reformanda* but the measure of reform is the Gospel understood in the Church's Tradition not political slogans. Among the human virtues besides prudence, Aquinas placed great emphasis on the virtue of justice. This virtue is in the human will and is a skill in taking full account in our decisions of the rights of others in the human community. As social animals we need each other to attain our own goals, not only as regards our physical health and security that we enjoy as individuals, but as regards family, society, and truth that are goods that are by their very nature common.

They are common in that, because they are chiefly spiritual, we can share them with others without any loss but very real gain to ourselves. This sharing, however, requires equality between persons as persons, and it requires cooperation among all so that each contributes her or his special gifts to the common good as it is the goal for all. Finally, justice requires that the common good be distributed according to the needs particular to each. Thus the virtue of justice sums up, as it were, all the means that are required for all of us to reach the true ultimate goal of human life. That is why the Bible often uses the term "righteousness," "justice," or "justification" to include all of morality.

Thus today for some "liberation theology" has taken the place of "moral theology" and commitment to the true ultimate end of life is spoken of as "the preferential option for the poor," meaning that we must all commit ourselves to bring about justice for those who suffer injustice. Hence liberation theology deals primarily with moral rather than dogmatic issues. It has drawn much from Marxist political theory, although that has now become largely passé. No wonder then, that, given my former Marxism and my Notre Dame Ph.D. in Political Science, liberation theology has great appeal for me. Nevertheless, for the same reasons, for me it arouses certain questions and suspicions with regards to elements in Marx's thought that I long ago worked through. At its best liberation theology is typified for me by one of its founders Gustavo Gutiérrez, with whom I had a brief acquaintance. I am delighted that Gutiérrez, who has done much to revive the memory of one of my heroes, the great Dominican "Defender of the Indians," Bartolomé de las Casas (1484-1566), has now himself entered our Order.[320]

As a teacher I want to insist that the worst of all forms of poverty is ignorance and especially ignorance of the Gospel. In our culture the very rich and well educated are in fact often extremely poor as regards knowledge of the Gospel, just as are the materially poor to whom the Gospel has not been preached or only preached badly. Thus I find the frequent statements made by activists that "the poor have much to teach us" misleading. This smacks of the Marxist delusion that the proletariat will learn the laws of historical materialism from the class struggle and become its real theoreticians.

What the poor can really teach us is to be humbly open to the Word of God. Yet only when the apostles Jesus has sent to them to proclaim the Word of God in its fullness can they be liberated from the poverty of ignorance into which we all, poor and rich, have fallen through sin. To think that the Holy Spirit will enlighten them simply because they are materially poor even if they have not received the teaching of an apostolic Church is contrary to all of Christian history. Without such preaching the poor became the prey of the worst heresies and superstitions. In my opinion, it is mere romanticism to suppose that the ignorant poor can reform society or the church by some special wisdom and virtue that is attributed to them simply by the fact that they are deprived of education, discipline, and material means.

Hence I prefer, as clearer and more honest, the term "advocacy for the poor" rather than "option for the poor," although the latter term occurs in some Magisterial documents The poor have needs and they have rights, but when they are unable to speak for themselves or be heard when they speak, then it is a Christian obligation to intercede for them with those in power to obtain their rights and have their needs met. No doubt we should help the poor to organize themselves and demand their own rights, but how they should do this depends entirely on the political situation. Injustice is seldom corrected by revolution, because revolution by its violence usually just piles one injustice on another. In history it is hard to name a single revolution that was truly an uprising of the oppressed that was successful in establishing social justice. Our own American Revolution, one of the few revolutions that did succeed, got its inspiration and leadership from the upper classes not from the poor.

I believe that the message of the Gospel is best preached to the poor in the manner chosen by Jesus himself and copied by St. Dominic in founding his mendicant friars. Preachers must be willing to share the conditions of the poor and hence speak from firsthand experience of the injustices that the poor suffer, thus demonstrating that the preachers are not in the service of the oppressors or acting for their own gain. St. Dominic first preached with a group of twelve Cistercian abbots. When their preaching had little effect, he said to them, "Send home your retinue and your horses, and like the apostles go on foot!" When they decided this was too much for them, Dominic walked alone but soon gathered about him the Order of Friars Preachers.

Dominic's advice is not easy for us friars today to apply, although some, like Chris Gaerets (d. 2001) and Dan Roach in Bolivia, have lived it to the letter. But I have usually lived in a community of friars who are university teachers or students. We live the lives of middle class professionals who travel far and wide in our cars and on the airlines and take expensive vacations. Although we put all we earn into the common fund and can use nothing of it except by consent of our community, our style of life is definitely middle class. St. Thomas Aquinas said that religious poverty is to be judged not by how much or how little of material goods are possessed in common, but by whether we have nothing that is not required by our mission and our search for holiness.[321] Although Dominicans are not as obsessed about debating "What is poverty?" as our Franciscans brothers and sisters, still I have heard endless discussion among us on this subject, but these debates have shed little light on how we can practically do better than try to apply the measure for poverty that our brother, Aquinas, gave us. Yet I also know only too well that I ought to personally apply that advice more honestly and completely in my own life.

When I was Regent of Studies for our Chicago Province I was very concerned to strengthen the preparation of our students in political ethics and tried to give them some experience of political and pastoral activism. To my great disillusionment the students who became most interested in these issues left the priesthood. Today most of the younger friars, as I listen to their conversations, still seem not very socially engaged, although they have at least one course on the Church's social teaching and spend a summer getting pastoral acquaintance with social problems. Strangely after Vatican

II, social movements in the Church in the United States were either wasted in such issues as support of the Marxist Sandinistas in Nicaragua or diverted into special black, feminist, and gay movements. I am proud to say, however, that our Chicago Province has succeeded in recruiting a fair number of African-Americans and our New Orleans Province has a fast growing number of Latino members, both native to the U. S. and immigrant.

Yet I must confess that I have had little involvement in the movements for justice for people of color, not from any lack of concern, but because in my opinion so many of their leaders are compounding the problem by trying in an artificial and divisive way to resist assimilation into our general culture. Certainly every national and racial group has a right to be proud of its good traditions and can make important contributions to our culture, but no group should cultivate its minority status. Just as the Church must enculturate its message, so minorities must somehow relate positively to the culture of the majority of the land they live in, as minorities have had to do in the past. In doing so they should try to retain and share with others what is special and fine in their culture, but they should not set themselves up over and against the majority culture, even when it seems that this culture rejects them. The presidential candidacy of Barack Obama indicates that this is a true possibility.

In particular I frankly believe that intermarriage is the only real and ultimate solution for the racism against persons of color that is so deeply engrained in American culture. This may be a wrongheaded view on my part, but I am afraid I have no other light to shed on the subject and do not know how I could influence these leaders to take another direction.

Yet liberation theology, besides its attack on the American faith in an unregulated free market economy, an attack with which I strongly agree, has too often fallen into the opposite errors of socialism and a false notion of "democracy," "equality" and even "anarchism." The social doctrine of the Church teaches that justice in society requires respect for political authority joined with subsidiarity, respect for private property, and also the "preferential option for the poor," in the sense of an "advocacy for the poor." From my great teacher at Notre Dame, Yves Simon, I learned why the common good of a community can never be achieved by anarchism, that is, by seeking to make political decisions only by consensus as Marx thought would be possible in a fully communist society. Aquinas shows that practical decisions seldom permit of a definitive, completely demonstrated decision. In choosing means to an end, each proposed choice usually presents both good points and bad points. No amount of dialogue, even among people of equal intelligence and equal good will, will necessarily produce agreement. Even the angels, Aquinas says, argue with each other about what to do.[322] Hence even among equals in a society there must be authoritative ways to arrive at common action for the common good. The members of the community who do not agree must obey that authority's ultimate decisions.

Such an authority can be vested in one person, in a select group of persons, or in the majority; but it cannot simply be left to the consensus of all. The best form of government, Aristotle said,[323] is ordinarily a "republic" in which each of these types of authority are combined as they are in our United States government with its president, legislature, and majority vote. We do not have a pure democracy, especially if that is understood as an anarchy in which minorities are free to refuse to obey majority decisions.

Like Aquinas says of Moses,[324] Jesus also designed his Church as a republic. It has the pope as head, the bishops as its select governing group, the laity as active participants in its sacraments and its mission. It is also from the laity as a whole that the leaders of the Church are called, not from a special class or dynasty. Contrary to the opinions of some scholars, I believe that historically it was Jesus himself who structured this Church in a way appropriate to its apostolic mission of teaching the Gospel. I am confirmed in this opinion by the example of St. Dominic who so wisely constructed his Order of Preachers. Yet I also know this well-built Church has in the course of history often suffered temporary deformations from the pressures and influences of contemporary civil politics. For Catholics the feminist question is entangled with the question of the ordination of women and that with the whole notion of "hierarchy" in the Church. How is a hierarchical Church to live in modern democracy? In the third millennium should we not have a more "democratic" ecclesiology? For a Dominican discussion group I wrote a paper entitled "The Priesthood of Christ and of the Baptized and Ordained,"[325] because some of the opinions I was hearing about our priestly vocation seemed to me based on false notions of hierarchy and equality in the Church.

The main points I made in this article from my studies and my own experience as a priest were the following. Scholars seem to agree that in the New Testament there is as yet no settled terminology for church leaders and the term priest (*hierous*) appears explicitly only in the Epistle to the Hebrews. Hence, we must go from what is most explicit in our data to what is less clear. The priesthood of the Old Testament was only an imperfect foreshadowing of the perfect priesthood of Christ who offers himself on the Cross. Hebrews speaks only obscurely of the Eucharist. But the Eucharistic texts of St. Paul and the Gospels make clear that the Eucharistic offering that continues in the Church as its central sacrificial act is a commemoration of Christ's priestly act on the Cross. Thus Christ's unique priesthood does not exclude but requires a continuing priesthood in the Church, provided this is understood to be only a participation in Christ's priesthood. This principle is reinforced by I Peter and Revelations which say that God's People are ""a chosen race, a royal priesthood" and by other texts that call them "a temple." Thus the teaching of Vatican II that the baptized as a community participate in the one priesthood of Christ is biblically solid.

Yet the People of God cannot be the Body of Christ without an organic structure. This requires leadership, although this leadership, like Christ's own leadership, must be one of service, not exploitation. A priest cannot be self-appointed, nor does the priest act only as a representative of the Church (*in persona ecclesiae*). The priest receives his priesthood from a special sacrament established by Christ, hence he acts not only in the name of the Church but in the name of Christ (*in persona Christi*). As Christ is the One Mediator between God and the People of God, so the priest he has ordained to represent him shares in his mediation. After his ascension Christ sent his Holy Spirit on the Twelve whom he had carefully prepared and to whom he gave the priestly power to pass on to the successors whom they ordain. Thus as Vatican II teaches, the ministerial priesthood resembles the general priesthood of the baptized since both are sacramentally conferred as participations in Christ's priesthood. Yet they differ "not just in degree but in kind." All the baptized are disciples of Christ, but the Sacrament of Holy Orders produces the ministerial priesthood as a servant leadership in the Church in order that the priesthood of the baptized as the Body of Christ can be realized in its communal life, worship, and cooperative mission.

It is in this context that the question of women's ordination arises. The question of whether there needs to be a feminist ethics and whether it should be based on liberation theology is another matter. As to that question, especially as it has been developed by Carol Gilligan as a theology of "caring,"[326] I will only point out that a Thomistic ethics must fully recognize that its principles are known not by discursive reason but as intuitively evident. Furthermore, it must acknowledge that our experience of embodiment and of bodily feelings play an essential role in ethical perception and decision, promoting good decision in concrete situations or hindering them. Without stereotyping the female personality, I believe that the intuitional acuity and strong empathy with which evolution has equipped women with for their maternal role, necessary to evolutionary survival of the species, enables them, beside their general scholarly competence that they have in common with male theologians, to make a special contribution to ethics.

Feminism raises another question that has so much concerned me, namely, the meaning of human "equality." In a recent article "An Educator's Vision,"[327] I wrote about my service at St. Xavier College, Chicago in the 1950s, under Sister Mary Josetta Butler, RSM, who was indeed a woman of power! I believe that at a conference of Dominican Sisters at Regina High School in Chicago I was one of the first of our Fathers to argue that since women are members of the Order of Preachers they too must be preachers, as St. Catherine of Siena, the second founder of our Order, certainly was and has been officially declared by Pope Paul VI in 1970 a Doctor of the Church. "Preaching" for us Dominicans has never been simply in the liturgy but has meant proclaiming the Gospel in every suitable situation, and this the active Sisters of the Third Order have always done. Thus it has always grieved me that when the issue of feminism became of general concern we Dominican men were so timid about discussing it openly in light of our theological tradition. Most either kept silent or gave uncritical support to the way the issue was being promoted in a one-sided manner.

As early as 1984, I submitted an article to our provincial magazine, *Spirituality Today*, in which I tried to discuss this topic. In it I recalled the neglected opinion of Aquinas that the Church in instituting the minor orders by dividing the diaconate into several distinct ministries was exercising its authority to change certain non-substantive aspects of the sacraments.[328] Hence, I suggested, the Church might have the power to ordain women at least to some type of diaconal role for which their special gifts may qualify them. The editor, however, rejected this article as too likely to offend both women and men Dominicans. The question is still under discussion by theologians and this discussion has lead me now to think I was mistaken on this issue.[329]

I also read, often with some exasperation, yet always trying to keep an open mind, a good deal of feminist literature. My interest in this topic was kept alive by my practical concerns for my Dominican Sisters who seemed to place such hopes in the idea—increasingly implausible to me—that the Church would soon yield to the feminist agitation for ordination. I was also troubled by the negative effect the debate seemed to be having on male vocations. But it also began to have for me a deep theoretical interest.

In 1992 I was honored by an invitation to deliver the annual McGivney lectures, previously given by John Finnis, Kenneth Schmitz, Elizabeth Anscombe, Ralph McInerny, and others at the John Paul II Institute for Marriage and Family in Washington DC. I regret to say my talks, that I hoped would arouse some debate, got little attention from the Catholic University of America students or faculty or the Dominicans at the House of Studies—let alone from those back in my own Province when they were published. I worked for some time revising these lectures, which finally appeared as a book *Justice in the Church: Gender and Participation* in 1996.[330] I must add my special gratitude to my friend Victor LaMotte, OP, formerly editor of the journal *Listening*. In spite of his wretched health, Victor had the patience to be a thorough reader of *Justice in the Church,* and also of *Living the Truth in Love,* and to make valuable suggestions for their revision. I have always regretted that he did not publish his own fine Ph.D. dissertation on the topic of analogy in metaphysics. When the MS. was sent by the publisher to readers, Avery Dulles, SJ (now Cardinal Dulles) commended it as the most thorough treatment of the topic to date. He has since published on the topic himself in essential agreement with my conclusions, but following a different line of argument, namely the history of the tradition.

He also suggested I give more attention to recent literature on the subject. Hence I added to the draft citations of *The Splendor of Truth* and the *Catechism of the Catholic Church* that had given me assurance that I was on the right track. I also included three rather long appendices. One of these is a survey of recent feminist literature and another deals with the most recent Vatican document on the subject, *Ordinatio Pastoralis*. A third analyses radical feminist theology as synthesized by Elizabeth A. Johnson in her book, *She Who Is*.[331]

Beth Johnson, formerly of The Catholic University of America and now of Fordham University, to me typifies the radical feminist position among Catholic Sisters. She is an attractive, gracious, and witty person whose is determined to be herself rather than fit the stereotype of one of our "good Sisters" of the past. Yet I found her well-written book to be largely based on the thought of two other more extreme feminists,[332] the formidable Scripture scholar, Elisabeth Schüssler Fiorenza and the polemical, patristic scholar Rosemary Radford Ruether. Schüssler Fiorenza seems to have renounced activism for women's ordination, because she considers priesthood as such a patriarchal, hierarchical tyranny.[333] Ruether, a leader of Woman-Church who, while deploring the tendentious scholarship of my former student, Matthew Fox, also expressed strong agreement with his "creation-centered spirituality" whose shortcomings I pointed out in Chapter 23. Johnson so emphasizes "negative" theology in its insistence on the ineffability of God that it becomes possible to project the political agenda of feminism on the blank screen of divine mystery. As sympathetic as I am to this agenda in so far as it seeks more just relations between men and women in today's society, I regard such speculations as lacking a critical theological or philosophical foundation for reasons I tried to explain in the lengthy review of *She Who Is* that I appended to the lectures in *Justice in the Church.*

I prepublished a version of the third lecture in *Justice in the Church*, as "Gender and the Priesthood of Christ: A Theological Reflection," in *The Thomist* in 1993[334] and later in 1995 summarized its argument for the popular press in "Notes Toward a Theology of Gender," in the *National Catholic Register* (1995)[335] and expounded it in an interview with John J. Myers, Bishop of Peoria, on the *Eternal Word Television Network.* That I would appear on Mother Angelica's programs and with this particular bishop, known for his vigorous conservatism, hardly commended me, or my views, to my opponents! Two scholars, both women, gave me favorable reviews, but in less prestigious journals than *Theological Studies* in which the reviewer, also a woman, said she didn't at all like it but didn't bother to inform readers of just what my line of argument was.

When at Boston College, I lectured on "Women's Participation in the Church," to a large, principally student, audience, organized by a faculty member and good friend Fr. Ron Tacelli, SJ, I was delighted at the open-minded reception it received. Yet the two faculty members asked to comment on it largely avoided my arguments and discussed other matters. One, Fr. Francis Sullivan, SJ, a specialist on the various level of authority of magisterial pronouncements, belabored the question whether *Ordinatio Pastoralis* was infallible, though at the beginning of my lecture, I had explicitly pointed out that my theological argument was independent of that issue. The other commentator, a noted biblical scholar, Pheme Perkins, said nothing about my use of the Bible, but discussed her personal experience of how effective women can be in parish ministry. A reporter for the student newspaper *The Observer* who interviewed me, asked me also about my Communist past, and gave his very accurate summary of my talk the sexy headline, "Fr. Ashley on Trotsky and Consecrated Virgins."[336]

In today's culture this issue is viewed by so many simply in terms of democratic individualism and equality of opportunity for all. What reason could there possibly be to exclude women from an office for which women can be just as qualified by intelligence and education as men? The answer seems so obvious that I have frequently heard sisters and priests assert, "There are no theological reasons against ordaining women. The tradition is entirely due to the patriarchy of the past, from which we should free ourselves and the Church." Thus women's ordination has joined contraception, clerical celibacy, and homophobia as the marks of John Paul II's betrayal of the "Spirit of Vatican II."

Therefore, in *Justice in the Church* I discuss the confusion that underlies much liberation theology between the personal equality of all human beings (including the unborn) in the Church and society, and the functional inequality and hierarchy of authority that is required by the just organization of any human community, notably, I might say, in the organization of any university. I then argue that the oppression of women by men, like the existence of poverty, is one of the great sad facts of the sinful history of the world, biblically acknowledged in Genesis 3 in the "curses" (evil consequences) on the disobedience of Adam and Eve. This tragic fact is amply manifested throughout the Bible and the history of the Church. But Jesus, in redeeming our sinful world, transcended whatever that is sinful in our history and restored the moral order as it was in God's original intention in creation, including the true character of human sexuality founded on the complementary and mutual relation of woman to man and man to woman. That is the aspect of a genuine "creation spirituality" that Fox neglected.

The family structure as God intended it in creation, therefore, is not oppressive, though it can be abused, but is essential for human flourishing. This fundamental structure, built into the very constitution of our bodies and psyches, fits woman to be the child-bearer and caretaker and the man to be the child-begetter, protector and provider in service of the woman in her childbearing and child care. As such the husband is, in light of the New Testament symbolism of the relation of Christ to the Church, the "head" of the family, as both St. Paul (I Cor 11:3; Eph 5: 23) and St. Peter (I Pt 3:1) taught. "Head" here does not mean possessor or oppressor, but the Christ-like servant priest of the *ecclesia domestica*, the household Church.

In view of this profound human familial relationship from which we learn what all other friendships should be like, it is understandable why in the Old Testament God sealed the covenant with his people by revealing himself to them by a masculine name, Yahweh. Hence the prophets speak of the covenant as the marriage of God (who, unlike pagan gods, has no goddess wife) to his people, e.g. Hosea 2:22. This is the way God chose to refute the pantheism of the Canaanites and of most religions not derived from Judaism and to assert true monotheism, a belief in one God who has created the world freely and has also given his higher creatures a share in his freedom. To speak of the Absolute as Goddess, as many cultures do, conveys the image of the identification of the world with the Goddess, as the child tends to be identified with the mother as the nurturing Same, while monotheism is best conveyed by the relational symbol of the Father as the powerful, but caring Other.

Thus, it becomes intelligible why Jesus also chose to make those who share his priesthood in the Church to be fathers and not mothers. This does not mean that the men are superior as persons to women, but that that some men are called to a special role of service in the Church resembling that of Jesus himself. Another, complementary role of service, the dignity of which is not less than that a priest's but in some ways greater, was given to Mary, Mother of God, the virgin contemplative in the Church, the new Eve, as Jesus is the New Adam. While the first Eve was born from Adam's side, the New Adam is born from Mary, in complete reciprocity. As the male priest is a sign to the whole Church of the continuing presence of Christ, so the female contemplative, bride of Christ, is a sign to the whole Church that anticipates the promised Kingdom of God.

Both these roles, that of the male priest and the female consecrated contemplative have a principally symbolic function in the Church in that the priest reminds the laity of Christ's presence with them and the contemplative reminds them that the goal of the Church is eternal not temporal life; "My kingdom does not belong to this world" (Jn 18:36). We all need such reminders. This complementary symbolism for a sacramental Church is not something so superficial that the Church can change it, since the sacramental symbols were chosen by God himself to reveal his loving purpose and to achieve the well-being of all, women and men alike, in the Church and in society. The Church can of course find new ways to make clear to our culture that women are full participants in the Church's life and it is to this that our efforts should be directed.

The age-old sin of male oppression will not be overcome by taking away from men their proper role of headship in the family and in the Church, but by teaching them that this headship is one of Christlike self-sacrifice, of chaste fidelity, and nonviolence. I say again that to me personally this issue is important primarily because it is another example of how our culture has the insane, anti-ecological ambition to destroy nature and substitute for it human inventions rather than to respect and perfect it. Nothing is more natural than the relations of man and wife, parents and children. Thus the fervid campaign for the ordination of women is just another misguided attack on the natural order. We must perfect the natural relationship of man and woman by freeing it of all that is sexist, preserving and enhancing its God-given complementarity that can alone produce genuine mutuality and equality.

TWO SMILING WOMEN

It took lovely Eve to deceive
stupid, lustful Adam
so afraid once more to be alone.
that he munched the other half of that
so fatal apple.

It took the New Eve
graciously to receive

within her destined womb
the Second Adam, nurse him at her breast ,
then see him hanging, bleeding, high against the darkened sky,
then, yes then
risen from that fatal tomb!

Chapter 25 - Listening and Longing

What Says the Bible?

I have begun each of the preceding chapters with one of the seven features that I said in Chapter 18 mark the spirituality of aging. In this chapter and the concluding chapter, I turn to the goal of true Christian spirituality, intimate union with God beyond this life. This goal is known to us only through the teaching of the Catholic Church that is based on the Sacred Scriptures as they are interpreted by the bishops of the Church headed by the successor of St. Peter in the light of living Sacred Tradition. As St. Peter wrote "Know this first of all, that there is no prophecy of scripture that is a matter of personal interpretation, for no prophecy ever came through human will; but rather human beings moved by the Holy Spirit spoke under the influence of God," (2 Pt 1:20-22).

Obviously it is not always easy to determine what this inspired preaching is. At present our Dominican Bible scholars seem fearful of seeming "politically incorrect" if they honestly present what the Bible says about sexuality and especially sexual asceticism. Therefore, I was surprised but pleased when William B. Farmer (now deceased) invited me to write an article on "The Bible and Sexuality" for the forthcoming *International Catholic Bible Commentary*[337] of which he was editor. I couldn't imagine why he asked me to do this. Had more competent scholars turned it down? In any case in my article I tried to avoid the influence of current ideologies and present the biblical teaching without flinching.

I knew Farmer only through his bold, persistent campaign to question the received view of modern exegetes that Mark was the earliest of the Synoptic Gospels, later used independently by Luke and Matthew along with a no longer extant source, Q. As an alternative to this standard theory, Farmer and the English Catholic scholar Bernard Orchard revived in modified form the older view, once supported by Catholic scholars, that Matthew is the first Gospel as indicated by its strongly Jewish-Christian perspective. Hence Luke was written later for formerly pagan Christians. Finally Mark was an attempt, probably sponsored by St. Peter for the sake of Church unity, to provide a short gospel that avoided the points where Matthew and Luke seemed discordant. John came still later. I have always been sympathetic to these efforts of Farmer and Orchard, but it seems to me dangerous to base Catholic theology on just any one of these hypotheses, including theirs, about the composition and dating of biblical writings. The available data on which such theories are based is very scanty and even when there is a standard "mainstream" position this remains insecure. To think that the words of St. Paul, because they were recorded earlier, are more inspired than the Gospel tradition of Jesus' words, goes contrary to the very notion of inspiration since the principal Author of all these biblical texts is the Holy Spirit who transcends time.

The principal contribution of historical criticism to theology seems to me mainly negative, that is, by its inconclusive scholarly debates it saves the theologian from trusting too much in what we can establish with historical certitude. Theologians, thus warned, will then base their work, as Vatican II urged,[338] on the religious message of the canonical Scriptures accepted by faith as the inerrant Word of God. This religious message of course depends in part on some historical facts. The Exodus and Covenant events on which Israel based its faith in Yahweh, the messianic hopes of Israel, its punishment for violating the covenant and its merciful restoration must have a true historical foundation. So must the main events of Jesus' life and teaching, including the institution of baptism and the Eucharist, his crucifixion, the firm witness of the apostles to his resurrection, the apostolic foundation and mission of the Church to all nations. Historical scholarship can support these basic facts, but theology receives even these on the basis of a reasonable faith, not merely on scholarly arguments.

In my article, however, I did not enter into these thorny thickets of exegesis but simply summarized what the Bible says about human sexuality, leaving the interpretation of this to the reader. That was what Farmer wanted and he accepted my article with praise, but with great embarrassment called me a year later to say that a feminist member of the editorial board had refused to agree to its publication. He had then showed it to other theologians, including two women, who could see nothing wrong in it. He had even suggested an additional article by another writer that might reflect another view more congenial to the objecting editor, but she remained adamant. The English edition of the commentary appeared without the article.

To my mind the greatest of all the many injustices to women was their exclusion from higher education. One source of this exclusion was the rabbinical prohibition against women's studying Torah. The story of Martha and Mary (Lk 10:38-42) shows that Jesus rejected this prohibition by praising Mary for her desire to lay aside domestic tasks to attentively meditate on his teaching. Only if study is open to women can they fully participate in civil and ecclesiastical life. Fortunately today many Catholic women are studying and teaching theology and they themselves, I am convinced, will in time correct the flaws in present feminist theory in the light of Jesus' Good News. Yet this first generation of women theologians has, in my opinion, often been seriously victimized by the dissenting opinions of the male theologians who have been their mentors.

Moreover, I believe that they will not be able to correct these mistakes until they have not only theological education but also an appropriate philosophical preparation that will enable them to adequately criticize current trends. While most priest theologians receive at least some philosophical training before taking up theological studies, at present most women start theological studies without such a philosophical preparation and are thus ill-prepared to read current theology with a critical eye. Any adequate spirituality must take gender differences and gender relationships into consideration. The fact that in 1970 Paul VI declared Sts. Catherine of Siena and Teresa of Avila and in 1997 John Paul II proclaimed St. Thérèse of Lisieux Doctors of the Church, women whose writings are on spirituality shows that the Church has now become especially sensitive on this issue.

Pondering the Right of Dissent from Church Teaching

For Catholics the feminist question is entangled with the question of ordination and that in turn with the whole notion of "hierarchy" in the church. Related to questions about priesthood is another topic that continues to engage my thinking on spirituality, the authority of the teaching of the pastors of the Church and especially its relation to the work of theologians, a topic which I have already touched on in the last chapter in connection with the Curran case. As far as I know the formal process for resolving conflicts between theologians and bishops set up in the NCCB document *Doctrinal Responsibilities* (1989) has not been employed often. Moreover suspicions that the bishops were not really serious about the enforcement of that document were raised by the new warning issued by NCCB Committee on Doctrine against the use of Richard McBrien's *Catholicism* for general instruction in the Catholic Faith. The Committee's new warning against *Catholicism* was occasioned by

McBrien's publication in 1996 of a revision of the work which had until then continued to be used with only minor revisions by many for college and adult teaching. This new *monitum* was given by the Committee only after correspondence with Fr. McBrien and was issued to make clear that the revised edition still had not adequately corrected the problems of which the Committee had originally complained. Furthermore, the Committee pointed out that *Doctrinal Responsibilities* concerns disagreements between a theologian and his own bishop, not to actions by the Conference as a whole. McBrien, on the other hand, felt that it was unjust that he not be afforded the full process.

This brings the question to a new phase. As is well known, it is not at all clear exactly what authority the NCCB has to issue doctrinal teaching in the name of all the bishops, since canonically this is proper only to a national synod. According to John Paul II, *Apostolos Suos,* "On the Theological and Juridical Nature of Episcopal Conferences" (1997), a National Catholic Bishops Conference is only authorized to make statements of a pastoral, not a doctrinal character lest the *de jure divino* authority of local bishops be weakened.[339] In the case of McBrien's *Catholicism* it seems that the Committee on Doctrine's action is in fact pastoral, since its letter went no further than to criticize the book as a suitable instrument for catechesis and adult education.

It is often alleged that theologians in the medieval universities were considered part of the Magisterium. This, however, was precisely because it was always assumed that no matter how much they differed among themselves they could not dissent from the bishops who had the right to dismiss and even excommunicate them if they did so. Thus, Catholics before Vatican II generally took for granted that whatever was taught in Church sponsored schools had to be consistent with official Church teaching and could usually be followed as a safe guide both in faith and morals. Vatican II said nothing to change this view and it has probably continued to prevail in the minds of the average priest and lay Catholic. Hence, the public media often quote the dissenting opinions of well-known Catholic theologians as evidence that such views, since they are at least tolerated by the bishops, have good standing in the Church. Thus it appears to the public that it is not the theologians who are to be blamed for being dissenters from episcopal authority. Rather it is the bishops who are to be blamed for being dissenters from the authority of the theologians!

As I said in discussing the Curran case, since Vatican II a paradigm shift has taken place in how the relation of theologians to the bishops is to be understood. Many younger theologians have picked up from their professors the idea that theologians speak only for themselves as members of a profession. While today theologians hope their work will be of service to the Church, they hold that their responsibility in this regard is only indirect and implies no control of their scholarly work or teaching by the Church as such. The official teaching of the Church is taken only as material for research. It must, of course, be presented objectively, but this presentation does not necessarily require any faith commitment on the part of the theologian whose approach should be primarily historical and critical. Thus, according to this current view, theology has the same standards of academic freedom as any other department of a university, and theologians' competence and fidelity to these standards is to be judged only by their academic peers.

Obviously to those who have this new notion of the responsibilities of a theologian, the action of Cardinal Ratzinger and of the Chancellor of The Catholic University of America in the Curran affair was an unjust violation of academic freedom. Yet to those who continue to accept the traditional view of the theologian's vocation, still evident even in recent Church documents, the removal of Curran was a responsible act of doctrinal supervision by the teaching authority of the Church essential for the identity and mission of a Catholic institution. Are these two views absolutely incompatible?

I believe that, although they appear flatly contradictory, some reconciliation or at least practical compromise between them is possible and even necessary in our culture, where a Catholic institution must operate in a largely secularized milieu as I have earlier discussed with regard to Catholic health services. This is why I have occasionally participated in the "Common Ground Initiative"[340] sponsored by the late Cardinal Bernadine in the hope of getting a fairer discussion of this very serious problem.

What is imperative is that the bishops make very clear to Catholics—and for theologians who accept this paradigm shift to concede—that "theology" as it is practiced today in our universities has no other authority than the learned arguments of the theologians. Therefore it cannot claim to serve as a direct guide to the faith and conscience of Catholics. Such a guide can be provided only by the bishops under the pope, who according to the Catholic faith are alone invested with apostolic authority. This distinction does not mean that theology will no longer serve the Church and contribute to the development of doctrine, but that its pronouncements as far as Catholic faith and commitment are concerned, always stand under the judgment of the Magisterium and cannot substitute for it as a "parallel magisterium."

There has been anguished discussion over the requirement by the Vatican document *Ex Corde Ecclesiae* (1990),[341] that all Catholic teachers of theology receive the "mandate" of the local bishop. In the U.S. situation this seems to many educators impractical and in fact few bishops want to take on any such responsibility, as I learned from their reluctance to accept my suggestion to include in the revised *Religious and Ethical Directives for Catholic Health Care Facilities* a formal process for dealing with bioethical questions.

Perhaps bishops might mandate certain theologians in their institutions of a dioceses who accept the traditional responsibility of adhering to Church teachings without dissent (at least in their role as teachers) so as to meet the needs of students who certainly have a right to a straight forward presentation and sympathetic defense of Church doctrines. Perhaps also an official distinction could be made between the responsibilities of teachers with respect to catechesis and graduate theological instruction. Undergraduates today are usually in need of and have a right to remedial catechesis. At the graduate level, on the other hand, Catholic students of theology have a responsibility to know already the essentials of the faith to which they are committed. Hence they are not so likely to confuse it with theological opinions that are worthwhile discussing but ought not to be followed in practice until approved by the Church's pastors.

In my opinion none of the three encyclicals, *Humanae Vitae* of Paul VI on contraception, and *The Splendor of Truth* and *The Gospel of Life* of John Paul II, solemnly (and hence infallibly) define these moral norms as requiring of Catholics the assent of divine faith. Nevertheless, they provide a very firm papal witness to the constant tradition of the Church. This makes evident that these norms have reached that stage of clarity in doctrinal development that renders theological dissent from them, to say the least, "rash" and their substantial change in the future extremely improbable or even impossible. This advanced degree of doctrinal development is also substantially embodied in the moral teaching of the *Catechism of the*

Catholic Church especially because it has also received the morally unanimous consent of the college of bishops who were consulted before its publication. The minor corrections made in the *editio typica* later published do not detract from this moral unanimity of the episcopal college.

In concluding this account of controversies about human rights and Church teaching in which I have been so much engaged during this time of my life I want to underline how absurd it is that "gay rights" is today commonly grouped together with the questions of the rights of the colored, of women, and of the laity in the Church on the ground that these are all matters of "equality." To my mind and in my experience with people they are utterly different questions. As to gay rights I have already related my experiences with Courage and my reflections on this subject. I also lectured in a lecture series on homosexuality, sponsored by the Jacques Maritain Institute of the University of Notre Dame that Ralph McInerny directs. This series was courageously designed and promoted by Randy Smith, who was completing his doctorate in medieval studies at that University and who now teaches at the University of St. Thomas in Houston.   Randy told me that he had felt that a counterbalance to the propaganda of a student group of gay activists at Notre Dame was urgent, since the theology department there seemed to be cowed by "political correctness" into silence about the Church's teaching on the subject. In this October, 1997 lecture "The Theology of Sexuality and Homosexuality" I tried to place this delicate topic in the context of a general view of why God made us sexual, since without that broader perspective the Christian understanding of homosexual orientation as a "disorder," and homosexual activity as immoral, makes no sense. I have also urged the Institute for the Psychological Sciences in Washington where, as I will relate later I taught in 2001-2002, to do research on this problem, not by immediately studying homosexuality, but by studying the psychology of successful heterosexual development ending in stable marriage and good parenthood. Until we understand human heterosexuality as it is ordered by human nature, we will never be able to understand how and why it can be tragically disordered.

Living the Truth in Love

If I have grown at all spiritually in my later years it has been through trying to be fair and objective in the controversies that I have, at such length, just related and by the patience required in writing articles and books. After having learned to use a desktop computer, much of my life has been spent in front of its screen. In writing the present memoir a computer accident caused me to lose the draft of the first three chapters that I had to reconstruct. I have nightmares that someday we may get all the books in the world on CDROM and then an accident will occur that will wipe them out more thoroughly than the burning of the Alexandrian Library wiped out ancient learning or the first Emperor of China tried to burn all its classical literature. Or perhaps instead so much information will become available to us by clicking a computer mouse that we will be overwhelmed by despair of learning anything. I remember also that neither wisdom loving Socrates nor my all wise and loving Lord Jesus ever wrote a book.

Yet between 1998 and 2001 I did a fair amount of writing on theological topics: "*Dei Verbum* and Christian Morals;"[342]; "Spirituality and Counseling;"[343] "John Paul II: Theologian of the Body of the Acting Person;"[344] seven articles for *The Encyclopedia of Monasticism*:[345] "Christianity: Overview," the "Christian Perspectives" parts on "Humor," "Death," "Asceticism," "Prayer," "Laicization of Spirituality," and "Life Cycle," also "Self-Mutilation;" and in bioethics: "What is a Human Person?;"[346] "Designer Babies or Gifts of God?;" and with Albert Moraczewski, OP, "Cloning, Aquinas, and the Embryonic Person;"[347] and I acted as a consultant for a high school textbook in religion.[348]

Yet with less teaching and traveling, I have been able to give more time to writing and my religious superiors seem to want to make this my principal form of preaching. Three recent books have been concerned with the Dominican tradition and have been inspired by my desire to help the all too few new candidates to our Dominican Family. One, already mentioned, *The Dominicans*,[349] is a brief history of how the four themes of preaching, community, liturgy, and study, which constitute the "spirit of the founder" of our Order, have been worked out in each of its eight centuries of life and mission. Another is *St. Thomas Aquinas: Selected Spiritual Writings*, translated by Fr. Matthew Rzeczkowski, OP, with my introduction and brief commentaries.[350] Most of these selections have never before been translated. The third book is *Spiritual Direction in the Dominican Tradition*,[351] which has a more practical and pastoral character.

While spiritual direction has not been my special work, I have over the years been a spiritual director to a number of both women and men. There is little new in these books that expound the thought of Aquinas, but I hope they will make available some of the results of the rich publications by Dominican scholars in the first half of this century with which younger people are not acquainted. I have also published an essay, "Spirituality and Counseling," in Robert Wicks, ed., *Handbook of Spirituality for Ministers.*[352]

I once told my former student Mark Latkovic that in my life I have had only two "big ideas" around which most of my writing has turned. One is the Lyceum theme about the relation of modern natural science to theology that includes the concept of the importance of the human body, which I got from Fr. William H. Kane, OP. I showed my continuing interest in this theme in an article "Astronomy as a Liberal Art"[353] in which I described how mathematical astronomy as one of the seven liberal arts functioned in classical and medieval education and what were its limitations as a true introduction to natural science. In another article, "Truth and Technology,"[354] I discussed Martin Heidegger's thesis that scientific technology is the logical outcome but also the death knell of philosophy as it originated with Plato and Aristotle. I argued that this is a false diagnosis and that the decline of philosophy in our times is due to the separation of philosophy from science because of the current defective philosophies of science. I developed this thesis more fully in another essay, "The End of Philosophy and the End of Physics: A Dead End."[355]

My other big idea is the relation of the person to the common good that I derived from Charles DeKoninck. Both views ultimately come from St. Thomas Aquinas. I tried to expound this theme in a work mainly the fruit of my teaching in Washington and is intended as a textbook for colleges and seminaries, *Living the Truth in Love: A Biblical Introduction to Moral Theology.*[356] It is a textbook and not a full treatise in the manner of Germain Grisez's *The Way of the Lord Jesus.*

For moral theology to be theology it must be based on the Word of God given us. According to Vatican II's, *Decree on Divine Revelation* (*Dei Verbum*) this Word is found in the Bible and the Sacred Tradition out of which the Bible arose and for which it is the privileged witness, the *norma normans* but not the exhaustively explicit expression of Sacred Tradition. Today many theologians want to add to this twin source of Revelation a third, "religious experience."

I think this is a mistake, hard to reconcile with *Dei Verbum*. The term "religious experience" is so vague as to be almost meaningless. If it means the unfolding and confirmation of the revelation entrusted to the Church (the *depositum fidei*) in our prayer and Christian living as we are guided by Christ's Holy Spirit in the Christian Community, then it is not a source of Revelation nor an addition to it. Rather it is the subjective appropriation or reception of the objective truth contained first in Sacred Scripture and Sacred Tradition.

Some feminist theologians seek to ground theology in "woman's experience." If they mean something other than their perception of how the Gospel given to the Church in Scripture and Tradition makes sense in the light of their discipleship of prayer and service, I fear they are the blind leading the blind. So are male theologians who try to ground theology on any foundation other than Scripture and Sacred Tradition. As I have already insisted, women and men, through their experience as sexual persons have somewhat different perspectives on the Gospel and different expressions of their perceptions of it. Yet it is one and the same Word of God known by both sexes through the same gift of faith and in the light of the same Holy Spirit.

Limits of research and of book length made it impossible for me to explore as I would have liked in *Living the Truth* the contributions of Sacred Tradition in the Church Fathers and great medieval theologians to moral theology. I had to limit myself (except for occasional citations of some Church Fathers and Aquinas) to the Scriptures themselves, although I am very conscious of the patristic riches that I had to pass over. What I tried to do in my revision of moral theology was twofold: first, I surveyed all the topics found in the pre-Vatican II manuals. While these manuals suffered from serious flaws, principally their voluntarism and casuistry, they also contained a rich fund of pastoral experience. To begin all over again to invent moral theology as some writers are attempting to do deprives students and other readers of the riches of doctrinal development and substitutes a thin soup of talk about "love" and pop psychology, with some floating chunks of liberation theology. Therefore, I shamelessly began with the outline of Dominicus Merkelbach's old manual of moral theology[357] and included all the topics of which he treats, although not attempting his elaborate detail and obsolete canonical data. From among the manualists I used Merkelbach, because by following Aquinas he had already largely escaped deontological voluntarism.

Second, I asked myself how all this fund of moral experience and analysis had arisen from the Bible. In the *Summa Theologiae* St. Thomas assumed that his readers were well acquainted with the Biblical text and did not systematically attempt to root his moral analysis exegetically, but merely cited the Bible when convenient. Yet these citations are not "proof-texts" in the manner of a "proof from Scripture" in the manuals. They are intended to recall to the reader the principal moral themes that run throughout the whole Bible and there have what is called today a "narrative", i.e. a concrete, developmental mode.

Theologians, therefore, need not attempt to "prove" the principles they derive from Scripture by direct exegetical work. They can rely on the work of current exegesis (avoiding extravagances and hypercriticism) for a primary reading of the text. Then, as the patristic and medieval theologians did, they can draw out those developing themes whose sense depends not simply on individual texts but on these texts in relation to the Canon as a whole. Thus within the Scriptures there is what is called today "intertextuality" with its "hermeneutic circle." This is what I tried to do, using particular texts to illustrate whence the Catholic Tradition has derived its understanding of God's Word.

The greatest difficulty I met in pursuing this program was how to relate the "theological" virtues of faith, hope, and love, central to the moral teaching of the New Testament, to the four "cardinal" virtues. These cardinal virtues are not listed anywhere in the Bible except in a single verse of the deuterocanonical Wisdom 8:7. "The fruits of her [Wisdom] works are virtues, for she teaches moderation and prudence, justice and fortitude, and nothing is more useful for men than these."

I found an answer to this problem when I realized that "prudence" is the practical aspect of "Wisdom" (Hebrew *hokma*, Greek *sophia*), certainly a fundamental biblical theme, and "Justice" is the biblical "righteousness" especially embodied in the Ten Commandments. These Commandments, on which the whole of the Bible's moral teaching rests, are the Law (*Torah*, instruction) which seals the Covenant of God with his People. Moreover, the Bible links "Faith" to "Wisdom" and the "Justice" of the Old Covenant to the "Love" of the New Covenant.

Thus the difficulty is reduced to the problem of "Fortitude" and "Temperance" and their link to "Hope." But "Fortitude" is the biblical theme of martyrdom, with its patience under trial, and "Temperance" the biblical theme of chastity and virginity that are so much praised in the New Testament. Fortitude and Temperance taken together embody that self-mastery and self-sacrifice of Jesus' celibacy and his Cross, the icon of traditional Christian asceticism. But can this asceticism, which to many seems depressive, be connected with theological Hope? A grand theme of the whole of Scripture—indeed more than a theme, a dimension—is its eschatology, its hope for the Coming Kingdom of God to which the pleasures of this world must be subordinated and its fears and pains heroically endured.

I also tried to make some of the ideas in *Living the Truth in Love* available to a wide public by agreeing to give a course of eight one-hour lectures in the work of the International Catholic University. This is a project of my friend Ralph McInerny of the University of Notre Dame and is based on lectures first presented on Mother Angelica's *Eternal Word Television Network*. How strange that a cloistered nun has created EWTN, one of the biggest television networks in the world! I was amazed at this odd combination of a traditional cloister and a very high-tech TV station located in a pinewoods suburb of Birmingham, Alabama. There I watched Mother Angelica in person give a live TV talk to a small and enthusiastic live audience, just like Oprah Winfrey, and answer the questions of callers-in. She managed an intimate, motherly presence ideal for the "tube." My Dominican brothers were shocked that I would appear on one of her programs, since many of them regard her as a Catholic fundamentalist of the most benighted type. I must say that her own penchant for excommunicating liberal Catholics and her refusal to enter into cooperation with the U.S. bishops or permit religious sisters in contemporary clothes on her programs seem to me wrongheaded. Yet liberal excesses have understandably provoked her and those who love her. Until the post-Vatican II Church achieves a better theological balance, her own excesses serve as a counterbalance.

Thus, this book *Living the Truth in Love* is my best try at a revision of moral theology for our times. It witnesses to my conviction that in such a revision we can do no better for systematic moral theory than use the four cardinal virtues to supply the framework for our obligations to self and neighbor and then coordinate these virtues with the theological virtues that relate directly to God. In this way the whole Christian life existentially revealed in Jesus' own life as he lived and perfected the Old Law and transformed it into the new, interior Law of the Holy Spirit can be systematically expounded and its realism and beauty manifested. This can be done in a way that is true to the Bible and true to the rich experience of the Church's centuries' old tradition of moral preaching and ministry of the Sacrament of Reconciliation. It can also be true to the needs of our time for moral healing, and true to a future when love and truth will finally have their victory in the Kingdom.

The Prayer He Taught Us To Pray

I don't know where I got this idea, but when I now pray the "prayer that Jesus taught us," I see that it has the following pattern that addresses the Holy Trinity and prays for the theological and cardinal virtues that enable the Christian to travel to the Trinity and escape the roadblocks set by Satan.

A.

1) to *God our Father, who art in heaven*, his utter transcendence as principle of all that has being, *Holy be your name"* (the prayer for faith)

2) to God the Son, *Thy kingdom come*, because he became Man to die on the Cross for us and lead us by his preaching and resurrection into the eternal kingdom of his Father.

3) to the Holy Spirit, *Thy Will be done*, since the Holy Spirit is the Love uniting Father and Son as One God, and the giver of the three theological virtues of Faith (Father), Hope (Son), and Charity (the Holy Spirit): *on earth as it is in heaven* which applies to all three of these petitions, since this is the work of the Church to be completed in the last days. This is what St. Paul means by "spirit" as contrasted to "soul," and "body" and as our goal.

B.

Give us this day our daily bread is a prayer for all the things we need in this life: physical goods, food, clothing, shelter, health and aids to attain the spiritual goods, knowledge by reason and faith and the sacraments be-ginning with Baptism and culminating in the Eucharist, to which especially correspond the cardinal virtue of Justice, the social virtue that makes us think of others and their needs. This what Paul means (1 Thess 5:23) by "soul" that mediates between "body" and "spirit" and pertains to the illuminative way of the spiritual life.

C.

1) *Forgive us our trespasses as we forgive those who trespass against us* pertains to the second cardinal virtue, Fortitude, which moderates our animal instinct to fight and struggle to attain our goals, but which can destroy our friendship with our neighbor. Yet it is also what helps us take up our cross and be martyred.

2) *Lead us not into temptation* pertains to the third cardinal virtue of Temperance, the control of our physical appetites for food, drink, sex, comfort, recreation in which the pursuit of sensual pleasure that naturally supports these instincts becomes the perverse and addictive, which are the source of the most common though not the serious sins

3) *But deliver us from evil* pertains to the chief of the cardinal virtues Prudence that helps us make good decisions so that we do not deceive ourselves. "Evil" is really the person Satan, and this is the last petition corresponding to the first petition to God the Father, since Satan deceived our first parents to the worst of all sins pride "You shall be as gods."

The first three petitions match the last three since Faith pertains especially to the Trinity, part A, while in reverse the last three in reverse pertain to the Holy Spirit (who protects us from the devil and pride); the Son who strengthens us in our weaknesses, and the Father who maintains the order of justice in the universe. Finally the theological virtues of Faith corresponds to Prudence, Hope to Fortitude and Temperance (since we control our passions in view of the ultimate happiness we hope for, and Charity to Justice since "love your neighbor as yourself" perfects our respect for others' rights.

Being Right vs. What's Left?

This concern with theological polarization in the Church and my feeling that, in spite of my desire to be independent of current ideologies, I was being pigeonholed by many of my peers as a "conservative," was heightened for me by another project in which I accidentally became involved. The last year in Washington I was interviewed by Mary Jo Weaver, formerly a professor at the seminary called "The Josephinum," and now at Indiana University. She is well known as an active feminist, but is also what I would describe as "a sturdy, native Catholic." She and Scott Appleby, editor of an important series of studies in the sociology of religion titled *Fundamentalism at the University of Chicago,* but now director of The Cushwa Center for the Study of American Religion at the University of Notre Dame, had received a large grant from the Lilly Endowment to study "conservative" Catholicism. This project was motivated by the neglect of the media to give the same attention to conservative Catholicism as it does to more liberal Catholics.

Mary Jo came to JP II during a preparatory year for the study that she was using to visit various Catholic institutions with a conservative reputation. As a result of her interview with me I was invited to participate as one of a group of scholars who met at the plush Conference Center of Indiana University in Indianapolis. These sessions, expertly chaired by Weaver and Appleby, included some fifteen scholars ranging from the conservative historian James Hitchcock of St. Louis University to Joseph Komonchak and William Dinges of Catholic University along with others of diverse views. These were among the most helpful and pleasant colloquia in which I have ever shared, very objective, open, cordial, and lively. The resulting twelve studies are published by Indiana University in the volume *Being Right: Conservative Catholicism in America.*358 Another group of participants is now studying liberal Catholics for a volume probably to be called *What's Left?* A third study of the middle-of-the-roaders may also be undertaken. The method of these studies is sociological rather than strictly theological.

My own essay in *Being Right* (somewhat compressed by the editors), "The Loss of Theological Unity: Pluralism, Thomism, and Catholic Morality"359 argues, as I have done elsewhere in the course of this memoir, that the decline of the influence of Thomism after Vatican II was not because it was out-of-date, because it could not serve the aims of the Council, but rather because the existential and transcendental Thomists, who dominated the pre-Vatican II period, gave it interpretations that rendered it irrelevant to current issues in a scientific, technological culture.

Retirement?

I have recounted my work as a consultant for the Committee on Doctrine as it continued for sometime after I left Washington and returned to St. Louis. The Committee recently decided (I believe for budgetary reasons) to have only two regular consultants, neither of whom is a specialist in moral theology. Hence I now serve only in an ad hoc capacity. On my return to St. Louis for a couple of years I continued teaching at Aquinas Institute of Theology, reverting to my old love, philosophy. Since, however, these courses could well be taught by younger, full time Dominican professors at Aquinas, I taught only an occasional course and not at Aquinas but at Kenrick Seminary or at the Center for Bioethics in the Medical School of St. Louis University. I did not regard this as retirement, however, since I was fully occupied in lecturing and the writing that I have already detailed in this chapter, as well as odd writing chores such as the twenty-five short articles in *Encyclopedia of Catholic*ism, edited by Richard A. McBrien.[360] and more recently three such articles to be published in the *Encyclopedia of Monasticism*, oddly enough .dealing with "Self Mutilation," "Death: Christian Perspectives," and "The Life Cycle."

In 1993 besides the continuing meetings of *Being Right* and the Committee on Doctrine, I gave workshops for priests in Atlanta, for teachers of religion in Shreveport, lectures to the Dominican novices in Denver, and talks at the Newman Center of Tulane University, in New Orleans and I have attended summer workshops on Thomism given by the Jacques Maritain Institute at Notre Dame. Thus I occasionally attended the annual meetings of the International Medieval Congress in Kalamazoo, the Catholic Theological Society of America, and the Jacques Maritain Association. I have also participated or lectured in meetings at various places including Sacred Heart Seminary, the Grisez Colloquium at Princeton, the Bishops' Medical Ethics Workshops in Dallas, a conference on bioethics in Cambridge, England, etc. I have given retreats to priests and to Dominican laity in Maryland.

During this time I made three remarkable trips abroad. The most significant was taken at the invitation of Fr. Thomas McDermott, then provincial of the newly autonomous Dominican Province of Nigeria and I will say more about this later. The other two trips were vacations with Fr. O'Rourke's group, one to Spain and the other to Northern Italy and down to Rome. I had thought of Spain as a romantic country, which it certainly is, but somehow also as "backward," which it is not. The high point of the trip was St. Dominic's birthplace, the village of Calaruegua north of Madrid and San Esteban in Salamanca, but Avila, Burgos Seville, Granada, Toledo all had their marvels. When I returned I read a good biography of Queen Isabella and marveled at her faith and statesmanship, even if seriously marred by her misguided expulsion of the Jews. The vast wheat fields of the high plateau of central Spain made me think of Oklahoma. On the Italian trip I was especially taken with the wonderful Scrovengi (or Arena) Chapel painted by Giotto in Padua, the little republic of San Marino, and the old abbey of Pompons, places that were new to me. In Padua at the tomb of St. Anthony I found a great crowd from every country praying and venerating the relics with great enthusiasm, but when we came to San Domenico's in Bologna, and the wonderful tomb of St. Dominic, I was chagrined to find only five people in the Church doing their spiritual reading!

One of most curious experiences of this time came when I was invited to New York to participate in Public Television's "Debates-Debates" program that ordinarily features political topics. I was told, however, that I was invited because of my book *Theologies of the Body*. When I asked what the topic was to be I was informed that it had been suggested by a recent article in *The Wall Street Journal* and was "Is Nudism God's Will?" I was to appear with a Protestant evangelical, and an Indian Jainist on the con side, and—believe it or not—three Catholics of rather conservative theological persuasions—on the pro side! It was an invitation that, curious as I am, I could not refuse. The program was well run and quite free of any snickering. In fact it seemed to be too serious.

Of the three Catholics that defended nudism, the first was an editor of a magazine devoted to the movement but who was blind. He claimed that being naked made him feel whole again. The second was a Trappist monk out of his cloister (legitimately, I suppose) and doing charitable work. He did not claim to practice nudism himself, but thought that we ought to respect the human body. The third was a rather Amazonian blonde Bavarian woman who works in her home nude at her computer as a translator. She spoke somewhat scornfully, "You Americans think of nudism as getting a suntan. Real nudists bicycle and cut down trees!" On my side the evangelical young man spoke earnestly of the biblical virtue of modesty, while the Jainist said that since his religion promoted nonviolence, he thought going nude in public in the United States was a kind of psychological violence and was therefore to be deplored. In my summation of our negative side of the debate I pointed out that the world religions had generally agreed that human sexuality requires moderation by discipline and has therefore taught that nudity is often inappropriate. The arguments our debaters had presented for it, I said, did not seem to outweigh this age-old religious view based on widespread human experience.

This visit to New York and wandering about its streets has made it again for me, even more than Chicago where I lived so long, the symbol of our current civilization for good and for ill. This theme of the wonder of a great city has obsessed me ever since I went to Chicago, and the following two poems show the development of my feelings and thoughts about it, as well as my stylistic experiments through the years. First comes a poem from my first encounter with Chicago (the "you" refers to a girl back in Blackwell to whom the poem was originally sent in my school days):

CITY AND COUNTRY

> I know streets and the buildings there
> are like holes in the side of the air
> and the people squint their dirty eyes.
> Every night is blank with cries,
> the girls the guys,
> the feet going by, they keep going by.
>
> Trees and long fields here and cattle,
> the cold clear rattle
> of a snake around a stone,
> hills going up,
> hills going down,
> there one man standing alone,
> and sighs of wings in the shade by water—
> these
> are for you beneath the trees.
>
> Street and feet and cries and I,
> skin of soot,
> dead bones, live fat under foot
> under each long foot
> streets and feet

repeat repeat
and the moon is faded when it comes
in magnificence of soot the trace of thumbs
for you alone beneath the trees

I, I,
    and now I know
    streets and buildings there.
    Yes hear the riveter of the brass sun
        impinge on the girders of the soft June air
        that there
            is the moon.

A second, recent poem refers to this New York visit for the Debates-Debates show and also my memories of walking the streets of Jerusalem where a workman from the small town of Nazareth had died. I hope I do not give away the poem by saying that for me the "hen" in the text is Jesus as symbolized by the Church.

TWO CITIES

As a hen gathers her young under her wings (Mt 23:37)

Down the Judaic ways of Manhattan
for fascinated hours I walked;
and footsore walked back here again
to Gramercy Park Hotel,
    where the street ended
    abruptly at closed gates,
    reflecting, amazed,
    on the towers,
    on the traffic,
    screeches, racket,
    a sort of silent roar,
    the fleeting sun, the rain,
    my face in a dirty pool—
    remembering rackety Jerusalem,
    walled against a pitiless sun.

Now I sing to myself:
    "Pity, pity

　　　　the city, the city
　　　　over it, over it
　　　　Jesus wept."

Oh the comings, the goings,
　　　　　　the sittings, the standing, the talking, the walking
　　　　　　the meetings, the matings, the conceptions and
　　　　　　abortions,
　　　　　　the birthings and dyings,
　　　　　　wheels within wheels,
　　　　　　false promises in neon,
　　　　　　towers on towers,
blind Sun, seeing all through the fog greyly!

Misery loves company,
　　　　　for our prison we built you, wall within wall,
　　　　　fearing the desert open to the very edge.

In the wild Jesus met the Devil,
but on angel-wings the Devil flew Him back
　　　　　to this highest tower
　　　　　of this temple
　　　　　built by greedy hands,
　　　　　here to your cruel heart,
　　　　　light blinded,
　　　　　noise deafened City!

Amidst this cruel traffic
what unlikely hen
spreading her motherly wings
will gather us homeless
　　　　　either there or here?

Chapter 26 - How Long, O Lord, How Long?

Gratitude

As I come to the end of this section on the spirituality of aging I am grateful that I have completed such a long task and especially grateful to all those who have encouraged my work. One person that has been of help to me in old age has been Dr. Mark Latkovic, a former student of mine in Washington, now a teacher at Sacred Heart Seminary in Detroit. He chose to write his doctoral dissertation under Prof. William May on my contribution to the post-Vatican II revision of moral theology. It is a privilege to have the results of my often scattered efforts synthesized by so able a young scholar.

Also one of the joys has been tutoring or assisting students without the formalities of the classroom. Thus at times I have tutored not only Dominican students in reading courses, but also a Jesuit, a Franciscan, and a Benedictine. I also served on the board of Sister René Merkes' defense of her doctoral thesis on "The Relation of the Infused and Acquired Virtues According to Aquinas" at Marquette University, for which I was a reader. One of the Dominicans I tutored in metaphysics was a very gifted African-American Dominican of our province, Duane Brown. Only a few months later in 1997 he died of leukemia at age 29, after giving us all a marvelous lesson of Christian courage in the face of so unexpected death. At the last Mass I attended with him in his hospital room, at the Kiss of Peace, he whispered to me, "I must return the books on metaphysics you lent me." I thank him for that lesson on good dying as I continue my own vigil, awaiting the Lord. Maranatha!

KAI EIDON ALLON AGGELON

"Then I saw another mighty angel come down from heaven wrapped in a cloud, with a halo around his head; his face was like the sun and his feet were like pillars of fire," (Rv 10:1)

I saw another angel
shadow more than flame.
Without praise or blame
quietly, quietly
with bent head,
he said
my name,

and into my heavy eyes
came tears
the weary tears of shame.

"It is time," he said,
"Time now to go."
Slowly, not looking back,
head bent,
knees slack,
into eternity
I went
beyond, beyond
our earth, our sea, the sky,
the future, the past,
knowing at last
now
what it is
to die.

By God's mercy, I have survived the turn of the millennium and I am still on my feet, but a bit wobblier. My health has changed little except, as I have said already, at the end of 1999 I had a heart bypass, hormonal treatment for prostate cancer, take a pill for diabetes, and I have also grown more deaf, so that I need hearing aids, and I take 9 pills every morning before Morning Prayer each day. For a while I had frequent attacks of a nauseating vertigo, similar to those my father had, and which I first had in the 1970s. This is due to what is called BPPV (benign proxysmal vertigo) caused by debris collected in my inner ears (I have heard a good many things good and bad) and is commoner in old age. It bothered me especially the spring of my 90th year, going on 91, but now at 95 I seldom feel it. My recovery from the heart surgery was quite easy and to try to stave off a recurrence I take three 10 minute walks five times a week but with a walking stick.

In 1998 I had celebrated my fiftieth year of ordination and delivered a vespers sermon at our Chicago Province's assembly. A couple of the brethren wrote me indignant letters because they thought I exploited the situation to push for my pet idea, namely, that our Dominican preaching today should be centered on catechizing our people with the Church's teaching as set out in the *Cate-*

chism of the Catholic Church. I will have more to say on that subject in this chapter. Since then I have heard increasing support for this opinion.

It was also made a great celebration for me by four unexpected events. First of all I was invited by Fr. Thomas McDermott, the provincial of our Dominican Province of Nigeria to preach the annual retreat there to the Dominicans, Fathers, Brothers, Sisters and the Dominican Laity. I was rather afraid to do it, but it turned out well. Coming and going, I laid over in Rome to rest. Lagos, where my plane landed, is a fearsome place of many millions who have recently come from the bush into this other vast wilderness of houses that are little more than shanties. I arrived at night and the car in which my brothers met me battled through heavy traffic on streets without traffic lights and lit mainly by flares in the market places along the highway. Yet our large Dominican church in Lagos is magnificent.

The retreat was held in the university town of Ibadan about a two hour drive from the coastal city of Lagos. The Dominican chapel and House of Studies are located a little out of town and are surrounded by a lush garden. A native artist designed the chapel. With a roof supported by great wooden pillars carved in African style, it is surrounded by a moat and is open to the air. My Nigerian brothers took very good care of me and I appreciated their reverence for an old priest, a reverence that, as I have mentioned before, is sometimes missing in our U.S. culture. I was especially touched when several recently professed friars asked to see me, and when I met with them said that they were about to begin their studies and could I give them any good advice on how to be good students!

The reason Fr. McDermott asked me to give the retreat surprised me. Some of the Dominicans had introduced the charismatic practice of praying over people for "deliverance from evil spirits." With Nigerians whose culture rests on ancestor worship and is to a degree obsessed by fear of evil spirits, witchcraft, and the power of curses, these deliverance sessions had proved immensely popular. The problem was, however, that the phenomena exhibited by those asking to be delivered are often extremely dramatic. The "possessed" fall writhing on the ground, vomit, and often in great detail name the spirits that are said to possess them. In one case told to me the possessed woman announced that she was filled with ten thousand female demons that had arisen from the Niger River.

Obviously such dramatic events may produce hysteria and copy-catting, mass suggestion. The pastoral question was whether to avoid such hysteria by stopping these deliverance sessions or not. To stop them might send people back to their witch doctors; to continue them might be giving into superstition. Why was I, who had no experience with such charismatic problems, asked to talk about them in the retreat? That they were real problems became evident from the many very thoughtful questions I received in two open discussions about them.

Fr. McDermott explained to me that as a student he had heard me talk about the existence of angels and devils and knew that I would take the problem seriously and not just reduce it to pop psychology, as he feared other preachers might do. So what did I say to them? I congratulated the Nigerians first on the fact that in their culture the awareness of the reality of the spiritual beings that surround us was still alive while Americans know of this reality only in the fancies of science fiction. Then I told them that theologically we must keep our attention fixed on Christ who has conquered Satan. To permit Satan to preoccupy us is to fall into his shrewd trap. Consequently while it was wholly proper for them to pray for deliverance, in doing so they must also seek to establish an atmosphere of confidence in the power of Christ and serenity, quiet, and peace, not of terrifying and suggestive drama. They should not take seriously the mouthings of the possessed that may simply express superstition or in fact be used by Satan to create panic.

Above all, I tried to explain, the work of Satan is not to be sought so much in such phenomena that manifest his wicked power, but in far subtler work. This is to be especially found in his clever way of setting people of good will against people of good will in fruitless and destructive conflict. It is this evil work of polarization that Satan has brought about in the Church in his ultimately futile attempt to frustrate the work of the Holy Spirit in Vatican II.

The second great celebration of my fiftieth anniversary was equally unexpected. At my very secular alma mater, the University of Chicago, a group of Catholics, led by Thomas Levergood and Professor Paul Griffiths have set up a Lumen Christi Institute whose purpose is to provide better Catholic intellectual fare for students. In addition to sponsoring successful public lectures for several years they had gained the cooperation of the Dean of the College to offer occasional accredited courses in Catholic studies at the University the where I did my undergraduate studies and M.A. and entered the Catholic Church. To my great delight they asked me to give a course for a quarter (the University runs on a quarter system) with the title "Aquinas, Creation, and Modern Science."

I lived for the time at the St. Pius V Priory in Chicago, a colorful Mexican parish that was itself a rich experience. I greatly enjoyed living there and look forward to perhaps ending my life there since it is the retirement home for our Chicago Province. Walking in the neighborhood I found a special pleasure in the several "dollar stores" that sell "seconds" because they also often have wonderful popular junk with a folk flavor. I was there during Holy Week and Easter and saw how thoroughly these Mexican American families with their numerous children seem at home in church.

Teaching in the University quadrangles that I knew in my youth and that are little changed—though for me they were filled with shadows—was strangely bittersweet. My dear friend Leo Shields, my fraternity brothers, Hutchins and Adler, my Marxist comrades stood about me as I looked into the fresh faces, attentive but perhaps a bit skeptical, of my students as I talked about Creation. According to Qoheleth "Vanity of vanities; there is nothing new under the sun." Certainly time can seem to stand still, a feeling I tried to express in the following poem:

THE MYTH OF THE ETERNAL RETURN

"The Pythagoreans teach that a day will come when you all will be gathered again, sitting in the very same places to listen, and I shall be telling you the same story once more."—Simplicius

Not that spring comes seldom
but that it comes again again
in the bare theater of morning
tragedies of women, comedies of men,

that it is all done over
that flames and leaves repeat
even the wind as usual
and the smells of night are sweet

as they were last year and ever
even now as it was then

this like the endless echo of your laughter
that it came and now comes after...
Will it come again, again?

At the end of my course at the University I gave a public lecture titled, "How the Liberal Arts Opened My American Mind," in which I recalled the Adler and Hutchins glory days. The contrast between the Ibadan and the University of Chicago experiences led me to write another poem:

AN EXPANDING UNIVERSE

Drum beats on the roof,
are the torrents from the eves of the Dominican's Ibadan
     chapel
into the garden moat, in the Nigerian rainy season,
     black ears attentive
to my poor, pale words
of angels and of demons. "Let not Satan 's armies
hold your fearful attention.
Fix your dark eyes
on Christ, the power, the wisdom of God Almighty."

The carillon of the hour
From Rockefeller's tower in the gray quadrangle
     of the U. of C.
after my aging absence of sixty years,
new ears so noncommittal
to my dry words:
God, Creation, angels, devils, us,
the puzzle of the Big Bang from nothing.

For Plato
we are shadows cast by a Sun that is alone The Real,
but I am no shadow
yet nothing but the reality of this pacing moment
there in Africa, here in Chicago
at that moment, at this moment
fleeting yet as tangible as one drop of rain
one drum beat vibrating.

like the gray quad here again just as it was then.
Yes there are indeed shadows, teachers, friends,
      comrades sixty years ago
carried away in the torrential flow of time,
but none were dreams and I am not a dream,
now not even a dream of a sleeping god.

Augustine said,
"Time is the moving shadow of eternity"
But more truly Thomas said, "Eternity is Now,
      but now shares in that Now ."
I said to my Chicago students, so young and I so old,
"Your world is real but only one drop in the ocean
      of the world of spirits.
Your world can be the door to a vista far more vast
      than the space that ever expands
from the original exploding atom.
Attentively they heard, wrote it down on the exam.
Did they feel the opening of the spiritual heavens
      that enclose us all?

I said to those their age there in hot Ibadan,
In that same year that marked my fiftieth year as priest
Looking into their dark, bright eyes, eager to learn,
"Do not fear the spirits invoked by witches' curses
since Christ has conquered all demonic fear.,
Thank God that your African horizons have not narrowed.
Not just space expands for you, but all reality,
      matter and spirit where for always
Love the Lover now waits at the center,
Risen in flesh fountain of the eternal torrent of the Spirit
In the Garden of Creation imprisoned
in the academic quadrangle's four gray walls
that hide the vaster world you Africans still touch.

In the Word made flesh
Eternity entered time and made us now, how really
our bodies are the temples they now are
like that timbered chapel in Ibadan carved in African style
alive with the audible vitality of drums and young, deep
voices

out of sun-drenched bodies swaying in God's praise,
the flood that cleans the world
to make it once again the Garden.
As time flows by and in each moment shares
    the reality of now
living and expanding into always Now
may Africa, once the Garden of our enfleshed spirit race
be in the Faith our fallen family's future!

The third great celebration was the gift of my colleague, Fr. Kevin O'Rourke, to whom I owe so much and in so many ways, who invited a group of friends and former students to celebrate with me. These included the Dominicans Fr. Albert S. Moraczweski, founder of the National Catholic Bioethics Center of which I was a Senior Fellow, Charles Bouchard, President of Aquinas Institute of Theology of which I am an emeritus professor, and Romanus Cessario of St. John's Seminary, Brighton, MA, who, among many other favors, obtained for me the invitation to be senior professor at the John Paul II Institute for Studies in Marriage and Family, and also Mark Johnson of Marquette University with whom I have often collaborated, and finally Sister Paula Jean Miller of the Center for Thomistic Studies, Houston, and Mark Latkovic of Sacred Seminary, Detroit, who were two of my former students.

Among these friends I especially want to mention Sister Renée Mirkes, OSF, editor of *NaPro Ethics*, Omaha, NE, who amused us at the gathering by singing a song she had composed and illustrated with a remarkably clever exhibit she had made. Such occasions are gratifying indeed but have furnished themes for sober meditations on how often I have failed to make the best use of the great opportunities that God and my fellow Dominicans and other friends have offered me. To complete my pleasure in all this Fr. Bouchard, in the name of Aquinas Institute of Theology where I had taught for so many years in 2001 graciously conferred on me an honorary degree and in 2007 members of the faculty did a Festschrift in my honor, edited by Richard A. Peddicord, OP, called, *In Medio Ecclesiae*.[361]

By this time I was ready to settle down to complete the book on metaphysics on which I was working, when still a fourth celebration came to me. In September 2001 I accepted an invitation of Fr. Augustine DiNoia, OP, to return for a year to Washington, DC For some years Augustine served very successfully as the Executive Sec-

retary of the Committee on Doctrine of the NCCB, to which I had also served as a consultant. When the American Polish community
under the leadership of Cardinal Maida, Archbishop of Detroit
endowed a magnificent new John Paul II Cultural Center in honor of
"their" pope John Paul II, Fr. DiNoia was chosen as the director of its
Forum. He was also a member of the International Theological
Commission.

The Center houses a museum with fascinating interactive catechetical exhibits for young people and an art museum to display
works from the Vatican Collection, as well as a special room dedicated to John Paul II's life and pontificate. On its top floor is the Cultural Forum that has offices for some ten visiting scholars and a fine
conference room where meetings and seminars of various sorts are
held. I was to work with Fr. DiNoia, Avery Dulles, SJ, and Professor
Kenneth Schmitz of the University of Toronto, in developing a plan
for the Forum. Fr. Dulles was made Cardinal and hence was not able
to join us, but during the year the plan was successfully finished and
approved by the Board of the Center. In the spring of 2002, however, Fr. DiNoia was called to Rome to be Undersecretary for the
Sacred Congregation of the Doctrine of the Faith and was then
transferred to be secretary of the Sacred Congregation for Worship
and consecrated Archbishop. While at the Cultural Center I made
new friends and am especially grateful to Ms. Karen King, Fr.
DiNoia's secretary, for her great assistance in my efforts there.

In the course of the year at the Center I took part in a seminar
on the thought of John Paul II and gave two lectures in the Christmas season on the angels, and in the spring semester took part in a
series of lectures on Christianity and Islam, in which twice I gave the
closing lecture. In this lecture I stressed the idea that unless Christians join a common cause with Muslims in proclaiming the Creator,
the God of Abraham, we Christians will find ourselves caught in the
middle between two great warring forces. On the one hand Muslims
will identify Christianity with the godless Secular Humanism of the
Western powers, and on the other hand, Secular Humanists will
identify Christianity with the religious fanaticism of some Muslims. I
was delighted that in the discussion following the second delivery of
the lecture an elderly and very impressive Muslim, head of some
Islamic society, rose to commend what I had said and to express
hopes for continuing discussion.

While at the Center I also took part in a symposium at Ave Maria
College in Michigan at which I read a paper "Jesus' Self-Knowledge

in Aquinas' Exposition of The Gospel According to St. John." I also lectured at Providence College, RI on "The Validity of Metaphysics," at the Newman Center at Yale, New Haven, CT on "Cloning and the Beginning of the Human Person," and at St. Charles Borromeo Seminary in Philadelphia, PA on "Organ Donation and Implantation." At the same time I was teaching at the Institute for Psychological Sciences in Arlington, VA.

At the end of May 2002 I returned to St. Louis, but was no longer assigned to St. Louis Bertrand Priory that since 1981 had been my community, but to the main Dominican community of brothers preparing for the priesthood at Aquinas Institute of Theology and many of their faculty, located in Jesuit Hall at the Jesuit sponsored St. Louis University. I said in the last chapter that as a Dominican I have always lived in a park and again I have the recently enlarged and beautified campus of the University for my walks. From the fifth floor of Jesuit Hall I overlook the beautiful campus of the University and in the distance to the east can see the St. Louis Gateway Arch. In the little park across the streets I watch people with their dogs.

I still do a little traveling, notably to Rome in 2003 to attend a conference at the "Angelicum" or University of St. Thomas run by Dominican Order. It concerned the teaching of philosophy in the Order and I presented a "Guide to Dominican Studies" that was commended in the next General Chapter but, to my disappointment, without any practical application. I also lectured for two weeks at the Center for Thomistic Studies at the University of St. Thomas in Huston. I was still teaching occasional classes and tutoring students. Fr. Kevin O'Rourke and I, with the assistance of Sister Jean DeBlois, CSJ, have prepared a 5th, much revised, edition of our *Health Care Ethics: A Theological Approach* finally published in 2006. In it we must deal with such new issues as the special health concerns of women, stem cell research, and controversies over the care of the dying.

More important from my point of view was the publication in 2006 of my *The Way Toward Wisdom: An Interdisciplinary and Contextual Introduction to Metaphysics* (University of Notre Dame Press, 2006) for the Center of Thomistic Studies, University of St. Thomas, Houston, TX 2006.

For the future I place great hope in the work of the Institute for Advanced Physics, Baton Rouge, LA, founded by a noted physicist, Dr. Anthony Rizzi, formerly on the faculty of The California Institute of Technology from which he resigned to devote full time to this project. Through the writings of Jacques Maritain, Rizzi discovered the realistic thought of St. Thomas Aquinas which he has studied profoundly and has come to agree with the Albertus Magnus Lyceum position that I have described earlier. This position which rejects any distinction between the philosophy of nature and natural science and treats mathematicized science as a dialectical portion of natural science itself. This provides a much more satisfactory statement of the relation between natural science based on reason and Christian faith based on revelation than current "Design Arguments," yet is not content with "dialogue," as is so much work on this subject, especially by Protestant writers such as Ian Barbour and authors favored by the Pendleton Foundation and the magazines *Zygyon* and *Theology and Science*.

Dr. Anthony Rizzi, in his lively introductory book *The Science Before Science: A Guide to Thinking in the 21st Century* Rizzi has explained this issue. He also grants certificates to physicists and philosophers who have passed an exam on this book, and since 2003 has held summer conferences at Notre Dame to prepare a standard textbook for those majoring in physics that will root current physics in truly empirical principles. I have spoken at these, including that of 2010. Rizzi has recently also published the first of a series of textbooks on science for science majors, *Physics for Realists* (2008) based on Thomistic principles and trained a number of young physicists. Unfortunately no Catholic university has yet adopted this approach.

Senile Sexuality

Science has much to say about the aging body. I use to hear Italian men in confession say, "Father, I did something natural." Sex is indeed a major feature of human personality and still has to be controlled even in old age where it plays a role in spirituality. As I reviewed this autobiography I have noted that in the first part that dealt with my conversion, I was very explicit about my early sexual sins. One of the editors thought I should remove this as rather scandalous, but I did not. I wrote there that after my conversion I have never fallen into those sins, thanks to the grace of God! It is evident that at that time my sexual impulses were bisexual and even tipped toward homosexuality.

My prostate surgery in 1992 relieved me of nocturnal emissions. Now at 95 I have noticed that although I remain somewhat bisexual and have to reject temptations to impure thoughts when I see attractive young people of both sexes, I am more inclined to normal attraction to the opposite sex. I was surprised at myself the other day in choir when I found that the beautiful face and figure of a young girl there in the chapel, especially her long dark hair that reminded me of my mother, kept obscuring my prayer!

Now when I see happy families I also realize how wonderful it is to have children. St. Thomas Aquinas says that is what God intended before original sin, although now, as Jesus exemplifies and St. Paul teaches, celibacy is to be preferred so as to devote all our energies to walking the path to everlasting life. Certainly I do not regret my celibate vows as they have given me great freedom of mind.

Return to St. Pius V Priory

Most of this vigil I have spent at my computer and have managed to write for publication, "How Theology Can Enrich Theology," " The Luminous Mysteries of the Rosary," "Healing for Freedom: A Christian Perspective on Personhood and Psychotherapy," and have translated the interesting commentary on the last chapter of proverbs *De Muliere Forti* (The Strong Woman) attributed to St. Albert the Great and a major article, "Albert the Great on the Cogitative Power," for a collection of essays on St. Albert edited by Irven M. Resnick and to be published by Brill; *Doctrinal Preaching: Trinitarian and Narrative*.

I have written but not yet found a publisher for *A Marian Ecclesiology* and revised my old lectorate thesis *Contemplation and Society*. I am now working on short books of meditations: *Four Newest Things: Death, Hell, Purgatory, Heaven* and *God the Carpenter's Holy Family*, and a pamphlet on vocations: *God Calls You, Me, Yes, Each and All*. I have also been reworking this autobiography that the University of Notre Dame Press considered for a year and then rejected as too long.

My increasingly poor hearing and my walking with a stick now discourage traveling, but I have managed last summer to get to Notre Dame to the Jacques Maritain conference to give a paper on my book *The Way Toward Wisdom* and to Xavier University in Chicago for our Provincial Assembly. Getting to St. Xav's where I had taught and engaged in the curricular program supported by the Albertus Magnus Lyceum from 1951-1962 seemed to bring me full circle. This year 2010 after being diagnosed as having heart failure I am going to that assembly again and am reassigned to St. Pius Priory in Chicago that is our Dominican infirmary and hope to keep writing there.

St. Pius V Priory is a solid five story building with a sixth floor solarium erected in 1940 by our former Provincial Edward Hughes at 1909 South Ashland Ave., nor far from downtown Chicago, as the provincial headquarters of the Province of St. Albert the Great of the Dominican Order. It is built next to an ugly redbrick parish church also named after St. Pius V. The Church is famous as a Shrine of St. Jude, Patron of Impossible Cases, about whom I am now (2012) writing a book. Ours is a highly Mexican neighborhood with wonderful murals on the old buildings and constant heavy traffic on Ashland.

Besides the Provincial and his staff, St. Pius V Priory is a retirement convent (or as we say "on limited service") for aged friars of whom there are at present twelve. We every day chant the Liturgy of the Hours and concelebrate the Eucharist in our priory chapel. The rest of the time is spent either in private prayer or in some individual work according to our physical and mental condition. If we become bedridden we are sent to the very fine Resurrection Health Care Center in the Chicago suburbs where at present there are five Dominican men. Here at the priory we are cared for by two fine nurses in active service, Alejandra Gallegos, born in Mexico, and Gladys Cardoso, born in Ecuador, and a staff of cooks and maintenance people. I am in fair shape physically, although I have mild heart failure, use a stout walking stick, and am very "hearing disadvantaged" with annoying, buzzing hearing aids.

When not at prayer or meals (I am diabetic) I slave away at my computer, writing books and articles, turning out a book about every five months. I have good friendships with the other members of the priory although my hearing aids are so often inadequate to their aged voices.

THE PLOT

Aristotle supposed the heavens are made
of a quintessential element
for eternity circling, circling, and et cetera.
Now we suppose it all began
with a so Big Bang, eventually
to spread into nothing but perhaps

a quantum wiggle
in a void.
Yet in the sea of random, chance events
we have emerged
only to lapse again
and wash away without a trace.

Yet when I look into your face, my friend
I know it is not so.
No doubt we have emerged
like actors on the stage
of a vast play
trying to remember what we are to say
and when to pause
to bring the drama to its close with wild applause
but the Playwright knows.

After the embarrassments of reviewing my own life, I need to sum up the journey already covered, since I still have at least a few more wobbly steps to take. The meaning of a Dominican's life must be in such a vision of the Truth that he has been given to attain, so I want to finish these recollections with a summary of the concerns on which my thinking is still focused. If you, patient readers (if there are any who have walked this far with me), find this last chapter is more sermonizing than autobiography, I must plead that the life story of any member of the Order of Preachers can only be one sermon after another!

Catholic spiritual writers are agreed that the spiritual life has three stages: first that of beginners or the purgatorial stage of overcoming mortal sins; second that of the mature Christian who is advancing in the acquisition of the virtues or illuminative stage; and third, the unitive stage of a confirmed union with God. According to many saints, such as John of the Cross, the second stage is divided from the first by the Dark Night of the Soul, a period of trial in which the person learns no longer to depend in prayer on the imagination. He claimed that among contemplative religious this can set in by the end of their novitiate. The third period is divided from the second by the profound trial of the Dark Night of the Spirit when the person is learning no longer to depend in prayer on abstract intellectual concepts of God but is becoming acutely aware of the utter transcendence of faith.

Thus this division results from the nature of the human person who is first animal, living by the senses and sense appetites but as Christian living by faith; second naturally human living by abstract intelligence and rational decisions but as a Christian living by hope; and third the person transformed by grace and living as a Christian by charity. This, of course, is a schema, since only a few young saints pass through these stages quickly. Most Christians tend to move a few steps forward and then a step or so backward but do not make rapid progress and are still so imperfect at death that they must pass through Purgatory before they can enter the Beatific Vision. Hence, just as in a cross-country journey the road may be very widening and require one to climb mountains and find one's way out of deep valleys, so one ought to keep going vigorously without worrying too much just where one is on the map so it is with the Christian Way.

Thus some days I think I have made progress and others I feel like I have fallen back. Certainly for me, even at 95, while hoping firmly by God's grace to reach the goal and be with him forever I must be ready for a long Purgatory in which he washes me clean in the fire of His love of much dirt that is all too evident. Yet I do think that as a religious I have been in the middle part of the journey for a long time. The scrupulosity that I mentioned and the theological depths of my meditation which frequently occur, plunge downward and lead to surprising insights that seem to me to have had intermittently the character of the Dark Night of the Soul and this has further darkened notably this last year.

Is that progress or just mental aging? I much more than ever rely on my baptismal commitment and my Eucharistic nourishment to get over discouragement. I am increasingly conscious of how self-centered I have been throughout my life as a teacher, loving my own learning, rather than sharing the truth or being concerned in my prayer for others. Since my time now must be short this frightens me, but I have confidence God can complete the work in me if I open to Him more.

For me God the Father has given the care that, as I have related, I missed in my earthly father and I cling to him especially in St. Joseph. My mother cared tenderly for me but also infected me with her neuroses, while Mary washes me in her own purity. I meditate on my Lord's five wounds and, as in the pictures of St. Dominic, embrace the foot of his Cross and like the Magdalene reach out to embrace the Lord's risen feet. This is still a vigil and my lamp burns low, but there is more than enough oil ready at hand. Above all as I write this I am aware of how good God has been to me...how very good!

President of AI 1968

After Vatican II

At Catholic U. 1992

Gray haired

Ralph Powell & Benedict Ashley, St. Louis

1986 Ben & Rusty

Pope John Paul II says, "Thank You."

Notes

[1] Richard Dawkins, *The God Delusion* (Boston: Houghton Mifflin, 2006); Daniel Dennett, *Breaking the Spell: Religion as a Natural Phenomenon* (London: Viking, 2006); Sam Harris, *Letter to a Christian Nation* (New York, Knopf, 2006); Christopher Hitchens, *God Is Not Great: How Religion Poisons Everything* (New York: Hatchette Book Group, 2007); Victor J. Stenger, *God: The Failed Hypothesis: How Science Shows that God Does not Exist* (Amherst, NY; Prometheus Books).

[2] *The Way Toward Wisdom: An Interdisciplinary and Contextual Introduction to Metaphysics* (University of Notre Dame Press for the Center of Thomistic Studies, University of St. Thomas, Houston, TX, 2006).

[3] See Neodesha, KS, City Profile, http://www.epodunk.com/cgi-bin/genInfo.php?locIndex=4881

[4] See Clyda Franks, *Ponca City and Kay County Boom Towns*, Images of America: Oklahoma (Tulsa, OK: Arcadia Pubs, 2002), Chapter 3, pp. 51-66. for a history of this town and region.

[5] See "Chickaskia River Near Blackwell," http://en.wikipedia.org/wiki/Chikaskia_River

[6] (1) Father: Arthur B. Ashley, 1880, born Lewiston, IL. Accountant; (2) Grandfather William D. Ashley, 1841, Pulaski County, Kentucky, wagon maker; (3) John Oliver Ashley, 1819 Pulaski County, KY Farmer, blacksmith, wagon maker; (4) John Ashley, Jr. 1794, ? North Carolina farmer; (5) John Ashley 1755 Mecklenburg, North Carolina, farmer; (6) Francis Ashley 1739, North Carolina; (7), John Plowman Ashley 1692 Lancaster County, Virgina; (8) Thomas A. Ashley 1660 Lancaster County, Virginia, Blacksmith; (9) John Ashley 1618, Lancaster, Gloucestershire, England, married Lady Jane Cooper and in about 1650 came to Virginia. His property was on Cedar Creek close to Wateree Reservoir in South Carolina, North of Columbia, S. C.; (10) William Ashley, 1600 Lincolshire Parish, England; (11) Anthony Ashley,1576 Wimbourne, St. Giles, Dorsetshire, England; (12) Anthony Ashley c. 1530 Fordingbridge, Hampshire, England; (13) Sir Henry of Wimborne St. Giles Dorset, England 1490; (14) Sir Hugh of Wimborne St. Giles Ashley 1465, Wimborne St. Giles, Dorset,; 15) Edmund of Wimbourne St. Giles Ashley, 1440 Dorset (16) Robert Ashley, 1415,Wiltshire, whose great, great grandfather, (20) was Benedict Ashley in the reign of Henry II and Edward I, c.1300.

[7] His father was the third William Moore in this country, born in Somerset County, Pennsylvania, March 1, 1807. His mother Mary Ann Holzople was of Dutch ancestry. They had four other sons besides Norman and three daughters. The second William Moore, my great-grandfather, was born 1782 in Pennsyl-

vania and married a woman of French descent, while the first William Moore, my great-great-great grandfather, was born in Ireland and came to Pennsylvania about 1765 when he was about twelve years old.

[8] Laura Jane was the daughter of Thomas McCormick Dawson (1836-1901) from Westmoreland County, Pennsylvania and Charity Jane Van Ausdall. This Charity Jane, my maternal great-grandmother, was born October 21, 1836, the daughter of Isaac Van Ausdall, a Methodist preacher and Esther Alter, a nurse. In her family was also the first woman preacher among the Pennsylvania Methodists, Helenor, known as "the Lady Preacher." The Alters also were friends of Alexander Campbell, once a Baptist but founder of the Disciples of Christ or Christian Church, in which my father was raised, a denomination founded to end denominationalism by having "No Name but Christ's, no Creed but the Bible." Esther Alter was daughter of John Alter and Helenor Sheetz who was a descendant of Peter Sheetz from South Switzerland, a watchmaker who made and lost a fortune in the island of San Domingo and then settled in Cumberland County, Pennsylvania in 1794. Esther Alter's father, John Alter was born Sept 13, 1771, the son of Johan Jacob Alter and Margaret Landis of Swiss ancestry. Johan, who fought in the Revolution, was the son of George Heinrich Alter who came from the Rhineland with his two sons Johan Jacob and George Friedrich, Jr. in 1750.

[9] This essay and other unpublished writings of mine are now in the "Ashley Archive" at the Institute for Psychological Sciences, Arlington, VA.

[10] *S. Th.,* I-II, q.89, a.6, c..

[11] She was Laura Abigail Clubb wife of I. M. Clubb, owner of the Clubb Hotel in Kaw City. Much of her collection is now in the Philbrook Art Museum in Tulsa. It is often forgotten that a Vice-President of the United States under Herbert Hoover was Charles Curtis 1860-1936), a Kansas Senator, whose mother was a Kaw Indian.

[12] I was most impressed by the landscape of Ralph A. Blakelock, 1847-1919 an artist of whom a writer for the U.S. Figge Art Museum, Davenport, Iowa, writes (http://www.figgeartmuseum.org/): " The artist sought to capture the Hudson River School style but could not find it within himself to seek the grand subject or the sweeping vista that focused on literal details of the landscape. Instead he turned inward, and, along with Albert Pinkham Ryder, represented to many twentieth-century critics, authentic American painting, untainted by European influence, both in method and in mind."

[13] New York: Simon and Schuster, 1987.

[14] Chicago: University of Chicago Press, 1991.

[15] With Charles van Doren, rev. ed., New York: Simon and Schuster, 1972.

[16] See http://en.wikipedia.org/wiki/Richard_McKeon and, Eugene Garver and Richard Buchanan, eds., *Pluralism in Theory and Practice: Richard McKeon and American Philosophy* (Nashville: Vanderbilt University Press, 2000).

[17] New York: Harcourt, Brace and Company, 1927.

[18] See http://en.wikipedia.org/wiki/Scott_Buchanan

[19] http://en.wikipedia.org/wiki/Stringfellow_Barr

[20] *The Annotated Alice: Alice's Adventures in Wonderland and Through the Looking Glass by Louis Carroll* (New York: C.N. Potter, 1960). See http://en.wikipedia.org/wiki/Martin_Gardner

[21] See http://en.wikipedia.org/wiki/Germain_Grisez and my objections to his moral system, "Integral Human Fulfillment According to Germain Grisez," *The Ashley Reader: Redeeming Reason* (Naples, FL: Sapientia Press of Ave Maria University, 2006), pp. 225-271.

[22] *The Higher Learning in America* (New Haven, CT: Yale University Press, 1936); *No Friendly Voice* (Westport, CT: Greenwood, 1968).

[23] Boston: Little, Brown and Co., 1989.

[24] Chicago: University of Chicago Press, 1991.

[25] Edited by John H. Hicks, with a Foreword by Studs Terkel (Berkeley: University of California Press, 1993).

[26] Spring, 1990, pp. 211-235; p. 211.

[27] *Ibid.,* p. 214.

[28] *University of Chicago Magazine* 59, Summer, 1977, pp. 23-25.

[29] I have not been able to check these references to Farrell and Mencken.

[30] Pp. 212 f.

[31] New York: Macmillan/Collier, 1992.

[32.] New York: Macmillan, 1992.

[33] See "Ohio's Hall of Fame: Janet Kalven" http://www.odjfs.state.oh.us/women/halloffame/bio.asp?ID=153

[34] See http://en.wikipedia.org/wiki/Charles_Hartshorne

[35] See http://en.wikipedia.org/wiki/R.S._Crane

[36] Chicago: University of Chicago Press, 1967.

[37] Chicago: University of Chicago Press, 1952.

[38] Chicago: University of Chicago Press, 1992. See http://www.imdb.com/title/tt0105265/

[39] An example of his many publications is Robert S. Brumbaugh, 1918-, *Western Philosophic Systems and their Cyclic Ttransformations*; foreword by George Kimball Plochmann (Carbondale : Southern Illinois University Press, c1992.

[40] Chicago: University of Chicago Press, 1963.

[41] See Wikipedia biography, Herbert Alexander Simon, 1916-2001: http://en.wikipedia.org/wiki/Herbert_Simon

[42] See http://lawprofessors.typepad.com/laborprof_blog/laborprofschool.html

[43] See http://en.wikipedia.org/wiki/Quincy_Wright

[44] Ellis died in 2000; see his biography in Wikipedia http://en.wikipedia.org/wiki/Ellis_B._Kohs

[45] http://en.wikipedia.org/wiki/Thornton_Wilder

[46] New York: Random House, 1935. On Stein see http://en.wikipedia.org/wiki/Gertrude_Stein

[47] New York: Limited Editions Club, 1962.

[48] London: Longmans Green, 1934.

[49] London: Longmans, Green, 1934.

[50]. New York: W. Morrow, 1983. See his Wikipedia biography: http://en.wikipedia.org/wiki/Martin_Gardner

[51] See http://en.wikipedia.org/wiki/Saul_Bellow

[52] A reprint of an obituary in *The New York Times* is at http://query.nytimes.com/gst/fullpage.html?res=990CE0DE1630F930A25757C0A963958260

[53] Chicago: 2nd ed. Aldine Press, 1972. See Loyd S. Etheredge, "Profile to appear in *American National Biography*, forthcoming from the Oxford University Press" http://web.mit.edu/m-i-t/profiles/profile_ithiel.html and "What Next? The Intellectual Legacy of Ithiel de Sola Pool" http://web.mit.edu/comm-forum/papers/etheredge.html

[54] My recollections of some of these Trotskyites is rather clouded and may not be entirely accurate. Steven J. Zipperstein, "The First Loves of Isaac Rosenfeld," in *Jewish Social Studies*, Volume 5, Numbers 1 & 2, available at http://www.jstor.org/discover/10.2307/4467539?uid=2134&uid=2&uid=70&uid=4&sid=21101458310251 has much information on Passin and Bellows.

[55] New York: New American Library, 1971. On Reedy see http://en.wikipedia.org/wiki/George_Reedy He died in 1999.

[56] On him see "The Two Frank Meyers," review by Ryan McMaken of the book by Kevin J. Smant, *Principles and Heresies: Frank S. Meyer and the Shaping of the American Conservative Movement* (ISI Books, 2000). http://en.wikipedia.org/wiki/Frank_Meyer_(political_philosopher)

[57] See http://en.wikipedia.org/wiki/Whittaker_Chambers

[58] New York: Random House, 1961, reprinted Westport CN: Greenwood Press, 1973.

[59] Richard Dawkins *The God Delusion* (note 1 above) neglects Aquinas' fuller and more strictly philosophical treatment of this First Way in the *Summa Contra Gentiles* I, 13 and badly summarizes it (p. 77) from the *Summa Theologiae* I, q. 2 as "Nothing moves without a prior mover: This leads us to a regress from which the only escape is God. Something had to make the first move, and that something we call God" and then says that it is "an entirely unwarranted assumption that God himself is immune to regress" or to endow this Mover with "the properties normally ascribed to God." Dawkins grants that some processes have a "terminator" such as cutting a piece of gold down to its atoms, but then says, "it is by no means clear that God provides a natural terminator to the re-

gresses of Aquinas" (pp. 78). Thus Dawkins ignores the fact that Aquinas' First Way only concludes to the existence of an Unmoved Mover, "which is what everybody means by 'God,'" not immediately and formally to God. Only after an immaterial Unmoved Mover has been formally proved to exist, does Aquinas use further arguments to prove that it must be a supremely intelligent and powerful personal being. Moreover Dawkins by stretching the term First Cause to include material terminators such as atoms ignores the fact that this would be to attempt a proof from material causality, which Aquinas denies to be possible. St. Thomas is not, like Dawkins, a reductionist for whom "to explain" always means to reduce a thing to its parts. I have treated this question in detail in detail my book *The Way Toward Wisdom* (Notre Dame: University of Notre Dame Press, 2006), pp. 61-131.

[60] The internet still carries much information on this man with a wonderful name: see "Count Alfred Habdank Skarbek Korzybski, Author of *Science and Sanity*, 1933" at http://evans-experientialism.freewebspace.com/korzybski.htm

[61] "A Psychological Model with a Spiritual Dimension," *Pastoral Psychology* (May, 1972): 31-40.

[62.] Petersham, MA: St. Bede's Publications, rev. ed, 1986.

[63] See *Nature, the Physician and the Family: The Collected Works of Herbert Ratner*, MD. Privately published, 1997. See the memorial on Dr. Ratner of the La Leche League (for breast nursing and a short biography http://www.medicineatmichigan.org/classnotes/notes.asp?nid=121

[64] On Janet's later role in the Grail Movement and Catholic feminism see her book *Women Breaking Boundaries: A Grail Journey, 1940-1995*. (Albany: State University of New York Press, 1999).

[65] Cleveland, Ohio: privately printed, 1936.

[66] Trained as a clinical psychiatrist he became a noted Trappist monk. See http://www.homeinsp.com/files/Fr_1.htm. On his conversion see his book *The Glory of Thy People* (New York; MacMillan, 1948).

[67] See http://en.wikipedia.org/wiki/Charles_De_Koninck

[68] I here paraphrase the opinion of Bernard E. Scott in his as yet unpublished *The Man I Called Father: A Meditative Memoir*, vol. 1, generously sent me in draft. If completed it will provide an intimate portrait of the later Schwartz. I have felt it best not to change my own recollections of him, except for chronology.

[69] "The Natural Mystical Experience and the Void," *Redeeming the Time* (London: G. Bles, The Centenary Press, 1943) pp. 225-255. The American edition (New York: Charles Scribner's Sons), has the title *Ransoming the Time.*

[70] See "God and the Brain" http://atheistempire.com/reference/brain/main.html

[71] *Dante* (New York: Dutton, 1923).

[72] Vatican I, *Dei Filius,* DS 3, 3013. Vatican II , *Lumen Gentium*, n. 8; *Catechism of the Catholic Church* #811-870. I have presented this argument in my book, *Choosing a Worldview and Value System: An Ecumenical Apologetics* (Staten Island, NY: Alba House, 2000).

[73] See biographical note http://www.bautz.de/bbkl/g/gredt_j_a.shtml

[74] *King's Pawn: the Memoirs of George H. Dunne* (Chicago: Loyola University Press, 1990).

[75] *The Dominican Bulletin*, (River Forest, IL) Winter 1950, pp. 14-16.

[76] E.g., *The Structure of Political Thought* (New York: McGraw-Hill, 1963).

[77] See note 74 above.

[78] See http://www.ncbcenter.org/ topic "About: History."

[79] See "Ryerson & Burnham Archives: Collection Descriptions: Childerly Chapel photograph album, c.1926-c.1930." http://www.artic.edu/aic/libraries/rbarchives/rbarchcoll.html

[80] See http://ethicscenter.nd.edu/about/inspires/yves-simon

[81] Yves Rene Marie Simon (1903-1961); see the work of his son Anthony O. Simon*, Acquaintance with the Absolute: The Philosophy of Yves R. Simon: Essays and Bibliography* (New York: Fordham University Press, 1998).

[82] See his biography (in German) on Wikipedia http://de.wikipedia.org/wiki/Waldemar_Gurian

[83] Notre Dame dissertation (Anne Arbor, MI: Edward Brothers, lithoprint, 1951).

[84] Notre Dame, IN, 1941.

[85] See F. A. Hermens, *Democracy or Anarchy? A Study of Proportional Representation* (Notre Dame, Ind.: Review of Politics, University of Notre Dame,

1941).

[86] Notre Dame: University of Notre Dame Press, 1947, 1972.

[87] Montreal: Edition de Université Laval, 1943.

[88] "In Defense of Jacques Maritain," *Modern Schoolman* 22 (May, 1945):183-208.

[89] "In Defense of St. Thomas," *Laval Philosophique et Theologique* 1 (2, 1945): 1-103.

[90] *Problems for Thomists: The Problem of Species* (St. Paul MN: College of St. Thomas, 1940).

[91] For more details see my "The River Forest School of Natural Philosophy", *Philosophy and the God of Abraham,* Essays in Memory of James A. Weisheipl, R. J. Long, ed. (Toronto: Pontifical Institute of Mediaeval Philosophy, 1991), pp. 1-16; "Thomism and the Transition from the Classical World-View to Historical-Mindedness," *The Future of Thomism*, D. W. Hudson and D. W. Moran, eds. (Notre Dame, IN: American Maritain Association, University of Notre Dame Press, 1992), pp. 109-122; and "The Loss of Theological Unity: Pluralism, Thomism, and Catholic Morality*," Being Right: Conservative Catholics in America*, M.J. Weaver and S. Appleby eds. (Bloomington/ Indianapolis: Indiana University Press, 1995), pp. 63-87.

[92] On Joseph Cardijn see See http://www.catholicauthors.com/cardijn.html

[93] See http://en.wikipedia.org/wiki/Henry_Rago

[94] See http://www.jewishaz.com/jewishnews/031219/pioneer.shtml

[95] See http://domcentral.org/dominican-priest-and-scupltor-thomas-mcglynn-a-mcglynn-album/

[96] Charles W. Ferguson, *Naked to Mine Enemies : The life of Cardinal Wolsey*, with a new introduction by A.L. Rowse (New York: Time, Inc., 1965).

[97] I think it was John Hunt, *The Ascent of Everest* (London; Hodder & Staughten, 1953).

[98] John Hersey, *Hiroshima* (New York, A. A. Knopf, 1946).

[99] *Perfectae Caritatis*, n. 2.

[100] See http://en.wikipedia.org/wiki/Louis_de_Montfort

[101] For more about Fr. Kane see his Festschrift, James A. Weisheipl, ed., *The Dignity of Science: Studies in the Philosophy of Science Presented to W.H. Kane, O.P.*, The Thomist Press, 1961.

[102] This is a major theme of my *The Way Toward Wisdom: An Indisciplinary and Intercultural Introduction to Metaphysics* (Notre Dame, IN: University of Notre Dame Press, 2006).

[103] First edition, St. Louis: The Pope John Center 1985; second edition with new introduction, Braintree, MA: The Pope John Center, 1995. This institution is now in Boston and called The National Catholic Bioethics Center.

[104] Note 101 above.

[105] On Poinsot see John Deely, *Four Ages of Understanding: The First Post-modern Survey of Philosophy from Ancient Times to the Turn of the Twentieth Century* (Toronto: University of Toronto, 2001), pp. 447-484.

[106] Reginald Garrigou-Lagrange, *De revelatione per Ecclesiam catholicam proposita* , 5th ed. revised (Rome, Desclée, 1950); the apologetic theory of this book seem to me the most profound avilable, although its second historical part is somewhat perfunctory. On Garrigou-Lagrange, whose reputation, obscured in the Vatican II period, is now recovering, see Richard Peddichord, OP, *The Sacred Monster of Thomism: Life & Legacy of Reginald Garrigou-Lagrange* (South Bend, IN: St. Augustine's Press, 2005).

[107] "The Christmas Star" Dec. 1943, pp 15-17; "Utopia and Myopia," Dec. 1946, pp. 18-29; "Meet My Mother," Autumn, 1947, pp. 1-3; "Materialism," Winter, 1947 pp. 21; "Pagan-like", Spring, 1947, pp. 4-7; "Principle or Compromise," Autumn, 1948 pp. 5-8.

[108] This argument is presented in detail in my book, *Choosing A Worldview and Value System: An Ecumenical Apologetics* (Staten Island, NY: Alba House, 2000).

[109] *Lumen Gentium*, n. 20.

[110] No. 32, 1 (Jan, 1958): pp. 1-31 and 2, (April, 1958): pp. 202-234.

[111] River Forest, IL: Albertus Magnus Lyceum, 1958.

[112] *Aristotle's Sluggish Earth*, (River Forest, IL: Albertus Magnus Lyceum,

1958). Previously in The *New Scholasticism* , 32, 2 (Part I: "Problematics of the De Caelo," 32 (1958), pp.1-31; Part II, "Media of Demonstration", pp. 202-234; the biological part was never published.

[113] See R. James Long ed., *Philosophy and the God of Abraham, Essays in Memory of James A. Weisheipl* (Pontifical Institute of Medieval Philosophy, Toronto, 1991).

[114] That is why my recent publication *The Way Toward Wisdom*, has the description in the title *An interdisciplinary and multicultural introduction to metaphysics* (South Bend IN: University of Notre Dame Press, 2006).

[115] *American Catholics and the Intellectual Life* (Chicago: Heritage Foundation, (1956).

[116] See Joan Glisky, IHM, "Sister Mary Emil Penet, IHM, http://ejournals.bc.edu/ojs/index.php/catholic/article/view/706 and Loran Ann Quinonez, and Mary Daniel Turner,. *The Transformation of American Sisters* (Philadelphia: Temple University Press, 1988). http://www.temple.edu/tempress/titles/814_reg.html

[117] For example: (1) "Science in Synthesis: A Study of Liberal Culture in A Scientific Age," Aquinas Newman Center of University of New Mexico, 1956; (2) education: "A Symposium of the Thomas More Association on the Catholic Contribution to American Intellectual Life," Rosary College, June 14-15, 1958; the Aquinas Lecture at St. Meinrad's Abbey, "The Seven Liberal Arts as Tools for Sacred Theology," March, 1960; and "Redesigning the Curriculum," College of St. Mary of the Springs, Columbus Ohio, Sept, 1960) and (3) art: "Dominican Subjects as Treated by Fra Angelico," Siena Heights College, Adrian, MI, Feb. 1956.

[118.] New York: Sheed and Ward, 4 vols. 1938-1942.

[119] *Friar Thomas D'Aquino* with corrigenda and addenda by James A. Weisheipl, OP (Washington, DC : Catholic University of America Press, 1983).

[120] This argument is discussed at length in *The Way Toward Wisdom,* cf. note 2 above, pp. 569.

[121] On the history of this see James A. Weisheipl, ed., *The Dignity of Science:Studies in the Philosophy of Science presented to W.H. Kane, O.P.* (Washington, DC: The Thomist Press, 1961), pp. 469-485).

[122] Pietro M. Passerini, OP (1597-1677).

[123] For much more serious efforts see the collections of essays cosponsored, with the commendation of Pope John Paul II, by the Vatican Observatory, Rome, and the Center for Theology and Natural Sciences, Berkeley, CA: *Physics, Philosophy and Theology: A Common Quest for Understanding*, R. J. Russell, W. R. Stoeger, SJ, George V Coyne SJ eds., 1988 and *Quantum Cosmology and the Laws of Nature: Scientific Perspectives on Divine Action*, R. J. Russell, N. Murphy, and C. J. Isham, eds. 2nd ed., 1996. Protestants have also made serious efforts as witnessed by the magazines *Zygon* http://www.zygonjournal.org and *Theology and Science* that is published by the Center for Theology and the Natural Sciences http://www.ctns.org/publications.html. I regret to say that in my opinion this work though valuable fails to get beyond "dialogue."

[124.] See http://books.google.com/books/about/Science_in_Synthesis.html?id=sFdOHAAA CAAJ.

[125] For Wallace's publications see http://www.innerexplorations.com/philtext/ww.htm

[126] See *Nature, the Physician and the Family: The Collected Works of Herbert Ratner*, M.D. Privately published, 1997. See the memorial on Dr. Ratner of the La Leche League (for breast nursing) http://whale.to/vaccine/tribute_to_dr.html

[127] His principal work is, *The General Science of Nature* (Milwaukee: Bruce, 1958).

[128] The *New Biology: Barbara McClintock and an emerging holistic science* (Chambersburg, PA : Published for the American Teilhard Association for the Future of Man by ANIMA Books, 1992).

[129] See, *Philosophy and the God of Abraham: Essays in Memory of James A. Weisheipl, O.P.*, ed. R. James Long (Toronto: PIMS, 1991).

[130] For his obituary see http://boards.ancestry.com/topics.obits2/2298/mb.ashx

[131] Published under the heading: "Problem: The Relation of Physical Activity to Essence and End", with a comment by Robert J, McCall, S.SJ, *American Catholic Philosophical Association Proceedings*, April 16, 1952, 185-197.

[132] The present decline of support for Gilson's views is well explained by Wayne J. Hankey, "From Metaphysics to History, from Exodus to Neoplatonism, from Scholasticism to Pluralism: the Fate of Gilsonian Thomism in English-speaking North America," See: http://classics.dal.ca/Faculty%20and%20Staff/Gilson.php

[133] Dubuque, IA: Wm. C. Brown Co., 1952.

[134] *The Two Cultures: A Second Look* (Cambridge: Cambridge University Press, 1964).

[135] See also see my "An Educator's Vision" in *The Quality of Mercy: A Festschrift in Honor of Sister Mary Josetta Butler, R.S.M., 1904-1995*, Claudette Dwyer ed. (Chicago: Sisters of Mercy of the Americas, Regional Community of Chicago, 1996), pp. 31-42.

[136] Oscar W. Perlmutter, C. M. Warner, and A. Ducan Yokum, "The St. Xavier Plan of Liberal Education," *Religious Education*, 50, 5 (1955), pp. 322 ff.

[137] John Paul II, *Fides et Ratio*, nn. 43-46.

[138] See Wilfred Niels Arnold http://onlinelibrary.wiley.com/doi/10.1016/S0307-4412%2897%2900097-6/abstract

[139] Dubuque, IA: The Priory Press, 1958.

[140] These texts were published by Priory Press, Dubuque, IA and were widely used in Catholic colleges.

[141] See Apostles' obituary http://query.nytimes.com/gst/fullpage.html?res=9C0CE7D9103EF933A15754C0A966958260

[142] *Aeterni Patris*, n. 31, cf. http://www.vatican.va/holy_father/leo_xiii/encyclicals/documents/hf_l-xiii_enc_04081879_aeterni-patris_en.html

[143] "The Lyceum for Natural Science," in *The Works of the Province of St.Albert the Great, 4th Provincial Meeting, 1952*, pp. 44-46); three papers issued by St. Xavier's in 1954 on "The Thomistic Ideal of Education;" "The Science of Mathematics;" "The Teaching of Poetics and of Fine Arts in their Relation to Intellectual Development"; articles "Integrated Education," *The Dominican Bulletin*, (Autumn, 1954) pp. 1-8); "The Role of the Philosophy of Nature in Catholic Liberal Education", *Proceedings of the American Catholic Philosophical Association*, Washington, DC, 1956; "Why a Liberal Arts Handbook," *Dominican Education Bulletin*, (Spring, 1959), pp. 17-20; "A New Curriculum of Christian Doctrine for Catholics Schools", *Religious Education* (July-August, 1961), pp. 1-7); "Why Study Nature in the Elementary School", *The Catholic Educator*, Nov, 1962, pp. 223-226); "On the Curriculum and Methods of the Philosophy

Program," in George F. McClean, ed., *Philosophy and the Integration of Contemporary Catholic Education*, (Washington, DC, Catholic University of America Press, 1962), pp. 320-323); "The Integration of Sacred Doctrine and Natural Science," *Proceedings of the Society of College Teachers of Sacred Doctrine*, 1962, pp. 24-28, with discussion, pp. 47-57.

[144] "Research into the Intrinsic Final Causes of Physical Things," *Proceedings of the American Catholic Philosophical Association, Are Thomists Selling Science Short?*" in the 1960 Lecture Series in the Philosophy of Science, Mt. St. Mary's Seminary of the West, Cincinnati, Ohio, 1960, 21 pp.; "The Thomistic Synthesis" (River Forest, Ill, St. Albertus Magnus Lyceum Publications, 1961); "Does Natural Science Attain Nature or only the Phenomena" in Vincent E. Smith, ed., *The Philosophy of Physics* (Jamaica, NY: St. John's University, 1961) pp. 63-82; "Variations on the Scholastic Theme: Thomism" in George McLean, O.M.I., ed., *Teaching Thomism Today* (Washington, DC, Catholic University of America Press, 1962). I also tried to extend this approach to the social sciences in "Social Pluralism in American Life Today" in *Proceedings of the ACPA*, 1959, pp. 109-116; "The Sociology of Knowledge and the Social Role of the Scientist," (River Forest, IL, Albertus Magnus Lyceum Publications, 1960); "A Social Science Founded on a Unified Natural Science" in James A. Weisheipl, ed., *The Dignity of Science: Studies in the Philosophy of Science presented to W.H. Kane, O.P.* (Washington, DC: The Thomist Press, 1961), pp. 469-485.

[145] Articles in *The New Catholic Encyclopedia* (New York: McGraw-Hill, 1967): "Christian Education, Papal Teaching on" (3: 637-8); "Education, II (Philosophy of) Historical Development, Ancient and Medieval" (5: 162-166); "Liberal Arts," (8:646-99); "Finality" in 2nd edition (5:723-27).

[146] *Cross and Crown* (later *Spirituality Today*) 12 (June, 1960), pp. 133-145, reissued as a *Cross and Crown Reprint*.

[147] See http://www.ai.edu/

[148] See brief note http://en.wikipedia.org/wiki/Germain_Grisez

[149] *Contraception and the Natural Law* (Milwaukee: Bruce, 1964); *Abortion: The Myths, the Arguments, the Realities* (Washington, DC: Corpus Books, 1970).

[150] See Eleanor Carlo, T.O.P., "Creative Preaching Through Art: The Dominican Contribution."

[151] The anonymous author was the Redemptorist Francis X. Murphy; see http://www.newyorker.com/archive/content/articles/050516fr_archive01. See his death notice http://www.alfonsiana.edu/In%20Memoriam/EN%20-%20IM%20Murphy.htm

[152] *The Mind of Santayana* (New York, NY: Greenwood Press, 1955, 1968).

[153] Raymund J. Nogar, OP, *The Lord of the Absurd* (Notre Dame, IN: University of Notre Dame Press, 1998, original 1966).

[154] Thomas O'Meara, OP, and Celestine D. Weisser, OP, eds., *Paul Tillich in Catholic Thought*; with an afterword by Paul Tillich (Dubuque, IA: Priory Press, 1964); "Karl Rahner, Theologian" in *Doctrine and Life* 17;"Theology and Philosophy as Presented in Paul Tillich's 'Gotteslehre.'" Doctoral Dissertation, Ludwig-Maximillian University, 1967.

[155] "The Late Heidegger's Omission of the Ontic-Ontological Structure of Dasein," in John Sallis, ed., Introduction, *Heidegger and the Path of Thinking* (Pittsburgh, PA: Duquesne University Press,1970).

[156] *Prophets of the West: An introduction to the philosophy of history* (New York: Holt, Rinehart, and Winston, 1970).

[157] "Teilhard de Chardin: Toward a Developmental and Organic Theology," *The Catholic Theological Society of America, Proceedings of the Thirty-Third Annual Convention* 33 (1978), pp. 143-47 and *A Theology of Jesus*. 4 vols. Vol. 1 and 2 (Wilmington DE.: Michael Glazier, 1986-7); Vol. 3 and 4 (Collegeville, MN: The Liturgical Press, 1992-1994).

[158] For example, *Crisis and Change: The Church in Latin America Today* (Maryknoll, NY: Orbis Books, 1988).

[159] See http://www.domcentral.org/oplaity/layspirit.htm

[160] *The image of God: The doctrine of St. Augustine and its influence* (Dubuque, IA: Priory Press, 1963).

[161] *The Indwelling of the Trinity : A Historico-Doctrinal Study of the Theory of St. Thomas Aquinas* (Dubuque, IA: Priory Press, 1955).

[162] See http://www.domcentral.org/study/aumann/default.htm

[163] See http://en.wikipedia.org/wiki/Benedict_T._Viviano_O.P.

[164] http://www.matthewfox.org/about-matthew-fox/

[165] See Ingrid H. Shafer, "Odd Man Out: A Modern Morality Play: Andrew Greeley, Joseph Cardinal Bernadin , Eugene Kennedy";

http://projects.usao.edu/~facshaferi/SALIERI.HTML

[166] See http://en.wikipedia.org/wiki/Menninger_Foundation

[167] On this question see my *The Way Toward Wisdom,* note 2 above, Chapters I-V.

[168] See J Ziegler, review of Ronald McCamy, *Out of a Kantian Chrysalis* (Pieterlen,
Switzerland: Peter Lang Publishing, 1998)
http://www.cts.org.au/1999/outofakantianchrysalis.htm

[169] On this see my *Healing for Freedom: A Christian Perspective on Personhood and Psychotherapy* to be published by the Institute for the Psychological Sciences, Arlington Virginia.

[170] *The Sexual Celibate*; complete and unabridged (New York : Image Books, 1979, 1974).

[171] See http://en.wikipedia.org/wiki/Charles_Curran_(theologian)

[172] See C. Cochini, SJ, *Apostolic Origins of Clerical Celibacy* (San Francisco, CA: Ignatius Press, 1990); R. Cholij, *Clerical Celibacy in East and West,* (Herefordshire, England: Fowler Wright, 1989) and Stefan Heid, *Zölibat in der frühen Kirche* (Paderborn: Ferdinand Schöningh Verlag, 1997); also Manfred Hauke*, Women in the Priesthood?* (San Francisco, CA: Ignatius Press,1993) on the theological reasons for exclusively male priesthood.

[173] See *Book of Constitutions and Ordinations of the Friars of the Order of Preachers* (LCO) http://www.op.org/en/official-documents

[174] M.-H.Vicaire, OP, *St. Dominic and His Times* (New York: McGraw-Hill, 1964).

[175.] See http://www.op.org/en/official-documents

[176] See http://www.ctu.edu/

[177] The present edition *Program of Priestly Formation*, 5th edition, National Conference of Catholic Bishops is available at http://www.usccb.org/vocations/

[178] On Moraczewski see note 18 above. On Institute see http://www.religionandhealth.org/about.htm

[179] See http://en.wikipedia.org/wiki/Joseph_Fletcher

[180] Privately published, Houston, 1972.

[181] In Kendig Brubaker Cully, *Does the Church Know How to Teach?* (New York: Macmillan, 1970), pp. 261-280.

[182] *Catholic Mind* (March 1971):pp. 29-33.

[183] *Review for Religious* (March 1971):1pp. 87-98; a longer version directed to Dominicans was published in *The Dominican Education Association Newsletter* (May 1970), pp. 4-14).

[184] *Review for Religious* (May 1972): 325-41.

[185] *Texas Catholic Herald*, Dec. 20, 1971).

[186] April-May, 1971, pp. 17-25.

[187] *Pastoral Psychology* (May 1972): 31-40.

[188] *Creative Intuition in Art and Poetry* (New York: Pantheon, 1953).

[189] *The Thomist*, 36 (April 1972): 199-230.

[190] This argument which I owe to Charles DeKoninck is developed in an essay, "The Existence of Created Pure Spirits," in *The Ashley Reader: Redeeming Reason* (Naples, FL.: Sapientia Press, 2006), pp. 47-60.

[191] See Thomas O'Meara, OP, *"Modern Art and the Sacred: The Prophetic Ministry of Alain Couturier, OP"* http://www.spiritualitytoday.org/spir2day/863814omeara.html

[192] See http://en.wikipedia.org/wiki/Mark_Rothko

[193] See http://en.wikipedia.org/wiki/Broken_Obelisk

[194] Often referred to as "The Menil Collection", see http://en.wikipedia.org/wiki/The_Menil_Collection

[195] See http://en.wikipedia.org/wiki/Ren%C3%A9_Magritte

[196] Donald E. Bloesch, *Essentials of Evangelical Theology,* 2 vols. in 1 (Peabody, MA: Hendricksons Publications, 2005).

[197] *A Broader Vision: Perspectives on Buddhism and the Christ* (Virginia Beach, VA: A.R.E. Press. 1995).

[198] Since then the Congregation for the Doctrine of the Faith has answered questions on this difficult subject put to it by the U. S. Bishops, see http://www.usccb.org/comm/archives/2007/07-143.shtml

[199] In John N. Deely and R. J. Nogar, eds., *The Problem of Evolution* (Appleton-Century-Crofts, 1973), pp. 265-85.

[200] *University of Dayton Journal* (Dayton, 1975).

[201] See http://www.amazon.com/Health-Care-Ethics-Fifth-Theological/dp/1589011163

[202] See http://www.ncbcenter.org/

[203] 1st edition 1978, 2nd 1982, 3rd 1989, 4th Georgetown University Press, 1997 and with Jean Deblois, CSJ, a much revised 5th edition 2005.

[204] 1st ed. 1986, St. Louis: Catholic Health Association; 2nd ed., Georgetown University Press, 1994.

[205] Dubuque, IA: Archdiocese of Dubuque, *Telegraph-Herald Press,* 1976.

[206] In *The New Technologies of Birth and Death* (St. Louis: Pope John Center, 1980), pp.80-97.

[207] In Donald G. McCarthy, ed*., Responsible Stewardship of Human Life,* Inquiries into Medical Ethics II (Houston, TX: The Institute of Religion and Human Development and St. Louis, MO, the Catholic Hospital Association, 1976), pp. 35-42.

[208] *Issues in Ethical Decision Making* (St. Louis: Pope John Center, no date).

[209] *Hospital Progress* (July 1978): pp. 78-81. *Humanae Vitae* is the papal encyclical condemning contraception, while *Human Sexuality* was a report of a committee of the American Catholic Theological Association dissenting from Church teaching on sexuality that was condemned by the National Catholic Bishops Conference.

[210] *Hospital Progress* (August, 1980): pp. 47-50.

[211] In D. G. McCarthy and A.S. Moraczewski, *An Ethical Evaluation of Fetal*

Experimentation (St. Louis, MO: Pope John Center, 1976), Appendix I, pp. 113-133. A much fuller discussion is in my essay Chapter 20, "When Does a Human Person begin to Exist?" *The Ashley Reader: Redeeming Reason* (Naples, FL: Sapientia Press, 2006), pp. 329-368.

[212] In J. Schoolar and C. Gaits, eds., *Research and the Psychiatric Patient* (New York: Brunner/Mazel, 1975).

[213] See http://domcentral.org/jordan-aumann-o-p-introduction/

[214] *Exchange* (Fall 1976), pp. 5-9.

[215] *Cross and Crown* 29 (September 1977), pp. 237-249.

[216] *The Thomist*, 42 (April 1978): 226-239 (a special number edited by Thomas O'Meara, OP).

[217] *Spirituality Today* 31, 2 (July 1979): pp. 121-136.

[218] Toronto: Pontifical Institute of Mediaeval Studies, 1980, pp. 73-102.

[219] *Omnis Terra* (March 1974): pp. 211-288.

[220] See http://fr.wikipedia.org/wiki/Ivan_Illich

[221] See http://en.wikipedia.org/wiki/Kensington_Runestone

[222] See http://www.naturalism.org/naturali.htm

[223] "Retirement or Vigil," *Review for Religious* (May, 1972): pp. 325-41.

[224] Rivka Felday, *Galileo and the Church: Political Inquisition or Critical Dialogue?* (Cambridge: University of Cambridge Press, 1955).

[225] See Piet Pennington de Vries, SJ, Dis*cernment of Spirits, According to the Life and Teachings of St. Ignatius of Loyola.* Translated by W. Dudok Van Heel (New York, Exposition Press, 1973).

[226] See http://en.wikipedia.org/wiki/G%C3%B6tz_Briefs

[227] See Raphael Simon, *The Glory of Thy People, the Story of a Conversion* with a preface by Fulton J. Sheen (Petersham, MA : St. Bede's Publications, 1986) for an account of the conversion of Simon, Schwartz and other Jews to Catholicism..

[228] Minneapolis, MN, Winston Press, 1980

[229] See http://www.ad2000.com.au/articles/1994/sep1994p14_835.html

[230] See Robert Henle, SJ,"Transcendental Thomism: A Critical Assessment," *in One Hundred Years of Thomism:* Aeterni Patris *and Afterwards,*" in V. Brezik, CSB, ed. (Houston, TX: Center for Thomistic Studies, University of St. Thomas, 1981), pp. 173-198.

[231] I have recently argued this in detail in a paper, "Fundamental Option And/Or Commitment to Ultimate End," for a Karl Rahner Society symposium at the national convention of the Catholic Theological Society of America, June 1996, now published in *The Ashley Reader: Redeeming Reason* (Naples, FL: Sapientia Press, 2006) revised and with the title "Can We Make a Fundamental Option?," pp. 203-224

[232] "The Church's Message to Artists and Scientists," keynote address for annual convention of the Fellowship of Catholic Scholars, San Francisco, August 25, 1987, published in their bulletin and later printed in *The Battle for the Catholic Mind,* ed. by William E. May and Kenneth D. Whitehead (South Bend, IN: St. Augustine's Press, 2001), pp.334-345.

[233] In *Technological Powers and the Person* (St. Louis: Pope John Center, 1983), pp.313-333.

[234] In *Mind and Brain* (St. Louis, MO: The Institute for the Theological Encounter with Science and Technology of St. Louis University, 1985).

[235] See http://en.wikipedia.org/wiki/Herbert_Simon

[236] *Theologies of the Body: Humanist and Christian* (St. Louis, MO: Pope John Center, 1985). 2nd edition, with a new introductory chapter has been published (1996) by the Pope John Center (Braintree, Mass), now National Catholic Bioethics Center, Philadelphia.

[237] *Thomistic Studies II* (Houston: University of St. Thomas, 1987).

[238] *The Thomist* 51, 3 (July, 1987): pp. 501-521.

[239] *Ethics and Medics*, Vol. 11, n. 3 (March, 1986), Houston, TX: Pope John Center.

[240] Ibid.

[241] Ibid., vol. 17, n. 4 (April, 1992).

[242] *The Thomist*, 1987, also in *Persona et Morale, Atti del I Congresso Internazionale di Teologia Morale*, Rome, 1986, (Milano: Edizione Ares, 1987).

[243] *Proceedings of the 41st Annual Convention of the Catholic Theological Society of America*, vol.41, 1986, pp. 47-50.

[244] On false mysticism in the Church see See Ronald A. Knox*, Enthusiasm: A Chapter in the History of Religion : With Special Reference to the XVII and XVIII Centuries* (Notre Dame, IN: University of Notre Dame, 1994); Quietism is treated pp. 231-287.

[245] In *Moral Theology Today: Certitude and Doubts* (St. Louis, MO: Pope John Center, 1984): pp. 46-63.

[246] *Health Care Ethics: A Theological Analysis* (co-authored with Kevin D. O'Rourke) 1st ed., 1978, St. Louis, MO: Catholic Health Association; 2nd ed., 1981; 3rd edition, 1989; 4th, rev. ed. (Washington, DC: Georgetown University Press, 1997); in Italian translation, 1993; 5th ed., 1993, greatly revised and with Jean Deblois, CSJ, as third co-author and the title as *Health Care Ethics: A Catholic Theological Analysis*, 2006 (Washington, DC: Georgetown University Press).

[247] See http://en.wikipedia.org/wiki/Josef_Fuchs_%28theologian%29

[248] Josef Fuchs, SJ, "The Absoluteness of Moral Terms," *Gregorianum*, 52 (1971): pp. 415-455.

[249] See http://www.ts.mu.edu/readers/content/get-past-articles.html   Search for: Richard McCormick, S.J., "Some Early Reactions to *Veritatis Splendor ,"Theological Studies, 1954.*

[250] Much of what follows about moral theory is taken from a lecture, "Values vs. Virtues: Kant and Aquinas," delivered at Lumen Christi the Catholic student center of the University of Chicago, Nov. 6, 1997.

[251] On McGuire and why a Catholic University retains him on its faculty see the two blogs by John McAdams http://mu-warrior.blogspot.com/2005/11/marquette-and-heretical-dan-maguire.html and http://mu-warrior.blogspot.com/2006/06/daniel-maguire-banned-by-milwaukee.html

[252.] *Hospital Progress*, April, 1985, pp. 50, 53, 66.

[253.] "Christian Moral Principles: a Review Discussion" of Germain Grisez's *The Way of the Lord Jesus*, vol. 1, "Christian Moral Principles," *The Thomist* 48, 3 (July, 1984): pp. 450-460.

[254] Aquinas, *Summa Theologiae* I-II, q. 82, a. 3.

[255] In *Human Sexuality and Personhood* (St. Louis, MO: Pope John Center, 1981), pp. 223-242

[256] Not published; it was for discussion at a reflection meeting of the National Catholic Bishops Conferences held at St .John's University, Collegeville, MN, June 12-23, 1982.

[257] In *The Family Today and Tomorrow* (Braintree, MA: Pope John Center, 1985), pp. 101-112.

[258] In Mark F. Schwartz, A.S. Moraczewski, and J.A. Monteleone, eds., *Sex and Gender* (St. Louis, MO: Pope John Center, 1983), pp. 1-47.

[259] See http://couragerc.net/ and Catholic Medical Association "Homosexuality and Hope." http://www.cathmed.org/issues_resources/publications/position_papers/homosexuality_and_hope/ with extensive bibliography.

[260] Elizabeth Moberley, *Homosexuality: A New Christian Ethic* (San Francisco, CA: Attic Press: 1983).

[261] Edited by Jeannine Grammick and Pat Furey (New York: Crossroad, 1988), pp. 105-111.

[262] *The Feminist Question: Feminist Theology in the Light of Christian Tradition* (Grand Rapids, MI: W. B. Eerdmans, 1994).

[263] Vol. 1, *Christian Moral Principles*, 1983, Chapter VI, note 17. Two other volumes have now appeared: Vol 2, *Living a Christian Life*, 1993 and Vol. 3, *Difficult Moral Questions,* 1997.

[264] In *Moral Truth and Moral Tradition: Essays in Honour of Peter Geach and Elizabeth Anscombe*, ed. by Luke Gormally (Dublin and Portland, OR: Four Courts Press, 1994), pp. 68-96. This is now available as "Integral Human Fulfillment According to Germain Grisez" in *The Ashley Reader,* note 10 above, pp. 225-270.

[265] In Robert P, George, ed., *Natural Law and Moral Inquiry: Ethics, Meta-physics, and Politics in the Work of Germain Grisez* (Washington, DC: Georgetown University Press, 1998).

[266] *The Way of the Lord Jesus*, vol. 1, pp.7-12.

[267] Sister Paul Jean Miller, *Marriage: the Sacrament of Divine-human Communion* (Quincy, IL: Franciscan Press, 1996).

[268] Note 103 above

[269] "The bishops as successors of the apostles, receive from the Lord, to whom all power is given in heaven and on earth, the mission of teaching all peoples, and of preaching the Gospel to every creature, so that all men may attain to salvation through faith, baptism, and the observance of the commandments (cf. Mt 28:18; Mk 16:15-16; Acts 26:17f.)." *Lumen Gentium*, n. 24

[270] Introduction and trans. by Leonard Swidler (New York: Paulist, 1992); cf. *Catholic World Report*, 2 (Nov. 1991): pp. 56-58.

[271] *Catholicism in Crisis* (June, 1985), pp. 14-15.

[272] "Thanks to his intuition as a brilliant physicist and by relying on different arguments, Galileo, who practically invented the experimental method, under-stood why only the sun could function as the centre of the world, as it was then known, that is to say, as a planetary system. The error of the theologians of the time, when they maintained the centrality of the earth, was to think that our understanding of the physical world's structure was, in some way, imposed by the literal sense of Sacred Scripture." Pope John Paul II, *L'Osservatore Romano* N. 44 (1264), Nov. 4, 1992. For his view on evolution as a factual certitude but capable of different explanations see his 1996 address to the Pontifical Acade-my of Sciences, http://www.ewtn.com/library/papaldoc/jp961022.htm

[273] In *The Future of Thomism*, ed. by Deal W. Hudson and Dennis Wm. Moran, Preface by Gerald A. McCool, SJ (Notre Dame, IN: American Maritain Association, distributed by the University of Notre Dame Press, 1992), pp. 109-122. Now in a much revised form in *The Ashley Reader,* note 10 above, "Transition to Historical-Mindedness," pp. 13-26.

[274] In *Semiotics 1991*, ed. by John Deely and Terry Prewitt (Lanham, MD: University Press of America, 1993), pp. 49-60.

[275] In R. James Long ed., *Philosophy and the God of Abraham, Essays in Memory of James A. Weisheipl* (Toronto: Pontifical Institute of Medieval Philosophy,

1991), pp. 1-16.

[276] In *Reproductive Technologies: Marriage and the Church* (St. Louis, MO: Pope John Center, 1980), pp.80-97.

[277] In *The Twenty-Fifth Anniversary of Vatican II: A Look Back and A Look Forward* (Braintree,MA: Pope John Center, 1990), pp.35-48.

[278] In *Catholic Conscience: Foundation and Formation*, (Braintree,MA : Pope John Center, 1991), pp. 39-58.

[279] In *The Interaction of Catholic Bioethics and Secular Society*. Proceedings of the Eleventh Bishops' Workshop, Dallas, Texas, ed. by Russell E. Smith (Braintree, MA: The Pope John Center, 1992), pp.163-180.

[280] *Ethics and Medics* 13, 3 (March, 1988)

[281] Ibid., 13, 8 (August, 1988).

[282] Ibid., 13, 1 (July, 1988).

[283] Ibid., 17, 4 (April, 1992).

[284] Written for a symposium sponsored by the Pope John Center and St. Joseph's Hospital, Houston, TX (1991).

[285] *Hospital Progress* (August, 1980): 47-50.

[286] A paper delivered at the Annual Thomist Colloquium, Dominican House of Studies, Washington, DC, 1986.

[287] In D.G. McCarthy and A.S. Moraczewski, eds., *Moral Responsibility in Prolonging Life Decisions* (St. Louis, MO: Pope John Center, 1981), pp. 116-123.

[288] "Holy Living and Holy Dying," *Origins* 19 (Sept. 14, 1989), pp. 241-248, is the Catholic-Methodist statement. It was rather unfortunate in my opinion that the Methodists then chose to publish a separate statement on the subject in their own name, although they certainly had the right to do so.

[289] In *Reproductive Technologies, Marriage, and the Church* (Braintree, MA: Pope John Center, 1987), pp.113-118.

[290] Ibid., pp. 159-165.

[291] *Spirituality Today* 33 (March, 1981), pp. 43-52.

[292] See the 13th century document "Dominic's Nine Ways of Prayer," http://www.fisheaters.com/stdominic9ways.html

[293] Collegeville, MN.: The Liturgical Press/Michael Glazier, 1991.

[294] In Sisters Mary Nona McGreal and Margaret Ormond, ed., *Common Life in the Spirit of St. Dominic* (River Forest, IL: Parable, 1990), pp.26-38 (co-authored with David Wright, OP).

[295] Collegeville, MN: The Liturgical Press/ Michael Glazier: 1991).

[296] Now available online at http://domcentral.org/the-dominicans-a-short-history/and http://domcentral.org/dominican-spirituality/

[297] *Review for Religious*, May, 1972, pp. 325-34.

[298] *Tractatus de Signis: The Semiotic of John Poinsot*, 1st ed. (bilingual): Interpretative arrangement by John Deely (Berkeley, CA: University of California Press, 1985). The title page reads "In consultation with Ralph Austin Powell," because Powell, hoping to further Deely's career, insisted on not being listed as co-editor. It is certain, however, the work would never have seen the light of day except for Deely who carried it through yet could not persuade Powell to take proper credit.

[299] Washington, DC, University Press of America, 1983.

[300] For the 5th edition (2009) see http://www.usccb.org/issues-and-action/human-life-and-dignity/health-care/upload/Ethical-Religious-Directives-Catholic-Health-Care-Services-fifth-edition-2009.pdf

[301] *The Sterilization Controversy: A New Crisis for the Catholic Hospital*? (New York: Paulist Press, 1977).

[302] This is the title of a book by a Catholic, Norman M. Ford (Cambridge: Cambridge University Press, 1988) that defended delayed hominization.

[303] With Albert S. Moraczewski, OP, in Peter J. Cataldo and Albert S. Moraczewski, OP, eds., *The Fetal Tissue Issue: Medical and Ethical Aspects* (Braintree, MA: Pope John Center, 1994).

[304] In D. G. McCarthy and A.S. Moraczewski, *An Ethical Evaluation of Fetal Experimentation* (St. Louis, MO: Pope John Center, 1976). Appendix I, pp. 113-

133.

[305] *The National Catholic Bioethics Quarterly*, 1 (2) 2001, pp. 189-202. These studies have been combined and further developed in Chapter 20 of *The Ashley Reader: Redeeming Reason* (Naples, FL: Sapientia Press, 2006).

[306] May 5, 1980 in *Vatican Council II: More Postconciliar Documents*, vol. 2, Autin Flannery, OP, ed. (Northport, NY: Costello Publishing Co., 1982), pp. 510-517.

[307.] In *Evangelium Vitae*, n. 65. John Paul II declared, "In harmony with the magisterium of my predecessors and in communion with the bishops of the Catholic Church, *I confirm that euthanasia is a grave violation of the law of God,* since it is the deliberate and morally unacceptable killing of a human person. This doctrine is based upon the natural law and upon the written word of God, is transmitted by the church's tradition and taught by the ordinary and universal magisterium." The italics are in the original.

[308] See http://www.vatican.va/roman_curia/congregations/cfaith/documents/rc_con_cfa ith_doc_19900524_theologian-vocation_en.html

[309] "What is Moral Theology," *Medics and Ethics*, Part I (July 1993), Part II, (August, 1993); 3-4.

[310] In Russell E. Smith, ed., *The Splendor of Truth and Health Care*, Proceedings of the 14th Workshop for Bishops, Dallas Texas, 1995 (Braintree, MA: The Pope John Center, 1996), pp. 98-110.

[311.] In Russell E. Smith, ed., *The Gospel of Life and the Vision of Health Care,* Proceedings of the Fifteenth Workshop of Bishops (Dallas, TX, Braintree, MA: The Pope John Center, 1997), pp. 10-16.

[312.] To be published in the workshop proceedings of 1997.

[313] First three editions, 1978, 1982, 1989 and a shorter text book version *Ethics of Health Care*, 1986, were published by The Catholic Health Association, St. Louis. A 4th edition, 1989 of the former work was published Washington, DC: Georgetown University Press with a textbook version *Ethics of Health Care in 2002* and a 5th much revised and briefer edition of the main work is now published by the latter press, 2006, coauthored with Jean DeBlois. CSJ, and with the subtitle *A Catholic Theological Analysis* and also a textbook edition of *Ethics of Health Care,* 2002. An Italian translation of the main work was published in 1993.

[314.] Robert H. Blank and Janna C. Merrick, eds. in chief (Westport, CT: Greenwood Press, 1996), pp. 119-121.

[315] *L'Osservatore Romano*, Weekly English Edition, n. 38, 23 Sept., 1998, pp.8-10.

[316] *Theological Investigations* (London, Baltimore, New York: (Dartman, Longman, and Todd/ Helicon/ Herder and Herder/ Seabury, Crossroad, 1961-1992), 23 vols. vol. 2, pp. 217-234)

[317] A paper for a symposium of the Karl Rahner Society at the national convention of the Catholic Theological Society of America, June 1996, *Philosophy and Theology* 10, 1, Jan, 1997, pp.113-141 now available in *The Ashley Reader*, note 10 above, 203-244, as "Can We make a Fundamental Option?"

[318] "Instruction on Certain Aspects of the Theology of Liberation," 1984 and "Instruction on Christian Freedom and Liberation," 1986.

[319] *Deus est Caritas*, 2006, http://www.vatican.va/holy_father/benedict_xvi/encyclicals/documents/hf_ben-xvi_enc_20051225_deus-caritas-est_en.html , nn. 26 ff.

[320] See brief biography Wikipedia http://www.answers.com/topic/gustavo-gutirrez. On Las Casas see http://en.wikipedia.org/wiki/Bartolom%C3%A9_de_Las_Casas

[321] *Summa Theologiae*, II-II, q.188, a. 7, ad 1.

[322] *Summa Theologiae*, I, q. 113, a. 8 c. commenting on Dan 10:13.

[323] *Politics* IV, 8, 1295a 25 sq.

[324] *Summa Theologiae*, I-II, q. 105, a. 1, c.

[325] "The Priesthood of Christ and the Priesthood of the Ordained," in Donald J. Goergen and Ann Garrido, eds., *The Theology of Priesthood* (Collegeville, MN: The Liturgical Press, 2000), pp. 139-164. Now included in *The Ashley Reader*, note 10 above, pp. 125-148.

[326] See http://en.wikipedia.org/wiki/Carol_Gilligan

[327] In *The Quality of Mercy: A Festschrift in Honor of Sister Mary Josetta Butler, RSM, 1904-1995*, Claudette Dwyer, ed. (Chicago: Sisters of Mercy of the Americas: Regional Community of Chicago, 1996), pp. 31-42.

[328] *Summa Theologiae*, III, Suppl. q. 37. A. 2 ad 2.

[329] See Phyllis Zagano, "Catholic Women Deacons," 2003, who favors their ordination. http://www.americamagazine.org/gettext.cfm?articleTypeID=1&textID=2778& issueID=422

[330] Washington, DC: The Catholic University of America Press, 1996. .

[331] *She Who Is: The Mystery of God in Feminist Theological Discourse* (New York: Crossroad, 1992).

[332] The book of Donna Stricken, *UnGodly Rage: The Hidden Face of Catholic Feminism* (San Francisco, CA: Igantius Press, 1991), while it is as fiercely polemical as the movement it criticizes provides a detailed factual account of a movement that seems now to have spent its fury. A German theologian Manfred Hauke, *God or Goddess? Feminist Theology: What Is It? Where Does It Lead?* (same publisher, 1995) gives a calmer analysis.

[333] See her speeches http://www.women-churchconvergence.org/

[334] *The Thomist*, 57, 3 (July, 1993):pp. 343-379.

[335] *National Catholic Register*, Dec. 31, 1995, p. 5.

[336] In *The Observer of Boston College*, vol 14, 9, Feb 5, 1997, pp. 13 and 12.

[337] *William R. Farmer, ed.; Armando Levoratti, Sean McEvenue, and David L. Dungan, assoc. eds., ; André LaCocque, Map Editor (Collegeville Mn: Liturgical Press, 1998).*

[338] "In Sacred Scripture, therefore, while the truth and holiness of God always remains intact, the marvelous 'condescension' of eternal wisdom is clearly shown, 'that we may learn the gentle kindness of God, which words cannot express, and how far He has gone in adapting His language with thoughtful concern for our weak human nature.' (11) For the words of God, expressed in human language, have been made like human discourse, just as the word of the eternal Father, when He took to Himself the flesh of human weakness, was in every way made like men." *Dei Verbum,* III, 13.

[339] See Michael Gilchrist, http://www.ad2000.com.au/articles/1998/sep1998p7_547.html

[340] See http://www.catholiccommonground.org/

341

http://www.vatican.va/holy_father/john_paul_ii/apost_constitutions/documents/
hf_jp-ii_apc_15081990_ex-corde-ecclesiae_en.html

342 *Catholic Dossier*, Jan-Feb. 2000, pp.22-28.

343 *Handbook of Spirituality for Ministers*, ed. by Robert J. Wicks (New York:
Paulist, 2000), pp. 656-670.

344 *Josephinum Journal of Theology*, 7, 1-2 (Summer 2000), pp. 31-45.

345 William M. Johnston, ed. (Chicago: Fitzroy Dearborn Pubs., 2000).

346 *NaProEthics* ,vol. 3, n. 4 (July, 1998), pp. 4-5.

347 *The National Catholic Bioethics Quarterly*, 1, 2 (Summer 2001), pp. 189-
202.

348 *Love's Revelation*, Gerard Lordan, ed. (River Forest, IL: Priory Press,
2001).

349 Collegeville, MN: The Liturgical Press/Michael Glazier, 1991.

350. Hyde Park, NY: New City Press, 1995.

351. New York: Paulist Press, 1995.

352 Vol. II, *Perspectives for the 21st Century* (New York: Paulist Press, 2000),
pp. 656-670.

353 *Semiotics 1991*, edited by John Deely and Terry Prewitt (Lanham, MD:
University Press of America, 1993), pp. 49-60.

354 American Catholic Philosophical Association Proceedings, *The Importance of
Truth*, 68 (1993): pp. 27-40.

355 In Roman T. Ciapalo, ed., *Postmodernism and Christian Philosophy*, with an
intro. by Jude P. Daugherty (Washington, DC: American Maritain Association,
The Catholic University of America Press, 1997), pp.12-22.

356 Staten Island, NY: Alba House, 1996; a popular summary is my article,
"Living in Christ," *Crisis*, 11, 6 (June 1993): pp. 23-26.

[357] *Summa Theologiae Moralis*, 3rd rev. ed., (Paris: Desclée de Brouwer, 1938).

[358] *Being Right: Conservative Catholics in America*, Mary Jo Weaver and R. Scott Appleby, eds.(Bloomington/Indianapolis: Indiana University Press, 1995).

[359] Ibid., pp. 63-87.

[360] San Francisco: Harper/Collins, 1995.

[361] *In Medio Ecclesiae : Essays in honor of Benedict M. Ashley, OP, on the occasion of his 90th birthday* by members of the faculty of Aquinas Institute of Theology; Richard A. Peddicord, ed. (Bloomington, IN.: Author House; 2007)

Made in the USA
Charleston, SC
10 April 2013